Hockey Scouting Report 2004

SHERRY ROSS

Sterling Publishing Co., Inc.
New York

For my family, my foundation.

Editing by Christine Kondo
Cover design by Peter Cocking
Cover photograph of Mario Lemieux by Bruce Bennett/Bruce Bennett Studios
Typesetting by MicroMega Designs

Library of Congress Cataloging-in-Publication Data

10 9 8 7 6 5 4 3 2 1

Published by Sterling Publishing Co., Inc.
387 Park Avenue South, New York, NY 10016
© 2003 by Michael A. Berger
Distributed in Canada by Sterling Publishing
c/o Canadian Manda Group, One Atlantic Avenue, Suite 105
Toronto, Ontario, Canada M6K 3E7
Distributed in Great Britain by Chrysalis Books
64 Brewery Road, London N7 9NT, England
Distributed in Australia by Capricorn Link (Australia) Pty. Ltd.
P.O. Box 704, Windsor, NSW 2756, Australia

Printed in Canada
All rights reserved

Sterling ISBN 1-4027-1034-8

SHERRY ROSS

Yrs. of NHL service: 25
Born: Randolph, NJ
Position: press box
Height: no way
Weight: you gotta be kidding
Uniform no.: DKNJ
Shoots: straight

LAST SEASON
Ross is the hockey columnist for the *New York Daily News*. She lives in New Jersey with her cats Madam Marie and Candy, and her horse Cody.

THE FINESSE GAME
The versatile veteran began her career in the 1978-79 season, covering the New York Rangers for the Morristown (N.J.) *Daily Record*. Overcoming the expected rookie mistakes, she moved on to cover hockey for the Bergen (N.J.) *Record*, *Newsday*, and *The National*. In 1992, she became the NHL's first female team broadcaster when she was hired by the New Jersey Devils as a radio color analyst. In 1994, she became the first woman to call a major professional men's team championship as the radio color analyst for the NHL broadcast of the Stanley Cup Finals.

As a freelance writer, Ross has contributed to *Sports Illustrated*, *Beckett Hockey Monthly*, the *Hockey News*, and the *Sporting News*. She is the secretary-treasurer for the Professional Hockey Writers Association. She also covers horse racing for the *Daily News*.

THE PHYSICAL GAME
Horseback riding, frequent trips to Walt Disney World, and as many Bruce Springsteen shows as the budget will allow help shake off rink rust.

THE INTANGIBLES
Although she has lost a step over the years, her enthusiasm keeps Ross in the game.

ACKNOWLEDGEMENTS
This copy of *HSR* in your hands will be the last one authored by yours truly after an association that began in 1991-92. I would like to think that the work on this book made me a better hockey writer. It certainly put me in touch with a vast network of sources, who will remain anonymous, and who so generously shared their wisdom and notes with me. The men (I don't know any female scouts yet) who do this job do so with a love for the game that is undying. Without them, these editions would never have made it to a bookshelf.

I would like to thank all of them, as well as Michael Berger, who is the Col. Sanders of this franchise. Michael created this book in the late '80s as a resource guide for writers and broadcasters. The audience has expanded to fantasy pool enthusiasts as well as fans in new markets like Tampa and Nashville who wanted to learn more about what makes a player tick. I have been told that several teams buy these guides for their scouts, which I hope is a reflection of how well we have done our job over the past decade-plus. Michael, thanks for the opportunity to do this.

My early co-author and former colleague, Frank Brown, now works for the NHL and has never failed to provide me with valuable resource material at crunch time. Thanks, Skinner.

We have done our best to include as many young players as possible in this year's edition. We missed Barret Jackman last season, for which we will never forgive ourselves, but writing this in July, long before the puck first drops in October, requires a crystal ball and the magic shop was fresh out.

As much as we welcome the new guys, we mourn the loss of some of the familiar faces. Roger Neilson, as gentle and dignified a man as you could ever hope to know, lost his battle with cancer in June. Referee Paul Stewart and New Jersey Devils defenseman Ken Daneyko have left the game, but they won't be far from the rink, thank goodness.

Kelly Dresser, my computer maven, is simply a genius. My Bruce friend and hockey colleague E.J. Hradek is always a source of information and encouragement. Christine Kondo showed no sign of a sophomore slump as she followed up her Calder Trophy-caliber performance with another determined editing job.

The deadline for this book happily coincides with the start of the E Street Band's 10-show stand at Giants Stadium. So I will now bid a fond farewell to Branko Radivojevic, and get ready to give Max Weinberg a standing ovation.

CONTENTS

POINT LEADERS

NHL Scoring Statistics 2002-2003

RANK	POS.	PLAYER	GP	G	A	PTS	+/-	PP	S	PCT
1.	C	PETER FORSBERG	75	29	77	106	52	8	166	17.5
2.	L	MARKUS NASLUND	82	48	56	104	6	24	294	16.3
3.	C	JOE THORNTON	77	36	65	101	12	12	196	18.4
4.	R	MILAN HEJDUK	82	50	48	98	52	18	244	20.5
5.	R	TODD BERTUZZI	82	46	51	97	2	25	243	18.9
6.	R	PAVOL DEMITRA	78	36	57	93	0	11	205	17.6
7.	R	GLEN MURRAY	82	44	48	92	9	12	331	13.3
8.	C	MARIO LEMIEUX	67	28	63	91	-25	14	235	11.9
9.	R	DANY HEATLEY	77	41	48	89	-8	19	252	16.3
10.	R	ZIGMUND PALFFY	76	37	48	85	22	10	277	13.4
11.	C	MIKE MODANO	79	28	57	85	34	5	193	14.5
12.	C	SERGEI FEDOROV	80	36	47	83	15	10	281	12.8
13.	L	PAUL KARIYA	82	25	56	81	-3	11	257	9.7
14.	R	MARIAN HOSSA	80	45	35	80	8	14	229	19.6
15.	R	ALEXANDER MOGILNY	73	33	46	79	4	5	165	20.0
16.	C	VACLAV PROSPAL	80	22	57	79	9	9	134	16.4
17.	C	VINCENT LECAVALIER	80	33	45	78	0	11	274	12.0
18.	R	DANIEL ALFREDSSON	78	27	51	78	15	9	240	11.3
19.	R	ALEX KOVALEV	78	37	40	77	-9	11	271	13.7
20.	R	JAROMIR JAGR	75	36	41	77	5	13	290	12.4
21.	R	BRETT HULL	82	37	39	76	11	12	262	14.1
22.	L	RAY WHITNEY	81	24	52	76	-26	8	235	10.2
23.	R	MIROSLAV SATAN	79	26	49	75	-3	11	240	10.8
24.	C	BRAD RICHARDS	80	17	57	74	3	4	277	6.1
25.	C	MATS SUNDIN	75	37	35	72	1	16	223	16.6
26.	C	BRENDAN MORRISON	82	25	46	71	18	6	167	15.0
27.	C	SAKU KOIVU	82	21	50	71	5	5	147	14.3
28.	R	MARTIN ST. LOUIS	82	33	37	70	10	12	201	16.4
29.	L	VYACHESLAV KOZLOV	79	21	49	70	-10	9	185	11.4
30.	C	ROBERT LANG	82	22	47	69	12	10	146	15.1
31.	L	BRENDAN SHANAHAN	78	30	38	68	5	13	260	11.5
32.	C	ANDREW CASSELS	79	20	48	68	-4	9	113	17.7
33.	D	AL MACINNIS	80	16	52	68	22	9	299	5.3
34.	L	ILYA KOVALCHUK	81	38	29	67	-24	9	257	14.8
35.	R	JAROME IGINLA	75	35	32	67	-10	11	316	11.1
36.	L	GEOFF SANDERSON	82	34	33	67	-4	15	286	11.9
37.	L	ALEX TANGUAY	82	26	41	67	34	3	142	18.3
38.	L	CORY STILLMAN	79	24	43	67	12	6	157	15.3
39.	D	SERGEI GONCHAR	82	18	49	67	13	7	224	8.0
40.	C	DOUG WEIGHT	70	15	52	67	-6	7	182	8.2
41.	C	OLLI JOKINEN	81	36	29	65	-17	13	240	15.0
42.	L	MARIAN GABORIK	81	30	35	65	12	5	280	10.7
43.	C	ALEXEI YASHIN	81	26	39	65	-12	14	274	9.5
44.	R	TEEMU SELANNE	82	28	36	64	-6	7	253	11.1
45.	R	MIKE JOHNSON	82	23	40	63	9	8	178	12.9

GP = games played; G = goals; A = assists; PTS = points; +/- = goals-for minus goals-against while player is on ice; PP = power-play goals; S = no. of shots; PCT = percentage of goals to shots; * = rookie

RANK	POS.	PLAYER	GP	G	A	PTS	+/-	PP	S	PCT
46.	D	NICKLAS LIDSTROM	82	18	44	62	40	8	175	10.3
47.	C	JEFF O'NEILL	82	30	31	61	-21	11	316	9.5
48.	L	RYAN SMYTH	66	27	34	61	5	10	199	13.6
49.	R	STEVE SULLIVAN	82	26	35	61	15	4	190	13.7
50.	C	VINCENT DAMPHOUSSE	82	23	38	61	-13	15	176	13.1
51.	R	ANSON CARTER	79	26	34	60	-11	10	193	13.5
52.	C	TODD WHITE	80	25	35	60	19	8	144	17.4
53.	C	TODD MARCHANT	77	20	40	60	13	7	146	13.7
54.	C	MICHAEL NYLANDER	80	17	43	60	3	7	161	10.6
55.	R	PETR SYKORA	82	34	25	59	-7	15	299	11.4
56.	R	MIKE KNUBLE	75	30	29	59	18	9	185	16.2
57.	R	BRIAN ROLSTON	81	27	32	59	1	6	281	9.6
58.	C	JEREMY ROENICK	79	27	32	59	20	8	197	13.7
59.	L	MARTIN HAVLAT	67	24	35	59	20	9	179	13.4
60.	C	CRAIG CONROY	79	22	37	59	-4	5	143	15.4
61.	C	PETR NEDVED	78	27	31	58	-4	8	205	13.2
62.	C	JOE SAKIC	58	26	32	58	4	8	190	13.7
63.	C	DANIEL BRIERE	82	24	34	58	-20	9	181	13.3
64.	R	SHANE DOAN	82	21	37	58	3	7	225	9.3
65.	C	STEVE RUCCHIN	82	20	38	58	-14	6	194	10.3
66.	C	ALEXEI ZHAMNOV	74	15	43	58	0	2	166	9.0
67.	C	PATRIK ELIAS	81	28	29	57	17	6	255	11.0
68.	C	PATRICK MARLEAU	82	28	29	57	-10	8	172	16.3
69.	R	SCOTT MELLANBY	80	26	31	57	1	13	132	19.7
70.	L	LADISLAV NAGY	80	22	35	57	17	8	209	10.5
71.	C	RON FRANCIS	82	22	35	57	-22	8	156	14.1
72.	R	PETER BONDRA	76	30	26	56	-3	9	256	11.7
73.	C	VIKTOR KOZLOV	74	22	34	56	-8	7	232	9.5
74.	L	KEITH TKACHUK	56	31	24	55	1	14	185	16.8
75.	L	JASON BLAKE	81	25	30	55	16	3	253	9.9
76.	R	JAMIE LANGENBRUNNER	78	22	33	55	17	5	197	11.2
77.	C	SCOTT GOMEZ	80	13	42	55	17	2	205	6.3
78.	D	SERGEI ZUBOV	82	11	44	55	21	8	158	7.0
79.	R	OWEN NOLAN	75	29	25	54	-3	13	221	13.1
80.	C	RADEK BONK	70	22	32	54	6	11	146	15.1
81.	C	CHRIS DRURY	80	23	30	53	-9	5	224	10.3
82.	C	ERIC LINDROS	81	19	34	53	5	9	235	8.1
83.	D	DAN BOYLE	77	13	40	53	9	8	136	9.6
84.	L	MARTIN GELINAS	81	21	31	52	-3	6	152	13.8
85.	C	DAYMOND LANGKOW	82	20	32	52	20	4	196	10.2
86.	R	MARK RECCHI	79	20	32	52	0	8	171	11.7
87.	L	JEFF FRIESEN	81	23	28	51	23	3	179	12.8
88.	C	MIKE YORK	71	22	29	51	-8	7	177	12.4
89.	R	TONY AMONTE	72	20	31	51	0	7	207	9.7
90.	C	MIKE COMRIE	69	20	31	51	-18	8	170	11.8
91.	C	STEVEN REINPRECHT	77	18	33	51	-6	2	146	12.3
92.	C	JOZEF STUMPEL	78	14	37	51	0	4	110	12.7
93.	C	PAVEL DATSYUK	64	12	39	51	20	1	82	14.6
94.	L	RICHARD ZEDNIK	80	31	19	50	4	9	250	12.4
95.	R	BILL GUERIN	64	25	25	50	5	11	229	10.9
96.	C	MARC SAVARD	67	17	33	50	-14	6	148	11.5
97.	D	MATHIEU SCHNEIDER	78	16	34	50	2	11	199	8.0
98.	C	KIP MILLER	72	12	38	50	-1	3	89	13.5
99.	C	ERIC BOGUNIECKI	80	22	27	49	22	3	117	18.8
100.	L	JERE LEHTINEN	80	31	17	48	39	5	238	13.0

GP = games played; G = goals; A = assists; PTS = points; +/- = goals-for minus goals-against while player is on ice; PP = power-play goals; S = no. of shots; PCT = percentage of goals to shots; * = rookie

GOAL LEADERS

ASSIST LEADERS

RANK	PLAYER	G	PLAYER	A
1.	MILAN HEJDUK	50	PETER FORSBERG	77
2.	MARKUS NASLUND	48	JOE THORNTON	65
3.	TODD BERTUZZI	46	MARIO LEMIEUX	63
4.	MARIAN HOSSA	45	PAVOL DEMITRA	57
5.	GLEN MURRAY	44	MIKE MODANO	57
6.	DANY HEATLEY	41	VACLAV PROSPAL	57
7.	ILYA KOVALCHUK	38	BRAD RICHARDS	57
8.	ZIGMUND PALFFY	37	MARKUS NASLUND	56
9.	ALEX KOVALEV	37	PAUL KARIYA	56
10.	BRETT HULL	37	RAY WHITNEY	52
11.	MATS SUNDIN	37	AL MACINNIS	52
12.	JOE THORNTON	36	DOUG WEIGHT	52
13.	PAVOL DEMITRA	36	TODD BERTUZZI	51
14.	SERGEI FEDOROV	36	DANIEL ALFREDSSON	51
15.	JAROMIR JAGR	36	SAKU KOIVU	50
16.	OLLI JOKINEN	36	MIROSLAV SATAN	49
17.	JAROME IGINLA	35	VYACHESLAV KOZLOV	49
18.	GEOFF SANDERSON	34	SERGEI GONCHAR	49
19.	PETR SYKORA	34	MILAN HEJDUK	48
20.	ALEXANDER MOGILNY	33	GLEN MURRAY	48
21.	VINCENT LECAVALIER	33	DANY HEATLEY	48
22.	MARTIN ST. LOUIS	33	ZIGMUND PALFFY	48
23.	KEITH TKACHUK	31	ANDREW CASSELS	48
24.	RICHARD ZEDNIK	31	SERGEI FEDOROV	47
25.	JERE LEHTINEN	31	ROBERT LANG	47
26.	BRENDAN SHANAHAN	30	ALEXANDER MOGILNY	46
27.	MARIAN GABORIK	30	BRENDAN MORRISON	46
28.	JEFF O'NEILL	30	VINCENT LECAVALIER	45
29.	MIKE KNUBLE	30	NICKLAS LIDSTROM	44
30.	PETER BONDRA	30	SERGEI ZUBOV	44
31.	PETER FORSBERG	29	CORY STILLMAN	43
32.	OWEN NOLAN	29	MICHAEL NYLANDER	43
33.	MARIO LEMIEUX	28	ALEXEI ZHAMNOV	43
34.	MIKE MODANO	28	SCOTT GOMEZ	42
35.	TEEMU SELANNE	28	JAROMIR JAGR	41
36.	PATRIK ELIAS	28	ALEX TANGUAY	41
37.	PATRICK MARLEAU	28	ALEX KOVALEV	40
38.	MARCO STURM	28	MIKE JOHNSON	40
39.	DANIEL ALFREDSSON	27	TODD MARCHANT	40
40.	RYAN SMYTH	27	DAN BOYLE	40
41.	BRIAN ROLSTON	27	ED JOVANOVSKI	40
42.	JEREMY ROENICK	27	BRETT HULL	39
43.	PETR NEDVED	27	ALEXEI YASHIN	39
44.	DAVE SCATCHARD	27	PAVEL DATSYUK	39
45.	MIROSLAV SATAN	26	BRENDAN SHANAHAN	38
46.	ALEX TANGUAY	26	VINCENT DAMPHOUSSE	38
47.	ALEXEI YASHIN	26	STEVE RUCCHIN	38
48.	STEVE SULLIVAN	26	KIP MILLER	38
49.	ANSON CARTER	26	ROBERT SVEHLA	38
50.	JOE SAKIC	26	MARTIN ST. LOUIS	37

P.I.M. LEADERS

RANK	PLAYER	MJR	PIM
1.	JODY SHELLEY	27	249
2.	REED LOW	20	234
3.	MATT JOHNSON	15	201
4.	WADE BELAK	18	196
5.	PETER WORRELL	19	193
6.	*BARRET JACKMAN	10	190
7.	ERIC BOULTON	18	178
8.	SCOTT MELLANBY	4	176
9.	JEFF ODGERS	17	171
10.	TIE DOMI	13	171
11.	KRZYSZTOF OLIWA	17	161
12.	DALE PURINTON	9	161
13.	DONALD BRASHEAR	11	161
14.	P.J. STOCK	16	160
15.	DARREN LANGDON	11	159
16.	SEAN AVERY	11	153
17.	SCOTT NICHOL	9	149
18.	CHRIS SIMON	8	148
19.	CHRIS NEIL	15	147
20.	ADAM MAIR	8	146
21.	BRAD FERENCE	10	146
22.	TODD BERTUZZI	2	144
23.	MATTHEW BARNABY	10	142
24.	SEAN HILL	1	141
25.	BRYAN MARCHMENT	9	141

P-PLAY LEADERS

PLAYER	PP
TODD BERTUZZI	25
MARKUS NASLUND	24
DANY HEATLEY	19
MILAN HEJDUK	18
MATS SUNDIN	16
PETR SYKORA	15
GEOFF SANDERSON	15
VINCENT DAMPHOUSSE	15
DAVE ANDREYCHUK	15
ANDY DELMORE	14
ALEXEI YASHIN	14
MARIAN HOSSA	14
MARIO LEMIEUX	14
KEITH TKACHUK	14
BRENDAN SHANAHAN	13
OLLI JOKINEN	13
SCOTT MELLANBY	13
OWEN NOLAN	13
JAROMIR JAGR	13
JOE THORNTON	12
GLEN MURRAY	12
BRETT HULL	12
TOMAS HOLMSTROM	12
MARTIN ST. LOUIS	12
PAUL KARIYA	11

GOALIE WIN LEADERS

RANK	PLAYER	W
1.	MARTIN BRODEUR	41
2.	PATRICK LALIME	39
3.	ED BELFOUR	37
4.	PATRICK ROY	35
5.	CURTIS JOSEPH	34
6.	J GIGUERE	34
7.	OLAF KOLZIG	33
8.	DAN CLOUTIER	33
9.	ROMAN CECHMANEK	33
10.	MARTY TURCO	31
11.	TOMMY SALO	29
12.	ROMAN TUREK	27
13.	MARC DENIS	27
14.	JOCELYN THIBAULT	26
15.	TOMAS VOKOUN	25
16.	DWAYNE ROLOSON	23
17.	MIKE DUNHAM	21
18.	CHRIS OSGOOD	21
19.	PASI NURMINEN	21
20.	JOSE THEODORE	20
21.	ROBERTO LUONGO	20
22.	EMMANUEL FERNANDE	19
23.	EVGENI NABOKOV	19
24.	FELIX POTVIN	17
25.	JOHN GRAHAME	17

GOALIE G.A.A. LEADERS

PLAYER	GAA
MARTY TURCO	1.72
ROMAN CECHMANEK	1.83
DWAYNE ROLOSON	2.00
MARTIN BRODEUR	2.02
PATRICK LALIME	2.16
PATRICK ROY	2.18
TOMAS VOKOUN	2.20
ROBERT ESCHE	2.20
EMMANUEL FERNANDE	2.24
ED BELFOUR	2.26
J GIGUERE	2.30
GARTH SNOW	2.31
JOCELYN THIBAULT	2.37
OLAF KOLZIG	2.40
DAN CLOUTIER	2.42
RON TUGNUTT	2.47
BRENT JOHNSON	2.47
CURTIS JOSEPH	2.49
MIKE DUNHAM	2.50
JOHN GRAHAME	2.52
KEVIN WEEKES	2.55
JAMIE STORR	2.55
MARTIN BIRON	2.56
ROMAN TUREK	2.57
FELIX POTVIN	2.66

ANAHEIM MIGHTY DUCKS

Players' Statistics 2001-2002

POS.	NO.	PLAYER	GP	G	A	PTS	+/-	PIM	PP	SH	GW	GT	S	PCT
L	9	PAUL KARIYA	82	25	56	81	-3	48	11	1	2	1	257	9.7
R	39	PETR SYKORA	82	34	25	59	-7	24	15	1	5	1	299	11.4
C	20	STEVE RUCCHIN	82	20	38	58	-14	12	6	1	4		194	10.3
C	77	ADAM OATES	67	9	36	45	-1	16	4		2		67	13.4
D	8	SANDIS OZOLINSH	82	12	32	44	-6	56	6		3		137	8.8
D	28	NICLAS HAVELID	82	11	22	33	5	30	4		5		169	6.5
R	32	STEVE THOMAS	81	14	16	30	10	53	1		4		118	11.9
R	23	*STANISLAV CHISTOV	79	12	18	30	4	54	3		2		114	10.5
L	12	MIKE LECLERC	57	9	19	28	-8	34	1		4		122	7.4
C	10	JASON KROG	67	10	15	25	1	12		1	1		92	10.9
C	44	ROB NIEDERMAYER	66	10	12	22	-10	57	3		1		125	8.0
D	3	KEITH CARNEY	81	4	18	22	8	65			1	2	87	4.6
C	19	ANDY MCDONALD	46	10	11	21	-1	14	3		1		92	10.9
L	18	PATRIC KJELLBERG	76	8	11	19	-9	16	2	1	2		95	8.4
C	26	SAMUEL PAHLSSON	34	4	11	15	10	18		1	2		28	14.3
D	24	RUSLAN SALEI	61	4	8	12	2	78					93	4.3
D	5	VITALY VISHNEVSKI	80	2	6	8	-8	76	1				65	3.1
D	2	FREDRIK OLAUSSON	44	2	6	8	0	22	2		1		38	5.3
C	11	MARC CHOUINARD	70	3	4	7	-9	40	1				52	5.8
R	4	LANCE WARD	65	3	2	5	-6	121			1		52	5.8
L	22	*ALEXEI SMIRNOV	44	3	2	5	-1	18			1		46	6.5
L	21	DAN BYLSMA	39	1	4	5	-1	12					23	4.3
L	25	KEVIN SAWYER	31	2	1	3	-2	115					11	18.2
D	34	*KURT SAUER	80	1	2	3	-23	74					50	2.0
L	44	*MIKE BROWN	16	1	1	2	0	44			1		8	12.5
R	38	ROB VALICEVIC	10	1		1	1	2			1		7	14.3
D	37	CHRIS O'SULLIVAN	2		1	1	0						3	
R	51	*JONATHAN HEDSTROM	4				-1						3	
L	14	*CAM SEVERSON	2				0	8					1	
G	35	J GIGUERE	65				0	8						
G	30	ILJA BRYZGALOV					0							
G	29	MARTIN GERBER	22				0							

GP = games played; G = goals; A = assists; PTS = points; +/- = goals-for minus goals-against while player is on ice; PIM = penalties in minutes; PP = power-play goals; SH = shorthanded goals; GW = game-winning goals; GT = game-tying goals; S = no. of shots; PCT = percentage of goals to shots; * = rookie

KEITH CARNEY

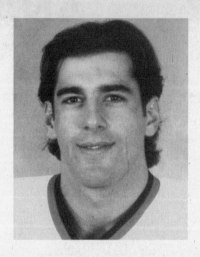

Yrs. of NHL service: 11
Born: Providence, R.I.; Feb. 3, 1970
Position: left defense
Height: 6-2
Weight: 211
Uniform no.: 3
Shoots: left

Career statistics:

GP	G	A	TP	PIM
729	36	137	173	700

1999-2000 statistics:

GP	G	A	TP	+/-	PIM	PP	SH	GW	GT	S	PCT
82	4	20	24	+11	87	0	0	1	0	73	5.5

2000-2001 statistics:

GP	G	A	TP	+/-	PIM	PP	SH	GW	GT	S	PCT
82	2	14	16	+15	86	0	0	0	0	65	3.1

2001-2002 statistics:

GP	G	A	TP	+/-	PIM	PP	SH	GW	GT	S	PCT
60	5	9	14	+14	30	0	0	1	0	66	7.6

2002-2003 statistics:

GP	G	A	TP	+/-	PIM	PP	SH	GW	GT	S	PCT
81	4	18	22	+8	65	0	0	1	2	87	4.6

LAST SEASON

Second on team in average ice time (22:33). Third on team in plus-minus. Missed one game due to coach's decision.

THE FINESSE GAME

Carney is quick and agile and he positions himself well defensively. He is a smart power-play point man who works on the second unit on the right side. He is among the NHL's better penalty killers, and he has good hockey sense and great anticipation. He reads the play well, is a fine skater, and moves the puck smoothly and quickly out of the zone. He is a very good shot-blocker.

Carney was considered an offensive defenseman when he first tried to break into the NHL, but he lacked the elite skills to succeed on that style alone. He has turned his finesse skills to his defensive advantage and emphasizes play in his own zone, though he is capable of contributing some offense. Anaheim routinely sent him out to face other team's top lines night after night, and Carney rose to the challenge with sometimes spectacular results. He was a poor man's Scott Stevens.

Carney complements an offensive partner well. He is not strictly stay-at-home, though. He just picks his spots wisely and conserves energy, which is smart considering how much ice time he logs.

THE PHYSICAL GAME

Carney is not a hitter, but he will get in the way of people. Instead of punishing, he ties up his man effectively. A well-conditioned athlete, he is an honest worker who is the last one off the ice in practice. He

has become an utterly reliable defenseman whose total package is far greater than the tallying of his assets individually. Carney is smaller than he plays, and Anaheim has to guard against him looking completely gaunt, as he did by the time his Cinderella team reached the Stanley Cup finals.

THE INTANGIBLES

Carney is a warrior and is the foundation of Anaheim's defense. Coaches can't find enough good things to say about him.

PROJECTION

His focus on defense will again limit Carney's total to around 20 points.

STANISLAV CHISTOV

Yrs. of NHL service: 1
Born: Chelyabinsk, Russia; Apr. 17, 1983
Position: left wing
Height: 5-10
Weight: 178
Uniform no.: 23
Shoots: right

Career statistics:

GP	G	A	TP	PIM
79	12	18	30	54

2002-2003 statistics:

GP	G	A	TP	+/-	PIM	PP	SH	GW	GT	S	PCT
79	12	18	30	+4	54	3	0	2	0	114	10.5

LAST SEASON

First NHL season. Tied for seventh among NHL rookies in points. Tied for eighth among NHL rookies in goals and assists. Missed three games due to coach's decision.

THE FINESSE GAME

Chistov is a dynamic little player whose lack of size should prove to be no drawback.

Chistov gets high marks in almost every talent category. He is an excellent skater, with acceleration and agility. He handles the puck at high tempo and through traffic. He has great hockey sense and vision. He is both a sniper and a playmaker. Chistov stands out even on a team with a lot of highly skilled players. Chistov is something special. He will try creative moves and is bold enough to beat even veteran defenseman with an outside move.

Chistov has drawn comparisons to teammate Paul Kariya, Pavel Bure, Sergei Samsonov, and Alexander Mogilny, yet he is not quite like any of those players. He may prove better than those stars, but in more of an all-around sense than as a record-setting scorer.

Anaheim broke Chistov in on a checking line which may have hurt his scoring chances and a run at the Calder Trophy but which will make him a better player in the long run. His astonishing moves will make people gasp, but his defensive gaffes won't.

THE PHYSICAL GAME

Much of Chistov's petite frame is filled up with heart. He is a game player as well as being a game-breaker. He's got grit.

THE INTANGIBLES

Chistov started learning English when he was 15 and his ease with the language has helped his transition. He is also pleasantly ego-free and that helped veteran teammates accept him readily.

PROJECTION

Ice time should start to increase for Chistov and with that, his point totals should increase. It wouldn't be a shock to see him hit 20 goals, 40 points in his sophomore season, and there will be bigger numbers to come.

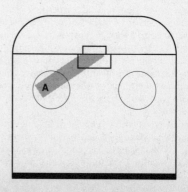

SERGEI FEDOROV

Yrs. of NHL service: 13
Born: Pskov, Russia; Dec. 13, 1969
Position: center
Height: 6-2
Weight: 200
Uniform no.: 91
Shoots: left

Career statistics:

GP	G	A	TP	PIM
908	400	554	954	587

1999-2000 statistics:

GP	G	A	TP	+/-	PIM	PP	SH	GW	GT	S	PCT
68	27	35	62	+8	22	4	4	7	0	263	10.3

2000-2001 statistics:

GP	G	A	TP	+/-	PIM	PP	SH	GW	GT	S	PCT
75	32	37	69	+12	40	14	2	7	1	268	11.9

2001-2002 statistics:

GP	G	A	TP	+/-	PIM	PP	SH	GW	GT	S	PCT
81	31	37	68	+20	36	10	0	6	0	256	12.1

2002-2003 statistics:

GP	G	A	TP	+/-	PIM	PP	SH	GW	GT	S	PCT
80	36	47	83	+15	52	10	2	11	0	281	12.8

LAST SEASON

Signed as free agent by Anaheim on July 19, 2003. Led Red Wings in assists, points, game-winning goals, and shots. Second on team in goals and short-handed goals. Missed two games with back injury.

THE FINESSE GAME

Fedorov likes to gear up from his own defensive zone, using his acceleration and balance to drive wide to his right, carrying the puck on his backhand and protecting it with his body. If the defenseman lets up at all, Fedorov is by him, pulling the puck quickly to his forehand. Nor is he by any means selfish. He has 360-degree vision of the ice and makes solid, confident passes right under opponents' sticks and smack onto the tape of his teammates'. His skating is nothing short of phenomenal. He can handle the puck while dazzling everyone with his blades.

Versatility is a Fedorov hallmark. In his career he has played left wing, center, and even defense. He fuels a power play and kills penalties. With his enormous package of offensive and defensive skills, he can go from checking his opponent's top center to powering the power play from shift to shift. Throughout his Detroit career, Fedorov may have been the team's top defensive center and he contributed big numbers offensively. He certainly kept the team viable last season while Steve Yzerman was absent.

Fedorov will swing behind the opposing net from left to right, fooling the defense into thinking he is going to continue to curl around, but he can quickly reverse with the puck on his backhand, shake his shadow, and wheel around for a shot or goalmouth pass. He does it all in a flash, and skating with the puck doesn't slow him down one whit.

THE PHYSICAL GAME

When you are as gifted as Fedorov, opponents will do all they can to hit you and hurt you. Although the wiry Fedorov is reluctant to absorb big hits or deliver any, he will leave the relative safety of open ice and head to the trenches when he is getting punished.

Much of his power is generated from his strong skating. For the most part, his defense is dominated by his reads, anticipation, and quickness in knocking down passes and breaking up plays. He is not much of a body checker, and he gets most of his penalties from stick and restraining fouls.

THE INTANGIBLES

Fedorov moves his equipment to Anaheim after spending his whole career with the Red Wings.

PROJECTION

Even though Anaheim will suffer from a Cup Final hangover and the loss of Paul Kariya to free agency, Fedorov should be good for 75 points. His supporting cast here is nowhere near as talented as in Detroit, though.

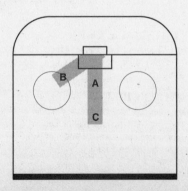

J. GIGUERE

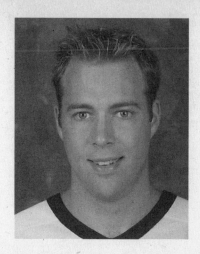

Yrs. of NHL service: 4
Born: Montreal, Que., May 16, 1977
Position: goalie
Height: 6-0
Weight: 185
Uniform no.: 35
Shoots:

Career statistics:

GP	MIN	GA	SO	GAA	A	PIM
182	10517	428	16	2.44	2	36

1999-2000 statistics:

GP	MIN	GAA	W	L	T	SO	GA	S	SAPCT	PIM
7	330	2.73	1	3	1	0	15	175	.914	2

2000-2001 statistics:

GP	MIN	GAA	W	L	T	SO	GA	S	SAPCT	PIM
34	2031	2.57	11	17	5	4	87	976	.911	8

2001-2002 statistics:

GP	MIN	GAA	W	L	T	SO	GA	S	SAPCT	PIM
53	3127	2.13	20	25	6	4	111	1384	.920	28

2002-2003 statistics:

GP	MIN	GAA	W	L	T	SO	GA	S	SAPCT	PIM
65	3775	2.30	34	22	6	8	145	1820	.920	8

LAST SEASON

Won 2003 Conn Smythe Trophy. Tied for second among NHL goalies in shutouts. Fifth among NHL goalies in wins. Career highs in wins and shutouts.

THE PHYSICAL GAME

After the kind of playoffs Giguere enjoyed, he merits a whole book instead of a single page. There has probably never been a more dominating performance by a goalie in the modern era. It was so impressive it earned Giguere the playoff MVP trophy despite the fact he didn't have a great final series and the Mighty Ducks lost out to the Devils in seven games.

Crucial to Giguere's development was the trade to Anaheim (in 2000) that teamed him with the goaltending goalie guru, Francois Allaire. Giguere learned his butterfly technique while a teenager attending one of Allaire's hockey camps. The biggest correction Allaire made was to get Giguere into the habit of keeping his torso upright when he drops to his knees. Allaire re-taught Giguere the basics. Instead of making everything so complicated, Giguere learned how better technique makes the game so much easier.

It helps that Giguere is a great athlete. Giguere is a good skater with quick post-to-post moves. He has sharp reflexes and controls his rebounds well. He has been compared to Patrick Roy, another Allaire protege, but Giguere doesn't resort to the flamboyant style (and mistakes) that sometimes hurt Roy's game. He's above average with both his blocker and glove hands. His puckhandling is okay but he has been coached to minimize his forays out of the crease and that is for the best. He's good with his stick for breaking up plays around the net.

Giguere used to become dehydrated in games to the point of illness, but pays better attention to conditioning, fluids, and nutrition. Now he can play all night, as he just about did in winning Game 1 of the playoffs in Detroit.

THE INTANGIBLES

Giguere is no fluke. He was considered a world-class goalie when he was drafted and it just took him awhile to find his way.

PROJECTION

Giguere has arrived, but we expect a few hiccups for the Ducks as they adjust to their new position as favorites instead of underdogs. He should reach 30 wins.

MIKAEL HOLMQVIST

Yrs. of NHL service: 0
Born: Stockholm, Sweden; June 8, 1979
Position: center
Height: 6-3
Weight: 189
Uniform no.: n.a.
Shoots: left

Career (European) statistics:

GP	G	A	TP	PIM
277	42	49	97	86

2002-2003 European statistics:

GP	G	A	TP	PIM
56	15	25	40	36

LAST SEASON

Will be entering first full NHL season. Appeared in 56 games with TPS Turku (Finnish Elite League), scoring 15-25 — 40 with 36 PIM.

THE FINESSE GAME

The first word scouts use when they talk about Holmqvist is "soft." Sometimes it's meant as a compliment, because he has wonderfully soft hands for making and accepting passes. Often it's meant in a more disparaging sense, because Holmqvist doesn't have any sandpaper in his game at all.

He is more of a reaction player than one who will make things happen. Holmqvist likes the big European rinks and might prove allergic to corners.

His talent can't be denied. He is a creative and intuitive player with great hockey sense. Holmqvist will be a better playmaker than scorer. His skating speed is NHL caliber.

THE PHYSICAL GAME

Holmqvist has good size and a long reach but doesn't play hard. Anaheim was hoping he would gain a little more serious muscle but it just looks like he has grown, period. He isn't very strong on his skates and can get shoved off the puck too readily.

THE INTANGIBLES

Anaheim has waited a long, long time for this first-round draft pick (in 1997) to blossom. He will have the best chance of any of the new faces to earn a starting job in training camp. There's a question as to whether he has the taste for the North American style of play. His work ethic remains a question mark.

PROJECTION

Holmqvist is at least a year away from becoming a top-six forward.

MIKE LECLERC

Yrs. of NHL service: 5
Born: Winnipeg, Man.; Nov. 10, 1976
Position: left wing
Height: 6-2
Weight: 208
Uniform no.: 12
Shoots: left

Career statistics:

GP	G	A	TP	PIM
281	53	75	128	247

1999-2000 statistics:

GP	G	A	TP	+/-	PIM	PP	SH	GW	GT	S	PCT
69	8	11	19	-15	70	0	0	2	0	105	7.6

2000-2001 statistics:

GP	G	A	TP	+/-	PIM	PP	SH	GW	GT	S	PCT
54	15	20	35	-1	26	3	0	3	2	130	11.5

2001-2002 statistics:

GP	G	A	TP	+/-	PIM	PP	SH	GW	GT	S	PCT
82	20	24	44	-12	107	8	0	4	0	178	11.2

2002-2003 statistics:

GP	G	A	TP	+/-	PIM	PP	SH	GW	GT	S	PCT
57	9	19	28	-8	34	1	0	4	0	122	7.4

LAST SEASON

Tied for fourth on team in game-winning goals. Missed 21 games due to knee injuries and surgery. Missed one game with elbow surgery. Missed three games due to coach's decision.

THE FINESSE GAME

Leclerc has a long reach with a lot of power on his shot, which is accurate and quickly released. He is un-selfish and wants to dish the puck off, though his coaches want him to shoot. He has very good vision and is at his best in-tight. On his best nights, Leclerc is a dominant player who skates, goes to the body, goes to the net, and creates space for his linemates.

Defensively aware, Leclerc works hard in all three zones. Skating is the only thing that might hold him back from becoming an elite power forward. He lacks quickness and acceleration, but has a long, strong stride once he gets in gear.

Leclerc had trouble with nagging injuries last sea-son which prevented him from getting in a groove. Leclerc's idol is Cam Neely, which is not a bad role model for a kid with size, touch, and a bit of a temper, as Leclerc appears to have.

THE PHYSICAL GAME

Leclerc uses his body well and he matches up well against other teams' rugged forwards because he's not awed by them and he's certainly not afraid to drop his gloves. He is starting to make his reputation and doesn't need to spend as much time in the penalty box. He fights to get into the quality scoring zones around the net.

THE INTANGIBLES

The benefit in adding players like Adam Oates and Petr Sykora to the lineup is that it allows Leclerc to settle into a comfortable second-line role while the two newcomers handle first-line duties.

Leclerc is intense and plays hard every night. He's a quiet kid and coachable; a good team player who will be an asset for years to come. Anaheim needs his physical presence up front. Leclerc was a restricted free agent after the season.

PROJECTION

A healthy Leclerc should score 20 goals and we might even see the big year we've been waiting for — 25 would do it.

ROB NIEDERMAYER

Yrs. of NHL service: 10
Born: Cassiar, B.C.; Dec. 28, 1974
Position: center
Height: 6-2
Weight: 204
Uniform no.: 44
Shoots: left

Career statistics:

GP	G	A	TP	PIM
641	117	191	308	541

1999-2000 statistics:

GP	G	A	TP	+/-	PIM	PP	SH	GW	GT	S	PCT
81	10	23	33	-5	46	1	0	4	0	135	7.4

2000-2001 statistics:

GP	G	A	TP	+/-	PIM	PP	SH	GW	GT	S	PCT
67	12	20	32	-12	50	3	1	0	0	115	10.4

2001-2002 statistics:

GP	G	A	TP	+/-	PIM	PP	SH	GW	GT	S	PCT
57	6	14	20	-15	49	1	2	1	1	87	6.9

2002-2003 statistics:

GP	G	A	TP	+/-	PIM	PP	SH	GW	GT	S	PCT
66	10	12	22	-10	57	3	0	1	0	125	8.0

LAST SEASON

Acquired from Calgary on March 11, 2003, for Mike Commodore and J-F Damphousse. Missed 11 games with sprained knee. Missed one game with flu. Missed two games due to coach's decision.

THE FINESSE GAME

Niedermayer is an excellent skater, better even than older brother Scott (a defenseman for the New Jersey Devils). Big and strong, Niedermayer has the speed to stay with some of the league's best power centers, but it wasn't until the trade to Anaheim late last season that he unleashed his power game. Suddenly Niedermayer started doing a Todd Bertuzzi impersonation, only with a higher hockey IQ.

He is a strong passer and an unselfish player, probably too unselfish. He controls the puck well at tempo and can beat a defender one-on-one. He has started to finish better and play with much more authority.

Niedermayer is solid on face-offs. His speed and size are his biggest assets, especially down low in his team's defensive zone. Anaheim played him as a right wing and that removed some defensive responsibility and might prove to be his future. He is a good two-way forward who needs to elevate his offensive game.

THE PHYSICAL GAME

Although not overly physical, Niedermayer has good size. He is an intelligent player and doesn't hurt his team by taking bad penalties. Niedermayer has had some struggles with concussions, which were actually career-threatening, and it took away some of his inclination to play a physical style, although he sure looked like a confident player again in the playoffs.

THE INTANGIBLES

Niedermayer is a quiet team leader. The change to Anaheim worked wonders. He thrives in the team defense system and looks like a new man.

PROJECTION

Niedermayer's point totals will remain modest, probably around 40 points if he keeps a job in Anaheim's top six.

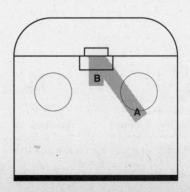

ADAM OATES

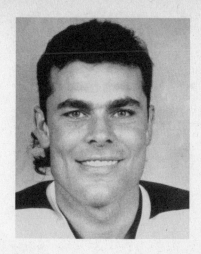

Yrs. of NHL service: 18
Born: Weston, Ont.; Aug. 27, 1962
Position: center
Height: 5-11
Weight: 190
Uniform no.: 77
Shoots: right

Career statistics:

GP	G	A	TP	PIM
1277	339	1063	1402	407

1999-2000 statistics:

GP	G	A	TP	+/-	PIM	PP	SH	GW	GT	S	PCT
82	15	56	71	+13	14	5	0	6	0	93	16.1

2000-2001 statistics:

GP	G	A	TP	+/-	PIM	PP	SH	GW	GT	S	PCT
81	13	69	82	-9	28	5	0	4	0	72	18.1

2001-2002 statistics:

GP	G	A	TP	+/-	PIM	PP	SH	GW	GT	S	PCT
80	14	64	78	-4	28	3	0	1	0	102	13.7

2002-2003 statistics:

GP	G	A	TP	+/-	PIM	PP	SH	GW	GT	S	PCT
67	9	36	45	-1	16	4	0	2	0	67	13.4

LAST SEASON

Third on Mighty Ducks in assists. Missed 15 games due to hand surgery.

THE FINESSE GAME

Passing is Oates' first instinct, though he has a fine shot with a precise touch. Taking more shots makes him a less predictable player, since the defense can't back off and anticipate the pass. He is one of the NHL's best playmakers because of his passing ability and his creativity. He is most effective down low where he can open up more ice, especially on the power play. He has outstanding timing and vision.

Oates remains one of the elite playmakers in the NHL, defying age. He uses a shorter-than-average stick and a minimal curve on his blade, the result being exceptional control of the puck. Although he's a right-handed shooter, his right wings have always been his preferred receivers. He can pass on the backhand but also carries the puck deep. He shields the puck with his body and turns to make the pass to his right wing.

Use of the backhand gives Oates a tremendous edge against all but the rangiest NHL defensemen. He forces defenders to reach in and frequently draws penalties when he is hooked or tripped. If defenders don't harass him, he then has carte blanche to work his passing magic.

Oates is definitely not one of those players stubborn to a fault. He will also play a dump-and-chase game if he is being shadowed closely, throwing the puck smartly into the opposite corner with just the right velocity to allow his wingers to get in on top of the defense.

He was seventh in the NHL in face-offs (57.8 per cent), which makes him an asset on penalty killing; a successful draw eats up 10 to 15 seconds on the clock.

THE PHYSICAL GAME

Oates is not a physical player but he doesn't avoid contact. He plays in traffic and will take a hit to make the play, and he's smart enough at this stage of his career to avoid the garbage. He's an intense player with a wiry strength, but he tends to wear down late in the season.

THE INTANGIBLES

Oates played a key role in Anaheim's roll to the Stanley Cup Finals. He was an unrestricted free agent after the season.

PROJECTION

Oates is at best a No. 2 center who can still help on special teams. Depending on where he signs, he should still be good for about 55 assist-heavy points.

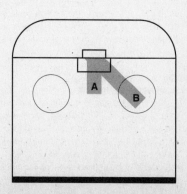

SANDIS OZOLINSH

Yrs. of NHL service: 11
Born: Riga, Latvia; Aug. 3, 1972
Position: left defense
Height: 6-3
Weight: 215
Uniform no.: 8
Shoots: left

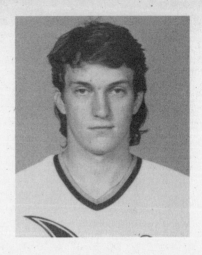

Career statistics:

GP	G	A	TP	PIM
743	153	356	509	554

1999-2000 statistics:

GP	G	A	TP	+/-	PIM	PP	SH	GW	GT	S	PCT
82	16	36	52	+17	46	6	0	1	0	210	7.6

2000-2001 statistics:

GP	G	A	TP	+/-	PIM	PP	SH	GW	GT	S	PCT
72	12	32	44	-25	71	4	2	2	0	145	8.3

2001-2002 statistics:

GP	G	A	TP	+/-	PIM	PP	SH	GW	GT	S	PCT
83	14	38	52	-7	58	3	0	1	0	172	8.1

2002-2003 statistics:

GP	G	A	TP	+/-	PIM	PP	SH	GW	GT	S	PCT
82	12	32	44	-6	56	6	0	3	0	137	8.8

LAST SEASON

Acquired from Florida with Lance Ward on January 30, 2003, for Matt Cullen, Pavel Trnka, and a fourth-round draft pick in 2003. Led team defensemen in points. Led team in average ice time (26:01). Tied for third on team in power-play goals. One of five Ducks to appear in all 82 games.

THE FINESSE GAME

Ozolinsh has good straightaway speed, but he can't make a lot of agile, pretty moves. Because he can't weave his way through a number of defenders, he has to power his way into open ice with the puck and drive the defenders back through intimidation. His speed often allows him to get back and help out on the odd-man rushes that he helps create, though Ozolinsh isn't always motivated to bother.

Ozolinsh is a pure "offenseman," but one who doesn't always recognize when it's safe to go. He sees only one traffic light, and it's stuck on green. He likes to start things by pressing in the neutral zone, where he will gamble and try to intercept cross-ice passes. His defense partner and the forwards will always have to be alert to guard against odd-man rushes back, because he doesn't recognize when it's a good time to be aggressive or when to back off.

He will start the breakout play with his smooth skating, then spring a teammate with a crisp pass. He can pass on his forehand or backhand, which is a good thing because he is all over the ice. He will follow up the play to create an odd-man rush, trail in for a drop pass, or drive to the net for a rebound.

Ozolinsh sometimes hangs on to the puck too long. He has a variety of shots, with his best being a one-timer from the off-side on the power play, where he slides into the back door on the weak side. He is not as effective when he works down low.

THE PHYSICAL GAME

Ozolinsh goes into areas of the ice where he gets hit a lot, but he is stronger than he looks. He is all business on the ice and pays the price to get the puck, but doesn't really have a taste for hitting, or the desire to keep his crease clean. He is undisciplined and will overstay his shift, which can force his defense partners to scramble. Anaheim kept a tighter rein on him in this department last season, and he responded by being +10 in 31 games after the trade.

THE INTANGIBLES

Ozolinsh remains a quirky, high-risk defenseman that we would not want on our side at crunch time.

PROJECTION

Ozolinsh will get his ice time, and will get his 45-50 points.

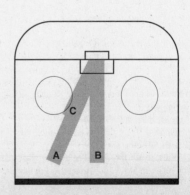

SAMI PAHLSSON

Yrs. of NHL service: 3
Born: Ornskoldsvik, Sweden; Dec. 17, 1977
Position: center
Height: 5-11
Weight: 212
Uniform no.: 26
Shoots: left

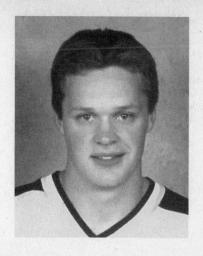

Career statistics:

GP	G	A	TP	PIM
190	14	30	44	64

2000-2001 statistics:

GP	G	A	TP	+/-	PIM	PP	SH	GW	GT	S	PCT
76	4	5	9	-14	20	1	1	1	0	59	6.8

2001-2002 statistics:

GP	G	A	TP	+/-	PIM	PP	SH	GW	GT	S	PCT
80	6	14	20	-16	26	1	1	0	0	99	6.1

2002-2003 statistics:

GP	G	A	TP	+/-	PIM	PP	SH	GW	GT	S	PCT
34	4	11	15	+10	18	0	1	2	0	28	14.3

LAST SEASON

Appeared in 13 games with Cincinnati (AHL), scoring 1-7 — 8 with 24 PIM. Missed one game due to coach's decision.

THE FINESSE GAME

Pahlsson has a solid, gritty all-around game. He is positionally sound and he is excellent on draws. His skating is NHL-caliber. He isn't breakaway-quick, but his anticipation will buy him a few steps every time.

Pahlsson has had trouble finding a role (he is now with his third organization). At his best, he is a third- or fourth-line energy guy who has some offensive upside. One of Pahlsson's weaknesses is that he is not going to be a big point-producer at the NHL level. When he isn't, he doesn't work harder to get out of the slump. He just sort of waits for the scoring touch to come back.

Pahlsson can forecheck with energy, force turnovers, and then has the ability to make something good happen with the puck by getting it to a team-mate. He isn't much of a finisher himself.

Pahlsson is a good penalty killer.

THE PHYSICAL GAME

Pahlsson is average height but solid, and he plays even bigger. He has a long reach; he digs in the corners and is tough. It's difficult to separate him from the puck. Pahlsson has a knack for taking ill-timed penalties.

THE INTANGIBLES

Pahlsson spent most of the season in the minors, but after his promotion he saw more playing time and re-sponsibility down the stretch and into the playoffs, which bodes well for him to earn a regular job this season. He was a restricted free agent after last season.

PROJECTION

Pahlsson has the potential to score 10 goals a season in a checking role. It doesn't sound like much, but he will make Anaheim a harder team to fight through — and that is no small compliment.

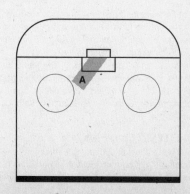

VACLAV PROSPAL

Yrs. of NHL service: 6
Born: Ceske-Budejovice, Czech Republic; Feb. 17, 1975
Position: center
Height: 6-2
Weight: 195
Uniform no.: 20
Shoots: left

Career statistics:

GP	G	A	TP	PIM
467	88	206	294	236

1999-2000 statistics:

GP	G	A	TP	+/-	PIM	PP	SH	GW	GT	S	PCT
79	22	33	55	-2	40	5	0	4	0	204	10.8

2000-2001 statistics:

GP	G	A	TP	+/-	PIM	PP	SH	GW	GT	S	PCT
74	5	24	29	-1	22	1	0	0	0	136	3.7

2001-2002 statistics:

GP	G	A	TP	+/-	PIM	PP	SH	GW	GT	S	PCT
81	18	37	55	-11	38	7	0	2	0	166	10.8

2002-2003 statistics:

GP	G	A	TP	+/-	PIM	PP	SH	GW	GT	S	PCT
80	22	57	79	+9	53	9	0	4	0	134	16.4

LAST SEASON

Signed as free agent by Anaheim. Led Lightning players in points. Tied for fourth in NHL in assists. Tied for team lead in assists. Career highs in points and assists. Second on team in plus-minus. Tied for second on team in shooting percentage. Third on team in goals. Tied for third on team in game-winning goals. Missed two games due to NHL suspension.

THE FINESSE GAME

Prospal has a power-play weapon, and it's not an overpowering shot: it's his ability to thread the puck through penalty killers to an open man. He has terrific hockey vision.

Prospal loves to score (his wrist shot and one-timers are accurate) and make plays. He had to learn to play without the puck, and he succeeded. His defensive game has also improved. His plus-minus was a career best. Prospal thinks the game well and is an unselfish player.

The only rap on Prospal is his skating ability, but it's NHL caliber and his view of the ice and his hockey sense compensate for any lack of pure speed. Prospal is very good on face-offs.

Prospal really seems to enjoy the game and is always one of the first players to hit the ice for practice. He has a very lively goal celebration dance which tends to tick off opponents (and his own goalies, in practice).

THE PHYSICAL GAME

Prospal is tall but lean and he loses an edge in one-on-one battles. Right now he gives the impression of being a little smaller than he is, but he's an eager player who will get involved. He got a little too involved when he cross-checked Ottawa's tough guy Chris Neil and was suspended by the league. Prospal is an emotional, high-energy player.

THE INTANGIBLES

Consistency, which had always eluded Prospal, found him last season. And just in time, too, since he became an unrestricted free agent and landed a big contract with the Mighty Ducks.

PROJECTION

Prospal is a legitimate 20-goal scorer. His point totals will always be heavily skewed towards assists.

STEVE RUCCHIN

Yrs. of NHL service: 9
Born: Thunder Bay, Ont.; July 4, 1971
Position: center
Height: 6-3
Weight: 211
Uniform no.: 20
Shoots: left

Career statistics:

GP	G	A	TP	PIM
534	133	256	389	128

1999-2000 statistics:

GP	G	A	TP	+/-	PIM	PP	SH	GW	GT	S	PCT
71	19	38	57	+9	16	10	0	2	2	131	14.5

2000-2001 statistics:

GP	G	A	TP	+/-	PIM	PP	SH	GW	GT	S	PCT
16	3	5	8	-5	0	2	0	0	0	19	15.8

2001-2002 statistics:

GP	G	A	TP	+/-	PIM	PP	SH	GW	GT	S	PCT
38	7	16	23	-3	6	4	0	1	0	57	12.3

2002-2003 statistics:

GP	G	A	TP	+/-	PIM	PP	SH	GW	GT	S	PCT
82	20	38	58	-14	12	6	1	4	0	194	10.3

LAST SEASON

Finalist for 2003 Masterton Trophy. Second on team in assists. Third on team in goals, points, and shots. Tied for third on team in power-play goals and game-winning goals. One of five Ducks to appear in all 82 games.

THE FINESSE GAME

Healthy for the first time in three seasons, Rucchin was one of the key reasons (along with the astounding goaltending of J-S Giguere) why the Ducks made it into the playoffs at all, let alone all the way to the Stanley Cup Finals.

Rucchin is a checking center whose finesse skills were so honed in the days when he was Anaheim's No. 1 center that he doesn't look out of place in a more offensive role. It all starts with his best asset, his size, along with his above-average skating and elite-level smarts which make him Anaheim's best all-around player. He grinds and digs the puck off the wall, and has the vision and the passing skills to find a breaking winger. He is patient and protects the puck well.

Rucchin is a bear on draws, and he is especially focused on a defensive-zone face-off. He can win a draw outright, or if he fails, tie up the opposing center to allow his teammates to get to the puck first.

THE PHYSICAL GAME

Rucchin is a defensive forward in a power forward's body. He can be a real force. He's strong and balanced, willing to forecheck hard and fight for the puck along the boards and in the corners. When he wins the puck, he's able to create a smart play with it. He has a long reach for holding off defenders and working the

puck one-handed, or reaching in defensively to knock the puck away from an attacker. He often matches up against other teams' big centers, and more often than not, shuts them down.

THE INTANGIBLES

Rucchin is physically and mentally tough. He not only overcame his own serious injuries, but coped with the death of his brother in the past year. He is a gamer, a leader, and one of the most intelligent and respected players in the NHL. Rucchin should be a Selke Trophy candidate.

PROJECTION

We doubted Rucchin's ability to bounce back from injuries and he showed us a thing or two. What we do expect this season, however, is a team-wide letdown akin to what Carolina suffered in 2002-03. Accordingly, we would expect Rucchin's totals to slump slightly to the 50-point range.

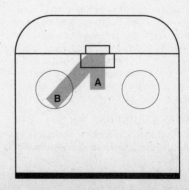

RUSLAN SALEI

Yrs. of NHL service: 7
Born: Minsk, Belarus; Nov. 2, 1974
Position: left defense
Height: 6-1
Weight: 205
Uniform no.: 24
Shoots: left

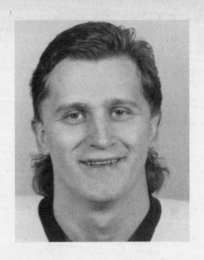

Career statistics:

GP	G	A	TP	PIM
434	21	50	71	511

1999-2000 statistics:

GP	G	A	TP	+/-	PIM	PP	SH	GW	GT	S	PCT
71	5	5	10	+3	94	1	0	0	0	116	4.3

2000-2001 statistics:

GP	G	A	TP	+/-	PIM	PP	SH	GW	GT	S	PCT
50	1	5	6	-14	70	0	0	0	0	73	1.4

2001-2002 statistics:

GP	G	A	TP	+/-	PIM	PP	SH	GW	GT	S	PCT
82	4	7	11	-10	97	0	0	1	0	96	4.2

2002-2003 statistics:

GP	G	A	TP	+/-	PIM	PP	SH	GW	GT	S	PCT
61	4	8	12	+2	78	0	0	0	0	93	4.3

PROJECTION

Salei will score in the 20-point range and can be expected to post healthy PIM totals.

LAST SEASON

Third on team in penalty minutes. Missed 21 games with back injuries.

THE FINESSE GAME

Salei is a fairly agile skater but he doesn't have great breakaway speed. He skates well backwards, is mobile, and is not easy to beat one-on-one.

Salei's defensive reads are very good, and he can kill penalties. He can handle some second-unit power-play time, although he lacks great offensive instincts. Salei moves the puck well and has an NHL-caliber point shot. He shoots well off the pass and his shots are high velocity.

Salei has become a much more disciplined player in recent years. He used to be something of a head-hunter, but he suffered a concussion of his own a few seasons ago and that seems to have settled him down.

THE PHYSICAL GAME

Salei, who made Mike Modano's list of dirtiest NHL players, has managed to get through two seasons without being suspended. Salei is mature, solidly built, and initiates a lot of contact. He is not afraid to hit anyone. He has a bit of a nasty streak that results in some cheap hits, but he can play it hard and clean, too. Salei will sometimes start running around and lose track of his man.

THE INTANGIBLES

Salei will probably again be a top-four defenseman, although the development of Kurt Sauer could cut into his ice time.

KURT SAUER

Yrs. of NHL service: 1
Born: St. Cloud, Minn.; Jan. 16, 1981
Position: left defense
Height: 6-4
Weight: 225
Uniform no.: 34
Shoots: left

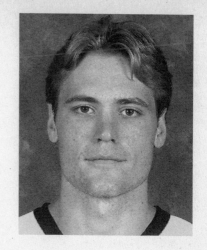

Career statistics:

GP	G	A	TP	PIM
80	1	2	3	74

2002-2003 statistics:

GP	G	A	TP	+/-	PIM	PP	SH	GW	GT	S	PCT
80	1	2	3	-23	74	0	0	0	0	50	2.0

LAST SEASON

First NHL season. Worst plus-minus on team. Missed two games due to personal reasons.

THE FINESSE GAME

Sauer is a stay-at-home defenseman and a punishing checker. He is also a project.

Sauer's reads and reactions are tested on a nightly basis and they are the areas where he needs the most work. Sauer is an intelligent player and playing for a teaching coach like Mike Babcock will prove to be a boon to his career. After the Mighty Ducks acquired Sandis Ozolinsh, Sauer became the partner for the high-risk forward.

Sauer's offensive contributions will be minimal. Although he has a decent slap shot, he is more likely to start backing out of the zone in a defensive mode than make a risky play.

He is developing into a sound penalty-killer. He pairs with Keith Carney on the penalty kill.

THE PHYSICAL GAME

Sauer is a big, strong specimen and he loves the physical element of the game. He initiates and he isn't intimdated by the name on the back of the sweater. He is fit and can handle a lot of minutes. In fact, he thrives on the workload.

THE INTANGIBLES

Sauer was drafted 88th overall in the 2000 draft but was never signed by Colorado and became a free agent. It's one of the few talent evaluation errors the Avs have made.

PROJECTION

We figure Sauer to be a top-four defenseman again for Anaheim this season. We would expect more than three points next season (he scored four in 20 playoff games), but he's not going to be in a scoring race with Al MacInnis.

PETR SYKORA

Yrs. of NHL service: 8
Born: Plzen, Czech Republic; Nov. 19, 1976
Position: right wing
Height: 6-0
Weight: 190
Uniform no.: 39
Shoots: left

Career statistics:

GP	G	A	TP	PIM
527	179	230	409	206

1999-2000 statistics:

GP	G	A	TP	+/-	PIM	PP	SH	GW	GT	S	PCT
79	25	43	68	+24	26	5	1	4	0	222	11.3

2000-2001 statistics:

GP	G	A	TP	+/-	PIM	PP	SH	GW	GT	S	PCT
73	35	46	81	+36	32	9	2	3	0	249	14.1

2001-2002 statistics:

GP	G	A	TP	+/-	PIM	PP	SH	GW	GT	S	PCT
73	21	27	48	+12	44	4	0	4	0	194	10.8

2002-2003 statistics:

GP	G	A	TP	+/-	PIM	PP	SH	GW	GT	S	PCT
82	34	25	59	-7	24	15	1	5	1	299	11.4

LAST SEASON

Tied for fourth in NHL in shots. Tied for sixth in NHL in power-play goals. Led team in goals, power-play goals, and shots. Tied for team lead in game-winning goals. Second on team in points and shooting percentage. Career high in goals. One of five Ducks to appear in all 82 games.

THE FINESSE GAME

Sykora has excellent hands in-tight, for passing or shooting. He defies the usual European stereotype of the reluctant shooter, because he's a goal-scorer, though he will go into streaks where he will pass up a low-percentage shot to work for a better one. His wrist shot is excellent. He also has adequate snap and slap shots. He was the best power-play sniper on Anaheim last season.

There are only a few things Sykora doesn't do well technically, but what really sets him apart is his intelligence. Playing against men as a 17-year-old in the IHL in 1994-95 obviously spurred his development, and taught him how to survive as a smaller player in the mean NHL. Sykora is a creative player, and dares to do things that other players wouldn't try.

Sykora is a fine skater with a fluid stride, and he accelerates in a few steps. He is quick on a straightaway, with or without the puck, and is also agile in his turns. He picks his way through traffic well, and would rather try to outfox a defender and take the shortest path to the net than drive wide.

He sees the ice well and is a heads-up passer with a great touch. His defensive play has improved, though he stills blows the occasional checking assignment, which always seems to occur at a crucial point. He can kill penalties because of his ability to read the play and his quickness.

THE PHYSICAL GAME

Sykora can't muck in the corners or along the boards, but don't expect him to be intimidated. He'll battle for the puck behind or in front of the net, but he is simply not a big, or mean, player. He is strong for his size and his skating provides him with good balance. His work ethic is strong.

THE INTANGIBLES

Sykora felt chafed for years under New Jersey's checking system. Anaheim's wasn't exactly footloose, but playing with a winger like Paul Kariya jazzed up Sykora's game like never before. Just in time, too, since he became a restricted free agent after the season.

PROJECTION

Sykora was shaken by the trade and started off slowly, but by the end of the season you could have sworn he'd been born in a pond. His production wasn't quite up to where we'd like to see it. Sykora has 70-point potential.

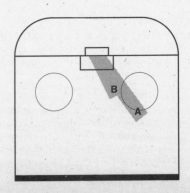

VITALY VISHNEVSKI

Yrs. of NHL service: 4
Born: Kharkov, Ukraine; Mar. 18, 1980
Position: left defense
Height: 6-2
Weight: 206
Uniform no.: 5
Shoots: left

Career statistics:

GP	G	A	TP	PIM
261	4	20	24	261

1999-2000 statistics:

GP	G	A	TP	+/-	PIM	PP	SH	GW	GT	S	PCT
31	1	1	2	0	26	1	0	0	0	17	5.9

2000-2001 statistics:

GP	G	A	TP	+/-	PIM	PP	SH	GW	GT	S	PCT
76	1	10	11	-1	99	0	0	0	0	49	2.0

2001-2002 statistics:

GP	G	A	TP	+/-	PIM	PP	SH	GW	GT	S	PCT
74	0	3	3	-10	60	0	0	0	0	54	0.0

2002-2003 statistics:

GP	G	A	TP	+/-	PIM	PP	SH	GW	GT	S	PCT
80	2	6	8	-8	76	0	1	0	0	65	3.1

LAST SEASON

Missed two games due to coach's decision.

THE FINESSE GAME

Vishnevski is an excellent skater with a long, powerful stride and good straightaway speed. He has good mobility and good balance. He has no trouble keeping pace with NHL-caliber skaters.

He has good size and strength, and plays a power game. Vishnevski is a warrior around the crease and along the wall.

Vishnevski has to improve his defensive reads. He moves the puck extremely well and is poised and composed under pressure. He doesn't have much offensive upside — he just wants to get the puck out of his zone and knock the stuffing out of anyone who tries to skate back in with it. Opponents are going to be hurried into a lot of quick decisions when they come down his side of the ice.

THE PHYSICAL GAME

A solid 200 pounds, Vishnevski is a mean hitter. Opponents hate him. He hits hard and he competes hard. He makes his teammates play stronger and braver around him. He plays better with better players and is a nice fit with a high-risk offensive defenseman. He is an even better skater than Scott Stevens, so expect to see a lot of West Coast versions of those Stevens-style body bombs. He is confident in his checking ability and seeks out big hits at the blueline and in the neutral zone. He will hit anyone, regardless of name, number, or salary rank. He is a bigger Darius Kasparaitis, and really gets under people's skin.

THE INTANGIBLES

Vishnevski is only 23, and still needs intensive coaching. He took a step backwards in his progress last season and lost playing time to Kurt Sauer and Niclas Havelid. Anaheim might use him as trade bait since a lot of teams have been lusting after him, plus he was a restricted free agent after last season.

PROJECTION

Vishnevski remains a project but one worth investing in. His point totals will barely break into double digits, but he should have triple-digit PIM.

ATLANTA THRASHERS

Players' Statistics 2001-2002

POS.	NO.	PLAYER	GP	G	A	PTS	+/-	PIM	PP	SH	GW	GT	S	PCT
R	15	DANY HEATLEY	77	41	48	89	-8	58	19	1	6		252	16.3
L	13	VYACHESLAV KOZLOV	79	21	49	70	-10	66	9	1	2		185	11.4
L	17	ILYA KOVALCHUK	81	38	29	67	-24	57	9		3		257	14.8
C	9	MARC SAVARD	67	17	33	50	-14	85	6		4		148	11.5
C	27	PATRIK STEFAN	71	13	21	34	-10	12	3		2	1	96	13.5
D	38	YANNICK TREMBLAY	75	8	22	30	-27	32	5		1		151	5.3
L	19	SHAWN MCEACHERN	46	10	16	26	-27	28	4	1	1		120	8.3
C	12	TONY HRKAC	80	9	17	26	-16	14	2		2		86	10.5
D	8	FRANTISEK KABERLE	79	7	19	26	-19	32	3	1	2		105	6.7
D	25	ANDY SUTTON	53	3	18	21	-8	114	1	1			65	4.6
L	23	LUBOS BARTECKO	37	7	9	16	3	8			1		54	13.0
D	36	DANIEL TJARNQVIST	75	3	12	15	-20	26	1				65	4.6
R	18	BRAD TAPPER	35	10	4	14	2	23	1		3	1	68	14.7
C	37	*DAN SNYDER	36	10	4	14	-4	34		1	1	1	41	24.4
D	4	CHRIS TAMER	72	1	9	10	-10	118					53	1.9
L	16	JEFF COWAN	66	3	5	8	-15	115					52	5.8
C	39	PER SVARTVADET	62	1	7	8	-11	8					47	2.1
C	3	*MARK HARTIGAN	23	5	2	7	-8	6	1				25	20.0
R	20	JEFF ODGERS	74	2	4	6	-13	171			1		48	4.2
L	7	CHRIS HERPERGER	27	4	1	5	-11	7					26	15.4
C	22	*KAMIL PIROS	3	3	2	5	4	2			1		8	37.5
D	43	*MIKE WEAVER	40		5	5	-5	20					21	
D	29	*KIRILL SAFRONOV	32	2	2	4	-10	14					21	9.5
L	10	YURI BUTSAYEV	16	2		2	-5	8					21	9.5
D	50	*JOE DIPENTA	3	1	1	2	3						2	50.0
D	2	*GARNET EXELBY	15		2	2	0	41					9	
R	6	*FRANCIS LESSARD	18		2	2	1	61					7	
L	45	*BENJAMIN SIMON	10		1	1	0	9					7	
R	11	JEAN-PIERRE VIGIER	13				-13	4					21	
C	28	*JEFF FARKAS	3				-1						5	
L	41	*SIMON GAMACHE	2				-1	2					3	
L	49	*ZDENEK BLATNY	4				-1						2	
D	47	*KURTIS FOSTER	2				-2						1	
D	44	UWE KRUPP	4				-2	10					1	
G	34	BYRON DAFOE	17				0							
D	28	TODD REIRDEN					0							
G	33	MILAN HNILICKA	21				0	2						
G	35	FREDERIC CASSIVI	2				0							
G	31	PASI NURMINEN	52				0	4						

GP = games played; G = goals; A = assists; PTS = points; +/- = goals-for minus goals-against while player is on ice; PIM = penalties in minutes; PP = power-play goals; SH = shorthanded goals; GW = game-winning goals; GT = game-tying goals; S = no. of shots; PCT = percentage of goals to shots; * = rookie

GARNET EXELBY

Yrs. of NHL service: 0
Born: Craik, Sask.; Aug. 16, 1981
Position: left defense
Height: 6-1
Weight: 210
Uniform no.: 2
Shoots: left

Career statistics:

GP	G	A	TP	PIM
15	0	2	2	41

2002-2003 statistics:

GP	G	A	TP	+/-	PIM	PP	SH	GW	GT	S	PCT
15	0	2	2	0	41	0	0	0	0	9	0.0

LAST SEASON

Will be entering first full NHL season. Appeared in 53 games for Chicago (AHL), scoring 3-6 — 9 with 140 PIM.

THE FINESSE GAME

Exelby is a stay-at-home defenseman. He prowls the front of his net and plows out the crease. Exelby takes pride in knowing he can be an intimidating factor. He is able to scare some attackers into giving up the puck.

Exelby needs to improve his own puck skills to take better advantage of opponents' mistakes. His skills are adequate, though, and his skating is NHL caliber, but not much better than that.

Exelby will become a mainstay on the power play. He is smart positionally. He will block shots willingly. He is really intense in a crunch-time situation.

THE PHYSICAL GAME

With his abrasive, physical style, Exelby is bound to become a fan favorite. He'll be "in" with his teammates, too, since he is quick to stand up for them. He will make opponents pay a price if they try to head-hunt Dany Heatley or Ilya Kovalchuk. Exelby is sometimes too eager to go hunting for hits himself and he takes himself out of position. His enthusiasm will have to be reined in a little. Exelby will use his stick too freely and takes bad penalties because of that.

Exelby missed some playing time in the minors because of a broken finger, which prevented him from playing in the AHL All-Star Game. He is a fit athlete and can handle a lot of minutes. Coach Bob Hartley has compared him to Adam Foote.

THE INTANGIBLES

The Thrashers were 9-4-1-1 with Exelby in the lineup after his March promotion from the minors. That's called making an impact.

PROJECTION

The way has been paved for Exelby to earn a starting job with the Thrashers this season. He is likely to be a top-four defenseman. His point totals will be small. His PIM totals will be large.

DANY HEATLEY

Yrs. of NHL service: 2
Born: Freiburg, Germany; Jan. 21, 1981
Position: right wing
Height: 6-3
Weight: 210
Uniform no.: 15
Shoots: left

Career statistics:

GP	G	A	TP	PIM
159	67	89	156	114

2001-2002 statistics:

GP	G	A	TP	+/-	PIM	PP	SH	GW	GT	S	PCT
82	26	41	67	-19	56	7	0	4	0	202	12.9

2002-2003 statistics:

GP	G	A	TP	+/-	PIM	PP	SH	GW	GT	S	PCT
77	41	48	89	-8	58	19	1	6	0	252	16.3

LAST SEASON

Third in NHL in power-play goals. Sixth in NHL in goals. Ninth in NHL in points. Led team in average ice time (21:57), goals, points, power-play goals, game-winning goals, and shooting percentage. Second on team in assists and shots. Missed five games with groin injury.

THE FINESSE GAME

A second-year player is simply not supposed to have his name up there in the stats with Mario Lemieux and Mike Modano. Tell that to Heatley, who followed up his 2002 Calder Trophy campaign with an unbelievable sophomore season.

Heatley is not a very fast or smooth skater, and he probably has just enough speed to qualify as NHL-caliber, but he makes it work. His chief assets are his willingness to shoot and his offensive instincts. He has a big point shot and is already a first-unit power-play man and a player who can take charge. In fact, he can dominate.

Heatley graduated to the NHL in a tough spot. The Thrashers didn't provide much support, so Heatley had to do everything himself. His all-around game is very advanced for a young player.

Heatley will produce even more if Atlanta can find a bona fide No. 1 center for him. He is a pure goal-scorer, with an assortment of shots. He has learned to go get the puck and has to do a lot of the work himself. Just wait 'til he gets someone to get the puck to him.

THE PHYSICAL GAME

Heatley is rugged and likes to drive to the net. He has worked hard to improve his strength and conditioning. He sure doesn't look like a boy among men.

THE INTANGIBLES

One really splendid thing about Heatley is that even with all his individual accolades, he hates losing. He won't just get used to it in Atlanta. He's going to try to change the culture. Heatley was named MVP at the NHL All-Star Game with a four-goal performance.

PROJECTION

If Atlanta gets the least bit competitive this season, Heatley will be a Hart Trophy candidate. He could flirt with 100 points. He is worth the price of admission.

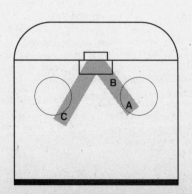

ILYA KOVALCHUK

Yrs. of NHL service: 2
Born: Tver, Russia; Apr. 15, 1983
Position: left wing
Height: 6-2
Weight: 220
Uniform no.: 17
Shoots: right

Career statistics:

GP	G	A	TP	PIM
146	67	51	118	85

2001-2002 statistics:

GP	G	A	TP	+/-	PIM	PP	SH	GW	GT	S	PCT
65	29	22	51	-19	28	7	0	4	1	184	15.8

2002-2003 statistics:

GP	G	A	TP	+/-	PIM	PP	SH	GW	GT	S	PCT
81	38	29	67	-24	57	9	0	3	0	257	14.8

LAST SEASON

Led team in shots. Second on team in goals and shooting percentage. Tied for second on team in power-play goals. Third on team in points. Tied for third on team in game-winning goals. Missed one game due to coach's decision.

THE FINESSE GAME

Kovalchuk is an explosive skater, a dynamic scorer and, did we mention, a gamebreaker?

Every offensive skill he possesses is world-class. Every time the puck is on his stick, he can make things happen. He has a very high confidence in his shot. Like the great snipers, he will shoot from angles that seem bizarre, and will usually get the shot on net. His release is quick, his selection varied, his aim accurate, his velocity rapid.

Kovalchuk's speed is intimidating. Defenders are forced to back off, and that only opens up more ice for him. He excels on the power play and in four-on-four, and will become a penalty killer and shorthanded threat. Actually, it seems like the other team is shorthanded whenever he's on the ice.

Kovalchuk's defensive play is nonexistent. That is what drives his coaches crazy.

THE PHYSICAL GAME

This kid's got attitude and an edge. He plays with a swagger. He's like that off the ice, too, which isn't exactly great news for his teammates. He's moody and he's not the most lovable guy on the team. They'll put up with him as long as he scores.

THE INTANGIBLES

Think of a young Pavel Bure, with just a little more size and a lot more snarl. We could stand for him to lose some of the selfishness, especially when it comes to taking bad retaliation penalties just because he feels like it.

PROJECTION

Kovalchuk will be a 60-goal scorer but the Thrashers are still lacking in centers who can help him get there, so we'd settle for a 40-goal season.

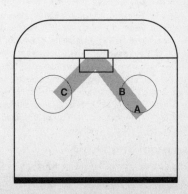

VYACHESLAV KOZLOV

Yrs. of NHL service: 10
Born: Voskresensk, Russia; May 3, 1972
Position: left wing
Height: 5-10
Weight: 185
Uniform no.: 13
Shoots: left

Career statistics:

GP	G	A	TP	PIM
724	232	275	507	458

1999-2000 statistics:

GP	G	A	TP	+/-	PIM	PP	SH	GW	GT	S	PCT
72	18	18	36	+11	28	4	0	3	0	165	10.9

2000-2001 statistics:

GP	G	A	TP	+/-	PIM	PP	SH	GW	GT	S	PCT
72	20	18	38	+9	30	4	0	5	1	187	10.7

2001-2002 statistics:

GP	G	A	TP	+/-	PIM	PP	SH	GW	GT	S	PCT
38	9	13	22	0	16	3	0	1	1	68	13.2

2002-2003 statistics:

GP	G	A	TP	+/-	PIM	PP	SH	GW	GT	S	PCT
79	21	49	70	-10	66	9	1	2	0	185	11.4

LAST SEASON

Led Thrashers in assists with career high. Second on team in points. Tied for second on team in power-play goals. Third on team in goals and shots. Missed three games due to NHL suspension.

THE FINESSE GAME

Kozlov has a very quick getaway step that allows him to jump into holes and openings. His darting style makes it impossible for defenders to chase him and easy for them to lose him.

Offensively, he can play as freewheeling as the team wants. He seems to materialize at the right place and at the right time. He can split the defense if it plays him too close, or drive the defense back with his speed and use the open ice to find a teammate. He has great control of the puck at high speed and plays an excellent transition game. Kozlov does not have to be coaxed into shooting, and he has a quick release — generally to the top corners of the net.

That said, there are also times when Kozlov can be frustrating to watch. He will hold the puck past the point when he either should make a play with it or make a pass. He then either loses control of it or takes himself to lesser ice. The reasonable speculation is that by holding the puck he is buying time for teammates to break into open ice; other times, he simply appears incapable of making a decision about what to do or he is trying to make the perfect play instead of a good-enough play more quickly.

THE PHYSICAL GAME

Just as a defender comes to hit him, Kozlov gets rid of the puck. Usually it goes to a teammate; sometimes it simply goes up for grabs. It would be easy to say Kozlov is like a quarterback who gets rid of the ball rather than getting sacked. More likely, he's taking the hit to create space for someone else by allowing the defender to take himself — and Kozlov — out of the play. Kozlov is not tall but he is solidly built. He's got a little mean streak, as proven by his suspension (for abuse of an official).

THE INTANGIBLES

Kozlov proved to be a good fit as the left wing on the Dany Heatley line with Atlanta. He was an unrestricted free agent after the season.

PROJECTION

Kozlov should be a 30-goal scorer if he ends up in as sweet a spot as he did last season.

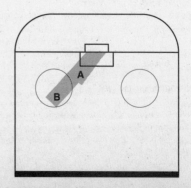

KARI LEHTONEN

Yrs. of NHL service: 0
Born: Helsinki, Finland; Nov. 16, 1983
Position: goaltender
Height: 6-3
Weight: 190
Uniform no.: n.a.
Catches: left

Career statistics:

GP	MIN	GA	SO	GAA	A	PIM
68	3877	124	9	1.92	n.a.	24

2001-2002 European statistics:

GP	MIN	GAA	W	L	T	SO	GA	S	SAPCT	PIM
23	1242	1.79	13	5	3	4	37	n.a.	n.a.	2

2002-2003 statistics:

GP	MIN	GAA	W	L	T	SO	GA	S	SAPCT	PIM
45	2635	1.98	23	14	6	5	87	n.a.	n.a.	22

LAST SEASON

Will be entering first NHL season. Drafted second overall in 2002.

THE PHYSICAL GAME

Lehtonen plays a hybrid stand-up/butterfly style and he has a good technical base. He is a good skater with quick feet for kick and pad saves, and a quick glove. If he goes down, Lehtonen recovers quickly for the rebound. He considers Patrick Roy the model for NHL goalies. Lehtonen, like Roy, keeps his torso upright when he goes to his knees to stop shots. Lehtonen, though, plays more stand-up than Roy did, and his style may compare more to that of Martin Brodeur, minus Brodeur's wizardry as a puckhandler. Lehtonen has good size and he knows how to use it. He doesn't flop around or make easy saves look hard. He gives the shooter very little net.

Lehtonen has excellent reflexes and reads plays well, although it will understandably take him time to adjust to North American rinks and the pace of the pro game. He will especially need to be able to find the puck through traffic.

Lehtonen is an average puckhandler. He hasn't had to use his stick much to break up plays around the net. It would surely be a plus if he could do so, but let's let him learn his angles first.

Lehtonen is tall but he's reedy. He is built along athletic lines, racy like a Thoroughbred. Goalies can't put on too much weight too soon without having the gain affect their playing style. Lehtonen will have to make sure he can handle the pace of an NHL game and the grind of a long season.

THE MENTAL GAME

Lehtonen is very mature for a young player. He's been able to rise to any challenge. He is very composed. His winning attitude carries over to his teammates. He seldom looks flustered, even under pressure.

THE INTANGIBLES

Atlanta would like to rush Lehtonen right into goal (wouldn't you, if your options were Pasi Nurminen, Milan Hnilicka, and Byron Dafoe?). If he isn't ready, though, he could play the first half in the minors.

PROJECTION

Lehtonen is awfully young to take on a starting role for a bad team, but the Thrashers need him awfully bad. If he plays a full season, 20 wins would be a reasonable start.

SHAWN MCEACHERN

Yrs. of NHL service: 11
Born: Waltham, Mass.; Feb. 28, 1969
Position: center / left wing
Height: 5-11
Weight: 200
Uniform no.: 19
Shoots: left

Career statistics:

GP	G	A	TP	PIM
801	237	279	516	408

1999-2000 statistics:

GP	G	A	TP	+/-	PIM	PP	SH	GW	GT	S	PCT
69	29	22	51	+2	24	10	0	4	1	219	13.2

2000-2001 statistics:

GP	G	A	TP	+/-	PIM	PP	SH	GW	GT	S	PCT
82	32	40	72	+10	62	9	0	1	1	231	13.9

2001-2002 statistics:

GP	G	A	TP	+/-	PIM	PP	SH	GW	GT	S	PCT
80	15	31	46	+9	52	5	0	3	0	196	7.7

2002-2003 statistics:

GP	G	A	TP	+/-	PIM	PP	SH	GW	GT	S	PCT
46	10	16	26	-27	28	4	1	1	0	120	8.3

LAST SEASON

Tied for worst plus-minus on team. Missed 36 games with groin and back injuries.

THE FINESSE GAME

McEachern can shift speeds and direction smoothly without losing control of the puck. He can play both left wing and center, but he is better as a winger because he doesn't use his linemates as well as a center should. An accurate shooter with a hard wrister, McEachern has a quick release on his slap shot, which he lets go after using his outside speed. He is strong on face-offs and is a smart penalty killer who pressures the puck carrier.

McEachern isn't overly creative. He doesn't have to be. His dangerous acceleration is what gives him his edge. He suffers from some tunnel vision, which negates some of the advantage of his speed. He skates with his head down, looking at the ice instead of the play around him. He is strong and fast, with straight-away speed, but he tends to expend his energy almost carelessly and has to take short shifts.

At the start of his career, McEachern looked like he was going to be one of those speedy third-line checking types without much finish. Instead, he has worked hard to polish his game and likes his role as a scorer and go-to guy. Many of his goals result from beating the defenders to loose pucks around the net. He has decent hands in-tight.

THE PHYSICAL GAME

Generally an open-ice player, McEachern will also pursue the puck with some diligence in the attacking zone. He is light, and although he can sometimes build up momentum with his speed for a solid bump, he loses most of the close-in battles for the puck. He's a yapper; many nights he can distract opponents, who want to rip his head off. McEachern has some quiet grit and plays through injuries, although he couldn't grit it out through the serious hurts that ended his season prematurely last year.

THE INTANGIBLES

McEachern is a versatile player who can fill a lot of roles with his speed. He was named Atlanta's captain upon his arrival in 2002.

PROJECTION

McEachern was on a 50-point pace before the injury.

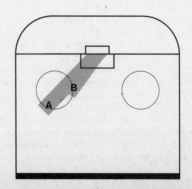

KIRILL SAFRONOV

Yrs. of NHL service: 1
Born: St. Petersburg, Russia; Feb. 26, 1981
Position: left defense
Height: 6-1
Weight: 210
Uniform no.: 29
Shoots: left

Career statistics:

GP	G	A	TP	PIM
35	2	2	4	16

2001-2002 statistics:

GP	G	A	TP	+/-	PIM	PP	SH	GW	GT	S	PCT
3	0	0	0	-5	2	0	0	0	0	2	0.0

2002-2003 statistics:

GP	G	A	TP	+/-	PIM	PP	SH	GW	GT	S	PCT
32	2	2	4	-10	14	0	0	0	0	21	9.5

LAST SEASON

First NHL season. Missed five games due to coach's decision. Appeared in 44 games with Chicago (AHL), scoring 4-15 — 19 with 29 PIM.

THE FINESSE GAME

A former first-round draft pick of the Phoenix Coyotes in 1999, it has taken time for Safronov's game to mature.

Safronov has developed into a two-way defenseman. He started off by concentrating in his own end of the ice, and it looked like he would develop into strictly a stay-at-home type, but he has some offensive upside. He plays a simple, low-risk game in the defensive zone. Intelligent and reliable, he is a strong and agile skater.

Safronov has good offensive instincts. He has a decent point shot. He is a sharp passer and will join the rush although not lead it. He could probably handle second-unit power-play time next season.

Safronov can be a little shaky mentally and may need some coddling by the coaching staff or a mentor teammate. He tends to get down on himself after a bad shift or a bad game.

THE PHYSICAL GAME

The Russian defenseman played junior hockey in Canada and has a taste for the North American style of play. He is not aggressive, but he is strong and rugged.

THE INTANGIBLES

Safronov was considered by some scouts to be the best defense prospect of his draft year. The defenseman class of 1999 included 2003 Calder Trophy winner Barrett Jackman.

PROJECTION

Safronov has the goods to become a top-four defenseman for Atlanta this season and can score in the 15-point range. We expect him to be conservative at the outset but his point totals will escalate as he becomes more relaxed.

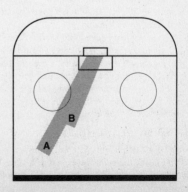

MARC SAVARD

Yrs. of NHL service: 6
Born: Ottawa, Ont.; July 17, 1977
Position: center
Height: 5-10
Weight: 185
Uniform no.: 9
Shoots: left

Career statistics:

GP	G	A	TP	PIM
376	86	166	252	277

1999-2000 statistics:

GP	G	A	TP	+/-	PIM	PP	SH	GW	GT	S	PCT
78	22	31	53	-2	56	4	0	3	1	184	12.0

2000-2001 statistics:

GP	G	A	TP	+/-	PIM	PP	SH	GW	GT	S	PCT
77	23	42	65	-12	46	10	1	5	2	197	11.7

2001-2002 statistics:

GP	G	A	TP	+/-	PIM	PP	SH	GW	GT	S	PCT
56	14	19	33	-18	48	7	0	3	1	140	10.0

2002-2003 statistics:

GP	G	A	TP	+/-	PIM	PP	SH	GW	GT	S	PCT
67	17	33	50	-14	85	6	0	4	0	148	11.5

LAST SEASON

Acquired from Calgary for Ruslan Zainullin on November 15, 2002. Second on team in game-winning goals. Third on team in assists and shooting percentage. Missed five games with groin injury. Missed one game with flu.

THE FINESSE GAME

Savard's size and skating will prevent him from ever playing a dominating game, but he clicked with Atlanta's budding superstar Dany Heatley, and that covered up for many flaws in Savard's game.

He is an intelligent playmaker whose points will always be heavier in assists than goals. He doesn't have a very quick or accurate shot. Savard really has a knack for delivering the puck to a guy who can do something dangerous with it, instead of passing just because he's tired of carrying it. He possesses good vision and instincts for the power play. A left-handed shot, he favors the attacking right-wing corner/half-boards for his "office." He will not even try one-on-one moves. He's a distributor.

Savard is not very quick off the mark and his speed is about average. He is pretty sturdy, well-balanced and strong on his skates, which makes his dives all the more comical. He is one of the most blatant actors in the game and draws a huge share of penalties. It's a wonder NHL referees haven't caught on to his act, because he's really terrible at it.

THE PHYSICAL GAME

Savard won't touch a soul with an intentional, clean hit. He is sneaky mean, however, and if he can, he'll pay you back. He is small and is targeted by a lot of bigger guys, so that's how he has learned to defend himself. He absorbs some pretty stiff hits without being the least bit intimidated. He is actually quite strong for his size. His defensive play will be limited to stick-checking.

THE INTANGIBLES

Savard was dealt, as we anticipated last season, but could hardly have ended in a better spot than being Heatley's setup man. It's a role tailor-made for him. Savard scored 16-31 — 47 in 57 games with Atlanta. He was a restricted free agent after the season.

PROJECTION

If Savard doesn't miss training camp or otherwise lose playing time in a prolonged contract dispute, and if he plays with Heatley again, career numbers are definitely in store, maybe in the 75-point range.

PATRIK STEFAN

Yrs. of NHL service: 4
Born: Pribham, Czech Republic; Sept. 16, 1980
Position: center
Height: 6-3
Weight: 205
Uniform no.: 27
Shoots: left

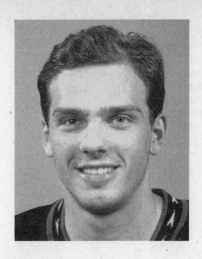

Career statistics:

GP	G	A	TP	PIM
268	35	78	113	86

1999-2000 statistics:

GP	G	A	TP	+/-	PIM	PP	SH	GW	GT	S	PCT
72	5	20	25	-20	30	1	0	0	0	117	4.3

2000-2001 statistics:

GP	G	A	TP	+/-	PIM	PP	SH	GW	GT	S	PCT
66	10	21	31	-3	22	0	0	1	0	93	10.8

2001-2002 statistics:

GP	G	A	TP	+/-	PIM	PP	SH	GW	GT	S	PCT
59	7	16	23	-4	22	0	1	0	0	67	10.4

2002-2003 statistics:

GP	G	A	TP	+/-	PIM	PP	SH	GW	GT	S	PCT
71	13	21	34	-10	12	3	0	2	1	96	13.5

PROJECTION

Stefan is still struggling to put his game together after suffering serious injuries, including concussions and a broken jaw, in his first three NHL seasons. His 13 goals were a career high last season. He is a low pool pick with a realistic estimate of no more than 20 goals.

LAST SEASON

Career highs in goals and points. Missed 11 games with fractured ankle.

THE FINESSE GAME

Every so often, Stefan has one of those special nights that remind everyone of his abilities. He is a tall skater whose stance is upright, allowing him to keep his head up to see all of the ice and all of his options. He uses a long stick for a long reach to beat defenders one-on-one in open ice. He loves to carry the puck and has drawn comparisons to Jaromir Jagr for his end-to-end ability.

Stefan needs to use his speed more and take the shortest route to the net on an odd-man rush, instead of fanning himself to the outside. Even if he doesn't score, he can draw the attention of the goalie and defensemen and create room for his linemates.

An excellent passer who can thread a puck through a crowd, he shoots well forehand and backhand and isn't shy about using his shot. He is good on draws and can run a power play.

THE PHYSICAL GAME

Stefan needs to use his body better. His history of injuries may lead to his lack of interest in a physical game, but he has to step it up and play harder; he has to go through people to get to the net or the puck.

THE INTANGIBLES

Atlanta thinks Stefan is the No. 1 center they need so desperately, but there are two flaws in that plan: 1. He's a better winger than center, and; 2. He's not a first-line forward.

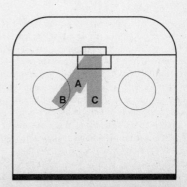

CHRIS TAMER

Yrs. of NHL service: 9
Born: Dearborn, Mich.; Nov. 17, 1970
Position: left defense
Height: 6-2
Weight: 205
Uniform no.: 4
Shoots: left

Career statistics:

GP	G	A	TP	PIM
606	19	59	78	1128

1999-2000 statistics:

GP	G	A	TP	+/-	PIM	PP	SH	GW	GT	S	PCT
69	2	8	10	-32	91	0	0	0	0	61	3.3

2000-2001 statistics:

GP	G	A	TP	+/-	PIM	PP	SH	GW	GT	S	PCT
82	4	13	17	-1	128	0	1	1	0	90	4.4

2001-2002 statistics:

GP	G	A	TP	+/-	PIM	PP	SH	GW	GT	S	PCT
78	3	3	6	-11	111	0	1	0	0	66	4.6

2002-2003 statistics:

GP	G	A	TP	+/-	PIM	PP	SH	GW	GT	S	PCT
72	1	9	10	-10	118	0	0	0	0	53	1.9

LAST SEASON

Second on team in penalty minutes. Missed three games with back injury. Missed two games due to NHL suspension. Missed five games due to coach's decision.

THE FINESSE GAME

Tamer is a conservative, stay-at-home defenseman. He has limited skating and stick skills, but he is smart enough to stay within his limitations and play a positional game.

He plays a poised game and learns from his mistakes. He does the little things well, chipping a puck off the boards or angling an attacker to the wall. He kills penalties, blocks shots, and finishes his checks.

Tamer is smart enough when he is firing from the point to make sure his shot doesn't get blocked. He will take something off his shot, or put it wide so the forwards can attack the puck off the end boards.

THE PHYSICAL GAME

Tamer doesn't nail people, but he has some strength and will use it to push people out of the crease, and he'll battle in the corners. He doesn't have the good skating base to be a punishing open-ice hitter, but he defends himself and sticks up for his teammates. He doesn't have a serious nasty side, but is often guilty of late hits and received an intent to injure suspension last season. Tamer is fearless in his shot-blocking.

Tamer is a well-conditioned athlete and he can handle a lot of ice time, despite dealing with asthma.

THE INTANGIBLES

Tamer has dropped out of Atlanta's top for defense. He will never be a star, but he gives solid support and can complement a more offensive player, like Frantisek Kaberle. His point production will be low, but he is an intelligent rearguard. Tamer is a quiet leader who will continue to help the next generation of Thrashers build toward the future.

PROJECTION

Tamer's points are a bonus. What he gives that counts are his efforts in the defensive zone, his guts, and, of course, his PIM.

BOSTON BRUINS

Players' Statistics 2001-2002

POS.	NO.	PLAYER	GP	G	A	PTS	+/-	PIM	PP	SH	GW	GT	S	PCT
C	19	JOE THORNTON	77	36	65	101	12	109	12	2	4	1	196	18.4
R	27	GLEN MURRAY	82	44	48	92	9	64	12		5	2	331	13.3
R	26	MIKE KNUBLE	75	30	29	59	18	45	9		4	1	185	16.2
R	12	BRIAN ROLSTON	81	27	32	59	1	32	6	5	5	1	281	9.6
C	16	JOZEF STUMPEL	78	14	37	51	0	12	4		2	1	110	12.7
D	34	BRYAN BERARD	80	10	28	38	-4	64	4		1		205	4.9
L	11	P.J. AXELSSON	66	17	19	36	8	24	2	2	1		122	13.9
D	44	NICHOLAS BOYNTON	78	7	17	24	8	99		1	2		160	4.4
D	46	JONATHAN GIRARD	73	6	16	22	4	21	2		2		123	4.9
D	6	DANIEL MCGILLIS	71	3	17	20	3	60	2			1	130	2.3
L	22	MICHAL GROSEK	63	2	18	20	2	71			1		74	2.7
L	10	MARTY MCINNIS	77	9	10	19	-11	38			1		121	7.4
R	20	MARTIN LAPOINTE	59	8	10	18	-19	87	1		1		110	7.3
L	36	*IVAN HUML	41	6	11	17	3	30			2		75	8.0
D	25	HAL GILL	76	4	13	17	21	56					114	3.5
L	17	ROB ZAMUNER	55	10	6	16	2	18	3		1		94	10.6
D	21	SEAN O'DONNELL	70	1	15	16	8	76			1		61	1.6
L	14	SERGEI SAMSONOV	8	5	6	11	8	2	1		3		23	21.7
C	42	P.J. STOCK	71	1	9	10	-5	160	1				38	2.6
D	32	DON SWEENEY	67	3	5	8	-1	24				1	55	5.4
D	18	IAN MORAN	78		8	8	-18	48					96	
D	23	SEAN BROWN	69	1	5	6	-6	117					39	2.6
R	37	*LEE GOREN	14	2	1	3	-2	7	2				15	13.3
C	29	*ANDY HILBERT	14		3	3	-1	7					22	
C	76	*KRIS VERNARSKY	14	1		1	-2	2					18	5.6
D	39	*ZDENEK KUTLAK	4	1		1	0						1	100.0
D	59	RICHARD BRENNAN	7		1	1	3	6					12	
L	43	*MARTIN SAMUELSSON	8		1	1	-1	2					3	
L	33	KRZYSZTOF OLIWA	42				-3	161					14	
D	28	*SHAONE MORRISONN	11				0	8					4	
D	64	JARNO KULTANEN	2				1						3	
C	63	MATT HERR	3				0						1	
G	30	JEFF HACKETT	36				0	2						
G	31	STEVE SHIELDS	36				0	8						
R	55	BRANTT MYHRES	1				0	31						
G	70	TIM THOMAS	4				0							
G	1	ANDREW RAYCROFT	5				0							

GP = games played; G = goals; A = assists; PTS = points; +/- = goals-for minus goals-against while player is on ice; PIM = penalties in minutes; PP = power-play goals; SH = shorthanded goals; GW = game-winning goals; GT = game-tying goals; S = no. of shots; PCT = percentage of goals to shots; * = rookie

P. J. AXELSSON

Yrs. of NHL service: 6
Born: Kungalv, Sweden; Feb. 26, 1975
Position: left wing
Height: 6-1
Weight: 175
Uniform no.: 11
Shoots: left

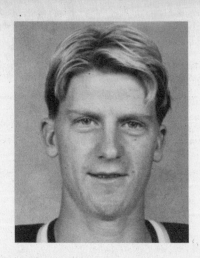

Career statistics:

GP	G	A	TP	PIM
465	57	96	153	147

1999-2000 statistics:

GP	G	A	TP	+/-	PIM	PP	SH	GW	GT	S	PCT
81	10	16	26	+1	24	0	0	4	0	186	5.4

2000-2001 statistics:

GP	G	A	TP	+/-	PIM	PP	SH	GW	GT	S	PCT
81	8	15	23	-12	27	0	0	2	0	146	5.5

2001-2002 statistics:

GP	G	A	TP	+/-	PIM	PP	SH	GW	GT	S	PCT
78	7	17	24	+6	16	0	2	0	0	127	5.5

2002-2003 statistics:

GP	G	A	TP	+/-	PIM	PP	SH	GW	GT	S	PCT
66	17	19	36	+8	24	2	2	1	0	122	13.9

LAST SEASON

Tied for second on team in shorthanded goals. Third on team in shooting percentage. Career highs in goals and points. Missed 10 games with back injuries. Missed four games with knee injury. Missed two games with flu.

THE FINESSE GAME

Axelsson is a role player who proudly tackles the job. He is a very fast skater. His hand skills are just about average, though he was a fairly decent scorer in the Swedish Elite League, and he doesn't fumble with the puck. His future in this league will be based less on his scoring than on his defensive ability. The Bruins keep expecting him to chip in more offensively, and they finally started to see more input last season. Axelsson plays mostly in a checking role but can function as a safety-valve winger with two offensive-minded guys.

Killing penalties is where he excels. Axelsson is a smart player with a real head for the game. He has the skills (especially skating) that stamp him as a bona fide NHLer. He does all the little things to help his team win. He chips pucks past point men, never stops skating, never stops fighting for the puck, and he thrives on big checking assignments against other teams' top lines.

Axelsson's primary asset is his work ethic.

THE PHYSICAL GAME

Axelsson is competitive, a solid checker who will finish all of his hits. He will stand up to big power forwards and won't be intimidated, despite the fact that he is the kind of tall but scrawny player that some big guys could use as a toothpick. Axelsson is not fun to play against.

THE INTANGIBLES

Axelsson is a catalyst. He contributes an honest 16 minutes every night. He is a low-risk, high-energy performer. Axelsson was a restricted free agent after last season.

PROJECTION

If Axelsson hadn't been injured, he might have cracked the 20-goal barrier. It will probably take that for him to receive the Selke Trophy recognition he deserves.

BRYAN BERARD

Yrs. of NHL service: 7
Born: Woonsocket, R.I.; March 5, 1977
Position: left defense
Height: 6-1
Weight: 195
Uniform no.: 34
Shoots: left

Career statistics:

GP	G	A	TP	PIM
452	46	173	219	359

1998-1999 statistics:

GP	G	A	TP	+/-	PIM	PP	SH	GW	GT	S	PCT
69	9	25	34	+1	48	4	0	5	1	135	6.7

1999-2000 statistics:

GP	G	A	TP	+/-	PIM	PP	SH	GW	GT	S	PCT
64	3	27	30	+11	42	1	0	0	0	98	3.1

2001-2002 statistics:

GP	G	A	TP	+/-	PIM	PP	SH	GW	GT	S	PCT
82	2	21	23	-1	60	0	0	0	0	132	1.5

2002-2003 statistics:

GP	G	A	TP	+/-	PIM	PP	SH	GW	GT	S	PCT
80	10	28	38	-4	64	4	0	1	0	205	4.9

LAST SEASON

Finalist for 2003 Masterton Trophy. Led team defense in points. Third on team in shots. Missed two games due to coach's decision.

THE FINESSE GAME

The loss of most of the vision in one of his eyes is often not noticeable, which is a testament to how hard Berard has worked to come back after his injury (the result of a high stick) in March, 2000.

Berard has incorporated elements of style from two other prominent American-born defensemen, Brian Leetch and Chris Chelios, but he has become his own man.

A terrific skater, Berard has top offensive instincts and a good shot from the point. He manages to get his shots through a majority of the time, which is one of Leetch's gifts.

Like Chelios, when Berard is on, he's in perpetual motion. He seldom stops trying to make things happen. He loves to create excitement and put pressure on his opponents. He is a high-risk, high-reward player. He wants the puck when the game is on the line.

Berard does have to play a little more conservatively because of vision loss (he is also required to wear a visor), but he remains a gambler at heart.

THE PHYSICAL GAME

When Berard wore down badly at the end of his comeback season with the Rangers in 2001-02, we were just as ready as Glen Sather to write him off. Instead, Berard signed a new deal with the Bruins, essentially his hometown team, and played another remarkable first half. He tailed off again in the second half of the season, although not as drastically as he did with the Rangers.

Berard is not overly physical but he will use his body to slow people down and he will get chippy.

THE INTANGIBLES

How much does Berard love the game? Enough that he traded in the security of an insurance payoff. Enough to risk the vision in his remaining good eye. Enough to make us root for him every shift.

PROJECTION

Boston's defense corps is slowly improving but expect Berard to remain a part of the core. Maybe he can flirt with 40 points again.

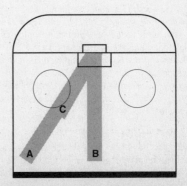

NICHOLAS BOYNTON

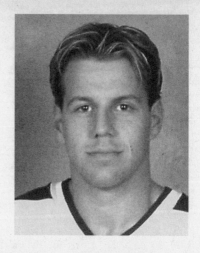

Yrs. of NHL service: 2
Born: Nobleton, Ont.; Jan. 14, 1979
Position: right defense
Height: 6-2
Weight: 210
Uniform no.: 44
Shoots: right

Career statistics:

GP	G	A	TP	PIM
164	11	31	42	206

1999-2000 statistics:

GP	G	A	TP	+/-	PIM	PP	SH	GW	GT	S	PCT
5	0	0	0	-5	0	0	0	0	0	6	-

2000-2001 statistics:

GP	G	A	TP	+/-	PIM	PP	SH	GW	GT	S	PCT
1	0	0	0	-1	0	0	0	0	0	1	0.0

2001-2002 statistics:

GP	G	A	TP	+/-	PIM	PP	SH	GW	GT	S	PCT
80	4	14	18	+18	107	0	0	1	0	136	2.9

2002-2003 statistics:

GP	G	A	TP	+/-	PIM	PP	SH	GW	GT	S	PCT
78	7	17	24	+8	99	0	1	2	0	160	4.4

LAST SEASON

Led team in average ice time (22:40). Career highs in goals, assists, and points. Missed two games with flu. Missed one game with hand injury. Missed one game due to coach's decision.

THE FINESSE GAME

He's no Ray Bourque, but Boynton is the most exciting defenseman the Bruins have developed in a long time. What is most impressive is that after a solid rookie campaign, Boynton continued to progress in his second full NHL season.

Boynton is an exceptional skater in all directions and he has good balance. It looked like Boynton was going to try to break in as an "offenseman," but he has dedicated himself to learning the defensive side of the game and is going to be a top pair, two-way defenseman for years to come.

Boynton is poised with the puck and makes crisp, calm outlet passes. He jumps up into the play intelligently. He doesn't have an elite shot but he has good lateral mobility along the blueline and that makes his slap shot more effective. Boynton is also clever enough to use the fake half-slap and pass.

Boynton just does everything well. He can separate the puck carrier from the puck. He makes the good first pass. Boynton takes on a lot of ice time and allowed the Bruins to trade Kyle McLaren. He plays against other team's top lines.

THE PHYSICAL GAME

Boynton has good size and coaches are going to expect him to be more aggressive. He isn't going to be a big banger, but he could develop along Wade Redden lines and be a player who makes sure he stays between the attacker and the net with his body.

THE INTANGIBLES

Boynton was diagnosed with diabetes three years ago and has had to learn how to balance that medical condition with trying to play at the pro level. Boynton is a gamer and is remarkably consistent.

PROJECTION

Boynton fell just shy of the 30 points we projected for him last season. We anticipate a slight bump up to the 35-point range.

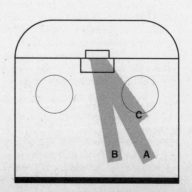

HAL GILL

Yrs. of NHL service: 6
Born: Concord, Mass.; Apr. 6, 1975
Position: right defense
Height: 6-7
Weight: 230
Uniform no.: 25
Shoots: left

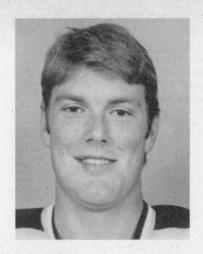

Career statistics:

GP	G	A	TP	PIM
464	17	61	78	365

1999-2000 statistics:

GP	G	A	TP	+/-	PIM	PP	SH	GW	GT	S	PCT
81	3	9	12	0	51	0	0	0	0	120	2.5

2000-2001 statistics:

GP	G	A	TP	+/-	PIM	PP	SH	GW	GT	S	PCT
80	1	10	11	-2	71	0	0	0	0	79	1.3

2001-2002 statistics:

GP	G	A	TP	+/-	PIM	PP	SH	GW	GT	S	PCT
79	4	18	22	+16	77	0	0	0	0	137	2.9

2002-2003 statistics:

GP	G	A	TP	+/-	PIM	PP	SH	GW	GT	S	PCT
76	4	13	17	+21	56	0	0	0	0	114	3.5

LAST SEASON

Led team in plus-minus. Matched career high in goals. Missed six games with finger injury.

THE FINESSE GAME

Gill is a defenseman who can be used in any game situation. He is at his best under pressure, poised and calm with the puck, and he is a better outlet passer now than ever. Gill does not panic easily.

Gill was not much of a scorer at the college level and he won't be in the NHL either, but his finesse skills serve him well in a defensive role. He makes the first pass on the breakout or gets the puck and moves it out of the zone. He does possess a huge shot from the point, though his lack of mobility along the blueline makes it a less effective scoring weapon. His puck movement is advanced.

Gill's only drawback is his skating. He has slow feet, which may keep him from becoming an elite defenseman, but every other facet of his game is Grade A. Gill is one of the tallest players in the NHL, and he uses his reach well.

THE PHYSICAL GAME

Gill competes hard every night. He is not intimidated by some of the league's tough customers and is one of the few defensemen in the East who can stay on his feet after a hit by someone like Bobby Holik. Gill is solid and imposing, and can intimidate with his size. He is strong on the boards, strong in the corners and he clears out the front of his net. He doesn't fight. He doesn't have to. He has a pretty long fuse, but don't confuse that with a lack of hockey courage. Gill is a gamer. The Bruins would like to see him initiate more, but that isn't his nature.

THE INTANGIBLES

How's this for a compliment? Jaromir Jagr called Gill the toughest player he competes against. Gill can handle a good amount of ice time and he always gets the assignments against other team's top lines. He was a restricted free agent after the season.

PROJECTION

Gill has matured into a top defensemen. He won't get much attention because he doesn't score a lot of points, and he doesn't make the splashy hits that draw attention to other defensive defensemen. If the Bruins ever get truly competitive, Gill may finally receive the acclaim he deserves.

JONATHAN GIRARD

Yrs. of NHL service: 4
Born: Joliette, Que.; May 27, 1980
Position: right defense
Height: 5-11
Weight: 192
Uniform no.: 46
Shoots: right

Career statistics:

GP	G	A	TP	PIM
150	10	34	44	46

1999-2000 statistics:

GP	G	A	TP	+/-	PIM	PP	SH	GW	GT	S	PCT
23	1	2	3	-1	2	0	0	0	0	17	5.9

2000-2001 statistics:

GP	G	A	TP	+/-	PIM	PP	SH	GW	GT	S	PCT
31	3	13	16	+2	14	2	0	1	0	42	7.1

2001-2002 statistics:

GP	G	A	TP	+/-	PIM	PP	SH	GW	GT	S	PCT
20	0	3	3	0	9	0	0	0	0	28	0.0

2002-2003 statistics:

GP	G	A	TP	+/-	PIM	PP	SH	GW	GT	S	PCT
73	6	16	22	+4	21	2	0	2	0	123	4.9

PROJECTION

Girard has been on the bubble for a few seasons and shouldn't approach camp thinking he has won a job. There will be a lot of jostling for positions. Girard's future is on a third-defense pair. He could score 25 points.

LAST SEASON

Career highs in goals, assists, and points. Missed nine games due to coach's decision.

THE FINESSE GAME

Girard broke into the pros as an "offenseman," but spent some time in the minors bolstering the defensive side of his game.

Boston was still trying to hammer home the point last season, which is why he was a healthy scratch on so many occasions. Girard has to play better positionally because he is not going to post the kind of spectacular numbers that will allow a team to over-look his defensive shortcomings.

Girard has good puck skills and he is a quick skater. He has the kind of lateral movement along the blueline that is the hallmark of elite point men. He has a major-league slap shot. He is also creative enough not to just blast the puck, but will try to fake a defender with a pseudo-slap and then pass the puck in deep for a one-timer by a teammate. Girard has very good offensive instincts.

THE PHYSICAL GAME

Girard is a slightly smaller than average defenseman who hasn't quite mastered the art of playing bigger. He should study tapes of Don Sweeny for guidance and inspiration. He is a fit athlete who can handle 20 minutes or more of ice time.

THE INTANGIBLES

Girard should see second-unit power-play time if he wins a job. He was a restricted free agent after the season.

JEFF JILLSON

Yrs. of NHL service: 2
Born: Providence, RI; July 24, 1980
Position: right
Height: 6-3
Weight: 220
Uniform no.: 5
Shoots: right

Career statistics:

GP	G	A	TP	PIM
74	5	19	24	38

2001-2002 statistics:

GP	G	A	TP	+/-	PIM	PP	SH	GW	GT	S	PCT
48	5	13	18	+2	29	3	0	2	0	47	10.6

2002-2003 statistics:

GP	G	A	TP	+/-	PIM	PP	SH	GW	GT	S	PCT
26	0	6	6	-7	9	0	0	0	0	22	0.0

LAST SEASON

Acquired from San Jose with Jeff Hackett on January 23, 2003, for Kyle McLaren and a fourth-round draft pick in 2004. Missed one game due to coach's decision. Appeared in 19 games with Cleveland (AHL), scoring 3-5 — 8 with 12 PIM. Appeared in 30 games with Providence (AHL), scoring 4-11 — 15 with 26 PIM.

THE FINESSE GAME

Jillson can become a solid two-way defenseman, although his game at present is heavily weighted offensively. He won't be an elite scoring defenseman, so he has to use his finesse skills better in his own end.

Jillson will eagerly get involved in the attack. Jillson is a righthanded shot, a valuable asset. He will cheat down to the circles for a one-timer or a slap shot. He has a good point shot.

Jillson needs to improve his skating, especially his foot speed, in order to become a full-timer. He also needs to improve his decision-making, which should evolve with more experience. He has improved at making the first pass out of the zone and tying up opposing players' sticks in the defensive zone. Jillson appears coachable and willing to learn from mistakes.

THE PHYSICAL GAME

Jillson took the college route to the NHL, which is unusual for a player with his kind of ferocious game. He is very competitive, and can be taken off his game when he gets too fired up. He has very good size and he uses it well. Jillson is a big, clean hitter, and isn't nasty.

THE INTANGIBLES

After the trade, Jillson finished up the season at Providence playing for Mike Sullivan, who became the new Bruins head coach. Jillson is expected to contend for a top-four job in training camp and should see power-play time.

PROJECTION

Jillson needs to prove he can stick at the NHL level. If he does, he should produce 30-35 points.

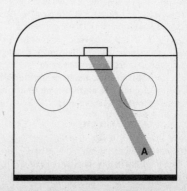

MARTIN LAPOINTE

Yrs. of NHL service: 10
Born: Ville Ste. Pierre, Que.; Sept. 12, 1973
Position: right wing
Height: 5-11
Weight: 200
Uniform no.: 20
Shoots: right

Career statistics:

GP	G	A	TP	PIM
679	133	155	288	1076

1999-2000 statistics:

GP	G	A	TP	+/-	PIM	PP	SH	GW	GT	S	PCT
82	16	25	41	+17	121	1	1	2	1	127	12.6

2000-2001 statistics:

GP	G	A	TP	+/-	PIM	PP	SH	GW	GT	S	PCT
82	27	30	57	+3	127	13	0	8	0	181	14.9

2001-2002 statistics:

GP	G	A	TP	+/-	PIM	PP	SH	GW	GT	S	PCT
68	17	23	40	+12	101	4	0	2	1	141	12.1

2002-2003 statistics:

GP	G	A	TP	+/-	PIM	PP	SH	GW	GT	S	PCT
59	8	10	18	-19	87	1	0	1	0	110	7.3

LAST SEASON

Worst plus-minus on team. Missed 17 games with foot injury. Missed five games with groin injury. Missed one game due to coach's decision.

THE FINESSE GAME

Everything about Lapointe's game stems more from what is between his ribs than what is between his ears. It all comes from the heart: the competitiveness, the drive that sends him to the net in the straightest line possible. If a defenseman or opposing forward — or goalie — happens to get knocked down in the process, that's their problem.

Lapointe's goals and assists result more from his acceleration than his speed. He doesn't have break-away speed, but his eagerness, his intensity, and his willingness to compete make him seem faster than he actually is. He doesn't have a great shot, though he has a nice, quick release and uses a wrist or snap shot as opposed to a big windup. Most of his goals are scored in the hard areas around the crease. He screens goalies, tips shots, and works for loose pucks.

Equally important, Lapointe does not let a stick-check slow him down. He'll pull a checker along like a boat tugging a water-skier. He'll steam into the play to create an odd-man rush, and he creates lots of options with a nice passing touch that prevents goalies from overplaying him to shoot.

THE PHYSICAL GAME

Lapointe wants to play, wants to win, and won't take an easy way out, which means a lot of opponents end up flat on the ice. He hits them all, big or small, and hits hard. He is low but wide, with a broad upper body and solid center of gravity that powers his physical game. He can be a menace in the corners and a force in front of the net.

There is a snarl in Lapointe's game, a fire that always seems close to the fuse. He takes a good share of over-emotional penalties. He wakes things up, and never lets opponents take the easy way out. He never lets himself take the easy way, either. Lapointe was a flashy scorer in junior but dedicated himself to learning how to check. His approach is summarized in his statement, "I'd rather change my role and have the team win instead of being a one-man show."

THE INTANGIBLES

Lapointe has never been the same player since he took all the money to sign as a free agent with Boston in 2001. Was it the big payday that hurt him? Or did his former Red Wings teammates make him look like a much better player than he was?

PROJECTION

For the second straight postseason, Lapointe has been ordinary. That is where he used to make his reputation. He HAS to score more than eight goals this season, doesn't he?

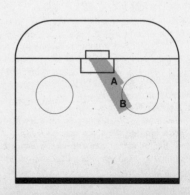

DANIEL MCGILLIS

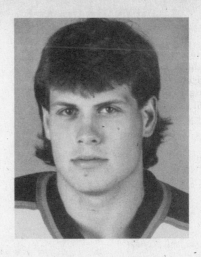

Yrs. of NHL service: 7
Born: Hawkesbury, Ont.; July 1, 1972
Position: left defense
Height: 6-2
Weight: 230
Uniform no.: 6
Shoots: left

Career statistics:

GP	G	A	TP	PIM
527	51	153	204	469

1999-2000 statistics:

GP	G	A	TP	+/-	PIM	PP	SH	GW	GT	S	PCT
68	4	14	18	+16	55	3	0	1	0	128	3.1

2000-2001 statistics:

GP	G	A	TP	+/-	PIM	PP	SH	GW	GT	S	PCT
82	14	35	49	+13	86	4	0	4	0	207	6.8

2001-2002 statistics:

GP	G	A	TP	+/-	PIM	PP	SH	GW	GT	S	PCT
75	5	14	19	+17	46	2	0	1	0	147	3.4

2002-2003 statistics:

GP	G	A	TP	+/-	PIM	PP	SH	GW	GT	S	PCT
71	3	17	20	+3	60	2	0	0	1	130	2.3

LAST SEASON

Acquired by San Jose from Philadelphia on December 6, 2003, for Marcus Ragnarsson. Acquired by Boston from San Jose on March 11, 2003, for a second-round draft pick in 2003. Missed five games with concussion.

THE FINESSE GAME

Not a quick skater, McGillis is strong and agile enough for his size. He uses his finesse skills in a defensive role — sweep-checks, poke-checks — but needs to improve his reads. He is a fearless shot-blocker and is consistently among his team's leaders in that department.

McGillis has some good offensive skills, but they are enhanced because of his physical play. He provides point production with an edge. McGillis does have a wickedly hard point shot, and can handle second-unit power-play time.

McGillis is better at playing a hard game and trying to shut opponents down than scoring himself. He applies most of his talents to the defensive aspect of the game.

THE PHYSICAL GAME

McGillis steps up and challenges, and he's a big, big hitter. He's not afraid to go after the stars. He has also developed a very sly nasty streak. Even two referees can't catch him in the act. He is quickly becoming a disliked, and not necessarily respected, opponent.

THE INTANGIBLES

Two trades in a year had to affect McGillis's mentally after starting his career and playing for so many years in Philadelphia. Now he gets another coaching change to start the season. If Mike Sullivan likes crunching defensemen, then they should get along just fine.

PROJECTION

McGillis should score in the 25-point range.

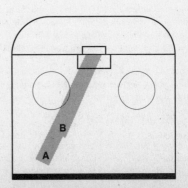

MARTY MCINNIS

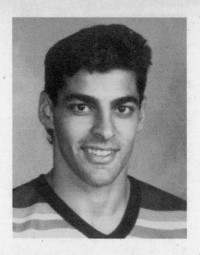

Yrs. of NHL service: 11
Born: Hingham, Mass.; June 2, 1970
Position: left wing
Height: 5-11
Weight: 187
Uniform no.: 10
Shoots: right

Career statistics:

GP	G	A	TP	PIM
796	170	250	420	330

1999-2000 statistics:

GP	G	A	TP	+/-	PIM	PP	SH	GW	GT	S	PCT
62	10	18	28	-4	26	2	1	2	0	129	7.8

2000-2001 statistics:

GP	G	A	TP	+/-	PIM	PP	SH	GW	GT	S	PCT
75	20	22	42	-21	40	10	0	1	0	136	14.7

2001-2002 statistics:

GP	G	A	TP	+/-	PIM	PP	SH	GW	GT	S	PCT
79	11	17	28	-15	33	2	0	1	0	157	7.0

2002-2003 statistics:

GP	G	A	TP	+/-	PIM	PP	SH	GW	GT	S	PCT
77	9	10	19	-11	38	0	0	1	0	121	7.4

LAST SEASON

Missed two games with knee injury. Missed three games due to coach's decision.

THE FINESSE GAME

The versatile McInnis does a lot of the little things adequately, but does nothing exceptionally. He is a smart positional player. McInnis is also smart and reliable defensively and he turns his checking work into scoring opportunities with quick passes. He is a very patient shooter but has little in his arsenal.

McInnis isn't fast but he is deceptive with his quick first few strides to the puck. He seems to be more aware of where the puck is than his opponents are, so while they're looking for the puck he's already heading towards it. McInnis can handle some second-unit power-play time.

McInnis is a good penalty killer because of his tenacity and anticipation. He reads plays well on both offense and defense. Playing the off-wing opens up his shot for a quick release; he's always a shorthanded threat. He's an ideal third-line forward because he can check and provide some offensive counterpunch.

THE PHYSICAL GAME

McInnis is not big or tough, but he is sturdy and will use his body to bump and scrap for the puck. He always tries to get in the way, though he loses a lot of battles in-tight to larger forwards because he is not that strong.

THE INTANGIBLES

McInnis can be used in a lot of situations and with many different line combinations. He is a useful role player to have around, although his plus-minus last year dreadful.

PROJECTION

A healthy McInnis should be good for 10 goals.

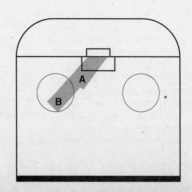

GLEN MURRAY

Yrs. of NHL service: 11
Born: Halifax, N.S.; Nov. 1, 1972
Position: right wing
Height: 6-3
Weight: 225
Uniform no.: 27
Shoots: right

Career statistics:

GP	G	A	TP	PIM
742	236	227	463	477

1999-2000 statistics:

GP	G	A	TP	+/-	PIM	PP	SH	GW	GT	S	PCT
78	29	33	62	+13	60	10	1	2	1	202	14.4

2000-2001 statistics:

GP	G	A	TP	+/-	PIM	PP	SH	GW	GT	S	PCT
64	18	21	39	+9	32	3	1	1	0	138	13.0

2001-2002 statistics:

GP	G	A	TP	+/-	PIM	PP	SH	GW	GT	S	PCT
82	41	30	71	+31	40	9	0	9	0	246	16.7

2002-2003 statistics:

GP	G	A	TP	+/-	PIM	PP	SH	GW	GT	S	PCT
82	44	48	92	+9	64	12	0	5	2	331	13.3

LAST SEASON

Led NHL in shots. Fifth in NHL in goals. Seventh in NHL in points. Led team in goals. Tied for team lead in power-play goals and game-winning goals. Second on team in average ice time (22:36), assists, and points. Career highs in goals, assists, and points. Only Bruin to appear in all 82 games.

THE FINESSE GAME

Who said there are no successful second acts? Murray turned what looked like a terribly lopsided trade in L.A.'s favor (the Jason Allison deal) into a splashy comeback. Murray started his career with the Bruins and left in a 1995 trade. He carried a "next Cam Neely" tag for a long time. Now that Murray is playing more consistently, that tag is no longer a drag. It's a compliment.

Murray is at his best on the right side, jamming in his forehand shots. He has good size and a top short game. He also has a quick release and, like a lot of great goal scorers, he just plain shoots. He doesn't even have to look at the net because he feels where the shot is going, and he protects the puck well with his body. Murray has also developed a wickedly fast slap shot and has developed confidence in this weapon. He is now more consistently using his speed and strength to get in better scoring position.

Murray is a lumbering skater and needs a good setup man. He has found one of the game's elite in center Joe Thornton. Thornton has great hands and patience with the puck and just waits on the cycle until Murray slides into a seam.

THE PHYSICAL GAME

On nights when he's playing well, Murray is leaning on people and making his presence felt. He'll bang. He pushes off defenders to get open for his quick release. Murray has stayed healthy over the past two seasons, which has gone a long way towards making him a confident attacker.

THE INTANGIBLES

Murray inherited the ice time and the pressure after Bill Guerin was traded and exceeded all expectations. Especially ours.

PROJECTION

Hoo boy, did we get this one wrong. We actually pegged Murray for a decrease in goals, when all he did was notch his first 40-goal season. What could possibly stop him from doing it again? Well, if Thornton's off-ice problems affect his on-ice performance, then Murray's totals will sag. Otherwise, he should post another 40-goal season.

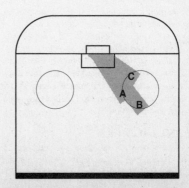

SEAN O'DONNELL

Yrs. of NHL service: 8
Born: Ottawa, Ont.; Oct. 13, 1971
Position: left defense
Height: 6-3
Weight: 230
Uniform no.: 21
Shoots: left

Career statistics:

GP	G	A	TP	PIM
611	20	109	129	1125

1999-2000 statistics:

GP	G	A	TP	+/-	PIM	PP	SH	GW	GT	S	PCT
80	2	12	14	+4	114	0	0	1	0	51	3.9

2000-2001 statistics:

GP	G	A	TP	+/-	PIM	PP	SH	GW	GT	S	PCT
80	4	13	17	0	161	1	0	2	0	67	6.0

2001-2002 statistics:

GP	G	A	TP	+/-	PIM	PP	SH	GW	GT	S	PCT
80	3	22	25	+27	89	1	0	2	0	112	2.7

2002-2003 statistics:

GP	G	A	TP	+/-	PIM	PP	SH	GW	GT	S	PCT
70	1	15	16	+8	76	0	0	1	0	61	1.6

LAST SEASON

Missed 11 games with knee injury. Missed one game due to coach's decision.

THE FINESSE GAME

O'Donnell has worked hard to rise above being a one-dimensional player, but his skating holds him back. He is not very good laterally and that results in him being beaten wide. He tries to line up someone and misses because he doesn't have the quickness to get there. O'Donnell has to really concentrate on playing a containment game.

He has some offensive input because he is alert and tries so hard, but O'Donnell is really at his best when he can play a stay-at-home style. He makes a suitable partner for a high-risk defenseman, although he runs into spells where he starts taking high-risk runs at people. His hand skills are average at best. He can make a decent outlet pass, but he tends to get a bit panicky under pressure.

O'Donnell's defensive reads are adequate. He has become a decent shot-blocker.

THE PHYSICAL GAME

O'Donnell is fearless. He is a legitimate tough guy who fights anybody. He hits hard. He uses his stick. He's a nasty customer. O'Donnell sticks up for his teammates, but often overreacts. He has a penchant for taking bad penalties.

THE INTANGIBLES

O'Donnell is a serviceable third-pair defenseman, but injuries forced the Bruins to move him up and he performed well for long stretches. O'Donnell is a great team guy, and he will fit in well with the team's younger defensemen.

PROJECTION

O'Donnell will provide toughness, and 20-25 points.

BRIAN ROLSTON

Yrs. of NHL service: 9
Born: Flint, Mich.; Feb. 21, 1973
Position: center
Height: 6-2
Weight: 205
Uniform no.: 12
Shoots: left

Career statistics:

GP	G	A	TP	PIM
654	171	213	384	183

1999-2000 statistics:

GP	G	A	TP	+/-	PIM	PP	SH	GW	GT	S	PCT
77	16	15	31	-12	18	5	0	6	0	206	7.8

2000-2001 statistics:

GP	G	A	TP	+/-	PIM	PP	SH	GW	GT	S	PCT
77	19	39	58	+6	28	5	0	4	0	286	6.6

2001-2002 statistics:

GP	G	A	TP	+/-	PIM	PP	SH	GW	GT	S	PCT
82	31	31	62	+11	30	6	9	7	0	331	9.4

2002-2003 statistics:

GP	G	A	TP	+/-	PIM	PP	SH	GW	GT	S	PCT
81	27	32	59	+1	32	6	5	5	1	281	9.6

LAST SEASON

Second in NHL in shorthanded goals. First on team in shorthanded goals. Tied for first on team in game-winning goals. Second on team in shots. Tied for third on team in shots. Missed one game with headaches.

THE FINESSE GAME

Rolston's game is speed. He is a fast, powerful skater who drives to the net and loves to shoot. He passes well on his forehand and backhand, and reads break-out plays by leading his man smartly.

The main difference in Rolston's game is that now he is converting the chances that he gets with his speed. Rolston has developed far more patience with his shot. He has a cannon from the top of the circles in, with a quick release. Where he once had a tendency to hurry his shots, now he waits. Rolston creates so many odd-man-rush opportunities, especially shorthanded ones, that not forcing the goalie to handle the puck is a sin. That is what was happening when he was pinging shots off the glass.

He is an aggressive penalty killer. He uses his quick getaway stride to pull away for shorthanded breaks. He takes some pride in this role, and works diligently. Although he doesn't like it, he has been shoehorned into the role of a defensive winger. He makes a highly effective shadow, as he is one of the few players with the size, skill, and smarts to match strides with a Jaromir Jagr or Pavel Bure.

Rolston plays center or wing, and plays the point well on the power play.

THE PHYSICAL GAME

Rolston will take a hit to make a play, and has taken the next step to start initiating fights for pucks. He can be intimidated, however, and lacks true grit. His better games come against skating clubs. He is durable; in part because he keeps himself out of areas where he can get hurt.

THE INTANGIBLES

Rolston has stepped up his game in every area and is a quality competitor. He is among the elite penalty killers in the NHL. Rolston was a restricted free agent after the season and has some pretty good ammo to take to the bargaining table.

PROJECTION

Despite a tough finish to the season in Boston, Rolston was one of the guys who never quit. He exceeded our downgraded projection for him last season, although we will repeat that for this year: 25 goals, 50 points.

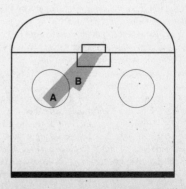

SERGEI SAMSONOV

Yrs. of NHL service: 6
Born: Moscow, Russia; Oct. 27, 1978
Position: left wing
Height: 5-8
Weight: 180
Uniform no.: 14
Shoots: right

Career statistics:

GP	G	A	TP	PIM
401	129	170	299	77

1999-2000 statistics:

GP	G	A	TP	+/-	PIM	PP	SH	GW	GT	S	PCT
77	19	26	45	-6	4	6	0	3	0	145	13.1

2000-2001 statistics:

GP	G	A	TP	+/-	PIM	PP	SH	GW	GT	S	PCT
82	29	46	75	+6	18	3	0	3	2	215	13.5

2001-2002 statistics:

GP	G	A	TP	+/-	PIM	PP	SH	GW	GT	S	PCT
74	29	41	70	+21	27	3	0	4	0	192	15.1

2002-2003 statistics:

GP	G	A	TP	+/-	PIM	PP	SH	GW	GT	S	PCT
8	5	6	11	+8	2	1	0	3	0	23	21.7

LAST SEASON

Missed 68 games with wrist injury and surgery. Missed six games with groin injury.

THE FINESSE GAME

Samsonov found an excellent linemate in Joe Thornton. It's like the quote about the pairing of Ginger Rogers and Fred Astaire — he gave them class and she gave them sex. Thornton provides the size and muscle and Samsonov brings the speed and touch.

Every time Samsonov has the puck there's a buzz because he makes things happen. He tries stickhandling moves and shots that other players don't even dream of. Here's what's scary: he can be even better. He is an absolute treat to watch. He is an outstanding skater. The puck doesn't slow him down a hair. He performs the hockey equivalent of a between-the-legs dribble, putting pucks between the legs (his or the defenders') and executing cutbacks. Samsonov is as nifty in tight spaces as he is in open ice.

Although small, Samsonov has the ability to be an explosive game-breaker. Think Pavel Bure, although Samsonov isn't quite yet in that league. But he has the kind of speed and talent that can bring a crowd out of its seats or fake a defenseman out of his skates.

He has outstanding quickness and breakaway speed. He uses all of the ice. Samsonov can get too in love with his skating. When he slumps, it's because of the Alexei Kovalev syndrome, when his idea of a great play is to try to go the length of the ice and through all five defenders before taking a shot, as if hockey were some kind of obstacle course. When he keeps the game simple and uses his linemates better,

he has more success. He is reliable enough defensively, and he is certainly no liability.

THE PHYSICAL GAME

Sturdily built, Samsonov is a little tank. He can't be scared off the play and he handles himself well in traffic and in tight spaces along the boards and in corners. Samsonov digs into every scrum. Samsonov believes that a small man can star in the NHL if he is good enough. He is.

THE INTANGIBLES

Injuries hit Samsonov hard for a second consecutive year. He was an unrestricted free agent after the season.

PROJECTION

Samsonov's assists will probably always be 10 higher than his goals. He should be a consistent 30-goal, 70-point player, especially if he plays with Thornton and if he can manage to stay in one piece.

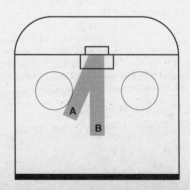

STEVE SHIELDS

Yrs. of NHL service: 6
Born: Toronto, Ont.; July 19, 1972
Position: goaltender
Height: 6-3
Weight: 215
Uniform no.: 31
Catches: left

Career statistics:

GP	MIN	GA	SO	GAA	A	PIM
225	12632	545	10	2.59	2	70

1999-2000 statistics:

GP	MIN	GAA	W	L	T	SO	GA	S	SAPCT	PIM
67	3797	2.56	27	30	8	4	162	1826	.911	29

2000-2001 statistics:

GP	MIN	GAA	W	L	T	SO	GA	S	SAPCT	PIM
21	1135	2.48	6	8	5	2	47	531	.911	2

2001-2002 statistics:

GP	MIN	GAA	W	L	T	SO	GA	S	SAPCT	PIM
33	1777	2.67	9	20	2	0	79	850	.907	4

2002-2003 statistics:

GP	MIN	GAA	W	L	T	SO	GA	S	SAPCT	PIM
36	2112	2.76	12	13	9	0	97	930	.896	8

LAST SEASON

Missed one game with flu.

THE PHYSICAL GAME

Shields's game has some major hiccups, the primary one is that he can't catch the puck. He never seems to track the puck coming all the way to his body, which is why he doesn't watch the puck go into his glove. He also loses it after it hits him elsewhere on his body, which is why he is prone to many bad rebounds. This sounds so elementary, but no one seems to have tried to straighten him out, and it's going to be a major trip-up. It may be a habit he picked up from playing with Dominik Hasek years ago in Buffalo. The difference is that Hasek was always able to keep track of the puck and stop second and third tries.

Shields is mobile and competitive, but he is a big goalie who looks like Darren Pang (who was a small goalie) in the net because of his technical shortcomings. He has a lot of raw skills but needs a full-time goalie coach.

THE MENTAL GAME

Shields is able to shake off bad games and come right back. He needs to be more consistent on a nightly basis. He can win some big games on pure adrenaline when the team doesn't play well in front of him.

THE INTANGIBLES

Boston handed him the No. 1 role last season, but Shields handled it about as well as he handled most pucks. The Bruins acquired Jeff Hackett late in the season, then lost him to free agency, leaving them again with Shields. If the Bruins don't acquire a goalie in the off-season, then Shields may have a shot to win the role again, although he will have to battle with prospect Andrew Raycroft.

PROJECTION

Shields isn't in the top echelon of goaltenders, and if the Bruins start the season with him as their No. 1, it's a pretty good indication they aren't terribly serious about being contenders, no matter what other personnel moves they make.

JOE THORNTON

Yrs. of NHL service: 6
Born: London, Ont.; July 2, 1979
Position: center
Height: 6-4
Weight: 220
Uniform no.: 19
Shoots: left

Career statistics:

GP	G	A	TP	PIM
432	137	211	348	513

1999-2000 statistics:

GP	G	A	TP	+/-	PIM	PP	SH	GW	GT	S	PCT
81	23	37	60	-5	82	5	0	3	0	171	13.5

2000-2001 statistics:

GP	G	A	TP	+/-	PIM	PP	SH	GW	GT	S	PCT
72	37	34	71	-4	107	19	1	5	0	181	20.4

2001-2002 statistics:

GP	G	A	TP	+/-	PIM	PP	SH	GW	GT	S	PCT
66	22	46	68	+7	127	6	0	5	1	152	14.5

2002-2003 statistics:

GP	G	A	TP	+/-	PIM	PP	SH	GW	GT	S	PCT
77	36	65	101	+12	109	12	2	4	1	196	18.4

LAST SEASON

Second in NHL assists. Third in NHL in points. Led team in assists, points, and shooting percentage. Tied for team lead in power-play goals. Second on team in goals. Tied for second on team in shorthanded goals. Third on team in average ice time (22:32), plus-minus, and penalty minutes. Tied for third on team in game-winning goals. Career highs in assists and points. Missed five games with elbow injury.

THE FINESSE GAME

Thornton has played for some tough coaches — Pat Burns, Mike Keenan — and each one left his mark. A lot was demanded of Thornton, and once Jason Allison was traded to L.A., Thornton was ready to take over as Boston's No.1 center. He has advanced to become one of the top-five centers in the league.

Thornton's assets are his exceptional vision of the ice and the hand skills to make things happen. He is so adept at finding holes and passing lanes that team-mates have to be alert when playing with him, because he will create something out of nothing. Sergei Samsonov was an ideal winger for him when he was healthy. Glen Murray, a stone finisher, also had great chemistry with Thornton, stepping up after Bill Guerin was lost to free agency in 2002.

Thornton loves to work the boards, corners, and front of the net. He needs to be prodded to keep his feet moving, though, as he often drifts into a bad habit of standing and waiting for things to happen. He needs to make things happen. Thornton's skating could use some improvement, but it's NHL calibre. He is steadily improving his work on draws. Last year's

percentage was 49.5. Thornton needs to shoot more.

He is so strong he can hold off a defender with one arm and still make a strong pass with the other. He plays with a confidence bordering on arrogance.

THE PHYSICAL GAME

Thornton plays with an edge and has a short fuse. He is a frequent target and he doesn't let too many misdeeds go unpunished. Opponents know it, and try to goad him. Thornton needs to learn how to play tough and stay out of the penalty box.

He also needs to learn to stay out of bars. Thornton faced criminal charges during the off-season for an altercation that involved a police officer.

THE INTANGIBLES

Thornton has arrived as a player but still has some growing up to do as a human. He's 24, young but no kid, and maturity may be the only element lacking in his game and his life.

PROJECTION

Thornton should be a steady 100-point producer now, and a future Hart Trophy candidate, assuming his off-ice woes don't bleed over onto the ice.

ROB ZAMUNER

Yrs. of NHL service: 11
Born: Oakville, Ont.; Sept. 17, 1969
Position: left wing
Height: 6-3
Weight: 203
Uniform no.: 17
Shoots: left

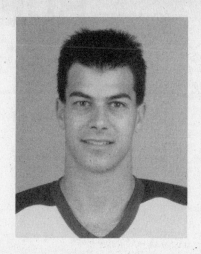

Career statistics:

GP	G	A	TP	PIM
741	135	167	302	451

1999-2000 statistics:

GP	G	A	TP	+/-	PIM	PP	SH	GW	GT	S	PCT
57	9	12	21	-6	32	0	1	0	0	103	8.7

2000-2001 statistics:

GP	G	A	TP	+/-	PIM	PP	SH	GW	GT	S	PCT
79	19	18	37	+7	52	1	2	4	1	123	15.4

2001-2002 statistics:

GP	G	A	TP	+/-	PIM	PP	SH	GW	GT	S	PCT
66	12	13	25	+6	24	1	2	0	0	98	12.2

2002-2003 statistics:

GP	G	A	TP	+/-	PIM	PP	SH	GW	GT	S	PCT
55	10	6	16	+2	18	3	0	1	0	94	10.6

LAST SEASON

Missed 22 games with broken foot. Missed three games with groin injury. Missed one game due to personal reasons. Missed one game due to coach's decision.

THE FINESSE GAME

Zamuner doesn't have great speed, but he compensates for it in other ways, including all-out effort, all the time. A complementary player, he is a grinder who can also handle the puck, and he has some hand skills. Lacking speed, he plays well positionally and takes away the attacker's angles to the net. He doesn't skate as well as many of today's third-line checking wingers, but he is smart enough.

Zamuner has pretty much become a penalty-killing specialist. He is a shorthanded threat because of his anticipation and work ethic, and he easily turns penalty-killing attempts into shorthanded counterattacks. He has a knack for scoring key goals.

Zamuner was a sniper at the minor-league level, but has not been able to have the same impact in the NHL. He has a decent touch for scoring or passing, but it's average at best.

THE PHYSICAL GAME

Zamuner had problems in the past with fitness, until he realized what a big edge he could have with better conditioning. He has good size and he uses it effectively; he is pesky and annoying to play against. On many nights he will be the most physically active forward, adding a real spark with his effort.

THE INTANGIBLES

There are a lot of things Zamuner can't do, but a coach who values what Zamuner can do will find him a valuable role player. Injuries made Zamuner a forgotten man with the Bruins last season.

PROJECTION

Zamuner is a checking winger who can provide a minimum of 15 goals a season.

BUFFALO SABRES

Players' Statistics 2001-2002

POS	NO.	PLAYER	GP	G	A	PTS	+/-	PIM	PP	SH	GW	GT	S	PCT
R	81	MIROSLAV SATAN	79	26	49	75	-3	20	11	1	3	1	240	10.8
C	48	DANIEL BRIERE	82	24	34	58	-20	62	9		4	1	181	13.3
R	12	*ALES KOTALIK	68	21	14	35	-2	30	4		2	2	138	15.2
R	17	JEAN-PIERRE DUMONT	76	14	21	35	-14	44	2		2		135	10.4
C	37	CURTIS BROWN	74	15	16	31	4	40	3	4	4		144	10.4
L	24	TAYLOR PYATT	78	14	14	28	-8	38	2				110	12.7
C	71	JOCHEN HECHT	49	10	16	26	4	30	2		2		145	6.9
C	18	TIM CONNOLLY	80	12	13	25	-28	32	6		2		159	7.5
D	45	DMITRI KALININ	65	8	13	21	-7	57	3	1		1	83	9.6
D	44	ALEXEI ZHITNIK	70	3	18	21	-5	85			1		138	2.2
D	51	BRIAN CAMPBELL	65	2	17	19	-8	20			1		90	2.2
C	22	ADAM MAIR	79	6	11	17	-4	146		1	1		83	7.2
D	3	JAMES PATRICK	69	4	12	16	-3	26	2		1		63	6.3
D	10	*HENRIK TALLINDER	46	3	10	13	-3	28	1				37	8.1
R	61	MAXIM AFINOGENOV	35	5	6	11	-12	21	2		2		77	6.5
D	4	RHETT WARRENER	50		9	9	1	63					47	
L	26	ERIC BOULTON	58	1	5	6	1	178					33	3.0
L	28	JASON BOTTERILL	17	1	4	5	1	14	1				20	5.0
D	74	JAY MCKEE	59		5	5	-16	49					44	
D	8	RORY FITZPATRICK	36	1	3	4	-7	16					29	3.4
C	16	CHRIS TAYLOR	11	1	3	4	-1	2					10	10.0
R	55	DENIS HAMEL	25	2		2	-4	17			1		41	4.9
R	19	*NORMAN MILLEY	8		2	2	-2	6					8	
R	15	*MILAN BARTOVIC	3	1		1	0						5	20.0
R	29	*JAROSLAV KRISTEK	6				-2	4					4	
D	21	RADOSLAV HECL	14				0	2					3	
D	6	DOUG HOUDA	1				-2	2					1	
D	33	*DOUG JANIK	6				1	2						
G	43	MARTIN BIRON	54				0	12						
G	35	MIKA NORONEN	16				0							
G	30	RYAN MILLER	15				0							
C	60	*PAUL GAUSTAD	1				0							
R	23	*SEAN MCMORROW	1				0							

GP = games played; G = goals; A = assists; PTS = points; +/- = goals-for minus goals-against while player is on ice; PIM = penalties in minutes; PP = power-play goals; SH = shorthanded goals; GW = game-winning goals; GT = game-tying goals; S = no. of shots; PCT = percentage of goals to shots; * = rookie

MAXIM AFINOGENOV

Yrs. of NHL service: 4
Born: Moscow, Russia; Sept. 4, 1979
Position: right wing
Height: 6-0
Weight: 190
Uniform no.: 61
Shoots: left

Career statistics:

GP	G	A	TP	PIM
259	56	65	121	171

1999-2000 statistics:

GP	G	A	TP	+/-	PIM	PP	SH	GW	GT	S	PCT
65	16	18	34	-4	41	2	0	2	0	128	12.5

2000-2001 statistics:

GP	G	A	TP	+/-	PIM	PP	SH	GW	GT	S	PCT
78	14	22	36	+1	40	3	0	5	0	190	7.4

2001-2002 statistics:

GP	G	A	TP	+/-	PIM	PP	SH	GW	GT	S	PCT
81	21	19	40	-9	69	3	1	0	0	234	9.0

2002-2003 statistics:

GP	G	A	TP	+/-	PIM	PP	SH	GW	GT	S	PCT
35	5	6	11	-12	21	2	0	2	0	77	6.5

PROJECTION

Afinogenov should be a consistent 25-goal scorer. He has to earn the ice time instead of thinking it is his due.

LAST SEASON

Missed 46 games with concussion. Missed one game due to coach's decision.

THE FINESSE GAME

Afinogenov is a powerful skater with explosive speed and excellent balance. He may have too much confidence in his puckhandling skills because he likes to take the scenic Alexei Kovalev route to the net — that is, the longest way and through as many defenders as possible. Fun, maybe. Effective, no.

Afinogenov needs to use his linemates better and be more of a give-and-go player. His shot isn't great. It's his intimidating speed and the quickness of his shot that gives him the offensive edge.

Afinogenov is a poverty-stricken version of Pavel Bure, an NHL star who thinks he doesn't need his teammates. If Afinogenov scored 50 goals, that might be forgivable. He sees absolutely no need to concern himself with team defense, either. He managed to be -12 in just 35 games.

THE PHYSICAL GAME

Afinogenov is not very big, but on the shifts where he turns on his intensity he can't be intimidated. He plays with determination in the attacking zone and has to learn to apply that to the rest of the ice.

THE INTANGIBLES

If he is going to play such a high-risk game, he will need to score more. The Sabres were probably relieved he came back at all after missing the first half of the season with a concussion suffered in a somewhat mysterious off-season accident.

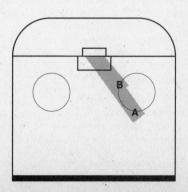

STEVE BEGIN

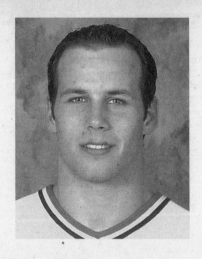

Yrs. of NHL service: 2
Born: Trois Rivieres, Que.; June 14, 1978
Position: center
Height: 5-11
Weight: 190
Uniform no.: 26
Shoots: left

Career statistics:

GP	G	A	TP	PIM
123	11	7	18	192

1999-2000 statistics:

GP	G	A	TP	+/-	PIM	PP	SH	GW	GT	S	PCT
13	1	1	2	-3	18	0	0	0	0	3	33.3

2000-2001 statistics:

GP	G	A	TP	+/-	PIM	PP	SH	GW	GT	S	PCT
4	0	0	0	0	21	0	0	0	0	3	0.0

2001-2002 statistics:

GP	G	A	TP	+/-	PIM	PP	SH	GW	GT	S	PCT
51	7	5	12	-3	79	1	0	0	1	65	10.8

2002-2003 statistics:

GP	G	A	TP	+/-	PIM	PP	SH	GW	GT	S	PCT
50	3	1	4	-7	51	0	0	1	0	59	5.1

LAST SEASON

Acquired by Buffalo with Chris Drury on July 3, 2003, for Steven Reinprecht and Rhett Warrener. Missed eight games with concussion. Missed six games with broken nose. Missed one game with flu. Missed 17 games due to coach's decision.

THE FINESSE GAME

Begin is not overly skilled, but he is a team player first, and that may net him a roster spot on the Sabres, who could use a guy with some oomph.

He could become a third-line player at best, although Begin will continue to be a fourth-line energy guy for the foreseeable future. He is versatile and can play any of the three forward positions.

Begin is strong in the corners. He will be one of those players who just skates up and down his wing. He will be a lot like Randy McKay was early in his career, although he doesn't have as much offensive upside as McKay because he is not as good a skater. His skating is NHL calibre but he lacks agility. He will get in on the forecheck and make his hits.

Begin doesn't have great hands or vision. He has a fairly heavy shot. Most of his goals will come from scaring people into giving him enough room and simply grinding it out around the net.

THE PHYSICAL GAME

A very rugged player, Begin is a throwback, a tough customer and a team man who will pay the price to win. He will come in and make his mark and keep other teams honest. His penalty minutes come from sticking up for teammates or to make a point. He is not an undisciplined player.

THE INTANGIBLES

Begin is a gritty depth guy. He was used more when Darryl Sutter took over as the Flames' coach in December. New coach Lindy Ruff may appreciate the same rugged qualities, which may help him earn more ice time this season, even in his fourth-line role.

PROJECTION

Players like Begin are an essential part of team chemistry. His points will be modest in a part-time role, but his penalty minutes are likely to be impressive.

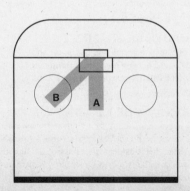

MARTIN BIRON

Yrs. of NHL service: 5
Born: Lac St. Charles, Que.; Aug. 15, 1977
Position: goaltender
Height: 6-2
Weight: 168
Uniform no.: 43
Catches: left

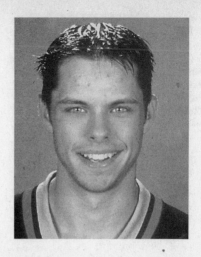

Career statistics:

GP	MIN	GA	SO	GAA	A	PIM
194	10802	435	15	2.42	2	26

1999-2000 statistics:

GP	MIN	GAA	W	L	T	SO	GA	S	SAPCT	PIM
41	2229	2.42	19	18	2	5	90	988	.909	6

2000-2001 statistics:

GP	MIN	GAA	W	L	T	SO	GA	S	SAPCT	PIM
18	918	2.55	7	7	1	2	39	427	.909	0

2001-2002 statistics:

GP	MIN	GAA	W	L	T	SO	GA	S	SAPCT	PIM
72	4085	2.22	31	28	10	4	151	1781	.915	8

2002-2003 statistics:

GP	MIN	GAA	W	L	T	SO	GA	S	SAPCT	PIM
54	3170	2.56	17	28	6	4	135	1468	.908	12

PROJECTION
Biron is on the hot seat in Buffalo. If Miller or Mika Noronen steps up and has a good camp, Biron could be trade bait unless he responds to the challenge. His role as the No. 1 goalie is in jeopardy.

LAST SEASON
Recorded 25 or more wins for second consecutive season.

THE PHYSICAL GAME
Biron was pretty much skin and bones when he was drafted, and has gradually built himself up to be able to handle the wear and tear of NHL goaltending. He is still on the ridiculously lean side, and will have to have his carbs on game days.

Like Martin Brodeur, whose personality Biron echoes, he is a hybrid goalie: not quite butterfly, not quite stand-up. His bent-over stance reminds onlookers of Mike Liut. His long legs take away the lower portion of the net which makes the butterfly work well for him. His recovery time is good, and if he does go down, he recovers his feet quickly. He will be aggressive with his stick, taking a Bill Smith-like whack at someone in his crease. Biron is average handling the puck.

THE MENTAL GAME
Succeeding Dominik Hasek put a great strain on Biron. Although he behaves like a pretty carefree guy, his lack of success last season obviously weighed heavily on him.

THE INTANGIBLES
Biron seemed hopelessly lost at times last season. He had trouble maintaining his focus and concentration. The fact that Buffalo has a strong goaltending prospect in Ryan Miller won't provide much comfort for him.

DANIEL BRIERE

Yrs. of NHL service: 5
Born: Gatineau, Que.; Oct. 6, 1977
Position: center
Height: 5-10
Weight: 181
Uniform no.: 48
Shoots: left

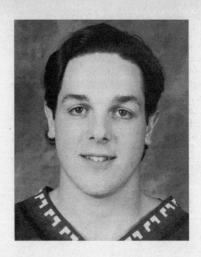

Career statistics:

GP	G	A	TP	PIM
272	77	81	158	158

1999-2000 statistics:

GP	G	A	TP	+/-	PIM	PP	SH	GW	GT	S	PCT
13	1	1	2	0	0	0	0	0	0	9	11.1

2000-2001 statistics:

GP	G	A	TP	+/-	PIM	PP	SH	GW	GT	S	PCT
30	11	4	15	-2	12	9	0	1	0	43	25.6

2001-2002 statistics:

GP	G	A	TP	+/-	PIM	PP	SH	GW	GT	S	PCT
78	32	28	60	+6	52	12	0	5	1	149	21.5

2002-2003 statistics:

GP	G	A	TP	+/-	PIM	PP	SH	GW	GT	S	PCT
82	24	34	58	-20	62	9	0	4	1	181	13.3

LAST SEASON

Acquired from Phoenix on March 11, 2003, with a third-round draft pick in 2004 for Chris Gratton and a fourth-round draft pick in 2004. Tied for Sabres' lead in game-winning goals. Second on team in goals, assists, points, power-play goals, shots, and shooting percentage. Only player on Sabres to appear in all 82 games.

THE FINESSE GAME

Briere is a pure goal-scorer, but what has turned him from a career minor leaguer to a bona fide major leaguer is his willingness to add other elements to his game instead of simply relying on his great shot. Briere kills penalties, wins draws, and works hard to get to loose pucks.

He has a great release on an accurate shot, but Briere's chief asset is as a playmaker. He is dynamite on the power play, with the extra space allowing him the extra half-second of time to make a play. He uses his time and space wisely. He has a great passing touch with the puck, plus terrific hockey sense and vision. He knows how to play this game.

Briere is an excellent, shifty skater, which serves him well in the offensive zone since players are forced to restrain him rather than hit him. Defensively, he has to use his skating and his hand skills to survive. He's outmuscled in any physical match-ups. The big knock on Briere is his lack of defensive awareness.

THE PHYSICAL GAME

Briere has improved his physical conditioning, but the coaching staff still has to watch his minutes because he plays hard and will wear down if he is overused.

Briere has to play with an edge, even if he is on the small side.

THE INTANGIBLES

Briere has been benched, paid his dues in the minors, and passed through the waiver wire and it made him more determined than ever to succeed at the NHL level. He was a big hit in Buffalo after the deal, with 12 points in 14 games.

PROJECTION

Briere should be a 30/30 man (30 goals, 30 assists) this season.

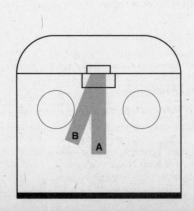

CURTIS BROWN

Yrs. of NHL service: 7
Born: Unity, Sask.; Feb. 12, 1976
Position: center
Height: 6-0
Weight: 197
Uniform no.: 37
Shoots: left

Career statistics:

GP	G	A	TP	PIM
474	100	131	231	258

1999-2000 statistics:

GP	G	A	TP	+/-	PIM	PP	SH	GW	GT	S	PCT
74	22	29	51	+19	42	5	0	4	1	149	14.8

2000-2001 statistics:

GP	G	A	TP	+/-	PIM	PP	SH	GW	GT	S	PCT
70	10	22	32	+15	34	2	1	0	0	105	9.5

2001-2002 statistics:

GP	G	A	TP	+/-	PIM	PP	SH	GW	GT	S	PCT
82	20	17	37	-4	32	4	1	5	0	171	11.7

2002-2003 statistics:

GP	G	A	TP	+/-	PIM	PP	SH	GW	GT	S	PCT
74	15	16	31	+4	40	3	4	4	0	144	10.4

LAST SEASON

Tied for third in NHL in shorthanded goals. Led team in plus-minus and shorthanded goals. Tied for team lead in game-winning goals. Missed five games with fractured ankle. Missed two games with knee injury. Missed one game due to coach's decision.

THE FINESSE GAME

Brown is a little cannonball, strong and quick on his skates and unafraid to get involved around the net. He is an excellent penalty killer, with terrific reads and anticipation, and the jump to pick off passes and turn them into shorthanded chances.

A converted left wing, Brown makes an ideal third-line forward. The Sabres are so thin in talent that sometimes he is bumped up to a top-six job. It's hard to fault a guy when he is playing out of position.

Brown has enough offensive skills to play on the top two lines, but his chief asset is his defensive ability. He is Selke Trophy caliber. Brown will create things with his speed on the forecheck and then use his skilled hands to make the tape-to-tape pass. He is a playmaker first. Brown's hockey sense and defensive awareness are exceptional.

THE PHYSICAL GAME

Brown is little, but plays with a bit of swagger. He isn't really tough — he just gives the impression that he won't back off. He is abrasive and annoying. He will wear down if he is overused.

THE INTANGIBLES

Brown is a valuable role player, but as a restricted free agent on a budget-conscious team, he could lure some trade offers.

PROJECTION

He will get a lot of ice time again. Brown should produce 40 points.

BRIAN CAMPBELL

Yrs. of NHL service: 2
Born: Strathroy, Ont.; May 23, 1979
Position: defense
Height: 6-0
Weight: 190
Uniform no.: 51
Shoots: left

Career statistics:

GP	G	A	TP	PIM
114	6	24	30	38

1999-2000 statistics:

GP	G	A	TP	+/-	PIM	PP	SH	GW	GT	S	PCT
12	1	4	5	-2	4	0	0	0	0	10	10.0

2000-2001 statistics:

GP	G	A	TP	+/-	PIM	PP	SH	GW	GT	S	PCT
8	0	0	0	-2	2	0	0	0	0	7	0.0

2001-2002 statistics:

GP	G	A	TP	+/-	PIM	PP	SH	GW	GT	S	PCT
29	3	3	6	0	12	0	0	0	0	30	10.0

2002-2003 statistics:

GP	G	A	TP	+/-	PIM	PP	SH	GW	GT	S	PCT
65	2	17	19	-8	20	0	0	1	0	90	2.2

PROJECTION

Campbell needs to show more and we anticipate he will. Expect an increase into the range of 30-35 points.

LAST SEASON

Missed 17 games due to coach's decision.

THE FINESSE GAME

The Sabres have been counting on Campbell to be the second coming of Phil Housley, but it's been a long time coming.

Campbell's future appears to be that of an offensively gifted, rushing, power-play quarterback, but all of that will depend on Campbell's continuing adjustment to pace of the NHL game.

Campbell is a slick, speedy skater. He really busts it from the neutral zone on the breakout. He's a strong puckhandler with good hockey sense and vision. Campbell needs to improve his play in his own end. He is not going to have the kind of elite numbers that will allow teams to overlook his defensive lapses.

Campbell has gotten a lot smarter about his reads. He knows when to jump into the play and when to stay back. Because he's not very physical, he is going to have to continue to work on his positional play.

THE PHYSICAL GAME

The knock on Campbell is his lack of size. He's about Housley-size, though, and he has the same red hair. A team can live with those drawbacks if Campbell can start putting up big numbers.

THE INTANGIBLES

Campbell isn't a top-four defenseman yet, but he could play his way onto the Sabres as a third-pair defender and pick up some increased power-play time.

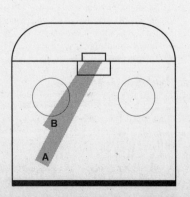

TIM CONNOLLY

Yrs. of NHL service: 4
Born: Syracuse, NY; May 7, 1980
Position: center
Height: 6-1
Weight: 182
Uniform no.: 18
Shoots: right

Career statistics:

GP	G	A	TP	PIM
325	46	99	145	152

1999-2000 statistics:

GP	G	A	TP	+/-	PIM	PP	SH	GW	GT	S	PCT
81	14	20	34	-25	44	2	1	1	1	114	12.3

2000-2001 statistics:

GP	G	A	TP	+/-	PIM	PP	SH	GW	GT	S	PCT
82	10	31	41	-14	42	5	0	0	0	171	5.8

2001-2002 statistics:

GP	G	A	TP	+/-	PIM	PP	SH	GW	GT	S	PCT
82	10	35	45	+4	34	3	0	3	0	126	7.9

2002-2003 statistics:

GP	G	A	TP	+/-	PIM	PP	SH	GW	GT	S	PCT
80	12	13	25	-28	32	6	0	2	0	159	7.5

LAST SEASON

Third on team in power-play goals and shots. Worst plus-minus on team. Missed two games due to NHL suspension.

THE FINESSE GAME

One area where Connolly improved dramatically last season was in trying to score goals. A little selfishness can go a long way, especially if a player takes a shot from a high-quality scoring area instead of trying to force a pass to a teammate who is in a worse spot. Connolly made better use of his teammates last season.

Connolly is an exceptional and exciting one-on-one player. He works the give-and-go well. Connolly has reminded some scouts of Steve Yzerman style-wise because of his ability to make plays at a very high tempo. Connolly has great confidence in his abilities. He is creative and not afraid to try new moves. A quick and agile skater with a low center of gravity, he maintains his control of the puck through traffic. He needs to be less of a perimeter player, however.

Connolly is a mainstay on the second-unit power play in Buffalo. He is smart and his anticipation is exceptional. As his game matures, he will also see more time killing penalties. His defensive play at even strength remains a project.

THE PHYSICAL GAME

Connolly needs to spend time in the weight room. He is pretty strong for his size already. Connolly has a bit of an attitude, which hasn't exactly endeared him to some veteran officials. He might not get the benefit of some penalty calls. He received a four-game NHL suspension (he will serve the remaining two at the start of this season) for high-sticking Garnet Exelby, which was more of a reactionary incident than an attempt to injure.

THE INTANGIBLES

Likely to be the No. 2 center behind Daniel Briere, Connolly will get to avoid some checking attention. Connolly was a restricted free agent after the season. He is still pretty immature emotionally and has some growing up to do.

PROJECTION

Connolly's production was way off last season. He should be in the 50-point range with his ability.

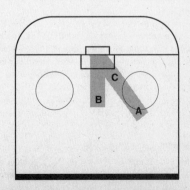

ANDY DELMORE

Yrs. of NHL service: 4
Born: LaSalle, Ont.; Dec. 26, 1976
Position: right defense
Height: 6-1
Weight: 200
Uniform no.: 5
Shoots: right

Career statistics:

GP	G	A	TP	PIM
239	41	53	94	74

1999-2000 statistics:

GP	G	A	TP	+/-	PIM	PP	SH	GW	GT	S	PCT
27	2	5	7	-1	8	0	0	1	0	55	3.6

2000-2001 statistics:

GP	G	A	TP	+/-	PIM	PP	SH	GW	GT	S	PCT
66	5	9	14	+2	16	2	0	0	0	119	4.2

2001-2002 statistics:

GP	G	A	TP	+/-	PIM	PP	SH	GW	GT	S	PCT
73	16	22	38	-13	22	11	0	3	0	175	9.1

2002-2003 statistics:

GP	G	A	TP	+/-	PIM	PP	SH	GW	GT	S	PCT
71	18	16	34	-17	28	14	0	6	0	149	12.1

LAST SEASON

Acquired by Buffalo on June 27, 2003, from Nashville for a third-round draft pick in 2004. Tied for first among NHL defensemen in goals. Led Predators defensemen in points. Led team in power-play goals and game-winning goals. Missed six games with shoulder injury. Missed three games with wrist injury. Missed four games due to coach's decision.

THE FINESSE GAME

Delmore is an excellent skater with a booming slap shot. That might be good enough to keep him in the league as a forward, but Delmore is a defenseman whose defensive reads are barely adequate. He needs a lot of work on his defensive game and needs to be paired with a reliable, stay-at-home defenseman who can almost act as an on-ice coach. Delmore has potential because of his offensive ability, but he is high, high risk. Nashville even used him at right wing last season just to keep his power-play acumen in the lineup.

Delmore can't be sent out to protect a lead late in a tight game because he is a defensive liability. But high risks can mean high rewards; he will use his blazing speed to rush the puck when other, more sensible, defensemen wouldn't. If it pays off with a goal, then Delmore is a hero. If not, he's a minus.

Delmore has a hard, accurate shot with a quick release, and is totally unafraid to gamble in-deep. He should be very afraid.

THE PHYSICAL GAME

Delmore is average in size for an NHL defenseman, but he is not in any way physical. He needs to be willing to use his body to at least tie up an opposing forward. Delmore has to get stronger and learn better body positioning. He will block shots. The past two seasons, Delmore has started off looking like he will attempt to play a better all-around game, but he usually lets it go to seed in the second half. He was benched for four of the last 10 games in Nashville, however.

THE INTANGIBLES

Delmore was tied with some pretty big names (Al MacInnis and Sergei Gonchar) for most goals scored by a defenseman last season, but has earned nowhere near the respect those two veterans have. Delmore must become a more complete player if he wants a long NHL career.

PROJECTION

Delmore's points were impressive but he needs to be less high-risk. Delmore can score 35 points and trim his plus-minus.

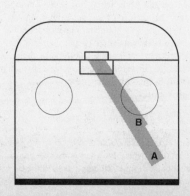

CHRIS DRURY

Yrs. of NHL service: 5
Born: Trumbull, Conn.; Aug. 20, 1976
Position: center
Height: 5-10
Weight: 180
Uniform no.: 18
Shoots: right

Career statistics:

GP	G	A	TP	PIM
394	108	167	275	222

1999-2000 statistics:

GP	G	A	TP	+/-	PIM	PP	SH	GW	GT	S	PCT
82	20	47	67	+8	42	7	0	2	0	213	9.4

2000-2001 statistics:

GP	G	A	TP	+/-	PIM	PP	SH	GW	GT	S	PCT
71	24	41	65	+6	47	11	0	5	1	204	11.8

2001-2002 statistics:

GP	G	A	TP	+/-	PIM	PP	SH	GW	GT	S	PCT
82	21	25	46	+1	38	5	0	6	0	236	8.9

2002-2003 statistics:

GP	G	A	TP	+/-	PIM	PP	SH	GW	GT	S	PCT
80	23	30	53	-9	33	5	1	5	2	224	10.3

LAST SEASON

Acquired by Buffalo with Steve Begin on July 3, 2003, for Steven Reinprecht and Rhett Warrener. Previously acquired by Calgary with Stephane Yelle from Colorado on October 1, 2002, for Dean McAmmond, Derek Morris, and Jeff Shantz. Missed one game with finger injury. Missed one game with groin injury.

THE FINESSE GAME

Drury has a wealth of assets, starting with his skating. He gets in on top of a goalie very quickly — and we mean right on top, because he is probably the best on the team at crease-crashing. He is able to control the puck while charging in. He knows where the net is and isn't afraid to get there by the shortest route possible, even though he isn't the biggest guy in the world.

Drury has quick and soft hands, and is a steady scorer. His effort is so consistent and that's what produces his points. He already has an advanced defensive side to his game. Even on nights when he isn't scoring, he is doing something to help his team win. He is a clever playmaker, but linemates can also pick up goals by following him to the net and feasting on the rebounds his efforts create.

He is capable of playing wing or center, but was used most often by Calgary in the middle. Drury is a smart player who quickly grasps any concepts the coaching staff pitch him.

THE PHYSICAL GAME

Small but sturdy, Drury doesn't back down an inch and is usually the player who makes the pre-emptive hit. He sure doesn't play little. Drury plays hard and competes every shift, whether it's the first minute of the game or the last.

THE INTANGIBLES

Remarkably poised and mature, with excellent leadership skills, Drury is probably a future captain. Buffalo will benefit from his leadership and he will be a top-two center with the Sabres.

PROJECTION

Drury didn't have much of a supporting cast in Calgary and the picture didn't improve much with the trade to Buffalo. He should be good for 25 goals on his own merits.

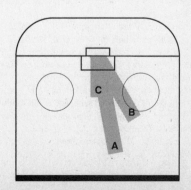

J. P. DUMONT

Yrs. of NHL service: 5
Born: Montreal, Que.; Apr. 1, 1978
Position: right wing
Height: 6-1
Weight: 205
Uniform no.: 17
Shoots: left

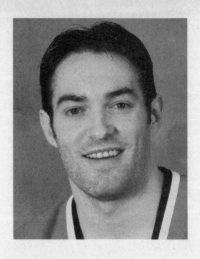

Career statistics:

GP	G	A	TP	PIM
303	79	84	163	168

1999-2000 statistics:

GP	G	A	TP	+/-	PIM	PP	SH	GW	GT	S	PCT
47	10	8	18	-6	18	0	0	1	0	86	11.6

2000-2001 statistics:

GP	G	A	TP	+/-	PIM	PP	SH	GW	GT	S	PCT
79	23	28	51	+1	54	9	0	5	0	156	14.7

2001-2002 statistics:

GP	G	A	TP	+/-	PIM	PP	SH	GW	GT	S	PCT
76	23	21	44	-10	42	7	0	3	1	154	14.9

2002-2003 statistics:

GP	G	A	TP	+/-	PIM	PP	SH	GW	GT	S	PCT
76	14	21	35	-14	44	2	0	2	0	135	10.4

LAST SEASON

Third on team in assists. Tied for third on team in points. Missed four games with flu. Missed one game with back injury. Missed one game due to coach's decision.

THE FINESSE GAME

Dumont has the knack of being in the right place at the right time. He does a lot of his work around the front of the net. A lot of goal-scorers play on the perimeter or look for the big, showy shot from somewhere. He's a guy that gets on the inside and doesn't mind the rough going.

He has all of the weapons needed to become a scorer in the NHL. Dumont is an instinctive shooter and playmaker who sees his options a step ahead of everyone else. He disguises his intentions well. Because he is unselfish with the puck, defenders may expect the pass. But he has an excellent wrist and slap shot, so you can't allow him to cruise to the net. He is pure hands.

Dumont goes through and around players like the breeze, with excellent puck control. His skating is NHL caliber. He has good acceleration for short bursts or rink-long sprints. He had to work on his conditioning and took power-skating lessons, so he is willing to work to improve his game. His hand-eye coordination for tip-ins and rebounds is outstanding.

As is typical with many slow-developing players, the knock on Dumont is his lack of intensity at times, but he is maturing. He is one of those rare players who finds the back of the net by any means possible.

THE PHYSICAL GAME

Dumont is tall but whippet-thin. He has an edge to his game, which he needs to show more on a consistent basis.

THE INTANGIBLES

Dumont had an up-and-down season in tough circumstances in Buffalo. He did perk up after newcomer Daniel Briere was put on his line.

PROJECTION

Dumont should be a 30-goal scorer.

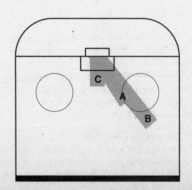

JOCHEN HECHT

Yrs. of NHL service: 4
Born: Mannheim, Germany; June 21, 1977
Position: center
Height: 6-1
Weight: 200
Uniform no.: 71
Shoots: left

Career statistics:

GP	G	A	TP	PIM
269	58	86	144	166

1999-2000 statistics:

GP	G	A	TP	+/-	PIM	PP	SH	GW	GT	S	PCT
63	13	21	34	+20	28	5	0	1	0	140	9.3

2000-2001 statistics:

GP	G	A	TP	+/-	PIM	PP	SH	GW	GT	S	PCT
72	19	25	44	+11	48	8	3	1	2	208	9.1

2001-2002 statistics:

GP	G	A	TP	+/-	PIM	PP	SH	GW	GT	S	PCT
82	16	24	40	+4	60	5	0	3	1	211	7.6

2002-2003 statistics:

GP	G	A	TP	+/-	PIM	PP	SH	GW	GT	S	PCT
49	10	16	26	+4	30	2	0	2	0	145	6.9

LAST SEASON

Missed 20 games with concussion. Missed 11 games with wrist injuries. Missed two games with knee injury.

THE FINESSE GAME

Hecht is a rangy forward who can handle all three forward positions. He is a good skater with a good passing touch, a playmaker more than a scorer. He plays with a straight-up stance that allows him to see everything. He stickhandles in close, and has a great move walking out from the corner or behind the net.

A very smart player with deceptive speed, Hecht will probably be a better winger since he isn't strong enough on draws to handle playing center full-time. He is a tough read for opposing defensemen because he doesn't do the same thing every time. He is quite unpredictable: he might try to beat a defender one-on-one on one rush and the next time chip the puck into the corner or work a give-and-go. He uses a lot of play selections. Hecht is far from a reluctant shooter.

Hecht plays with drive. He doesn't quit. He's never going to be the big star on a team but he's going to be a big part of a team. Hecht was originally touted as a power forward when he broke in with the Blues but it's doubtful he will develop along those lines. Hecht is a guy who will show up to play every night. He can kill penalties and add depth to the Sabres.

THE PHYSICAL GAME

Physical play doesn't bother Hecht, but he doesn't initiate it. He has to get a lot stronger and learn to play in the dirty areas of the ice. He doesn't mind sticking his nose in. Hecht is well-conditioned and can handle 18 minutes of ice time a night.

THE INTANGIBLES

Hecht is an underrated forward, the kind of guy you need to watch every night to appreciate. Hecht got off to a good start before injuries hit. He finished the season playing with Daniel Briere and J.P. Dumont.

PROJECTION

Hecht should be a 20-goal scorer as a top-six forward with the Sabres.

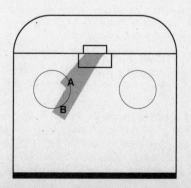

DMITRI KALININ

Yrs. of NHL service: 3
Born: Cheljabinsk, Russia; July 22, 1980
Position: defense
Height: 6-2
Weight: 215
Uniform no.: 45
Shoots: left

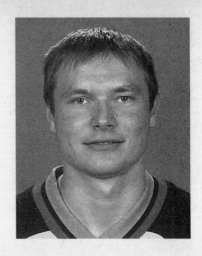

Career statistics:

GP	G	A	TP	PIM
206	14	42	56	125

1999-2000 statistics:

GP	G	A	TP	+/-	PIM	PP	SH	GW	GT	S	PCT
4	0	0	0	0	4	0	0	0	0	3	0.0

2000-2001 statistics:

GP	G	A	TP	+/-	PIM	PP	SH	GW	GT	S	PCT
79	4	18	22	-2	38	2	0	0	0	88	4.5

2001-2002 statistics:

GP	G	A	TP	+/-	PIM	PP	SH	GW	GT	S	PCT
58	2	11	13	-6	26	0	0	0	0	67	3.0

2002-2003 statistics:

GP	G	A	TP	+/-	PIM	PP	SH	GW	GT	S	PCT
65	8	13	21	-7	57	3	1	0	1	83	9.6

Zhitnik would open up some ice time. Ideally, he will mature into a steady, everyday second-pair defenseman.

PROJECTION

He should earn a full-time role and score 25-30 points.

LAST SEASON

Second on team in average ice time (21:40). Missed seven games with shoulder injury. Missed one game with flu. Missed nine games due to coach's decision. Appeared in one game with Rochester (AHL), scoring 0-0 — 0.

THE FINESSE GAME

Kalinin is an excellent skater with good mobility and lateral movement. He has the ability to rush the puck out of the defensive zone, or make an outlet pass. Kalinin seems to make the right decision either way. He doesn't get panicky and is able to quickly make the proper decision.

Kalinin is smart and has a good grasp of the game. He is a hard worker, and he is consistent, especially for a younger player. Kalinin had to persevere through some injuries early in his junior career, and he seems to appreciate what it takes to hold an NHL job.

Kalinin has a decent shot from the point but he prefers to be a stay-at-home defenseman and it's not likely he will ever get too involved in the power play. He is a good penalty killer.

THE PHYSICAL GAME

Kalinin has good size and strength and is able to battle in a one-on-one situation. He takes the body well, but he isn't a huge hitter.

THE INTANGIBLES

Kalinin's benchings came at the start of the season. Buffalo is getting well-stocked on defense and he will have to fight even harder for a top-four job this season, although the anticipated departure of Alexei

ALES KOTALIK

Yrs. of NHL service: 1
Born: Jindrichuv Hradec, Czech Republic; Dec. 23, 1978
Position: right wing
Height: 6-1
Weight: 217
Uniform no.: 12
Shoots: right

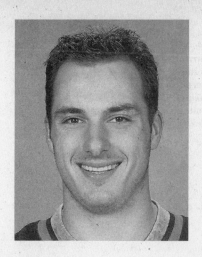

Career statistics:

GP	G	A	TP	PIM
81	22	17	39	32

2001-2002 statistics:

GP	G	A	TP	+/-	PIM	PP	SH	GW	GT	S	PCT
13	1	3	4	-1	2	0	0	0	0	21	4.8

2002-2003 statistics:

GP	G	A	TP	+/-	PIM	PP	SH	GW	GT	S	PCT
68	21	14	35	-2	30	4	0	2	2	138	15.2

LAST SEASON

First NHL season. Second among NHL rookies in goals. Third among NHL rookies in shooting percentage. Fourth among NHL rookies in points. Tied for fourth among NHL rookies in power-play goals. Fifth among NHL rookies in shots. Led team in shooting percentage. Third on team in goals. Tied for third on team in points. Missed six games due to coach's decision. Missed three games with flu. Appeared in eight games with Rochester (AHL), scoring 0-2 — 2 with 4 PIM.

THE FINESSE GAME

Kotalik is a power forward in the making, which is something Buffalo could use after trading away Vaclav Varada.

Kotalik has excellent tools. He is a good skater who is agile in traffic. He has wonderful hands and a good scoring instinct. It's rare to see a player have a high shot total and a high shooting percentage. Usually a player sacrifices attempts for accuracy or vice versa. Not only does Kotalik get a healthy share of scoring chances, but he converts on them as well.

Kotalik's defensive game is pretty sound. He is versatile and can play either right wing or center although his future is probably on the wing.

THE PHYSICAL GAME

Buffalo would like Kotalik to play with more of an edge. He's a decent size but isn't very aggressive. Kotalik won't shy away from contact, but he needs to initiate more.

THE INTANGIBLES

Kotalik improved as the season wore on, and was one of the top rookies of last season. He is second on the Sabres' depth chart behind Miroslav Satan.

PROJECTION

Kotalik had a strong second half when a lot of other first-year NHLers fade. It's a promising sign for the upcoming season.

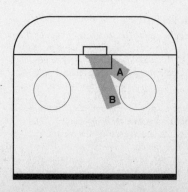

JAY MCKEE

Yrs. of NHL service: 7
Born: Kingston, Ont.; Sept. 8, 1977
Position: left defense
Height: 6-4
Weight: 212
Uniform no.: 74
Shoots: left

Career statistics:

GP	G	A	TP	PIM
464	10	67	77	372

1999-2000 statistics:

GP	G	A	TP	+/-	PIM	PP	SH	GW	GT	S	PCT
78	5	12	17	+5	50	1	0	1	0	84	6.0

2000-2001 statistics:

GP	G	A	TP	+/-	PIM	PP	SH	GW	GT	S	PCT
74	1	10	11	+9	76	0	0	0	0	62	1.6

2001-2002 statistics:

GP	G	A	TP	+/-	PIM	PP	SH	GW	GT	S	PCT
81	2	11	13	+18	43	0	0	1	0	50	4.0

2002-2003 statistics:

GP	G	A	TP	+/-	PIM	PP	SH	GW	GT	S	PCT
59	0	5	5	-16	49	0	0	0	0	44	0.0

PROJECTION

McKee is a steady regular but don't count on him for more than 10 points.

LAST SEASON

Missed 22 games with knee injuries. Missed one game with flu.

THE FINESSE GAME

McKee has been studiously applying his skills to the defensive aspects of his game for so long now that the offensive part of the game — what little he had — has completely atrophied. Considering his skill level, he could be more of a two-way defenseman but seems to have found his comfort zone in the defensive zone.

McKee is a strong skater, which powers his open-ice hits. He has good acceleration and quickness to carry the puck out of the zone. He gets involved in the attack because of his skating, but he doesn't have elite hands or playmaking skills. He succeeds when he is paired with a more offensive-minded partner.

He has sharp hockey sense and plays an advanced positional game. McKee routinely handles the checking assignments against other teams' top forwards.

THE PHYSICAL GAME

McKee has good size and is wiry and tough, if a little on the lean side. He doesn't have much of a mean streak. McKee knows he has to hit to be effective. He just doesn't do it with much relish.

THE INTANGIBLES

McKee is one of the most valuable Sabres. He continues to mature as a player and as a leader. He was a restricted free agent after the season.

TAYLOR PYATT

Yrs. of NHL service: 3
Born: Thunder Bay, Ont.; Aug. 19, 1981
Position: left wing
Height: 6-4
Weight: 222
Uniform no.: 24
Shoots: left

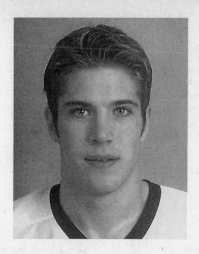

Career statistics:

GP	G	A	TP	PIM
204	28	38	66	112

2000-2001 statistics:

GP	G	A	TP	+/-	PIM	PP	SH	GW	GT	S	PCT
78	4	14	18	-17	39	1	0	2	0	86	4.7

2001-2002 statistics:

GP	G	A	TP	+/-	PIM	PP	SH	GW	GT	S	PCT
48	10	10	20	+4	35	0	0	0	1	61	16.4

2002-2003 statistics:

GP	G	A	TP	+/-	PIM	PP	SH	GW	GT	S	PCT
78	14	14	28	-8	38	2	0	0	0	110	12.7

LAST SEASON

Third on team in shooting percentage. Missed four games with concussion.

THE FINESSE GAME

Pyatt is a power forward who doesn't play with a lot of power — think of a poor man's John LeClair, and that's Pyatt.

Pyatt has great hands. He is strong and he has a knack for the net. He has a good wrist and slap shot. Since Pyatt is usually so worried about the guy he was checking in his defensive role, he never felt very comfortable stretching himself offensively. He will. He tends to score in streaks and then go into scoring droughts, but consistency should come along in time.

Pyatt is a very good skater. If he ever decides to drive with more force to the net he will be just about unstoppable. He doesn't initiate contact. He will ward people off when they're trying to hang on to him but he should be bulling towards the net and making people scatter.

Pyatt hustles and plays with energy. He is aware defensively. He can be sent out to protect a one-goal lead. He is strong along the wall and in the corners. He backchecks diligently.

THE PHYSICAL GAME

Pyatt finishes poised in traffic. He is very strong on his skates, well-balanced, and tough to knock down. He will be a factor on the power play, since he willingly goes to the net to battle for rebounds, deflections, and screens.

THE INTANGIBLES

Players of Pyatt's ilk take longer to develop. From what Buffalo has seen of him so far, they are willing to be patient.

PROJECTION

Pyatt showed an improved scoring touch but he really needs to turn it up a notch and break through the 20-goal barrier.

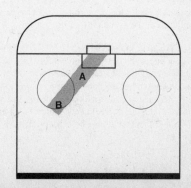

MIROSLAV SATAN

Yrs. of NHL service: 8
Born: Topolcany, Slovakia; Oct. 22, 1974
Position: left wing
Height: 6-3
Weight: 190
Uniform no.: 81
Shoots: left

Career statistics:

GP	G	A	TP	PIM
622	230	232	462	247

1999-2000 statistics:

GP	G	A	TP	+/-	PIM	PP	SH	GW	GT	S	PCT
81	33	34	67	+16	32	5	3	5	1	265	12.5

2000-2001 statistics:

GP	G	A	TP	+/-	PIM	PP	SH	GW	GT	S	PCT
82	29	33	62	+5	36	8	2	4	1	206	14.1

2001-2002 statistics:

GP	G	A	TP	+/-	PIM	PP	SH	GW	GT	S	PCT
82	37	36	73	+14	33	15	5	5	0	267	13.9

2002-2003 statistics:

GP	G	A	TP	+/-	PIM	PP	SH	GW	GT	S	PCT
79	26	49	75	-3	20	11	1	3	1	240	10.8

LAST SEASON

Led team in points for sixth season. Led team in goals, assists, power-play goals, and shots. Third on team in average ice time (21:23) and game-winning goals. Career highs in assists and points. Missed three games with hip injury.

THE FINESSE GAME

Satan has terrific breakaway speed, which allows him to pull away from many defenders. Satan will lapse into bad nights where he gambles and plays a riskier game, but he is a fairly conscientious two-way player.

Not shy about shooting, Satan keeps his head up and looks for his shooting holes, and is accurate with a wrist and snap shot. He sees his passing options and will sometimes make the play, but he is the sniper on whatever line he is playing and prefers to take the shot himself. The majority of his assists will come as a result of his scoring attempts. One fault is his tendency to hold on to the puck too long.

Satan has been a moody sort in the past but he was committed and consistent most of last season.

THE PHYSICAL GAME

Not being huge, and being the prime checking objective on a team that isn't exactly loaded with offensive options takes its toll on Satan at crunch time. With Buffalo's financial concerns, the burden is likely to get heavier on Satan before it gets lighter. Satan has a wiry strength, and shouldn't be as intimidated as he appears to be.

THE INTANGIBLES

Satan was the subject of a lot of trade interest at the March deadline, but with a new owner on board, maybe Satan can be re-signed (he was an unrestricted free agent) and be the centerpiece of Buffalo's return to respectability. That he carved out the kind of numbers he did last season in such a depressing atmosphere and with little aid shows how talented a player Satan is. He scored only two goals after the trade deadline, however.

PROJECTION

Goals, goals, goals — forget playmaking. Satan wants to score. He could be a 40-goal scorer if he had the right setup guy.

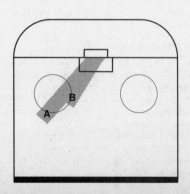

ALEXEI ZHITNIK

Yrs. of NHL service: 11
Born: Kiev, Ukraine; Oct. 10, 1972
Position: left defense
Height: 5-11
Weight: 215
Uniform no.: 44
Shoots: left

Career statistics:

GP	G	A	TP	PIM
814	77	291	368	928

1999-2000 statistics:

GP	G	A	TP	+/-	PIM	PP	SH	GW	GT	S	PCT
74	2	11	13	-6	95	1	0	0	0	139	1.4

2000-2001 statistics:

GP	G	A	TP	+/-	PIM	PP	SH	GW	GT	S	PCT
78	8	29	37	-3	75	5	0	1	1	149	5.4

2001-2002 statistics:

GP	G	A	TP	+/-	PIM	PP	SH	GW	GT	S	PCT
82	1	33	34	-1	80	1	0	0	0	150	0.7

2002-2003 statistics:

GP	G	A	TP	+/-	PIM	PP	SH	GW	GT	S	PCT
70	3	18	21	-5	85	0	0	1	0	138	2.2

THE INTANGIBLES

At $3.75 million, can the Sabres afford to keep him, especially since he becomes an unrestricted free agent after this season?

PROJECTION

Zhitnik's absolute top end is 30 points.

LAST SEASON

Led team in average ice time (26:32). Third on team in penalty minutes.

THE FINESSE GAME

Zhitnik has a bowlegged skating style that ex-coach Barry Melrose once compared to Bobby Orr's. Zhitnik is no Orr, but he was born with skates on. He has speed, acceleration, and lateral mobility.

Zhitnik simply isn't an elite offensive defenseman, no matter how hard the Sabres try to pretend he is. It's like that Joan Cusack line from "Working Girl." You can dance around in your underwear and sing, but it doesn't make you Madonna.

Zhitnik needs to develop his lateral movement better; he needs to use all of the blueline and stop his shots from getting blocked. He has a good, hard shot, and he keeps it low for deflections in front. He still likes to think about going on the attack before his own end is cleaned up, and will occasionally make the risky play. Overall, though, he plays defense reasonably well and gets matched against other team's top lines. He gets into position, takes away the passing lanes, and plays a strong transition game.

THE PHYSICAL GAME

Zhitnik plays sensibly and doesn't take bad penalties very often. His two-game suspension last season (for kneeing Jan Hlavac) was uncharacteristic. His lower-body strength is impressive. He can really unload on some checks. Zhitnik is very fit and is able to just gobble up minutes.

CALGARY FLAMES

Players' Statistics 2001-2002

POS.	NO.	PLAYER	GP	G	A	PTS	+/-	PIM	PP	SH	GW	GT	S	PCT
R	12	JAROME IGINLA	75	35	32	67	-10	49	11	3	6	1	316	11.1
C	22	CRAIG CONROY	79	22	37	59	-4	36	5		2		143	15.4
C	18	CHRIS DRURY	80	23	30	53	-9	33	5	1	5	2	224	10.3
L	23	MARTIN GELINAS	81	21	31	52	-3	51	6		3	1	152	13.8
D	32	TONI LYDMAN	81	6	20	26	-7	28	3				143	4.2
C	11	STEPHANE YELLE	82	10	15	25	-10	50	3		3		121	8.3
L	19	OLEG SAPRYKIN	52	8	15	23	5	46	1		1		116	6.9
R	17	CHRIS CLARK	81	10	12	22	-11	126	2		2	1	156	6.4
L	10	DAVE LOWRY	34	5	14	19	4	22	1				40	12.5
D	6	BOB BOUGHNER	69	3	14	17	5	126			1		62	4.8
D	4	*JORDAN LEOPOLD	58	4	10	14	-15	12	3				78	5.1
R	16	SHEAN DONOVAN	65	5	7	12	-8	37		1	1		88	5.7
D	3	DENIS GAUTHIER	72	1	11	12	5	99			1		50	2.0
D	28	ROBYN REGEHR	76		12	12	-9	87					109	
C	40	SCOTT NICHOL	68	5	5	10	-7	149		1			66	7.6
R	24	BLAKE SLOAN	67	2	8	10	-5	28					56	3.6
D	8	PETR BUZEK	44	3	5	8	-6	14	3				48	6.3
D	21	ANDREW FERENCE	38	1	7	8	-15	42	1				39	2.6
R	7	*CHUCK KOBASEW	23	4	2	6	-3	8	1		1		29	13.8
L	27	CRAIG BERUBE	55	2	4	6	-6	100			1		21	9.5
L	26	STEVE BEGIN	50	3	1	4	-7	51			1		59	5.1
C	15	*BLAIR BETTS	9	1	3	4	3					1	16	6.3
D	42	*MICKI DUPONT	16	1	2	3	-5	4					27	3.7
D	5	*STEVE MONTADOR	50	1	1	2	-9	114					64	1.6
D	2	MIKE COMMODORE	6		1	1	2	19					5	
R	43	LADISLAV KOHN	3		1	1	1	2					3	
D	51	RICK MROZIK	2				0						2	
R	38	ROBERT DOME	1				0						1	
G	1	ROMAN TUREK	65				0	14						
G	33	JAMIE MCLENNAN	22				0	14						
D	36	*MIKE MOTTAU	4				-1							

GP = games played; G = goals; A = assists; PTS = points; +/- = goals-for minus goals-against while player is on ice; PIM = penalties in minutes; PP = power-play goals; SH = shorthanded goals; GW = game-winning goals; GT = game-tying goals; S = no. of shots; PCT = percentage of goals to shots; * = rookie

CRAIG CONROY

Yrs. of NHL service: 7
Born: Potsdam, N.Y.; Sept. 4, 1971
Position: center
Height: 6-2
Weight: 197
Uniform no.: 22
Shoots: right

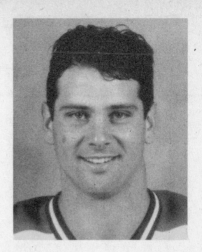

Career statistics:

GP	G	A	TP	PIM
546	110	183	293	293

1999-2000 statistics:

GP	G	A	TP	+/-	PIM	PP	SH	GW	GT	S	PCT
79	12	15	27	+5	36	1	2	3	0	98	12.2

2000-2001 statistics:

GP	G	A	TP	+/-	PIM	PP	SH	GW	GT	S	PCT
83	14	18	32	+2	60	0	4	2	0	133	10.5

2001-2002 statistics:

GP	G	A	TP	+/-	PIM	PP	SH	GW	GT	S	PCT
81	27	48	75	+24	32	7	2	4	1	146	18.5

2002-2003 statistics:

GP	G	A	TP	+/-	PIM	PP	SH	GW	GT	S	PCT
79	22	37	59	-4	36	5	0	2	0	143	15.4

LAST SEASON

Led team in assists for second consecutive season. Led team in shooting percentage. Second on team in points. Third on team in goals. Tied for third on team in power-play goals. Missed three games with foot injuries.

THE FINESSE GAME

Conroy was a scorer at the minor-league level and college, but was pigeonholed as a defensive player when he got his first NHL break in the St. Louis system. He was so good at it that he became a Selke Trophy candidate, and it looked like he was doomed to being thought of as a one-dimensional player.

A trade to Calgary, a lot of confidence, and a guy named Jarome Iginla changed all that. Conroy's speed fit in well with Iginla (another good skater, Martin Gelinas, completes the trio). Conroy can play against other teams' top lines because he is so good defensively, but now he is also able to exploit top-line players whose own defensive awareness is far less keen than Conroy's.

Using his speed, size, and anticipation, Conroy kills penalties well. He is a smart player who can make the little hook or hold to slow down an opponent without getting caught. He has quick hands and is good on draws. His hands are much better than the average checking center's. He's reliable in all key situations: defending a lead, in the closing minutes of a period, and killing penalties at crucial times. Conroy is outstanding on draws and ranked eighth in the NHL last season (56.99 per cent).

THE PHYSICAL GAME

Conroy isn't mean, but he is tough in a quiet way. He uses his size well and accepts checking roles against elite players without being intimidated. He is relentless on every shift and has a great work ethic.

THE INTANGIBLES

Conroy is at best a No. 2 center who handles No. 1 responsibility in Calgary. He is as important to the Flames in the room as he is on the ice.

PROJECTION

We correctly projected a "slip" to 60 points for Conroy last season and think 55-60 points will be his target again this season.

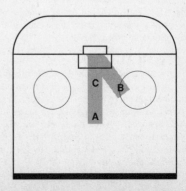

SHEAN DONOVAN

Yrs. of NHL service: 8
Born: Timmins, Ont.; Jan. 22, 1975
Position: right wing
Height: 6-2
Weight: 200
Uniform no.: 16
Shoots: right

Career statistics:

GP	G	A	TP	PIM
536	67	68	135	348

1999-2000 statistics:

GP	G	A	TP	+/-	PIM	PP	SH	GW	GT	S	PCT
51	5	7	12	-17	26	1	0	1	0	66	7.6

2000-2001 statistics:

GP	G	A	TP	+/-	PIM	PP	SH	GW	GT	S	PCT
63	12	11	23	-14	47	1	3	1	0	93	12.9

2001-2002 statistics:

GP	G	A	TP	+/-	PIM	PP	SH	GW	GT	S	PCT
61	8	7	15	-21	44	1	0	2	0	82	9.8

2002-2003 statistics:

GP	G	A	TP	+/-	PIM	PP	SH	GW	GT	S	PCT
65	5	7	12	-8	37	0	1	1	0	88	5.7

LAST SEASON

Acquired from Pittsburgh on March 11, 2003, for Mathias Johansson and Micki Dupont. Missed 11 games with broken foot. Missed one game due to travel.

THE FINESSE GAME

Donovan has big-league speed but lacks the hand skills to make the best use of it. His quickness and powerful stride allow him to shift directions with agility. And he doesn't waste energy. He knows where he is supposed to be positioned and reads plays well. He has good anticipation, which stamps him as a strong penalty killer, though he is not a shorthanded scoring threat yet because of his lack of moves on a breakaway.

Donovan may never be a great point producer because of his lack of scoring or playmaking touch. He could earn a steady job as a third-line checking winger, but has to become more consistent in his nightly effort. He isn't fazed by facing some of the league's better wingers, and has the skating ability to shadow almost anyone.

THE PHYSICAL GAME

Donovan is always busy making hits. He brings a lot of energy to a game when he is in the mood. He doesn't have much of a mean streak but shows an occasional willingness to agitate. He needs to get under his opponents' skin a little more. He takes the body but doesn't punish people. He is well-conditioned and has good stamina. He doesn't get pushed off the puck easily.

THE INTANGIBLES

A player with Donovan's kind of speed can have a comfortable, 10-year NHL career, but he'll only be successful if he can add more scoring and intensity. He has few games when he is a real presence, and that's the tease. Donovan scored 1-2 — 3 in 13 games after the joining the Flames. He became a restricted free agent at the end of the season.

PROJECTION

All speed, no finish. He is a long shot to get much more than 25 points.

DENIS GAUTHIER

Yrs. of NHL service: 5
Born: Montreal, Que.; Oct. 1, 1976
Position: left defense
Height: 6-2
Weight: 210
Uniform no.: 3
Shoots: left

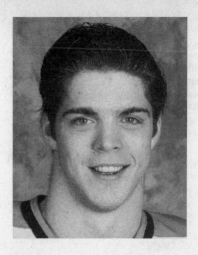

Career statistics:

GP	G	A	TP	PIM
304	12	30	42	402

1999-2000 statistics:

GP	G	A	TP	+/-	PIM	PP	SH	GW	GT	S	PCT
39	1	1	2	-4	50	0	0	0	0	29	3.4

2000-2001 statistics:

GP	G	A	TP	+/-	PIM	PP	SH	GW	GT	S	PCT
62	2	6	8	+3	78	0	0	0	0	33	6.1

2001-2002 statistics:

GP	G	A	TP	+/-	PIM	PP	SH	GW	GT	S	PCT
66	5	8	13	+9	91	0	1	2	0	76	6.6

2002-2003 statistics:

GP	G	A	TP	+/-	PIM	PP	SH	GW	GT	S	PCT
72	1	11	12	+5	99	0	0	1	0	50	2.0

LAST SEASON

Tied for team lead in plus-minus. Missed five games with concussion. Missed one game due to NHL suspension.

THE FINESSE GAME

Gauthier must be French for "keep your head up or I will take it off if you have it down." Gauthier is a powerful and fierce hitter. Anyone on the receiving end of a Gauthier check knows he has been rocked. He is especially good at catching people coming across the middle of the ice head down. Gauthier has the timing and the knack for it. One of his role models is Dave Manson. Another is Scott Stevens. Ouch. What Gauthier has to learn is to try not to kill someone on every rush, but to pick his spots better. There are times when a simple take-out is the right play.

A good skater, he is strong and balanced on his skates. Lower-body strength and speed power his hitting. He is capable of hitting in open ice because of his mobility. Gauthier doesn't mind hitting the big names, either.

Gauthier won't take off on many rushes. He prefers to skate the puck out of his zone or make the outlet pass or the bank off the boards. He is the epitome of a stay-at-home defenseman.

Gauthier improved in his defensive reads and positioning, and he is still maturing and improving.

THE PHYSICAL GAME

He doesn't fight, but Gauthier is a burr. He is always annoying people, always sticking his nose in and he'll be as snarky as David Spade while he does it. He is an agitator who always gets people worried about him,
and he relishes going after other teams' stars. Gauthier is in excellent physical condition. He can handle a lot of ice time.

THE INTANGIBLES

Gauthier moved up into a top-four role with Calgary last season and is likely to stick there.

PROJECTION

Gauthier will have minor point totals (10-15) and major penalty minutes (around 100 at least).

MARTIN GELINAS

Yrs. of NHL service: 14
Born: Shawinigan, Que.; June 5, 1970
Position: left wing
Height: 5-11
Weight: 195
Uniform no.: 23
Shoots: left

Career statistics:

GP	G	A	TP	PIM
976	252	268	520	614

1999-2000 statistics:

GP	G	A	TP	+/-	PIM	PP	SH	GW	GT	S	PCT
81	14	16	30	-10	40	3	0	0	0	139	10.1

2000-2001 statistics:

GP	G	A	TP	+/-	PIM	PP	SH	GW	GT	S	PCT
79	23	29	52	-4	59	6	1	4	0	170	13.5

2001-2002 statistics:

GP	G	A	TP	+/-	PIM	PP	SH	GW	GT	S	PCT
72	13	16	29	-1	30	3	0	1	1	121	10.7

2002-2003 statistics:

GP	G	A	TP	+/-	PIM	PP	SH	GW	GT	S	PCT
81	21	31	52	-3	51	6	0	3	1	152	13.8

LAST SEASON

Second on team in power-play goals and shooting percentage. Third on team in assists. Tied for third on team in game-winning goals. Missed one game due to coach's decision.

THE FINESSE GAME

Gelinas plays a grinding game on the dump-and-chase. Much of his scoring is generated by his forechecking, with the majority of his goals tap-ins from about five feet out. He is strong along the boards and in front of the net. He is not a natural scorer, but he has good instincts and works hard for his chances. He is a good penalty killer.

Gelinas is ideally a third-line winger on a deeper team. With the Flames he ended up on the first line with Jarome Iginla. Even though the Flames' star had a tough season, Gelinas was able to benefit with his highest assist total since 1996-97.

Gelinas is an energetic player who provides momentum-changing shifts. He's not a goal-scorer, though, and gets into trouble when he starts thinking and playing like one. The less fancy, the better. He is not at all creative and can't help a power play much, although he will probably draw power-play time.

THE PHYSICAL GAME

Gelinas is a small player and seems to get himself into situations where he just gets flattened. He has very thick thighs, which power his skating and his body checks and his work in the corners. He doesn't get intimidated, but he does get wiped out of the play and he needs to be smarter about jumping in and out of holes, paying the price only when necessary.

THE INTANGIBLES

Gelinas left a Stanley Cup final team (Carolina) in 2002 to sign with a team that has a long shot (at best) of even qualifying. Not all players grab for the bucks or the glory: Gelinas chose Calgary because his wife would be happiest with him playing there.

PROJECTION

Gelinas surprised us with 20 goals last season. Assuming he keeps the same role with the Flames and stays on Iginla's line, he should be good for another 20 goals and 45-50 points.

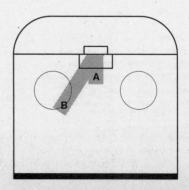

JAROME IGINLA

Yrs. of NHL service: 7
Born: Edmonton, Alberta; July 1, 1977
Position: right wing
Height: 6-1
Weight: 200
Uniform no.: 12
Shoots: right

Career statistics:

GP	G	A	TP	PIM
545	209	221	430	338

1999-2000 statistics:

GP	G	A	TP	+/-	PIM	PP	SH	GW	GT	S	PCT
77	29	34	63	0	26	12	0	4	0	256	11.3

2000-2001 statistics:

GP	G	A	TP	+/-	PIM	PP	SH	GW	GT	S	PCT
77	31	40	71	-2	62	10	0	4	3	229	13.5

2001-2002 statistics:

GP	G	A	TP	+/-	PIM	PP	SH	GW	GT	S	PCT
82	52	44	96	+27	77	16	1	7	2	311	16.7

2002-2003 statistics:

GP	G	A	TP	+/-	PIM	PP	SH	GW	GT	S	PCT
75	35	32	67	-10	49	11	3	6	1	316	11.1

LAST SEASON

Tied for second in NHL in shots. Led team in goals, points, power-play goals, shorthanded goals, game-winning gals, and shots. Second on team in assists. Third on team in average ice time (21:25) and shooting percentage. Missed five games with hip/groin strain. Missed two games with torn shoulder muscle.

THE FINESSE GAME

Iginla doesn't have great speed but he's smart and energetic. He is a savvy two-way forward, and made his way in the NHL on his defense first. The scoring touch came later, which is the reverse for most young players and is one of the reasons why he was able to step into the NHL with such success. He has a veteran's understanding of the game at a young age. We had our doubts that Iginla would become a great goal-scorer, but he proved us wrong. Iginla struggled last season with injuries but he still managed to come close to 40 goals.

Iginla does his best work in the corners and in front of the net. He is strong, and doesn't mind the trench warfare. In fact, he thrives on it. Iginla plays well in all three zones. He's a power forward who plays both ends of the rink, and there aren't many players with that description in the NHL.

Iginla played with Craig Conroy and Martin Gelinas as linemates last year. They're no all-stars, but they're swift and smart and they all clicked.

THE PHYSICAL GAME

Gritty, powerful, and aggressive, Iginla will take a hit to make a play but, even better, he will initiate the hits. He has a mean streak and will have to control himself at the same time he is proving his mettle around the NHL — a fine line to walk, especially since teams target him now.

THE INTANGIBLES

Pressure for Iginla came in the form of a fat new contract and fat numbers from the previous season (52 goals) to try to live up to. He fell short. But remember that Iginla played hurt pretty much from training camp, was the focus of opposing team's checkers every game, and still managed to score 35 goals.

Not only a terrific player, Iginla is cognizant of his duty as a role model. He conducts himself professionally off the ice as well as on. He is the best ambassador for the NHL since Wayne Gretzky.

PROJECTION

Can Iginla return to 50-goal status? And will he do it with the Flames or another team? We think he'll flirt with 50 and be in a new uniform by March.

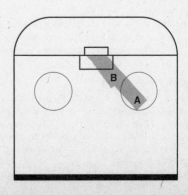

CHUCK KOBASEW

Yrs. of NHL service: 0
Born: Osoyoos, BC; Apr. 17, 1982
Position: right wing
Height: 5-11
Weight: 195
Uniform no.: 7
Shoots: right

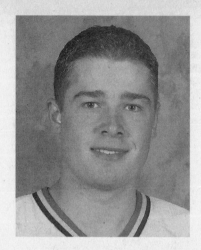

Career statistics:

GP	G	A	TP	PIM
23	4	2	6	8

2002-2003 statistics:

GP	G	A	TP	+/-	PIM	PP	SH	GW	GT	S	PCT
23	4	2	6	-3	8	1	0	1	0	29	13.8

LAST SEASON

Will be entering first full NHL season. Missed eight games due to coach's decision. Appeared in 48 games with Saint John (AHL), scoring 21-12 — 33 with 61 PIM.

THE FINESSE GAME

Kobasew is a two-way forward whose biggest asset is his brain. Anything else — his skating, hands, shot, or size — fails to draw anyone's attention, but he's a smart player. His skating is NHL caliber, but not outstanding. Kobasew's effort is what will allow him to outskate lazier players.

Kobasew has decent hands in-tight around the net. He may turn into one of the most opportunistic scorers on the Flames. He is a dogged forechecker. His goal totals will always outweigh his assists. Kobasew will be an asset on the power play because of his work ethic around the net.

Few players this young step into the league (assuming Kobasew does this year) with as advanced an all-around game. He is sharp in all three zones. He knows what his defensive assignments are and finishes his checks. He will go into the corners.

Kobasew has been a good penalty killer in college and in junior.

THE PHYSICAL GAME

Kobasew isn't very big and he lacks a physical presence, but he's quietly tough. Kobasew wins a lot of puck battles simply because he wants it more than the other guy.

THE INTANGIBLES

Kobasew started the season with the Flames but wasn't quite ready for the NHL pace and was sent to the minors in mid-December. Given all of the turmoil around the parent team, (Darryl Sutter took over as head coach after Kobasew's demotion) it was probably the best move.

At every level he has played at so far, Kobasew has been a winner and a crunch-time player. You will notice him most in the last minutes of a game, whether his team needs to protect a lead or needs a goal. Scouts think he may develop along Jere Lehtinen lines, and he's got a little Adam Graves in him as well. He could end up as the No. 2 right wing behind Jarome Iginla. He is a money player who will have his biggest nights in the biggest games.

PROJECTION

If Kobasew can nab a top-six job, it would be no shock to see him score 15 goals in his rookie season. The Flames have him pegged as a second-line winger. He looks like a complete player.

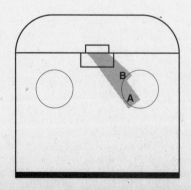

JORDAN LEOPOLD

Yrs. of NHL service: 1
Born: Golden Valley, Minn,; Aug. 3, 1980
Position: defense
Height: 6-1
Weight: 193
Uniform no.: 4
Shoots: left

Career statistics:

GP	G	A	TP	PIM
58	4	10	14	12

2002-2003 statistics:

GP	G	A	TP	+/-	PIM	PP	SH	GW	GT	S	PCT
58	4	10	14	-15	12	3	0	0	0	78	5.1

LAST SEASON

First NHL season. Missed four games with concussion. Missed six games with shoulder bruise. Missed nine games due to coach's decision. Appeared in three games with Saint John (AHL), scoring 1-2 — 3 with 0 PIM.

THE FINESSE GAME

Leopold is a highly skilled offensive defenseman who could develop into a major point-producer in the NHL. He is a smooth skater with excellent balance and lateral movement. He has a small turning radius. Leopold likes to carry the puck but he will quickly learn he can't get away with the same things at the pro level that he did in college. The players here are more advanced, and the play happens much faster.

Leopold will adjust. He is poised and confident with the puck. If he doesn't rush it, he will be able to move it with an accurate pass. He has very good hockey vision and sense.

Leopold lacks a screaming point shot, but he has a quick release. He will probably develop into a point man who can quarterback a power play. Leopold is the kind of defenseman who will be able to exploit other players' defensive weaknesses when he plays against opponents' top lines, as he will eventually do.

THE PHYSICAL GAME

Leopold does not have much of a physical presence. He plays a containment game and will outthink his opponents rather than outmuscle them. Leopold pays close attention to his conditioning and can handle a lot of minutes.

THE INTANGIBLES

Leopold is good enough that the Flames felt comfortable in trading Derek Morris. Leopold's rookie season started off rough, with a concussion, and he had an erratic first half. He played well after his late January recall from a short stint in the minors. If Leopold is not a top-four defenseman in the first part of the season, he is likely to be one by the All-Star break.

PROJECTION

The Flames are likely to start Leopold off conservatively, although within a few seasons he is likely to score in the 40-point range.

TONI LYDMAN

Yrs. of NHL service: 3
Born: Lahti, Finland; Sept. 25, 1977
Position: left defense
Height: 6-1
Weight: 200
Uniform no.: 32
Shoots: left

Career statistics:

GP	G	A	TP	PIM
222	15	58	73	110

2000-2001 statistics:

GP	G	A	TP	+/-	PIM	PP	SH	GW	GT	S	PCT
62	3	16	19	-7	30	1	0	0	0	80	3.8

2001-2002 statistics:

GP	G	A	TP	+/-	PIM	PP	SH	GW	GT	S	PCT
79	6	22	28	-8	52	1	0	0	0	126	4.8

2002-2003 statistics:

GP	G	A	TP	+/-	PIM	PP	SH	GW	GT	S	PCT
81	6	20	26	-7	28	3	0	0	0	143	4.2

LAST SEASON

Led team in average ice time (25:46). Led team defensemen in points. Missed one game with flu.

THE FINESSE GAME

A good skater and puckhandler, Lydman learned a lot from playing with Phil Housley when that veteran was with the Flames. Unfortunately, last season Lydman was afflicted with making a lot of the high-risk passes that Housley is so (in)famous for.

Lydman is a very smart hockey player with good hockey sense and good positioning. Lydman isn't exactly an offenseman. He is more of a two-way defenseman, more like ex-teammate Tommy Albelin — one of the most underrated NHL journeymen — but Lydman is more highly skilled in all respects. He makes a good first pass. Lydman can jump into the play and has a good shot.

Occasionally Lydman tries to do too much, and the coaches have to remind him to get back to basics and make the simple plays.

Lydman seems to have the grit to compete on a nightly basis. He is a stronger, braver Calle Johansson.

THE PHYSICAL GAME

Lydman is a quiet competitor who won't run you over but won't get out of the way, either. He will battle until the end. He has decent size, is strong along the wall, and is a good enough skater to surprise an opponent with an open-ice body check, which he is not too timid to throw. Playing with the gritty Bob Boughner has inspired Lydman to add a physical element.

THE INTANGIBLES

Lydman initially had problems adjusting to North American hockey (smaller ice surface, the redline) but he has shown steady progress since recovering from a concussion. He can handle 20+ minutes a night as part of Calgary's young defense corps. You might not even notice him while he's getting the job done.

PROJECTION

Lydman can be a 30- to 35-point scorer this season.

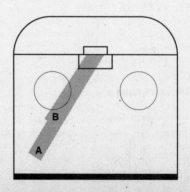

ROBYN REGEHR

Yrs. of NHL service: 4
Born: Recife, Brazil; Apr. 19, 1980
Position: left defense
Height: 6-2
Weight: 210
Uniform no.: 28
Shoots: left

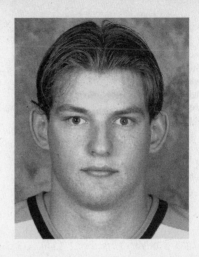

Career statistics:

GP	G	A	TP	PIM
281	8	28	36	296

1999-2000 statistics:

GP	G	A	TP	+/-	PIM	PP	SH	GW	GT	S	PCT
57	5	7	12	-2	46	2	0	0	0	64	7.8

2000-2001 statistics:

GP	G	A	TP	+/-	PIM	PP	SH	GW	GT	S	PCT
71	1	3	4	-7	70	0	0	0	0	62	1.6

2001-2002 statistics:

GP	G	A	TP	+/-	PIM	PP	SH	GW	GT	S	PCT
77	2	6	8	-24	93	0	0	0	0	82	2.4

2002-2003 statistics:

GP	G	A	TP	+/-	PIM	PP	SH	GW	GT	S	PCT
76	0	12	12	-9	87	0	0	0	0	109	0.0

LAST SEASON

Second on team in average ice time (22:45). Missed six games with rib injury.

THE FINESSE GAME

Regehr seems to have lost none of his skating ability after suffering past injuries to both of his legs. He has a good first step for a big guy. His skating is strong and well-balanced. He is defense-oriented, but with his heads-up passing and intelligence, he keys many breakouts that lead to scoring chances. Even though his name might not show up on the scoresheet, check the videotape and you'll find that four or five passes back, the play originated with Regehr. He does not get involved in the rush himself. When parked on the point, he has a decent slap shot, but it is hardly his best skill, and it's not the reason why he's in the lineup.

Regehr seems to learn with each passing week about positioning, reads, and dealing with the speed of the game. There are steps forward and back, and Regehr often had to sit out a game or a shift before finding his consistency again.

Regehr plays in all defensive situations, five-on-five, and killing penalties. He does not and will not see any power-play time. Regehr is still finding his way, and sometimes plays like he's afraid to make mistakes instead of allowing his game to flow naturally. Last season saw him take the next step in becoming a confident top-pair defenseman.

THE PHYSICAL GAME

Regehr has NHL size. He's strong but not a fighter. He won't go out and try to beat people up, but he is tough to play against because he hits. He finishes his checks and pins players to the boards. He resembles a young Rod Langway. Regehr needs to be more aggressive, which will probably develop as he gains more confidence.

THE INTANGIBLES

Quite simply, Regehr is going to be a stud — a big, powerful, defensive defenseman and franchise foundation for years to come. He still needs polish and, at 23, is experiencing growing pains. He has the potential to be the next Adam Foote (coincidentally, Regehr was drafted by Colorado but went to Calgary in the 2000 Theo Fleury trade). If a trophy for the best defensive defenseman is ever created, Regehr will be an instant contender. Regehr is one of the first players opposing teams ask about when they come shopping in Calgary. Regehr was a restricted free agent after last season, but if the Flames trade him, they might as well just fold the franchise.

PROJECTION

Regehr will never score many goals, but he will prevent a lot of them from being scored. If he gets 15 points a season, that will be a high-end output.

ROMAN TUREK

Yrs. of NHL service: 6
Born: Pisek, Czech. Republic; May 21, 1970
Position: goaltender
Height: 6-3
Weight: 215
Uniform no.: 1
Catches: right

Career statistics:

GP	MIN	GA	SO	GAA	A	PIM
310	18064	694	24	2.31	11	30

1999-2000 statistics:

GP	MIN	GAA	W	L	T	SO	GA	S	SAPCT	PIM
67	3960	1.95	42	15	9	7	129	1470	.912	4

2000-2001 statistics:

GP	MIN	GAA	W	L	T	SO	GA	S	SAPCT	PIM
54	3232	2.28	24	18	10	6	123	1248	.901	6

2001-2002 statistics:

GP	MIN	GAA	W	L	T	SO	GA	S	SAPCT	PIM
69	4081	2.53	30	28	11	5	172	1839	.906	4

2002-2003 statistics:

GP	MIN	GAA	W	L	T	SO	GA	S	SAPCT	PIM
65	3822	2.57	27	29	9	4	164	1679	.902	14

LAST SEASON

Missed nine games with broken finger.

THE PHYSICAL GAME

Turek went from being a goalie who gave his team a chance to win every night to an erratic goalie who cost his team any chance to win.

Turek is one of the biggest, widest goalies in the NHL. And that's before he puts his pads on. Turek maximizes his size. He plays a hybrid half-butterfly, half-standup style. It's much like Martin Brodeur's, although Turek isn't quite as athletic as Brodeur. He is very good low, flaring out his legs to take away the bottom part of the net. And because he keeps his torso upright, he takes away the top part of the net. Turek doesn't have to go a mile out to cut down the angle on a shooter, and he is always confident he's in the right spot. He can play mind games with shooters as well as any goalie in the NHL.

He likes to handle the puck, and uses his stick very well. Turek takes away a shooter's options. He can get across the net quickly and use his flexibility and his big frame.

Turek seldom leaves bad rebounds. Pucks just seem to get absorbed in him. He is sometimes overly aggressive on plays around the net, though, so that when quick rebounds come, he is not always in position to recover well.

THE MENTAL GAME

We're not at all sure where Turek's head was last season. He had no threat to his No. 1 position and Calgary rewarded him with a contract extension in 2001-02.

THE INTANGIBLES

Calgary is stuck with a No. 1 goalie who not only isn't in the NHL's elite, but isn't even up to lowered expectations any more. Maybe Darryl Sutter can find a goalie guru to straighten him out.

PROJECTION

Turek is too unpredictable to project for many more than 25 wins.

RHETT WARRENER

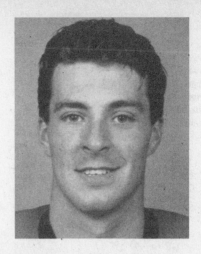

Yrs. of NHL service: 8
Born: Shaunavon, Sask.; Jan. 27, 1976
Position: left defense
Height: 6-2
Weight: 217
Uniform no.: 4
Shoots: right

Career statistics:

GP	G	A	TP	PIM
483	13	56	69	660

1999-2000 statistics:

GP	G	A	TP	+/-	PIM	PP	SH	GW	GT	S	PCT
61	0	3	3	+18	89	0	0	0	0	68	0.0

2000-2001 statistics:

GP	G	A	TP	+/-	PIM	PP	SH	GW	GT	S	PCT
77	3	16	19	+10	78	0	0	2	0	103	2.9

2001-2002 statistics:

GP	G	A	TP	+/-	PIM	PP	SH	GW	GT	S	PCT
65	5	5	10	+15	113	0	0	1	1	66	7.6

2002-2003 statistics:

GP	G	A	TP	+/-	PIM	PP	SH	GW	GT	S	PCT
50	0	9	9	+1	63	0	0	0	0	47	0.0

LAST SEASON

Acquired from Buffalo with Steven Reinprecht on July 3, 2003, for Chris Drury and Steve Begin. Missed eight games with concussion. Missed 10 games with foot injury. Missed three games with abdominal injury. Missed seven games with groin injury. Missed two games due to coach's decision.

THE FINESSE GAME

Warrener's game is heavily slanted to defense. He has a foundation of good hockey sense, completed by his size and firm passing touch. He plays a simple game, wins a lot of the one-on-one battles, and sticks within his limitations. His defensive reads are quite good. He plays his position well and moves people out from in front of the net. He blocks shots, and he can start a quick transition with a breakout pass.

Warrener struggles a bit with his foot speed. His turns and lateral movement are okay, but he lacks quickness and acceleration, which hampers him from becoming a more effective two-way defenseman. This flaw also leads to him taking a lot of clutch-and-grab type penalties.

He is smart. Warrener is a reasonably sound second-pair defenseman, who has often been shoved into the role of a top-two, which is beyond his ability.

THE PHYSICAL GAME

He likes the aggressive game, but sometimes Warrener gets a little too rambunctious and gets out of position. However, that is to be expected from a player looking to make an impact. He's a solid hitter but doesn't make the open-ice splatters. Warrener is not a self-starter. He needs someone to stay on him about his conditioning and his effort.

THE INTANGIBLES

When Warrener is paired with a stay-at-home type, he gets more involved in the attack. He can be the defensive partner, too, if he is teamed with a more offensive defenseman. Warrener is being projected as a partner for Robyn Regher in Calgary.

Warrener is an underrated player, one of those players who does so many little things well that you don't notice him until he's out of the lineup, which he was too frequently again last season. Was there a part of his body that didn't hurt last year? Warrener is a quiet leader.

PROJECTION

Warrener won't win any Norris Trophies, but he is an everyday defenseman who provides 20 points a year.

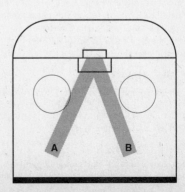

STEPHANE YELLE

Yrs. of NHL service: 8
Born: Ottawa, Ont.; May 9, 1974
Position: center
Height: 6-1
Weight: 190
Uniform no.: 11
Shoots: left

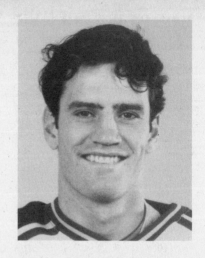

Career statistics:

GP	G	A	TP	PIM
587	64	104	168	302

1999-2000 statistics:

GP	G	A	TP	+/-	PIM	PP	SH	GW	GT	S	PCT
79	8	14	22	+9	28	0	1	1	0	90	8.9

2000-2001 statistics:

GP	G	A	TP	+/-	PIM	PP	SH	GW	GT	S	PCT
50	4	10	14	-3	20	0	1	0	0	54	7.4

2001-2002 statistics:

GP	G	A	TP	+/-	PIM	PP	SH	GW	GT	S	PCT
73	5	12	17	+1	48	0	1	1	0	71	7.0

2002-2003 statistics:

GP	G	A	TP	+/-	PIM	PP	SH	GW	GT	S	PCT
82	10	15	25	-10	50	3	0	3	0	121	8.3

LAST SEASON

Acquired from Colorado with Chris Drury on October 1, 2002, for Deam McAmmond, Derek Morris, and Jeff Shantz. Tied for third on team in game-winning goals. Only Flame to appear in all 82 games.

THE FINESSE GAME

Yelle is an intelligent player who reads the play extremely well. It's his knowledge of the game that has made him an NHL player. His other skills are average: he's a good skater, but he sees the ice in terms of his defensive role. Yelle just doesn't think offense. He's a player you want on the ice to kill penalties or to protect a lead, or sometimes just to go out and play a smart shift to settle a team down.

Yelle doesn't have quick hands, and as a result, has a lot of off-nights on draws. He doesn't have the hands to get involved in the offense. He isn't even a real shorthanded threat because he doesn't have breakaway speed and will make the safe play instead of the prettier high-risk one. He kills penalties but has to be paired with a better-skating partner.

Yelle is a blue-collar forward. His nightly effort is consistently strong.

THE PHYSICAL GAME

Yelle is a tall and stringy-looking athlete with toothpicks for legs. He handles himself well, because even though he doesn't look strong he finds a way to get the puck out. He is usually pretty durable.

THE INTANGIBLES

Yelle is a smart player and works diligently, which compensates for some of his other flaws. He's one of those players you don't notice much until he's out of the lineup. He plays an important role for Calgary because Craig Conroy, who would normally be used as a checking-line center, plays on the top line and that gives Yelle the defensive assignments. Yelle was an unrestricted free agent after last season.

PROJECTION

Yelle's absolute top end is 15 goals, though he is more likely to score goals in single digits. His value is as a defensive forward.

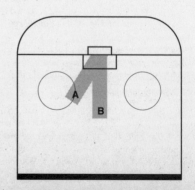

CAROLINA HURRICANES

Players' Statistics 2001-2002

POS.	NO.	PLAYER	GP	G	A	PTS	+/-	PIM	PP	SH	GW	GT	S	PCT
C	92	JEFF O'NEILL	82	30	31	61	-21	38	11		7	2	316	9.5
C	10	RON FRANCIS	82	22	35	57	-22	30	8	1	1		156	14.1
C	17	ROD BRIND'AMOUR	48	14	23	37	-9	37	7	1			110	12.7
R	19	RADIM VRBATA	76	16	19	35	-7	18	6		4	1	215	7.4
D	22	SEAN HILL	82	5	24	29	4	141	1				188	2.7
L	26	ERIK COLE	53	14	13	27	1	72	6	2	3		125	11.2
L	20	JAN HLAVAC	61	10	16	26	-10	28	6		1	1	123	8.1
C	63	JOSEF VASICEK	57	10	10	20	-19	33	4		1		87	11.5
C	14	KEVYN ADAMS	77	9	9	18	-8	57					169	5.3
R	27	CRAIG ADAMS	81	6	12	18	-11	71	1		1		107	5.6
D	6	BRET HEDICAN	72	3	14	17	-24	75	1		1		113	2.7
L	47	*RYAN BAYDA	25	4	10	14	-5	16			1		49	8.2
L	62	*JAROSLAV SVOBODA	48	3	11	14	-5	32	1				63	4.8
R	55	*PAVEL BRENDL	50	5	8	13	5	6	1		1		94	5.3
D	21	DAVID TANABE	68	3	10	13	-27	24	2				104	2.9
D	7	NICLAS WALLIN	77	2	8	10	-19	71			2		69	2.9
D	4	AARON WARD	77	3	6	9	-23	90			1		66	4.5
D	25	*BRUNO ST. JACQUES	24	2	5	7	-4	14					19	10.5
L	37	*TOMAS KURKA	14	3	2	5	1	2					22	13.6
C	12	CRAIG MACDONALD	35	1	3	4	-3	20					43	2.3
C	15	HAROLD DRUKEN	16	1	3	4	0	2					15	6.7
L	11	JEFF DANIELS	59		4	4	-9	8					41	
L	39	*BRAD DEFAUW	9	3		3	-2	2	1		1		19	15.8
R	42	*JEFF HEEREMA	10	3		3	-2	2	1				16	18.8
C	46	*MICHAEL ZIGOMANIS	19	2	1	3	-4		1	1			19	10.5
R	36	*JESSE BOULERICE	48	2	1	3	-2	108				1	12	16.7
D	71	*TOMAS MALEC	41		2	2	-5	43					30	
L	52	*DAMIAN SURMA	1	1		1	0						1	100.0
D	28	STEVE HALKO	6					1					5	
L	29	MIKE WATT	5				-1						2	
G	1	ARTURS IRBE	34				0	4						
G	80	KEVIN WEEKES	51				0	2						
G	30	PATRICK DESROCHERS	6				0							
L	16	TOMMY WESTLUND	3				0							

GP = games played; G = goals; A = assists; PTS = points; +/- = goals-for minus goals-against while player is on ice; PIM = penalties in minutes; PP = power-play goals; SH = shorthanded goals; GW = game-winning goals; GT = game-tying goals; S = no. of shots; PCT = percentage of goals to shots; * = rookie

KEVYN ADAMS

Yrs. of NHL service: 4
Born: Washington, D.C.; Oct. 8, 1974
Position: center
Height: 6-1
Weight: 195
Uniform no.: 14
Shoots: right

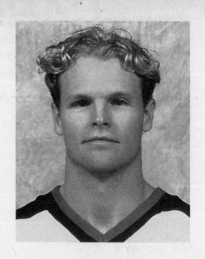

Career statistics:

GP	G	A	TP	PIM
290	31	46	77	200

1999-2000 statistics:

GP	G	A	TP	+/-	PIM	PP	SH	GW	GT	S	PCT
52	5	8	13	-7	39	0	0	0	0	70	7.1

2000-2001 statistics:

GP	G	A	TP	+/-	PIM	PP	SH	GW	GT	S	PCT
78	11	18	29	+3	54	0	0	3	0	105	10.5

2001-2002 statistics:

GP	G	A	TP	+/-	PIM	PP	SH	GW	GT	S	PCT
77	6	11	17	-5	43	0	0	2	0	108	5.6

2002-2003 statistics:

GP	G	A	TP	+/-	PIM	PP	SH	GW	GT	S	PCT
77	9	9	18	-8	57	0	0	0	0	169	5.3

LAST SEASON

Missed five games with abdominal strain.

THE FINESSE GAME

Originally a first-round draft pick by Boston (1993), Adams is a classic example of how time, patience — and expansion — can finally result in a pretty good living as an NHL journeyman. The Hurricanes are Adams's fifth NHL team, which explains the "journey" part of that. He may have finally found a home.

One of Adams's calling cards is that he's a good face-off man. With Brind'Amour missing nearly half the season due to injury, Adams stepped up as best he could to fill in the void.

Strong on his skates, Adams gets involved in the high-traffic areas. He plays a very sound defensive game. He doesn't score much, but he is not afraid to shoot. His points evolve from effort more than talent.

THE PHYSICAL GAME

Adams has good size but he is not imposing. He maximizes his strength by playing a quietly aggressive game, especially in his puck battles.

THE INTANGIBLES

Everything started to click in his first full season with the Hurricanes, and Adams has probably netted a full-time job on the checking line.

PROJECTION

Adams can contribute quality minutes as a third-line checking center and role player. His top end is probably around 30 points.

RYAN BAYDA

Yrs. of NHL service: 1
Born: Saskatoon, Sask.; Dec. 9, 1980
Position: left wing
Height: 5-11
Weight: 185
Uniform no.: 47
Shoots: left

Career statistics:

GP	G	A	TP	PIM
25	4	10	14	16

2002-2003 statistics:

GP	G	A	TP	+/-	PIM	PP	SH	GW	GT	S	PCT
25	4	10	14	-5	16	0	0	1	0	49	8.2

LAST SEASON

Will be entering first full NHL season. Appeared in 53 games with Lowell (AHL), scoring 11-32 — 43 with 32 PIM.

THE FINESSE GAME

In each of the last two seasons, the Hurricanes have been able to work a solid young player into their lineup. Two years ago, it was Erik Cole. After Cole was lost to injury in January last year, Bayda was promoted from the minors.

Bayda is a smart and poised player with the puck. He has good offensive instincts. No less an expert than Ron Francis has praised his hockey sense. Bayda has quick hands, an accurate shot, and doesn't have to be encouraged to shoot. He is also a good playmaker with keen vision.

Bayda is a very good skater, with good agility and balance. His play away from the puck is advanced for a young player. He is an aggressive forechecker.

THE PHYSICAL GAME

Bayda is on the small side, but he plays with grit and intensity. There are frequent nights when he will have a lot more hits than the bigger guys on his team. Bayda is surprisingly effective along the boards and in the corners. Most nights his face looks like he's been in a knife fight.

THE INTANGIBLES

Bayda toyed with the idea of turning pro in 2001 but wisely opted to play another year of college at North Dakota. The coaching he received there has helped his development. He is projected as a top-six forward for the Hurricanes and fit in nicely with Francis and Jeff O'Neill after his February recall last season. Bayda handled a lot of minutes for a first-year pro.

PROJECTION

Bayda will still be an official rookie this season since he played one game under the limit last year. The experience will only help. He has been an effective scorer at every level and a 15-goal rookie season wouldn't be out of the question.

BOB BOUGHNER

Yrs. of NHL service: 8
Born: Windsor, Ont.; Mar. 8, 1971
Position: right defense
Height: 6-0
Weight: 203
Uniform no.: 6
Shoots: right

Career statistics:

GP	G	A	TP	PIM
535	14	46	60	1240

1999-2000 statistics:

GP	G	A	TP	+/-	PIM	PP	SH	GW	GT	S	PCT
73	3	4	7	-11	166	1	0	1	0	40	7.5

2000-2001 statistics:

GP	G	A	TP	+/-	PIM	PP	SH	GW	GT	S	PCT
58	1	3	4	+18	147	0	0	0	0	46	2.2

2001-2002 statistics:

GP	G	A	TP	+/-	PIM	PP	SH	GW	GT	S	PCT
79	2	4	6	+9	170	0	0	0	0	58	3.5

2002-2003 statistics:

GP	G	A	TP	+/-	PIM	PP	SH	GW	GT	S	PCT
69	3	14	17	+5	126	0	0	1	0	62	4.8

LAST SEASON

Tied for team lead in plus-minus. Tied for second on team in penalty minutes. Missed 11 games with thumb injury. Missed two games with wrist injury.

THE FINESSE GAME

Boughner gets the most out of his talent. He's a defensive defenseman who plays a conservative game, but competes hard every night and maxes out his modest skills.

Boughner can still draw the occasional assignment against other teams' top lines, but Calgary has a good young starting four and Boughner gets to play in a comfortable role as a fifth or sixth defenseman and penalty killer. That puts him in a better position to succeed.

He doesn't have great hands, so Boughner doesn't get involved much in the offense. He doesn't (or shouldn't) try to make the first pass out of the zone. He has to be reminded to keep it simple and just bang the puck off the glass. Playing on a good-skating team like Calgary allows Boughner to make more low-risk passes and not try to do too much on his own. Boughner is a good fit here.

THE PHYSICAL GAME

Boughner is very aggressive and loves to hit. His teammates appreciate the way he pays the price and stands up for them.

THE INTANGIBLES

Boughner is surrounded by so many young defensemen that you have to hope his agent built a babysitting bonus into his contract. This is one of those steady, experienced character guys that always seem in such short supply and high demand. Boughner knows his role here and is willing to help. He suffered a cut tendon in his wrist that ended his season with two games left, but it was not believed to be career-threatening.

PROJECTION

Boughner will see third-pair ice time, add toughness and poise, and maybe score a few points here and there.

PAVEL BRENDL

Yrs. of NHL service: 1
Born: Opocno, Czech Rep.; Mar. 23, 1981
Position: right wing
Height: 6-1
Weight: 204
Uniform no.: 55
Shoots: right

Career statistics:

GP	G	A	TP	PIM
58	6	8	14	8

2001-2002 statistics:

GP	G	A	TP	+/-	PIM	PP	SH	GW	GT	S	PCT
8	1	0	1	-1	2	0	0	0	0	6	16.7

2002-2003 statistics:

GP	G	A	TP	+/-	PIM	PP	SH	GW	GT	S	PCT
50	5	8	13	+5	6	1	0	1	0	94	5.3

LAST SEASON

Acquired from Philadelphia with Bruno St. Jacques on February 7, 2003, for Sami Kapanen and Ryan Bast. Missed 19 games with knee surgery.

THE FINESSE GAME

One scout said that three things happen when Brendl shoots the puck: he misses the net, he hits the goalie, or he scores. In other words, the goalie is virtually helpless and finds it almost impossible to make the save unless Brendl's shot finds him.

Brendl has a heavy wrist and slap shot. His skating is a sticking-point, though. He is strong and balanced on his skates but his foot speed is suspect. Brendl also isn't the game's most advanced defensive player.

As good a sniper as he is, Brendl also has wonderful hands for passing.

THE PHYSICAL GAME

Brendl has excellent size and the desire to take the puck to the net in traffic. He is poised under fire and can shoot or make a play in a throng of defenders. Brendl is still getting used to the notion that the guys who bounced off him in junior are smaller and not as strong as the pros who will now try to stop him on a nightly basis. Brendl tends to get discouraged early in a game if things aren't going his way, and sulks rather than trying to find more and better ways of getting the job done.

Brendl has a history of being extremely lax in his conditioning and paying virtually no attention to nutrition. He really needs a babysitter.

THE INTANGIBLES

Brendl is now with his third organization in just the last three years, and you have to wonder where his head is at. It certainly looks like the motivation to become an NHL star will have to come from somewhere else — a coach, a mentoring veteran player — since Brendl isn't a self-starter. Mark Recchi and Keith Primeau made Brendl their project in the middle of the season in Philadelphia and Brendl woke up for about a month only to be traded to Carolina. He had only one assist in eight games with the Hurricanes before suffering a season-ending knee injury.

It's far too early to give up on a 22-year-old. Maybe Ron Francis and Rod Brind'Amour can finish what Recchi and Primeau started.

PROJECTION

Brendl will have to work hard to come back from knee surgery. "Work" is a four-letter word to him. If he gets it in gear, a 20-goal season would not be out of the question, but that's a big "if."

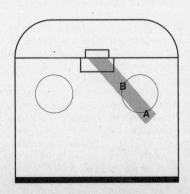

ROD BRIND'AMOUR

Yrs. of NHL service: 14
Born: Ottawa, Ont.; Aug. 9, 1970
Position: center / left wing
Height: 6-1
Weight: 202
Uniform no.: 17
Shoots: left

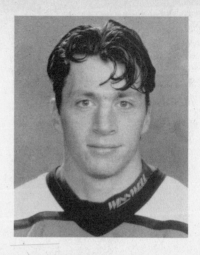

Career statistics:

GP	G	A	TP	PIM
1031	339	534	873	848

1999-2000 statistics:

GP	G	A	TP	+/-	PIM	PP	SH	GW	GT	S	PCT
45	9	13	22	-13	26	4	1	1	0	87	10.3

2000-2001 statistics:

GP	G	A	TP	+/-	PIM	PP	SH	GW	GT	S	PCT
79	20	36	56	-7	47	5	1	5	0	163	12.3

2001-2002 statistics:

GP	G	A	TP	+/-	PIM	PP	SH	GW	GT	S	PCT
81	23	32	55	+3	40	5	2	5	1	162	14.2

2002-2003 statistics:

GP	G	A	TP	+/-	PIM	PP	SH	GW	GT	S	PCT
48	14	23	37	-9	37	7	1	0	0	110	12.7

LAST SEASON

Second on team in average ice time (23:45) and shooting percentage. Third on team in points and power-play goals. Missed 34 games with hand injury.

THE FINESSE GAME

Versatility and dependability are among Brind'Amour's trademarks. He is one of the best two-way centers in the league. He wins face-offs. He checks. He has the strength, speed, and stride to handle every defensive aspect of the game; the grit and desire to earn the loose pucks; the temperament and credibility to be on the ice in the last minute.

Brind'Amour may not beat many players one-on-one in open ice, but he outworks defenders along the boards and uses a quick burst of speed to drive to the net. He's a playmaker in the mucking sense, with scoring chances emerging from his commitment. He is a better player at center than wing, and he likes playing the middle best, though he can handle either assignment.

Brind'Amour has a long, powerful stride with a quick first step to leave a defender behind; his hand skills complement the skating assets. He drives well into a shot on the fly, and has a quick-release snap shot and a strong backhand.

When Brind'Amour does not have the puck he works ferociously to get it back. An excellent penalty killer, and the center the Hurricanes send out if they are two men short. Brind'Amour thinks nothing of blocking shots, despite the injury risk. He is outstanding on draws and ranked 10th in the NHL in face-offs last season (56.52 per cent).

THE PHYSICAL GAME

A king in the weight room, Brind'Amour uses his size well and is a strong skater. He can muck with the best in the corners and along the boards. He will carry the puck through traffic in front of the net and battle for position for screens and tip-ins. He is among the hardest workers on the team, even in practice, and is always striving to improve his game. Brind'Amour isn't mean, but he is quietly tough.

THE INTANGIBLES

The fact that Brind'Amour ended up third in scoring on Carolina despite missing almost half the season shows not only how weary the Hurricanes were last season, but what a treasure Brind'Amour is. The team was lost without him and missed the playoffs after going to the finals the previous season. Brind'Amour is a coach's dream because he can be deployed in any situation and will provide trustworthy work.

PROJECTION

Brind'Amour was on a pace to score 24 goals before his season-ending injury, and 20-25 is his expected range.

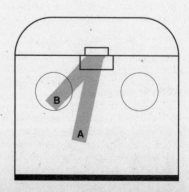

ERIK COLE

Yrs. of NHL service: 2
Born: Oswego, NY; Nov. 6, 1978
Position: left wing
Height: 6-0
Weight: 200
Uniform no.: 26
Shoots: left

Career statistics:

GP	G	A	TP	PIM
134	30	37	67	107

2001-2002 statistics:

GP	G	A	TP	+/-	PIM	PP	SH	GW	GT	S	PCT
81	16	24	40	-10	35	3	0	2	0	159	10.1

2002-2003 statistics:

GP	G	A	TP	+/-	PIM	PP	SH	GW	GT	S	PCT
53	14	13	27	+1	72	6	2	3	0	125	11.2

LAST SEASON

Led team in shorthanded goals. Third on team in game-winning goals and plus-minus. Missed 29 games with broken fibula.

THE FINESSE GAME

Cole showed no signs of a sophomore slump. After an impressive rookie season (in which he proved to be one of Carolina's most impressive playoff performers in the team's run to the Stanley Cup Finals in 2002), Cole was on a pace to improve on his freshman marks before he suffered on broken leg on Jan. 30.

Cole is an impact player. He is a swift and sure skater with good agility. He goes into traffic with or without the puck. He is a good puckhandler. Cole has the makings of a good power forward, if not an elite one. He forechecks aggressively and is always on the hunt for the puck, trying to make something good happen.

Cole has a variety of shots, including an effective backhand. He works down low and behind the net and in all the dirty areas in order to score. He lacks the touch to get into the 30-goal range. Cole is versatile enough to play all three forward positions, although he is likely to succeed as a left winger. He can work both special teams.

The stats don't begin to tell the Cole story.

THE PHYSICAL GAME

Cole is a dynamic player. He brings a flair to every shift. He is an enthusiastic and effective body-checker. He is rambunctious and intense. He needs to learn to improve his fitness level so that he can bring the same energy every night.

THE INTANGIBLES

Cole has a very mature game and his work ethic quickly earned him respect on a largely veteran team. As some of those vets are traded away or retire, Cole is going to become part of the nucleus of the next gen-eration. Cole has a well-rounded game and on a night when he isn't scoring, he will be performing the less glamorous tasks to help his team win. Cole has never had anything handed to him at any stage of his career and isn't about to start taking the NHL for granted.

PROJECTION

Cole was on a 20-goal pace before the injury ended his season and we would anticipate at least that many goals from him this year.

RON FRANCIS

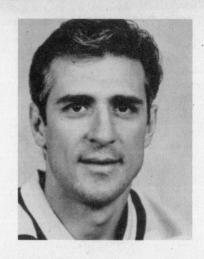

Yrs. of NHL service: 22
Born: Sault Ste. Marie, Ont.; Mar. 1, 1963
Position: center
Height: 6-3
Weight: 200
Uniform no.: 10
Shoots: left

Career statistics:

GP	G	A	TP	PIM
1651	536	1222	1758	965

1999-2000 statistics:

GP	G	A	TP	+/-	PIM	PP	SH	GW	GT	S	PCT
78	23	50	73	+10	18	7	0	4	0	150	15.3

2000-2001 statistics:

GP	G	A	TP	+/-	PIM	PP	SH	GW	GT	S	PCT
82	15	50	65	-15	32	7	0	4	0	130	11.5

2001-2002 statistics:

GP	G	A	TP	+/-	PIM	PP	SH	GW	GT	S	PCT
80	27	50	77	+4	18	14	0	5	2	165	16.4

2002-2003 statistics:

GP	G	A	TP	+/-	PIM	PP	SH	GW	GT	S	PCT
82	22	35	57	-22	30	8	1	1	0	156	14.1

LAST SEASON

Led team in assists and shooting percentage. Second on team in goals, points, and power-play goals. One of three Hurricanes to appear in all 82 games.

THE FINESSE GAME

Francis is a veteran two-way center who can still put some points on the board, especially with the manpower advantage. Technically, he is a choppy skater who gets where he has to be with a minimum amount of style. His understanding of the game is key because he has great awareness of his positioning. He gets loads of ice time, so he has learned to pace himself to conserve energy. There are few useless bursts of speed. He is one of the game's smartest players.

Francis is a face-off artist, although he fell out of the league's top 10 last season. He is still the guy you would want your money on for a crucial draw, especially in the defensive zone. On rare nights when he is struggling with an opposing center, he'll tinker with his changes in the neutral zone, then save what he has learned for a key draw deep in either zone. Just as a great scorer never shows a goalie the same move twice in a row, Francis never uses the same technique twice in succession. He has good hand-eye coordination and uses his body well. Few players win their draws as outright as he does on a consistent basis.

When he focuses on a defensive role, Francis has the vision to come out of a scramble into an attacking rush. He anticipates passes, blocks shots, then springs an odd-man breakout with a smart play.

Francis doesn't have a screamingly hard shot, nor is he a flashy player. He works from the center of the ice, between the circles, and has a quick release on a one-timer. He can kill penalties or work the point on the power play with equal effectiveness. He complements any kind of player.

THE PHYSICAL GAME

Not a big, imposing hitter, Francis will still use his body to get the job done. He will bump and grind and go into the trenches. Back on defense, he can function as a third defenseman. On offense, you will find him going into the corners or heading for the front of the net for tips and rebounds.

He will be 41 by the end of this season. Francis keeps himself in great shape and is remarkably durable.

THE INTANGIBLES

The player the Hurricanes drafted in the first round this year, Eric Staal, has been described as a young Ron Francis. Good thing, because the old Ron Francis is just about done.

This could be Francis's final season. If the Hurricanes are out of a playoff spot by March, he would make a great rental for a playoff-bound team.

PROJECTION

We anticipated a decline in production off of his 75-point season in 2001-02, but the dropoff was even steeper than expected. Francis can be realistically counted on for 55 points, since Carolina doesn't figure to be much improved.

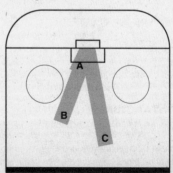

BRET HEDICAN

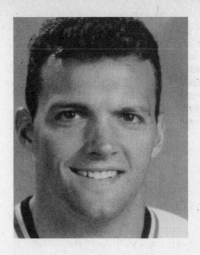

Yrs. of NHL service: 11
Born: St. Paul, Minn.; Aug. 10, 1970
Position: left defense
Height: 6-2
Weight: 205
Uniform no.: 6
Shoots: left

Career statistics:

GP	G	A	TP	PIM
717	40	170	210	629

1999-2000 statistics:

GP	G	A	TP	+/-	PIM	PP	SH	GW	GT	S	PCT
76	6	19	25	+4	68	2	0	1	0	58	10.3

2000-2001 statistics:

GP	G	A	TP	+/-	PIM	PP	SH	GW	GT	S	PCT
70	5	15	20	-7	72	4	0	1	0	104	4.8

2001-2002 statistics:

GP	G	A	TP	+/-	PIM	PP	SH	GW	GT	S	PCT
57	5	11	16	-1	22	0	0	1	0	85	5.9

2002-2003 statistics:

GP	G	A	TP	+/-	PIM	PP	SH	GW	GT	S	PCT
72	3	14	17	-24	75	1	0	1	0	113	2.7

LAST SEASON

Third on team in average ice time (23:01). Missed 10 games due to concussion.

THE FINESSE GAME

Hedican is among the best-skating defensemen in the NHL. He has a nice, deep knee bend and his fluid stride provides good acceleration; each stride eats up lots of ice. His steady balance allows him to go down to one knee and use his stick to challenge passes from the corners. He uses quickness, range, and reach to make a confident stand at the blueline.

Hedican happily uses his speed with the puck to drive down the wing and create trouble in the offensive zone. He also varies the attack. He seems to prefer the left-wing boards, but will also take the right-wing route to try to make plays off the backhand.

He is a good enough stickhandler to try one-on-one moves. He is eager to jump into the play. He will never be a great point getter or playmaker because he doesn't think the game well enough, but he tries to help his team on the attack. He is a better player in the playoffs, when he doesn't think as much and lets his natural instincts rule.

Hedican knows that if an attacker beats him, he will be able to keep up with him and steer him to bad ice. He is the perfect guy to pick up the puck behind the net and get it to the redline and start the half-court game. He doesn't always just put his head down and go, either. He will move up the middle and look for a pass to a breaking wing, though he is guilty of some giveaways at the most inopportune times.

THE PHYSICAL GAME

Hedican has decent size but not a great deal of strength or toughness. He won't bulldoze in front of the net, but prefers to tie people up and go for the puck. He is more of a stick checker than a body checker, though he will sometimes knock a player off the puck at the blueline, control it and make a smart first pass. He prefers to use body positioning to nullify an opponent rather than initiate hard body contact.

THE INTANGIBLES

Injuries again derailed Hedican last season. He suffered the concussion in mid-December and missed playing time again in January because of it.

PROJECTION

Hedican hasn't taken the next step yet, and still has an offensive upside. He should score around 30 points, assuming he is fully recovered from the injury.

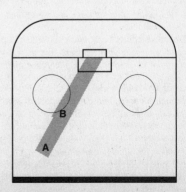

SEAN HILL

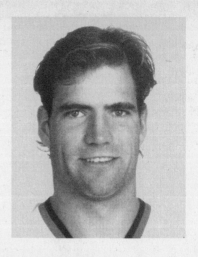

Yrs. of NHL service: 11
Born: Duluth, Minn.; Feb. 14, 1970
Position: right defense
Height: 6-0
Weight: 203
Uniform no.: 22
Shoots: right

Career statistics:

GP	G	A	TP	PIM
602	44	161	205	702

1999-2000 statistics:

GP	G	A	TP	+/-	PIM	PP	SH	GW	GT	S	PCT
62	13	31	44	+3	59	8	0	2	0	150	8.7

2000-2001 statistics:

GP	G	A	TP	+/-	PIM	PP	SH	GW	GT	S	PCT
48	1	10	11	+5	51	0	0	0	0	47	2.1

2001-2002 statistics:

GP	G	A	TP	+/-	PIM	PP	SH	GW	GT	S	PCT
72	7	26	33	0	89	4	0	2	0	145	4.8

2002-2003 statistics:

GP	G	A	TP	+/-	PIM	PP	SH	GW	GT	S	PCT
82	5	24	29	+4	141	1	0	0	0	188	2.7

LAST SEASON

Led team in average ice time (24:20) and penalty minutes. Led team defensemen in points. Second on team in plus-minus. Third on team in assists and shots. One of three Hurricanes to appear in all 82 games.

THE FINESSE GAME

The eye of the hurricane logo on the front of the Carolina jersey is like Superman's "S" to Hill. With the Hurricanes, he is a stud No. 1 defenseman. Anywhere else, he is probably best on the third defense pair. Don't ask us to explain it. We can't.

A good skater, Hill is agile, strong, and balanced, if not overly fast. He can skate the puck out of danger or make a smart first pass. He learned defense in the Montreal system, but has since evolved into more of a specialty-team player. Hill sees significant power play-time in Carolina even though the team has much better offensive defensemen.

Hill has a good point shot and good offensive sense. He likes to carry the puck and start things off a rush, or he will jump into the play.

Hill's best quality is his competitiveness. He will hack and whack at puck carriers like an annoying terrier ripping and nipping your socks and ankles.

THE PHYSICAL GAME

For a smallish player, Hill gets his share of points by playing bigger than his size. He has a bit of a mean streak, and though he certainly can't overpower people, he is a solidly built player who doesn't get pushed around easily. Hill is a willing hitter.

Hill hurts his team by taking ill-timed and unnecessary penalties.

THE INTANGIBLES

Hill is a No. 1 defenseman in Carolina, which is well beyond his modest talent.

PROJECTION

A poor-man's MacInnis, Hill doesn't have elite skills, but he can chip in 25-30 points and will probably be close to triple digits in PIM again.

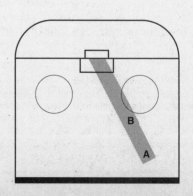

JAN HLAVAC

Yrs. of NHL service: 4
Born: Prague, Czech Republic; Sept. 20, 1976
Position: left wing
Height: 6-0
Weight: 185
Uniform no.: 20
Shoots: left

Career statistics:

GP	G	A	TP	PIM
284	73	90	163	82

1999-2000 statistics:

GP	G	A	TP	+/-	PIM	PP	SH	GW	GT	S	PCT
67	19	23	42	+3	16	6	0	2	0	134	14.2

2000-2001 statistics:

GP	G	A	TP	+/-	PIM	PP	SH	GW	GT	S	PCT
79	28	36	64	+3	20	5	0	6	0	195	14.4

2001-2002 statistics:

GP	G	A	TP	+/-	PIM	PP	SH	GW	GT	S	PCT
77	16	15	31	+9	18	1	0	3	1	132	12.1

2002-2003 statistics:

GP	G	A	TP	+/-	PIM	PP	SH	GW	GT	S	PCT
61	10	16	26	-10	28	6	0	1	1	123	8.1

PROJECTION

Maybe Hlavac's 28-goal season in New York was a fluke. We would downgrade him to 20 goals until proven otherwise.

LAST SEASON

Acquired by Carolina with Harold Druken from Vancouver on November 1, 2002, for Darren Langdon and Marek Malik. Missed two games with knee injury. Missed 14 games with broken finger.

THE FINESSE GAME

Where did this guy's game go?

Hlavac is capable of being a dynamic, top-level scorer. Hlavac is a good stickhandler who can move the puck at a high tempo. He has good anticipation and acceleration. He is occasionally guilty of over-handling the puck. Hlavac has a good scoring touch and needs to shoot more.

Hlavac forechecks intelligently and creates plays off the turnovers. He is a very good passer and play-maker and has good defensive awareness. Hlavac needs to play on a team that has a heavy European flavor to its offense, but even that might not be enough to bring him back around.

THE PHYSICAL GAME

Hlavac is strong on his skates, even though he isn't very big. He is sturdy and has a quiet toughness to him.

THE INTANGIBLES

Carolina failed to qualify Hlavac, making him an un-restricted free agent. He has never recaptured the confidence he had with Petr Nedved and Radek Dvorak a few season ago with the Rangers when he scored 28 goals. Hlavac played on four teams in the last three seasons, which didn't help his comfort level.

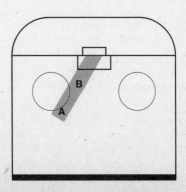

TOMAS MALEC

Yrs. of NHL service: 1
Born: Skalica, Slovakia; May 13, 1982
Position: left defense
Height: 6-2
Weight: 193
Uniform no.: 71
Shoots: left

Career statistics:

GP	G	A	TP	PIM
41	0	2	2	43

2002-2003 statistics:

GP	G	A	TP	+/-	PIM	PP	SH	GW	GT	S	PCT
41	0	2	2	-5	43	0	0	0	0	30	0.0

LAST SEASON

First NHL season. Missed seven games due to coach's decision. Appeared in 30 games with Lowell (AHL), scoring 0-4 — 4 with 50 PIM.

THE FINESSE GAME

Malec is a two-way defenseman with some offensive upside. He is an excellent skater, both forwards and backwards. Malec is able to get involved in an offensive play and then recover quickly to prevent his partner from being outnumbered.

As a power-play quarterback, Malec's involvement will be more as a passer than a shooter. He has good lateral mobility along the blueline to set up an effective point shot, even if it's not a blue darter, but he is more intent on finding an open man with a pass.

Malec will start up a number of his team's attacks with a smart rush out of the zone. He loves to carry the puck. He excels at the transition game.

Defensively, Malec takes up the passing lanes with his stick and plays smart positionally. Malec's game is pretty complete and all it will take is more experience. Undrafted in 2000, Malec decided to come to North America and play junior hockey, which helped him catch on as a free agent.

THE PHYSICAL GAME

Malec is just a shade on the small side but he plays with an edge. He has something of a mean streak when he's provoked. He is naturally competitive.

THE INTANGIBLES

There are a lot of things the Hurricanes do that baffle us. Playing Malec as a left wing is just one of those.

PROJECTION

Malec should break in on the third defense pair in Carolina with a future as a No. 4. He should see some power-play time and can score in the 20-point range.

DANIIL MARKOV

Yrs. of NHL service: 6
Born: Moscow, Russia; July 11, 1976
Position: left defense
Height: 6-1
Weight: 190
Uniform no.: 55
Shoots: left

Career statistics:

GP	G	A	TP	PIM
336	19	82	101	240

1999-2000 statistics:

GP	G	A	TP	+/-	PIM	PP	SH	GW	GT	S	PCT
59	0	10	10	+13	28	0	0	0	0	38	-

2000-2001 statistics:

GP	G	A	TP	+/-	PIM	PP	SH	GW	GT	S	PCT
59	3	13	16	+6	34	1	0	2	0	49	6.1

2001-2002 statistics:

GP	G	A	TP	+/-	PIM	PP	SH	GW	GT	S	PCT
72	6	30	36	-7	67	4	0	1	0	103	5.8

2002-2003 statistics:

GP	G	A	TP	+/-	PIM	PP	SH	GW	GT	S	PCT
64	4	16	20	+2	36	2	0	0	1	105	3.8

LAST SEASON

Acquired from Phoenix on June 21, 2003, with a fourth-round draft pick in 2003 for David Tanabe and Igor Knyazev. Second on Coyotes in average ice time (23:16). Missed 17 games with fractured forearm. Missed one game with flu.

THE FINESSE GAME

Markov is pretty sound positioning-wise, and he is a good skater. Markov has become a lot smarter about recognizing his offensive chances — he loves that part of the game — and is lower-risk defensively.

Markov makes a good first pass. Once he gets the puck he is looking to go up-ice for a play, which not all defensemen do, and a stick-to-stick pass gets him out of trouble. His frequent injuries keep him from getting in a real groove.

Markov has added an edge to his game, rather than just relying on his skills. He can be as irritating as former teammate Claude Lemieux, and he will plow over an opponent (or a referee) in his pursuit of the puck. His enthusiasm is contagious. His teammates love playing with him because of his zest for the game.

THE PHYSICAL GAME

Markov isn't very big but he brings a little edge and a little chippiness to his game. He's a bit brash and cocky. He has some grit and steps up his game in big spots. Markov tends to get hit with a nagging injury season after season.

His teammates and coach appreciate Markov's toughness.

THE INTANGIBLES

While David Tanabe may have more offensive upside, we think Carolina got the better of this deal. Markov will be a top-pair defenseman for the Hurricanes. Markov was a restricted free agent after the season.

PROJECTION

Markov should score 40 points in an increased role with his new team if he can avoid injuries.

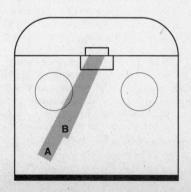

JEFF O'NEILL

Yrs. of NHL service: 8
Born: Richmond Hill, Ont.; Feb. 23, 1976
Position: center
Height: 6-1
Weight: 190
Uniform no.: 92
Shoots: right

Career statistics:

GP	G	A	TP	PIM
606	184	198	382	492

1999-2000 statistics:

GP	G	A	TP	+/-	PIM	PP	SH	GW	GT	S	PCT
80	25	38	63	-9	72	4	0	7	0	189	13.2

2000-2001 statistics:

GP	G	A	TP	+/-	PIM	PP	SH	GW	GT	S	PCT
82	41	26	67	-18	106	17	0	5	2	242	16.9

2001-2002 statistics:

GP	G	A	TP	+/-	PIM	PP	SH	GW	GT	S	PCT
76	31	33	64	-5	63	11	0	6	1	272	11.4

2002-2003 statistics:

GP	G	A	TP	+/-	PIM	PP	SH	GW	GT	S	PCT
82	30	31	61	-21	38	11	0	7	2	316	9.5

LAST SEASON

Tied for second in NHL in shots. Led team in goals for third consecutive season. Led team in points, power-play goals, game-winning goals, and shots. Second on team in assists. One of three Hurricanes to appear in all 82 games.

THE FINESSE GAME

O'Neill continues to be a study in frustration. Following his career year in 2000-01, there was great optimism that O'Neill had put all the pieces of the puzzle together. But still his intensity slacks off at times and he doesn't maintain an involved game. Even O'Neill himself will admit it is taking him a long time to mature.

An excellent skater, with balance, speed, acceleration, and quickness, he has a good sense of timing and is patient with his passes. He doesn't have a big-time release but he has a decent one-timer. Now he has confidence in his shots, and is taking more one-timers and looking to shoot more, when in past seasons he thought pass first. O'Neill was among the league leaders in shots on goal last season, so he has made the transition to sniper.

O'Neill likes to carry the puck down the left-wing boards to protect the puck, and with his speed he is able to blow by defensemen. He does not follow this move up by driving to the net. Defensively, he has to remind himself not to leave the zone before the puck does. He is often too anxious to counterattack before his team has control, as his -21 will attest.

THE PHYSICAL GAME

O'Neill could always be in better shape. He is considered something of a soft player, whose effort and intensity don't come up to his skill level. O'Neill has been inspired by teammate Ron Francis to be a more consistent and dedicated player, but he could still bring it up a notch. Francis will probably only play one more season and then it will be up to O'Neill to become a leader by example.

THE INTANGIBLES

O'Neill went on a scoring spurt right after Sami Kapanen was traded in early February, then slumped at the end of the season. There is just something about O'Neill that makes you feel there's some gas left in the tank.

PROJECTION

O'Neill has scored at least 30 goals and 60 points in each of the last three seasons, which is pretty good unless you think he should be scoring 40 goals and 80 points, which we do.

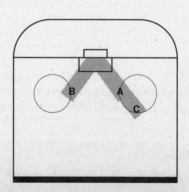

JOSEF VASICEK

Yrs. of NHL service: 3
Born: Havlickuv Brod, Czech Republic; Sept. 12, 1980
Position: center
Height: 6-4
Weight: 200
Uniform no.: 63
Shoots: left

Career statistics:

GP	G	A	TP	PIM
211	32	40	72	139

2000-2001 statistics:

GP	G	A	TP	+/-	PIM	PP	SH	GW	GT	S	PCT
76	8	13	21	-8	53	1	0	0	0	103	7.8

2001-2002 statistics:

GP	G	A	TP	+/-	PIM	PP	SH	GW	GT	S	PCT
78	14	17	31	-7	53	3	0	3	0	117	12.0

2002-2003 statistics:

GP	G	A	TP	+/-	PIM	PP	SH	GW	GT	S	PCT
57	10	10	20	-19	33	4	0	1	0	87	11.5

LAST SEASON

Third on team in shooting percentage. Missed 25 games with back injury.

THE FINESSE GAME

Vasicek's back injury occurred in October, and he never got his game going all season. He is still in pursuit of consistency. There are nights when he competes hard and looks like he can dominate a game. Other nights someone needs to light a fire under him.

Vasicek is a good skater with good balance. He has good acceleration for a big guy and can get in quickly on the forecheck.

He has terrific hockey instincts, especially on offense. He has good passing skills and is more of a playmaker than a scorer. He doesn't shoot enough.

THE PHYSICAL GAME

Vasicek is tall and still filling out. He needs to use his body better because he could be much more of a physical factor. He doesn't initiate enough, and he can be intimidated. He has a long reach which he puts to good use defensively.

THE INTANGIBLES

Vasicek is a quiet leader. He was named captain of his team in junior, which is a pretty rare honor for a European player. He was a restricted free agent after the season.

PROJECTION

There is so much potential here in such a big package that we are reluctant to quit on Vasicek just yet. If he is 100 per cent this season, he should be up in the 40-point range, with an emphasis on assists.

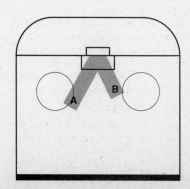

KEVIN WEEKES

Yrs. of NHL service: 4

Born: Toronto, Ont.; Apr. 4, 1975

Position: goaltender

Height: 6-0

Weight: 195

Uniform no.: 80

Catches: left

Career statistics:

GP	MIN	GA	SO	GAA	A	PIM
211	11323	574	13	3.04	2	6

1999-2000 statistics:

GP	MIN	GAA	W	L	T	SO	GA	S	SAPCT	PIM
20	987	2.86	6	7	4	1	47	461	.898	0

2000-2001 statistics:

GP	MIN	GAA	W	L	T	SO	GA	S	SAPCT	PIM
61	3378	3.14	20	33	3	4	177	1742	.898	4

2001-2002 statistics:

GP	MIN	GAA	W	L	T	SO	GA	S	SAPCT	PIM
19	830	2.89	3	9	0	2	40	511	.916	0

2002-2003 statistics:

GP	MIN	GAA	W	L	T	SO	GA	S	SAPCT	PIM
51	2965	2.55	14	24	9	5	126	1438	.912	2

PROJECTION

Weekes will play around 60-65 games and can probably win 25 games, but it will be a struggle because the Hurricanes figure to be one of the NHL's weaker teams.

LAST SEASON

Missed eight games with a concussion.

THE PHYSICAL GAME

Weekes has good size and is good stand-up goalie. He has toned down his aggressive play which has improved his game. He is strong positionally. Weekes is very athletic, so when he has to rely on his reflexes in a scramble, he can compete for the save.

Weekes is a very good skater. He likes to come out of his net to handle the puck. While he's not great at it, his passing skills are quite passable, and a considerable upgrade over Arturs Irbe. He uses his stick well to poke away rebounds and loose pucks.

Weekes is strong with both his glove and blocker on high shots. He is smart and coachable.

THE MENTAL GAME

Weekes finally won back a No. 1 starting role last season. He's had to learn to be more patient, which might have been the most valuable asset his former partner Irbe imparted to him. Weekes has been eager for the No. 1 role ever since he lost it after only one season in Tampa Bay (as a result of the Lightning acquiring Nikolai Khabibulin). Weekes is highly competitive.

THE INTANGIBLES

Carolina wasted little time in re-signing Weekes (who became a restricted free agent after the season) to a new contract, which shows their faith in him. He will give them a chance to win some games, but he is not the kind of goalie a team would ride into the playoffs.

GLEN WESLEY

Yrs. of NHL service: 16
Born: Red Deer, Alta.; Oct. 2, 1968
Position: left defense
Height: 6-1
Weight: 205
Uniform no.: 2
Shoots: left

Career statistics:

GP	G	A	TP	PIM
1173	124	376	500	859

1999-2000 statistics:

GP	G	A	TP	+/-	PIM	PP	SH	GW	GT	S	PCT
78	7	15	22	-4	38	1	0	0	2	99	7.1

2000-2001 statistics:

GP	G	A	TP	+/-	PIM	PP	SH	GW	GT	S	PCT
71	5	16	21	-2	42	3	0	0	0	92	5.4

2001-2002 statistics:

GP	G	A	TP	+/-	PIM	PP	SH	GW	GT	S	PCT
77	5	13	18	-8	56	1	0	0	1	88	5.7

2002-2003 statistics:

GP	G	A	TP	+/-	PIM	PP	SH	GW	GT	S	PCT
70	1	10	11	-2	44	1	0	0	0	77	1.3

LAST SEASON

Signed as free agent by Carolina on July 8, 2003. Previously acquired by Toronto from Carolina on March 9, 2003, for a second-round draft pick in 2004. Missed 12 games with foot injuries.

THE FINESSE GAME

Wesley simply isn't the 40-point player he was years ago in Boston. He is at best a No. 4 defenseman at this stage of his career. He has toiled in the one to two slot for Carolina because the team is so thin defensively, but if some of the younger players continue to progress, it will allow Wesley to slide back in a lesser role and put him in a position to succeed.

Wesley has solid, but not elite, skills. He is very good with the puck. He clicks on the power play because he knows when to jump into the holes. He has good but not great offensive instincts, which means he thinks rather than reacts when gauging when to pinch, rush, pass the puck, and back off. He is a decent skater who is not afraid to veer into the play deep. He seldom gets trapped there. He has a good slap shot from the point and snap shot from the circle.

You could count on two hands the number of times Wesley has been beaten one-on-one during his career, and there are very few defensemen you can say that about. He makes defensive plays with confidence and is poised even when outnumbered in the rush. He has to keep his feet moving. Wesley is reliable and does his job with a minimum of fuss.

THE PHYSICAL GAME

Wesley is not a bone-crunching defenseman, but neither was Jacques Laperriere, and he's in the Hall of Fame. We're not suggesting that Wesley is in that class, only that you don't have to shatter glass to be a solid checker, which he is. He's not a mean hitter, but he will execute a takeout check and not let his man get back into the play.

He is also sly about running interference for his defense partner, allowing him time to move the puck and giving him confidence that he won't get hammered by a forechecker.

THE INTANGIBLES

Wesley was injured during his stint with the Leafs but did play well when he was able to return in the playoffs. Carolina received a second-round draft pick for the rental and only had to give him a $250,000 raise to re-sign him as a free agent. Pretty slick.

PROJECTION

At 35, Wesley is tailing off. He can be expected to score in the 20-point range.

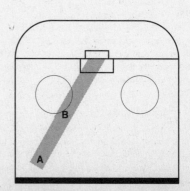

CHICAGO BLACKHAWKS

Players' Statistics 2001-2002

POS.	NO.	PLAYER	GP	G	A	PTS	+/-	PIM	PP	SH	GW	GT	S	PCT
R	26	STEVE SULLIVAN	82	26	35	61	15	42	4	2	3		190	13.7
C	13	ALEXEI ZHAMNOV	74	15	43	58	0	70	2	3	1		166	9.0
L	55	ERIC DAZE	54	22	22	44	10	14	3		5		170	12.9
L	19	KYLE CALDER	82	15	27	42	-6	40	7		2		164	9.1
C	39	*TYLER ARNASON	82	19	20	39	7	20	3		6		178	10.7
R	14	THEOREN FLEURY	54	12	21	33	-7	77	1		3	1	124	9.7
L	28	MARK BELL	82	14	15	29	0	113		2			127	11.0
D	43	NATHAN DEMPSEY	67	5	23	28	-7	26	1		2		124	4.0
C	11	ANDREI NIKOLISHIN	60	6	15	21	-3	26		1			73	8.2
L	17	CHRIS SIMON	71	12	8	20	-7	148	2		2	1	88	13.6
C	20	MIKE EASTWOOD	70	3	13	16	-5	32	1				39	7.7
D	42	JON KLEMM	70	2	14	16	-9	44	1		1		74	2.7
D	25	ALEXANDER KARPOVTSEV	40	4	10	14	-8	12	3		1		36	11.1
D	8	STEVE POAPST	75	2	11	13	14	50					49	4.1
C	22	IGOR KOROLEV	48	4	5	9	-1	30	1		1		32	12.5
L	50	*IGOR RADULOV	7	5		5	-3	4	3				14	35.7
L	34	JASON STRUDWICK	48	2	3	5	-4	87					19	10.5
D	5	STEVE MCCARTHY	57	1	4	5	-1	23					55	1.8
R	49	*SHAWN THORNTON	13	1	1	2	-4	31					15	6.7
D	44	*BURKE HENRY	16		2	2	-13	9					25	
D	46	TODD GILL	5		1	1	3						9	
L	15	GARRY VALK	16		1	1	0	6					9	
D	4	SAMI HELENIUS	15		1	1	4	34					7	
C	16	PETER WHITE	6		1	1	0						2	
R	23	RYAN VANDENBUSSCHE	22				0	58					7	
C	53	*BRETT MCLEAN	2				-1						1	
L	33	LOUIE DEBRUSK	4				0	7						
G	31	CRAIG ANDERSON	6				0							
G	30	MARC LAMOTHE					0							
G	29	STEVE PASSMORE	11				0	4						
G	41	JOCELYN THIBAULT	62				0	4						
G	30	MICHAEL LEIGHTON	8				0							

GP = games played; G = goals; A = assists; PTS = points; +/- = goals-for minus goals-against while player is on ice; PIM = penalties in minutes; PP = power-play goals; SH = shorthanded goals; GW = game-winning goals; GT = game-tying goals; S = no. of shots; PCT = percentage of goals to shots; * = rookie

TYLER ARNASON

Yrs. of NHL service: 1
Born: Oklahoma City, Okla.; Mar. 16. 1979
Position: center
Height: 5-11
Weight: 210
Uniform no.: 39
Shoots: left

Career statistics:

GP	G	A	TP	PIM
103	22	21	43	24

2001-2002 statistics:

GP	G	A	TP	+/-	PIM	PP	SH	GW	GT	S	PCT
21	3	1	4	-3	4	0	0	0	0	19	15.8

2002-2003 statistics:

GP	G	A	TP	+/-	PIM	PP	SH	GW	GT	S	PCT
82	19	20	39	+7	20	3	0	6	0	178	10.7

LAST SEASON

First NHL season. Named to NHL All-Rookie Team. Led NHL rookies and team in game-winning goals. Led NHL rookies in shots. Tied for second among NHL rookies in points. Third among NHL rookies in goals. Sixth among NHL rookies in assists. One of four Blackhawks to appear in all 82 games.

THE FINESSE GAME

Arnason plays with a lot of confidence and poise and is very strong on the puck. He likes to shoot — he had 10 shots on goal in an early-season game against Carolina — and he has a quick and accurate release. Arnason's wingers have learned to just drive to the net, because he will usually get a shot through and create chances for a deflection or a rebound.

Arnason possesses excellent vision, hands, and has a great feel for the game. He is a good skater but will fall into a bad habit of cruising and he sometimes has to be nudged to keep his feet moving.

Arnason saw ice time on the power play, penalty killing and late in close games. He protects the puck well with his body. He is learning to play with the same kind of intensity in the defensive zone that he shows in the attacking zone.

THE PHYSICAL GAME

Arnason reported to Blackhawks training camp in 2001 overweight and out of shape. Arnason needed to do some growing up and dedicate himself to becoming a pro. Minor league coach Trent Yawney and a personal trainer helped introduce Arnason to the weight room (he lost 20 pounds but added muscle) and cleaned up his eating habits. They also performed an attitude adjustment that helped Arnason make such a splash last season.

THE INTANGIBLES

Arnason was among the favorites for the Calder Trophy until a sluggish final quarter derailed his chances.

PROJECTION

Arnason is a top-six forward and may take over the No. 1 center's job from Alexei Zhamnov this season. As long as Arnason doesn't forget all of his hard-learned lessons, a step up to 25 goals, 50 points would be laudable.

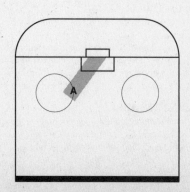

MARK BELL

Yrs. of NHL service: 2
Born: St. Paul's, Ont.; Aug. 5, 1980
Position: center/left wing
Height: 6-3
Weight: 198
Uniform no.: 28
Shoots: left

Career statistics:

GP	G	A	TP	PIM
175	26	32	58	241

2000-2001 statistics:

GP	G	A	TP	+/-	PIM	PP	SH	GW	GT	S	PCT
13	0	1	1	0	4	0	0	0	0	14	0.0

2001-2002 statistics:

GP	G	A	TP	+/-	PIM	PP	SH	GW	GT	S	PCT
80	12	16	28	-6	124	1	0	1	0	120	10.0

2002-2003 statistics:

GP	G	A	TP	+/-	PIM	PP	SH	GW	GT	S	PCT
82	14	15	29	0	113	0	2	0	0	127	11.0

PROJECTION

Bell will probably continue to see most of his time on the third line but he has more offensive upside. We expect a bump to 20 goals, 35 points this season.

LAST SEASON

Second NHL season. Second on team in penalty minutes. Tied for second on team in shorthanded goals. One of four Blackhawks to appear in all 82 games.

THE FINESSE GAME

Bell is a terrific puckhandler and passer, a natural point-producer who is always looking to make things happen in the offensive zone. He has a hard slap shot and a strong wrister. He has good hand-eye coordination for tipping pucks in front of the net. He also has good hockey sense, good vision, and good instincts — there is almost nothing negative about his offensive game.

Bell is a smooth, fluid skater who is very strong on his skates. He can put on a good burst of speed to beat a defender wide. He uses his speed to establish an aggressive forechecking game, and he can quickly make a turnover into a scoring chance.

His defensive game will need work, as will his proficiency on face-offs (he improved to 52.5 per cent last season). He can be used to kill penalties.

THE PHYSICAL GAME

Bell is tall and strong and is still adding muscle. He suffered two concussions several years ago and it might have taken him time to regain confidence in his physical play, because he didn't start asserting himself well until last season. Now Bell is establishing a real physical presence and is playing without fear.

THE INTANGIBLES

The Blackhawks could use a few more guys who play with Bell's edge. He was probably Chicago's unsung hero last season. Bell has a very bright future.

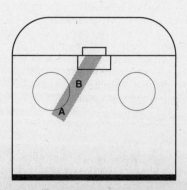

KYLE CALDER

Yrs. of NHL service: 3
Born: Mannville, Alta.; Jan. 5, 1979
Position: center
Height: 5-11
Weight: 180
Uniform no.: 19
Shoots: left

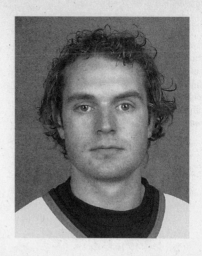

Career statistics:

GP	G	A	TP	PIM
214	38	74	112	103

1999-2000 statistics:

GP	G	A	TP	+/-	PIM	PP	SH	GW	GT	S	PCT
8	1	1	2	-3	2	0	0	0	0	5	20.0

2000-2001 statistics:

GP	G	A	TP	+/-	PIM	PP	SH	GW	GT	S	PCT
43	5	10	15	-4	14	0	0	1	0	63	7.9

2001-2002 statistics:

GP	G	A	TP	+/-	PIM	PP	SH	GW	GT	S	PCT
81	17	36	53	+8	47	6	0	3	0	133	12.8

2002-2003 statistics:

GP	G	A	TP	+/-	PIM	PP	SH	GW	GT	S	PCT
82	15	27	42	-6	40	7	0	2	0	164	9.1

PROJECTION

We thought Calder would break through the 20-goal barrier last season but he slumped badly (only one goal in the last 28 games) at the end of a dismal season for everyone in Chicago. We'll expect 20 this season.

LAST SEASON

Led team in power-play goals. Third on team in assists. One of four Blackhawks to appear in all 82 games.

THE FINESSE GAME

Calder has good offensive instincts. He is a heady player, too, and the defensive part of his game is pretty well advanced for such a young player.

He sees the ice well and finds the open man. Calder has a very nice scoring touch and has a lot of confidence in his shot. It's an accurate shot with a quick release, and he works hard to get to the high-percentage scoring areas.

Calder's skating is not great. It's NHL caliber, but it's something he is still going to have to work on. He is slippery, though, and a defender who thinks he has Calder corralled may be surprised when he wriggles his way out and finds open space for a shot.

THE PHYSICAL GAME

Calder is tough along the boards. He is small and needs to get a little thicker in his upper body to win puck battles and not get shoved out of the crease easily. He is gritty and has become more consistent in his effort. Calder tried awfully hard to lead the Blackhawks by example last season, but there weren't many people willing to follow.

THE INTANGIBLES

Calder's progress has been gradual but continues on the upswing, which is a very positive sign. He is a top-six forward in Chicago. Calder has a terrific work ethic and is a favorite with the coaches.

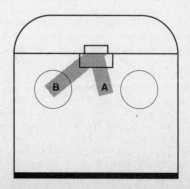

ERIC DAZE

Yrs. of NHL service: 8
Born: Montreal, Que.; July 2, 1975
Position: left wing
Height: 6-6
Weight: 234
Uniform no.: 55
Shoots: left

Career statistics:

GP	G	A	TP	PIM
581	222	165	387	174

1999-2000 statistics:

GP	G	A	TP	+/-	PIM	PP	SH	GW	GT	S	PCT
59	23	13	36	-16	28	6	0	1	1	143	16.1

2000-2001 statistics:

GP	G	A	TP	+/-	PIM	PP	SH	GW	GT	S	PCT
79	33	24	57	+1	16	9	1	8	2	205	16.1

2001-2002 statistics:

GP	G	A	TP	+/-	PIM	PP	SH	GW	GT	S	PCT
82	38	32	70	+17	36	12	0	5	1	264	14.4

2002-2003 statistics:

GP	G	A	TP	+/-	PIM	PP	SH	GW	GT	S	PCT
54	22	22	44	+10	14	3	0	5	0	170	12.9

LAST SEASON

Secone on team in goals and game-winning goals. Third on team in points, plus-minus, shots, and shooting percentage. Tied for third on team in power-play goals. Missed five games with ankle infection. Missed five games with groin injury. Missed 18 games with back injuries and surgery.

THE FINESSE GAME

Although the most impressive thing about Daze is his size, it is his skating ability that sets him apart from other lumbering big men. He isn't a speed demon, but he skates well enough to not look out of place with faster linemates.

Daze keeps his hands close together on his stick and is able to get a lot on his shot with very little backswing. Daze's best weapon is his one-timer, which may be one of the most unstoppable shots in the NHL. Daze keeps his stick on the ice and always seems to be poised to take the shot. He has excellent hands for shooting or scoring, and is an adept stickhandler who can draw defenders to him and then slip a pass through to a teammate. He sets screens on the power play. He has good hockey vision and an innate understanding of the game. His defensive game has improved dramatically. He is now a very solid two-way forward.

Daze excels when he drives wide, protects the puck and takes it to the net. Very few defensemen can handle him when he does, but he frequently stops working and moving his feet. When he stands around rooted to one spot on the power play, he is useless. Daze played left wing most of the season and that is his preferred side, although he can play the right.

THE PHYSICAL GAME

Daze doesn't back down, but he doesn't show much initiative either. He is not a typical power forward. There will be the occasional night when he tries to run guys over, but those games are infrequent. He doesn't have the strength or the taste for it. Daze has a long reach — he can pass or shoot the puck even when a defenseman thinks he has him all wrapped up and under control. He doesn't have much of a mean streak.

THE INTANGIBLES

Daze had back surgery during training camp and suffered some recurring back kinks after returning, along with a few other nagging injuries. Daze also suffered from the loss of Tony Amonte.

PROJECTION

Daze could be a 40-goal scorer if he had a better supporting cast. That won't happen unless he is traded (which is quite likely to happen). If he stays with Chicago, look for a 30-goal season.

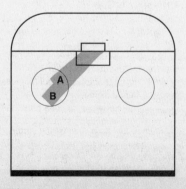

ALEXANDER KARPOVTSEV

Yrs. of NHL service: 10
Born: Moscow, Russia; Feb. 25, 1974
Position: left defense
Height: 6-3
Weight: 215
Uniform no.: 25
Shoots: left

Career statistics:

GP	G	A	TP	PIM
563	34	146	180	408

1999-2000 statistics:

GP	G	A	TP	+/-	PIM	PP	SH	GW	GT	S	PCT
69	3	14	17	+9	54	3	0	0	0	51	5.9

2000-2001 statistics:

GP	G	A	TP	+/-	PIM	PP	SH	GW	GT	S	PCT
53	2	13	15	-4	39	1	0	0	0	52	3.8

2001-2002 statistics:

GP	G	A	TP	+/-	PIM	PP	SH	GW	GT	S	PCT
65	1	9	10	+10	40	0	1	0	0	40	2.5

2002-2003 statistics:

GP	G	A	TP	+/-	PIM	PP	SH	GW	GT	S	PCT
40	4	10	14	-8	12	3	0	1	0	36	11.1

LAST SEASON

Third on team in average ice time. Tied for third on team in power-play goals. Missed 13 games with fractured cheek and orbital bone. Missed 18 games with fractured right ankle. Missed 10 games due to foot injuries. Missed one game with flu.

THE FINESSE GAME

Ask Karpovtsev, "What did you have for dinner last night, Alex?" and he is likely to answer, "Pucks." If there was a shot-blocking contest at the NHL All-Star Game, Karpovtsev would be reigning champ. It's one of the reasons why he misses so much playing time. Many of his injuries, like his fractured cheek bone last season, result from his shot-blocking attempts.

Karpovtsev has decent puck-carrying skills and the good sense to move the puck quickly, but displays the defensive defenseman's mindset of getting to the redline and dumping the puck into the corner or making a short outlet pass. Under pressure behind his net, he tends to whack the puck around the boards, a play that often gets picked off.

The strength of Karpovtsev's skating game is best reflected in his terrific lateral movement. He covers acres of ground with a huge stride and a long reach, has excellent balance, turns nicely in both directions, and boasts a fair amount of quickness and agility. He has a quick first step to the puck.

Karpovtsev does show, at times, a good instinct for seeing a better passing option than the obvious in the attacking zone. He has an effective, hard shot from the point, and his accuracy has improved.

THE PHYSICAL GAME

A crease clearer and shot-blocker, Karpovtsev is far more comfortable and poised in front of his net than when he chases to the corners or sideboards. Once he gets away from the slot, with or without the puck, he loses either confidence or focus or both, which can lead to unforced errors or turnovers. Still, he is an effective weapon against a power forward. He can tie up the guy in front, lean on him, and hit and skate.

Karpovtsev has become increasingly fragile and less willing to throw his body at other people. He still seems willing to hurl himself in front of shots, but he's either very unlucky or not very good at timing his slides. The puck is supposed to hit his equipment, not bone or a vital organ.

THE INTANGIBLES

Karpovtsev is useful when he plays, but his spending more time in the emergency room than on the ice will probably have Chicago trying to move him.

PROJECTION

Last season we said, "Here is a prediction: Karpovtsev's number of games missed will be higher than his points scored." The tally: 42 games missed, 14 points scored. We'll book that wager again.

JON KLEMM

Yrs. of NHL service: 8
Born: Cranbrook, B.C.; Jan. 8, 1970
Position: right defense
Height: 6-2
Weight: 200
Uniform no.: 42
Shoots: right

Career statistics:

GP	G	A	TP	PIM
560	35	86	121	298

1999-2000 statistics:

GP	G	A	TP	+/-	PIM	PP	SH	GW	GT	S	PCT
73	5	7	12	+26	34	0	0	0	0	64	7.8

2000-2001 statistics:

GP	G	A	TP	+/-	PIM	PP	SH	GW	GT	S	PCT
78	4	11	15	+22	54	2	0	2	0	97	4.1

2001-2002 statistics:

GP	G	A	TP	+/-	PIM	PP	SH	GW	GT	S	PCT
82	4	16	20	-3	42	2	0	1	0	111	3.6

2002-2003 statistics:

GP	G	A	TP	+/-	PIM	PP	SH	GW	GT	S	PCT
70	2	14	16	-9	44	1	0	1	0	74	2.7

PROJECTION

Klemm can give you a reliable performance on defense game after game and produce 20 points.

LAST SEASON

Second on team in average ice time (21:57). Missed 12 games with hand injury.

THE FINESSE GAME

Klemm is hardly a No. 1 defenseman, but that is how the 'Hawks utilize him.

Klemm's finesse skills are good enough that he can be used up front in a pinch. His defensive skills are good enough that he can be paired with a high-risk offensive defenseman, either a young kid or a more experienced roamer.

Klemm is an all-purpose defenseman who does everything the team asks of him. His skating is average, but he plays within his limitations. When he's moved up front, he fills the role of a grinding winger. On defense, he is as steady and low-risk as they come, without doing anything truly special. What Klemm does is provide stability and instill confidence in his teammates.

THE PHYSICAL GAME

Klemm doesn't go looking for hits. He eliminates his man but doesn't have the explosive drive from his legs to make powerful highlight hits. Klemm stays in good condition and handled a lot of ice time last season without breaking down.

THE INTANGIBLES

Klemm is a sportswriter's nightmare because he's so quiet, yet he's appreciated by his coaches and teammates for his willingness to do anything for the team. He really is best slotted as a second-pair defenseman, though.

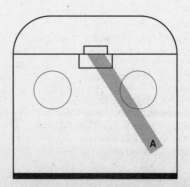

STEVE MCCARTHY

Yrs. of NHL service: 3
Born: Trail, B.C.; Feb. 3, 1981
Position: left defense
Height: 6-0
Weight: 197
Uniform no.: 5
Shoots: left

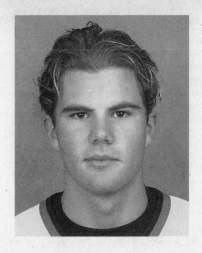

Career statistics:

GP	G	A	TP	PIM
109	2	10	12	37

1999-2000 statistics:

GP	G	A	TP	+/-	PIM	PP	SH	GW	GT	S	PCT
5	1	1	2	0	4	1	0	0	0	4	25.0

2000-2001 statistics:

GP	G	A	TP	+/-	PIM	PP	SH	GW	GT	S	PCT
44	0	5	5	-7	8	0	0	0	0	32	0.0

2001-2002 statistics:

GP	G	A	TP	+/-	PIM	PP	SH	GW	GT	S	PCT
3	0	0	0	-1	2	0	0	0	0	2	0.0

2002-2003 statistics:

GP	G	A	TP	+/-	PIM	PP	SH	GW	GT	S	PCT
57	1	4	5	-1	23	0	0	0	0	55	1.8

PROJECTION

McCarthy played much steadier after his mid-December call-up and should battle for a top-four job with Chicago this season. If he scores in the 20-point range that would be a positive next step.

LAST SEASON

Appeared in 19 games with Norfolk (AHL), scoring 1-6 — 7 with 14 PIM. Missed four games due to coach's decision.

THE FINESSE GAME

McCarthy has major-league speed, acceleration, balance, and agility. He is tough to beat one-on-one. He is a tape-to-tape passer. He still has trouble with the pace of the NHL game and needs to improve his decision-making. McCarthy needs to quickly recognize when it is safe to make an outlet pass out of his zone or whether it is wiser to make the boring play and chip it safely off the boards.

Everyone has focused on McCarthy's offense but what he has had to do is concentrate on his defense. McCarthy could become a poor man's Scott Niedermayer, able to apply his finesse skills in the defensive zone and contribute offensively.

McCarthy can handle power-play quarterbacking duties. He has a hard and accurate point shot.

THE PHYSICAL GAME

McCarthy is on the wiry side and needs to develop more upper-body strength. He has to add a more physical element to his game, as Niedermayer quietly does.

THE INTANGIBLES

McCarthy has not developed at the pace the 'Hawks had hoped but he's only 22 and it's way to soon to give up on him. McCarthy was a restricted free agent at the end of last season.

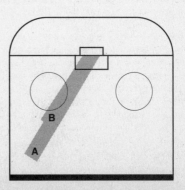

ANDREI NIKOLISHIN

Yrs. of NHL service: 9
Born: Vorkuta, Russia; March 25, 1973
Position: left wing / center
Height: 6-0
Weight: 213
Uniform no.: 11
Shoots: left

Career statistics:

GP	G	A	TP	PIM
579	88	180	268	246

1999-2000 statistics:

GP	G	A	TP	+/-	PIM	PP	SH	GW	GT	S	PCT
76	11	14	25	+6	28	0	2	2	0	98	11.2

2000-2001 statistics:

GP	G	A	TP	+/-	PIM	PP	SH	GW	GT	S	PCT
81	13	25	38	+9	34	4	0	2	1	145	9.0

2001-2002 statistics:

GP	G	A	TP	+/-	PIM	PP	SH	GW	GT	S	PCT
80	13	23	36	-1	40	1	0	0	0	143	9.1

2002-2003 statistics:

GP	G	A	TP	+/-	PIM	PP	SH	GW	GT	S	PCT
60	6	15	21	-3	26	0	1	0	0	73	8.2

LAST SEASON

Acquired from Chicago on June 21, 2003, for a fourth-round draft pick in 2004. Previously acquired by Chicago from Washington with Chris Simon on November 1, 2002, for Michael Nylander, a third-round draft pick in 2003, and a conditional third-round draft pick in 2004. Missed 13 games with a knee injury. Missed eight games due to contract dispute.

THE FINESSE GAME

Nikolishin sees the ice well and is a gifted playmaker. Unfortunately, last season he fell back into his old habit of forcing plays instead of taking shots himself. When he does that, he becomes an entirely predictable player and much too easy to defend against. He fits best with a finishing winger who can convert his slippery passes.

Nikolishin has become more of a defensive-minded forward, which means it's less likely he will earn a spot on the top-two lines. He backchecks, blocks shots, and kills penalties.

He does a good job on draws — no doubt learning from former teammate Adam Oates has helped him. Nikolishin studies his opponents well and reacts to them, winning a majority of his draws by countering what the other player is doing.

Nikolishin is a strong skater with a powerful stride, and he makes some of the tightest turns in the league. His great talent is puckhandling, but like many Europeans he tends to hold on to the puck too long and leave himself open for hits.

THE PHYSICAL GAME

Nikolishin is extremely strong on his skates and likes to work in the corners for the puck. He is tough to knock off balance and has a low center of gravity. He has adapted smoothly to the more physical style of play in the NHL, and although he isn't very big, he will plow into heavy players while going for the puck. When he puts his mind to it, he is one of the tougher defensive forwards in the league.

THE INTANGIBLES

Nikolishin was injured shortly after being traded to Chicago. Nikolishin can be well-spotted in a part-time and penalty-killing role. He's a valuable player to have on hand, but with Colorado loaded at center, it's hard to figure where Nikolishin will get any even-strength ice time.

PROJECTION

Nikolishin seems content to let his defensive game carry him. He has proven before that he can put up some numbers, but it's likely he will slouch to the 30-point range.

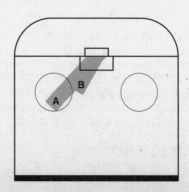

TUOMO RUUTU

Yrs. of NHL service: 0
Born: Vantaa, Finland; Feb. 16, 1983
Position: center
Height: 6-1
Weight: 201
Uniform no.: n.a.
Shoots: left

Career (European) statistics:

GP	G	A	TP	PIM
128	30	42	72	179

2001-2002 European statistics:

GP	G	A	TP	PIM
51	7	16	23	69

2002-2003 European statistics:

GP	G	A	TP	PIM
30	12	15	27	24

LAST SEASON

Will be entering first NHL season. Appeared in 30 games with Helsinki (Finland), scoring 12-15 — 27 with 24 PIM.

THE FINESSE GAME

The next Peter Forsberg? Nice to start off an NHL career without any pressure.

Ruutu is supposed to be the Next Great Thing in the NHL. Or maybe that's the Next Grate Thing, since the first quality anyone mentions in discussing Ruutu is his ability to drive opponents over the edge with his abrasive play. Ruutu is a hellacious forechecker. He is quick on the puck, and strong, and forces turnovers and errant passes.

Ruutu is smart and knows what to do with the puck after he's caused a ruckus. He heads for the open spots on the ice with a choppy skating stride that always makes it looks like he's churning to get from Point A to Point B. He lacks breakaway speed but he's really effective in ploughing through traffic.

Ruutu is smart. He kills penalties. He will be able to handle shifts against other team's star lines because nothing intimidates him.

Ruutu works hard around the net for his goals. Although he's not a great finisher, he will get more than his share through effort. He has already been compared to Forsberg, Claude Lemieux, Adam Deadmarsh, and Michael Peca, but Ruutu will be his own man.

THE PHYSICAL GAME

Talk about making an impact. Ruutu will not arrive meekly in the NHL. Ruutu plays a very mature game. He is gritty and aggressive. He is mentally tough and he will do all of the little things to help his team win. He blocks shots, plays the body, hacks and whacks, and seldom plays a quiet shift.

THE INTANGIBLES

Chicago traded Andrei Nikolishin in anticipation of opening up a roster spot at center for Ruutu this season. During the summer, however, they were still haggling over a contract. Ruutu would have to accept the capped rookie salary structure but was holding out for some hefty incentive clauses. He would be any coach's dream — but even more so if that coach happens to be a Sutter. Ruutu has a big heart and wants to make an impact in the NHL.

PROJECTION

Ruutu may not light it up just yet. Forsberg scored 15 goals in his first season. We'd take that as a jumping-off point.

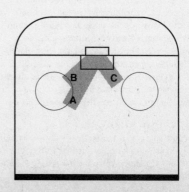

STEVE SULLIVAN

Yrs. of NHL service: 7
Born: Timmins, Ont.; July 6, 1974
Position: center/right wing
Height: 5-9
Weight: 160
Uniform no.: 26
Shoots: right

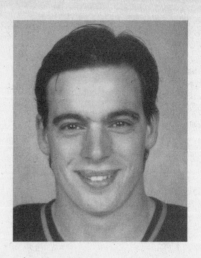

Career statistics:

GP	G	A	TP	PIM
517	151	225	376	332

1999-2000 statistics:

GP	G	A	TP	+/-	PIM	PP	SH	GW	GT	S	PCT
80	22	43	65	+19	56	2	1	6	0	180	12.2

2000-2001 statistics:

GP	G	A	TP	+/-	PIM	PP	SH	GW	GT	S	PCT
81	34	41	75	+3	54	6	8	3	1	204	16.7

2001-2002 statistics:

GP	G	A	TP	+/-	PIM	PP	SH	GW	GT	S	PCT
78	21	39	60	+23	67	3	0	8	2	155	13.6

2002-2003 statistics:

GP	G	A	TP	+/-	PIM	PP	SH	GW	GT	S	PCT
82	26	35	61	+15	42	4	2	3	0	190	13.7

LAST SEASON

Led team in goals, points, plus-minus, shots, and shooting percentage. Second on team in assists, power-play goals, and shorthanded goals. Tied for third on team in game-winning goals. One of four Blackhawks to appear in all 82 games.

THE FINESSE GAME

Sullivan brings a center's vision to the right-wing position. He has terrific speed, hands, sense, and anticipation. Playing wing, he doesn't have to be down low on defensive-zone coverage, and the trade-off of using a smaller player along the boards still works out in his and Chicago's favor.

One advantage to being as small as Sullivan is that you are closer to the puck than a lot of your rivals. Sullivan complicates matters by using a short stick — short even by his standards — to keep the puck in his feet. He draws penalties by protecting the puck so well. Foes usually have to foul him to get it. He is able to maintain control of the puck because it is so close to his body. He wants the puck and likes to shoot. He will scrap around the net for loose pucks.

Sullivan is quick and smart enough to get himself out of pending jams, but he does not have elite skills and has to apply himself constantly. He is strictly an offensive threat, almost a specialty player. This is particularly true on the penalty-killing unit.

THE PHYSICAL GAME

You can't survive in the NHL if you are small and soft. Sullivan plays with fire. He had a slow start to the season but finished well in what was yet another troubled season in Chicago.

THE INTANGIBLES

Sullivan is a No. 2 (at best) right wing functioning as a No. 1 for the Blackhawks.

PROJECTION

Sullivan should be regarded realistically as a 20-goal, 60-point guy.

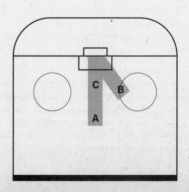

JOCELYN THIBAULT

Yrs. of NHL service: 10
Born: Montreal, Que.; Jan. 12, 1975
Position: goaltender
Height: 5-11
Weight: 170
Uniform no.: 41
Catches: left

Career statistics:

GP	MIN	GA	SO	GAA	A	PIM
522	29656	1329	35	2.69	3	16

1999-2000 statistics:

GP	MIN	GAA	W	L	T	SO	GA	S	SAPCT	PIM
60	3438	2.76	25	26	7	3	158	1679	.906	2

2000-2001 statistics:

GP	MIN	GAA	W	L	T	SO	GA	S	SAPCT	PIM
66	3844	2.81	27	32	7	6	180	1711	.895	2

2001-2002 statistics:

GP	MIN	GAA	W	L	T	SO	GA	S	SAPCT	PIM
67	3838	2.49	33	23	9	6	159	1626	.902	2

2002-2003 statistics:

GP	MIN	GAA	W	L	T	SO	GA	S	SAPCT	PIM
62	3650	2.37	26	28	7	8	144	1690	.915	4

LAST SEASON

Tied for second among NHL goalies in shutouts. Missed nine games due to post-concussion syndrome.

THE PHYSICAL GAME

Thibault is a small netminder whose technique makes him look even smaller. He is a butterfly-style goalie, but when he goes to his knees he doesn't keep his torso upright (as Patrick Roy always did so splendidly), and that costs Thibault a big chunk of net.

Because he plays deep in his net, Thibault does not challenge shooters. He relies on his reflexes, which, happily for him, happen to be excellent. He is a battler and doesn't give up on a puck, but he creates problems for himself by making the easy saves more difficult than they would be if his fundamentals were better. He has a good glove hand and quick feet, and he is a good skater with lateral mobility.

Thibault has improved his stickhandling, and how he directs his rebounds. He is not very strong on his stick, which means he fails to make key poke-checks or knock-away, cross-crease passes.

THE MENTAL GAME

Thibault's workload was reduced by necessity because of his season-ending injury, but the Blackhawks would be wise to plan on starting him in around 60 games. He is an active goalie, and a small one. Thibault weighs about 160 pounds after an all-you-can-eat buffet, and his athletic style takes a lot out of him. Mentally and physically, he is not an elite No. 1 goalie and probably never will be, but he is all the team has for now and he works extremely hard.

THE INTANGIBLES

The second-half collapse of the Blackhawks was hardly Thibault's fault. Given the way people quit in front of him, his numbers were more than respectable.

PROJECTION

As anticipated, Chicago fell back to earth a little last season and Thibault's win total was just where we expected it to be. He is likely to win 25-28 games.

ALEXEI ZHAMNOV

Yrs. of NHL service: 11
Born: Moscow, Russia; Oct. 1, 1970
Position: center
Height: 6-1
Weight: 200
Uniform no.: 13
Shoots: left

Career statistics:

GP	G	A	TP	PIM
740	237	436	673	610

1999-2000 statistics:

GP	G	A	TP	+/-	PIM	PP	SH	GW	GT	S	PCT
71	23	37	60	+7	61	5	0	7	0	175	13.1

2000-2001 statistics:

GP	G	A	TP	+/-	PIM	PP	SH	GW	GT	S	PCT
63	13	36	49	-12	40	3	1	3	0	117	11.1

2001-2002 statistics:

GP	G	A	TP	+/-	PIM	PP	SH	GW	GT	S	PCT
77	22	45	67	+8	67	6	0	3	0	173	12.7

2002-2003 statistics:

GP	G	A	TP	+/-	PIM	PP	SH	GW	GT	S	PCT
74	15	43	58	0	70	2	3	1	0	166	9.0

LAST SEASON

Led team in assists and shorthanded goals. Second on team in points. Missed eight games with hand injuries.

THE FINESSE GAME

Zhamnov's game is puck control. He can carry it at top speed or work the give-and-go. The Russian is a crafty playmaker and is not too unselfish. He has an accurate if not overpowering shot. He gets his wrist shot away quickly, and he shoots it with his feet still moving, which few players can do. As well, he can blast off the pass, or manoeuvre until he has a screen and then wrist it. He will try to score from "bad" angles. He is cool and patient with the puck, and he turns harmless-looking plays into dangerous scoring chances. On the power play, he works the left point or, if used low, can dart in and out in front of the goalie, using his soft hands for a tip.

Defensively, Zhamnov is sound and is frequently used against other teams' top forward lines. He is a dedicated backchecker and never leaves the zone too quickly.

Zhamnov simply isn't an elite player, no matter how much the 'Hawks pretend.

THE PHYSICAL GAME

Zhamnov will bump to prevent a scoring chance or go for a loose puck, but body work is not his forte. The knock on Zhamnov is his lack of physical play, but he works hard and competes. He is strong and fights his way through traffic in front of the net to get to a puck when he wants to. He needs to do a better job of tying up the opposing center on face-offs, since he wins few draws cleanly.

THE INTANGIBLES

Zhamnov just doesn't have the presence or the drive to be a true No. 1 center under these circumstances, but that's where he stands on the team's depth chart.

PROJECTION

Checking pressure and a generally glum atmosphere in Chicago will probably mean a 15-goal, 60-point season for Zhamnov.

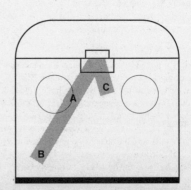

COLORADO AVALANCHE

Players' Statistics 2001-2002

POS.	NO.	PLAYER	GP	G	A	PTS	+/-	PIM	PP	SH	GW	GT	S	PCT
C	21	PETER FORSBERG	75	29	77	106	52	70	8		2		166	17.5
R	23	MILAN HEJDUK	82	50	48	98	52	32	18		4	1	244	20.5
L	40	ALEX TANGUAY	82	26	41	67	34	36	3		5	2	142	18.3
C	19	JOE SAKIC	58	26	32	58	4	24	8		1		190	13.7
C	28	STEVEN REINPRECHT	77	18	33	51	-6	18	2	1	1		146	12.3
D	53	DEREK MORRIS	75	11	37	48	16	68	9		7		191	5.8
D	4	ROB BLAKE	79	17	28	45	20	57	8	2	3		269	6.3
D	7	GREG DE VRIES	82	6	26	32	15	70			2		112	5.3
D	52	ADAM FOOTE	78	11	20	31	30	88	3		2		106	10.4
L	44	BATES BATTAGLIA	83	6	19	25	-19	100	1	1	2		123	4.9
D	41	MARTIN SKOULA	81	4	21	25	11	68	2				93	4.3
L	37	DEAN MCAMMOND	41	10	8	18	1	10	2		2		72	13.9
L	29	ERIC MESSIER	72	4	10	14	-2	16		1	1		52	7.7
D	20	BRYAN MARCHMENT	81	2	12	14	2	141					84	2.4
R	13	DAN HINOTE	60	6	4	10	4	49			3		65	9.2
R	12	MIKE KEANE	65	5	5	10	0	34		1	1	1	35	14.3
C	10	SERGE AUBIN	66	4	6	10	-2	64			1		62	6.4
C	22	*VACLAV NEDOROST	42	4	5	9	8	20	1				35	11.4
C	11	JEFF SHANTZ	74	3	6	9	-12	35			2		68	4.4
C	32	*RIKU HAHL	42	3	4	7	3	12					61	4.9
R	27	SCOTT PARKER	43	1	3	4	6	82					20	5.0
L	9	BRAD LARSEN	6		3	3	3	2					6	
D	2	BRYAN MUIR	32		2	2	3	19					9	
D	6	*D.J. SMITH	34	1		1	2	55					7	14.3
D	24	CHRIS MCALLISTER	33		1	1	4	47					13	
R	50	BRIAN WILLSIE	12		1	1	0	15					12	
C	45	STEVE BRULE	2				0						2	
C	38	*CHARLIE STEPHENS	2				0						1	
G	33	PATRICK ROY	63				0	20						
D	39	*JEFF PAUL	2				0	7						
G	1	DAVID AEBISCHER	22				0	4						
C	36	*STEVE MOORE	4				0							

GP = games played; G = goals; A = assists; PTS = points; +/- = goals-for minus goals-against while player is on ice;
PIM = penalties in minutes; PP = power-play goals; SH = shorthanded goals; GW = game-winning goals; GT =
game-tying goals; S = no. of shots; PCT = percentage of goals to shots; * = rookie

BATES BATTAGLIA

Yrs. of NHL service: 6
Born: Chicago, Ill.; Dec. 13, 1975
Position: left wing
Height: 6-2
Weight: 205
Uniform no.: 44
Shoots: left

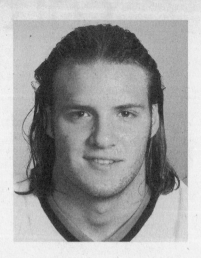

Career statistics:

GP	G	A	TP	PIM
415	64	92	156	291

1999-2000 statistics:

GP	G	A	TP	+/-	PIM	PP	SH	GW	GT	S	PCT
77	16	18	34	+20	39	3	0	3	0	86	18.6

2000-2001 statistics:

GP	G	A	TP	+/-	PIM	PP	SH	GW	GT	S	PCT
80	12	15	27	-14	76	2	0	3	0	133	9.0

2001-2002 statistics:

GP	G	A	TP	+/-	PIM	PP	SH	GW	GT	S	PCT
82	21	25	46	-6	44	5	1	2	3	167	12.6

2002-2003 statistics:

GP	G	A	TP	+/-	PIM	PP	SH	GW	GT	S	PCT
83	6	19	25	-19	100	1	1	2	0	123	4.9

LAST SEASON

Acquired from Carolina on March 11, 2003, for Radim Vrbata. Second on Avs in penalty minutes. Worst plus-minus on team. Appeared in 83 games due to trade.

THE FINESSE GAME

Battaglia is a good skater who is strong on the puck. He has had to drill hard to perfect most of his skills, because he is not a natural. His first strides are a bit sluggish, but he has a strong stride once he gets moving.

He goes hard to the net to create his scoring chances. He moves the puck alertly and plays smart positional hockey. He won't gamble or try to do anything fancy with the puck, which makes it easy for other grinders to play with him. He has a good head for the game, and the heart, too.

Battaglia is versatile and can play all three forward positions. He is a natural center but will probably be used on the wing because of Colorado's depth there. He is skilled enough to take an occasional spin on one of the top lines but he can't keep it up for long. A third-line role suits Battaglia just fine.

THE PHYSICAL GAME

Battaglia has good size and is willing to use it. He works hard and his enthusiasm alone will bug other players. A Chicago native, he grew up emulating Jeremy Roenick. He'll never have Roenick's scoring touch, but he'll bring the nonstop work ethic of a young Roenick every night.

THE INTANGIBLES

Battaglia has a solid, 10-year NHL future in store as a third-line forward. He'll bring energy to every shift. He has relaxed into his role without assuming a comfort zone. Battaglia had a terrible start in Carolina (along with the rest of his team, after going to the finals in 2002), and he failed to have the impact in Colorado (1-5 — 6 in 13 games) the Avs had hoped for. He had a mediocre playoffs, which was the biggest disappointment because he usually steps up his game in bigger spots.

PROJECTION

Battaglia's 21-goal season in 2001-02 looks like an aberration. He needs to contribute around 10-15 in his third-line role.

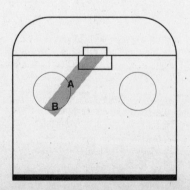

ROB BLAKE

Yrs. of NHL service: 13
Born: Simcoe, Ont.; Dec. 10, 1969
Position: right defense
Height: 6-4
Weight: 225
Uniform no.: 4
Shoots: right

Career statistics:

GP	G	A	TP	PIM
829	173	367	540	1174

1999-2000 statistics:

GP	G	A	TP	+/-	PIM	PP	SH	GW	GT	S	PCT
77	18	39	57	+10	112	12	0	5	0	327	5.5

2000-2001 statistics:

GP	G	A	TP	+/-	PIM	PP	SH	GW	GT	S	PCT
67	19	40	59	+3	77	10	0	2	1	267	7.1

2001-2002 statistics:

GP	G	A	TP	+/-	PIM	PP	SH	GW	GT	S	PCT
75	16	40	56	+16	58	10	0	2	0	229	7.0

2002-2003 statistics:

GP	G	A	TP	+/-	PIM	PP	SH	GW	GT	S	PCT
79	17	28	45	+20	57	8	2	3	0	269	6.3

LAST SEASON

Led team in average ice time (26:21), shorthanded goals, and shots. Tied for third on team in power-play goals. Missed two games with back spasms. Missed one game with groin injury.

THE FINESSE GAME

Lower-body strength is the key to Blake's open-ice hitting, along with, of course, his skating. Blake is one of the best open-ice hitting defensemen in the league. Blake is a powerful skater, quick, and agile with good balance. He steps up and challenges at the blueline, and has great anticipation. He's also quite bold, forcing turnovers at the blueline with his body positioning and quick stickwork. He is brave but not brash in his decision making.

Blake has finesse skills that make an impact in any zone on the ice. He works the point on the power play and has a good, low shot, which he rifles off the pass. He has quality hand skills and is not afraid to skip in deep to try to make something happen. It's not so much that Blake is smart about his pinches — he really is rather indiscriminate about going on the attack — but he works up such a head of steam and he is so fearsome a hitter that players tend to scatter out of his way, and that gives him the confidence to force the play deep in the offensive zone. Blake has sharp enough passing skills to use a backhand pass across the goalmouth.

Blake rarely goes a game without getting at least one shot on goal, and he had a nine-shot game last season. Not only does he take shots, he blocks them as well. Blake is also among the best in the league at that foolhardy skill.

THE PHYSICAL GAME

Blake is among the hardest hitters in the league. He has a nasty streak and will bring up his gloves and stick them into the face of an opponent when he thinks the referees aren't watching. He can dominate with his physical play. When he does, he opens up a lot of ice for himself and his teammates. Blake sees the major checking duties against other teams' top lines. Blake is fit and handles a ton of ice time.

THE INTANGIBLES

Blake will turn 34 this season which doesn't make him a fossil, but he has a lot of hockey mileage on him. It looks like the Avs will still be counting on him for 26-27 minutes of ice time per game, though.

PROJECTION

Blake should still score in the 45-point range.

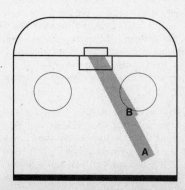

ADAM FOOTE

Yrs. of NHL service: 12
Born: Toronto, Ont.; July 10, 1971
Position: right defense
Height: 6-2
Weight: 215
Uniform no.: 52
Shoots: right

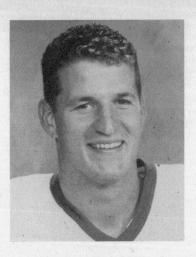

Career statistics:

GP	G	A	TP	PIM
726	47	157	204	1053

1999-2000 statistics:

GP	G	A	TP	+/-	PIM	PP	SH	GW	GT	S	PCT
59	5	13	18	+5	98	1	0	2	0	63	7.9

2000-2001 statistics:

GP	G	A	TP	+/-	PIM	PP	SH	GW	GT	S	PCT
35	3	12	15	+6	42	1	1	1	0	59	5.1

2001-2002 statistics:

GP	G	A	TP	+/-	PIM	PP	SH	GW	GT	S	PCT
55	5	22	27	+7	55	1	1	0	0	85	5.9

2002-2003 statistics:

GP	G	A	TP	+/-	PIM	PP	SH	GW	GT	S	PCT
78	11	20	31	+30	88	3	0	2	0	106	10.4

LAST SEASON

Second on team in average ice time. Third on team in penalty minutes. Career high in goals. Missed two games with groin injury. Missed two games with hamstring injury.

THE FINESSE GAME

Foote has great foot speed and quickness, especially for a player considered a big, tough guy. Defensively, he's strong in his coverage as a stay-at-home type, but he's not creative with the puck, probably his major deficiency. Still, all of the Avalanche defensemen are encouraged to jump into the attack and Foote eagerly does so when given the chance. He is gaining confidence in that facet of the game and it is reflected in his rising point totals, but it would be wrong to start thinking of him as an offensive defenseman. He is becoming more of a two-way player. Foote is wise in his pinches and knows when to drive to the slot, and he has a useful shot. He won't take wild chances.

Foote usually skates the puck out of his zone and is less likely to find the man for an outlet pass. There are few defensemen in the league who can match him in getting the first few strides in and jumping out of the zone. He is an excellent penalty killer.

Foote was the most consistent Avs defenseman last season.

THE PHYSICAL GAME

Foote is big, solid, and uses his body well. He plays the man, not the puck. He is highly aggressive in his defensive zone. Anyone trying to get to the net through Foote will pay a price. He plays it smart and takes few bad penalties. In recent seasons, he has stepped up his physical play and he dishes out some powerful checks. He has good lower-body strength and drives his body upwards, resulting in a heavy impact with his unfortunate target. Foote can fight when provoked and stands up for his teammates. Foote is the Avs' most physically dominant defenseman. He was able to stay healthy last season, which made a huge difference.

THE INTANGIBLES

Foote is a warrior, an excellent two-way defenseman whose offensive skills are a few notches below elite class. He is one of the more underrated blueliners around. What sets him apart is his competitiveness. He thrives on the challenge of playing against other teams' top forwards. If a team needs to protect a lead late in the game, it couldn't do much better than having Foote digging in.

PROJECTION

Foote plays a defense-first game but can still score 25 to 30 points, which is a golden combination.

PETER FORSBERG

Yrs. of NHL service: 8
Born: Ornskoldsvik, Sweden; July 20, 1973
Position: center
Height: 6-0
Weight: 205
Uniform no.: 21
Shoots: left

Career statistics:

GP	G	A	TP	PIM
541	198	488	686	514

1999-2000 statistics:

GP	G	A	TP	+/-	PIM	PP	SH	GW	GT	S	PCT
49	14	37	51	+9	52	3	0	2	0	105	13.3

2000-2001 statistics:

GP	G	A	TP	+/-	PIM	PP	SH	GW	GT	S	PCT
73	27	62	89	+23	54	12	2	5	0	178	15.2

2001-2002 statistics:

Did not play in NHL in 2001-02

2002-2003 statistics:

GP	G	A	TP	+/-	PIM	PP	SH	GW	GT	S	PCT
75	29	77	106	+52	70	8	0	2	0	166	17.5

LAST SEASON

Won 2003 Hart Trophy. Won 2003 Art Ross Trophy. Named to NHL First All-Star Team. Led NHL in assists and points. Tied for NHL lead in plus-minus. Second on team in goals. Third on team in shooting percentage. Tied for third on team in power-play goals. Missed two games with groin injury. Missed three games with neck injury. Missed one game with flu. Missed one game with charley horse.

THE FINESSE GAME

Forsberg is an amazingly strong skater. When he has the puck, any time he falls down a penalty should probably be called — unless, of course, he's diving, which he's not above doing. He's that solid on his feet. Forsberg is a smooth skater with explosive speed and can accelerate while carrying the puck. He has excellent vision of the ice and is a sublime playmaker. One of the few knocks on him is that he doesn't shoot enough. Forsberg's shot total is low for someone who sees as much ice time as he does. He works most effectively down between the circles with a wrist or backhand shot off the rush, and does his best work in traffic. There's a lot of Gordie Howe about him.

Forsberg protects the puck as well as anybody in the league. He is so strong he can control the puck with one arm while fending off a checker and still make an effective pass. His passing is nearly as good as teammate Joe Sakic's. He can be off-balance with his head down, digging the puck out of his skates, yet still put a pass on a teammate's stick. The Swede seems to be thinking a play or two ahead of everyone else on the ice and has an amazing sense of every player's position.

Forsberg is used in all game situations: power play, penalty killing, and four-on-four. His skill level is world class in every department.

THE PHYSICAL GAME

Forsberg is tough to knock down. He loves contact and dishes out more than he receives. He has a wide skating base and great balance. He can be cross-checked when he's on his backhand and still not lose control of the puck. Jaromir Jagr may be the only other player who can do that.

Forsberg has a cockiness that many great athletes carry like an aura. He dares people to try to intimidate him. His drive to succeed helps him handle the cheap stuff and keep going. He's got a mean streak too: bringing his stick up into people's faces. He also takes abuse and is a frequent target of cheap hits. He plays equally hard on any given inch of the ice. His physical game sometimes goes over the top and robs him of his offensive game, which is why rivals are so eager to engage him.

THE INTANGIBLES

Everyone who was wondering how Forsberg would rebound from missing an entire NHL season (2001-02) was part sabbatical, part medical) had all of their questions answered quickly. Forsberg was as hungry and dazzling as ever, but he left the Avs dangling at the end of last season with a question about whether he would return or play in Sweden this year. Forsberg was a restricted free agent after the season.

PROJECTION

We projected a 90-point season for Forsberg. He exceeded that. The Avs seem to be a team in flux so we would caution against expecting a repeat of his 106-point year and again project 90 points.

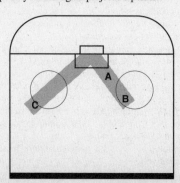

MILAN HEJDUK

Yrs. of NHL service: 5
Born: Usti-nad-Labem, Czech Republic; Feb. 14, 1976
Position: right wing
Height: 5-11
Weight: 185
Uniform no.: 23
Shoots: right

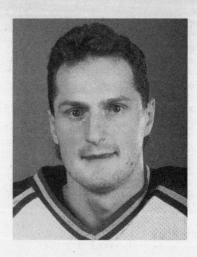

Career statistics:

GP	G	A	TP	PIM
388	162	179	341	134

1999-2000 statistics:

GP	G	A	TP	+/-	PIM	PP	SH	GW	GT	S	PCT
82	36	36	72	+14	16	13	0	9	2	228	15.8

2000-2001 statistics:

GP	G	A	TP	+/-	PIM	PP	SH	GW	GT	S	PCT
80	41	38	79	+32	36	12	1	9	0	213	19.3

2001-2002 statistics:

GP	G	A	TP	+/-	PIM	PP	SH	GW	GT	S	PCT
62	21	23	44	0	24	7	1	5	1	139	15.1

2002-2003 statistics:

GP	G	A	TP	+/-	PIM	PP	SH	GW	GT	S	PCT
82	50	48	98	+52	32	18	0	4	1	244	20.5

LAST SEASON

Won 2003 Rocket Richard Trophy. Named to NHL First All-Star Team. Led NHL in goals and shooting percentage. Tied for NHL lead in plus-minus. Fourth in NHL in points and power-play goals. Led team in power-play goals. Second on team in points, game-winning goals, and shots. One of four Avs to appear in all 82 games.

THE FINESSE GAME

No less an authority than Joe Sakic, his linemate, has declared that Hejduk has the best hands on the Avs. Hejduk is a finisher. His release is deadly quick and accurate. Hejduk rarely shoots the puck wide of the net. He knows where the puck is going, but the goaltenders don't. Most importantly, he is willing to pay the price around the net to score. He has excellent speed and vision, and he is outstanding on the power play. He has great stamina and can handle of lot of ice time.

Hejduk has great hockey sense and has gotten steadily better season by season. He knows where to find the open ice. As soon as he has the puck, he has a shot away with a quick release.

Hejduk has tremendous foot speed. It took him awhile at the start of his career to adjust to the pace of the NHL game but he is a totally uptempo player now. He finds the openings and has the kind of acceleration to burst through seams. He drives to the net for screens and rebounds. He can't plant himself there since he lacks the size, but he will jump in and out of holes and takes the pounding.

Hejduk is always in a good position offensively and defensively.

THE PHYSICAL GAME

Hejduk is small but has a solid build. He doesn't stay out of the high-traffic areas. He won't be intimidated. He plays the game with great gusto and determination. Hejduk seems fully recovered from an abdominal injury that prevented him from playing his game in 2001-02.

THE INTANGIBLES

Hejduk's upbeat attitude makes him popular in the Avs' dressing room. He has earned his respect as one of the quiet leaders. Even winning the Richard trophy for leading the league in goals is unlikely to raise his profile much, and that's fine with him.

PROJECTION

We underestimated Hejduk last season and projected a measly 35 goals for him. Given his ability, and consistency, he should flirt with 50 goals again this year.

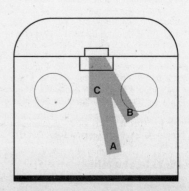

PAUL KARIYA

Yrs. of NHL service: 9
Born: North Vancouver, B.C.; Oct. 16, 1974
Position: left wing
Height: 5-10
Weight: 176
Uniform no.: 9
Shoots: left

Career statistics:

GP	G	A	TP	PIM
606	300	369	669	213

1999-2000 statistics:

GP	G	A	TP	+/-	PIM	PP	SH	GW	GT	S	PCT
74	42	44	86	+22	24	11	3	3	0	324	13.0

2000-2001 statistics:

GP	G	A	TP	+/-	PIM	PP	SH	GW	GT	S	PCT
66	33	34	67	-9	20	18	3	3	0	230	14.4

2001-2002 statistics:

GP	G	A	TP	+/-	PIM	PP	SH	GW	GT	S	PCT
82	32	25	57	-15	28	11	0	8	1	289	11.1

2002-2003 statistics:

GP	G	A	TP	+/-	PIM	PP	SH	GW	GT	S	PCT
82	25	56	81	-3	48	11	1	2	1	257	9.7

LAST SEASON

Signed by Colorado as free agent on July 3, 2003. Led Mighty Ducks in assists and points. Second on team in goals, power-play goals, and shots. One of five Mighty Ducks to appear in all 82 games. Has played in 195 consecutive regular-season games.

THE FINESSE GAME

A magician with the puck, Kariya can make a play when it looks as if there are no possible options. He likes to use the net for protection, like his idol Wayne Gretzky, and make passes from behind the goal line. His release on his shot is excellent.

One of the best skaters in the NHL, Kariya is so smooth and fluid his movements appear effortless. He's also explosive, with a good change of direction; he can turn a defender inside out on a one-on-one rush. His speed is a weapon, since he forces defenders to play off him for fear of being burnt, and that opens the ice for his playmaking options. He combines his skating with no-look passes that are uncanny.

Kariya uses his speed defensively. He's quick on the backcheck to break up passes. He kills penalties by hounding the point men and pressuring them into making bad passes, which he then turns into scoring chances.

Kariya is a low-maintenance superstar. He has worked on his weaknesses. He's stronger on the puck, less fancy in his passing, and more willing to shoot.

THE PHYSICAL GAME

Kariya has powerful thighs and legs and has improved his upper-body strength. He is something of a workout nut — so much so that he actually has to scale back his off-season conditioning. Kariya has a concussion history, which made the big hit by New Jersey's Scott Stevens in the Cup finals so terrifying. Kariya recovered well enough to score a goal just a few shifts later.

THE INTANGIBLES

Anaheim took a calculated risk by not qualifying Kariya's $10 million salary and he shocked them (and the hockey world) by signing as a free agent with the Avs for only $1.2 million. He'll be reunited there with Teemu Selanne. More intriguingly, for the first time in his career Kariya will play with elite-class centers in Joe Sakic or Peter Forsberg. He didn't have a great playoffs with Anaheim, but now he'll have the best supporting cast this side of the Canadian Olympic hockey team. The weight of the whole team won't be on him here, and that will make a difference.

PROJECTION

If Kariya plays 80 games and doesn't score 100 points, we'll be shocked.

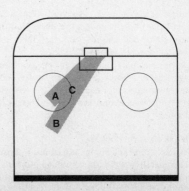

DEREK MORRIS

Yrs. of NHL service: 6
Born: Edmonton, Alta.; Aug. 24, 1978
Position: right defense
Height: 5-11
Weight: 200
Uniform no.: 53
Shoots: right

Career statistics:

GP	G	A	TP	PIM
418	45	166	211	453

1999-2000 statistics:

GP	G	A	TP	+/-	PIM	PP	SH	GW	GT	S	PCT
78	9	29	38	+2	80	3	0	2	0	193	4.7

2000-2001 statistics:

GP	G	A	TP	+/-	PIM	PP	SH	GW	GT	S	PCT
51	5	23	28	-15	56	3	1	4	0	142	3.5

2001-2002 statistics:

GP	G	A	TP	+/-	PIM	PP	SH	GW	GT	S	PCT
61	4	30	34	-4	88	2	0	1	0	166	2.4

2002-2003 statistics:

GP	G	A	TP	+/-	PIM	PP	SH	GW	GT	S	PCT
75	11	37	48	+16	68	9	0	7	0	191	5.8

LAST SEASON

Acquired from Calgary with Dean McAmmond and Jeff Shantz on October 1, 2002, for Chris Drury and Stephane Yelle. Led team in game-winning goals. Led team defensemen in points. Second on team in power-play goals. Third on team in average ice time (23:49) and shots. Missed seven games with eye injury.

THE FINESSE GAME

Morris possesses all the high-level skills, but what truly sets him apart from the other defensemen of his generation is his brain. Morris has a real grasp of the technical part of the game. He is a thinker and understands hockey thoroughly. He could be a future All-Star, and this might be the year when it all comes together for him.

Morris plays in all game situations, on the first penalty-killing unit, and on the first power-play unit. He is a fan of Paul Coffey, and he possesses the kind of skating that brings to mind his role model. Morris is better defensively, however, and will become a better all-round player. He handles the puck well in an uptempo game and may develop into the kind of defenseman who can take over a game.

Morris needs only to improve his one-on-one play and get a little stronger to continue on the path to becoming an elite defenseman. He is occasionally prone to a defensive breakdown, but he learns from his mistakes.

THE PHYSICAL GAME

Morris has improved his stamina and needs to maintain a serious strength and conditioning program. He is not very big, but he is strong. You can't run him over and he gets a lot of power from his legs for hitting and moving people out of the front of the net.

THE INTANGIBLES

As expected Morris was traded last season. With the deal coming so close to the start of the season, it was a little disconcerting for Morris, especially since he waded into such a veteran room. Morris gained confidence as the year progressed and really stepped it up in the playoffs. With Greg deVries gone, Morris will inherit more ice time and responsibility. This season will be his coming-out party.

PROJECTION

As Morris continues to mature he will gain confidence in his offensive game without losing anything from his defense. There is a 60-point season in his not-too-distant future.

JOE SAKIC

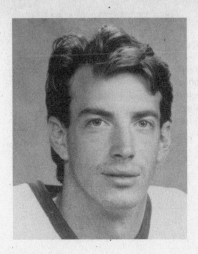

Yrs. of NHL service: 15
Born: Burnaby, B.C.; July 7, 1969
Position: center
Height: 5-11
Weight: 195
Uniform no.: 19
Shoots: left

Career statistics:

GP	G	A	TP	PIM
1074	509	806	1315	440

1999-2000 statistics:

GP	G	A	TP	+/-	PIM	PP	SH	GW	GT	S	PCT
60	28	53	81	+30	28	5	1	5	0	242	11.6

2000-2001 statistics:

GP	G	A	TP	+/-	PIM	PP	SH	GW	GT	S	PCT
82	54	64	118	+45	30	19	3	12	2	332	16.3

2001-2002 statistics:

GP	G	A	TP	+/-	PIM	PP	SH	GW	GT	S	PCT
82	26	53	79	+12	18	9	1	4	1	260	10.0

2002-2003 statistics:

GP	G	A	TP	+/-	PIM	PP	SH	GW	GT	S	PCT
58	26	32	58	+4	24	8	0	1	0	190	13.7

LAST SEASON

Tied for third on team in goals and power-play goals. Missed 24 games with ankle and foot injuries.

THE FINESSE GAME

Sakic is one of the game's best playmakers. It's not a secret that he has also become one of the game's best shooters, and he isn't shy about it. How do you defend against him? Try to keep the puck far, far away. Sakic's ability to visualize while speeding through the offensive zone is exceptional. He is slippery, and will spin off a defender and get a shot away. Either that, or he will find one of his linemates.

Sakic has one of the most explosive first steps in the league. He finds and hits the holes in a hurry — even with the puck — to create his chances. He uses a stick shaft with a little "whip"' in it that makes his shots more lethal. He has a terrific wrist shot and snap shot and one of the quickest releases in the game.

Sakic's most impressive gift, however, is his great patience with the puck. He will hold it until the last minute, when he has drawn the defenders to him and opened up ice, creating time and space for his linemates. This makes him a gem on the power play, where he works down low and just off the half-boards on the right wing. He can also play the point.

Sakic is a scoring threat whenever he is on the ice because he can craft a dangerous scoring chance out of a situation that looks innocent. He is lethal trailing the rush. He takes a pass in full stride without slowing, then dekes and shoots before the goalie can even flinch. He is smart defensively, and is a good face-off man, too. Even if he's tied up, he uses his skates to kick the puck free.

THE PHYSICAL GAME

Sakic is not a physical player, but he is stronger than he looks. He uses his body to protect the puck when he is carrying deep; you have to go through him to get it. He will try to keep going through traffic or along the boards with the puck, and often squirts free with it because he is able to maintain control and balance. He creates turnovers with his quickness and hands, not by initiating contact.

THE INTANGIBLES

Sakic is 34 and is at the age where ice time and injuries take a toll. If Peter Forsberg isn't back, there will be a huge burden placed on Sakic that he will try to shoulder but which may become too heavy. He is still one of the game's great forwards.

PROJECTION

Sakic is a point-a-game player.

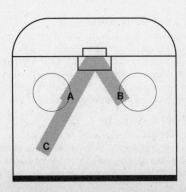

PHILIPPE SAUVE

Yrs. of NHL service: 0
Born: Buffalo, N.Y.; Feb. 27, 1980
Position: goaltender
Height: 6-0
Weight: 180
Uniform no.: 31
Catches: left

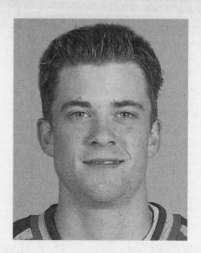

Career minor league statistics:

GP	MIN	GA	SO	GAA	A	PIM
157	8706	345	14	2.38	-	-

2002-2003 minor league statistics:

GP	MIN	GAA	W	L	T	SO	GA	S	SAPCT	PIM
60	3394	134.00	26	20	12	5	2.37	-	-	-

LAST SEASON

Will be entering first NHL season. Appeared in 60 games with Hershey (AHL), with a record of 26-20-12, five shutouts, and a 2.37 GAA.

THE PHYSICAL GAME

Sauve is a technically sound goalie whose style is a butterfly/standup hybrid. He is very athletic. He has good size and uses it to good advantage because of his technique. He is seldom overaggressive in challenging the shooter. Sauve will hold his angles and let the puck hit him, which is the easiest way to play this game. Sauve keeps his focus and watches the puck at all times. He follows the puck well and doesn't get frantic because he always seems to know where the puck is.

Sauve is aggressive in using his stick. He isn't a great puckhandler, like Martin Brodeur, but in Brodeur fashion he will use his stick to break up passes and plays around the net.

Sauve is very flexible for split saves and his legs take up a lot of the lower portion of the net when he does. His recovery is good for the second attempt. Like Mike Richter, he has an uncanny ability to best shooters in a breakaway situation, probably because he allows the shooter to make the first move and Sauve doesn't bite on a fake.

THE MENTAL GAME

The big question mark is Sauve's mental preparedness. We don't know if he's a big-game goalie because there haven't been many instances where he has been in a big game yet. He is competitive, but he has also lost his composure in some minor league playoff games by getting too revved up.

THE INTANGIBLES

Sauve is the son of a goalie (former NHLer Bob, who is now a player agent), so he knows about pressure. Trying to succeed a legend like the retired Patrick Roy will be, well, trying. Just ask Martin Biron how tough it was to follow Dominik Hasek in Buffalo. The battle for the No. 1 job will be between incumbent backup David Aebischer and Sauve, unless Colorado makes a surprising move to acquire a veteran goalie in the off-season.

PROJECTION

Sauve will probably start the season as Aebischer's backup, or might even get sent back to the minors if Colorado decides he needs to play more regularly. But he is projected as the Avs' No. 1 goalie by midseason.

TEEMU SELANNE

Yrs. of NHL service: 11
Born: Helsinki, Finland; July 3, 1970
Position: right wing
Height: 6-0
Weight: 204
Uniform no.: 8
Shoots: right

Career statistics:

GP	G	A	TP	PIM
801	436	483	919	303

1999-2000 statistics:

GP	G	A	TP	+/-	PIM	PP	SH	GW	GT	S	PCT
79	33	52	85	+6	12	8	0	6	2	236	14.0

2000-2001 statistics:

GP	G	A	TP	+/-	PIM	PP	SH	GW	GT	S	PCT
73	33	39	72	-7	36	12	0	7	1	233	14.2

2001-2002 statistics:

GP	G	A	TP	+/-	PIM	PP	SH	GW	GT	S	PCT
82	29	25	54	-11	40	9	1	8	0	202	14.4

2002-2003 statistics:

GP	G	A	TP	+/-	PIM	PP	SH	GW	GT	S	PCT
82	28	36	64	-6	30	7	0	5	1	253	11.1

LAST SEASON

Signed as free agent by Colorado on July 3, 2003. Led Sharks in points and shots. Tied for team lead in goals. Second on team in assists and game-winning goals. One of six Sharks to appear in all 82 games.

THE FINESSE GAME

Selanne is a big fan of fast sports cars. That's not surprising, because he plays like one. He has Porsche Turbo speed. He gets down low and then simply explodes past defensemen, even when starting from a standstill. He gets tremendous thrust from his legs and has quick feet. Acceleration, balance, smooth change of gears, it's all there.

Everything you could ask for in a shot is there as well. He employs all varieties of attacks and is equally comfortable on either wing. He can collect a pass at top speed while barely breaking stride.

Selanne is constantly in motion. If his first attempt is stopped, he'll pursue the puck behind the net, make a pass and circle out again for a shot. He is almost impossible to catch and is tough to knock down because of his balance. He will set up on the off-wing on the power play and can score on the backhand. His shot is not especially hard, but it is quick and accurate.

He doesn't just try to overpower with his skating, Selanne also outwits opponents. He has tremendous hockey instincts and vision, and is as good a playmaker as a finisher. He has a reputation for being selfish with the puck.

THE PHYSICAL GAME

Teams set out to bump and grind Selanne from the first shift, and he has to fight his way through the junk. When the referees are slow on the whistle, he takes matters into his own hands, usually with his stick. He is one of the toughest players in the league, European or otherwise. He is big and uses his strength along the wall, but he takes a beating.

THE INTANGIBLES

Selanne is reunited with Paul Kariya in Colorado, and they'll have two world-class centers to play with. Both he and Kariya have something missing from their resumes — a Stanley Cup.

PROJECTION

Selanne and Kariya have great chemistry and Selanne may flirt with 40 goals this season.

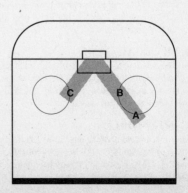

MARTIN SKOULA

Yrs. of NHL service: 4
Born: Litvinov, Czech Republic; Oct. 28, 1979
Position: left defense
Height: 6-2
Weight: 195
Uniform no.: 41
Shoots: left

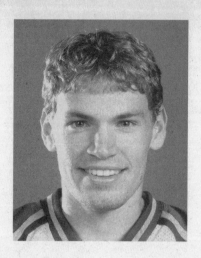

Career statistics:

GP	G	A	TP	PIM
325	25	72	97	168

1999-2000 statistics:

GP	G	A	TP	+/-	PIM	PP	SH	GW	GT	S	PCT
80	3	13	16	+5	20	2	0	0	0	66	4.5

2000-2001 statistics:

GP	G	A	TP	+/-	PIM	PP	SH	GW	GT	S	PCT
82	8	17	25	+8	38	3	0	2	0	108	7.4

2001-2002 statistics:

GP	G	A	TP	+/-	PIM	PP	SH	GW	GT	S	PCT
82	10	21	31	-3	42	5	0	1	0	100	10.0

2002-2003 statistics:

GP	G	A	TP	+/-	PIM	PP	SH	GW	GT	S	PCT
81	4	21	25	+11	68	2	0	0	0	93	4.3

PROJECTION

Skoula should continue to score in the 25-point range while paying more attention to his defensive play. He is a solid top-four defenseman now, and will get that role now that the Avs have lost free agent Greg de Vries (another underrated defenseman).

LAST SEASON

Missed one game with bruised shoulder.

THE FINESSE GAME

Skoula has the skills to excel in his own end. He is reliable and poised with the puck. Skoula's problems emerge when he doesn't have the puck. He will lapse into the bad habit of chasing behind the net and losing his checking assignment. His defensive lapses, though, have become far more infrequent.

Skoula's natural offensive instincts are excellent. He reacts quickly to plays and understands game situations well. Skoula is a wonderful skater both forwards and backwards. He has a long, smooth, natural stride. He is quick and efficient. He handles the puck well and has nice hands for making or receiving passes. He has good hockey vision, and is a heads-up player. He plays a good transition game.

Skoula improved in the second half of the season which indicates he might be getting it. Skoula is often overlooked on a team of stars, but he is developing into a reliable defenseman.

THE PHYSICAL GAME

Skoula is big and well-built. He isn't a mean hitter, but he registers meaningful takeouts. He needs to attend to his conditioning. Skoula is probably going to start getting more ice time this season.

THE INTANGIBLES

Calgary took Robyn Regehr instead of Skoula in the Theo Fleury deal in 1999. The Flames probably made the right choice, but the way Skoula is coming along, it seems there was no wrong choice.

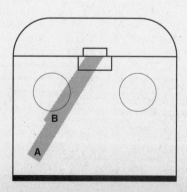

KARLIS SKRASTINS

Yrs. of NHL service: 4
Born: Riga, Latvia; July 9, 1974
Position: left defense
Height: 6-1
Weight: 212
Uniform no.: 3
Shoots: left

Career statistics:

GP	G	A	TP	PIM
307	13	41	54	130

1999-2000 statistics:

GP	G	A	TP	+/-	PIM	PP	SH	GW	GT	S	PCT
59	5	6	11	-7	20	1	0	2	0	51	9.8

2000-2001 statistics:

GP	G	A	TP	+/-	PIM	PP	SH	GW	GT	S	PCT
82	1	11	12	-12	30	0	0	1	0	66	1.5

2001-2002 statistics:

GP	G	A	TP	+/-	PIM	PP	SH	GW	GT	S	PCT
82	4	13	17	-12	36	0	0	1	1	84	4.8

2002-2003 statistics:

GP	G	A	TP	+/-	PIM	PP	SH	GW	GT	S	PCT
82	3	10	13	-18	44	0	1	0	0	86	3.5

LAST SEASON

Acquired from Nashville for future considerations on July 1, 2003. Second on Predators in average ice time (20:17). Tied for worst plus-minus on team. One of five Predators to appear in all 82 games. Has appeared in 269 consecutive games, the third-longest active ironman streak in the NHL.

THE FINESSE GAME

Skrastins is a steady, stay-at-home defenseman. He is a good penalty killer and worked on the Predators' top unit. He will probably see a similar role with Colorado. He blocks a lot of shots and plays a sound positional game. Skrastins is the player you want on the ice to help you protect a lead, except the Preds had precious few.

He is strong, mobile, and has decent hockey sense. His offensive upside is minimal, though he handles the puck well and is poised. He concentrates on the defensive aspects of his game.

Colorado's defense being deeper than Nashville's, Skrastins can settle into a more complementary role rather than handling the top-pair defense duties he had with the Predators. He is very underrated because he doesn't have the flashy point totals.

THE PHYSICAL GAME

Skrastins is a horse. He plays a lot of minutes against other teams' top players, and does so aggressively. He takes the body, blocks a lot of shots, and takes away a lot of passing and shooting lanes. Skrastins plays hurt. He hasn't missed a game in three seasons but that doesn't mean he never felt ouchy.

THE INTANGIBLES

The coaches love his energy and attitude. Nashville was looking to open up some salary room (Skrastins was an unrestricted free agent after last season) and the Avs needed someone to replace Greg de Vries, which made this move a natural for both parties.

PROJECTION

Skrastins isn't likely to score more than 20 points, but he will be a steady defenseman in Colorado.

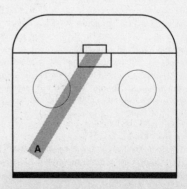

ALEX TANGUAY

Yrs. of NHL service: 4
Born: Ste-Justine, Que.; Nov. 21, 1979
Position: center/left wing
Height: 6-0
Weight: 190
Uniform no.: 40
Shoots: left

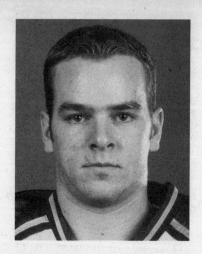

Career statistics:

GP	G	A	TP	PIM
310	83	160	243	131

1999-2000 statistics:

GP	G	A	TP	+/-	PIM	PP	SH	GW	GT	S	PCT
76	17	34	51	+6	22	5	0	3	1	74	23.0

2000-2001 statistics:

GP	G	A	TP	+/-	PIM	PP	SH	GW	GT	S	PCT
82	27	50	77	+35	37	7	1	3	0	135	20.0

2001-2002 statistics:

GP	G	A	TP	+/-	PIM	PP	SH	GW	GT	S	PCT
70	13	35	48	+8	36	7	0	2	0	90	14.4

2002-2003 statistics:

GP	G	A	TP	+/-	PIM	PP	SH	GW	GT	S	PCT
82	26	41	67	+34	36	3	0	5	2	142	18.3

LAST SEASON

Second on team in plus-minus, game-winning goals, and shooting percentage. Third on team in assists and points. Tied for third on team in goals. One of four Avs to appear in all 82 games.

THE FINESSE GAME

Tanguay is a strong skater with breakaway speed. He can embarrass a defenseman who doesn't realize how quick Tanguay is. He is nearly as fast with the puck as without it. He is absolutely dynamic. He loves to have the puck but he isn't selfish and is a good playmaker. Tanguay has to continually be urged by his coaches to shoot more. It's frustrating to have a guy with this much ability not even average two shots a game, but maybe playing with Milan Hejduk has something to do with that.

Tanguay has the natural sixth sense of scoring that cannot be taught. He finds the open space in front of the net, or the loose puck seems to materialize on his stick. He has played the wing for most of his first three NHL seasons, but he is a natural center, and his play-making skill complements that of linemate Joe Sakic.

Tanguay needs to continue to develop the defensive aspect of his game, but he has pretty good awareness of his responsibility and it won't take him long to become proficient. He likes his team to rely on him and he will develop into a player who can be used in all game situations.

THE PHYSICAL GAME

Tanguay goes willingly into the combat zones. He is aggressive and creative, a combination that gives him the hockey courage to play in the dirty areas of the ice

and the vision and hands to make something good happen for his team. Tanguay isn't big but he is highly competitive and will do what it takes to win. He is in good shape and handles a lot of minutes.

THE INTANGIBLES

Tanguay still needs to develop confidence in his shot. He is becoming a money player.

PROJECTION

Last season we predicted a 70-point season for Tanguay and he just missed. That is a logical target for him again this year.

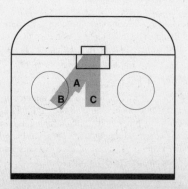

RADIM VRBATA

Yrs. of NHL service: 2
Born: Mlada Boleslav, Czech Republic; June 13, 1981
Position: right wing
Height: 6-1
Weight: 185
Uniform no.: 19
Shoots: right

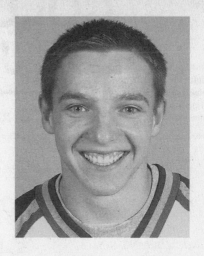

Career statistics:

GP	G	A	TP	PIM
128	34	31	65	32

2001-2002 statistics:

GP	G	A	TP	+/-	PIM	PP	SH	GW	GT	S	PCT
52	18	12	30	+7	14	6	0	3	0	112	16.1

2002-2003 statistics:

GP	G	A	TP	+/-	PIM	PP	SH	GW	GT	S	PCT
76	16	19	35	-7	18	6	0	4	1	215	7.4

LAST SEASON

Acquired from Colorado for Bates Battaglia on March 11, 2003. Second on team in game-winning goals and shots. Third on team in goals. Missed two games with flu.

THE FINESSE GAME

Vrbata is an excellent skater. Vrbata has a goal-scorer's mentality and a goal-scorer's shot. He has a quick release and darts around to find open areas of the ice to get open for a pass.

Vrbata was a part of the Avs Stanley Cup championship team in 2001. While it was a small role (he appeared in only nine playoff games), it was a valuable learning experience and it also helped his confidence. As a rookie, Vrbata had a higher goals-per-game average than stars like Peter Forsberg, Chris Drury, and Joe Sakic did in their first seasons.

THE PHYSICAL GAME

Vrbata needs to get stronger and grittier. He is average-sized but can't afford to play like an even smaller man. Maybe playing with a workaholic like Rob Brind'Amour will be an inspiration.

THE INTANGIBLES

Vrbata might have felt a little lost in Colorado's veteran system, but he perked up considerably after the trade with five goals in 10 games. He will be a top-six forward for Carolina.

PROJECTION

Assuming Vrbata can get decent ice time in 60-65 games, he should be in the 20- to 25-goal range.

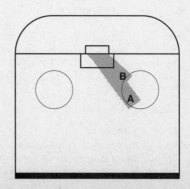

COLUMBUS BLUE JACKETS

Players' Statistics 2001-2002

POS	NO	PLAYER	GP	G	A	PTS	+/-	PIM	PP	SH	GW	GT	S	PCT
L	14	RAY WHITNEY	81	24	52	76	-26	22	8	2	2	1	235	10.2
C	25	ANDREW CASSELS	79	20	48	68	-4	30	9	1	5		113	17.7
L	8	GEOFF SANDERSON	82	34	33	67	-4	34	15	2	2		286	11.9
R	9	DAVID VYBORNY	79	20	26	46	12	16	4	1	4		125	16.0
D	3	JAROSLAV SPACEK	81	9	36	45	-23	70	5		1		166	5.4
C	16	MIKE SILLINGER	75	18	25	43	-21	52	9	3	3		128	14.1
L	61	*RICK NASH	74	17	22	39	-27	78	6		2		154	11.0
C	28	TYLER WRIGHT	70	19	11	30	-25	113	3	2	3		108	17.6
L	20	LASSE PIRJETA	51	11	10	21	-4	12	2		2		80	13.8
D	23	*DERRICK WALSER	53	4	13	17	-9	34	3		2		86	4.7
D	44	ROSTISLAV KLESLA	72	2	14	16	-22	71					89	2.2
C	19	SEAN PRONGER	78	7	6	13	-26	72	1				67	10.4
D	22	LUKE RICHARDSON	82		13	13	-16	73					56	
C	21	ESPEN KNUTSEN	31	5	4	9	-15	20	3		1		28	17.9
R	24	HANNES HYVONEN	36	4	5	9	-11	22					48	8.3
R	41	*MATT DAVIDSON	34	4	5	9	-12	18					28	14.3
D	42	*DUVIE WESTCOTT	39		7	7	-3	77					27	
R	43	DAVID LING	35	3	2	5	-6	86					37	8.1
L	45	JODY SHELLEY	68	1	4	5	-5	249					39	2.6
D	27	DARREN VAN IMPE	14	1	1	2	-6	10		1		1	11	9.1
D	34	J-LUC GRAND-PIERRE	41	1		1	-6	64					32	3.1
D	7	SCOTT LACHANCE	61		1	1	-20	46					35	
D	33	JAMIE ALLISON	48		1	1	-15	99					23	
L	26	*ANDREJ NEDOROST	12		1	1	-6	4					10	
R	11	KEVIN DINEEN	4				0	12					7	
R	15	*KENT MCDONELL	3				-1						4	
D	17	*PAUL MANNING	8				0	2					4	
D	37	DARREL SCOVILLE	2				0	4					1	
G	35	JEAN LABBE	11				0	2						
G	30	MARC DENIS	77				0	6						
L	12	MATHIEU DARCHE	1				-1							
C	38	*BLAKE BELLEFEUILLE	3				0							

GP = games played; G = goals; A = assists; PTS = points; +/- = goals-for minus goals-against while player is on ice; PIM = penalties in minutes; PP = power-play goals; SH = shorthanded goals; GW = game-winning goals; GT = game-tying goals; S = no. of shots; PCT = percentage of goals to shots; * = rookie

ANDREW CASSELS

Yrs. of NHL service: 13
Born: Bramalea, Ont.; July 23, 1969
Position: center
Height: 6-1
Weight: 185
Uniform no.: 25
Shoots: left

Career statistics:

GP	G	A	TP	PIM
926	194	500	694	370

1999-2000 statistics:

GP	G	A	TP	+/-	PIM	PP	SH	GW	GT	S	PCT
79	17	45	62	+8	16	6	0	1	0	109	15.6

2000-2001 statistics:

GP	G	A	TP	+/-	PIM	PP	SH	GW	GT	S	PCT
66	12	44	56	+1	10	2	0	1	0	104	11.5

2001-2002 statistics:

GP	G	A	TP	+/-	PIM	PP	SH	GW	GT	S	PCT
53	11	39	50	+5	22	7	0	1	0	64	17.2

2002-2003 statistics:

GP	G	A	TP	+/-	PIM	PP	SH	GW	GT	S	PCT
79	20	48	68	-4	30	9	1	5	0	113	17.7

LAST SEASON

Led team in game-winning goals and shooting percentage. Second on team in assists and points. Tied for second on team in power-play goals. Tied for third on team in goals. Missed three games with elbow injury.

THE FINESSE GAME

When it comes to hockey smarts, Cassels is a member of Mensa. He is an intelligent player with terrific hockey instincts, who knows when to recognize passing situations, when to move the puck and who to move it to. He has a good backhand pass in traffic and is almost as good on his backhand as his forehand. He is a veteran who lends a lot of expertise to the young Columbus power play and he's an effective setup man for the young Rick Nash.

Cassels just hates to shoot. He won't do it much, and although he has spent a great deal of time practicing it, his release is just not NHL caliber. He needs to play with a finisher, like Nash or Geoff Sanderson. They are different kind of finishers, but Cassels can feather a pass to Sanderson on the rush or find Nash in a crowd. Cassels is patient and draws defenders to him on the give-and-go. He is among the best backhand passers in the league. He has quick hands and can swipe a shot off a bouncing puck in midair. He doesn't always fight through checks to get the kind of shots he should, which is why he was never a bona fide No. 1 NHL center.

A mainstay on both specialty teams, Cassels has improved on draws. He backchecks and blocks shots. He has good speed but lacks one-step quickness. He has improved his puckhandling at a high tempo.

THE PHYSICAL GAME

To complement his brains, Cassels needs brawn. He does not force his way through strong forechecks and traffic around the net. He tends to get nicked up and run down late in the season or during a tough stretch.

THE INTANGIBLES

Cassels became a free agent on July 1 but Columbus quickly re-signed the useful veteran. Cassels has a history of overachieving on weak teams. His 68 points were the most since 1992-93 with Hartford.

PROJECTION

Cassels can score another 60 assist-heavy points in the right situation, which he seems to have landed in again as the No. 1 center for Columbus.

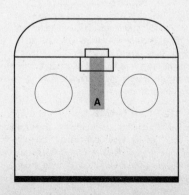

MARC DENIS

Yrs. of NHL service: 4
Born: Montreal, Que.; Aug. 1, 1977
Position: goaltender
Height: 6-0
Weight: 190
Uniform no.: 30
Catches: left

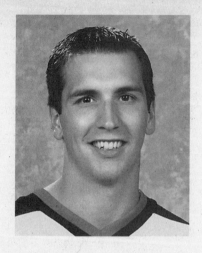

Career statistics:

GP	MIN	GA	SO	GAA	A	PIM
179	10156	515	9	3.04	1	8

1999-2000 statistics:

GP	MIN	GAA	W	L	T	SO	GA	S	SAPCT	PIM
23	1203	2.54	9	8	3	3	51	618	.917	6

2000-2001 statistics:

GP	MIN	GAA	W	L	T	SO	GA	S	SAPCT	PIM
32	1830	3.25	6	20	4	0	99	940	.895	2

2001-2002 statistics:

GP	MIN	GAA	W	L	T	SO	GA	S	SAPCT	PIM
42	2335	3.11	9	24	5	1	121	1197	.899	2

2002-2003 statistics:

GP	MIN	GAA	W	L	T	SO	GA	S	SAPCT	PIM
77	4511	3.09	27	41	8	5	232	2404	.903	6

LAST SEASON

Set NHL goalie record for minutes played in a season. Career high in wins.

THE PHYSICAL GAME

Denis is a good stand-up goalie whose technique has improved in the past two seasons. Denis made his most dramatic advance in his positioning. Denis now anticipates the shot, so he's not meeting the puck at a certain point, he's already there when the puck arrives.

With all the practice time he's devoted, Denis thinks less and is more in the flow of the game. He is less robotic. There were times he seemed almost lackadaisical because he was doing everything so text-book. Now he's not afraid to hit the ice and scramble his arms and legs all over to make a save. Denis is not afraid to let his natural ability take over.

Sound and reliable, Denis also improved his quickness and flexibility with the pads. That's important, because tall goalies have a tendency to be a little clumsy and vulnerable low. He is in better position to make the second saves. He moves well and is well-balanced. Denis keeps his knees bent instead of playing straight-legged as he used to, when he was slower and more predictable. Now he has a good base to react and get power from.

THE MENTAL GAME

Denis is confident but coachable. He shows a hunger and a desire to get better and better. Columbus has a good goalie coach in Rick Wamsley (all teams should invest so wisely). Having Ron Tugnutt around for a few seasons as a mentor was also a plus. It wouldn't

hurt (on several fronts) for Columbus to acquire another veteran backup.

THE INTANGIBLES

Denis was once in Colorado's system and considered the successor to Patrick Roy. He isn't in that elite class yet, but he's done nothing wrong.

PROJECTION

Denis was ridiculously overworked last season. It's amazing he held up as well as he did, but he really needs his workload trimmed back to around 66-68 starts. He did far better than the 20-win we projected for him last season. He should be good for at least 25 and will have a solid save percentage to accompany that. Denis is a solid No. 1 goalie, and he gives his team a chance to win every night.

ROSTISLAV KLESLA

Yrs. of NHL service: 2
Born: Novy Jicin, Czech Republic; Mar. 21, 1982
Position: left defense
Height: 6-3
Weight: 206
Uniform no.: 44
Shoots: left

Career statistics:

GP	G	A	TP	PIM
155	12	22	34	151

2000-2001 statistics:

GP	G	A	TP	+/-	PIM	PP	SH	GW	GT	S	PCT
8	2	0	2	-1	6	0	0	0	0	10	20.0

2001-2002 statistics:

GP	G	A	TP	+/-	PIM	PP	SH	GW	GT	S	PCT
75	8	8	16	-6	74	1	0	0	1	102	7.8

2002-2003 statistics:

GP	G	A	TP	+/-	PIM	PP	SH	GW	GT	S	PCT
72	2	14	16	-22	71	0	0	0	0	89	2.2

LAST SEASON

Missed eight games with sprained shoulder. Missed one game with flu. Missed one game due to coach's decision.

THE FINESSE GAME

Klesla learns something every day. He gets a little smarter, a little bolder. He pays close attention to the veterans on the team and his coaches. Early on in his rookie season, Klesla was too aggressive, and he tried plays he could make with ease in junior but which smart NHL players were just waiting to pounce on. So Klesla stopped trying to force fancy plays, adjusted to major-league speed, and steeled himself for the physical battles.

Klesla isn't a pure offensive defenseman. He uses his finesse skills in a defensive role, taking away passing lanes and playing well positionally. It will be impossible to confine Klesla to a role on a trapping team, and it's likely the Blue Jackets will learn simply to design their game plan around him.

Klesla will be a threat on the power play and especially four-on-four. He is considered the closest thing to a "rover" since Bobby Orr revolutionized the defenseman's role. He is an effortless skater, with a smooth change of direction, tight turning radius, and acceleration. He has excellent breakaway speed with or without the puck.

THE PHYSICAL GAME

Klesla is never going to be a punishing hitter, but he could develop along the lines of a Scott Niedermayer, who uses his secure skating to make his take-out hits. Like Niedermayer, Klesla has a long fuse but, when provoked, will show a surprising mean streak. He won't be intimidated. Klesla handles a lot of ice time.

THE INTANGIBLES

You can hang his sweater in the locker now, because he's here to stay. There will still be a lot of growing pains. He will be in the Blue Jackets' top four this season and for years to come. He's a quiet guy, and confident without being cocky.

PROJECTION

Klesla's offensive numbers should improve to 25-30 points as he gets more secure and the team slowly gets better around him.

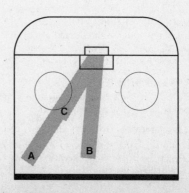

ESPEN KNUTSEN

Yrs. of NHL service: 3
Born: Oslo, Norway; Jan. 12, 1972
Position: center
Height: 5-11
Weight: 188
Uniform no.: 21
Shoots: left

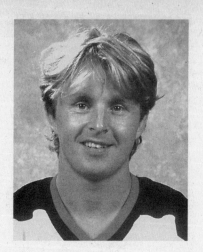

Career statistics:

GP	G	A	TP	PIM
174	27	77	104	97

2000-2001 statistics:

GP	G	A	TP	+/-	PIM	PP	SH	GW	GT	S	PCT
66	11	42	53	-3	30	2	0	0	0	62	17.7

2001-2002 statistics:

GP	G	A	TP	+/-	PIM	PP	SH	GW	GT	S	PCT
77	11	31	42	-28	47	5	2	1	0	102	10.8

2002-2003 statistics:

GP	G	A	TP	+/-	PIM	PP	SH	GW	GT	S	PCT
31	5	4	9	-15	20	3	0	1	0	28	17.9

LAST SEASON

Missed 39 games with hernia surgery. Missed 12 games with sprained wrist.

THE FINESSE GAME

Knutsen is something of a power-play specialist, which is a luxury for a developing team like Columbus. He is a good skater and is creative. He has terrific hockey vision.

Knutsen has improved in doing the dirty work in his own end of the ice, taking hits to make plays, and recognizing that his defense can be just as important as his offense. Knutsen will take a beating along the walls. He is good with the puck in tight quarters.

He excels as a power-play quarterback. He doesn't shoot much. He is the brains of the outfit, alert to Geoff Sanderson or another willing sniper and able to thread them a pass.

THE PHYSICAL GAME

Knutsen is small and needs to get a bit thicker for the battles along the wall and in front of the net. He wants the puck and works harder for it in the offensive zone than in his own end. Knutsen is very secure on his skates and is tough to knock off the puck.

Knutsen is tough mentally and physically. He shakes off injuries like rainwater and almost always returns to the lineup faster than expected.

THE INTANGIBLES

Injuries virtually washed out the season for Knutsen, who can be an effective two-way player.

PROJECTION

Knutsen may start losing some ice time to some younger players, so we would keep scoring expectations around 40 points.

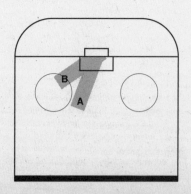

SCOTT LACHANCE

Yrs. of NHL service: 11
Born: Charlottesville, Va.; Oct. 22, 1972
Position: left defense
Height: 6-1
Weight: 215
Uniform no.: 7
Shoots: left

Career statistics:

GP	G	A	TP	PIM
742	31	108	139	523

1999-2000 statistics:

GP	G	A	TP	+/-	PIM	PP	SH	GW	GT	S	PCT
57	0	6	6	-4	22	0	0	0	0	41	-

2000-2001 statistics:

GP	G	A	TP	+/-	PIM	PP	SH	GW	GT	S	PCT
76	3	11	14	+5	46	0	0	0	0	55	5.4

2001-2002 statistics:

GP	G	A	TP	+/-	PIM	PP	SH	GW	GT	S	PCT
81	1	10	11	+15	50	0	0	0	0	48	2.1

2002-2003 statistics:

GP	G	A	TP	+/-	PIM	PP	SH	GW	GT	S	PCT
61	0	1	1	-20	46	0	0	0	0	35	0.0

LAST SEASON

Missed 12 games with sprained ankle. Missed nine games with back injuries.

THE FINESSE GAME

Lachance's whole career has been a tease. He seems to have so many things going for him that it only seemed a matter of time before he put it all together. Now time has passed him by.

Lachance has decent hockey sense. He moves the puck well although he has a tendency to get panicky under pressure, which made him a strange pickup for Columbus, a team that had to know it was going to have its share of on-ice turbulence.

He is one of the few defensemen with the patience to outsmart a trapping team. His skating, however, doesn't allow him to do some of the things an elite defensemen would do to turn that knowledge into counterattacking offense. His feet are really heavy.

THE PHYSICAL GAME

During play he will try hard to eliminate his man, but once the whistle blows, Lachance backs off from confrontation. That prevented Lachance from ever staking out his turf the way more assertive defensemen do. Lachance takes up space. That's about it.

THE INTANGIBLES

As well as the free agent signing of Luke Richardson worked out for the Blue Jackets, the signing of Lachance in 2002 produced the opposite result. He gave the team minutes, but never really hit it off well with Rostislav Klesla. Columbus is committed to Lachance again this season, so unless there is a surprise out of training camp, Lachance will get his minutes.

PROJECTION

Only one point in 60 games? For a guy that broke into the league as an offensive defenseman?

TREVOR LETOWSKI

Yrs. of NHL service: 4
Born: Thunder Bay, Ont.; Apr. 5, 1977
Position: center
Height: 5-10
Weight: 176
Uniform no.: 10
Shoots: right

Career statistics:

GP	G	A	TP	PIM
326	48	67	115	109

1999-2000 statistics:

GP	G	A	TP	+/-	PIM	PP	SH	GW	GT	S	PCT
82	19	20	39	+2	20	3	4	3	0	125	15.2

2000-2001 statistics:

GP	G	A	TP	+/-	PIM	PP	SH	GW	GT	S	PCT
77	7	15	22	-2	32	0	1	3	0	110	6.4

2001-2002 statistics:

GP	G	A	TP	+/-	PIM	PP	SH	GW	GT	S	PCT
75	9	16	25	+4	19	1	0	0	0	108	8.3

2002-2003 statistics:

GP	G	A	TP	+/-	PIM	PP	SH	GW	GT	S	PCT
78	11	14	25	+8	36	1	1	2	0	136	8.1

LAST SEASON

Signed as free agent by Columbus on July 3, 2003. Missed one game with flu. Missed three games due to coach's decision.

THE FINESSE GAME

Letowski is a shorthanded specialist. He is a small player with good quickness. He devoted himself to the defensive aspects of the game even as a junior, which probably accounts for his low draft position (174th overall in 1996), though he did have seasons of 99 and 108 points after his draft year. After paying his dues in the minors, he has turned into one of those nifty little forwards who could find an NHL job with any team, although his job will always be on the line because he's not a special player.

Letowski has good anticipation and makes excellent reads in his forechecking. He pressures the points on the power play to harry them into making bad passes, which he can then convert into shorthanded scoring chances. He is an opportunistic scorer with soft hands and a good, patient shot. He is average on face-offs. Letowski is versatile and played a lot of right wing last season.

Columbus already has a sound defensive system in place, so Letowski should slide right in. He may also see some second-unit power-play time. He's a smart player.

THE PHYSICAL GAME

Letowski has a big heart in a small frame. He is very competitive and not shy about going after the puck in the corners, though he lacks the strength for one-on-one battles. He tends to wear down and can't handle too many minutes a night.

THE INTANGIBLES

The Canucks failed to qualify Letowski, which made him an unrestricted free agent. He is likely to continue in a third- or fourth-line role.

PROJECTION

Letowski has some offensive upside but realistic totals for him would be 15 goals and 15 assists.

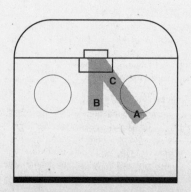

TODD MARCHANT

Yrs. of NHL service: 9

Born: Buffalo, N.Y.; Aug. 12, 1973

Position: center

Height: 5-10

Weight: 178

Uniform no.: 26

Shoots: left

Career statistics:

GP	G	A	TP	PIM
679	136	207	343	490

1999-2000 statistics:

GP	G	A	TP	+/-	PIM	PP	SH	GW	GT	S	PCT
82	17	23	40	+7	70	0	1	0	2	170	10.0

2000-2001 statistics:

GP	G	A	TP	+/-	PIM	PP	SH	GW	GT	S	PCT
71	13	26	39	+1	51	0	4	2	1	113	11.5

2001-2002 statistics:

GP	G	A	TP	+/-	PIM	PP	SH	GW	GT	S	PCT
82	12	22	34	+7	41	0	3	1	0	124	9.7

2002-2003 statistics:

GP	G	A	TP	+/-	PIM	PP	SH	GW	GT	S	PCT
77	20	40	60	+13	48	7	1	3	1	146	13.7

LAST SEASON

Signed as free agent by Columbus on July 3, 2003. Led Oilers in assists with career high. Second on team in points and shooting percentage. Tied for second on team in plus-minus. Tied for third on team in goals and power-plays goals. Missed four games due to virus.

THE FINESSE GAME

A speed merchant, Marchant is a strong one-on-one player with zippy outside speed. His quick hand skills keep pace with his feet, and he is particularly adept at tempting the defender with the puck, then dragging it through the victim's legs. He then continues to the net for his scoring chances.

Marchant is opportunistic, and, with his pace, reminds scouts of a young Theo Fleury. Production-wise, he has a long way to go to match Fleury's scoring touch. He will never be an elite scorer because he doesn't have the hands.

Marchant is smart, sees the ice well, and is a solid playmaker as well as shooter. He is no puck hog. He is an excellent penalty killer and a shorthanded threat because of his speed.

Marchant excels on face-offs and ranked sixth in the NHL (58 per cent) in that category last season.

THE PHYSICAL GAME

Teammates have nicknamed him "Mighty Mouse," as Marchant is fearless in the face of bigger, supposedly tougher, opposition. He hurls his body at larger foes. He is irritating to play against, because a big lug like Derian Hatcher looks foolish trying to chase down and swat a little-bitty guy like Marchant.

Marchant is average size but his grit makes him look bigger. He sacrifices his body, but you wonder how long his body will last under the stress he puts it through. He is well-conditioned and can handle a lot of ice time. The mental toughness is there, too. He will take a hit to make a play but has to get smarter about picking his spots in order to survive. Edmonton is a very mobile team and Marchant's lack of size is not as much of a detriment as it could be on other teams.

THE INTANGIBLES

Marchant made a surprising choice in signing with the young Blue Jackets (for five years at $2.9 million per). He will give them much-needed depth at center.

PROJECTION

Marchant is a role player with a big heart. His top end is 20 goals, which he nailed last season and should again this year. You might even speculate he'll go higher than that because of the prime ice time he'll get in Columbus.

RICK NASH

Yrs. of NHL service: 1
Born: Brampton, Ont.; June 16, 1984
Position: left wing
Height: 6-3
Weight: 188
Uniform no.: 61
Shoots: left

Career statistics:

GP	G	A	TP	PIM
74	17	22	39	78

2002-2003 statistics:

GP	G	A	TP	+/-	PIM	PP	SH	GW	GT	S	PCT
74	17	22	39	-27	78	6	0	2	0	154	11.0

LAST SEASON

Finalist for 2003 Calder Trophy. Named to NHL All-Rookie Team. Led NHL rookies in power-play points (16). Second among NHL rookies in power-play goals and shots. Tied for second among NHL rookies in points. Tied for third among NHL rookies in assists. Fourth among NHL rookies in goals. Tied for fourth among NHL rookies in shooting percentage. Worst plus-minus on team. Missed four games with back injury. Missed three games with hip pointer. Missed one game with concussion.

THE FINESSE GAME

Nash is a power forward in the making, and he is at his best down low. He makes the greatest impact in the dirty areas around the crease, especially on the power play. His skating, though, is the question mark. It may be marginally NHL caliber, but no one thought Luc Robitaille was a great skater either (600 goals later, it's still a deficiency).

What makes Nash seem faster is that he wants to get to where the puck is. Nash forechecks aggressively. He is able to get in on the puck carrier and he happily wades into the wars in the corners, along the boards, and in front of the net. Nash had a slow start to the season when he looked like he couldn't wait to get rid of the puck. He finished the season much more relaxed with the puck on his stick.

Nash is a combination of finesse and power. He has a great wrist shot, accurate and with a quick release. Nash can also shoot off the fly (as fast as he flies, anyway). He needs to work on his play away from the puck.

THE PHYSICAL GAME

Nash has shown up when the game is on the line. He is competitive and intense. Some scouts have compared him to a young Brendan Shanahan. Nash is still on the skinny side, but remember he's only 19.

THE INTANGIBLES

It takes an exceptional 18-year-old to step in and make an impact in his first NHL season. Nash is that good. He is also a humble kid, readily accepted by older teammates, and well-respected by the coaching staff. Don't mistake his low-key demeanor for a lack on confidence. Nash wants to be the go-to guy, which he will be in Columbus for a long time.

PROJECTION

Nash will be a first-line player in his second season. Isn't that rushing it? Yep. But we thought enough of Nash to project 35 points in his rookie season. Even if he hits a sophomore slump, he may cruise past 45 points next season. Nash seems to be too good to be true, but we believe he is.

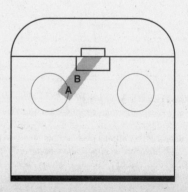

LUKE RICHARDSON

Yrs. of NHL service: 16
Born: Ottawa, Ont.; Mar. 26, 1969
Position: left defense
Height: 6-3
Weight: 210
Uniform no.: 22
Shoots: left

Career statistics:

GP	G	A	TP	PIM
1183	31	142	173	1877

1999-2000 statistics:

GP	G	A	TP	+/-	PIM	PP	SH	GW	GT	S	PCT
74	2	5	7	+14	140	0	0	1	0	50	4.0

2000-2001 statistics:

GP	G	A	TP	+/-	PIM	PP	SH	GW	GT	S	PCT
82	2	6	8	+23	131	0	1	0	0	75	2.7

2001-2002 statistics:

GP	G	A	TP	+/-	PIM	PP	SH	GW	GT	S	PCT
72	1	8	9	+18	102	0	0	0	0	65	1.5

2002-2003 statistics:

GP	G	A	TP	+/-	PIM	PP	SH	GW	GT	S	PCT
82	0	13	13	-16	73	0	0	0	0	56	0.0

LAST SEASON

Second on team in average ice time (23:31). One of two Blue Jackets to appear in all 82 games.

THE FINESSE GAME

Richardson is a good skater with lateral mobility and balance, but not much speed. He overcomes his skating flaws by taking up as much space as he can with his size. Richardson has learned to play a more conservative style as he has gotten older and it has made him less of a liability.

Richardson can't carry the puck and doesn't jump up into the rush well. He is best paired with a puck-carrying partner so he can just make the dish and play stay-at-home. He seldom uses his point shot, which is merely adequate.

Richardson doesn't always know when to stay in front of his net and when to challenge in the corners. The less he tries to do, the better. Richardson has become less of a headhunter and doesn't run around looking for the big hit. He is a smart and willing shot-blocker.

THE PHYSICAL GAME

Richardson is the kind of player you hate to play against but love to have on your side. He hits to hurt and is an imposing presence on the ice. He scares people. When he checks, he separates the puck carrier from the puck and doesn't let the man back into the play. When he is on the ice, his teammates play a bit bigger and braver. He also plays hurt. Richardson isn't shy about dropping his gloves, either.

THE INTANGIBLES

We didn't think that the signing of Richardson as a free agent was money well spent by Columbus in 2002, but he proved us wrong. Richardson was asked to do way too much, but he always performed to the best of his ability. His character has proven perfect for a team trying to break in some younger kids. Richardson has proven to be a steadying influence on a still-growing team.

PROJECTION

Richardson's role is as a physical stay-at-home defender. His point totals will remain low (10 to 15 points), even with the increased ice time.

GEOFF SANDERSON

Yrs. of NHL service: 12
Born: Hay River, N.W.T.; Feb. 1, 1972
Position: left wing
Height: 6-0
Weight: 190
Uniform no.: 8
Shoots: left

Career statistics:

GP	G	A	TP	PIM
848	300	276	576	355

1999-2000 statistics:

GP	G	A	TP	+/-	PIM	PP	SH	GW	GT	S	PCT
67	13	13	26	+4	22	4	0	3	0	136	9.6

2000-2001 statistics:

GP	G	A	TP	+/-	PIM	PP	SH	GW	GT	S	PCT
68	30	26	56	+4	46	9	0	7	0	199	15.1

2001-2002 statistics:

GP	G	A	TP	+/-	PIM	PP	SH	GW	GT	S	PCT
42	11	5	16	-15	12	5	0	2	0	112	9.8

2002-2003 statistics:

GP	G	A	TP	+/-	PIM	PP	SH	GW	GT	S	PCT
82	34	33	67	-4	34	15	2	2	0	286	11.9

LAST SEASON

Tied for sixth in NHL in power-play goals. Led team in goals, power-play goals, and shots. Tied for second on team in shorthanded goals. Third on team in plus-minus. One of two Blue Jackets to appear in all 82 games.

THE FINESSE GAME

Maybe it's age, maybe it's wisdom, maybe it's just the fact that he needs to catch his breath now and again, but the result is that the veteran Sanderson has learned how to vary the pace of his skating instead of going full-tilt every time. When he plays a pure speed game, Sanderson is too far ahead of the game and his teammates. With his better sense of timing and his ability to accelerate into holes, Sanderson revived what had been a flagging career.

Sanderson takes a lot of shots. He can drive wide on a defenseman or open up space by forcing the defense to play back off him. He doesn't score often off the rush because he doesn't have a heavy shot. He can create chaos off the rush, though, and finish up by getting open in the slot for a pass.

He has a superb one-timer on the power play, where he likes to score on his off-wing in the deep right slot. Sanderson has become a better all-round player: he is more intelligent in his own end and his checking is more consistent. He can also kill penalties. His speed makes him a shorthanded threat.

THE PHYSICAL GAME

Sanderson is wiry but gets outmuscled. Although his speed keeps him clear of a lot of traffic, he has to battle when the room isn't there.

THE INTANGIBLES

Sanderson finally got to enjoy a healthy season, and that was the biggest reason for the upswing in his production.

PROJECTION

Columbus is slowly shedding itself of some older players and working with their kids, but Sanderson is expected to remain a top-six forward for another season. He's a 30-goal scorer if he continues to have the same luck avoiding injuries that he did last season.

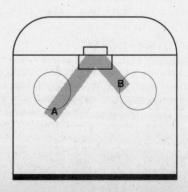

MIKE SILLINGER

Yrs. of NHL service: 11
Born: Regina, Sask.; June 29, 1971
Position: center
Height: 5-11
Weight: 196
Uniform no.: 16
Shoots: right

Career statistics:

GP	G	A	TP	PIM
753	153	221	374	439

1999-2000 statistics:

GP	G	A	TP	+/-	PIM	PP	SH	GW	GT	S	PCT
80	23	29	52	-30	102	8	3	2	0	146	15.8

2000-2001 statistics:

GP	G	A	TP	+/-	PIM	PP	SH	GW	GT	S	PCT
68	16	25	41	-11	48	1	0	2	0	119	13.4

2001-2002 statistics:

GP	G	A	TP	+/-	PIM	PP	SH	GW	GT	S	PCT
80	20	23	43	-35	54	8	0	5	0	150	13.3

2002-2003 statistics:

GP	G	A	TP	+/-	PIM	PP	SH	GW	GT	S	PCT
75	18	25	43	-21	52	9	3	3	0	128	14.1

LAST SEASON

Led team in shorthanded goals. Tied for second on team in power-play goals. Tied for third on team in game-winning goals. Missed five games with groin injury. Missed two games with shoulder injury.

THE FINESSE GAME

One of the drawbacks to this veteran's career is his size, but Sillinger is not without his assets. He is a clever player with a knack for positioning himself in the attacking zone. And he has a good shot with a quick release.

Sillinger is an energetic skater with speed and balance. His one-step acceleration is good. He plays well in traffic, uses his sturdy form to protect the puck, and he has sharp hand-eye coordination. Sillinger is a smart penalty killer and a shorthanded threat, as well as an ace on face-offs. Sillinger is the top face-off man for Columbus.

Expansion was tailor-made for guys like Sillinger. He has worked hard to make the most of what might be a last chance, and could be in a position to be picked up by a contender come playoff time.

THE PHYSICAL GAME

Sillinger is small but burly. He is tough to budge from in front of the net because of his low center of gravity. He is not feisty or aggressive. He keeps himself in good condition and over the past few seasons has missed very few games due to injuries.

THE INTANGIBLES

Sillinger is a special-teams specialist. He kills penalties, is a shorthanded threat, works the open ice on the power play and can fill in (short-term) on the top two lines in a pinch. He is a grinder, a role player, and a leader by example. In short, a nice fit on a team that is trying to mold its future.

PROJECTION

Sillinger just missed our 20-goal prediction on the nose due to injuries. He is likely to continue in a similar role for the Blue Jackets and we'd expect 20 from him this season. Until Columbus gets better, Sillinger will be among its front-line forwards.

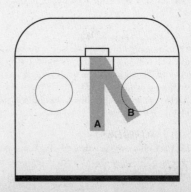

JAROSLAV SPACEK

Yrs. of NHL service: 5
Born: Rokycany, Czech Republic; Feb. 11, 1974
Position: left defense
Height: 5-11
Weight: 206
Uniform no.: 3
Shoots: left

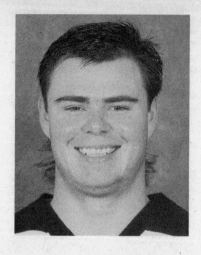

Career statistics:

GP	G	A	TP	PIM
362	34	106	140	232

1999-2000 statistics:

GP	G	A	TP	+/-	PIM	PP	SH	GW	GT	S	PCT
82	10	26	36	+7	53	4	0	1	0	111	9.0

2000-2001 statistics:

GP	G	A	TP	+/-	PIM	PP	SH	GW	GT	S	PCT
62	7	19	26	+3	28	3	0	1	0	106	6.6

2001-2002 statistics:

GP	G	A	TP	+/-	PIM	PP	SH	GW	GT	S	PCT
74	5	13	18	-4	53	1	1	2	0	93	5.4

2002-2003 statistics:

GP	G	A	TP	+/-	PIM	PP	SH	GW	GT	S	PCT
81	9	36	45	-23	70	5	0	1	0	166	5.4

Spacek was able to stay healthy and if he does so again, should score in the 40-point range.

LAST SEASON

Led team in average ice time (24:47). Led team defensemen in points. Third on team in shots. Career highs in assists and points. Missed one game due to personal reasons.

THE FINESSE GAME

Spacek is an agile skater. He is good one-on-one and even defending against a two-on-one. He moves the puck very well and has some offensive upside.

Spacek uses his finesse skills in a defensive manner, positioning himself intelligently and anticipating plays. He kills penalties, and can handle some power-play chores. He is a smart passer and executes the give-and-go well. Last season, Columbus gave him the chance to show off his offensive talent and he responded with a career high in points.

Spacek is asked to shoulder much more responsibility in Columbus than he should for his level of ability. That's likely to be the case for him again this season.

THE PHYSICAL GAME

Spacek is not a big hitter, and he isn't very large, but his positional play is good and he steps up to stop people in the neutral zone. Spacek was overused last season (on the top power-play unit, killing penalties, and opposing other team's top lines) and he was worn down late in the season.

THE INTANGIBLES

Spacek was Columbus' best defenseman last season.

PROJECTION

DAVID VYBORNY

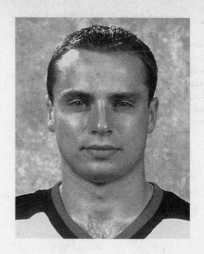

Yrs. of NHL service: 3
Born: Jihlava, Czech Republic; Jan. 22, 1975
Position: right wing
Height: 5-10
Weight: 189
Uniform no.: 9
Shoots: left

Career statistics:

GP	G	A	TP	PIM
233	46	63	109	44

2000-2001 statistics:

GP	G	A	TP	+/-	PIM	PP	SH	GW	GT	S	PCT
79	13	19	32	-9	22	5	0	1	0	125	10.4

2001-2002 statistics:

GP	G	A	TP	+/-	PIM	PP	SH	GW	GT	S	PCT
75	13	18	31	-14	6	6	0	2	0	103	12.6

2002-2003 statistics:

GP	G	A	TP	+/-	PIM	PP	SH	GW	GT	S	PCT
79	20	26	46	+12	16	4	1	4	0	125	16.0

LAST SEASON

Led team in plus-minus. Second on team in game-winning goals. Third on team in shooting percentage. Tied for third on team in goals. Career highs in goals, assists, and points. Missed three games due to coach's decision.

THE FINESSE GAME

Vyborny is a small forward with extreme quickness, speed, and balance. He is a dangerous offensive player with goal-scoring and playmaking abilities. He has good hockey sense and is especially smart around the net. Vyborny earned time on the first power-play unit.

Vyborny isn't a one-way forward. He has very good defensive awareness. Vyborny's +12 (a team record) is just an amazing statistic on this team, where no other player managed to avoid being minus for the season. He is very patient with the puck.

THE PHYSICAL GAME

Vyborny is small but he checks with intensity. He is fit and has shown a solid work ethic.

THE INTANGIBLES

We weren't alone in giving up on Vyborny after a dismal sophomore season. Vyborny was so discouraged that he was reportedly thinking of quitting the NHL to play in Europe. Vyborny wanted to prove something here, and he has.

PROJECTION

From under the radar to a top-six forward. There should be another 20-goal season in Vyborny's immediate future.

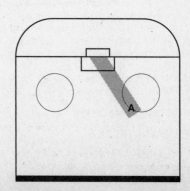

RAY WHITNEY

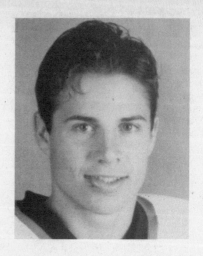

Yrs. of NHL service: 11
Born: Fort Saskatchewan, Alta.; May 8, 1972
Position: left wing / center
Height: 5-10
Weight: 175
Uniform no.: 14
Shoots: right

Career statistics:

GP	G	A	TP	PIM
633	191	301	492	197

1999-2000 statistics:

GP	G	A	TP	+/-	PIM	PP	SH	GW	GT	S	PCT
81	29	42	71	+16	35	5	0	3	2	198	14.6

2000-2001 statistics:

GP	G	A	TP	+/-	PIM	PP	SH	GW	GT	S	PCT
46	10	24	34	-17	30	5	0	0	0	120	8.3

2001-2002 statistics:

GP	G	A	TP	+/-	PIM	PP	SH	GW	GT	S	PCT
67	21	40	61	-22	12	6	0	3	0	210	10.0

2002-2003 statistics:

GP	G	A	TP	+/-	PIM	PP	SH	GW	GT	S	PCT
81	24	52	76	-26	22	8	2	2	1	235	10.2

LAST SEASON

Led Blue Jackets in assists, points, and game-winning goals. Career highs in assists and points. Second on team in goals and shots. Tied for second on team in shorthanded goals. Third on team in average ice time (21:00). Missed one game with flu.

THE FINESSE GAME

Whitney is not a fast skater, but he is shifty in tight quarters and that makes him very tough to check. He likes to cut to the middle of the ice and use his forehand. He is dangerous every shift.

Savvy and determined, Whitney compensates for his lack of speed with a keen sense of anticipation. He jumps into the right spot simply by knowing before his checker does that it's the right place to be. That makes him appear quicker than he really is.

Whitney is poised in traffic and well-balanced on his feet. He has exceptionally good hands for passing and shooting. He can lift a backhand shot when he is practically on top of the goalie. And he has a deceptive shot because he does not telegraph whether he is going to pass or shoot. Whitney is especially effective on the power play. He tied for the league lead in power-play assists (34) last season.

Because he can't win the battles on the boards, Whitney needs to play with a grinder on his wing.

THE PHYSICAL GAME

Whitney is small, but he plays a wily game. A center of his ability and size needs to be protected with a tough winger and defenseman in his five-man unit, but Whitney brings so much to the game that a team can make room for him. He is remarkably durable for his size.

THE INTANGIBLES

Whitney couldn't have picked a better time to post career numbers in several categories, since he became an unrestricted free agent after last season.

PROJECTION

Whitney has the ability to be a consistent 20-goal, 45-assist scorer in the right circumstances.

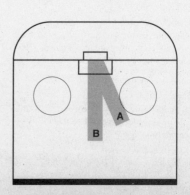

TYLER WRIGHT

Yrs. of NHL service: 9
Born: Canora, Sask.; Apr. 6, 1973
Position: center
Height: 6-0
Weight: 190
Uniform no.: 28
Shoots: right

Career statistics:

GP	G	A	TP	PIM
502	68	55	123	740

1999-2000 statistics:

GP	G	A	TP	+/-	PIM	PP	SH	GW	GT	S	PCT
50	12	10	22	+4	45	0	0	1	0	68	17.6

2000-2001 statistics:

GP	G	A	TP	+/-	PIM	PP	SH	GW	GT	S	PCT
76	16	16	32	-9	140	4	1	2	1	141	11.4

2001-2002 statistics:

GP	G	A	TP	+/-	PIM	PP	SH	GW	GT	S	PCT
77	13	11	24	-40	100	4	0	1	1	120	10.8

2002-2003 statistics:

GP	G	A	TP	+/-	PIM	PP	SH	GW	GT	S	PCT
70	19	11	30	-25	113	3	2	3	0	108	17.6

LAST SEASON

Second on team in penalty minutes and shots. Tied for second on team in shorthanded goals. Third on team in game-winning goals. Career high in goals. Missed one game with concussion. Missed nine games with a broken hand. Missed one game with flu. Missed one game with thigh injury.

THE FINESSE GAME

Wright brings to mind the prototypical agitators like Keith Acton and Ken Linseman. Playing in his third-line capacity, Wright will stir things up but be on the outside of the pile after everyone else has jumped in, admiring what he started. He is consistent in his effort, too. It's rare when he takes a night or a shift off.

Wright doesn't have a lot of finish around the net. He is not a natural goal-scorer. He has to work hard for everything he gets.

He's a quick and shifty skater, and handles the puck fine, but he does not have a big-league shot. His added dimension is as a penalty killer.

THE PHYSICAL GAME

Always in someone's face, Wright loves to try to distract other teams' top players — even from the bench. Yap, yap, yap. He's started to back up some of his chatter with points now, which is even more infuriating for opponents. He'll get slapped around a little because he's not much of a fighter. He's the human equivalent of a Jack Russell terrier.

THE INTANGIBLES

Wright is an enthusiastic and energetic player who adds something to a team's chemistry. He is well-liked by fans and teammates. He is a good leader for a team that is just starting to create an identity.

PROJECTION

Despite an early-season concussion, Wright was off to the best start of his career (8-4 — 17 in 15 games) before he broke his hand in November. He was still able to post the kind of numbers we had projected for him over a full season. He should become a reliable (and feisty) 20-goal scorer.

DALLAS STARS

Players' Statistics 2001-2002

POS.	NO.	PLAYER	GP	G	A	PTS	+/-	PIM	PP	SH	GW	GT	S	PCT
C	9	MIKE MODANO	79	28	57	85	34	30	5	2	6		193	14.5
D	56	SERGEI ZUBOV	82	11	44	55	21	26	8		2		158	7.0
R	13	BILL GUERIN	64	25	25	50	5	113	11		2	1	229	10.9
L	26	JERE LEHTINEN	80	31	17	48	39	20	5		3	2	238	13.0
C	44	JASON ARNOTT	72	23	24	47	9	51	7		6	1	169	13.6
L	10	BRENDEN MORROW	71	21	22	43	20	134	2	3	4	2	105	20.0
R	48	SCOTT YOUNG	79	23	19	42	24	30	5	1	4	1	237	9.7
C	77	PIERRE TURGEON	65	12	30	42	4	18	3		5	1	76	15.8
C	14	STU BARNES	81	13	26	39	-11	28	4	1	3		149	8.7
R	11	ULF DAHLEN	63	17	20	37	11	14	9		1		100	17.0
D	5	DARRYL SYDOR	81	5	31	36	22	40	2		1		132	3.8
C	39	*NIKO KAPANEN	82	5	29	34	25	44		1	1		80	6.3
D	2	DERIAN HATCHER	82	8	22	30	37	106	1	1	2		159	5.0
D	43	PHILIPPE BOUCHER	80	7	20	27	28	94	1	1	3	1	137	5.1
R	32	CLAUDE LEMIEUX	68	8	12	20	-12	44	1	1		1	119	6.7
L	18	ROB DIMAIO	69	10	9	19	18	76			2		81	12.3
D	4	LYLE ODELEIN	68	7	4	11	7	82					78	9.0
C	27	MANNY MALHOTRA	59	3	7	10	-2	42			1		62	4.8
D	17	STEPHANE ROBIDAS	76	3	7	10	15	35			1		47	6.4
L	29	*STEVE OTT	26	3	4	7	6	31					25	12.0
D	24	RICHARD MATVICHUK	68	1	5	6	1	58			1		59	1.7
L	22	KIRK MULLER	55	1	5	6	-6	18					48	2.1
R	28	DAVID OLIVER	6		3	3	1	2					5	
D	3	JOHN ERSKINE	16	2		2	1	29					12	16.7
R	47	AARON DOWNEY	43	1	1	2	1	69					14	7.1
G	31	RON TUGNUTT	31				0							
G	30	COREY HIRSCH	2				0							
C	32	JIM MONTGOMERY	1				0							
G	35	MARTY TURCO	55				0	16						

GP = games played; G = goals; A = assists; PTS = points; +/- = goals-for minus goals-against while player is on ice; PIM = penalties in minutes; PP = power-play goals; SH = shorthanded goals; GW = game-winning goals; GT = game-tying goals; S = no. of shots; PCT = percentage of goals to shots; * = rookie

JASON ARNOTT

Yrs. of NHL service: 10
Born: Collingwood, Ont.; Oct. 11, 1974
Position: center
Height: 6-4
Weight: 225
Uniform no.: 44
Shoots: right

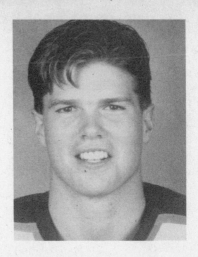

Career statistics:

GP	G	A	TP	PIM
670	223	288	511	831

1999-2000 statistics:

GP	G	A	TP	+/-	PIM	PP	SH	GW	GT	S	PCT
76	22	34	56	+22	51	7	0	4	0	244	9.0

2000-2001 statistics:

GP	G	A	TP	+/-	PIM	PP	SH	GW	GT	S	PCT
54	21	34	55	+23	75	8	0	3	2	138	15.2

2001-2002 statistics:

GP	G	A	TP	+/-	PIM	PP	SH	GW	GT	S	PCT
73	25	20	45	+2	65	10	0	3	0	197	12.7

2002-2003 statistics:

GP	G	A	TP	+/-	PIM	PP	SH	GW	GT	S	PCT
72	23	24	47	+9	51	7	0	6	1	169	13.6

LAST SEASON

Tied for team lead in game-winning goals. Missed nine games with ankle sprain. Missed one game with knee injury.

THE FINESSE GAME

For a player of his size, Arnott has tremendous skill. As a skater he has speed, balance, a long stride, plus agility in turning to either side. He has also added muscle to his frame, without losing any edge in his skating. He has a booming cannon of a shot, either on the fly or as a one-timer, and can be used at the point on the power play. Arnott also smoothly switches off with a winger on the half-boards.

Arnott's major flaw is that he is so skilled for a big guy that some nights he likes to take the easy way out. He should be a more effective power forward than he is, but he is easily sucked into a perimeter game. Arnott is a decent passer, though he is better getting the puck late and deep. His timing with passes is fine, as he holds onto the puck until a teammate is in the open. He is average on draws on a good night, and some nights really struggles. Arnott does have a knack for scoring timely goals (like his OT Cup-clincher for New Jersey over Dallas in 2000).

Arnott is far more effective as a center than a wing. Coaches like to use him on the wing because of his size and because of the lessened defensive responsibility, but Arnott seems more focused when he plays in the middle. He's also a lot happier playing there, and Arnott does tend to sulk. He does not have a lot of hockey smarts.

THE PHYSICAL GAME

Arnott has shown that he's willing to pay a physical price, but not on a consistent basis. You would really like to see a guy this powerful be more assertive. He was able to stay healthy last season, with only a couple of minor dings.

THE INTANGIBLES

Arnott may never achieve anywhere near the harmony he had with Patrik Elias and Petr Sykora in their two great seasons in New Jersey.

PROJECTION

Since Arnott has yet to find his real niche with the Stars, we'll keep his projection on the low side, around 25 goals and 50 points.

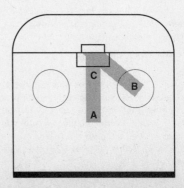

STU BARNES

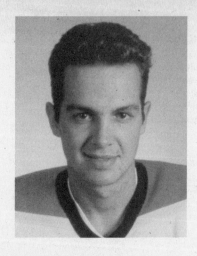

Yrs. of NHL service: 12
Born: Spruce Grove, Alta.; Dec. 25, 1970
Position: center
Height: 5-11
Weight: 180
Uniform no.: 14
Shoots: right

Career statistics:

GP	G	A	TP	PIM
820	210	274	484	310

1999-2000 statistics:

GP	G	A	TP	+/-	PIM	PP	SH	GW	GT	S	PCT
82	20	25	45	-3	16	8	2	2	0	137	14.6

2000-2001 statistics:

GP	G	A	TP	+/-	PIM	PP	SH	GW	GT	S	PCT
75	19	24	43	-2	26	3	2	5	0	160	11.9

2001-2002 statistics:

GP	G	A	TP	+/-	PIM	PP	SH	GW	GT	S	PCT
68	17	31	48	+6	26	5	0	4	1	127	13.4

2002-2003 statistics:

GP	G	A	TP	+/-	PIM	PP	SH	GW	GT	S	PCT
81	13	26	39	-11	28	4	1	3	0	149	8.7

LAST SEASON

Acquired from Buffalo on March 10, 2003, for Mike Ryan and a second-round draft pick in 2003.

THE FINESSE GAME

Barnes pursues the puck intelligently and finishes his checks. He employs these traits at even strength, killing penalties, or on the power play. He reads the play coming out of the zone and uses his anticipation to pick off passes. He plays with great enthusiasm. He has sharply honed puck skills and offensive instincts which he puts to effective use on the power play. He has good quickness and can control the puck in traffic. He uses a slap shot or a wrist shot in-tight.

Few of the quality chances that come Barnes's way get wasted. He has a quick release and is accurate with his shot. One of his favorite plays is using his right-handed shot for a one-timer on the power play.

Barnes has a good work ethic. His effort overcomes his deficiency in size. He's clever and plays a smart small-man's game. He plays all three forward positions. He tends to get into scoring slumps, but never quits working to try to snap out of them.

THE PHYSICAL GAME

Barnes is not big but he gets in the way. He brings a little bit of grit to the lineup, but what really stands out is his intensity and spirit. He can energize his team with one gutsy shift. He always keeps his feet moving and draws penalties. He gets outmuscled down low.

Barnes seemed completely recovered from a concussion which ended his 2001-02 season with the Sabres.

THE INTANGIBLES

Some players do not shoulder responsibility well. Barnes does, and will get a chance to do it over a full season with the Stars. He is the epitome of a player who leads by example. What we have always admired about Barnes is how he steps it up in the playoffs.

PROJECTION

Realistically, 20 goals is the right target for Barnes, who will be allowed to settle in as a role player with the Stars and not be expected to carry the scoring load as he did in Buffalo.

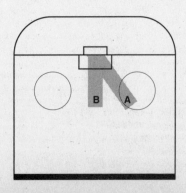

JOHN ERSKINE

Yrs. of NHL service: 2
Born: Ajax, Ont.; June 26, 1980
Position: defense
Height: 6-4
Weight: 215
Uniform no.: 3
Shoots: left

Career statistics:

GP	G	A	TP	PIM
49	2	1	3	91

2001-2002 statistics:

GP	G	A	TP	+/-	PIM	PP	SH	GW	GT	S	PCT
33	0	1	1	-8	62	0	0	0	0	16	0.0

2002-2003 statistics:

GP	G	A	TP	+/-	PIM	PP	SH	GW	GT	S	PCT
16	2	0	2	+1	29	0	0	0	0	12	16.7

LAST SEASON

Missed six games due to coach's decision. Appeared in 52 games with Utah (AHL), scoring 2-8 — 10 with 274 PIM.

THE FINESSE GAME

Erskine has been described as a poor man's Derian Hatcher. Given that the Stars no longer have the rich man's version, it's time for Erskine to step up.

Erskine is built along Hatcher lines. He's tall and lanky and a little raw. One of his biggest flaws is his skating. It's borderline awful. He will need to improve his foot speed just to be able to maintain his positioning. The less he does, the better. Erskine really needs to keep the game simple and force the attackers to come into his zone. Few people will dare because Erskine is powerful and kind of scary.

Erskine makes a smart first pass out of the zone. He could develop into a serviceable stay-at-home defenseman and a solid anchor for a more mobile and offensive-minded partner.

THE PHYSICAL GAME

Erskine is mean, menacing, and he is a real threat if the gloves come off. He actually had to fill out his frame a little over the past two years and he's still doing so. He brings a lot of energy to the ice.

THE INTANGIBLES

Erskine's progress has been slow and he might have been targeted for another year in the minors (or become trade bait) if Dallas hadn't lost Hatcher to free agency. Now the Stars really need him, and Erskine will get every chance to win a job in training camp.

PROJECTION

Erskine has never been much of a point-getter at any level and his offensive production is bound to be minimal. He could reap some penalty minutes for you, if your pool includes that stat.

BILL GUERIN

Yrs. of NHL service: 11
Born: Wilbraham, Mass.; Nov. 9, 1970
Position: right wing
Height: 6-2
Weight: 210
Uniform no.: 13
Shoots: right

Career statistics:

GP	G	A	TP	PIM
797	281	273	554	1149

1999-2000 statistics:

GP	G	A	TP	+/-	PIM	PP	SH	GW	GT	S	PCT
70	24	22	46	+4	123	11	0	2	0	188	12.8

2000-2001 statistics:

GP	G	A	TP	+/-	PIM	PP	SH	GW	GT	S	PCT
85	40	45	85	+7	140	11	1	5	0	289	13.8

2001-2002 statistics:

GP	G	A	TP	+/-	PIM	PP	SH	GW	GT	S	PCT
78	41	25	66	-1	91	10	1	7	0	355	11.6

2002-2003 statistics:

GP	G	A	TP	+/-	PIM	PP	SH	GW	GT	S	PCT
64	25	25	50	+5	113	11	0	2	1	229	10.9

LAST SEASON

Led team in power-play goals. Second on team in penalty minutes. Third on team in goals, points, and shots. Missed 18 games due to thigh injury and surgery.

THE FINESSE GAME

Guerin's brash confidence was just what the Stars need to restore some lost swagger after their non-playoff season in 2002. But the free agent signee couldn't seal the deal for Dallas in the playoffs because of a blood clot in his thigh which required surgery. Guerin did return to play four postseason games, but he was clearly not the same effective Guerin he had been for the first three-quarters of the season.

Guerin has a terrifying slap shot, a wicked screamer that he unleashes off the wing in full flight. He has gotten smarter about mixing up his shots, using a wrister or snap shot for a one-timer instead of going into a full windup.

Guerin becomes ineffective when he stops playing like a power forward and dances on the perimeter, playing an east-west instead of north-south game. His speed and power are potent weapons but he needs to drive down the right wing and force the defense back with his speed. When he backs off and takes the easier route to the off-wing, his scoring chances decrease drastically in quality.

Hockey sense and creativity are lagging a tad behind his other attributes, but Guerin is a conscientious player. He is aware defensively and has worked hard at that part of the game, though he will still lose his checking assignments and start running around in the defensive zone.

THE PHYSICAL GAME

The more physical the game is, the more Guerin gets involved. He is big, strong and tough in every sense of the word; he's useless when he plays otherwise.

The kind of game Guerin is going to have can usually be judged in the first few shifts. He can play it clean or mean, with big body checks or the drop of a glove. He will move to the puck carrier and battle for control until he gets it, and he's hard to knock off his skates.

In front of the net, Guerin digs hard. He works to establish position and has the hand skills to make something happen when the puck gets to his stick. He can routinely handle 20 minutes a night when he's 100 per cent.

THE INTANGIBLES

Guerin quickly found a compatible linemate in Mike Modano, and the two formed one of the league's best forward duos until Guerin's injury.

PROJECTION

Guerin would have likely scored around 32-35 goals if he had not been injured. The big question is whether Guerin will be the same after the thigh surgery or if it will have the same detrimental effect it did on Cam Neely's career.

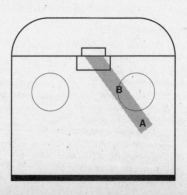

NIKO KAPANEN

Yrs. of NHL service: 1
Born: Hattula, Finland; Apr. 29, 1978
Position: center
Height: 5-9
Weight: 180
Uniform no.: 39
Shoots: left

Career statistics:

GP	G	A	TP	PIM
91	5	30	35	46

2001-2002 statistics:

GP	G	A	TP	+/-	PIM	PP	SH	GW	GT	S	PCT
9	0	1	1	-1	2	0	0	0	0	3	0.0

2002-2003 statistics:

GP	G	A	TP	+/-	PIM	PP	SH	GW	GT	S	PCT
82	5	29	34	+25	44	0	1	1	0	80	6.3

LAST SEASON

First NHL season. Led NHL rookies in assists and plus-minus. Fifth among NHL rookies in points. One of three Stars to appear in all 82 games.

THE FINESSE GAME

Dallas teammate Sergei Zubov has likened Kapanen to Igor Larionov, perhaps one of the brainiest centers of all time. That is a huge compliment to Kapanen, an unheralded rookie who became the Stars' top checking center last season.

Kapanen does so many of the little things well. He has good speed and understands the game well. He positions himself with a defense-first mentality because he knows what so few players seem to be able to grasp — that offense can spring from defense. Kapanen is often matched against other team's top lines, and can feast on their mistakes.

Kapanen has a good passing touch with the puck. He is more of a playmaker than a scorer. Kapanen lacks a shot that is a worthy scoring weapon.

THE PHYSICAL GAME

Kapanen is a small guy, and since he plays on a line with another smallish forward in Brenden Morrow, he is the loser in most physical battles against other big centers. He plays hard, though.

THE INTANGIBLES

Kapanen was expected to play last season in the minors. Instead, he won a job in training camp and never missed a game in the regular season. Kapanen solidified the Stars' third line and was so consistent all season that a sophomore slump appears to be a non-issue. He was accepted readily by a veteran team, which is a credit to his work ethic and attitude.

PROJECTION

Kapanen doesn't need to earn a job this fall, but he needs to keep playing with the same hunger he demonstrated last season. In a regular role again, he should deliver 35-40 points.

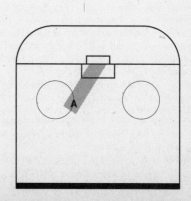

JERE LEHTINEN

Yrs. of NHL service: 8
Born: Espoo, Finland; June 24, 1973
Position: left wing
Height: 6-0
Weight: 200
Uniform no.: 26
Shoots: right

Career statistics:

GP	G	A	TP	PIM
510	144	171	315	114

1999-2000 statistics:

GP	G	A	TP	+/-	PIM	PP	SH	GW	GT	S	PCT
17	3	5	8	+1	0	0	0	1	0	29	10.3

2000-2001 statistics:

GP	G	A	TP	+/-	PIM	PP	SH	GW	GT	S	PCT
74	20	25	45	+14	24	7	0	1	1	148	13.5

2001-2002 statistics:

GP	G	A	TP	+/-	PIM	PP	SH	GW	GT	S	PCT
73	25	24	49	+27	14	7	1	4	2	198	12.6

2002-2003 statistics:

GP	G	A	TP	+/-	PIM	PP	SH	GW	GT	S	PCT
80	31	17	48	+39	20	5	0	3	2	238	13.0

LAST SEASON

Won 2003 Selke Trophy. Fourth in NHL in plus-minus. Led team in plus-minus for second consecutive season. Led team in goals with career high. Led team in shots. Missed two games with hip injury.

THE FINESSE GAME

Lehtinen is the smartest positional player on the Stars. He is remarkably astute and so honest and reliable that other players, almost through osmosis, have to come on-board. He also has the high-level skills to complement players like Mike Modano and Bill Guerin, acting as their defensive safety valve and also being able to convert scoring chances.

As much as Modano did on his own to become a superior two-way center, much of that progress can be traced to his teaming with Lehtinen. Modano returned the favor by enhancing the Finn's latent offensive ability. Both players are more complete because of the other, and they've had some of their best games as linemates. He always plays with his head up.

Lehtinen's skating is well above adequate. He's not really top flight, but he has enough quickness and balance to play with highly skilled people. He controls the puck well and is an unselfish playmaker.

Lehtinen has become much better at finishing. He has a good shot with a quick release, and as his team-leading shot total indicates, he has gained confidence in pulling the trigger. In fact, Lehtinen's goals-to-shots ratio was nearly 2:1, which is surprising for a player who is not goal-crazy.

No matter how much fun Lehtinen has scoring, though, he seems to take far more pride in playing against other team's top lines. Last year's Selke Trophy was his second.

THE PHYSICAL GAME

Is there a loose puck that Lehtinen ever loses a battle for? He is so strong on the puck. He protects it and won't be intimidated, and he competes along the boards. He completes his checks and never stops trying. He can handle a good amount of ice time and averaged 18:47 in ice time last season.

THE INTANGIBLES

Lehtinen is as reliable a forward as there is in the league. He is one player a coach never has to concern himself with.

PROJECTION

Lehtinen is a steady 45- to 50-point producer whose plus-minus will probably always exceed his goal total.

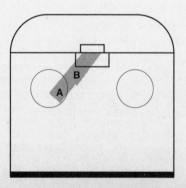

MANNY MALHOTRA

Yrs. of NHL service: 5
Born: Mississauga, Ont.; May 18, 1980
Position: center/left wing
Height: 6-2
Weight: 215
Uniform no.: 27
Shoots: left

Career statistics:

GP	G	A	TP	PIM
281	23	29	52	137

1999-2000 statistics:

GP	G	A	TP	+/-	PIM	PP	SH	GW	GT	S	PCT
27	0	0	0	-6	4	0	0	0	0	18	-

2000-2001 statistics:

GP	G	A	TP	+/-	PIM	PP	SH	GW	GT	S	PCT
50	4	8	12	-10	31	0	0	2	0	46	8.7

2001-2002 statistics:

GP	G	A	TP	+/-	PIM	PP	SH	GW	GT	S	PCT
72	8	6	14	-4	47	0	1	1	0	60	13.3

2002-2003 statistics:

GP	G	A	TP	+/-	PIM	PP	SH	GW	GT	S	PCT
59	3	7	10	-2	42	0	0	1	0	62	4.8

LAST SEASON

Missed 23 games due to coach's decision.

THE FINESSE GAME

Malhotra is a versatile player who may turn into a young Rod Brind'Amour — able to check, work on the power play, centre or wing, give a team a lead or protect it. Malhotra can bring so many things to a team. He just hasn't been able to put it all together yet, and his career is reaching the make-or-break stage.

Malhotra is a two-way center, although he has been used most often on the wing. He will never be a big-time scorer — his shot is not an awesome weapon — but by working to get in position and dig for short-range chances, he will get his share. He also has a terrific first step and reads offensive plays well. He has to read plays better defensively. He has a very young game yet. He will make his niche on the defensive side and has to develop his offense a bit more.

Malhotra's play is fuelled by will and determination. In fact, he might need to become a little less intense in practices and games in order to relax and get a better feel for the game.

THE PHYSICAL GAME

Malhotra is big and strong and likes to play a physical game, but he needs to bulk up a bit more to play against the big boys, against whom he still looks a bit coltish. He makes big hits and churns up pucks on the forecheck. He has been described as an ultimate team player and a kid who thrives on hard work and improving himself. He's a low-maintenance player.

THE INTANGIBLES

The change of scene from New York to Dallas did not kick-start Malhotra's career, as we thought it might. He has to find his niche in Dallas, or he will be on the move again.

PROJECTION

Malhotra should become a solid third-line forward, but he is probably two or three seasons away from becoming a defensive forward who can also produce 20 goals. We'd be happy with 10.

RICHARD MATVICHUK

Yrs. of NHL service: 11
Born: Edmonton, Alta.; Feb. 5, 1973
Position: left defense
Height: 6-2
Weight: 215
Uniform no.: 24
Shoots: left

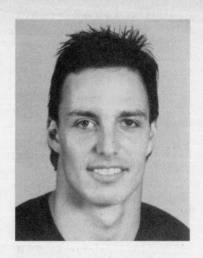

Career statistics:

GP	G	A	TP	PIM
658	37	109	146	548

1999-2000 statistics:

GP	G	A	TP	+/-	PIM	PP	SH	GW	GT	S	PCT
70	4	21	25	+7	42	0	0	1	0	73	5.5

2000-2001 statistics:

GP	G	A	TP	+/-	PIM	PP	SH	GW	GT	S	PCT
78	4	16	20	+5	62	2	0	1	0	85	4.7

2001-2002 statistics:

GP	G	A	TP	+/-	PIM	PP	SH	GW	GT	S	PCT
82	9	12	21	+11	52	4	0	2	0	109	8.3

2002-2003 statistics:

GP	G	A	TP	+/-	PIM	PP	SH	GW	GT	S	PCT
68	1	5	6	+1	58	0	0	1	0	59	1.7

LAST SEASON

Missed 14 games due to fractured fibula.

THE FINESSE GAME

Matvichuk has found his niche as a mobile, two-way defenseman. He is a good skater with a long stride, who skates well backwards and pivots in either direction. He has started to get involved more in the attack, and is capable of doing that to a degree. He has the hand skills and instincts to play with the offensive players up to a certain point, but that is not a high priority for him. He uses his hockey skills defensively. If his partner wants to go, Matvichuk will make sure to stay at home.

He has a low, hard, accurate shot from the point. Matvichuk makes smart, crisp passes and uses other players well. He can play either side defensively, which is an asset.

Matvichuk wants the ice time when the team needs a calm, defensive presence on the ice. He kills penalties and is one of the Stars' best shot-blockers.

THE PHYSICAL GAME

Matvichuk knows the importance of strength and aerobic training and wants to add even more muscle to stay competitive, since he was a little light by today's NHL standards. He's a hack-and-whack kind of mean guy, not a fighter. He occasionally gets into a mode where he starts fishing for the puck and has to be reminded to take the body. Matvichuk did this on a much more consistent basis last season, maybe because he was able to stay healthy.

Because he plays so hard and blocks so many shots, Matvichuk is subject to great wear and tear. He is tough, though, and plays through injuries.

THE INTANGIBLES

Matvichuk lost his hold on his top-four status in Dallas and his play and his confidence began to slip as a result. Like the other defensemen on the team, his role may be thrown out of whack since the Stars lost Derian Hatcher to free agency. Matvichuk went into the off-season as a restricted free agent.

PROJECTION

Matvichuk has become a confident and capable defenseman whose point totals will stay modest.

MIKE MODANO

Yrs. of NHL service: 14
Born: Livonia, Mich.; June 7, 1970
Position: center
Height: 6-3
Weight: 205
Uniform no.: 9
Shoots: left

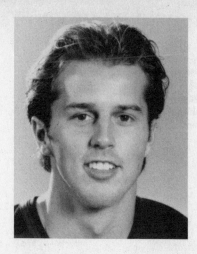

Career statistics:

GP	G	A	TP	PIM
1025	444	618	1062	664

1999-2000 statistics:

GP	G	A	TP	+/-	PIM	PP	SH	GW	GT	S	PCT
77	38	43	81	0	48	11	1	8	3	188	20.2

2000-2001 statistics:

GP	G	A	TP	+/-	PIM	PP	SH	GW	GT	S	PCT
81	33	51	84	+26	52	8	3	7	1	208	15.9

2001-2002 statistics:

GP	G	A	TP	+/-	PIM	PP	SH	GW	GT	S	PCT
78	34	43	77	+14	38	6	2	5	0	219	15.5

2002-2003 statistics:

GP	G	A	TP	+/-	PIM	PP	SH	GW	GT	S	PCT
79	28	57	85	+34	30	5	2	6	0	193	14.5

LAST SEASON

Tied for fourth in NHL in assists. Tied for 10th in NHL in points. Led team in assists and points. Tied for team lead in game-winning goals. Second on team in goals and shorthanded goals. Third on team in average ice time (20:52), plus-minus, and shooting percentage. Missed three games due to concussion. Played 1,000th NHL game. Scored 1,000th NHL point.

THE FINESSE GAME

Despite playing against other team's top lines almost every night, Modano managed to his post his highest point production since 1994. Is he that good an all-around player? Only one of the best in the game.

Like Steve Yzerman, Modano learned that shaving 20 points off his scoring resume was worth it to make his team better. Modano has been part of one Cup team and has been to the finals one other time.

Modano has terrific speed and skills, to go along with a strong physique. Modano has also gotten mentally tougher over the years. He has a work ethic that sets an example to everyone else on the Stars. When there is a lot of open ice, he's a thrilling player to watch. He has outstanding offensive instincts and great hands, and he is a smooth passer and a remarkable skater in all facets.

Modano makes other players around him better, which is the mark of a superstar. His speed and agility with the puck leave defenders mesmerized and open up ice for his linemates.

Modano has become a top penalty killer. His anticipation and quick hands help him intercept passes. By going to a straighter stickblade he has improved his face-offs, and become so reliable defensively that he is thrown onto the ice in the closing minutes of a period or game.

THE PHYSICAL GAME

Modano is not a physical player, but he isn't soft. He plays through injuries, and in his own way Modano is strong and tough — maybe not aggressive and feisty, but questions about his hockey courage have been quelled forever. He is a gamer.

THE INTANGIBLES

Modano responded to the challenge after the Stars missed the playoffs in 2002. He carried the scoring freight for Dallas in the postseason, but obviously missed his right wing Bill Guerin, who was forced to miss most of the playoffs with a thigh injury.

PROJECTION

Modano would have cracked the 90-point barrier we predicted for him last season if Guerin had stayed healthy. We'd expect nothing less than another 90-point season from him.

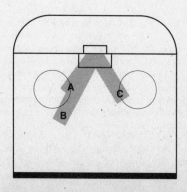

BRENDEN MORROW

Yrs. of NHL service: 4
Born: Carlyle, Sask.; Jan. 16, 1979
Position: left wing
Height: 5-11
Weight: 200
Uniform no.: 10
Shoots: left

Career statistics:

GP	G	A	TP	PIM
289	72	83	155	452

1999-2000 statistics:

GP	G	A	TP	+/-	PIM	PP	SH	GW	GT	S	PCT
64	14	19	33	+8	81	3	0	3	0	113	12.4

2000-2001 statistics:

GP	G	A	TP	+/-	PIM	PP	SH	GW	GT	S	PCT
82	20	24	44	+18	128	7	0	6	0	121	16.5

2001-2002 statistics:

GP	G	A	TP	+/-	PIM	PP	SH	GW	GT	S	PCT
72	17	18	35	+12	109	4	0	3	0	102	16.7

2002-2003 statistics:

GP	G	A	TP	+/-	PIM	PP	SH	GW	GT	S	PCT
71	21	22	43	+20	134	2	3	4	2	105	20.0

LAST SEASON

Led team in penalty minutes for third consecutive season. Tied for second in NHL in shooting percentage. Led team in shooting percentage for second consecutive season. Led team in shorthanded goals. Career high in goals. Missed nine games with chest injury. Missed one game with charley horse. Missed one game with groin injury.

THE FINESSE GAME

This is Dallas, so we have to start with defense. No kid in the Stars' system gets a chance to play with the big boys unless he has good defensive awareness and yes, it remained the same after the coaching change to Dave Tippett. Morrow was smart enough to understand that and built his game with a solid defensive foundation.

Now it's time to raise the roof. Morrow isn't very tall, but he is stocky and very strong on his skates and tough to knock off-balance. He is a very crafty, creative, and skilful puckhandler.

Morrow is a dedicated forechecker. Offensively, he will plunge into the slot and force a defender to take him down. In his own zone, he backchecks and positions himself well. He works well with the extra space on the power play and has a knack for scoring the big goal.

Morrow is growing along power forward lines, and he has a good veteran to learn from in Bill Guerin.

THE PHYSICAL GAME

Morrow isn't afraid to play with a little edge. He can be annoying, and he will often have other players chasing him and trying to slap him down like a bug.

He retaliates, too, and has added some serious muscle and strength to a good-sized frame.

THE INTANGIBLES

A hard worker, Morrow is a nice two-way forward who can have a long and steady career in his role. He wants to stay here and will do what it takes.

PROJECTION

Morrow will never put up spectacular numbers, but he works hard enough and is skilled enough to start getting into the 50-point range on a consistent basis.

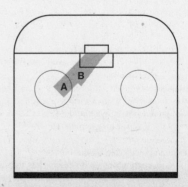

LYLE ODELEIN

Yrs. of NHL service: 13
Born: Quill Lake, Sask.; July 21, 1968
Position: right defense
Height: 5-11
Weight: 210
Uniform no.: 4
Shoots: left

Career statistics:

GP	G	A	TP	PIM
947	46	189	235	2178

1999-2000 statistics:

GP	G	A	TP	+/-	PIM	PP	SH	GW	GT	S	PCT
73	2	22	24	-9	123	1	0	1	0	89	2.2

2000-2001 statistics:

GP	G	A	TP	+/-	PIM	PP	SH	GW	GT	S	PCT
81	3	14	17	-16	118	1	0	0	0	104	2.9

2001-2002 statistics:

GP	G	A	TP	+/-	PIM	PP	SH	GW	GT	S	PCT
77	2	16	18	-28	93	0	0	0	0	86	2.3

2002-2003 statistics:

GP	G	A	TP	+/-	PIM	PP	SH	GW	GT	S	PCT
68	7	4	11	+7	82	0	0	0	0	78	9.0

LAST SEASON

Acquired by Dallas from Chicago on March 10, 2003, for Sami Helenious and future considerations. Missed 10 games with ankle injury. Missed four games due to coach's decision.

THE FINESSE GAME

Defense is Odelein's forte. He is very calm with the puck and able to wait until a player is on top of him, then carry the puck or find an open man. His skating is average at best, but he keeps himself out of trouble by playing a conservative game and not getting caught out of position. An attacker who comes into Odelein's piece of the ice will have to pay the price by getting through him.

Odelein's finesse skills are modest at best, but he has developed sufficient confidence to get involved in the attack if needed. He prefers to limit his contribution to shots from the point.

Odelein deserves credit for having moulded himself into more than an overachieving goon. Odelein remains an utterly fearless shot-blocker.

THE PHYSICAL GAME

Odelein is a banger, a limited player who knows what his limits are, stays within them, and plays effectively as a result. He's rugged and doesn't take chances. He takes the man at all times in front of the net and he plays tough. Heavy but not tall, he gives the impression of being a much bigger man. He will fight, but not very well.

Odelein can be taken off his game easily and gets caught up in yapping matches, which does his game no good. Odelein has become less of an impact player over the past several seasons.

THE INTANGIBLES

Odelein appeared in only two playoff games for the Stars. He became an unrestricted free agent after the season. He is a depth guy on a strong team and a third-pair defenseman at best on a worse one.

PROJECTION

Odelein will give you minutes on the ice and in the box. He won't give you points, but that's not what he's there for.

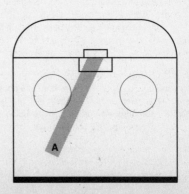

DARRYL SYDOR

Yrs. of NHL service: 11
Born: Edmonton, Alta.; May 13, 1972
Position: right defense
Height: 6-1
Weight: 205
Uniform no.: 5
Shoots: left

Career statistics:

GP	G	A	TP	PIM
863	82	323	405	598

1999-2000 statistics:

GP	G	A	TP	+/-	PIM	PP	SH	GW	GT	S	PCT
74	8	26	34	+6	32	5	0	1	0	132	6.1

2000-2001 statistics:

GP	G	A	TP	+/-	PIM	PP	SH	GW	GT	S	PCT
81	10	37	47	+5	34	8	0	1	0	140	7.1

2001-2002 statistics:

GP	G	A	TP	+/-	PIM	PP	SH	GW	GT	S	PCT
78	4	29	33	+3	50	2	0	0	0	183	2.2

2002-2003 statistics:

GP	G	A	TP	+/-	PIM	PP	SH	GW	GT	S	PCT
81	5	31	36	+22	40	2	0	1	0	132	3.8

LAST SEASON

Third on team in assists. Missed one game with shoulder injury.

THE FINESSE GAME

Sydor's offensive game can kick in at any time. He has a fine shot from the point and can handle power-play time. He has good sense for jumping into the attack and controls the puck ably when carrying it, though he doesn't always protect it well with his body. He makes nice outlet passes and has good vision of the ice. He can rush with the puck or play dump-and-chase. In his own zone, he has developed into a safe, reliable defender.

Sydor is yet another player whose game was offense-heavy before joining a defensively-conscious organization. As a result, he has become a more well-rounded player.

A very strong skater with balance and agility and excellent lateral movement, Sydor can accelerate well and changes directions easily. Not a dynamic defenseman, but better than average, he can be used up front during injury emergencies. Sydor has never been a spectacular player, but he's a pretty steady one.

THE PHYSICAL GAME

Sydor wants and needs to establish more of a physical presence. He is intense and has to be reined in. He has learned that sometimes going nowhere is better than trying to go everywhere. He competes hard and could still get stronger.

THE INTANGIBLES

Sydor is a top-four defenseman on one of the best defensive teams in the league, which is a worthy accomplishment. If the Stars don't re-sign Derian Hatcher, however, there may be trouble in Texas.

PROJECTION

Sydor should score in the 35-40 points range again.

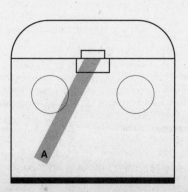

MARTY TURCO

Yrs. of NHL service: 3
Born: Sault Ste. Marie, Ont.; Aug. 13, 1975
Position: goaltender
Height: 5-11
Weight: 183
Uniform no.: 35
Catches: left

Career statistics:

GP	MIN	GA	SO	GAA	A	PIM
112	5988	185	12	1.85	3	38

2000-2001 statistics:

GP	MIN	GAA	W	L	T	SO	GA	S	SAPCT	PIM
26	1266	1.90	13	6	1	3	40	532	.925	12

2001-2002 statistics:

GP	MIN	GAA	W	L	T	SO	GA	S	SAPCT	PIM
31	1519	2.09	15	6	2	2	53	670	.921	10

2002-2003 statistics:

GP	MIN	GAA	W	L	T	SO	GA	S	SAPCT	PIM
55	3203	1.72	31	10	10	7	92	1359	.932	16

LAST SEASON

Finalist for 2003 Vezina Trophy. Named to NHL Second All-Star Team. Led NHL goalies in goals-against average with career best. Best GAA by NHL goalie in post-WWII era. Led NHL goalies in save percentage and assists (4). Tied for fifth among NHL goalies in shutouts. Missed 18 games with ankle injury. Missed one game due to NHL suspension.

THE PHYSICAL GAME

Turco is very aggressive and sometimes adventurous when playing the puck out of his net. He won't just play the puck or settle it down to leave it conservatively for a defenseman behind his net, but he is more often than not trying to make a play. He is not above trying to deke or out-stickhandle a forechecker. Sometimes this gets him into a predicament, but even if he gets burned, Turco is never shy about trying it again. Teams have to adjust their attack against Dallas, the way they have for years against New Jersey's Martin Brodeur, because of Turco's puckhandling ability.

Turco is wonderfully athletic but he does not rely on sheer reflex to stop pucks. He is always well-positioned for the first shot, square to the shooter, and doesn't have his feet moving at the wrong times. Turco plays as if he is in complete control of what is going on in the defensive zone. He is almost never panicky or lazy. Goaltending coach Andy Moog has taught Turco well about technique and patience.

Turco is fearsome in guarding his crease. He will machete away at the legs of opposing forwards, and served a one-game suspension last season for high-sticking Peter Forsberg.

THE MENTAL GAME

If Turco had any reservations about taking over the No. 1 role for Ed Belfour (who left as a free agent in 2002), he never let it show. His Dallas teammates picked up on that vibe and never missed a beat themselves, playing with confidence in front of him. Ron Tugnutt was an excellent choice to back up Turco, because he is very supportive of the No. 1 netminder.

Turco has a kind of cockiness that borders on arrogance. It shows in his body language and it's a great quality in a goaltender when he can back it up with saves, which Turco can.

THE INTANGIBLES

Turco lost three overtime games in the playoff series against Anaheim, and his psyche may suffer some damage from that. From what we've seen of Turco so far, however, it will just make him a more determined player this season. Turco was a restricted free agent in the off-season and will be earning much more than the $850,000 he was paid last season.

PROJECTION

Those stingy GAA and save percentage numbers will be hard to match, but Turco is no fluke. He should tally 30-35 wins.

PIERRE TURGEON

Yrs. of NHL service: 16
Born: Rouyn, Que.; Aug. 28, 1969
Position: center
Height: 6-1
Weight: 199
Uniform no.: 77
Shoots: left

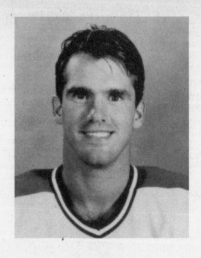

Career statistics:

GP	G	A	TP	PIM
1139	480	754	1234	390

1999-2000 statistics:

GP	G	A	TP	+/-	PIM	PP	SH	GW	GT	S	PCT
52	26	40	66	+30	8	8	0	3	0	139	18.7

2000-2001 statistics:

GP	G	A	TP	+/-	PIM	PP	SH	GW	GT	S	PCT
79	30	52	82	+14	37	11	0	6	1	171	17.5

2001-2002 statistics:

GP	G	A	TP	+/-	PIM	PP	SH	GW	GT	S	PCT
66	15	32	47	-4	16	7	0	1	1	121	12.4

2002-2003 statistics:

GP	G	A	TP	+/-	PIM	PP	SH	GW	GT	S	PCT
65	12	30	42	+4	18	3	0	5	1	76	15.8

LAST SEASON

Third on Stars in game-winning goals. Missed 14 games with ankle surgery. Missed three games with hip strain.

THE FINESSE GAME

Turgeon never seems to be looking at the puck, yet he is always in perfect control of it. Turgeon has a style unlike just about anyone else in the NHL. He's not a fast skater, but he can deke a defender or make a sneaky-Pete surprise pass. He is tough to defend against, because if you aren't aware of where he is on the ice or don't deny him the pass, he can kill a team with several moves.

Turgeon can slow or speed up the tempo of a game. He lacks breakout speed, but because he is slippery and can change speeds so smoothly, he's deceptive. His control with the puck down low is remarkable. He protects the puck well with the body and has good anticipation; he reads plays well and is patient with the puck. He is fairly good on draws.

Although best known for his playmaking, Turgeon has an excellent shot. He will curl out from behind the net with a wrist shot, shoot off the fly from the right wing, (his preferred side of the ice) or stand off to the side of the net on a power play and reach for a redirection of a point shot. He doesn't have a bazooka shot, but he uses quick, accurate wrist and snap shots. He has to create odd-man rushes — this is when he is at his finest.

THE PHYSICAL GAME

Turegon isn't very aggressive or big, and injuries seem to have taken the heart out of him. He doesn't compete the way he once did.

THE INTANGIBLES

Dallas signed free agent Scott Young in 2002 to try to revive Turgeon. While Young brought a spark back to his own game, he couldn't help Turgeon's. Turgeon was put on waivers by Dallas with no takers and became an unrestricted free agent after the season.

PROJECTION

Turgeon's years in Dallas were among the worst of his career. No matter where he ends up, we would expect little more than 15 goals, 50 points out of him.

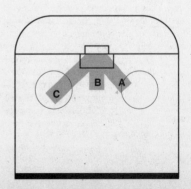

SCOTT YOUNG

Yrs. of NHL service: 14
Born: Clinton, Mass.; Oct. 1, 1967
Position: right wing
Height: 6-1
Weight: 200
Uniform no.: 48
Shoots: right

Career statistics:

GP	G	A	TP	PIM
1049	316	376	692	382

1999-2000 statistics:

GP	G	A	TP	+/-	PIM	PP	SH	GW	GT	S	PCT
75	24	15	39	+12	18	6	1	7	1	244	9.8

2000-2001 statistics:

GP	G	A	TP	+/-	PIM	PP	SH	GW	GT	S	PCT
81	40	33	73	+15	30	14	3	7	1	321	12.5

2001-2002 statistics:

GP	G	A	TP	+/-	PIM	PP	SH	GW	GT	S	PCT
67	19	22	41	+11	26	5	0	1	0	210	9.1

2002-2003 statistics:

GP	G	A	TP	+/-	PIM	PP	SH	GW	GT	S	PCT
79	23	19	42	+24	30	5	1	4	1	237	9.7

LAST SEASON

Second on team in shots. Missed two games due to NHL suspension. Missed one game with hip injury.

THE FINESSE GAME

Young is a hockey machine. He has a very heavy shot that surprises a lot of goalies, and he loves to fire it off the wing. He can also one-time the puck low on the face-off, or he'll battle for pucks and tips in front of the net. He's keen to score and always goes to the net with his stick down, ready for the puck, though he is not a great finisher. Young has a bit of tunnel vision, and doesn't really see his teammates or use them as well as he might. But he has tremendous confidence in his ability to score.

With all of that in mind, his defensive awareness is even more impressive. He reads plays in all zones equally well and has good anticipation. If Young is not scoring, he will be doing a lot of the little things that help make his team better.

Young is a fast skater, which, combined with his reads, makes him a sound forechecker. He will often outrace defensemen to get pucks and avoid icings, and his speed allows him to recover when he gets over-zealous in the attacking zone.

THE PHYSICAL GAME

Young's lone drawback is that he is not a physical player. He will do what he has to do in battles along the boards in the defensive zone, but he's more of a defensive force with quickness and hand skills. He's not a pure grinder, but will bump and get in the way. He drew his suspension last season for high-sticking Jaroslav Spacek of the Columbus Blue Jackets.

THE INTANGIBLES

Young is the kind of player who wanted to prove the Stars didn't make a mistake by signing him to a free agent deal in 2002. He emerged as one of the team's unsung heroes last season. He is a character person as well as an ultra-reliable performer. Players with great wheels like Young tend to last a long time, so expect him to flash his ability for another season or two.

PROJECTION

Young fell just two goals shy of the 25 we projected for him in a big bounce-back season. We would expect another 20-25.

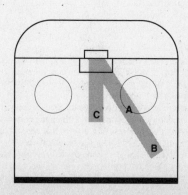

SERGEI ZUBOV

Yrs. of NHL service: 11
Born: Moscow, Russia; July 22, 1970
Position: right defense
Height: 6-1
Weight: 200
Uniform no.: 56
Shoots: right

Career statistics:

GP	G	A	TP	PIM
779	116	449	565	233

1999-2000 statistics:

GP	G	A	TP	+/-	PIM	PP	SH	GW	GT	S	PCT
77	9	33	42	-2	18	3	1	3	0	179	5.0

2000-2001 statistics:

GP	G	A	TP	+/-	PIM	PP	SH	GW	GT	S	PCT
79	10	41	51	+22	24	6	0	1	1	173	5.8

2001-2002 statistics:

GP	G	A	TP	+/-	PIM	PP	SH	GW	GT	S	PCT
80	12	32	44	-4	22	8	0	2	0	198	6.1

2002-2003 statistics:

GP	G	A	TP	+/-	PIM	PP	SH	GW	GT	S	PCT
82	11	44	55	+21	26	8	0	2	0	158	7.0

LAST SEASON

Fourth among NHL defensemen in points. Led team defensemen in points for sixth consecutive season. Second on team in average ice time (25:50), assists, and points. Third on team in power-play goals. One of three Stars to appear in all 82 games.

THE FINESSE GAME

There have probably been coaches who would have liked to wring more emotion out of Zubov in his NHL career. It hasn't happened yet, and it's not about to. Zubov is as coldly analytical a top defenseman as you can find. He plays the percentages, not the numbers of the jerseys coming at him. To Zubov, hockey is chess and math, angles and probabilities.

Zubov is not considered one of the game's elite defensemen, possibly because of the lack of passion that so many other greats share. He is just a notch below those Norris Trophy winners, though, because of assets such as vision, intelligence, and skill.

Zubov never looks down at the puck when he's skating with it, but always knows where the puck is. Zubov is at least as good as the majority of NHL forwards on the breakaway. He has a lifelong habit of waiting for the best percentage shot, though, and has often frustrated his teammates by passing up scoring chances. When the reasonable option is to dump and chase, Zubov would rather hang on to the puck at the blueline and try to make a play, which leads to the majority of his turnovers.

Zubov will occasionally thwart his teammates when he slows things down with the puck on a rush or breakout while the rest of the team has already taken off like racehorses. He has strong lateral acceleration, but he is also educated enough to keep his skating stride for stride with the wing trying to beat him to the outside. So many other defensemen speed up a couple of strides, then try to slow their men with stick-checks. Zubov will use his reach, superior body positioning, or his agility to force the play and compel the puck carrier to make a decision. But he doesn't always search out the right man or, when he does, he doesn't always eliminate the right man. A team has to live with that because Zubov's offensive upside is huge.

THE PHYSICAL GAME

Zubov is not physical, but he is solidly built and will take a hit to make a play. He can give a team a lot of minutes and not wear down physically.

His boyhood idol was Viacheslav Fetisov, and that role model should give you some idea of Zubov's style. He gets his body in the way with his great skating, then strips the puck when the attacker finds no path to the net. He doesn't initiate much, but doesn't mind getting hit to make a play.

THE INTANGIBLES

Mentally, Zubov will still lose his focus and is capable of the most astounding giveaways. He can often atone with a terrific offensive play, but his lapses keep him from being rated among the league's best. There will be much more pressure placed on Zubov this season since the Stars lost Derian Hatcher to free agency.

PROJECTION

As the Stars' reigning offensive defenseman, Zubov should again account for close to 60 points.

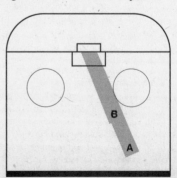

DETROIT RED WINGS

Players' Statistics 2001-2002

POS.	NO.	PLAYER	GP	G	A	PTS	+/-	PIM	PP	SH	GW	GT	S	PCT
C	91	SERGEI FEDOROV	80	36	47	83	15	52	10	2	11		281	12.8
R	17	BRETT HULL	82	37	39	76	11	22	12	1	4	1	262	14.1
L	14	BRENDAN SHANAHAN	78	30	38	68	5	103	13		6		260	11.5
D	5	NICKLAS LIDSTROM	82	18	44	62	40	38	8	1	4		175	10.3
C	13	PAVEL DATSYUK	64	12	39	51	20	16	1		1	1	82	14.6
D	23	MATHIEU SCHNEIDER	78	16	34	50	2	73	11		1		199	8.0
L	40	*HENRIK ZETTERBERG	79	22	22	44	6	8	5	1	4		135	16.3
C	8	IGOR LARIONOV	74	10	33	43	-7	48	5		3		50	20.0
L	96	TOMAS HOLMSTROM	74	20	20	40	11	62	12		2		109	18.3
L	18	KIRK MALTBY	82	14	23	37	17	91		4	1		116	12.1
C	33	KRIS DRAPER	82	14	21	35	6	82		1	2		142	9.9
L	20	LUC ROBITAILLE	81	11	20	31	4	50	3			1	148	7.4
D	15	JASON WOOLLEY	76	6	20	26	11	51	1		2		81	7.4
R	25	DARREN MCCARTY	73	13	9	22	10	138	1		2		129	10.1
D	11	MATHIEU DANDENAULT	74	4	15	19	25	64	1				74	5.4
D	24	CHRIS CHELIOS	66	2	17	19	4	78		1	1		92	2.2
C	21	BOYD DEVEREAUX	61	3	9	12	4	16			1		72	4.2
D	55	*DMITRI BYKOV	71	2	10	12	1	43	1				58	3.4
D	27	PATRICK BOILEAU	25	2	6	8	8	14			1		18	11.1
C	19	STEVE YZERMAN	16	2	6	8	6	8	1		1		13	15.4
C	29	*JASON WILLIAMS	16	3	3	6	3	2	1			1	20	15.0
D	2	JIRI FISCHER	15	1	5	6	0	16					19	5.3
D	3	*JESSE WALLIN	32		1	1	-2	19					23	
C	23	STACY ROEST	2				0						2	
G	31	CURTIS JOSEPH	61				0	4						
G	34	MANNY LEGACE	25				0	2						

GP = games played; G = goals; A = assists; PTS = points; +/- = goals-for minus goals-against while player is on ice; PIM = penalties in minutes; PP = power-play goals; SH = shorthanded goals; GW = game-winning goals; GT = game-tying goals; S = no. of shots; PCT = percentage of goals to shots; * = rookie

CHRIS CHELIOS

Yrs. of NHL service: 19
Born: Chicago, Ill.; Jan. 25, 1962
Position: right defense
Height: 6-1
Weight: 190
Uniform no.: 24
Shoots: right

Career statistics:

GP	G	A	TP	PIM
1326	176	717	893	2634

1999-2000 statistics:

GP	G	A	TP	+/-	PIM	PP	SH	GW	GT	S	PCT
81	3	31	34	+48	103	0	0	0	0	135	2.2

2000-2001 statistics:

GP	G	A	TP	+/-	PIM	PP	SH	GW	GT	S	PCT
24	0	3	3	+4	45	0	0	0	0	26	0.0

2001-2002 statistics:

GP	G	A	TP	+/-	PIM	PP	SH	GW	GT	S	PCT
79	6	33	39	+40	126	1	0	1	0	128	4.7

2002-2003 statistics:

GP	G	A	TP	+/-	PIM	PP	SH	GW	GT	S	PCT
66	2	17	19	+4	78	0	1	1	0	92	2.2

LAST SEASON

Second on team in average ice time (24:14). Missed 14 games with leg injuries. Missed one game with broken finger.

THE FINESSE GAME

Whatever the team needs, Chelios will bleed to give. He can become a top offensive defenseman, pinching boldly at every opportunity. Or he can create offense off the rush, make a play through the neutral zone or quarterback the power play from the point. He has a good, low, hard slap shot. He is not afraid to skate in deep, where he can handle the puck well and use a snap shot or wrist shot with a quick release.

If defense is needed, Chelios will rule in his own zone. He is extremely confident and poised with the puck and doesn't overhandle it, though he has slowed down a step. He wants to get the puck away from his net by the most expedient means possible. He is aggressive in forcing the puck carrier to make a decision by stepping up. He also steps up in the neutral zone to break up plays with his stick.

Chelios is an instinctive player. When he is on his game, he reacts and makes plays few other defensemen can. When he struggles, which is seldom, he is back on his heels. He tries to do other people's jobs and becomes undisciplined.

Chelios has excellent anticipation and is a strong penalty killer. He's a mobile, smooth skater with good lateral movement. He is seldom beaten one-on-one, and he's even tough facing a two-on-one. In his mind, he can do anything. He usually does.

THE PHYSICAL GAME

At age 42, Chelios should not be handling the ice time and demands of a No. 2 defenseman. That he is still able to do so, and perform at such a high caliber, gives you an idea of how dedicated Chelios is to his conditioning. Chelios is not that big but plays like an enormous defenseman. He is mean, tough and physical, strong and solid on his skates, and fearless.

THE INTANGIBLES

Chelios is at the hockey age where injuries are tougher to overcome. Expect him to spend a lot of time on the sidelines again this season.

PROJECTION

Chelios can no longer afford to play the game full-throttle, but he doesn't know any other way. A modest expectation would be 60 games played and 25-30 points in what will probably be this warrior's final season.

PAVEL DATSYUK

Yrs. of NHL service: 2
Born: Sverdlovsk, Russia; July 20, 1978
Position: center
Height: 5-11
Weight: 180
Uniform no.: 13
Shoots: left

Career statistics:

GP	G	A	TP	PIM
134	23	63	86	20

2001-2002 statistics:

GP	G	A	TP	+/-	PIM	PP	SH	GW	GT	S	PCT
70	11	24	35	+4	4	2	0	1	0	79	13.9

2002-2003 statistics:

GP	G	A	TP	+/-	PIM	PP	SH	GW	GT	S	PCT
64	12	39	51	+20	16	1	0	1	1	82	14.6

LAST SEASON

Third on team in plus-minus and shooting percentage. Tied for third on team in assists. Missed 18 games with sprained knee.

THE FINESSE GAME

Datsyuk is just the kind of young player the Red Wings needed to inject some youth into a creaky roster. He is one of the younger generation of Russian stars who have come along in the post-Viktor Tikhonov era but still possess the qualities of intelligence and puck control.

Datsyuk is a terrific skater. He has the best lateral movement on the team, and when the team includes forwards such as Sergei Fedorov and Steve Yzerman, that is high praise. He is a great one-on-one player, and has the kind of dynamic moves that lift fans out of their seats. Datsyuk can beat players one-on-one. If they are mesmerized by the puck and don't play the body, Datsyuk will burn them.

He has the kind of hand skills that can make opposing players look silly. He is patient and has great hockey vision. He is dangerous with the puck in any area of the ice.

Datsyuk is a better playmaker than scorer. He had a 1:3 ratio between his goals and assists, and didn't take enough shots. This might have something to do with playing with a winger who has the goal-scoring stature of Brett Hull. Datsyuk will need to develop more confidence in his own scoring ability to take his game to the next level. Datsyuk reminds scouts of a smaller and (only slightly) less cerebral Igor Larionov.

Datsyuk can develop into an effective penalty killer. His defensive game needs polish. He has worked on playing a smarter positional game and also needs to improve his face-offs.

THE PHYSICAL GAME

Datsyuk is on the small side and doesn't have much of a physical presence. He needs to get stronger to survive in the NHL.

THE INTANGIBLES

Datsyuk recovered well from his midseason knee injury and was part of a successful line with Hull and rookie Henrik Zetterberg after the All-Star break. He is modest, coachable, and well-liked on a veteran team.

PROJECTION

We predicted a top-six role and a 50-point season for Datsyuk last year. If he hadn't been injured, he would have scored closer to 60, which is what we'll be looking for from him this season.

JIRI FISCHER

Yrs. of NHL service: 4
Born: Horovice, Czech Republic; July 31, 1980
Position: left defense
Height: 6-5
Weight: 225
Uniform no.: 2
Shoots: left

Career statistics:

GP	G	A	TP	PIM
202	4	29	33	187

1999-2000 statistics:

GP	G	A	TP	+/-	PIM	PP	SH	GW	GT	S	PCT
52	0	8	8	+1	45	0	0	0	0	41	0.0

2000-2001 statistics:

GP	G	A	TP	+/-	PIM	PP	SH	GW	GT	S	PCT
55	1	8	9	+3	59	0	0	0	0	64	1.6

2001-2002 statistics:

GP	G	A	TP	+/-	PIM	PP	SH	GW	GT	S	PCT
80	2	8	10	+17	67	0	0	1	0	103	1.9

2002-2003 statistics:

GP	G	A	TP	+/-	PIM	PP	SH	GW	GT	S	PCT
15	1	5	6	0	16	0	0	0	0	19	5.3

LAST SEASON

Missed 67 games due to knee injury and surgery.

THE FINESSE GAME

For such a tall skater, Fischer doesn't look a bit gangly. He is strong on his skates and has a long stride. It doesn't take him long to get into stride, either. He is well-coordinated and agile in his turns.

Fischer has a low panic point and is confident with the puck. Soft hands for giving or receiving make him a good passer. He has some faith in his ability to skate the puck out and is willing to get involved in the rush, though he can be expected to focus on the defensive part of the game as he continues to break in.

Fischer will get some second-unit power-play and penalty-killing stints. His reach makes him a natural shorthanded threat, since he takes up a lot of ice. He has a decent point shot, though his release isn't quick. One-on-one he is just about impossible to best because a skater has to go a long way to get around him.

Fischer has often drawn comparisons to Rob Blake, but he may not have Blake's scoring touch.

THE PHYSICAL GAME

Fischer is very tall but not thick or heavy. He needs to develop more muscle for the battles along the wall and in front of the net. He can use his long reach to wrap up and neutralize an attacker. He has a latent mean streak. Opponents will quickly learn not to take liberties with him. Fischer works hard and can handle a healthy dose of ice time. If he comes back healthy, he will take a lot of the burden off of some of Detroit's older defensemen.

THE INTANGIBLES

Fischer will be returning from reconstructive knee surgery, which means it may take the first quarter of the season for him to recover the conditioning and confidence he needs to compete as one of Detroit's top two defensemen. He is still a work in progress.

PROJECTION

Fischer does not have a lot of offensive upside. Twenty points would be a peak year.

DOMINIK HASEK

Yrs. of NHL service: 11
Born: Pardubice, Czech Republic; Jan. 29, 1965
Position: goaltender
Height: 5-11
Weight: 180
Uniform no.: 39
Catches: left

Career statistics:

GP	MIN	GA	SO	GAA	A	PIM
581	33745	1254	61	2.23	14	112

1999-2000 statistics:

GP	MIN	GAA	W	L	T	SO	GA	S	SAPCT	PIM
35	2066	2.21	15	11	6	3	76	937	.919	12

2000-2001 statistics:

GP	MIN	GAA	W	L	T	SO	GA	S	SAPCT	PIM
67	3904	2.11	37	24	4	11	137	1726	.921	22

2001-2002 statistics:

GP	MIN	GAA	W	L	T	SO	GA	S	SAPCT	PIM
64	3872	2.17	41	15	8	5	140	1654	.915	8

2002-2003 statistics:

Did not play in NHL

LAST SEASON

Did not play in NHL.

THE PHYSICAL GAME

Nobody in the NHL has worse technique or better leg reflexes than Hasek. His foot speed is simply tremendous. He wanders and flops and sprawls, but he stops the puck. Usually, what Hasek sees, he stops, and to him the puck seems to be moving more slowly than it does for most other goalies. He tracks it from the shooter's stick into his glove or body, and he always seems to be in control, even when he's flopping like a trout.

Hasek is adept at directing his rebounds away from onrushing attackers. Hasek instructs his defensemen to get out of the way so he can see the shot.

Hasek plays deeper in his net than most modern-day goalies. It's a carryover from his European training and there isn't much sense in mucking with it now. His puckhandling is subpar.

Hasek has the single most bizarre habit of any NHL goalie we've seen. In scrambles around the net, he abandons his stick entirely and grabs the puck with his blocker hand. Opponents will moan that he seems to drop the stick in the way of a skater battling for the loose puck around the crease. Quite a coincidence.

THE MENTAL GAME

Hasek is competitive and unflappable. He never, ever gives up on a puck until it's in the net. His unorthodox style takes some getting used to, but at least most of the Red Wings have seen it before (and newcomer Derian Hatcher played with Ed Belfour, who isn't exactly by-the-book).

Hasek is cagey. When he dives, when he blows up over an opponent's nudge, it's all calculated. He doesn't mind taking penalties around the net if it makes an attacker more wary. He gets away with a lot of obstruction calls because he is so poor at handling hard-arounds that he just throws a body-block at a forechecker behind the net instead, then looks deeply offended when he is bumped.

THE INTANGIBLES

After a year off, and after winning his Cup in 2002, will Hasek return with the same fire? That's the $8 million question.

PROJECTION

Detroit is so solid defensively and is going to be so ticked off after being bumped off in the first round of the playoffs that Hasek should be good for 35-38 wins.

DERIAN HATCHER

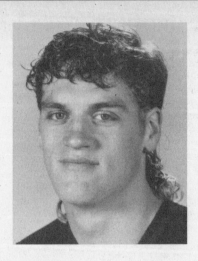

Yrs. of NHL service: 12
Born: Sterling Heights, Mich.; June 4, 1972
Position: left defense
Height: 6-5
Weight: 235
Uniform no.: 2
Shoots: left

Career statistics:

GP	G	A	TP	PIM
827	71	223	294	1380

1999-2000 statistics:

GP	G	A	TP	+/-	PIM	PP	SH	GW	GT	S	PCT
57	2	22	24	+6	68	0	0	0	0	90	2.2

2000-2001 statistics:

GP	G	A	TP	+/-	PIM	PP	SH	GW	GT	S	PCT
80	2	21	23	+5	77	1	0	2	0	97	2.1

2001-2002 statistics:

GP	G	A	TP	+/-	PIM	PP	SH	GW	GT	S	PCT
80	4	21	25	+12	87	1	0	0	2	111	3.6

2002-2003 statistics:

GP	G	A	TP	+/-	PIM	PP	SH	GW	GT	S	PCT
82	8	22	30	+37	106	1	1	2	0	159	5.0

LAST SEASON

Signed as free agent by Detroit on July 3, 2003. Finalist for 2003 Norris Trophy. Named to NHL Second All-Star Team. Fifth in NHL in plus-minus. Led Stars in average ice time (25:51). Second on team in plus-minus. Third on team in penalty minutes. One of three Stars to appear in all 82 games.

THE FINESSE GAME

Hatcher is among the game's most underrated defensemen, although he is likely to get more notice now that he has signed a big contract with Detroit. He plays in all key situations and has developed confidence in his decision-making process. His skating is labored, so he lets the play come to him. He is sturdy and well-balanced, though the fewer strides he has to take the better.

He has very good hands for a big man, and has a good head for the game. Hatcher is fairly effective from the point on the power play — not because he has a big, booming slap shot, but because he has a good wrist shot and will get the puck on net quickly. He will join the rush eagerly once he gets into gear (his first few strides are sluggish), and he handles the puck nicely. Hatcher will not get suckered into playing too deep in the attacking zone often, as it's a chore for him to recover defensively.

Hatcher plays hard in every zone, every night. His skills are just a shade below elite level but he takes steps forward every season as a leader. He is a character player, one his teammates look to for setting the tempo and seizing control of a game.

THE PHYSICAL GAME

This man is a big force. Hatcher has a mean streak when provoked and is a punishing hitter who relishes the physical aspect of the game. But he is also smart enough to realize that he's a target and opponents want to take him off his game. It's a huge detriment to his team when he is in the box, and not just because he is one of their key penalty killers. He plays physically every night and demands respect and room. He's fearless. He's also a big horse and eats up all the ice time a coach wants to give him. The more work he gets, the better.

THE INTANGIBLES

Hatcher is a Michigan boy and that may have played a part in his decision to sign with his favorite boyhood team. We also suspect a five-year, $30 million deal was an effective lure. He joins a defense in Detroit loaded with studs: Nicklas Lidstrom, Chris Chelios, Mathieu Schneider, Jiri Fischer, and now Hatcher.

PROJECTION

Hatcher is the defenseman you want on your team when you have to win a clutch game. He can provide 30 points and invaluable leadership.

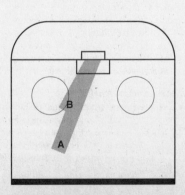

TOMAS HOLMSTROM

Yrs. of NHL service: 7
Born: Pitea, Sweden; Jan 23, 1973
Position: left wing
Height: 6-0
Weight: 200
Uniform no.: 96
Shoots: left

Career statistics:

GP	G	A	TP	PIM
474	81	125	206	349

1999-2000 statistics:

GP	G	A	TP	+/-	PIM	PP	SH	GW	GT	S	PCT
72	13	22	35	+4	43	4	0	1	0	71	18.3

2000-2001 statistics:

GP	G	A	TP	+/-	PIM	PP	SH	GW	GT	S	PCT
73	16	24	40	-12	40	9	0	2	0	74	21.6

2001-2002 statistics:

GP	G	A	TP	+/-	PIM	PP	SH	GW	GT	S	PCT
69	8	18	26	-12	58	6	0	1	0	79	10.1

2002-2003 statistics:

GP	G	A	TP	+/-	PIM	PP	SH	GW	GT	S	PCT
74	20	20	40	+11	62	12	0	2	0	109	18.3

LAST SEASON

Led team in shooting percentage. Tied for second on team in power-play goals. Career high in goals. Missed five games with chest injuries. Missed three games with flu.

THE FINESSE GAME

Holmstrom has a toothless grin and a gutsy game. He plays in the hard five feet outside the crease, sometimes inside it, and drives goalies wild. He has such a good shooting percentage because he takes most of his scoring chances from inside a very tight perimeter.

With the desire and work ethic of every low draft pick to ever make it to the NHL (257th in 1994), Holmstrom is a rough-cut stone. That makes him even more important, because he provides an element of grit along the wall and in front of the net on nights when the rest of his high-profile teammates might get the urge to play too fancy.

This Swede has style, too, and can score in the clutch. He has an excellent close-range shot. If anything, he needs to shoot more. He is also a smart passer. Holmstrom doesn't have great hands but he doesn't quit digging for loose pucks. He is a power-play mainstay because of his ability to screen and distract defensemen.

Holmstrom is usually trapped so deep inside the offensive zone that his teammates are left playing a man down at the other end of the ice. Last season he worked hard to improve his defensive awareness.

THE PHYSICAL GAME

Stocky and strong on his skates, Holmstrom can take a bloody pounding and get right back in the trenches to position himself for a pass. What is most impressive is how he is able to provoke the attacks without getting penalized himself. He rarely takes a bad penalty. The fact that he bounces back with a jack-o'-lantern smile is especially infuriating to opponents.

THE INTANGIBLES

Holmstrom is usually at his best in the postseason, although none of the Red Wings had anything to celebrate after their first-round sweep last year. He was better than usual during the regular season, and was probably Detroit's unsung hero.

PROJECTION

Don't expect much more than 15-20 goals from Holmstrom in the regular season. His value increases dramatically in April and May.

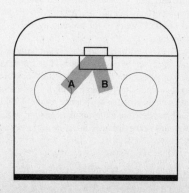

BRETT HULL

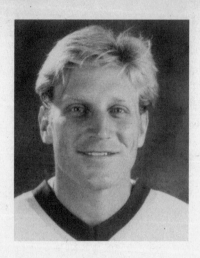

Yrs. of NHL service: 16
Born: Belleville, Ont.; Aug. 9, 1964
Position: right wing
Height: 5-11
Weight: 203
Uniform no.: 17
Shoots: right

Career statistics:

GP	G	A	TP	PIM
1183	716	606	1322	446

1999-2000 statistics:

GP	G	A	TP	+/-	PIM	PP	SH	GW	GT	S	PCT
79	24	35	59	-21	43	11	0	3	0	223	10.8

2000-2001 statistics:

GP	G	A	TP	+/-	PIM	PP	SH	GW	GT	S	PCT
79	39	40	79	+10	18	11	0	8	1	219	17.8

2001-2002 statistics:

GP	G	A	TP	+/-	PIM	PP	SH	GW	GT	S	PCT
82	30	33	63	+18	35	7	1	4	2	247	12.1

2002-2003 statistics:

GP	G	A	TP	+/-	PIM	PP	SH	GW	GT	S	PCT
82	37	39	76	+11	22	12	1	4	1	262	14.1

LAST SEASON

Led team in goals. Second on team in points and shots. Tied for second on team in assists, power-play goals, and shorthanded goals. One of four Red Wings to appear in all 82 games.

THE FINESSE GAME

All those years when Hull was whining about being defensively handcuffed in Dallas probably added several lucrative years to his career by making Hull a better all-around player. Make no mistake, though, scoring goals is what Hull still does best and enjoys most. He remains a shooter first. His shot is seldom blocked — he gets it away so quickly the defense doesn't have time to react — and his shots have tremendous velocity, especially his one-timers from the tops of the circles in.

Hull is always working to get himself in position for a pass but doesn't look like he's working. He sort of drifts into open ice and before a defender can react, he is firing off any kind of shot accurately. He usually moves to his off-wing on the power play. He can play the point but is a better asset down low.

An underrated playmaker who can thread a pass through traffic right onto the tape, Hull will find the open man because he has soft hands and good vision. When the opponent overplays him, he makes smart decisions about whether to shoot or pass.

Hull plays well in all three zones and has excellent instincts that serve him well in whatever he desires to apply them.

THE PHYSICAL GAME

Hull is compact and when he wants to hit, it's a solid check. He was healthy again last season, and that makes a huge difference in his play. He is not as physically involved as he was when he was scoring goals at an absurd rate, but he will bump people.

THE INTANGIBLES

This will probably be the last hurrah for Hull, who will want to go out with a bang. He may not have the support he's used to, however, given the unsettled contract situation with Steve Yzerman and Sergei Fedorov going to the Anaheim Mighty Ducks in the off-season.

PROJECTION

Hull is still a big-time player. We would expect 55-60 points.

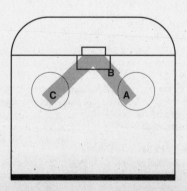

CURTIS JOSEPH

Yrs. of NHL service: 13
Born: Keswick, Ont.; Apr. 29, 1967
Position: goaltender
Height: 5-11
Weight: 190
Uniform no.: 31
Catches: left

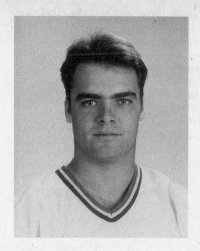

Career statistics:

GP	MIN	GA	SO	GAA	A	PIM
767	44688	2056	41	2.76	29	90

1999-2000 statistics:

GP	MIN	GAA	W	L	T	SO	GA	S	SAPCT	PIM
63	3801	2.49	36	20	7	4	158	1854	.915	14

2000-2001 statistics:

GP	MIN	GAA	W	L	T	SO	GA	S	SAPCT	PIM
68	4100	2.39	33	27	8	6	163	1907	.915	8

2001-2002 statistics:

GP	MIN	GAA	W	L	T	SO	GA	S	SAPCT	PIM
51	3065	2.23	29	17	5	4	114	1210	.906	10

2002-2003 statistics:

GP	MIN	GAA	W	L	T	SO	GA	S	SAPCT	PIM
61	3566	2.49	34	19	6	5	148	1676	.912	4

LAST SEASON

Tied for fifth in NHL in wins.

THE PHYSICAL GAME

Nothing Joseph does is by the book. He always looks unorthodox and off-balance, but he is one of those hybrid goalies whose success can't be argued with.

Joseph positions himself well, angling out to challenge the shooter. He is one of the best goalies against the breakaway in the NHL. He goes to his knees quickly, but bounces back to his skates fast for the rebound. He tends to keep rebounds in front of him. His glove hand is outstanding.

A strong, if bizarre, stickhandler, Joseph has to move his hands on the stick, putting the butt-end into his catching glove and lowering his blocker. His favourite move is a weird backhand whip off the boards. He is a good skater who moves out of his cage confidently to handle the puck.

His lateral movement is flawed. He uses his stick to harass anyone who camps on his doorstep. He's not Billy Smith, but he's aggressive with his whacks. Joseph gets into technical slumps, which seem to sprout from fatigue. You can judge this by the way he starts to play too deep in his net.

THE MENTAL GAME

Detroit did a good job of pacing Joseph and keeping him to under 65 games. Joseph should have benefited from that and been a better and more relaxed goalie, but it seemed to have the opposite effect. Did he see backup Manny Legace as a threat?

THE INTANGIBLES

Joseph didn't bring Detroit the Cup after his free-agent signing, so the Wings went out and sweet-talked Dominik Hasek out of retirement. That meant Joseph would be on the move during the summer, or else he would become an $8 million backup. Contenders should beware, since Joseph has proven himself only as a good goalie on bad teams.

PROJECTION

Whoever ends up with Joseph will need to ration his starts. It's impossible to guess how many wins he'll get without knowing where he is going to play.

NICKLAS LIDSTROM

Yrs. of NHL service: 12
Born: Vasteras, Sweden; Apr. 28, 1970
Position: left defense
Height: 6-2
Weight: 185
Uniform no.: 5
Shoots: left

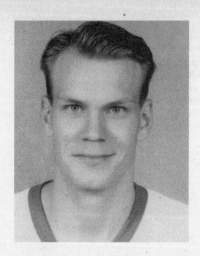

Career statistics:

GP	G	A	TP	PIM
935	163	525	688	258

1999-2000 statistics:

GP	G	A	TP	+/-	PIM	PP	SH	GW	GT	S	PCT
81	20	53	73	+19	18	9	4	3	0	218	9.2

2000-2001 statistics:

GP	G	A	TP	+/-	PIM	PP	SH	GW	GT	S	PCT
82	15	56	71	+9	18	8	0	0	0	272	5.5

2001-2002 statistics:

GP	G	A	TP	+/-	PIM	PP	SH	GW	GT	S	PCT
78	9	50	59	+13	20	6	0	0	0	215	4.2

2002-2003 statistics:

GP	G	A	TP	+/-	PIM	PP	SH	GW	GT	S	PCT
82	18	44	62	+40	38	8	1	4	0	175	10.3

LAST SEASON

Won 2003 Norris Trophy. Finalist for 2003 Lady Byng Trophy. Named to NHL First All-Star Team. Led NHL in average ice time (29:20). Third among NHL defensemen in points. Third in NHL in plus-minus. Led team defensemen in points. Led team in plus-minus. Second on team in assists. Tied for third on team in game-winning goals. One of four Red Wings to appear in all 82 games.

THE FINESSE GAME

Lidstrom is an excellent skater with good vision of the ice. He prefers to look for the breakout pass, rather than carry the puck, and he has a superb point shot that stays low and accurate. His work at the point on the power play has improved significantly through the years. He is as good as anyone in the league at sensing bodies going down to block his shots and still managing to somehow get the puck through them.

Lidstrom's rink management is solid, his decision-making is almost flawless, and his passing — especially to set up one-timers — is tape-to-tape.

Defensively, he uses exceptional anticipation to position himself perfectly. He is almost impossible to beat one-on-one, even two-on-one, in open ice. He neatly breaks up passes with a quick stick. He kills penalties and willingly blocks shots. He also plays either side — an underrated asset — and is dependable in the closing minutes of a tight period or game.

THE PHYSICAL GAME

Lidstrom truly perseveres. He does not take the body much and depends on his wits more than hard hits. Something he learned early in his career was if you aren't a punishing physical defenseman, then you need to play a sound positional game to excel in the NHL.

With body positioning and stick positioning, he leaves opposing puck carriers no place to go and no alternative but to give up the puck — usually to him. He finds a way to tie up the opponent's stick. He has stepped up his physical play. He's not a bruising hitter, but puck carriers are wary of him because he makes them pay a price. He won't be intimidated; many teams have tried and failed with that tactic.

He has little fear of contact and will accept a hit to make a play. It is a tribute to his style that he can play with quiet toughness and still be a Lady Byng candidate. This is how the game is meant to be played.

Lidstrom has added enough muscle to become a wiry, strong athlete who can handle an astounding amount of quality ice time. He wastes little energy and his innate talent maximizes his stamina.

THE INTANGIBLES

He is simply one of the best who has ever played this position. The Norris Trophy win was his third.

PROJECTION

Lidstrom has consistently made noises about going home to play in Sweden, so there is a good chance this will be his last season in the NHL. We expect him to bow out with another 60-point, Norris Trophy-caliber performance.

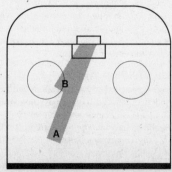

KIRK MALTBY

Yrs. of NHL service: 10
Born: Guelph, Ont.; Dec. 22, 1972
Position: left wing
Height: 6-0
Weight: 180
Uniform no.: 18
Shoots: right

Career statistics:

GP	G	A	TP	PIM
638	88	90	178	565

1999-2000 statistics:

GP	G	A	TP	+/-	PIM	PP	SH	GW	GT	S	PCT
41	6	8	14	+1	24	0	2	1	0	71	8.5

2000-2001 statistics:

GP	G	A	TP	+/-	PIM	PP	SH	GW	GT	S	PCT
79	12	7	19	+16	22	1	3	3	0	119	10.1

2001-2002 statistics:

GP	G	A	TP	+/-	PIM	PP	SH	GW	GT	S	PCT
82	9	15	24	+15	40	0	1	5	0	108	8.3

2002-2003 statistics:

GP	G	A	TP	+/-	PIM	PP	SH	GW	GT	S	PCT
82	14	23	37	+17	91	0	4	1	0	116	12.1

LAST SEASON

Tied for third in NHL in shorthanded goals. Led team in shorthanded goals. Third on team in penalty minutes. One of four Red Wings to appear in all 82 games.

THE FINESSE GAME

Maltby's skating helps keep him in position defensively. He is seldom caught up-ice. He plays well without the puck, understands the game and is coachable. He kills penalties effectively and blocks shots.

Maltby isn't overly creative, but he works tirelessly along the boards and in the corners to keep the puck alive. He has an average wrist and snap shot, yet has enough moves to be a threat when his team is shorthanded. Most of his goals are of the opportunistic type. He jumps on loose pucks and creates turnovers with his forechecking. Maltby was able to contribute a little more offensively last season without taking anything away from his defense.

Astute hockey sense stamps Maltby as a two-way winger. He is one of those key role players that a successful team simply can't live without.

THE PHYSICAL GAME

There are few nights when you don't notice Maltby is on the ice. He has good speed and he loves to flatten people with clean, hard hits. He is not very big, but he is solid and won't back down from a challenge. He draws more than his fair share of penalties, either by forcing opponents to pull him down or by aggravating them enough that they take a whack at him.

Maltby's power emanates from his lower-body drive. He is strong and balanced and will punish with his hits. His work ethic and conditioning are strong.

He wants to win the races for loose pucks.

THE INTANGIBLES

Maltby is a role player who takes great pride in that designation. He provides jump, energy, and intelligence to any lineup. Those are especially prized assets come playoff time.

PROJECTION

Maltby exceeded our goal expectation but 15 would be his absolute top end. Teams don't employ a Maltby for purely offensive purposes.

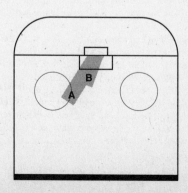

DARREN MCCARTY

Yrs. of NHL service: 10
Born: Burnaby, B.C.; April, 1972
Position: right wing
Height: 6-1
Weight: 215
Uniform no.: 25
Shoots: right

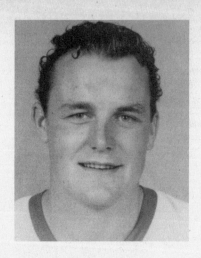

Career statistics:

GP	G	A	TP	PIM
600	113	149	262	1225

1999-2000 statistics:

GP	G	A	TP	+/-	PIM	PP	SH	GW	GT	S	PCT
24	6	6	12	+1	48	0	0	1	0	40	15.0

2000-2001 statistics:

GP	G	A	TP	+/-	PIM	PP	SH	GW	GT	S	PCT
72	12	10	22	-5	123	1	1	3	1	118	10.2

2001-2002 statistics:

GP	G	A	TP	+/-	PIM	PP	SH	GW	GT	S	PCT
62	5	7	12	+2	98	0	0	1	2	74	6.8

2002-2003 statistics:

GP	G	A	TP	+/-	PIM	PP	SH	GW	GT	S	PCT
73	13	9	22	+10	138	1	0	2	0	129	10.1

LAST SEASON

Led team in penalty minutes. Missed nine games with elbow infection.

THE FINESSE GAME

McCarty isn't the greatest skater. He has an awkward stride and his first few steps are rather slow, but he is strong on his skates and his acceleration is serviceable. He has decent finishing skills to go with a physical aspect. His balance is underrated. He absorbs (or delivers) hard hits from (to) some of the biggest skaters in the league, but hardly ever staggers.

McCarty has the poise to execute the consummate pro move: follow up a great play with a good one. He can deke a defender with an inside-outside move, then go backhand-forehand to finish the play with a huge goal — providing a huge boost to his team while utterly deflating the opposition.

McCarty has decent hands and will score the majority of his goals in-tight. He is not terribly creative but stays with a basic power game and is solid on the forecheck.

He is a righthanded shot but often plays the left side and protects the puck well. McCarty has worked to make himself a suitable linemate for Detroit's more skilled players. Although he is a mainstay on the Grind Line, he will act as a bodyguard if moved alongside some of the name players and doesn't look out of place. He also stirs things up in the corners to dig the puck out for his center's playmaking. He reads off his linemates and reacts well to situations.

THE PHYSICAL GAME

Mean, big, strong, tough and fearless — all the ingredients are there, along with the desire to throw his body at any player or puck he can reach. If a game is off to a quiet start, look for McCarty to wake everyone up. He forechecks and backchecks fiercely, and tries to go through players, not just to them.

McCarty is not a great fighter but he is willing. He's intelligent in picking his spots. His teammates know he is always there to back them up.

THE INTANGIBLES

Teams were cutting corners everywhere after last season but the Wings thought enough of McCarty to re-sign him before he became a free agent. McCarty is a valuable player on team full of MVPs. He plays with huge heart and brings an edge to the rink every night. The Red Wings are a smaller team in many ways when he is out of the lineup.

PROJECTION

He plays so hard and has become a little brittle in recent years, though, so we wouldn't expect much more than 70 games — and 20 points — out of him. We still want him on our side.

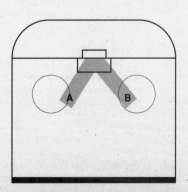

MATHIEU SCHNEIDER

Yrs. of NHL service: 14
Born: New York, N.Y.; June 12, 1969
Position: left defense
Height: 5-10
Weight: 192
Uniform no.: 23
Shoots: left

Career statistics:

GP	G	A	TP	PIM
914	154	352	506	907

1999-2000 statistics:

GP	G	A	TP	+/-	PIM	PP	SH	GW	GT	S	PCT
80	10	20	30	-6	78	3	0	1	1	228	4.4

2000-2001 statistics:

GP	G	A	TP	+/-	PIM	PP	SH	GW	GT	S	PCT
73	16	35	51	0	56	7	1	2	2	183	8.7

2001-2002 statistics:

GP	G	A	TP	+/-	PIM	PP	SH	GW	GT	S	PCT
55	7	23	30	+3	68	4	0	0	0	123	5.7

2002-2003 statistics:

GP	G	A	TP	+/-	PIM	PP	SH	GW	GT	S	PCT
78	16	34	50	+2	73	11	0	1	0	199	8.0

LAST SEASON

Acquired from Los Angeles on March 11, 2003, for Sean Avery, Maxim Kuznetsov, a first-round draft pick in 2003, and a second-round draft pick in 2004. Sixth among NHL defensemen in points. Third on team in average ice time.

THE FINESSE GAME

Schneider is an excellent skater, plus he's deceptively strong for his size. He sees the ice and moves the puck well coming out of his own end, and is capable of controlling the pace. He is a good two-way defenseman with the offensive skills to get involved in the attack and to work the point on the power play. A major concern has always been his positional play, but he is a much lower-risk player than he was early in his career.

Strong, balanced, and agile, Schneider lacks breakaway speed but he is quick with his first step and he changes directions smoothly. He can carry the puck but he does not lead many rushes. He gets the puck out of the corner quickly. Schneider makes good defensive decisions.

Schneider is good on the point. He does more with the puck than just drill a shot, though he has a tendency to get his shots blocked when he is slow on the release. He handles the puck well and looks for the passes down low. Given the green light, he is likely to get involved down low more often. He has the skating ability to recover quickly when he takes a chance.

THE PHYSICAL GAME

Schneider is a poor-man's version of Chris Chelios (now his Detroit teammate), and plays with a lot more intensity than people tend to give him credit for. He is not a big hitter, because he is rather small by today's NHL-defenseman standards. Schneider will battle the opposition's big forwards. He's extremely strong on his feet. He's also great at making the first pass, but he is not flashy, so he doesn't stand out. Schneider does have a knack for taking dumb penalties, often at the most inopportune moments.

Schneider's objective is to play a containment game and move the puck quickly and intelligently out of the zone. He is often matched against other teams' top scoring lines and always tries to do the job. He is best when paired with a physical defenseman. He has a tendency to hit high and gets penalties because of it.

THE INTANGIBLES

The Red Wings paid dearly to acquire Schneider for the repeat run at the Cup, but Schneider was a non-factor as the Red Wings were stunned by a first-round sweep by Anaheim. He comes into camp with a little extra pressure to prove that the high price tag was worth it.

PROJECTION

Schneider should be able to duplicate his 50-point season.

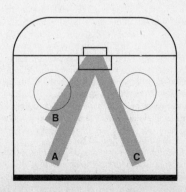

BRENDAN SHANAHAN

Yrs. of NHL service: 16
Born: Mimico, Ont.; Jan. 23, 1969
Position: left wing
Height: 6-3
Weight: 218
Uniform no.: 14
Shoots: right

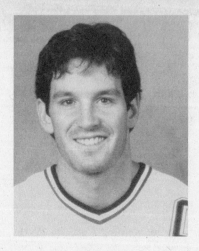

Career statistics:

GP	G	A	TP	PIM
1186	533	565	1098	2156

1999-2000 statistics:

GP	G	A	TP	+/-	PIM	PP	SH	GW	GT	S	PCT
78	41	37	78	+24	105	13	1	9	1	283	14.5

2000-2001 statistics:

GP	G	A	TP	+/-	PIM	PP	SH	GW	GT	S	PCT
81	31	45	76	+9	81	15	1	7	1	278	11.1

2001-2002 statistics:

GP	G	A	TP	+/-	PIM	PP	SH	GW	GT	S	PCT
80	37	38	75	+23	118	12	3	7	3	277	13.4

2002-2003 statistics:

GP	G	A	TP	+/-	PIM	PP	SH	GW	GT	S	PCT
78	30	38	68	+5	103	13	0	6	0	260	11.5

LAST SEASON

Led team in power-play goals. Second on team in penalty minutes and game-winning goals. Third on team in points and shots. Missed four games due to coach's decision.

THE FINESSE GAME

Shanahan is as good as he is because he works hard at it. The release on his shot is instantaneous, and he practices his one-timers religiously to maintain that touch. Shanahan can convert shots from imperfect feeds because of his drills. He beats goaltenders from a distance, and a lot of players can't because they don't have enough velocity on their shot. Shanahan works to get into a high-percentage scoring area and shoots with power and accuracy. He has wonderfully soft hands for nifty goalmouth passes.

On the power play, he is one of the best at staying just off the crease, waiting for a shot to come from the point, then timing his arrival at the front of the net for the moving screen, the tip, or the rebound. He can get a lot on his shot even when the puck is near his feet because of his short backswing and strong wrists.

Skating is one of Shanahan's few flaws. He isn't quick, isn't agile, and he often looks awkward with the puck. Most of the time he's better off making the hit that frees the puck, then passing it to a teammate and breaking to a spot, because he can score from anywhere. Shanahan doesn't skate very well backwards, and that gives him some defensive problems with Detroit's left-wing lock system.

THE PHYSICAL GAME

The dilemma for rival teams: If you play Shanahan aggressively, it brings out the best in him. If you lay off and give him room, he will kill you with his skills.

Shanahan spent his formative NHL years establishing his reputation by dropping his gloves with anybody who challenged him, but he has gotten smarter without losing his tough edge. Shanahan may have a longer fuse, but players around the league are aware of his reputation and know he is capable of snapping on any given night.

He takes or makes a hit to create a play. He's willing to eat glass to make a pass, but would rather strike the first blow. He does that by using his strength to fight through checks to get himself in a position to score. He sees the puck, goes and gets it, and puts it towards the front of the net.

THE INTANGIBLES

Other than his willingness to hit or to scrap, no aspect of his game is elite. But Shanahan is there when you need him to make a play that will win it for you, to say the right thing in the dressing room, or to orchestrate the Stanley Cup hand-off. And he's always there for the fans. Shanahan is one of the NHL's most popular players. Shanahan is the behind-the-scenes captain of the Red Wings.

PROJECTION

Shanahan came close to the 70 points we projected for him last season. He should come close to that number again, although he is reaching the age (34) where his production will start to slide.

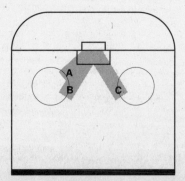

STEVE YZERMAN

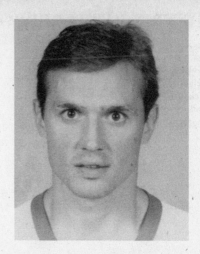

Yrs. of NHL service: 20
Born: Cranbrook, B.C.; May 9, 1965
Position: center
Height: 5-11
Weight: 185
Uniform no.: 19
Shoots: right

Career statistics:

GP	G	A	TP	PIM
1378	660	1010	1670	860

1999-2000 statistics:

GP	G	A	TP	+/-	PIM	PP	SH	GW	GT	S	PCT
78	35	44	79	+28	34	15	2	6	1	234	15.0

2000-2001 statistics:

GP	G	A	TP	+/-	PIM	PP	SH	GW	GT	S	PCT
54	18	34	52	+4	18	5	0	7	0	155	11.6

2001-2002 statistics:

GP	G	A	TP	+/-	PIM	PP	SH	GW	GT	S	PCT
52	13	35	48	+11	18	5	1	5	0	104	12.5

2002-2003 statistics:

GP	G	A	TP	+/-	PIM	PP	SH	GW	GT	S	PCT
16	2	6	8	+6	8	1	0	1	0	13	15.4

LAST SEASON

Won 2003 Masterton Trophy. Missed 66 games with knee surgery.

THE FINESSE GAME

Yzerman is one of the three most complete forwards in the NHL, with Peter Forsberg and Mike Modano. Yzerman is outstanding on draws. He is a great penalty killer because of his speed and anticipation.

A sensational skater, Yzerman zigs and zags all over the ice, spending very little time in the middle. It's hard to fully assess how much the reconstructive knee surgery and rehab cost him, since Yzerman came back later than expected and was only able to play 16 regular season games and four in the playoffs as Detroit was swept. He has great balance and quick feet, and is adroit at kicking the puck up onto his blade for a shot in one seamless motion. He's also strong for an average-sized forward. He protects the puck well with his body and has the arm strength for wraparound shots and off-balance shots through traffic.

Yzerman prefers to stickhandle down the right side of the ice. In addition to using his body to shield the puck, he uses the boards to protect it. If a defender starts reaching in with his stick, he usually ends up pulling Yzerman down for a penalty.

THE PHYSICAL GAME

Yzerman sacrifices his body in the right circumstances and thinks nothing of diving to block a shot. He pays the price along the boards and around the net, and he's deceptively strong. Yzerman knows he isn't big enough to be an intimidating hitter, but he gets his body and stick in the way and at least makes the puck carrier change direction abruptly. He simply does not give up on a play, and he plays all 200 feet of the rink.

THE INTANGIBLES

Doctors urged Yzerman to retire but he worked his way back last season and is expected to play one more year. He was an unrestricted free agent but is likely to re-sign with Detroit.

PROJECTION

There are too many red flags here, including the injury and the departure of Sergei Fedorov, to expect too much production out of Yzerman. He is also likely to take some nights off to save himself for the playoffs. He is not a point-a-game player anymore. He's more like a half-point-a-game player.

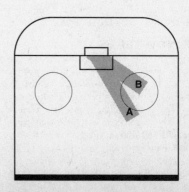

HENRIK ZETTERBERG

Yrs. of NHL service: 1
Born: Njurunda, Sweden; Oct. 9, 1980
Position: left wing
Height: 5-11
Weight: 176
Uniform no.: 40
Shoots: left

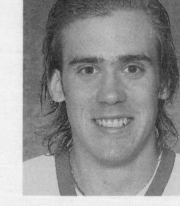

Career statistics:

GP	G	A	TP	PIM
79	22	22	44	8

2002-2003 statistics:

GP	G	A	TP	+/-	PIM	PP	SH	GW	GT	S	PCT
79	22	22	44	+6	8	5	1	4	0	135	16.3

LAST SEASON

Finalist for 2003 Calder Trophy. Named to NHL All-Rookie Team. Led NHL rookies in points, goals, and shooting percentage. Tied for third among NHL rookies in assists and power-play goals. Second on team in shooting percentage. Third on team in goals. Tied for third on team in game-winning goals. Missed three games with knee injury.

THE FINESSE GAME

Even though Zetterberg was the rookie scoring leader, what was most impressive about him was his defensive awareness. This is surprising because the knock on him in his draft year was his defensive play. Detroit's system has always demanded that its players be responsible in all zones, and his mature game allowed Detroit to hand him a lot of quality ice time.

Zetterberg is highly skilled in all areas. His hockey sense is probably his best asset. He has good hands for passing, but he is not a pure playmaker. He will take his scoring opportunities and has a good wrist shot. Zetterberg can make plays through traffic.

He has NHL speed, quickness, and agility. He is versatile and can play left wing or center.

THE PHYSICAL GAME

Zetterberg isn't very big nor is he aggressive. He isn't scared of contact, though. He has a solid, compact build and is very strong on his skates.

THE INTANGIBLES

Although everyone on the Wings seems about 50 years old, every season Detroit actually works in a young star or two. Given the fact that they tend to draft low every season because of their excellent regular-season record, the scouts have been earning their money. Zetterberg was a late-round gem (210th overall in 1999) who should secure a second-line role for Detroit this season.

PROJECTION

Expect Zetterberg to improve on his rookie marks and move into 50-point range.

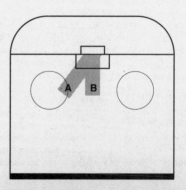

EDMONTON OILERS

Players' Statistics 2001-2002

POS.	NO.	PLAYER	GP	G	A	PTS	+/-	PIM	PP	SH	GW	GT	S	PCT
L	94	RYAN SMYTH	66	27	34	61	5	67	10		3	1	199	13.6
C	26	TODD MARCHANT	77	20	40	60	13	48	7	1	3	1	146	13.7
C	16	MIKE YORK	71	22	29	51	-8	10	7	2	4		177	12.4
C	89	MIKE COMRIE	69	20	31	51	-18	90	8		6		170	11.8
R	20	RADEK DVORAK	75	10	25	35	-6	30	3			1	166	6.0
C	10	SHAWN HORCOFF	78	12	21	33	10	55	2		3		98	12.2
L	18	ETHAN MOREAU	78	14	17	31	-7	112	2	3	2	1	137	10.2
C	19	MARTY REASONER	70	11	20	31	19	28	2	2			102	10.8
R	83	*ALES HEMSKY	59	6	24	30	5	14			1		50	12.0
D	2	ERIC BREWER	80	8	21	29	-11	45	1		1		147	5.4
R	15	BRAD ISBISTER	66	13	15	28	-9	43	2		3	1	119	10.9
D	24	STEVE STAIOS	76	5	21	26	13	96	1	3			126	4.0
C	28	*JASON CHIMERA	66	14	9	23	-2	36		1	4	1	90	15.6
L	7	DANIEL CLEARY	57	4	13	17	5	31			1		89	4.5
C	34	*FERNANDO PISANI	35	8	5	13	9	10	1				32	25.0
R	27	GEORGES LARAQUE	64	6	7	13	-4	110			2		46	13.0
D	21	JASON SMITH	68	4	8	12	5	64			1		93	4.3
C	37	BRIAN SWANSON	44	2	10	12	-7	10	1		1		67	3.0
D	23	CORY CROSS	37	2	7	9	16	24	1		1		29	6.9
D	32	SCOTT FERGUSON	78	3	5	8	11	120					45	6.7
D	5	*ALEXEI SEMENOV	46	1	6	7	-7	58					33	3.0
C	33	JIRI DOPITA	21	1	5	6	-4	11			1		23	4.3
R	14	*JANI RITA	12	3	1	4	2						18	16.7
D	47	*MARC-ANDRE BERGERON	5	1	1	2	2	9					5	20.0
C	36	*JARRET STOLL	4		1	1	-3						5	
D	29	KARI HAAKANA	13				-2	4					2	
G	35	TOMMY SALO	65				0	4						
G	30	JUSSI MARKKANEN	22				0	2						
D	12	*BOBBY ALLEN	1				0							
G	1	TY CONKLIN					0							

GP = games played; G = goals; A = assists; PTS = points; +/- = goals-for minus goals-against while player is on ice; PIM = penalties in minutes; PP = power-play goals; SH = shorthanded goals; GW = game-winning goals; GT = game-tying goals; S = no. of shots; PCT = percentage of goals to shots; * = rookie

ERIC BREWER

Yrs. of NHL service: 5
Born: Vernon, B.C.; Apr. 17, 1979
Position: left defense
Height: 6-3
Weight: 220
Uniform no.: 2
Shoots: left

Career statistics:

GP	G	A	TP	PIM
327	27	61	88	195

1999-2000 statistics:

GP	G	A	TP	+/-	PIM	PP	SH	GW	GT	S	PCT
26	0	2	2	-11	20	0	0	0	0	30	0.0

2000-2001 statistics:

GP	G	A	TP	+/-	PIM	PP	SH	GW	GT	S	PCT
77	7	14	21	+15	53	2	0	2	0	91	7.7

2001-2002 statistics:

GP	G	A	TP	+/-	PIM	PP	SH	GW	GT	S	PCT
81	7	18	25	-5	45	6	0	2	0	165	4.2

2002-2003 statistics:

GP	G	A	TP	+/-	PIM	PP	SH	GW	GT	S	PCT
80	8	21	29	-11	45	1	0	1	0	147	5.4

LAST SEASON

Led team in average ice time (24:55). Missed two games due to shoulder injury.

THE FINESSE GAME

Brewer has a little cockiness to him that shows an innate awareness of and supreme faith in his skill level. It will get him in trouble sometimes, but it will also encourage him to try some of the high-risk moves that only elite players make. Brewer can make them, and the Oilers want him to. They will live with the mistakes (and as his -11 shows, he still makes plenty of them).

Brewer can be used in all game situations. He can control games the way Scott Niedermayer does with the Devils. He has the skating and puck control to dominate. He's an excellent skater with quick acceleration and lateral movement. And like Niedermayer, the bigger the games are, the more Brewer steps up his game. He might have been Edmonton's top playoff performer for the second straight year.

Brewer is highly self-critical. He may be tougher on himself than the most exacting coach. The Oilers have to make sure someone on their coaching staff helps Brewer ride out some of the tough stretches before his on-ice play takes a hit. Brewer has a very mature, analytical approach to the game. He has matured to the point where he understands this is a job, and he wants to improve.

THE PHYSICAL GAME

Brewer is very strong in the defensive zone. He has good size and he likes to hit. He's smart in his own end. He's durable and in great condition. Brewer is the complete package.

THE INTANGIBLES

Coach Craig MacTavish has said openly he thinks Brewer can be a "spectacular" defenseman. Maybe that show of faith is just what Brewer needed. Brewer is a character player.

PROJECTION

Brewer has more offensive upside. We thought last season would be the year he would bump it up to 40 points, but that didn't happen, so we'll lower our standards a bit to 35 points.

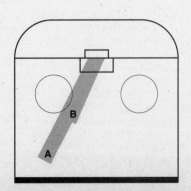

MIKE COMRIE

Yrs. of NHL service: 3
Born: Edmonton, Alta.; Sept. 11, 1980
Position: center
Height: 5-9
Weight: 175
Uniform no.: 89
Shoots: left

Career statistics:

GP	G	A	TP	PIM
192	61	72	133	149

2000-2001 statistics:

GP	G	A	TP	+/-	PIM	PP	SH	GW	GT	S	PCT
41	8	14	22	+6	14	3	0	1	0	62	12.9

2001-2002 statistics:

GP	G	A	TP	+/-	PIM	PP	SH	GW	GT	S	PCT
82	33	27	60	+16	45	8	0	5	3	170	19.4

2002-2003 statistics:

GP	G	A	TP	+/-	PIM	PP	SH	GW	GT	S	PCT
69	20	31	51	-18	90	8	0	6	0	170	11.8

LAST SEASON

Led team in game-winning goals. Second on team in power-play goals. Third on team in assists and shots. Tied for third on team in goals and points. Worst plus-minus on team. Missed 13 games with fractured right thumb.

THE FINESSE GAME

Comrie has to get a lot of ice time to be effective. He has a terrific instinct and passion for the game on top of good puckhandling, skating, and passing skills. He is a natural goal-scorer and a confident one; he wants the puck in key situations. He doesn't have a big shot, but it's a deceptive one, and a goalie never knows if Comrie will pass or shoot because he is equally adept at both. He stars on the power play, but he's not all offense. He has an advanced defensive game.

Comrie anticipates well. The puck always seems to be around him, and nothing on the ice ever seems to catch him by surprise. He's a very good positional player, which a little guy has to be.

Comrie was simply not the same player after suffering his hand injury early in the second half of the season. Comrie had 14 goals in 41 games before the January injury but only six in 28 after returning.

THE PHYSICAL GAME

He's small, but spunky. Comrie gets back up even faster than he's knocked down. He isn't intimidated. He knows how to pick his spots while darting in and out of traffic, but he is fearless in going into the corners or in front of the net. Other teams singled him out for punishment a lot last season, and Comrie often battled back with his own shots. He will even jump in to stick up for a teammate.

THE INTANGIBLES

Comrie arrived much sooner than anticipated. His work ethic is exemplary. He was a restricted free agent during the off-season, though, and a subject of frequent trade rumors.

PROJECTION

Comrie was close to our anticipated 30-goal pace before the fractured thumb. He should return to the ranks of the 30-goal scorers this season.

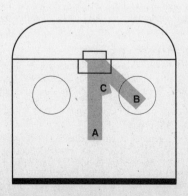

RADEK DVORAK

Yrs. of NHL service: 8
Born: Tabor, Czech Republic; Mar. 9, 1977
Position: left wing
Height: 6-1
Weight: 194
Uniform no.: 20
Shoots: right

Career statistics:

GP	G	A	TP	PIM
604	138	196	334	192

1999-2000 statistics:

GP	G	A	TP	+/-	PIM	PP	SH	GW	GT	S	PCT
81	18	32	50	+5	16	2	1	1	0	157	11.5

2000-2001 statistics:

GP	G	A	TP	+/-	PIM	PP	SH	GW	GT	S	PCT
82	31	36	67	+9	20	5	2	3	0	230	13.5

2001-2002 statistics:

GP	G	A	TP	+/-	PIM	PP	SH	GW	GT	S	PCT
65	17	20	37	-20	14	3	3	1	0	210	8.1

2002-2003 statistics:

GP	G	A	TP	+/-	PIM	PP	SH	GW	GT	S	PCT
75	10	25	35	-6	30	3	0	0	1	166	6.0

PROJECTION

Dvorak should be at least a 20-goal scorer this season.

LAST SEASON

Acquired from N.Y. Rangers with Cory Cross on March 11, 2003, for Anson Carter and Ales Pisa. Missed four games with knee injury. Missed three games due to concussion. Missed one game with back spasms.

THE FINESSE GAME

Dvorak has exceptional speed and is fast skater who fits right on a fleet Oilers team after the trade. He bursts down the wing and will mix up the defense by sometimes driving wide and sometimes cutting through the middle. He takes the puck with him at a high tempo and creates off the rush.

Dvorak lacks a true goal-scorer's mentality. He tends to over-pass. He has become a more complete player by adding defensive awareness to his game. Dvorak is very conscientious. He is a fine penalty killer because of his speed and anticipation.

With all of the pace to his game, people tend to have high expectations for Dvorak. Except for his 31-goal season with the Rangers in 2000-01, Dvorak has failed to deliver.

THE PHYSICAL GAME

Dvorak has very strong legs, which power his explosive skating. While he is not a hitter, he will fight for the puck on the forecheck, and he's not a bit intimidated by physical play.

THE INTANGIBLES

Dvorak is getting yet another chance in Edmonton. He showed a glimpse of what may come by scoring four goals and four assists in only 12 games with the Oilers.

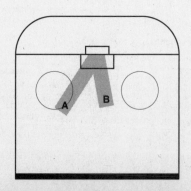

ALES HEMSKY

Yrs. of NHL service: 1
Born: Pardubice, Czech republic; Aug. 13, 1983
Position: right wing
Height: 6-0
Weight: 191
Uniform no.: 83
Shoots: right

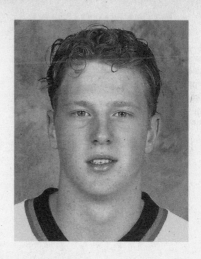

Career statistics:

GP	G	A	TP	PIM
59	6	24	30	14

2002-2003 statistics:

GP	G	A	TP	+/-	PIM	PP	SH	GW	GT	S	PCT
59	6	24	30	+5	14	0	0	1	0	50	12.0

LAST SEASON

First NHL season. Second among NHL rookies in assists. Tied for seventh among NHL rookies in points. Missed three games with abdominal strain. Missed 20 games due to coach's decision.

THE FINESSE GAME

Hemsky has magical hands, which are his primary asset. He is at his best in open ice, especially on the power play. He can make things happen there. Hemsky is creative and has 360-degree vision, or at least it seems like he does. He is always seeing the moves open up a bit ahead of everyone else. He can totally fool a defender who thinks he has him contained only to see Hemsky make or take the toughest pass. He embarrasses goalies with a toe-drag move.

Hemsky doesn't shoot as much as he should. When he does, he has a nice release, although there is not a lot of juice behind his shot. He has reminded some observers of Milan Hejduk.

Hemsky has good speed and handles the puck in keeping with his feet. He can attack one-on-one and turn a defender inside-out. Hemsky barely looks like he's trying and the next thing you know, he's at Mach speed. He has a lovely, fluid stride.

Hemsky's biggest flaw, and it's a serious one, is that he wants to be a perimeter player. Gifted guys who want to succeed in the NHL have to pay the price by going into traffic. Hemsky wants to take the scenic route.

THE PHYSICAL GAME

So now the question is, how badly does Hemsky want stardom in the NHL? He has to fight for the puck, fight for his space, and not look so scared. Hemsky is not a small guy, but there are too many nights when he plays like one. He needs a rink diagram to find the corners.

THE INTANGIBLES

So much talent, but what is he going to do with it? Inquiring minds want to know.

PROJECTION

Hemsky could score another pretty, assist-heavy 30 points and spend nights in the press box. Or he could become a 50-point impact player in his second season. The decision is all his.

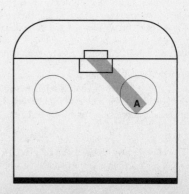

BRAD ISBISTER

Yrs. of NHL service: 6
Born: Edmonton, Alberta; May 7, 1977
Position: right wing
Height: 6-4
Weight: 227
Uniform no.: 15
Shoots: right

Career statistics:

GP	G	A	TP	PIM
358	83	82	165	463

1999-2000 statistics:

GP	G	A	TP	+/-	PIM	PP	SH	GW	GT	S	PCT
64	22	20	42	-18	100	9	0	1	1	135	16.3

2000-2001 statistics:

GP	G	A	TP	+/-	PIM	PP	SH	GW	GT	S	PCT
51	18	14	32	-19	59	7	1	4	0	129	13.9

2001-2002 statistics:

GP	G	A	TP	+/-	PIM	PP	SH	GW	GT	S	PCT
79	17	21	38	+1	113	4	0	2	0	142	12.0

2002-2003 statistics:

GP	G	A	TP	+/-	PIM	PP	SH	GW	GT	S	PCT
66	13	15	28	-9	43	2	0	3	1	119	10.9

LAST SEASON

Acquired from N.Y. Islanders with Raffi Torres on March 11, 2003, for Janne Niinimaa and a conditional second-round draft pick in 2003. Missed 14 games due to ankle injuries.

THE FINESSE GAME

Isbister is not creative, but he fits in well in a strong forechecking scheme because he plays up and down his left wing. He is a solid skater with straightaway speed and quickness. He has excellent acceleration from the blueline in, and he cuts to the net. His ankle injuries hindered him in this area last season.

A decent passer when he has a little time, his hand skills are a shade below average. Unlike more creative players, he tends not to see more than one option. His goals will come from driving to the net, which he needs to do with more authority if he is ever going to be effective.

With better hands and a quicker shot, Isbister could be a power forward in the making. He certainly tries to play like a power forward, and those do take a little longer to develop. That's probably why the Islanders waited so long before finally dealing him.

THE PHYSICAL GAME

Isbister is strong, able to fend off a defender with one arm and keep going. He protects the puck well. He is an enthusiastic forechecker and likes to be the first man in. He will take or make a hit to make a play happen. He has an aggressive nature and will aggravate a lot of players by making them eat glass. He has to be more consistent in his effort on a nightly basis.

THE INTANGIBLES

The Oilers seem to think Isbister can become the next Todd Bertuzzi. This is like looking at a big hunk of marble and thinking it could be Michelangelo's "David." Sure, it could happen, but it's going to take an awful lot of chiselling. Isbister scored 3-2 — 5 in 13 games with the Oilers after the trade but had a dismal playoffs.

PROJECTION

Isbister needs to step up his game and his production to around 25 goals.

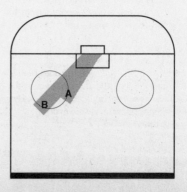

ETHAN MOREAU

Yrs. of NHL service: 7
Born: Huntsville, Ont.; Sept. 22, 1975
Position: left wing
Height: 6-2
Weight: 211
Uniform no.: 18
Shoots: left

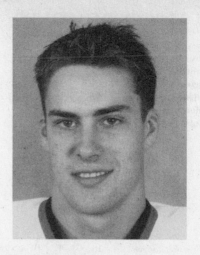

Career statistics:

GP	G	A	TP	PIM
523	85	79	164	637

1999-2000 statistics:

GP	G	A	TP	+/-	PIM	PP	SH	GW	GT	S	PCT
73	17	10	27	+8	62	1	0	3	0	106	16.0

2000-2001 statistics:

GP	G	A	TP	+/-	PIM	PP	SH	GW	GT	S	PCT
68	9	10	19	-6	90	0	1	3	0	97	9.3

2001-2002 statistics:

GP	G	A	TP	+/-	PIM	PP	SH	GW	GT	S	PCT
80	11	5	16	+4	81	0	2	1	1	129	8.5

2002-2003 statistics:

GP	G	A	TP	+/-	PIM	PP	SH	GW	GT	S	PCT
78	14	17	31	-7	112	2	3	2	1	137	10.2

LAST SEASON

Led team in shorthanded goals. Second on team in penalty minutes. Career high in points. Missed two games with flu. Missed one game with a cold. Missed one game due to coach's decision.

THE FINESSE GAME

Moreau doesn't attract a lot of attention on a team of skilled skaters, but he is one of those gritty guys a team needs in order to succeed. What does it take to win? A hit? A penalty kill? A fight? He will do whatever it takes to try to turn the tide in his team's favor.

Moreau is an intelligent, safe player with good hockey sense. He is a third-line winger who can also play center in a pinch, although he is better suited on left wing. He is not a natural scorer but has to work for his goals. His scoring touch improves with effort (funny how that works).

A long reach and a long stick allow Moreau to get his strong wrist shots away around a defenseman who may think he has Moreau tied up. Defensively, he's on his way because he has an understanding of positional play. He's a budding power forward who goes to the net hard. Moreau is a solid penalty killer and a shorthanded scoring threat.

THE PHYSICAL GAME

Moreau has good size and strength and is starting to develop more of a presence. He finishes his checks, especially around the net. There is a latent aggressive streak that has been emerging with more ice time and confidence. He works hard, is strong in the corners, and is willing take a hit to make a play.

THE INTANGIBLES

Former coach Craig Hartsburg compared Moreau to a young Bob Gainey, both for his playing style and budding leadership ability. Moreau is very well-liked by his teammates and his coaches and he has some good leadership qualities.

PROJECTION

Moreau can carve out a steady career as a third-line checker who can also produce 15 or so goals a year.

MARTY REASONER

Yrs. of NHL service: 4
Born: Rochester, NY; Feb. 26, 1977
Position: center
Height: 6-1
Weight: 190
Uniform no.: 19
Shoots: left

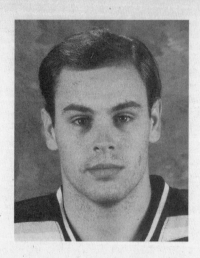

Career statistics:

GP	G	A	TP	PIM
217	34	55	89	111

1999-2000 statistics:

GP	G	A	TP	+/-	PIM	PP	SH	GW	GT	S	PCT
32	10	14	24	+9	20	3	0	0	0	51	19.6

2000-2001 statistics:

GP	G	A	TP	+/-	PIM	PP	SH	GW	GT	S	PCT
41	4	9	13	-5	14	0	0	0	0	65	6.2

2001-2002 statistics:

GP	G	A	TP	+/-	PIM	PP	SH	GW	GT	S	PCT
52	6	5	11	0	41	3	0	2	0	66	9.1

2002-2003 statistics:

GP	G	A	TP	+/-	PIM	PP	SH	GW	GT	S	PCT
70	11	20	31	+19	28	2	2	0	0	102	10.8

LAST SEASON

Led team in plus-minus. Tied for second on team in shorthanded goals. Career highs in goals, assists, and points. Missed one game with flu. Missed eight games due to coach's decision. Appeared in two games with Hamilton (AHL), scoring 0-2 — 2.

THE FINESSE GAME

Reasoner is a playmaker and most effective when he attacks in straight lines. When he starts to zig-zag, he slows down and loses his speed. Reasoner has such good hands and vision that he is able to bring the puck in with his deceptive speed and force the defenders to commit.

He has terrific hockey sense. Reasoner may not possess all the tools to be a top-six forward, though. He can handle power-play duty, and his five-on-five play improved enough last season to earn him the right to get some power-play ice.

Reasoner has started doing more of the little things that help his team win a game, and he was rewarded with more ice time last season because of that. He did very well on draws, for example. Reasoner may finally be getting it.

THE PHYSICAL GAME

Reasoner is average size and has never shown a knack for the physical part of the game. He can't afford to be a perimeter player. He could afford to work on his upper-body strength and his skating.

THE INTANGIBLES

Reasoner had another sub par training camp and began the season watching from the press box. Despite a brief stint in the minors, Reasoner was able to work his way back into the coaches' good graces and was a regular by the playoffs, albeit as a role player. Reasoner was a restricted free agent during the off-season and is a prime candidate to be shipped out.

PROJECTION

Reasoner needs to come into camp — wherever that might be for him this year — ready to battle for a job in the top nine. He is mostly a set-up guy, and could score 30 points again in the right spot.

JANI RITA

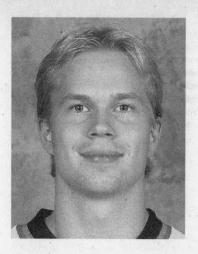

Yrs. of NHL service: 0
Born: Helsinki, Finland; July 25, 1981
Position: right wing
Height: 6-1
Weight: 206
Uniform no.: 14
Shoots: right

Career statistics:

GP	G	A	TP	PIM
13	3	1	4	0

2001-2002 statistics:

GP	G	A	TP	+/-	PIM	PP	SH	GW	GT	S	PCT
1	0	0	0	0	0	0	0	0	0	0	0.0

2002-2003 statistics:

GP	G	A	TP	+/-	PIM	PP	SH	GW	GT	S	PCT
12	3	1	4	+2	0	0	0	0	0	18	16.7

LAST SEASON

Will be entering first full NHL season. Appeared in 64 games with Hamilton (AHL), scoring 21-27 — 48 with 18 PIM.

THE FINESSE GAME

For all of those Oiler fans old enough to remember Esa Tikkanen in his prime, here comes his clone. Rita is Tikkanen with offensive upside.

Rita is a swift skater with a homing instinct on the puck on the forecheck. One of his weaknesses is his lack of hockey vision. Once he creates the turnover, he isn't very adept at knowing what to do next.

When he plays a simple power game, driving to the net, Rita has less time to think and is more effective. He has a very nice passing touch but because he isn't very sophisticated in his playmaking, he does less damage than he ought to. Rita doesn't always protect the puck well, either.

Rita will probably start out as a defensive winger, but his "Wow!" factor and his shot will get him some power-play time.

THE PHYSICAL GAME

Rita is tough, gritty, and honest. He will give a complete effort every night. He loves to play the game and it's apparent he loves to agitate. He isn't huge, but he plays big, and will take some abuse around the net to create a disturbance in front of the goalie. He is strong along the wall and in the corners.

THE INTANGIBLES

Edmonton's low-budget approach to every season relies on their hungry kids coming through. Rita will be given every chance to make an impact in training camp. He's going to be a lot of fun to watch.

PROJECTION

Rita will probably start out on the third line, but he has second-line potential and could be a 25-goal scorer in a season or two. A first season of 10-15 goals would be a great start.

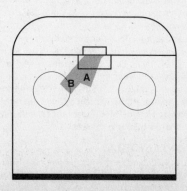

TOMMY SALO

Yrs. of NHL service: 7
Born: Surahammar, Sweden; Feb. 1, 1971
Position: goaltender
Height: 5-11
Weight: 173
Uniform no.: 35
Catches: left

Career statistics:

GP	MIN	GA	SO	GAA	A	PIM
477	27645	1177	34	2.55	6	65

1999-2000 statistics:

GP	MIN	GAA	W	L	T	SO	GA	S	SAPCT	PIM
70	4164	2.33	27	28	3	2	162	1875	.914	8

2000-2001 statistics:

GP	MIN	GAA	W	L	T	SO	GA	S	SAPCT	PIM
73	4364	2.46	36	25	12	8	179	1856	.904	4

2001-2002 statistics:

GP	MIN	GAA	W	L	T	SO	GA	S	SAPCT	PIM
69	4035	2.22	30	28	10	6	149	1713	.913	2

2002-2003 statistics:

GP	MIN	GAA	W	L	T	SO	GA	S	SAPCT	PIM
65	3814	2.71	29	27	8	4	172	1708	.899	4

LAST SEASON

Missed two games with groin strain.

THE PHYSICAL GAME

Salo took a step back last season, losing some of the form and technique that made him an effective if not elite-level NHL goalie. Salo has to play a more aggressive style, coming out to the top of his crease and beyond to challenge shooters. When he does that, he looks so much larger in the net. He is one of the smaller No. 1 goalies in the league in an era when goalies just keep getting taller and wider.

When the action is in-tight, Salo is excellent on low shots. He has adjusted to playing pucks through traffic, which is one of the biggest adjustments for European goalies. He has quick feet but is not a great skater. Salo needs to continually work on his lateral movement. He does have a problem with being bumped. He is out of the paint a lot and he's not very big, so on nights when the referees are lenient about calling goalie interference, Salo can be at a distinct disadvantage.

Salo has a bad habit of not holding his stick at a proper angle. When he gets into this slump he might as well not bother playing with a stick at all. He has a quick glove and tends to try and catch everything instead of using other parts of his body. Since he doesn't use his stick well, he will try to cover up on every loose puck for face-offs. Better stickhandling work would elevate his game a notch.

Salo's reflexes are outstanding. Few goalies in the league use their stick-side blocker better than Salo.

THE MENTAL GAME

The big knock on Salo has always been his lack of concentration, and that, along with his physical game, deteriorated last season.

THE INTANGIBLES

Salo may be challenged by backup Jussi Markkanen (or anyone else who might show up with a hot training camp) for at least a co-No. 1 role this season, especially after an unimpressive playoffs (3.15 GAA).

PROJECTION

Salo is no sure bet to get close to 30 wins this season, and would be a risky pool pick. He faces a lot of shots behind a wide-open Oilers system.

ALEXEI SEMENOV

Yrs. of NHL service: 1
Born: Moscow, Russia; Apr. 10, 1981
Position: left defense
Height: 6-6
Weight: 210
Uniform no.: 5
Shoots: left

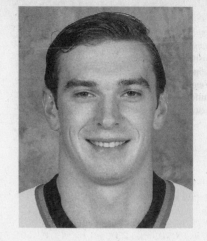

Career statistics:

GP	G	A	TP	PIM
46	1	6	7	58

2002-2003 statistics:

GP	G	A	TP	+/-	PIM	PP	SH	GW	GT	S	PCT
46	1	6	7	-7	58	0	0	0	0	33	3.0

LAST SEASON

First NHL season. Appeared in 37 games with Hamilton (AHL), scoring 4-3 — 7 with 45 PIM.

THE FINESSE GAME

Semenov is a tall drink of water, but for a towering guy he has surprisingly good agility and a tighter turning radius than one might expect. Despite that, he would still work best paired with a mobile partner.

Semenov won't take a lot of risks. He plays a conservative game, and with his size he is wise in letting the play come to him. He takes up a lot of space on the ice, and when he doesn't overcommit, he forces attackers to try to go through him. Good luck.

Semenov's defensive reads are good and he is a heads-up player. He probably won't have much of an impact offensively. He has a hard, heavy shot, but doesn't get it away quickly. He was a pretty good scorer in junior, but the pace of the NHL game may blunt his effectiveness at this level.

THE PHYSICAL GAME

There won't be many easy shifts against Semenov. Not only is he rangy and strong, he's mean, too. He will bulldoze guys away from the front of the net. He will develop into a solid penalty killer. Semenov can handle a lot of minutes. He is still listed at 210 pounds, but it looks like he's added at least 10 pounds since his draft year (1999).

THE INTANGIBLES

Semenov came to Canada from Russia in 1998 to play junior hockey and get acclimated to the lifestyle and the style of play in North America. That has not only helped his transition, but it showed his commitment to carving out an NHL career. He played well after his late December call-up.

PROJECTION

Semenov should win a full-time job this year and is likely to be in the Oilers' top four from the start of the season. His points will be in the 10-15 range but his PIM totals may be triple digits.

JASON SMITH

Yrs. of NHL service: 10
Born: Calgary, Alta.; Nov. 2, 1973
Position: right defense
Height: 6-3
Weight: 210
Uniform no.: 21
Shoots: right

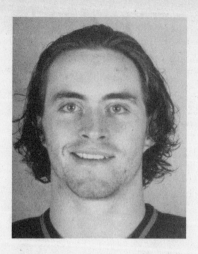

Career statistics:

GP	G	A	TP	PIM
642	26	85	111	681

1999-2000 statistics:

GP	G	A	TP	+/-	PIM	PP	SH	GW	GT	S	PCT
80	3	.11	14	+16	60	0	0	1	0	96	3.1

2000-2001 statistics:

GP	G	A	TP	+/-	PIM	PP	SH	GW	GT	S	PCT
82	5	15	20	+14	120	1	1	0	0	140	3.6

2001-2002 statistics:

GP	G	A	TP	+/-	PIM	PP	SH	GW	GT	S	PCT
74	5	13	18	+14	103	0	1	1	0	85	5.9

2002-2003 statistics:

GP	G	A	TP	+/-	PIM	PP	SH	GW	GT	S	PCT
68	4	8	12	+5	64	0	0	1	0	93	4.3

LAST SEASON

Third on team in average ice time (21:46). Missed 12 games with separated shoulder.

THE FINESSE GAME

Smith has a low-key personality and will never be the kind of defenseman who can control a game. He can, however, keep a game from getting out of hand with his cool work in the defensive zone. He has improved his defensive reads greatly, and is better at moving the puck. His panic point seems to improve every season.

Smith has gained confidence and has more poise and presence. He sacrifices his body to make hits and block shots. Smith is his own harshest critic. He doesn't give himself enough credit. He is the kind of player who needs to have the coaches give him a pat on the back or he will worry he's not doing enough.

Offensively, Smith won't make anyone forget Brian Leetch. He has a fairly heavy shot but it has little movement on it. He's not very creative, and he doesn't gamble. However, he can kill penalties, though he'll get into trouble against a team that cycles well down low.

THE PHYSICAL GAME

Smith is a solid hitter with a latent mean streak. His takeouts are effective along the boards and in front of the net. He's not as good in open ice because his mobility is not exceptional. He has a fairly long fuse but is a capable fighter. He has a high pain threshold and consistently plays hurt. He is fit and capable of handling a lot of minutes.

THE INTANGIBLES

Smith is emerging as a quiet leader. He's a little insecure, but wants to learn and will work hard to improve. He is very coachable. He will work best paired with an offensive defenseman, and appreciates it when he is given the task of trying to stop the other team's top line. He has developed into a reliable top-four defenseman and penalty killer.

Smith was a restricted free agent during the off-season.

PROJECTION

Smith is evolving into a reliable crunch-time player, but his numbers will never be gaudy. He can get 20 points a season, which seems to be his max.

RYAN SMYTH

Yrs. of NHL service: 8
Born: Banff, Alta.; Feb. 21, 1976
Position: left wing
Height: 6-1
Weight: 195
Uniform no.: 94
Shoots: left

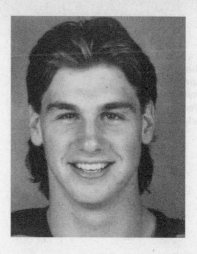

Career statistics:

GP	G	A	TP	PIM
560	175	196	371	441

1999-2000 statistics:

GP	G	A	TP	+/-	PIM	PP	SH	GW	GT	S	PCT
82	28	26	54	-2	58	11	0	4	1	238	11.8

2000-2001 statistics:

GP	G	A	TP	+/-	PIM	PP	SH	GW	GT	S	PCT
82	31	39	70	+10	58	11	0	6	1	245	12.6

2001-2002 statistics:

GP	G	A	TP	+/-	PIM	PP	SH	GW	GT	S	PCT
61	15	35	50	+7	48	7	1	5	1	150	10.0

2002-2003 statistics:

GP	G	A	TP	+/-	PIM	PP	SH	GW	GT	S	PCT
66	27	34	61	+5	67	10	0	3	1	199	13.6

LAST SEASON

Led team in goals, points, power-play goals, and shots. Second on team in assists and shooting percentage. Missed 15 games with shoulder injuries.

THE FINESSE GAME

Smyth is not a great, fluid skater, so he has to keep his feet moving. He does, with great energy that lifts his bench and the fans. He gets behind the opponent's defense with great consistency, driving to the net on a nightly basis and he's never more determined than when the stakes are high, as in the playoffs. Smyth may be the hardest-working player on the Oilers.

Smyth possesses little subtlety. Most of his goals come from the hash marks in, and probably half of them aren't the result of his shots, but tip-ins and body bounces. That's an art in itself, because Smyth has a knack for timing his moves to the net, along with a shooter's release. He has a long reach for getting to rebounds and is strong on his stick for deflections. He gets himself in the right place and is always aware of where the pass or the point shot is coming from. He has an advantage because his instincts and his reaction time are usually quicker than anyone else's.

Smyth is at a disadvantage when he is forced to shoot or make a play because he doesn't have a quick release. When he carries the puck, he doesn't have much sense of what to do with it.

THE PHYSICAL GAME

Smyth isn't built like a power forward, but when he is playing with bravado he sure tries to play like one. Smyth is one of the best forwards in the league along the wall. He uses his feet well to keep the puck alive.

He is a pesky net-crasher and can be an irritating presence. He doesn't throw bombs, but he is a willing thrasher along the boards and gets good leg drive for solid hits. He's not a fighter, yet he won't back down.

THE INTANGIBLES

For the second straight season, Smyth had to deal with a serious injury that cost him a quarter of the season. Other than that, there is nothing to dislike about this winger. Smyth was a restricted free agent during the off-season.

PROJECTION

As anticipated, Smyth returned to near the 30-goal mark. His target is between 30-35 goals.

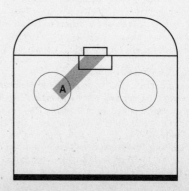

JARRET STOLL

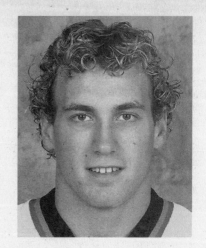

Yrs. of NHL service: 0
Born: Melville, Sask.; June 24, 1982
Position: center
Height: 6-1
Weight: 199
Uniform no.: 36
Shoots: right

Career statistics:

GP	G	A	TP	PIM
4	0	1	1	0

2002-2003 statistics:

GP	G	A	TP	+/-	PIM	PP	SH	GW	GT	S	PCT
4	0	1	1	-3	0	0	0	0	0	5	0.0

LAST SEASON

Will be entering first NHL season. Appeared in 76 games with Hamilton (AHL), scoring 21-33 — 54 with 86 PIM.

THE FINESSE GAME

Stoll's skating is what has held him back from reaching the NHL sooner, but the time in the minors has helped him become a better two-way player. He lacks breakaway speed, but his skating will probably be NHL caliber. Just don't expect anything dynamic.

Although he is considered a defensive forward and is likely to break in on the third line in just that role, Stoll knows what to do with the puck around the net. He is not flamboyant in any area. Stoll does have some confidence in his shot. He has a quick release and is accurate with both his wrist and snap shots. He will dig to get into high-percentage scoring areas. Assuming he does take on a checking role, he will be able to capitalize on the turnovers that high-octane first lines can be prone to.

Stoll is smart and competitive. Scouts like him more for the overall package rather than for any single skill.

THE PHYSICAL GAME

Stoll plays with an edge. He knows it takes a physical price to play in the NHL and he's willing to pay it. He had only a brief taste of the majors in his call-up by the Oilers last season, but he appears to be physically and mentally ready. Stoll is naturally competitive.

THE INTANGIBLES

How can Edmonton afford to lose Todd Marchant to free agency? When they have a youngster like Stoll ready to step in.

PROJECTION

Stoll will eventually become a third-line center who can produce 15-20 goals. It might even happen right off the bat.

MICHAEL YORK

Yrs. of NHL service: 4
Born: Pontiac, Mich.; Jan. 3, 1978
Position: center
Height: 5-10
Weight: 185
Uniform no.: 16
Shoots: right

Career statistics:

GP	G	A	TP	PIM
313	82	111	193	64

1999-2000 statistics:

GP	G	A	TP	+/-	PIM	PP	SH	GW	GT	S	PCT
82	26	24	50	-17	18	8	0	4	2	177	14.7

2000-2001 statistics:

GP	G	A	TP	+/-	PIM	PP	SH	GW	GT	S	PCT
79	14	17	31	+1	20	3	2	4	0	171	8.2

2001-2002 statistics:

GP	G	A	TP	+/-	PIM	PP	SH	GW	GT	S	PCT
81	20	41	61	+7	16	3	0	6	1	218	9.2

2002-2003 statistics:

GP	G	A	TP	+/-	PIM	PP	SH	GW	GT	S	PCT
71	22	29	51	-8	10	7	2	4	0	177	12.4

LAST SEASON

Second on team in assists and shots. Tied for second on team in shorthanded goals. Tied for third on team in points, power-play goals, and assists. Missed one game due to headaches. Missed seven games with fractured wrist.

THE FINESSE GAME

York is small but he finds a way to get the job done. He is fast enough to be first on the puck and will take a hit to make a play. He has good hands and vision. York finds a way to get the puck on net. He doesn't have a dangerous shot, but he knows by getting some action going in front of the goalie, a scoring chance may develop. York doesn't find anything embarrassing in scoring or assisting on garbage goals.

York has a decent wrister that he releases quickly and accurately, and a soft passing touch. Plus he's smart. York adjusted much better in his first full season in Edmonton after being disappointed by a draft-deadline trade from the Rangers late in the 2001-02 season. One thing readily apparent to the Edmonton coaching staff is that York makes players around him better, and that doesn't show up in his stats.

York is reliable, consistent, and can be used in every conceivable game situation with the possible exception of a bench-clearing brawl.

THE PHYSICAL GAME

York is small and needs to play a smarter small-man's game. He is a high-energy player and forechecks hard every shift, which tends to wear him out. He is remarkably durable and plays through a lot of dings without a complaint. He's a quiet guy, and well-respected by his teammates.

THE INTANGIBLES

York is not a star by any means, but he is a 10-year NHLer and a complementary player who can fit in on any hockey team. His size is his only drawback.

PROJECTION

York will be an integral part of the Oilers again this season and should get 55-60 points if he can stay intact.

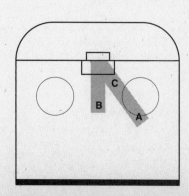

FLORIDA PANTHERS

Players' Statistics 2001-2002

POS.	NO.	PLAYER	GP	G	A	PTS	+/-	PIM	PP	SH	GW	GT	S	PCT
C	12	OLLI JOKINEN	81	36	29	65	-17	79	13	3	6		240	15.0
C	25	VIKTOR KOZLOV	74	22	34	56	-8	18	7	1	1	1	232	9.5
L	22	KRISTIAN HUSELIUS	78	20	23	43	-6	20	3		3	3	187	10.7
L	18	MARCUS NILSON	82	15	19	34	2	31	7	1			187	8.0
C	16	MATT CULLEN	80	13	20	33	-8	34	3	1	2		131	9.9
R	39	IVAN NOVOSELTSEV	78	10	17	27	-16	30	1			1	115	8.7
C	27	*JAROSLAV BEDNAR	67	5	22	27	1	18	2		1	2	95	5.3
L	14	NIKLAS HAGMAN	80	8	15	23	-8	20	2				132	6.1
C	9	*STEPHEN WEISS	77	6	15	21	-13	17			2		87	6.9
D	4	*JAY BOUWMEESTER	82	4	12	16	-29	14	2			2	110	3.6
D	6	ANDREAS LILJA	73	4	11	15	13	70					72	5.6
D	56	IVAN MAJESKY	82	4	8	12	-18	92			2		52	7.7
D	7	PAVEL TRNKA	46	3	9	12	1	30	1				58	5.2
D	34	MATHIEU BIRON	34	1	8	9	-18	14		1			52	1.9
L	32	STEPHANE MATTEAU	52	4	4	8	-9	27					47	8.5
R	21	DENIS SHVIDKI	23	4	2	6	-7	12	2		1		29	13.8
L	8	PETER WORRELL	63	2	3	5	-14	193					52	3.8
L	29	JEFF TOMS	8	2	2	4	2	4			1		12	16.7
C	19	BYRON RITCHIE	30		3	3	-4	19					29	
D	5	BRANISLAV MEZEI	11	2		2	-2	10			1		10	20.0
D	55	IGOR ULANOV	56	1	1	2	7	39					20	5.0
R	23	JURAJ KOLNIK	10		1	1	1						14	
L	38	*ERIC BEAUDOIN	15		1	1	-7	25					11	
D	29	IGOR KRAVCHUK	7		1	1	-3	4					8	
L	24	DARCY HORDICHUK	28				-2	97					7	
R	26	PIERRE DAGENAIS	9				-1	4					5	
R	15	JIM CAMPBELL	1				0						3	
D	28	JAMIE RIVERS	1				-2	2					2	
G	1	ROBERTO LUONGO	65				0	4						
G	30	JANI HURME	28				0	2						
D	33	*KYLE ROSSITER	3				-2							

GP = games played; G = goals; A = assists; PTS = points; +/- = goals-for minus goals-against while player is on ice; PIM = penalties in minutes; PP = power-play goals; SH = shorthanded goals; GW = game-winning goals; GT = game-tying goals; S = no. of shots; PCT = percentage of goals to shots; * = rookie

JAROSLAV BEDNAR

Yrs. of NHL service: 2
Born: Prague, Czech Republic; Nov. 8, 1976
Position: center
Height: 5-11
Weight: 198
Uniform no.: 27
Shoots: right

Career statistics:

GP	G	A	TP	PIM
89	9	24	33	26

2001-2002 statistics:

GP	G	A	TP	+/-	PIM	PP	SH	GW	GT	S	PCT
22	4	2	6	-4	8	1	0	2	0	20	20.0

2002-2003 statistics:

GP	G	A	TP	+/-	PIM	PP	SH	GW	GT	S	PCT
67	5	22	27	+1	18	2	0	1	2	95	5.3

LAST SEASON

Acquired from Los Angeles with Andreas Lilja on November 26, 2002, for Dmitry Yushkevich and a fifth-round draft pick in 2003. First NHL season. Tied for third among NHL rookies in assists. Tied for 10th among NHL rookies in points. Third on team in plus-minus. Missed one game due to illness.

THE FINESSE GAME

Bednar makes some beautiful goals and passes. His finesse moves have been compared to Martin Rucinsky, but this guy's got more determination to his game than Rucinsky had.

Bednar has an excellent wrist shot. He is a sleek, fast, well-balanced skater with speed and acceleration.

Bednar plays more of a traditional North American game — less of an East-West game than a lot of Europeans. Bednar needs to improve his defensive play and his consistency.

THE PHYSICAL GAME

Bednar doesn't initiate hits but he will fight his way through checks. He can be very strong along the boards, when he plays with determination — which isn't every night.

THE INTANGIBLES

Bednar was an overage draft pick by the Los Angeles Kings in 2001. The Kings hoped he could move right into their lineup, but he had to be sent to the minors to develop his all-around game. He played well, but erratically, after the trade to Florida, which is a team with a heavy European flavor. All five of his goals (in 52 games) came with the Panthers. He needs to show more if he is to win a job on one of the top two lines.

PROJECTION

Bednar may have 30-goal potential, as some scouts have said, but he is 26 and those goals better start coming soon.

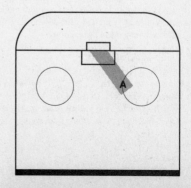

MATHIEU BIRON

Yrs. of NHL service: 3
Born: Lac-St. Charles, Que.; Aug. 29, 1980
Position: right defense
Height: 6-6
Weight: 226
Uniform no.: 43
Shoots: right

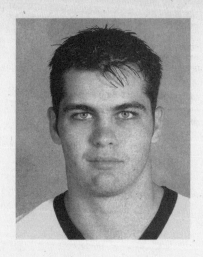

Career statistics:

GP	G	A	TP	PIM
144	5	13	18	76

1999-2000 statistics:

GP	G	A	TP	+/-	PIM	PP	SH	GW	GT	S	PCT
60	4	4	8	-13	38	2	0	2	0	70	5.7

2000-2001 statistics:

GP	G	A	TP	+/-	PIM	PP	SH	GW	GT	S	PCT
14	0	1	1	+2	12	0	0	0	0	10	0.0

2001-2002 statistics:

GP	G	A	TP	+/-	PIM	PP	SH	GW	GT	S	PCT
36	0	0	0	-16	12	0	0	0	0	35	0.0

2002-2003 statistics:

GP	G	A	TP	+/-	PIM	PP	SH	GW	GT	S	PCT
34	1	8	9	-18	14	0	1	0	0	52	1.9

LAST SEASON

Acquired from Columbus on October 4, 2002, for Petr Tenkrat. Third on team in average ice time. Missed eight games due to coach's decision. Appeared in 43 games with San Antonio (AHL), scoring 3-8 — 11 with 58 PIM.

THE FINESSE GAME

Biron didn't get a great start to his pro career in the Islanders organization and has bounced around a lot since. Only 23, he may just be starting to put the pieces together.

Biron has all of the desired skills in a solid NHL defenseman. He skates well for a big guy. He has a long, smooth stride with good acceleration, and he's tight in his turns.

He has an excellent shot. He has a nice touch with the puck for passing or shooting, but has to improve his speed in moving the puck, yet not be hasty. He is still guilty of some ghastly giveaways. He should develop more poise and confidence with the puck. If he does, he could earn second unit power-play time. Biron can also be used to kill penalties.

THE PHYSICAL GAME

Biron has picked up his hitting. He has good size and needs to make the most of it. He is well-balanced and hard to knock off his feet. He has to initiate more, but he is very at home when the hitting picks up. He needs to develop more lower-body strength to pack a bigger wallop in his checks.

THE INTANGIBLES

Biron started the season in coach Mike Keenan's doghouse and was banished to the minors. He played regularly after his late January call-up and was rewarded with increased ice time. He should come into training camp with a shot at winning a job on the second defense pair. Biron has a good attitude that doesn't seem to have been permanently scarred by some of his struggles to find a home.

PROJECTION

Big defensemen take longer to graduate. Biron will be worth the wait. He needs to learn defense first, but he has good offensive upside and could score in the 20-point range.

JAY BOUWMEESTER

Yrs. of NHL service: 1
Born: Edmonton, Alta.; Sept. 27, 1983
Position: defense
Height: 6-4
Weight: 210
Uniform no.: 4
Shoots: left

Career statistics:

GP	G	A	TP	PIM
82	4	12	16	14

2002-2003 statistics:

GP	G	A	TP	+/-	PIM	PP	SH	GW	GT	S	PCT
82	4	12	16	-29	14	2	0	0	2	110	3.6

LAST SEASON

First NHL season. Named to NHL All-Rookie Team. Worst plus-minus on team. One of three Panthers to appear in all 82 games.

THE FINESSE GAME

Despite playing on a non-playoff team and struggling defensively at times, Bouwmeester took a big step forward last season.

What is most impressive about Bouwmeester is his skating. It's no wonder he drew comparisons to Bobby Orr and Paul Coffey in his draft year (2002, when he was taken third overall). He is fast and agile, with quick acceleration. He skates so effortlessly that he is usually moving faster than it looks.

Bouwmeester has a cannon point shot, either a slapper or a one-timer, and a nice passing touch. His hockey sense and vision are very advanced. On defense, Bouwmeester is poised and has an instinctive feel for being in the right place at the right time. He carries the puck with confidence and makes smart decisions. He jumps into the rush alertly.

Most of his ice time came in crucial game situations, such as against other team's top lines, and trying to protect a rare Florida lead.

THE PHYSICAL GAME

Coach Mike Keenan, who was a key part of Chris Pronger's development, has already likened Bouwmeester to the St. Louis star in his attitude and mannerisms. Bouwmeester is already six-foot-four and he will continue to fill out his frame, which was already pretty solid and had him looking like a man among boys in junior. But now he is a boy among men, and he has to be willing to pay the physical price. He is not a punishing hitter. Bouwmeester isn't overly tough, and he doesn't fight. He is pretty fit although he tailed off at the end of the season, which is no surprise for a first-year pro.

THE INTANGIBLES

Bouwmeester has a very low-key personality. His modesty, which seems genuine, should help him blend in with older teammates, but Keenan might want him to be more assertive. His quiet demeanor has some detractors saying Bouwmeester lacks a passion for the game.

Bouwmeester would benefit from a veteran partner to mentor him, but it's a young corps in Florida, so it looks like he will have to do it himself.

PROJECTION

Bouwmeester's situation in Florida prevented him from earning Calder Trophy consideration, but all in all it proved to be a satisfying debut at a tough position. Bouwmeester will probably contribute a little more offensively, maybe around 25 points.

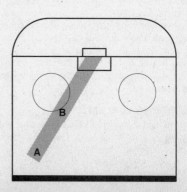

VALERI BURE

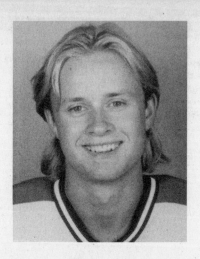

Yrs. of NHL service: 8
Born: Moscow, Russia; June 13, 1974
Position: right wing
Height: 5-10
Weight: 185
Uniform no.: 20
Shoots: right

Career statistics:

GP	G	A	TP	PIM
553	152	196	348	195

1999-2000 statistics:

GP	G	A	TP	+/-	PIM	PP	SH	GW	GT	S	PCT
82	35	40	75	-7	50	13	0	6	1	308	11.4

2000-2001 statistics:

GP	G	A	TP	+/-	PIM	PP	SH	GW	GT	S	PCT
78	27	28	55	-21	26	16	0	2	0	276	9.8

2001-2002 statistics:

GP	G	A	TP	+/-	PIM	PP	SH	GW	GT	S	PCT
31	8	10	18	-3	12	2	0	1	0	100	8.0

2002-2003 statistics:

GP	G	A	TP	+/-	PIM	PP	SH	GW	GT	S	PCT
51	5	23	28	-13	10	3	0	2	0	161	3.1

LAST SEASON

Acquired on waivers from St. Louis on June 25, 2003. Acquired by St. Louis on March 11, 2003, from Florida with a conditional third-round draft pick in 2004 for Mike Van Ryn. Missed 20 games with knee surgery. Missed 12 games with broken wrist.

THE FINESSE GAME

While a dynamic player, Bure struggles with the team concept. Bure has a great sense of anticipation and wants the puck every time he's on the ice. And, he can make things happen, though he sometimes tries to force the action rather than let the game flow naturally. He gets carried away in his pursuit of the puck and gets caught out of position, whereas if he just showed patience the puck would come to him.

Bure works well down low on the power play, but will also switch off and drop back to the point. He shows supreme confidence in his shot and scoring ability, and is very tough to defend against one-on-one.

He has good hands to go along with his speed and seems to get a shot on goal or a scoring chance on every shift. He is smart and creative, and can make plays as well as finish. Where Bure has to raise his game most is in the clutch, which is something he has never done.

THE PHYSICAL GAME

Bure is strong for his size and has to be more willing to pay the price. He has to keep a little grit in his game to succeed.

THE INTANGIBLES

Bure has had three knee surgeries in the past two seasons. Florida essentially loaned him to St. Louis for five games and got Mike Van Ryn all for a third-round draft pick, but they've also reacquired the final year of Bure's contract at (gulp) $3.1 million.

PROJECTION

Bure seems to be the kind of player who needs everything to go right for him to have a big season. Nothing ever does.

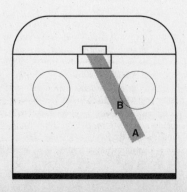

MATT CULLEN

Yrs. of NHL service: 6
Born: Virginia, Minn.; Nov. 2, 1976
Position: center
Height: 6-0
Weight: 205
Uniform no.: 16
Shoots: left

Career statistics:

GP	G	A	TP	PIM
457	71	141	212	190

1999-2000 statistics:

GP	G	A	TP	+/-	PIM	PP	SH	GW	GT	S	PCT
80	13	26	39	+5	24	1	0	1	0	137	9.5

2000-2001 statistics:

GP	G	A	TP	+/-	PIM	PP	SH	GW	GT	S	PCT
82	10	30	40	-23	38	4	0	1	0	159	6.3

2001-2002 statistics:

GP	G	A	TP	+/-	PIM	PP	SH	GW	GT	S	PCT
79	18	30	48	-1	24	3	1	4	0	164	11.0

2002-2003 statistics:

GP	G	A	TP	+/-	PIM	PP	SH	GW	GT	S	PCT
80	13	20	33	-8	34	3	1	2	0	131	9.9

PROJECTION

Cullen scored 6-6 — 12 in 30 games with Florida after the trade. He needs to show a bit more than that, although his top end isn't much above 45 points. To accomplish that, though, he will have to win a full-time job in training camp.

LAST SEASON

Acquired from Anaheim on January 30, 2003, with Pavel Trnka and a fourth-round draft pick in 2003 for Sandis Ozolinsh and Lance Ward. Third on team in game-winning goals and shooting percentage.

THE FINESSE GAME

Cullen has good speed and a good slap shot, and he handles the puck well in traffic. He is also willing to drive into the high-density areas of the ice. What he lacks is a soft pair of hands to finish off the plays.

Cullen is a better playmaker than goal-scorer. He needs to play with finishers but he also has to have the confidence to take the shot himself rather than try to force a bad pass.

An intelligent player with good hockey vision, Cullen has acceptable defensive awareness. It's an area he needs to work on, though, because right now it is tough to tell if Cullen will develop into a checking forward or a safety-valve center (think: Steve Rucchin) who can play with more talented but higher-risk linemates.

THE PHYSICAL GAME

Cullen is strong and fast and he has an aggressive streak to complement his work ethic. He plays hard every shift. Cullen has to judge situations better and not go full-tilt unless there is a chance of some reward, or else he tends to wear down physically.

THE INTANGIBLES

Cullen is a character player who can be appreciated for his teamwork as well as his skills.

NIKLAS HAGMAN

Yrs. of NHL service: 2
Born: Espoo, Finland; Dec. 5, 1979
Position: left wing
Height: 6-0
Weight: 200
Uniform no.: 14
Shoots: left

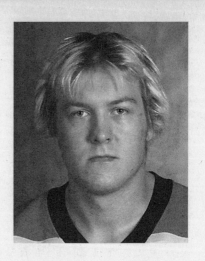

Career statistics:

GP	G	A	TP	PIM
158	18	33	51	28

2001-2002 statistics:

GP	G	A	TP	+/-	PIM	PP	SH	GW	GT	S	PCT
78	10	18	28	-6	8	0	1	2	0	134	7.5

2002-2003 statistics:

GP	G	A	TP	+/-	PIM	PP	SH	GW	GT	S	PCT
80	8	15	23	-8	20	2	0	0	0	132	6.1

LAST SEASON

Missed two games due to coach's decision.

THE FINESSE GAME

Some players survive the trial by fire that a tough coach like Mike Keenan brings to the team. Hagman didn't.

It's surprising because Hagman would seem to be Keenan's type of player. He is quick on the forecheck and he finishes all of his hits, even though he isn't all that big. Hagman simply gives you everything he has. Keenan wanted more.

Hagman has great hockey sense. Add that to his good skating and a really nice set of hands, and the possibilities await. Florida might try to play him as a third-liner again, but he is too undersized for that.

Hagman is a very good penalty killer, but he shouldn't be pegged as a mere defensive forward.

THE PHYSICAL GAME

Hagman's major drawback is his lack of size, but he doesn't let that interfere with his style of play.

THE INTANGIBLES

Hagman should be due for a bounce-back season after his promising freshman campaign. He may benefit from a change of scenery or a change of coach. There would be a number of teams eager to take him off Florida's hands. He is a role player with some upside.

Hagman has second-line potential, although he might not ever be a huge scorer. Hagman is a character guy. Think of a slightly less physical Dallas Drake, with better hands.

PROJECTION

Hagman fell well below the 15-20 goals we projected for him last season. Last season was a step backwards. This season will help determine Hagman's future.

KRISTIAN HUSELIUS

Yrs. of NHL service: 2
Born: Osterhaninge, Sweden; Nov. 10, 1978
Position: left wing
Height: 6-1
Weight: 190
Uniform no.: 22
Shoots: left

Career statistics:

GP	G	A	TP	PIM
157	43	45	88	34

2001-2002 statistics:

GP	G	A	TP	+/-	PIM	PP	SH	GW	GT	S	PCT
79	23	22	45	-4	14	6	1	3	0	169	13.6

2002-2003 statistics:

GP	G	A	TP	+/-	PIM	PP	SH	GW	GT	S	PCT
78	20	23	43	-6	20	3	0	3	3	187	10.7

LAST SEASON

Second on team in game-winning goals and shooting percentage. Third on team in goals, assists, and points. Tied for third on team in shots. Missed three games with knee injury. Missed one game due to coach's decision.

THE FINESSE GAME

Huselius is a heady player who uses his linemates well. He senses the holes and jumps into them for scoring chances, and has decent hands to take advantage of the opportunities. Huselius may be the best stickhandler on the Panthers.

Florida was concerned about how Huselius would adapt to the smaller North American ice surfaces after excelling in Sweden. Huselius made the transition effortlessly. He plays an uptempo game.

Huselius needs to play on one of the top two lines to be effective.

THE PHYSICAL GAME

Huselius isn't a big forward, but he has decent size. He needs to apply himself more physically and produce a better effort on a nightly basis.

THE INTANGIBLES

Huselius was a finalist for the 2002 Calder Trophy and followed up his dynamic rookie campaign with a quietly effective sophomore season. Huselius didn't seem to be one of coach Mike Keenan's favorites, and his ice time suffered because of that.

PROJECTION

Huselius should have moved forward from his rookie year, but the backslide was hardly devastating. He could easily rebound with 25 goals this season.

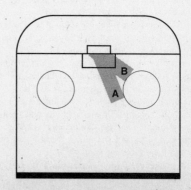

OLLI JOKINEN

Yrs. of NHL service: 5
Born: Kuopio, Finland; Dec. 5, 1978
Position: center
Height: 6-3
Weight: 205
Uniform no.: 12
Shoots: left

Career statistics:

GP	G	A	TP	PIM
395	71	81	152	413

1999-2000 statistics:

GP	G	A	TP	+/-	PIM	PP	SH	GW	GT	S	PCT
82	11	10	21	0	80	1	2	3	0	138	8.0

2000-2001 statistics:

GP	G	A	TP	+/-	PIM	PP	SH	GW	GT	S	PCT
78	6	10	16	-22	106	0	0	0	0	121	5.0

2001-2002 statistics:

GP	G	A	TP	+/-	PIM	PP	SH	GW	GT	S	PCT
80	9	20	29	-16	98	3	1	0	1	153	5.9

2002-2003 statistics:

GP	G	A	TP	+/-	PIM	PP	SH	GW	GT	S	PCT
81	36	29	65	-17	79	13	3	6	0	240	15.0

LAST SEASON

Led team in goals, points, power-play goals, short-handed goals, game-winning goals, shots, and shooting percentage. Second on team in average ice time (22:01) and assists. Third on team in penalty minutes. Missed one game with flu.

THE FINESSE GAME

Maybe Mike Keenan is a coaching genius. Jokinen, who a little more than a year ago was close to quitting the NHL and preparing to return to his native Finland to play, instead set career-best marks in almost every category. If there was a trophy for Most Improved Player in the NHL, it would have to go to Jokinen.

The journey from the fourth line to the first line was facilitated by Keenan who had the faith to put Jokinen out shift after shift, even after mistakes, which was something Jokinen had not experienced with his other head coaches. That started after Keenan took over from Duane Sutter, and gave Jokinen a head start in last year's training camp.

Maybe confidence was all Jokinen was missing. As the third overall draft pick (by Los Angeles in 1997), Jokinen felt intense pressure to score from the get-go, but when the points didn't come, criticism mounted. Jokinen was traded to the Islanders and then to the Panthers, losing his game along the way.

Now the budding power forward is beginning to blossom. He has considerable creativity and strength. He has become a better finisher than a playmaker, and has become more selfish, which is not a bad thing when you have a scoring touch.

Defensively Jokinen needs work (a lot), but

Keenan was probably willing to let that go last season to groom Jokinen's offensive touch.

THE PHYSICAL GAME

Jokinen was far more consistent in his physical play last season than ever before. He plays hard, uses his solid build, and won't be intimidated. He has a slightly nasty side that he needs to let loose more often, especially now that he is facing opponents' top checking lines. He can be chippy and annoying to play against.

THE INTANGIBLES

How will Jokinen respond now that the attention is focused on him again, and what will he do if Keenan doesn't return as the Panthers coach? Jokinen was a restricted free agent after the season, and couldn't have made a more spectacular case for a raise.

PROJECTION

When a player makes such a quantum leap in production (his previous season-high in goals was 11), it is hazardous to expect him to repeat it next season. However, Jokinen is a player that was pegged as this kind of performer in his draft year, so it would not be unreasonable to expect a repeat showing.

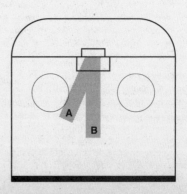

VIKTOR KOZLOV

Yrs. of NHL service: 8
Born: Togliatti, Russia; Feb. 14, 1975
Position: center
Height: 6-5
Weight: 225
Uniform no.: 25
Shoots: right

Career statistics:

GP	G	A	TP	PIM
540	119	214	333	152

1999-2000 statistics:

GP	G	A	TP	+/-	PIM	PP	SH	GW	GT	S	PCT
80	17	53	70	+24	16	6	0	2	0	223	7.6

2000-2001 statistics:

GP	G	A	TP	+/-	PIM	PP	SH	GW	GT	S	PCT
51	14	23	37	-4	10	6	0	2	0	139	10.1

2001-2002 statistics:

GP	G	A	TP	+/-	PIM	PP	SH	GW	GT	S	PCT
50	9	18	27	-16	20	6	0	1	0	143	6.3

2002-2003 statistics:

GP	G	A	TP	+/-	PIM	PP	SH	GW	GT	S	PCT
74	22	34	56	-8	18	7	1	1	1	232	9.5

LAST SEASON

Led team in average ice time (22:35) and assists. Second on team in goals, points, and shots. Career high in goals. Tied for second on team in power-play goals. Missed eight games due to abdominal injury.

THE FINESSE GAME

Kozlov is a beautiful skater for his size. He has the moves of a 150-pounder, with quickness and agility. He holds his own with faster linemates, but playing on a line with a power forwards suits his game better.

Kozlov has learned to come off the boards much quicker. As a huge right-handed shooter attacking the left side, he has a move that — dare we say it — makes him look like Mario Lemieux. He can undress a defender with his stickhandling and create a scoring chance down low. He has a keen sense of timing and pace, and is one of the top stickhandlers in the league.

Kozlov had three injury-plagued seasons which set back his development and confidence. He loves to shoot and has regained his confidence in his shot. He has an accurate wrist shot with a quick release. It is so strong that he can beat a goalie with an unscreened wrister from 40 feet out and the netminder won't be to blame. Kozlov is strong on the puck and strong shooting the puck. The defense sags off him and opens up room for linemates as well as himself.

He won't float and he has defensive principles. He won't hang at the redline, and he is an attentive backchecker. With deceptively quick acceleration for a player of his size, he excels at the transition game. Kozlov needs to learn to protect the puck better by keeping it closer to his feet. He often makes it too easy for a defender to strip the puck from him.

THE PHYSICAL GAME

Kozlov's physique makes him sturdy in contact, and when he goes down on a hook or a hold, nine times out of ten it's a dive. Although he has a long reach, Kozlov doesn't care to play the body defensively, though offensively he will work with the puck to get in front of the net and into scoring position. He handles the puck well in traffic, and has added some muscle.

THE INTANGIBLES

Kozlov will become a key ingredient if the Panthers hope to become playoff contenders. He was a restricted free agent during the off-season.

PROJECTION

Kozlov showed signs of life last season but this well hasn't been tapped yet. He has 80-point skill but we'd take a jump into the 70s this season.

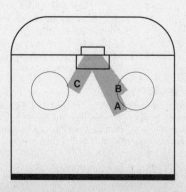

LUKAS KRAJICEK

Yrs. of NHL service: 1
Born: Prostejov, Czech Republic; Mar. 11, 1983
Position: defense
Height: 6-2
Weight: 182
Uniform no.: 29
Shoots: left

Career statistics:

GP	G	A	TP	PIM
5	0	0	0	0

2001-2002 statistics:

GP	G	A	TP	+/-	PIM	PP	SH	GW	GT	S	PCT
5	0	0	0	0	0	0	0	0	0	3	0.0

2002-2003 statistics:

Did not play in NHL

LAST SEASON

Will be entering first NHL season. Appeared in 52 games with Peterborough (OHL), scoring 11-42 — 53 with 42 PIM.

THE FINESSE GAME

Krajicek has world-class offensive skills. His skating and hands are exceptional. He is developing into a second-pair defenseman who will always be high-risk. His development is one of the reasons why the Panthers felt comfortable in trading away Sandis Ozolinsh.

Krajicek is poised with the puck, intelligent, and has good vision. All of his efforts, though, are concentrated on creating scoring chances.

Everything about Krajicek's game is attractive, except for his gambling passes, his ill-advised pinches, and his tendency to get trapped deep while the other team skates back on an odd-man rush.

THE PHYSICAL GAME

Krajicek isn't the least bit physical. The Panthers wisely sent him back for another year of junior hockey to get stronger and to be more prepared for playing against rugged players.

THE INTANGIBLES

Krajicek underwent off-season shoulder surgery which probably means he won't be able to win a starting role with the Panthers right off of training camp. We would be surprised if he isn't with the big club by the second half. Krajicek has been compared to Phil Housley for his up-tempo offensive game.

PROJECTION

Krajicek has a lot of offensive potential, but he's a defensive project. If he makes the team, he could score 30 points. He could also be -30. We can promise this: He won't be boring.

ANDREAS LILJA

Yrs. of NHL service: 2
Born: Landskrona, Sweden; July 13, 1975
Position: left defense
Height: 6-3
Weight: 222
Uniform no.: 6
Shoots: left

Career statistics:

GP	G	A	TP	PIM
101	5	15	20	96

2000-2001 statistics:

GP	G	A	TP	+/-	PIM	PP	SH	GW	GT	S	PCT
2	0	0	0	-2	4	0	0	0	0	1	0.0

2001-2002 statistics:

GP	G	A	TP	+/-	PIM	PP	SH	GW	GT	S	PCT
26	1	4	5	+3	22	1	0	0	0	12	8.3

2002-2003 statistics:

GP	G	A	TP	+/-	PIM	PP	SH	GW	GT	S	PCT
73	4	11	15	+13	70	0	0	0	0	72	5.6

PROJECTION

The steady Lilja will again be one of Florida's top-four defensemen, but he won't produce much offensively. His limit may be 20 points.

LAST SEASON

Acquired from Los Angeles with Jaroslav Bednar on November 26, 2002, for Dmitry Yushkevich and a fifth-round draft pick in 2003. Led team in plus-minus. Missed two games with foot injury. Missed one game with hand injury.

THE FINESSE GAME

The Panthers lost Robert Svehla (to a brief "retirement," when he was traded to Toronto), but gained, via trade, Lilja. The unheralded acquisition merely became Florida's steadiest defenseman.

Lilja is hardly flamboyant, but he is complete. He is fundamentally sound in all of the defensive basics. He does the little things well and adapts to any game situation.

Lilja doesn't have much offensive instinct, but he has a good shot from the point. He drills it, and puts the puck in play for tips and rebounds. He won't gamble in deep.

Most of his finesse skills are used in a defensive mode. Lilja plays a sound positional game and has a quick first step to the puck.

THE PHYSICAL GAME

Lilja is a big guy but he's not a banger. He is confident, but not very aggressive. He does a good job of tying up his man and he has a long reach.

Lilja had trouble adjusting to the NHL grind but has become better conditioned.

THE INTANGIBLES

With barely 100 NHL career games, Lilja is pretty much the grand old man of the Florida defense. He was a little mentally lost in the last month or so of the season, probably because of the lack of playoff hope.

ROBERTO LUONGO

Yrs. of NHL service: 3
Born: Montreal, Que.; Apr. 4, 1979
Position: goaltender
Height: 6-3
Weight: 205
Uniform no.: 1
Catches: left

Career statistics:

GP	MIN	GA	SO	GAA	A	PIM
194	10577	481	16	2.73	1	8

1999-2000 statistics:

GP	MIN	GAA	W	L	T	SO	GA	S	SAPCT	PIM
24	1292	3.25	7	14	1	1	70	730	.904	0

2000-2001 statistics:

GP	MIN	GAA	W	L	T	SO	GA	S	SAPCT	PIM
47	2628	2.44	12	24	7	5	107	1333	.920	2

2001-2002 statistics:

GP	MIN	GAA	W	L	T	SO	GA	S	SAPCT	PIM
58	3030	2.77	16	33	4	4	140	1653	.915	2

2002-2003 statistics:

GP	MIN	GAA	W	L	T	SO	GA	S	SAPCT	PIM
65	3627	2.71	20	34	7	6	164	2011	.918	4

LAST SEASON

Career high in wins. Missed three games with back spasms. Missed one game with bruised knee.

THE PHYSICAL GAME

Luongo is very tall and plays a butterfly style that completely takes away the top part of the net from shooters. So they try to go five-hole. Guess what? Luongo has really, really big pads (he'll be victimized if the NHL ever carries through with an equipment crackdown), fast legs, and good flexibility.

Luongo has a tendency to try to use his feet too much to kick out the puck, and he can leave some bad rebounds. Improved confidence in using his stick and controlling the puck for his defensemen will be a help. Luongo doesn't have to be Martin Brodeur. He just needs to give his defense a chance to play the puck.

Luongo's one glaring weakness is his lack of lateral movement. He needs to concentrate on improving his footwork because it won't take NHL shooters very long to figure out how to jerk him from post to post. Luongo has to avoid staying deep in his net. He is a terrific athlete.

THE MENTAL GAME

Luongo's game still has same flaws, but he is starting to believe in himself as a No. 1 goalie and that confidence is rubbing off on his teammates. Luongo is going to face another long season because of the youth of the team, but Luongo is starting to handle the mental ups and downs of the game better, staying competitive but on an even keel.

Luongo is very likable and has a great deal of presence and poise.

THE INTANGIBLES

Luongo played behind the 29th-ranked offense in the league and still gave his team a chance to win the game on many nights. He was clearly the Panthers' MVP last season.

PROJECTION

Luongo just hit the 20-win mark we projected for him last season. Considering the struggles of the team, that is an impressive number. We'll look for a slight improvement on that this season, but only by three or four wins.

MARCUS NILSON

Yrs. of NHL service: 3
Born: Balsta, Sweden; Mar. 1, 1978
Position: left wing
Height: 6-2
Weight: 195
Uniform no.: 18
Shoots: right

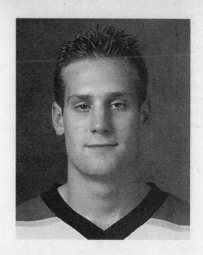

Career statistics:

GP	G	A	TP	PIM
258	42	65	107	167

1999-2000 statistics:

GP	G	A	TP	+/-	PIM	PP	SH	GW	GT	S	PCT
9	0	2	2	+2	2	0	0	0		6	-

2000-2001 statistics:

GP	G	A	TP	+/-	PIM	PP	SH	GW	GT	S	PCT
78	12	24	36	-3	74	0	0	2	0	141	8.5

2001-2002 statistics:

GP	G	A	TP	+/-	PIM	PP	SH	GW	GT	S	PCT
81	14	19	33	-14	55	6	1	2	0	147	9.5

2002-2003 statistics:

GP	G	A	TP	+/-	PIM	PP	SH	GW	GT	S	PCT
82	15	19	34	+2	31	7	1	0	0	187	8.0

PROJECTION

Until he proves otherwise, Nilson's max is probably 30 points, which he achieved last season.

LAST SEASON

Second on team in plus-minus. Tied for second on team in power-play goals. Tied for third on team in shots. One of three Panthers to appear in all 82 games.

THE FINESSE GAME

Nilson is a two-way player who has concentrated more on his defense (he was one of only three plus players among the Panthers' regulars), but he can produce more than he has thus far.

Nilson has very good hockey sense, a good passing touch and is a playmaker first. It behoves him to play with a finisher.

Nilson's chief flaw is his skating. He is pretty awkward and doesn't have great speed. We tend to think of all Europeans as being great skaters. Nilson is a glaring exception.

THE PHYSICAL GAME

Nilson is on the quiet side, not aggressive, but he's actually pretty gritty. Quietly tough, he played the last month of the season with a bad shoulder and didn't miss a game.

Nilson has increased his leg strength. He is strong along the boards and shows an increased desire to battle for the puck.

THE INTANGIBLES

Nilson continued to see considerable playing time on one of Florida's top-two lines (often with Viktor Kozlov) but we are starting to suspect Nilson's future is as a third-line checking winger who can add a soupcon of offense.

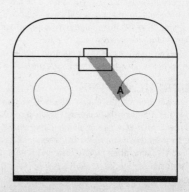

IVAN NOVOSELTSEV

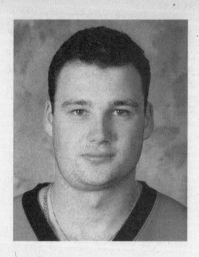

Yrs. of NHL service: 3
Born: Golitsino, Russia; Jan. 23, 1979
Position: right wing
Height: 6-1
Weight: 210
Uniform no.: 39
Shoots: left

Career statistics:

GP	G	A	TP	PIM
200	28	40	68	98

1999-2000 statistics:

GP	G	A	TP	+/-	PIM	PP	SH	GW	GT	S	PCT
14	2	1	3	-3	8	2	0	0	0	8	25.0

2000-2001 statistics:

GP	G	A	TP	+/-	PIM	PP	SH	GW	GT	S	PCT
38	3	6	9	-5	16	0	0	0	0	34	8.8

2001-2002 statistics:

GP	G	A	TP	+/-	PIM	PP	SH	GW	GT	S	PCT
70	13	16	29	-10	44	1	1	5	0	109	11.9

2002-2003 statistics:

GP	G	A	TP	+/-	PIM	PP	SH	GW	GT	S	PCT
78	10	17	27	-16	30	1	0	0	1	115	8.7

LAST SEASON

Career high in assists. Missed one game with facial injury. Missed one game with back injury. Missed two games due to coach's decision.

THE FINESSE GAME

Novoseltsev is a left-handed shot who plays the right wing. This opens up his forehand for one-timers. He plays a reckless style and is always looking for the net. He also has blinding speed and the ability to pick up the puck behind his own net and go end-to-end. He intimidates with his speed, driving defensemen back on their heels before he cuts inside or outside. His wrist shot is his favorite weapon. He needs to work to get into position to take more and better shots. Novoseltsev also needs to develop the desire to force his way into the play when room does not open up for him. He plays too much of a perimeter game.

The usual red flag attached to Novoseltsev is his lack of defensive awareness. He can also be a bit selfish with the puck and doesn't always use his teammates well. The Panthers have tried to hammer this into him but it's been slow to take hold.

Expectations were extremely high early in his career, but they have been scaled back drastically.

THE PHYSICAL GAME

Novoseltsev doesn't get overly involved in physical play. He is a bigger than average-sized player who plays much smaller. Once in awhile Novoseltsev will drive to the crease for a scoring chance. It would improve his game dramatically if he did it on a more consistent basis.

THE INTANGIBLES

Novoseltsev is maddeningly inconsistent. Florida is starting to add some North American-style forwards to the lineup, and while he was a top-six forward last season, Novoseltsev could be on the bubble unless he has a strong training camp.

PROJECTION

The only thing Novoseltsev does is score, and if he's not doing that, he's worthless in the lineup. Novoseltsev needed to score 20 goals last season to prove he belonged in the NHL. He didn't do that, and his stock has plummeted.

MIKE VAN RYN

Yrs. of NHL service: 2
Born: London, Ont.; May 14, 1979
Position: right defense
Height: 6-1
Weight: 190
Uniform no.: 43
Shoots: right

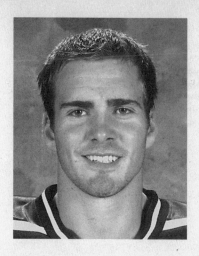

Career statistics:

GP	G	A	TP	PIM
69	2	11	13	26

2000-2001 statistics:

GP	G	A	TP	+/-	PIM	PP	SH	GW	GT	S	PCT
1	0	0	0	-2	0	0	0	0	0	1	0.0

2001-2002 statistics:

GP	G	A	TP	+/-	PIM	PP	SH	GW	GT	S	PCT
48	2	8	10	+10	18	0	0	1	0	52	3.8

2002-2003 statistics:

GP	G	A	TP	+/-	PIM	PP	SH	GW	GT	S	PCT
20	0	3	3	+3	8	0	0	0	0	21	0.0

LAST SEASON

Acquired from St. Louis on March 11, 2003, for Valeri Bure and a conditional draft pick in 2004. Appeared in 33 games with Worcester (AHL), scoring 2-8 — 10 with 16 PIM. Appeared in 11 games with San Antonio (AHL), scoring 0-3 — 3 with 20 PIM.

THE FINESSE GAME

Van Ryn needs to keep the game simple. He was projected as an impact offensive defenseman, but it's pretty clear that isn't going to happen, even though Van Ryn has very good skating skills. It has taken a long time (three years in the minors) for him to stop trying to do it all himself, the way he could in junior and college. Van Ryn will have to shed his high-risk tendencies to play in the NHL.

Van Ryn was such a dominant skater at lesser levels that he was able to rush the puck all the time and outskate other players. When he got to the pro level, he found that players could angle him off and force him to cough up the puck. He wasn't able to have much success until he learned the give and go, the short outlet pass, the safe route.

Van Ryn is projected as a top-four defenseman in Florida, where he will probably see significant special teams assignments. He has a good, low, accurate shot from the point and will make a solid if not elite power-play quarterback.

THE PHYSICAL GAME

Van Ryn is still filling out to NHL size. He has an aggressive streak in him. He willingly clears out the front of his net and just has to get a little stronger for those wars. He's an intense player.

THE INTANGIBLES

Van Ryn went back to junior after two years of college, and an arbiter freed his rights from New Jersey. Van Ryn became a free agent and made the cash grab, which was great for his bank account. But he missed out on playing for a system that is just about unparalleled in developing young defensemen, and that has hurt his career, maybe permanently. Florida coach Mike Keenan was instrumental in shaping up Chris Pronger's career. Maybe he can bolster Van Ryn's.

PROJECTION

Van Ryn could score 20 points and will continue to develop all aspects of his game.

STEPHEN WEISS

Yrs. of NHL service: 1
Born: Toronto, On.; Apr. 3, 1983
Position: center
Height: 5-11
Weight: 183
Uniform no.: 9
Shoots: left

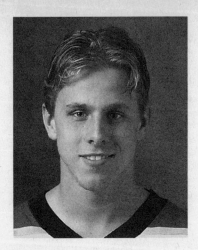

Career statistics:

GP	G	A	TP	PIM
84	7	16	23	17

2001-2002 statistics:

GP	G	A	TP	+/-	PIM	PP	SH	GW	GT	S	PCT
7	1	1	2	0	0	1	0	0	0	15	6.7

2002-2003 statistics:

GP	G	A	TP	+/-	PIM	PP	SH	GW	GT	S	PCT
77	6	15	21	-13	17	0	0	2	0	87	6.9

LAST SEASON

First NHL season. Third on team in game-winning goals. Missed five games with fractured toe.

THE FINESSE GAME

Weiss looked terribly out of place on the Panthers last season. Another year in junior might have done wonders for his development, and the Panthers just have to hope they didn't ruin Weiss (the fourth overall pick in the 2001 draft) by rushing him.

Weiss has posted nice numbers in junior, but he's going to be more than just a one-way center. He has some flair, but he's no prima donna. He backchecks diligently and will likely turn into one of Florida's better face-off guys once he adapts to the NHL.

Scouts think he might develop into a Steve Yzerman-type, a player who has the skill level to score 100 points but who will settle for 80 because he will dedicate himself to a two-way game. He has the heads and the hands for the game.

Weiss has a fluid skating stride, very efficient and with good acceleration.

THE PHYSICAL GAME

Weiss will need to improve his upper-body strength. He will probably never get bulky, but he can be wiry-tough. Weiss must also keep up his conditioning for the NHL grind.

THE INTANGIBLES

Weiss played on the third line most of last season but is going to develop into a top-six forward. He seems to have desire and a good attitude. Confidence will be a factor since he is a young player on a very young team and could use a mentor. He was a captain in junior and possesses obvious leadership qualities.

PROJECTION

Weiss has the potential to be a No. 1 center in Florida in a few seasons. As his playing time increases, so will his production. We aren't ready to give up on this kid yet. He's the goods.

If he wins a full-time role this year, it would be no shock to see him score 35 points.

LOS ANGELES KINGS

Players' Statistics 2001-2002

POS.	NO.	PLAYER	GP	G	A	PTS	+/-	PIM	PP	SH	GW	GT	S	PCT
R	33	ZIGMUND PALFFY	76	37	48	85	22	47	10	2	5	.	277	13.4
D	44	JAROSLAV MODRY	82	13	25	38	-13	68	8		1		205	6.3
C	32	DEREK ARMSTRONG	66	12	26	38	5	30	2		1		106	11.3
C	25	ERIC BELANGER	62	16	19	35	-5	26		3	1		114	14.0
L	24	*ALEXANDER FROLOV	79	14	17	31	12	34	1		3		141	9.9
C	41	JASON ALLISON	26	6	22	28	9	22	2		3	1	46	13.0
D	17	LUBOMIR VISNOVSKY	57	8	16	24	2	28	1		1		85	9.4
C	22	IAN LAPERRIERE	73	7	12	19	-9	122	1	1	1		85	8.2
R	28	ADAM DEADMARSH	20	13	4	17	2	21	4		1		55	23.6
L	42	MIKKO ELORANTA	75	5	12	17	-15	56	1		1		96	5.2
C	27	ERIK RASMUSSEN	57	4	12	16	-1	28			1		75	5.3
C	19	SEAN AVERY	51	6	9	15	7	153			2		59	10.2
R	29	BRAD CHARTRAND	62	8	6	14	-10	33		1	2		64	12.5
D	26	*JOSEPH CORVO	50	5	7	12	2	14	2				84	5.9
R	57	STEVE HEINZE	27	5	7	12	-5	12	1				44	11.4
L	23	CRAIG JOHNSON	70	3	6	9	-13	22					87	3.4
C	13	*MICHAEL CAMMALLERI	28	5	3	8	-4	22	2		2		40	12.5
D	63	BRAD NORTON	53	3	3	6	1	97					19	15.8
D	3	AARON MILLER	49	1	5	6	-7	24					34	2.9
D	14	MATTIAS NORSTROM	82		6	6	0	49					63	
C	11	STEVE KELLY	15	2	3	5	-6				1		14	14.3
C	31	*JARED AULIN	17	2	2	4	-3		1				21	9.5
L	43	JONATHAN SIM	22	1	2	3	-4	19					39	2.6
D	6	MAXIM KUZNETSOV	56		3	3	1	54					33	
D	5	*TOMAS ZIZKA	10		3	3	-4	4					12	
D	38	CHRIS MCALPINE	21		2	2	-4	24					15	
C	51	CHRIS SCHMIDT	10		2	2	-1	5					10	
C	52	*JERRED SMITHSON	22		2	2	-5	21					9	
L	49	*RYAN FLINN	19	1		1	0	28					13	7.7
D	53	JASON HOLLAND	2		1	1	1							
D	37	*KIP BRENNAN	19				0	57					6	
C	62	*SCOTT BARNEY	5				-1						5	
R	55	PAVEL ROSA	2				-1						4	
C	58	DEREK BEKAR	6				-1	4					4	
G	39	FELIX POTVIN	42				0	4						
L	12	KEN BELANGER	4				0	17						
G	1	JAMIE STORR	39				0	8						
G	45	TRAVIS SCOTT					0							
G	35	CRISTOBAL HUET	12				0							

GP = games played; G = goals; A = assists; PTS = points; +/- = goals-for minus goals-against while player is on ice; PIM = penalties in minutes; PP = power-play goals; SH = shorthanded goals; GW = game-winning goals; GT = game-tying goals; S = no. of shots; PCT = percentage of goals to shots; * = rookie

JASON ALLISON

Yrs. of NHL service: 10
Born: North York, Ont.; May 29, 1975
Position: center
Height: 6-3
Weight: 215
Uniform no.: 41
Shoots: right

Career statistics:

GP	G	A	TP	PIM
486	137	288	425	365

1999-2000 statistics:

GP	G	A	TP	+/-	PIM	PP	SH	GW	GT	S	PCT
37	10	18	28	+5	20	3	0	1	1	66	15.2

2000-2001 statistics:

GP	G	A	TP	+/-	PIM	PP	SH	GW	GT	S	PCT
82	36	59	95	-8	85	11	3	6	0	185	19.5

2001-2002 statistics:

GP	G	A	TP	+/-	PIM	PP	SH	GW	GT	S	PCT
73	19	55	74	+2	68	5	0	2	2	139	13.7

2002-2003 statistics:

GP	G	A	TP	+/-	PIM	PP	SH	GW	GT	S	PCT
26	6	22	28	+9	22	2	0	3	1	46	13.0

LAST SEASON

Third on team in average ice time (21:35) and plus-minus. Missed 23 games with knee injuries. Missed 33 games with cervical strain/hip pointer/concussion.

THE FINESSE GAME

Allison had become one of the best centers in the NHL, and one of its most underrated, but the injuries he suffered last season were major and they cast doubt as to whether he can rise to the elite level again.

Allison is among the best players in the league from the top of the circles in. He isn't flashy, he isn't brawny, but he is savvy, resolute, and highly skilled. Allison is a player capable of dominating games. He is strong on the puck, skates well, has excellent vision and sure, soft hands to put passes where they need to go. He is the complete package offensively.

Allison faces top checkers every shift and still excels. He makes players on his line better, and seems to adjust to whatever linemates are on his flanks. He moved from East Coast to West and didn't miss a beat. Allison is, night in and night out, one of the best forwards on the ice, especially on the power play. He excels with his down-low playmaking.

The puck follows Allison around the rink. He has great patience, uncanny hockey sense and is one of the top ten centers in the league when he is at the top of his game. Although his impact is predominantly on offense, he is often put on the ice to protect leads late in games, so his defense is hardly suspect.

THE PHYSICAL GAME

Allison hates to lose, and that gives him his great competitive edge. Allison is not quite as strong or tough as some of the league's best power forwards, but he goes through traffic and makes plays despite the checking attention focused on him. He is hungry to score and will pay the price to do so, as he showed last season.

THE INTANGIBLES

Allison is a big question mark because of injuries.

PROJECTION

If Allison is healthy, an assist-heavy 100 points would be a given. Pool players should steer clear unless there are some promising reports out of training camp. L.A.'s reacquisition of Jozek Stumpel looks like an insurance move in case Allison can't start the season.

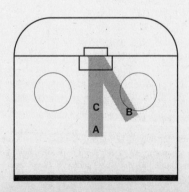

JARED AULIN

Yrs. of NHL service: 0
Born: Calgary, Alberta; Mar. 15, 1982
Position: center
Height: 6-0
Weight: 180
Uniform no.: 31
Shoots: right

Career statistics:

GP	G	A	TP	PIM
17	2	2	4	0

2002-2003 statistics:

GP	G	A	TP	+/-	PIM	PP	SH	GW	GT	S	PCT
17	2	2	4	-3	0	1	0	0	0	21	9.5

LAST SEASON

Will be entering first full NHL season. Missed two games with bruised left elbow. Appeared in 44 games with Manchester (AHL), scoring 12-32 — 44 with 21 PIM.

THE FINESSE GAME

Aulin has very nice hand skills and is an intelligent player, but is his skating good enough to keep up in the NHL?

Not only does Aulin have to keep pace, but because he isn't a very big player, he needs to find an extra gear so that he can gain the extra few steps he needs to get a jump on bigger opponents. At the moment, Aulin doesn't have it, but he was expected to work on his skating during the off-season to improve his foot speed. He is mobile but not at all quick.

Aulin has very good playmaking ability but doesn't possess any great scoring weapons. The majority of his points will come on assists.

THE PHYSICAL GAME

Aulin is definitely on the small and light-framed side and has had problems with injuries because of that. He needs to work on his upper-body strength and coaches would love to see a little more passion in his game.

THE INTANGIBLES

Injuries slowed his development in the minors, but he should be given a chance in training camp to win a starting job with the Kings. He showed some promising signs in his midseason call-up. Aulin is one of the players who came to the Kings in the 2001 Rob Blake deal with Colorado. He is an upbeat guy who will make a great addition to a room, provided he can play.

PROJECTION

His role as a top-six forward is no cinch, so keep expectations low (in the range of 20 assist-heavy points) for Aulin's first season.

ROMAN CECHMANEK

Yrs. of NHL service: 3
Born: Gottwaldov, Czech Republic, Mar. 2, 1971
Position: goaltender
Height: 6-3
Weight: 187
Uniform no.: 32
Catches: left

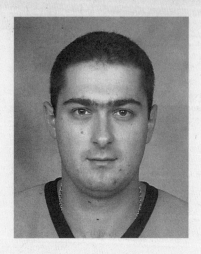

Career statistics:

GP	MIN	GA	SO	GAA	A	PIM
163	9384	306	20	1.96	1	22

2000-2001 statistics:

GP	MIN	GAA	W	L	T	SO	GA	S	SAPCT	PIM
59	3431	2.01	35	15	6	10	115	1464	.921	4

2001-2002 statistics:

GP	MIN	GAA	W	L	T	SO	GA	S	SAPCT	PIM
46	2603	2.05	24	13	6	4	89	1131	.921	10

2002-2003 statistics:

GP	MIN	GAA	W	L	T	SO	GA	S	SAPCT	PIM
58	3350	1.83	33	15	10	6	102	1368	.925	8

LAST SEASON

Acquired from Philadelphia on May 27, 2003, for a second-round draft pick in 2004. Second among NHL goalies in goals-against average. Tied for third among NHL goalies in save percentage. Missed three games with groin injury.

THE PHYSICAL GAME

Cechmanek makes the easy look difficult, which is exactly the opposite of what most teams want in a goaltender.

Cechmanek is limited in his lateral movement. Teams who play an east-west game can jerk him from post to post and find an opening. It also appears he doesn't always know where the puck is after he makes the initial save. Cechmanek overchallenges, often seeming to come out to the top of the circle, and it's a wonder he knows where the net is behind him. He probably just figures that anything shot towards him, he's going to be able to reach.

Cechmanek is so fundamentally unsound that if he weren't so big and so competitive, he never would have made it to this level. He takes up a lot of the net, and when he squares to the shooter, there is very little daylight for even the most gifted sniper to find.

Cechmanek covers the bottom half of the net as well as any goalie in the league. He is the only goalie who intentionally plays pucks off his head. OK, his head is protected by a helmet, but it's still weird.

He's more difficult to beat in-close: he slides his paddle along the ice to close holes. But he will allow bad long-range goals. His tendency to drop quickly makes him vulnerable to high shots on the corners. You'll see teams coming over the blueline and firing shots on him from above the circles.

THE MENTAL GAME

Cechmanek hates to lose, and on his best nights he plays a very focused game. But when things are going badly, Cechmanek is quick to pull up stakes rather than battle on.

THE INTANGIBLES

GM Bob Clarke finally gave up on Cechmanek, trading him after yet another disappointing playoffs by citing Cechmanek's tendency to pitch a shutout one night and allow soft goals the next. Strange that Clarke didn't realize this when everyone else in the league did, and signed him to a three-year, $10 million contract extension in January 2002. At least Clarke found another sucker in the L.A. Kings, who will discover that Cechmanek may be an upgrade from Felix Potvin, but not by much when it comes to crunch time.

PROJECTION

Cechmanek will be happy and secure in his new role as the No. 1 goalie in L.A. He'll get his share of shutouts and maybe around 28 wins, and will be his usual bizarre self should the Kings make the playoffs.

JOSEPH CORVO

Yrs. of NHL service: 1
Born: Oak Park, Ill.; June 20, 1977
Position: right defense
Height: 6-0
Weight: 205
Uniform no.: 26
Shoots: right

Career statistics:

GP	G	A	TP	PIM
50	5	7	12	14

2002-2003 statistics:

GP	G	A	TP	+/-	PIM	PP	SH	GW	GT	S	PCT
50	5	7	12	+2	14	2	0	0	0	84	5.9

LAST SEASON

First NHL season. Appeared in 26 games with Manchester (AHL), scoring 5-7 — 12 with 14 PIM.

THE FINESSE GAME

Corvo was able to play well as an offensive defenseman in the minors, and the Kings have hopes he will help fill the scoring void left after the trade of Mathieu Schneider.

Corvo certainly has good skills in the attacking zone, good enough that the Kings once flirted with the idea of converting him to forward. He is a very good skater and stickhandler. He can run a power play but isn't elite enough to be a first-unit quarterback.

Corvo has worked on his positional play and his defensive shortcomings in the minors. Since his point totals aren't going to be enough to compensate for many giveaways, he will have to continue his schooling.

THE PHYSICAL GAME

Corvo is average-sized but doesn't play a very physical game. He would need to play with a stay-at-home, physical partner to be most effective.

THE INTANGIBLES

Corvo missed all of the 1999-2000 season in a contract dispute. Principles are admirable, but the year off cost Corvo some valuable development time, and since he wasn't a blue chipper to begin with, he had to prove himself to Kings' management with little margin for error.

There are a slew of defense prospects ready to step up to grab jobs this fall. Corvo has a little bit of a jump thanks to the NHL experience he gained last season, but he can't take this opportunity for granted. Based on last season, we'd expect 20-25 points if he wins a full-time job.

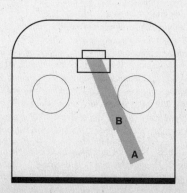

ADAM DEADMARSH

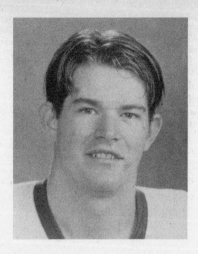

Yrs. of NHL service: 9
Born: Trail, B.C.; May 10, 1975
Position: right wing
Height: 6-0
Weight: 195
Uniform no.: 28
Shoots: right

Career statistics:

GP	G	A	TP	PIM
567	184	189	373	819

1999-2000 statistics:

GP	G	A	TP	+/-	PIM	PP	SH	GW	GT	S	PCT
71	18	27	45	-10	106	5	0	4	0	153	11.8

2000-2001 statistics:

GP	G	A	TP	+/-	PIM	PP	SH	GW	GT	S	PCT
57	17	15	32	+1	63	7	0	2	1	126	13.5

2001-2002 statistics:

GP	G	A	TP	+/-	PIM	PP	SH	GW	GT	S	PCT
76	29	33	62	+8	71	12	0	5	0	139	20.9

2002-2003 statistics:

GP	G	A	TP	+/-	PIM	PP	SH	GW	GT	S	PCT
20	13	4	17	+2	21	4	0	1	0	55	23.6

LAST SEASON

Third on team in power-play goals. Missed 61 games with a concussion. Missed one game with sprained wrist.

THE FINESSE GAME

Deadmarsh is feisty, tough, and can work in a checking role, but he can also play on a top line and score off the chances he creates with his defense and not look out of place. His game is incredibly mature. He is reliable enough to be put out on the ice to protect a lead in the late minutes of a game, because he'll do what it takes to win.

Deadmarsh is capable of playing in every situation. He's not as skilled as many top NHL forwards, but he has a meanness and a toughness about him. He's relentless in finishing his checks. He's very strong on the puck, very strong on the boards, and he's one of the faster players in the NHL in a power package. Although better at center than wing, he is versatile enough to handle either role.

Deadmarsh doesn't have to be the glamor guy, but that doesn't mean he provides unskilled labor. He has dangerous speed and quickness, and a nice scoring touch to convert the chances he creates off his forechecking. He doesn't play a complex game. He's a basic up-and-down winger. He excels as a dedicated penalty killer and has developed into a real force on the power play.

THE PHYSICAL GAME

Deadmarsh always finishes his checks. He has a strong work ethic with honest toughness. He never backs down from a challenge and issues some of his own. He isn't a dirty player, but he will fight when challenged or stand up for his teammates.

THE INTANGIBLES

Some players are never the same after a serious concussion, which is what ended Deadmarsh's season prematurely. Since so much of his game is based on playing with a snarl, he can't afford to be a hesitant, perimeter player. The Kings missed not only his skill but his leadership last year.

PROJECTION

Deadmarsh was on pace for a 40-goal season before the concussion. It's impossible to predict how he will recover until he starts playing NHL games again.

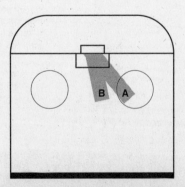

ALEXANDER FROLOV

Yrs. of NHL service: 1
Born: Moscow, Russia; June 19, 1982
Position: left wing
Height: 6-4
Weight: 191
Uniform no.: 24
Shoots: right

Career statistics:

GP	G	A	TP	PIM
79	14	17	31	34

2001-2002 European statistics:

GP	G	A	TP	PIM
43	18	12	30	16

2002-2003 statistics:

GP	G	A	TP	+/-	PIM	PP	SH	GW	GT	S	PCT
79	14	17	31	+12	34	1	0	3	0	141	9.9

LAST SEASON

First NHL season. Sixth among NHL rookies in points. Tied for seventh among NHL rookies in goals. Second on team in plus-minus. Tied for second on team in game-winning goals. Third on team in goals and shots. Missed two games with facial laceration. Missed one game due to coach's decision.

THE FINESSE GAME

Frolov is going to develop into a solid two-way power forward. He can play either left wing or center but is likely to develop as a winger where he has fewer concerns defensively.

Frolov is a finisher by nature. He has a goal-scorer's mentality. Put the puck on Frolov's stick anywhere near the net and a high-percentage scoring opportunity will result.

He protects the puck well. He is a tough guy to take off the puck. Frolov is strong one-on-one. He showed very good defensive awareness for a rookie and played well away from the puck.

THE PHYSICAL GAME

Frolov has the size and strength to play the pro game. There is a slight question as to whether he has the mental toughness, but he showed some positive signs last season.

THE INTANGIBLES

Frolov slumped at the end of the season (one goal in the last 11 games), but that is not uncommon for a player getting his first taste of a full North American schedule. Frolov handled a lot of minutes and might have worn down a little.

PROJECTION

We gave a 30-point projection for Frolov's rookie season and he came through. Now the issue for him will be developing the consistency and the conditioning to handle a full season as a top-six forward, which is what the Kings believe he is destined for. Don't expect a huge leap in production, but if he improves to the 40-point range he wil be on the right course.

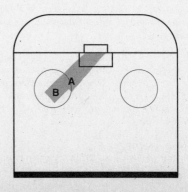

TIM GLEASON

Yrs. of NHL service: 0
Born: Southfield, Mich.; Jan. 29, 1983
Position: left defense
Height: 6-1
Weight: 201
Uniform no.: n.a.
Shoots: left

Career (junior) statistics:

GP	G	A	TP	PIM
214	37	114	151	225

2002-2003 junior statistics:

GP	G	A	TP	PIM
45	7	31	38	75

LAST SEASON

Acquired from Ottawa with future considerations on March 11, 2003, for Bryan Smolinski. Will be entering first NHL season. Appeared in 45 games with Windsor (OHL), scoring 7-31 — 38 with 75 PIM.

THE FINESSE GAME

Gleason has all the makings of a solid two-way NHL defenseman. His offensive skills, especially his fluid stride and effortless acceleration, are what caught the attentions of scouts first.

He is an excellent skater who can go end-to-end on a rush. His hand skills match his foot speed. If he gets involved low in the offensive zone, he is fast enough to recover and barrel back on defense. Gleason loves taking risks.

Gleason will produce most of his points from his speed. He may not develop into an elite-level point man on the power play because he doesn't have a very quick release on his slap shot, and he has trouble with one-timers.

THE PHYSICAL GAME

Not overly big by today's standards, Gleason is an honestly tough customer. He has a mean edge to his game, and has times when he snaps and can be scary-nasty. He will have to curb his temper, because he tends to take bad penalties that can cost his team. Gleason needs to play with attitude but not be selfish about his actions.

THE INTANGIBLES

Ottawa wasn't happy with the progress he showed in his final year of junior. That and the Senators' depth on defense made him trade bait, but he should be a good fit in L.A. He will probably need a firm hand from the coaching staff.

PROJECTION

Gleason is considered one of the blue chip prospects from the 2001 draft, and this could prove to be one steal of a deal for the Kings, who gave up a rent-a-player to get him. The Kings will give him every chance to make their roster in training camp, but if he starts the season in the minors, expect to see him by Christmas.

IAN LAPERRIERE

Yrs. of NHL service: 9
Born: Montreal, Que.; Jan. 19, 1974
Position: center
Height: 6-1
Weight: 201
Uniform no.: 22
Shoots: right

Career statistics:

GP	G	A	TP	PIM
633	68	114	182	1184

1999-2000 statistics:

GP	G	A	TP	+/-	PIM	PP	SH	GW	GT	S	PCT
79	9	13	22	-14	185	0	0	1	0	87	10.3

2000-2001 statistics:

GP	G	A	TP	+/-	PIM	PP	SH	GW	GT	S	PCT
79	8	10	18	+5	141	0	0	0	0	60	13.3

2001-2002 statistics:

GP	G	A	TP	+/-	PIM	PP	SH	GW	GT	S	PCT
81	8	14	22	+5	125	0	0	3	0	89	9.0

2002-2003 statistics:

GP	G	A	TP	+/-	PIM	PP	SH	GW	GT	S	PCT
73	7	12	19	-9	122	1	1	1	0	85	8.2

LAST SEASON

Second on team in penalty minutes. Missed three games due to knee surgery. Missed two games with back injury. Missed four games with cervical strain.

THE FINESSE GAME

Laperriere is the hardest, smartest player on the Kings, and he really stepped up his game when Jason Allison was lost to injury. Laperriere grew up watching Guy Carbonneau in Montreal, and he studied well. Laperriere knows how to win a draw between his feet. He uses his stick and his body to make sure the opposing center doesn't get the puck. He gets his bottom hand way down on the stick and tries to win draws on his backhand. He gets very low to the ice on draws.

The knock on Laperriere earlier in his career was his skating, but he has improved tremendously in that department. Although he'll never be a speed demon, he doesn't look out of place at the NHL level. He always tries to take the extra stride when he is backchecking so he can make a clean check, instead of taking the easy way out and committing a lazy hooking foul. He wins his share of races for the loose puck.

Laperriere is ever willing to use the backhand, either for shots or to get the puck deep. He is reliable defensively. He has little offensive instinct but gets his points off effort. He is best suited as a third-line checking forward.

THE PHYSICAL GAME

Laperriere is an obnoxious player who really battles for the puck. Although smallish, he has absolutely no fear of playing in the "circle" that extends from the lower inside of the face-off circles to behind the net.

He will pay any price. In fact, he often functioned as a bodyguard for Ziggy Palffy last season. He's an energy guy and a momentum changer. He thrives on being the first man in on the forecheck. Laperriere has suffered some serious head injuries in past seasons but remains a soldier undaunted.

He shows a ton of heart. He is essential to team chemistry. Laperriere channels his aggressions and takes few cheap penalties. He knows he can hurt his team by taking unnecessary calls.

THE INTANGIBLES

Laperriere adds true grit to the lineup despite his small size, which is his major flaw and the only one he can't do anything to change. His nightly effort puts a lot of bigger guys to shame. He is one of L.A.'s most consistent and popular forwards.

PROJECTION

Laperriere's skills are limited, but what he does, he does very well. His top range appears to be 25 points.

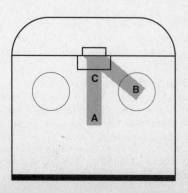

MATTIAS NORSTROM

Yrs. of NHL service: 9
Born: Mora, Sweden; Jan. 2, 1972
Position: left defense
Height: 6-2
Weight: 211
Uniform no.: 14
Shoots: left

Career statistics:

GP	G	A	TP	PIM
610	9	91	100	471

1999-2000 statistics:

GP	G	A	TP	+/-	PIM	PP	SH	GW	GT	S	PCT
82	1	13	14	+22	66	0	0	0	0	62	1.6

2000-2001 statistics:

GP	G	A	TP	+/-	PIM	PP	SH	GW	GT	S	PCT
82	0	18	18	+10	60	0	0	0	0	59	0.0

2001-2002 statistics:

GP	G	A	TP	+/-	PIM	PP	SH	GW	GT	S	PCT
79	2	9	11	-2	38	0	0	0	0	42	4.8

2002-2003 statistics:

GP	G	A	TP	+/-	PIM	PP	SH	GW	GT	S	PCT
82	0	6	6	0	49	0	0	0	0	63	0.0

LAST SEASON

Third on team in average ice time (21:30). One of two Kings to appear in all 82 games.

THE FINESSE GAME

Norstrom has established himself as a major physical presence and seems to rise to every challenge the Kings give him. He's a good skater, though he is still a little creaky in his pivots and turns. He does have straight-ahead speed, to a degree, thanks to a long stride. Along the boards he delivers strong, and frequent, hits.

Norstrom's foot skills outdistance his hand skills. He can make a decent pass but mostly he'll keep things simple with the puck — smacking it around the boards if he gets into trouble, rather than trying to make a play.

For so large a player, Norstrom uses a surprisingly short stick that cuts down on his reach defensively and limits some of his offensive options. However, he feels his responsibility is to break down the play, rather than create it. He will pinch down the boards occasionally, but only to drive the puck deeper, not to take the puck and make a play. He won't jump into the play on offense.

THE PHYSICAL GAME

Norstrom lives inside his opponent's jersey. He is hard-nosed. When he hits, you feel it. He is willing to do what it takes to help his team win. He is solidly built and likes to throw big, loud hits. He sacrifices his body by blocking shots. When Norstrom misses a game because of an injury, then he is really hurt, because he plays through a lot of pain.

He knows what he's good at. Norstrom has tremendously powerful legs and is strong on his skates. He has confidence in his power game and has developed a great enthusiasm for the physical aspect. Norstrom does it all without spending a lot of time in the box, which is pretty amazing when you watch how hard he plays.

THE INTANGIBLES

Norstrom is the Kings captain, which means a lot to him, especially as a European player. Maybe it's because he plays like a North American.

Norstrom is a hard-working athlete who loves to practise; a player valued more for his character than for his abilities, which are average. He is a defensive-style defenseman who will give his coach what's asked for, but he won't try to do things that will put the puck, or the team, in trouble. He is a steady player who routinely draws assignments against other teams' top lines. He's a real throwback.

PROJECTION

Norstrom will continue to get a large chunk of ice time, but his lack of offensive skills limit him to 15 points at best.

ZIGMUND PALFFY

Yrs. of NHL service: 9
Born: Skalica, Slovakia; May 5, 1972
Position: left wing
Height: 5-10
Weight: 183
Uniform no.: 33
Shoots: left

Career statistics:

GP	G	A	TP	PIM
607	302	328	630	298

1999-2000 statistics:

GP	G	A	TP	+/-	PIM	PP	SH	GW	GT	S	PCT
64	27	39	66	+18	32	4	0	3	1	186	14.5

2000-2001 statistics:

GP	G	A	TP	+/-	PIM	PP	SH	GW	GT	S	PCT
73	38	51	89	+22	20	12	4	8	0	217	17.5

2001-2002 statistics:

GP	G	A	TP	+/-	PIM	PP	SH	GW	GT	S	PCT
63	32	27	59	+5	26	15	1	6	1	161	19.9

2002-2003 statistics:

GP	G	A	TP	+/-	PIM	PP	SH	GW	GT	S	PCT
76	37	48	85	+22	47	10	2	5	0	277	13.4

LAST SEASON

Tied for 10th in NHL in points. Led team in goals, assists, points, plus-minus, power-play goals, game-winning goals, and shots. Second on team in average ice time (22:26), shorthanded goals, and shooting percentage. Missed six games with groin injuries.

THE FINESSE GAME

As trade rumors heated up last season, so did Palffy. Guess he really wants to stay in L.A., which is good news for the Kings, since he was their best player in a season ruined by injuries.

Palffy has elite, intellectual instincts with the puck and great vision. He has the confidence, and the arrogance, to try moves that only world-class players can execute. He is a game-breaker.

He has deceptive quickness. An elusive skater with a quick first step, he is shifty and can handle the puck while dancing across the ice. He won't burn around people, but when there's an opening he can get to it in a hurry. Sometimes a defender will let up on him for a fraction of a second, and when he does, Palffy has gained a full stride. His anticipation is what sets him apart.

Palffy has excellent hands for passing or shooting. He is one of the best snipers in the game. He is an aggressive penalty killer, always gambling for the shorthanded break, and is a constant threat.

THE PHYSICAL GAME

Palffy has a little bit of an edge to him. He's got the magic ingredient that sets the superior smaller players apart from the little guys who can't make the grade. He's not exactly a physical specimen, either. One player said of Palffy, "He's as unathletic a superstar as you'll ever find."

There are nights when Palffy coasts, and he has to be reminded by his coaches to produce more of a two-way effort. It has a magical effect on the Kings bench when he does.

Decidedly on the small side, Palffy can't afford to get into any battles in tight areas where he'll get crunched. He can jump in and out of holes and pick his spots, and he often plays with great spirit. He never puts himself in a position to get bowled over, but he has become less of a perimeter player and is more willing to take the direct route to the net, which has paid off in more quality scoring chances. He's not really a soft player. He won't go into the corner if he's going to get massacred, but he's not against hacking an opponent because he wants the puck.

THE INTANGIBLES

The Kings reacquired his pal Jozef Stumpel during the off-season, which can only improve Palffy's mood.

PROJECTION

If Jason Allison had stayed healthy, maybe Palffy would have hit the 50-goal mark last season. He is still capable of doing so.

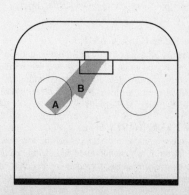

JOZEF STUMPEL

Yrs. of NHL service: 10
Born: Nitra, Slovakia; June 20, 1972
Position: center
Height: 6-3
Weight: 225
Uniform no.: 16
Shoots: right

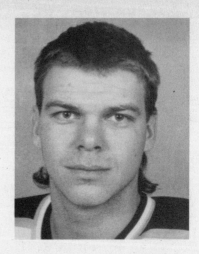

Career statistics:

GP	G	A	TP	PIM
694	143	368	511	171

1999-2000 statistics:

GP	G	A	TP	+/-	PIM	PP	SH	GW	GT	S	PCT
57	17	41	58	+23	10	3	0	7	1	126	13.5

2000-2001 statistics:

GP	G	A	TP	+/-	PIM	PP	SH	GW	GT	S	PCT
63	16	39	55	+20	14	9	0	6	0	95	16.8

2001-2002 statistics:

GP	G	A	TP	+/-	PIM	PP	SH	GW	GT	S	PCT
81	8	50	58	+22	18	1	0	3	0	100	8.0

2002-2003 statistics:

GP	G	A	TP	+/-	PIM	PP	SH	GW	GT	S	PCT
78	14	37	51	0	12	4	0	2	1	110	12.7

LAST SEASON

Acquired from Boston on June 20, 2003, for a fourth-round draft pick in 2003 and a second-round draft pick in 2004. Third on Bruins in assists. Missed three games with wrist injury. Missed one game with hip injury.

THE FINESSE GAME

Stumpel is a setup man and he needs to play with a stone finisher, because he overpasses. Stumpel has good hand skills which allow him to compensate for his skating, up to a point. He also has a deft scoring touch and is a passer with a good short game. He is very patient. He uses his feet well to keep the puck alive, to kick it up onto his stick, or to keep it in the attacking zone.

He also has keen hockey sense. But he does not shoot nearly enough, and that isn't likely to change at this point in his career.

Stumpel doesn't have much sand in his game and achieves everything with finesse.

THE PHYSICAL GAME

Stumpel is quite powerfully built, but he doesn't play to his size. He can be intimidated, and teams go after him early. He goes into the corners and bumps and protects the puck with his body, but when the action gets really fierce he backs off.

THE INTANGIBLES

Los Angeles reacquired Stumpel for the sole purpose of reuniting him with his good friend Ziggy Palffy, with whom Stumpel has played the best hockey of his career. The Kings may also worry that Jason Allison

will not be fully recovered from his injuries of last season. While Palffy is a No. 1 NHL right winger, Stumpel is not a true top NHL center. Palffy may just be talented enough to hoist him up another notch on a lot of nights, though.

PROJECTION

Stumpel will score 50 assists, 60 points, but you may not be able to find him when you really need him. He is not a crunch-time player.

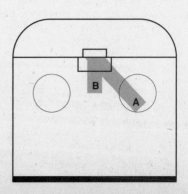

LUBOMIR VISNOVSKY

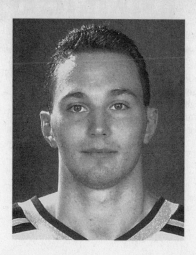

Yrs. of NHL service: 3
Born: Topolcany, Slovakia; Aug. 11, 1976
Position: left defense
Height: 5-10
Weight: 183
Uniform no.: 17
Shoots: left

Career statistics:

GP	G	A	TP	PIM
210	19	65	84	78

2000-2001 statistics:

GP	G	A	TP	+/-	PIM	PP	SH	GW	GT	S	PCT
81	7	32	39	+16	36	3	0	3	0	105	6.7

2001-2002 statistics:

GP	G	A	TP	+/-	PIM	PP	SH	GW	GT	S	PCT
72	4	17	21	-5	14	1	0	2	0	95	4.2

2002-2003 statistics:

GP	G	A	TP	+/-	PIM	PP	SH	GW	GT	S	PCT
57	8	16	24	+2	28	1	0	1	0	85	9.4

LAST SEASON

Missed 12 games with sprained knee. Missed 11 games with back injuries. Missed one game with sprained ankle. Missed one game with flu.

THE FINESSE GAME

Visnosvky started off the season regaining the form that saw him selected to the 2001 NHL All-Rookie Team, but a series of nagging injuries short-circuited what could have been a big bounce-back season. Even with those setbacks, there are enough good signs that tag him as a top-four defenseman for the Kings.

Visnovsky is an undersized defenseman with oversized offensive skills. He will never be an elite scoring defenseman, although there have been several small blueliners who have been able to have a major impact. He doesn't have quite the skating level for that. Visnovsky is a poor man's Brian Rafalski.

Visnovsky did show more power in his skating last year, and moved his feet instead of just coasting around. He needs to avoid getting pinned along the wall, because he isn't strong enough to win a battle. If he's skating, he's effective.

Visnovsky has a good shot from the point but is better used as a set-up man. He has good lateral mobility along the blueline and that increases his options. He moves the puck smartly.

THE PHYSICAL GAME

Visnovsky looks a lot smaller than advertised. Again, to make a Rafalski comparison, the New Jersey defenseman is very thick through his torso and can absorb some punishment, while Visnovsky is more slender. He is surrounded by some physical defense mates which makes his small stature less detrimental than it could be on some other teams. But when he gets in one-on-one situations, he is simply swamped.

THE INTANGIBLES

Visnovsky has matured a little physically and a lot more mentally. He seems settled in his personal life and that has made him calmer in his professional life.

PROJECTION

We liked what we saw of Visnovsky last season. If he can manage to avoid the injury jinx, expect him to see a lot of first-unit power-play ice time and a point increase to 40.

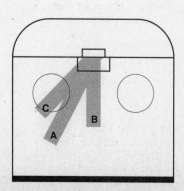

MINNESOTA WILD

Players' Statistics 2001-2002

POS.	NO.	PLAYER	GP	G	A	PTS	+/-	PIM	PP	SH	GW	GT	S	PCT
L	10	MARIAN GABORIK	81	30	35	65	12	46	5	1	8		280	10.7
L	11	PASCAL DUPUIS	80	20	28	48	17	44	6		4	1	183	10.9
C	7	CLIFF RONNING	80	17	31	48	-6	24	8		5		171	9.9
L	15	ANDREW BRUNETTE	82	18	28	46	-10	30	9		2	3	97	18.5
C	33	SERGEI ZHOLTOK	78	16	26	42	1	18	3		2	2	153	10.4
C	37	WES WALZ	80	13	19	32	11	63			4		115	11.3
L	24	ANTTI LAAKSONEN	82	15	16	31	4	26	1	2	4	2	106	14.1
D	17	FILIP KUBA	78	8	21	29	0	29	4	2	1		129	6.2
C	34	JIM DOWD	78	8	17	25	-1	31	3	1	2		78	10.3
R	18	RICHARD PARK	81	14	10	24	-3	16	2	2	3	1	149	9.4
C	96	*PIERRE-MARC BOUCHARD	50	7	13	20	1	18	5		1		53	13.2
D	20	ANDREI ZYUZIN	67	4	13	17	-8	36	2				113	3.5
D	5	BRAD BOMBARDIR	58	1	14	15	15	16	1				55	1.8
D	2	WILLIE MITCHELL	69	2	12	14	13	84		1	1		67	3.0
L	28	JEREMY STEVENSON	32	5	6	11	6	69	1		1		29	17.2
D	77	LUBOMIR SEKERAS	60	2	9	11	-12	30	1		1		50	4.0
D	55	NICK SCHULTZ	75	3	7	10	11	23			1		70	4.3
R	16	BILL MUCKALT	8	5	3	8	5	6					13	38.5
L	12	MATT JOHNSON	60	3	5	8	-8	201			1		24	12.5
D	23	JASON MARSHALL	45	1	5	6	4	69					40	2.5
C	14	DARBY HENDRICKSON	28	1	5	6	-3	8					34	2.9
L	19	*STEPHANE VEILLEUX	38	3	2	5	-6	23	1				52	5.8
R	27	*KYLE WANVIG	7	1		1	0	13					5	20.0
C	25	*RICKARD WALLIN	4	1		1	1				1		1	100.0
D	4	BRAD BROWN	57		1	1	-1	90					10	
D	3	LADISLAV BENYSEK	14				-3	8					7	
L	9	HNAT DOMENICHELLI	1				0						1	
G	35	EMMANUEL FERNANDEZ	35				0	6						
G	31	DIETER KOCHAN	1				0							
G	30	DWAYNE ROLOSON	50				0	4						
L	6	JEAN-GUY TRUDEL	1				0	2						
D	38	CURTIS MURPHY	1				0							

GP = games played; G = goals; A = assists; PTS = points; +/- = goals-for minus goals-against while player is on ice; PIM = penalties in minutes; PP = power-play goals; SH = shorthanded goals; GW = game-winning goals; GT = game-tying goals; S = no. of shots; PCT = percentage of goals to shots; * = rookie

PIERRE-MARC BOUCHARD

Yrs. of NHL service: 1
Born: Sherbrooke, Que.; Apr. 27, 1984
Position: center
Height: 5-10
Weight: 165
Uniform no.: 96
Shoots: left

Career statistics:

GP	G	A	TP	PIM
50	7	13	20	18

2002-2003 statistics:

GP	G	A	TP	+/-	PIM	PP	SH	GW	GT	S	PCT
50	7	13	20	+1	18	5	0	1	0	53	13.2

LAST SEASON

First NHL season. Missed 19 games due to coach's decision.

THE FINESSE GAME

Having seen what a little guy like Cliff Ronning can do offensively in the NHL, Minnesota is not going to be prejudiced against another teeny center.

Bouchard is a truly dynamic package of talent. He is a quick and evasive skater who can do a lot of things with the puck at a high pace. He has great vision, passing skills, and hockey sense. Anyone playing on his wing has to stay alert because Bouchard is the kind of playmaker who can make something out of nothing. He works the give and go, he has the confidence to try to beat a defender one-on-one, he can slither a perfect flat pass for a one-timer, and he has the patience to draw a defender to him and then find an open teammate for an odd-man scoring rush. Bouchard can control the tempo of a shift.

Bouchard needs to develop more confidence in his shot. He has a decent wrister although he will always primarily be a setup man.

His other drawback (other than lack of size) is a need to improve his understanding of his checking assignments. He looks a little aimless in his own zone. He knows right where everything is at the other end, though.

THE PHYSICAL GAME

Bouchard is small and also has a pretty light frame. It may be hard for him to bulk up without having the added weight affect his sublime skating.

THE INTANGIBLES

Minnesota allowed Bouchard to play for Canada in the World Junior Championships at midseason. Bouchard had been in and out of the lineup but after the tournament was a healthy scratch in only four of the last 40 games. He saw limited playoff action.

PROJECTION

The expected departure of Ronning may be the opportunity Bouchard needs. He could be a 40-point scorer (heavy on the assists). He is going to be a real fun player to watch.

ANDREW BRUNETTE

Yrs. of NHL service: 8
Born: Sudbury, Ont.; Aug. 24, 1973
Position: left wing
Height: 6-1
Weight: 210
Uniform no.: 15
Shoots: left

Career statistics:

GP	G	A	TP	PIM
460	106	189	295	154

1999-2000 statistics:

GP	G	A	TP	+/-	PIM	PP	SH	GW	GT	S	PCT
81	23	27	50	-32	30	9	0	2	1	107	21.5

2000-2001 statistics:

GP	G	A	TP	+/-	PIM	PP	SH	GW	GT	S	PCT
77	15	44	59	-5	26	6	0	4	1	104	14.4

2001-2002 statistics:

GP	G	A	TP	+/-	PIM	PP	SH	GW	GT	S	PCT
81	21	48	69	-4	18	10	0	2	1	106	19.8

2002-2003 statistics:

GP	G	A	TP	+/-	PIM	PP	SH	GW	GT	S	PCT
82	18	28	46	-10	30	9	0	2	3	97	18.5

LAST SEASON

Led team in power-play goals and shooting percentage. Third on team in goals. Tied for third on team in assists. One of two Wild players to appear in all 82 games.

THE FINESSE GAME

Brunette has an excellent short game, from the hash marks down. He has very good hands. He is able to make a pass in a small space. He is effective along the boards because he is so elusive.

Although Brunette is not an NHL-caliber skater, he is able to prove that he is an NHL-caliber scorer. Brunette is like a Dave Andreychuk in miniature. He has excellent soft hands for flicking in pucks out of midair, making deflections, scooping up rebounds. Brunette will not be scoring goals off the rush.

The problem with being a smaller Andreychuk is that Brunette does not have the same reach the big 500-goal scorer does. And he will not be able to stretch around defensemen or lean on his stick in front of the net the way Andreychuk did in his prime.

Brunette possesses a goal-scorer's mentality and expansion has given him the chance to prove it in Atlanta and now in Minnesota. Brunette has good hockey vision and excels on the power play.

THE PHYSICAL GAME

Brunette is not afraid to take his lumps around the net. He has a power-forward's build and has a little bit of an edge. To use an Andreychuk comparison again, he has a pretty long fuse and he has to be provoked before he'll snap. Brunette is tough along the boards and is willing to fight for the puck in all the dirty areas of the ice.

THE INTANGIBLES

Brunette will be one of Minnesota's top two left wings and one of its top power-play weapons.

PROJECTION

Brunette will continue to see prime ice time with Minnesota, and should score 20 goals and 50 points.

PASCAL DUPUIS

Yrs. of NHL service: 2
Born: Laval, Que.; Apr. 7, 1979
Position: left wing
Height: 6-0
Weight: 195
Uniform no.: 11
Shoots: left

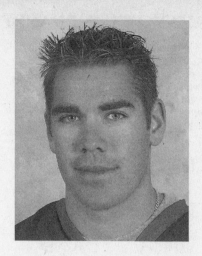

Career statistics:

GP	G	A	TP	PIM
160	36	40	76	64

2000-2001 statistics:

GP	G	A	TP	+/-	PIM	PP	SH	GW	GT	S	PCT
4	1	0	1	0	4	1	0	0	0	8	12.5

2001-2002 statistics:

GP	G	A	TP	+/-	PIM	PP	SH	GW	GT	S	PCT
76	15	12	27	-10	16	3	2	0	0	154	9.7

2002-2003 statistics:

GP	G	A	TP	+/-	PIM	PP	SH	GW	GT	S	PCT
80	20	28	48	+17	44	6	0	4	1	183	10.9

LAST SEASON

Led team in plus-minus. Second on team in goals and shots. Third on team in power-play goals. Tied for third on team in assists and game-winning goals. Missed one game with knee injury. Missed one game due to coach's decision.

Dupuis, a free agent signing in 2000, has evolved into Minnesota's No. 1 left winger, although that's a pretty lofty role for him. There is really nothing outstanding about his game, but the total package and the effort he puts out every night made him a suitable partner for Minnesota's brilliant right wing, Marian Gaborik.

Dupuis is average in almost every department although his skating is above NHL caliber. What sets Dupuis apart is how hard he works. He's gritty and earnest on the forecheck.

Defensively aware, Dupuis is savvy enough so that coach Jacques Lemaire doesn't hesitate to leave him out against other team's top lines when the Wild is on the road and Lemaire can't get the last change.

THE PHYSICAL GAME

Dupuis is not very big but he is gritty and has a solid work ethic. He is tailor-made for a style like the Wild's and for a coach like Lemaire.

THE INTANGIBLES

Dupuis is one of those quiet, effective two-way forwards who can have a steady 10-year NHL career. He had a respectable playoffs.

PROJECTION

Dupuis is a second-line left wing on a team that doesn't have a bona fide first-line left wing. He would do well to repeat his production of last season. We think those numbers are pretty much his top end.

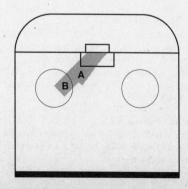

EMMANUEL FERNANDEZ

Yrs. of NHL service: 4
Born: Etobicoke, Ont.; Aug. 27, 1974
Position: goaltender
Height: 6-0
Weight: 185
Uniform no.: 35
Catches: left

Career statistics:

GP	MIN	GA	SO	GAA	A	PIM
154	8693	365	8	2.52	3	18

1999-2000 statistics:

GP	MIN	GAA	W	L	T	SO	GA	S	SAPCT	PIM
24	1353	2.13	11	8	3	1	48	603	.920	2

2000-2001 statistics:

GP	MIN	GAA	W	L	T	SO	GA	S	SAPCT	PIM
42	2461	2.24	19	17	4	4	92	1147	.920	6

2001-2002 statistics:

GP	MIN	GAA	W	L	T	SO	GA	S	SAPCT	PIM
44	2463	3.05	12	24	5	1	125	1157	.892	4

2002-2003 statistics:

GP	MIN	GAA	W	L	T	SO	GA	S	SAPCT	PIM
35	1979	2.24	19	13	2	2	74	972	.924	6

PROJECTION

Fernandez will again battle with Roloson for the right to be Minnesota's No. 1 goalie, so expect him to get fewer than 50 starts and around 22 wins.

LAST SEASON

Matched career high in wins. Missed 10 games with knee injury.

THE PHYSICAL GAME

Fernandez plays an athletic, scrambling style that is a good fit for an inexperienced club. He is a very active goalie out of his net, and that takes some of the heat off his defensemen. Minnesota's top pair would be Nos. 6 and 7 on a good team, so the more help they can get from their goalie, the better.

He has uncanny flexibility and quick reactions. His lateral movement is exceptional. Fernandez is one of the best goalies in the league at pushing off to get across from post to post. He is really good down low.

Fernandez has a quirky personality. But he worked hard during his many years as backup to Ed Belfour in Dallas to earn the respect of his teammates, who might otherwise not have been eager to follow him into battle.

THE MENTAL GAME

Fernandez has higher highs but lower lows than his partner Dwayne Roloson, which is why coach Jacques Lemaire didn't hesitate to switch goalies in the playoffs, a highly unusual strategy. Consistency continues to elude Fernandez (who is Lemaire's nephew, by the way).

THE INTANGIBLES

This might be Fernandez's last chance to prove he is a No. 1 goalie in the NHL. Fernandez was a restricted free agent after the season.

MARIAN GABORIK

Yrs. of NHL service: 3
Born: Trencin, Slovakia; Feb. 14, 1982
Position: left wing
Height: 6-1
Weight: 183
Uniform no.: 10
Shoots: left

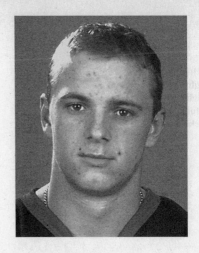

Career statistics:

GP	G	A	TP	PIM
230	78	90	168	112

2000-2001 statistics:

GP	G	A	TP	+/-	PIM	PP	SH	GW	GT	S	PCT
71	18	18	36	-6	32	6	0	3	0	179	10.1

2001-2002 statistics:

GP	G	A	TP	+/-	PIM	PP	SH	GW	GT	S	PCT
78	30	37	67	0	34	10	0	4	1	221	13.6

2002-2003 statistics:

GP	G	A	TP	+/-	PIM	PP	SH	GW	GT	S	PCT
81	30	35	65	+12	46	5	1	8	0	280	10.7

LAST SEASON

Led team in goals for second consecutive season. Led team in assists, points, game-winning goals, and shots. Missed one game with flu.

THE FINESSE GAME

The mark of a truly special player is whether he elevates the game of anyone who plays with him. Wayne Gretzky did. Mario Lemieux does. So does Gaborik.

Gaborik may never be an elite goal-scorer but he is a threat every time he has the puck. He can have a pretty successful career scoring consistently in the 30-goal range, which he has hit twice already in his remarkable young career. Gaborik works hard on his flaws, like one-timers, which have improved and which will make him a more dangerous weapon on the power play. Curiously, he is not a very effective power-play scorer.

He has explosive speed, in the Pavel Bure/Alexander Mogilny class, but he uses his teammates better than those two stars ever did. He has a heavy shot but it's just a touch shy of being the kind of tool that can make him a 50-goal scorer in the future.

Gaborik's game is pretty complete and mature. He is satisfying a very demanding coach in Jacques Lemaire with his defensive play. Gaborik is very smart and is always looking to break a linemate out of the zone for a scoring rush.

Gaborik has developed tremendous confidence. He believes he can have an impact on the outcome of a game and does what he can to back that up. He wants to improve. He wants to be a leader. His work habits are impeccable.

THE PHYSICAL GAME

Young and still filling out, Gaborik will never be a power player, but he is sturdy enough to stand up under everyday NHL abuse.

THE INTANGIBLES

Think of how long it took Joe Thornton and Vincent Lecavalier to hit their best strides and you can really appreciate what Gaborik has accomplished in only three seasons. Lemaire has proven to be an ideal coach for him, since he's a patient teacher and never put any pressure on Gaborik to achieve certain numbers. Gaborik will keep getting better. Gaborik starred in the playoffs as the Wild reached the Western Conference Finals.

Gaborik was a restricted free agent after the season and will be going into his first contract battle.

PROJECTION

Gaborik should become a consistent 65-70 point scorer, although this year may be a struggle if the Wild is affected by a post-playoff hangover.

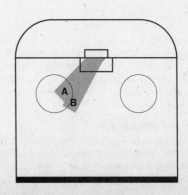

DARBY HENDRICKSON

Yrs. of NHL service: 8
Born: Richfield, Minn.; Aug. 28, 1972
Position: center
Height: 6-1
Weight: 195
Uniform no.: 14
Shoots: left

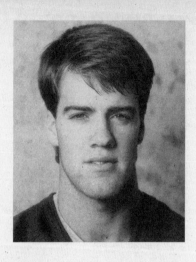

Career statistics:

GP	G	A	TP	PIM
484	63	61	124	358

1999-2000 statistics:

GP	G	A	TP	+/-	PIM	PP	SH	GW	GT	S	PCT
40	5	4	9	-3	14	0	1	1	0	39	12.8

2000-2001 statistics:

GP	G	A	TP	+/-	PIM	PP	SH	GW	GT	S	PCT
72	18	11	29	+1	36	3	1	1	1	114	15.8

2001-2002 statistics:

GP	G	A	TP	+/-	PIM	PP	SH	GW	GT	S	PCT
68	9	15	24	-22	50	2	2	1	0	79	11.4

2002-2003 statistics:

GP	G	A	TP	+/-	PIM	PP	SH	GW	GT	S	PCT
28	1	5	6	-3	8	0	0	0	0	34	2.9

PROJECTION

Hendrickson's ice time may suffer this season as the Wild improve. We wouldn't expect much more than 20 points.

LAST SEASON

Missed 45 games with fractured left forearm. Missed two games with concussion. Missed seven games due to coach's decision.

THE FINESSE GAME

Hendrickson is a two-way forward with better-than-average skills for a checking role. He is a good, quick skater in small areas. He is clever with the puck and will look to make a pass rather than shoot.

He is defensively alert, and has pretty much lost confidence in his offensive game. He's coachable and can play any forward position, which is a plus.

Hendrickson works hard and gives an honest effort that maximizes his modest skills. He is an in-between forward, since he isn't big enough to play an effective power game, but his skills aren't elite enough for him to be considered a pure finesse playmaker. Hendrickson is an efficient penalty killer.

THE PHYSICAL GAME

Hendrickson has a feisty side, and isn't afraid to get involved with some of the league's tougher players (like Keith Tkachuk), if not the heavyweights. When he's not dinged up, he digs in and plays in-your-face hockey, which gets him more ice time. Injuries took their toll on him last season, although he rebounded with a pretty gutsy effort in the playoffs.

THE INTANGIBLES

Hendrickson is an honest third-line center or winger on his best night. He is Jacques Lemaire's kind of player. He loves playing in his home state.

FILIP KUBA

Yrs. of NHL service: 3
Born: Ostrava, Czech Republic; Dec. 29, 1976
Position: left defense
Height: 6-3
Weight: 205
Uniform no.: 17
Shoots: left

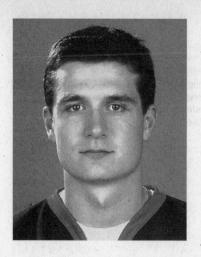

Career statistics:

GP	G	A	TP	PIM
233	23	67	90	91

1999-2000 statistics:

GP	G	A	TP	+/-	PIM	PP	SH	GW	GT	S	PCT
13	1	5	6	-3	2	1	0	1	0	16	6.3

2000-2001 statistics:

GP	G	A	TP	+/-	PIM	PP	SH	GW	GT	S	PCT
75	9	21	30	-6	28	4	0	4	1	141	6.4

2001-2002 statistics:

GP	G	A	TP	+/-	PIM	PP	SH	GW	GT	S	PCT
62	5	19	24	-6	32	3	0	1	0	101	4.9

2002-2003 statistics:

GP	G	A	TP	+/-	PIM	PP	SH	GW	GT	S	PCT
78	8	21	29	0	29	4	2	1	0	129	6.2

LAST SEASON

Led team defensemen in points for third consecutive season. Led team in average ice time (23:55). Tied for team lead in shorthanded goals. Missed four games with bruised foot.

THE FINESSE GAME

The Wild have given Kuba plenty of chances to fail and, more often than not, he hasn't. Coach Jacques Lemaire showed faith in him by putting him back out even after he had a bad shift, and the result is that Kuba has cut back on his bad nights. He was one of the Wild's most consistent performers from December on last season.

Kuba is at heart a defensive defensemen, but he can make at least a modest contribution offensively. He would have slightly bettered his previous season's numbers if he hadn't missed nearly a quarter of a season with his hand injury. Kuba has a very hard shot from the point, but he's got a "wild thing" in him and he is frequently wide off the glass. He would do better to take a little velocity off the shot and just make sure it's on target.

He handles all game situations with the Wild: five-on-five, four-on-four, power play, and penalty killing. He plays the point on the first power-play unit.

THE PHYSICAL GAME

Kuba is a very well-conditioned athlete. Kuba does not play the body much. He has a big wingspan, though, and makes good use of the poke-check. He also blocks shots.

THE INTANGIBLES

Kuba had a slow start to the season which may have had something to do with concerns about a new contract (which was signed in November). The Wild coaches loved Kuba's attitude. He has evolved into their No. 1 defenseman.

PROJECTION

Kuba could improve to 35 points, but it's a mistake to think he can carry much more of an offensive load than that.

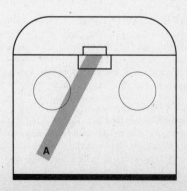

ANTTI LAAKSONEN

Yrs. of NHL service: 4
Born: Tammela, Finland; Oct. 3, 1973
Position: left wing
Height: 6-0
Weight: 180
Uniform no.: 24
Shoots: left

Career statistics:

GP	G	A	TP	PIM
284	50	54	104	76

1999-2000 statistics:

GP	G	A	TP	+/-	PIM	PP	SH	GW	GT	S	PCT
27	6	3	9	+3	2	0	0	1	0	23	26.1

2000-2001 statistics:

GP	G	A	TP	+/-	PIM	PP	SH	GW	GT	S	PCT
82	12	16	28	-7	24	0	2	1	0	129	9.3

2001-2002 statistics:

GP	G	A	TP	+/-	PIM	PP	SH	GW	GT	S	PCT
82	16	17	33	-5	22	0	0	1	0	104	15.4

2002-2003 statistics:

GP	G	A	TP	+/-	PIM	PP	SH	GW	GT	S	PCT
82	15	16	31	+4	26	1	2	4	2	106	14.1

PROJECTION

Laaksonen should again be a mainstay on the third line and can chip in 15-18 goals in a largely defensive role.

LAST SEASON

Tied for team lead in shorthanded goals. Second on team in shooting percentage. Tied for third on team in game-winning goals. One of two Wild players to appear in all 82 games.

THE FINESSE GAME

Laaksonen became acclimated to North American life by playing college hockey, and spent an apprenticeship in the minors before expansion provided him with a shot at his first full-time NHL job.

He has average skills and above-average intelligence. Laaksonen is a role player with good defensive awareness. He can be given a checking assignment against other teams' top lines and will do the job.

Laaksonen rarely makes a bad decision with the puck. He did nice work with Selke Trophy finalist Wes Walz on the checking line and kills penalties. He is quietly becoming a very good defensive forward who can chip in some key goals.

THE PHYSICAL GAME

Laaksonen is average-sized, but is willing to get his body in the way. He's tough to take out of the lineup. Laaksonen has appeared in 251 consecutive games and has appeared in every Wild regular-season game since they first dropped the puck in St. Paul.

THE INTANGIBLES

Laaksonen is coach Jacques Lemaire's kind of player: an intelligent and diligent checking forward and penalty killer.

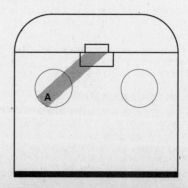

JASON MARSHALL

Yrs. of NHL service: 8
Born: Cranbrook, B.C.; Feb. 22, 1971
Position: right defense
Height: 6-2
Weight: 200
Uniform no.: 23
Shoots: right

Career statistics:

GP	G	A	TP	PIM
479	15	41	56	944

1999-2000 statistics:

GP	G	A	TP	+/-	PIM	PP	SH	GW	GT	S	PCT
55	0	3	3	-10	88	0	0	0	0	41	-

2000-2001 statistics:

GP	G	A	TP	+/-	PIM	PP	SH	GW	GT	S	PCT
55	3	4	7	-13	122	2	1	1	0	43	7.0

2001-2002 statistics:

GP	G	A	TP	+/-	PIM	PP	SH	GW	GT	S	PCT
80	5	6	11	-8	148	1	0	0	0	73	6.8

2002-2003 statistics:

GP	G	A	TP	+/-	PIM	PP	SH	GW	GT	S	PCT
45	1	5	6	+4	69	0	0	0	0	40	2.5

LAST SEASON

Missed 14 games with concussion. Missed three games with eye injury. Missed 20 games due to coach's decision.

THE FINESSE GAME

Marshall is big and mobile with good puck skills. He has been slow to come to hand, mostly from having to learn the mental discipline of playing his position, and odds are we've seen the best of what he has to offer.

Minnesota converted him from a defenseman to a right wing with mixed results. The intention appears to be to mold him into a mucker and a power-play specialist who will dig in around the net for rebounds and deflections. Marshall tried, but he just doesn't have the hands or instincts to be very effective. He is an adequate skater.

Marshall can be his own worst enemy. If he makes a mistake he is very hard on himself. He doesn't have much confidence in his game and doesn't take well to benchings or to challenges to his job.

THE PHYSICAL GAME

Marshall is big and likes to play a physical game. He sticks up for his teammates and will take the initiative to set a physical tone. He is a hard worker and shows up most nights. He can have games where he gets headstrong and starts running around out of position, committing sins of commission rather than omission.

THE INTANGIBLES

Marshall's concussion was obviously a factor, since he has to play a rambunctious, high-energy game to be effective. No doubt coach Jacques Lemaire was think-

ing of his old New Jersey Devils Crash Line of Bobby Holik, Randy McKay, and Mike Peluso when he groomed Marshall for the move up front.

PROJECTION

Marshall will be hard-pressed to get points in the double digits, but his PIM will be close to 150 if he is healthy and sees some fourth-line ice time. Minnesota makes more use of its fourth line than other teams.

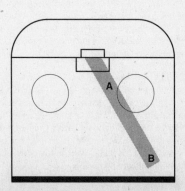

WILLIE MITCHELL

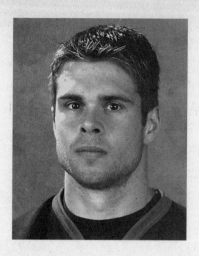

Yrs. of NHL service: 3
Born: Fort McNeill, B.C.; Apr. 23, 1977
Position: defense
Height: 6-3
Weight: 205
Uniform no.: 2
Shoots: left

Career statistics:

GP	G	A	TP	PIM
172	6	31	37	192

1999-2000 statistics:

GP	G	A	TP	+/-	PIM	PP	SH	GW	GT	S	PCT
2	0	0	0	+1	0	0	0	0	0	2	-

2000-2001 statistics:

GP	G	A	TP	+/-	PIM	PP	SH	GW	GT	S	PCT
33	1	9	10	+4	40	0	0	0	0	30	3.3

2001-2002 statistics:

GP	G	A	TP	+/-	PIM	PP	SH	GW	GT	S	PCT
68	3	10	13	-16	68	0	0	1	0	67	4.5

2002-2003 statistics:

GP	G	A	TP	+/-	PIM	PP	SH	GW	GT	S	PCT
69	2	12	14	+13	84	0	1	1	0	67	3.0

LAST SEASON

Third on team in plus-minus and penalty minutes. Career high in points. Missed five games with bruised ribs. Missed eight games with concussion.

THE FINESSE GAME

Mitchell is a stay-at-home defenseman who may have a little offensive upside. Mitchell is a decent skater for his size. He is strong on his skates but has only average speed and agility. He has to continue to learn the art of positioning. Mitchell knows he needs to keep the game simple and play within his limitations, and he is able to do so on most nights. He has improved his defensive reads.

Because of his limited skating skills it helps Mitchell to be paired with a mobile partner.

Mitchell has a hard slap shot from the point with a slow release, but doesn't have much hockey sense or vision to do much with it other than put his head down and shoot. There isn't one outstanding aspect of Mitchell's game, but there are a lot of little things that add up. He is eager to please and has a strong work ethic. Mitchell doesn't take many steps back but keeps getting gradually better.

THE PHYSICAL GAME

Mitchell is a tough customer. He played in the playoffs though a jaw injury that required a face shield and with a fractured wrist. He is a brave shot-blocker as well. He's a strong guy and is starting to assert himself as a physical presence. He will fight if he has to but that is really not his game. Mitchell is a hard bodychecker without being punishing.

THE INTANGIBLES

Defensemen like Mitchell take a few years to develop. He's 26 and about to hit his prime. He showed more consistency last season even while battling through nagging injuries. He should be in the Wild's top four. Mitchell was a restricted free agent after the season.

PROJECTION

Mitchell won't get more than 20 points, and he remains a project with a few rough edges.

CLIFF RONNING

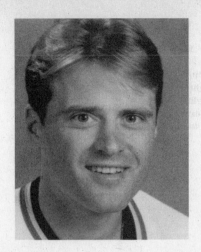

Yrs. of NHL service: 16
Born: Vancouver, B.C.; Oct. 1, 1965
Position: center
Height: 5-8
Weight: 165
Uniform no.: 7
Shoots: left

Career statistics:

GP	G	A	TP	PIM
1097	297	548	845	451

1999-2000 statistics:

GP	G	A	TP	+/-	PIM	PP	SH	GW	GT	S	PCT
82	26	36	62	-13	34	7	0	2	0	248	10.5

2000-2001 statistics:

GP	G	A	TP	+/-	PIM	PP	SH	GW	GT	S	PCT
80	19	43	62	+4	28	6	0	4	0	237	8.0

2001-2002 statistics:

GP	G	A	TP	+/-	PIM	PP	SH	GW	GT	S	PCT
81	19	35	54	0	32	5	0	0	2	199	9.5

2002-2003 statistics:

GP	G	A	TP	+/-	PIM	PP	SH	GW	GT	S	PCT
80	17	31	48	-6	24	8	0	5	0	171	9.9

LAST SEASON

Second on Wild in assists, power-play goals, and game-winning goals. Tied for second on Wild in points. Third on Wild in shots. Missed two games due to coach's decision.

THE FINESSE GAME

Ronning's forte is not scoring goals but creating chances for his wingers. He lets bigger linemates attract defenders so that he can dipsy-doodle with the puck. He's quick, shifty, and smart (he has to be smart, otherwise he'll be flattened along the boards like an advertisement).

Ronning likes to work from behind the net, using the cage as a shield and daring defenders to chase him. Ronning plays hockey like a game of chicken. He is a tempting target, and even smaller-sized defensemen fantasize about smashing him to the ice, but he keeps himself out of trouble by dancing in and out of openings and finding free teammates. He also works well off the half-boards on the power play.

A quick thinker and unpredictable, Ronning can curl off the wall into the slot, pass to the corners or the point and jump to the net, or beat a defender wide at the top of the circle and feed a teammate coming into the play late. He's not afraid of going into traffic. And as good a passer and playmaker as he is, Ronning isn't shy about pulling the trigger.

Ronning puts a lot of little dekes into a compact area and opens up the ice with his bursts of speed and his fakes. Unless the defense can force him along the wall and contain him, he's all over the ice trying to make things happen. He has not yet lost a step in his skating.

THE PHYSICAL GAME

No one asks jockeys to tackle running backs. Ronning is built for speed and deception. He is smart enough to avoid getting crunched and talented enough to compensate for his lack of strength. He has skills and a huge heart and competes hard every night.

Ronning is so small that usually the best he can do is tug at an opponent like a pesky little brother. He gets involved with his stick, hooking at a puck carrier's arm, and digging at the puck in a player's skates. He keeps the puck in his skates when he protects it, so that a checker will often have to pull Ronning down to get at the puck, which creates a power play. He is pretty durable for a small guy, and pays great attention to his physical fitness.

THE INTANGIBLES

Ronning had a positive impact in Minnesota, playing a key role in Marian Gaborik's development, and helping the Wild reach the playoffs in the franchise's third year of existence. He became an unrestricted free agent after last season.

PROJECTION

Ronning can still put up an assist-heavy 50 points in the right situation.

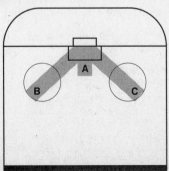

NICK SCHULTZ

Yrs. of NHL service: 2
Born: Regina, Sask.; Aug. 25, 1982
Position: left defense
Height: 6-0
Weight: 187
Uniform no.: 55
Shoots: left

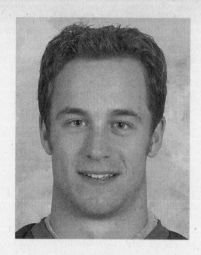

Career statistics:

GP	G	A	TP	PIM
127	7	13	20	37

2001-2002 statistics:

GP	G	A	TP	+/-	PIM	PP	SH	GW	GT	S	PCT
52	4	6	10	0	14	1	0	1	0	47	8.5

2002-2003 statistics:

GP	G	A	TP	+/-	PIM	PP	SH	GW	GT	S	PCT
75	3	7	10	+11	23	0	0	1	0	70	4.3

LAST SEASON

Second NHL season. Missed seven games due to coach's decision.

THE FINESSE GAME

After a really awful defensive start that had the Wild considering a demotion to the minors, Schultz turned his game around well enough that he was selected to play in the NHL's Young Stars game in January. Second-year struggles aren't unexpected for a young defenseman, but Schultz had a few nights that were just short of catastrophic before he straightened out his game.

Schultz is a very good skater who excels at the transition game. He is not fast and lacks one-step speed, but he is smooth and fluid in his pivots. He is poised with the puck. He can handle second-unit power-play time. He doesn't have a great shot but he reads the play well and will find passing lanes.

Don't expect big numbers from Schultz. He uses his finesse skills mostly in a defensive capacity. Schultz makes good breakout passes. He's smart and a coachable student.

THE PHYSICAL GAME

Schultz is below-average size by today's NHL defenseman standards. He needs to be nagged to keep a sandpaper element in his game. It doesn't come naturally to him but he won't succeed in the NHL without it. Schultz will take a hit to make a play but needs to initiate more.

THE INTANGIBLES

In the first half of the season, Minnesota was careful not to put too much pressure on Schultz by putting him out against other team's top forwards. Schultz grew to accept more responsibility and became the kind of reliable defenseman who could be put on the ice late in the game to protect a lead. What's most important about Schultz is that he wants to be that kind of player.

PROJECTION

Schultz is still going to suffer through some growing pains, but we envision him as a second-pair defenseman this season. He will never be a big point producer, but he could score in the 20-point range.

WES WALZ

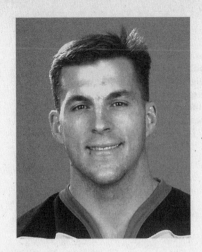

Yrs. of NHL service: 9
Born: Calgary, Alta.; May 15, 1970
Position: center
Height: 5-10
Weight: 180
Uniform no.: 37
Shoots: right

Career statistics:

GP	G	A	TP	PIM
395	68	102	170	214

2000-2001 statistics:

GP	G	A	TP	+/-	PIM	PP	SH	GW	GT	S	PCT
82	18	12	30	-8	37	0	7	3	0	152	11.8

2001-2002 statistics:

GP	G	A	TP	+/-	PIM	PP	SH	GW	GT	S	PCT
64	10	20	30	0	43	0	2	5	0	97	10.3

2002-2003 statistics:

GP	G	A	TP	+/-	PIM	PP	SH	GW	GT	S	PCT
80	13	19	32	+11	63	0	0	4	0	115	11.3

LAST SEASON

Finalist for 2003 Selke Trophy. Third on team in shooting percentage. Tied for third on team in game-winning goals. Missed one game with flu. Missed one game due to coach's decision.

THE FINESSE GAME

Defensive play was a Walz weakness early in his career. Now it is his career. His defensive awareness allows him to read plays and he turns the other team's mistakes into scoring chances. He pursues pucks instead of turning away, and doesn't break out of the zone prematurely. He is consistent in his effort. Walz takes great pride in the checking part of the game, but he also has a knack for scoring timely goals.

Walz has a lot of ability in a little package. His best asset is his speed; it gives him one-step quickness on a defender and a head start on breakaways. His shot is not scary, but it's accurate and he has a quick release.

He is a better playmaker than scorer. He keeps the puck alive in corners and threads a pass to teammates. Most of his scoring chances come in-tight.

THE PHYSICAL GAME

It was his size that handicapped him in winning a full-time NHL job with better teams. With the game expanding and opening to more finesse-oriented players, Walz can now thrive.

THE INTANGIBLES

Walz spent four years playing in Switzerland waiting for a chance to break back into the NHL and he has made the most of it.

PROJECTION

Walz has become such a defensive ace that the Wild used him successfully against the much bigger and stronger Peter Forsberg in the playoffs. The postseason brought out the best in Walz. Walz will again figure in as the primary checking center for the Wild. He can score 15-20 goals in his defensive role.

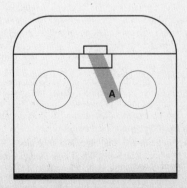

KYLE WANVIG

Yrs. of NHL service: 1
Born: Calgary, Alta.,; Jan. 29, 1981
Position: right wing
Height: 6-2
Weight: 219
Uniform no.: 27
Shoots: right

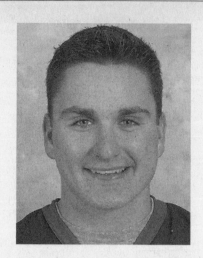

Career statistics:

GP	G	A	TP	PIM
7	1	0	1	13

2002-2003 statistics:

GP	G	A	TP	+/-	PIM	PP	SH	GW	GT	S	PCT
7	1	0	1	0	13	0	0	0	0	5	20.0

LAST SEASON

Will be entering first full NHL season. Appeared in 56 games with Houston (AHL), scoring 12-16 — 28 with 130 PIM.

THE FINESSE GAME

When you're as big as Wanvig, is finesse really an issue? Of course, because Wanvig has to have good hands to make the best use of the chances that will come his way by planting himself around the net.

Wanvig has good scoring instincts. He has a really nice touch around the net, which is where he is going to score most of his goals. Go ahead and call him a garbageman. So was Phil Esposito. From father out, he blasts a pretty serious slap shot.

Wanvig's biggest issue is his lack of foot speed. He's so big that it takes him a few churning strides to get up to full speed. It's a little scary when he does because he can bowl people over. He's not very agile but he is well-balanced on his skates.

Two flaws that plague a lot of young players — consistency and defensive awareness — will be the main areas Wanvig will need to work on.

THE PHYSICAL GAME

Wanvig likes contact. He'll drop 'em for a fight but that's not really why he's out there. He will need to establish a reputation to earn his room on the ice, but he doesn't need to take senseless penalties. He will be of far more value to Minnesota on the power play than creating one for the other team.

THE INTANGIBLES

Wanvig is one of those rough-edged power forwards whose game will need a few seasons in the NHL to mature.

PROJECTION

If Wanvig can make the team as a second-line right wing, he should get second-unit power-play time. A great first season would mean 15 goals.

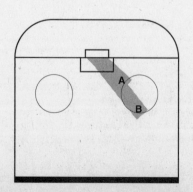

ANDREI ZYUZIN

Yrs. of NHL service: 6
Born: Ufa, Russia; Jan. 21, 1978
Position: left defense
Height: 6-1
Weight: 215
Uniform no.: 20
Shoots: left

Career statistics:

GP	G	A	TP	PIM
293	20	50	70	280

1999-2000 statistics:

GP	G	A	TP	+/-	PIM	PP	SH	GW	GT	S	PCT
34	2	9	11	-11	33	0	0	0	0	47	4.3

2000-2001 statistics:

GP	G	A	TP	+/-	PIM	PP	SH	GW	GT	S	PCT
64	4	16	20	-8	76	2	1	1	1	92	4.3

2001-2002 statistics:

GP	G	A	TP	+/-	PIM	PP	SH	GW	GT	S	PCT
47	1	4	5	-5	31	1	0	0	0	61	1.6

2002-2003 statistics:

GP	G	A	TP	+/-	PIM	PP	SH	GW	GT	S	PCT
67	4	13	17	-8	36	2	0	0	0	113	3.5

LAST SEASON

Acquired from New Jersey on waivers on November 4, 2002. Third on team in average ice time (21:36). Missed one game with flu. Missed 24 games due to coach's decision.

THE FINESSE GAME

Zyuzin is an offensive-minded defenseman, with the kind of speed and anticipation that should prevent him from being too much of a liability. He could prove to be the kind of player who can dictate the tempo of a game, or break it wide open with one end-to-end rush. He doesn't seem to possess the exceptional lateral movement along the blueline that sets a defenseman like Brian Leetch apart from most of his NHL brethren, but Zyuzin has a big upside.

He doesn't take his offensive chances blindly; he knows what the score is. He takes a chance when his team needs a goal. And when he needs to stay back on defense, he will. He will also get burned once in awhile, but he makes smart choices.

He is a fast skater with quick acceleration and balance. He handles the puck well at a high pace and can either pass or shoot. He's a smart playmaker, but one who will not pass up a golden scoring opportunity. He has a hard point shot and will become a good power-play quarterback.

THE PHYSICAL GAME

Zyuzin is not a physical player. He has adequate size but will need a streak of Chris Chelios-like aggressiveness to make the best use of his ability. He does have a desire to excel, and if it means stepping up his game physically, he will probably be able to make

that transition. He plays with a lot of energy.

THE INTANGIBLES

Zyuzin struggled to find his place with three different teams (San Jose, Tampa Bay, and New Jersey) but may have finally found his niche in Minnesota. He became a restricted free agent after the season.

PROJECTION

Zyuzin should score 25 points in a full-time role, if he gets one.

MONTREAL CANADIENS

Players' Statistics 2001-2002

POS.	NO.	PLAYER	GP	G	A	PTS	+/-	PIM	PP	SH	GW	GT	S	PCT
C	11	SAKU KOIVU	82	21	50	71	5	72	5	1	5		147	14.3
L	20	RICHARD ZEDNIK	80	31	19	50	4	79	9		2	1	250	12.4
C	94	YANIC PERREAULT	73	24	22	46	-11	30	7		4		145	16.5
C	38	JAN BULIS	82	16	24	40	9	30			2		160	10.0
D	79	ANDREI MARKOV	79	13	24	37	13	34	3		2		159	8.2
D	43	PATRICE BRISEBOIS	73	4	25	29	-14	32	1		1		105	3.8
R	37	NIKLAS SUNDSTROM	80	7	19	26	-1	30			1		71	9.9
R	24	ANDREAS DACKELL	73	7	18	25	-5	24			1		74	9.4
R	82	DONALD AUDETTE	54	11	12	23	-7	19	4		4	1	118	9.3
D	52	CRAIG RIVET	82	7	15	22	1	71	3		2		118	5.9
L	90	JOE JUNEAU	72	6	16	22	-10	20			2		88	6.8
R	21	RANDY MCKAY	75	6	13	19	-14	72	2			1	52	11.5
C	71	MIKE RIBEIRO	52	5	12	17	-3	6	2				57	8.8
L	25	CHAD KILGER	60	9	7	16	-4	21			1		60	15.0
R	27	MARIUSZ CZERKAWSKI	43	5	9	14	-7	16	1				77	6.5
L	81	*MARCEL HOSSA	34	6	7	13	3	14	2		1		51	11.8
D	54	PATRICK TRAVERSE	65		13	13	-9	24					63	
D	5	STEPHANE QUINTAL	67	5	5	10	-4	70					73	6.8
R	17	JASON WARD	8	3	2	5	3						10	30.0
D	28	KARL DYKHUIS	65	1	4	5	-5	34					24	4.2
D	51	FRANCIS BOUILLON	24	3	1	4	-2	4		1			30	10.0
L	22	BILL LINDSAY	19		2	2	-1	23					7	
D	8	*MICHAEL KOMISAREK	21		1	1	-6	28					26	
L	32	GORDIE DWYER	28		1	1	-3	96					10	
D	65	*RON HAINSEY	21				-1	2					12	
L	26	SYLVAIN BLOUIN	19				-3	47					4	
D	36	*FRANCOIS BEAUCHEMIN	1				-1						1	
G	41	ERIC FICHAUD					0							
G	60	JOSE THEODORE	57				0	6						
G	30	MATHIEU GARON	8				0							

GP = games played; G = goals; A = assists; PTS = points; +/- = goals-for minus goals-against while player is on ice; PIM = penalties in minutes; PP = power-play goals; SH = shorthanded goals; GW = game-winning goals; GT = game-tying goals; S = no. of shots; PCT = percentage of goals to shots; * = rookie

DONALD AUDETTE

Yrs. of NHL service: 12
Born: Laval, Que.; Sept. 23, 1969
Position: right wing
Height: 5-8
Weight: 190
Uniform no.: 82
Shoots: right

Career statistics:

GP	G	A	TP	PIM
684	251	237	488	546

1999-2000 statistics:

GP	G	A	TP	+/-	PIM	PP	SH	GW	GT	S	PCT
63	19	24	43	+2	57	1	1	4	0	162	11.7

2000-2001 statistics:

GP	G	A	TP	+/-	PIM	PP	SH	GW	GT	S	PCT
76	34	45	79	-2	76	14	1	3	2	225	15.1

2001-2002 statistics:

GP	G	A	TP	+/-	PIM	PP	SH	GW	GT	S	PCT
33	5	13	18	+3	20	3	0	3	0	82	6.1

2002-2003 statistics:

GP	G	A	TP	+/-	PIM	PP	SH	GW	GT	S	PCT
54	11	12	23	-7	19	4	0	4	1	118	9.3

LAST SEASON

Tied for second on team in game-winning goals. Missed one game with virus. Missed 16 games due to coach's decision. Appeared in 11 games with Hamilton (AHL), scoring 5-5 — 10 with 8 PIM.

THE FINESSE GAME

A bustling forward who barrels to the net at every opportunity, Audette is eager and feisty down low and has good hand skills. He also has keen scoring instincts, along with the quickness to make good things happen. His feet move so fast (with a choppy stride) that he doesn't look graceful, but he can really get moving and he has good balance.

A scorer first, Audette has a great top-shelf shot, which he gets away quickly and accurately. He can also make a play, but he will do this at the start of a rush. Once he is inside the offensive zone and low, he wants the puck. Considering his scoring touch, though, his selfishness can be forgiven.

Audette is at his best on the power play. He is savvy enough not to just stand around and take punishment. He times his jumps into the space between the left post and the bottom of the left circle. Audette is not very big, yet he makes his living around the net by smartly jumping in and out of the holes.

Audette steps up his game with the pressure.

THE PHYSICAL GAME

Opponents hate Audette, which he takes as a great compliment. He runs goalies, yaps, and takes dives — then goes out and scores on the power play after the opposition has taken a bad penalty.

Though he isn't as diligent coming back, Audette will forecheck and scrap for the puck. He's not very big, but around the net he plays like he's at least a six-footer. He keeps jabbing and working away until he is bowled over by an angry defender.

THE INTANGIBLES

Audette suffered a gruesome forearm/wrist injury in 2001-02 that required delicate surgery to repair. He was still showing the effects of this injury last season. His role is now that of a part-timer and virtual power-play specialist.

PROJECTION

You can't help but be impressed with Audette's perseverance, but it's unlikely he'll get the ice time to return to 20-goal status.

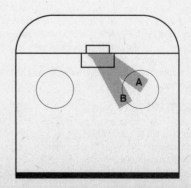

PATRICE BRISEBOIS

Yrs. of NHL service: 12
Born: Montreal, Que.; Jan. 27, 1971
Position: right defense
Height: 6-2
Weight: 203
Uniform no.: 43
Shoots: right

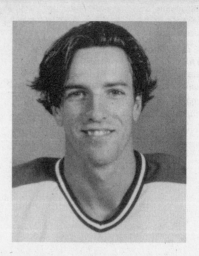

Career statistics:

GP	G	A	TP	PIM
720	75	236	311	479

1999-2000 statistics:

GP	G	A	TP	+/-	PIM	PP	SH	GW	GT	S	PCT
54	10	25	35	-1	18	5	0	2	2	88	11.4

2000-2001 statistics:

GP	G	A	TP	+/-	PIM	PP	SH	GW	GT	S	PCT
77	15	21	36	-31	28	11	0	4	0	178	8.4

2001-2002 statistics:

GP	G	A	TP	+/-	PIM	PP	SH	GW	GT	S	PCT
71	4	29	33	+9	25	2	1	1	0	95	4.2

2002-2003 statistics:

GP	G	A	TP	+/-	PIM	PP	SH	GW	GT	S	PCT
73	4	25	29	-14	32	1	0	1	0	105	3.8

LAST SEASON

Led team in average ice time. Second on team in assists. Missed eight games due to coach's decision. Missed one game with groin injury.

THE FINESSE GAME

Brisebois has some nice offensive skills, but he doesn't have the hockey sense to combine them in a complete package so he can be an elite-level defenseman. He has a decent first step to the puck, plus a good stride with some quickness, though he won't rush end-to-end. He carries the puck with authority but will usually take one or two strides and look for a pass, or else make the safe dump out of the zone. He steps up in the neutral zone to slow an opponent's rush. He is a good outlet passer.

Brisebois plays the point well enough to be on the first power-play unit. He lacks the rink vision and lateral movement that mark truly successful point men. He has a good point shot, though, with a sharp release, and he keeps it low and on target. He doesn't often venture to the circles on offense — when he does he has the passing skills and the shot to make something happen. And grant him this, he is always trying to make something good happen.

Brisebois has become less undisciplined and plays his position more calmly.

THE PHYSICAL GAME

Brisebois continues to pay the price physically. Although not a punishing hitter, he is strong and will make take-outs. He doesn't have a mean streak, so he has to dedicate himself to taking the body.

THE INTANGIBLES

The loveliness of Paris got Brisebois into a lot of trouble last season when he was spotted there while being given some time off by the club. Brisebois was supposedly nearly traded to New Jersey just prior to the trade deadline, and he's a sure bet to be shopped vigorously by the Habs. The development of some of their younger defensemen will hasten his departure.

PROJECTION

Brisebois probably needs a change of scene. He would be a capable second-pair defenseman on a stronger team. He has been a No. 1 for Montreal for years, but that is well beyond his scope. Expect 35-40 points if he gets moved.

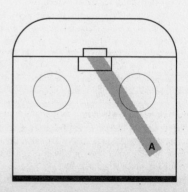

JAN BULIS

Yrs. of NHL service: 6
Born: Paradubice, Czech Republic; Mar. 18, 1978
Position: center
Height: 6-2
Weight: 201
Uniform no.: 38
Shoots: left

Career statistics:

GP	G	A	TP	PIM
328	51	101	152	118

1999-2000 statistics:

GP	G	A	TP	+/-	PIM	PP	SH	GW	GT	S	PCT
56	9	22	31	+7	30	0	0	1	0	92	9.8

2000-2001 statistics:

GP	G	A	TP	+/-	PIM	PP	SH	GW	GT	S	PCT
51	5	18	23	-1	26	1	0	0	0	61	8.2

2001-2002 statistics:

GP	G	A	TP	+/-	PIM	PP	SH	GW	GT	S	PCT
53	9	10	19	-2	8	1	0	3	0	87	10.3

2002-2003 statistics:

GP	G	A	TP	+/-	PIM	PP	SH	GW	GT	S	PCT
82	16	24	40	+9	30	0	0	2	0	160	10.0

LAST SEASON

Second on team in plus-minus and shots. Tied for third on team in assists. Career highs in goals, assists, and points. One of three Canadiens to appear in all 82 games.

THE FINESSE GAME

Bulis has decent size, skating, and skills to stamp him as a future top forward. He handles the puck well through traffic and in the open at high tempo.

More of a playmaker than a scorer, Bulis is not a pure passer. He has a quick release on his wrist shot and will take the shot if that is his better option, rather than try to force the pass. He has a good slap shot, too. His shot was clocked at close to 90 m.p.h. in his first year of junior.

Bulis plays a smart positional game and is defensively astute. He is a well-conditioned athlete and has a lot of stamina to handle the ice time and travel. He is very good on draws.

THE PHYSICAL GAME

Bulis brings an infectious enthusiasm, whether it's to a game or a practice session. He is one of those players who looks like he is simply having a great time playing hockey, but he is also serious about the sport. Bulis has a solid work ethic and is the kind of player coaches don't have to waste time motivating. He isn't aggressive, but he is stocky and strong on his skates. He can compete in a physical game and he likes to hit.

THE INTANGIBLES

The biggest single reason for Bulis's breakthrough season is that he was able to stay healthy. This was the

Bulis a lot of people have been waiting to see.

PROJECTION

Last season we said, "He is capable of scoring 40 points over a full season," which is precisely what happened. His top end probably isn't much higher than that.

ANDREAS DACKELL

Yrs. of NHL service: 7
Born: Gavle, Sweden; Dec. 29, 1972
Position: right wing
Height: 5-11
Weight: 194
Uniform no.: 24
Shoots: right

Career statistics:

GP	G	A	TP	PIM
553	87	151	238	152

1999-2000 statistics:

GP	G	A	TP	+/-	PIM	PP	SH	GW	GT	S	PCT
82	10	25	35	+5	18	0	0	1	1	99	10.1

2000-2001 statistics:

GP	G	A	TP	+/-	PIM	PP	SH	GW	GT	S	PCT
81	13	18	31	+7	24	1	0	3	0	72	18.1

2001-2002 statistics:

GP	G	A	TP	+/-	PIM	PP	SH	GW	GT	S	PCT
79	15	18	33	-3	24	2	3	2	0	83	18.1

2002-2003 statistics:

GP	G	A	TP	+/-	PIM	PP	SH	GW	GT	S	PCT
73	7	18	25	-5	24	0	0	1	0	74	9.4

PROJECTION

Dackell can handle a second-line role as a safety-valve winger, but because of his lack of scoring touch, he is better suited as a third-line checking forward. Don't bank on much more than 10 goals from him.

LAST SEASON

Missed nine games due to coach's decision.

THE FINESSE GAME

Dackell has good hockey sense and is sound defensively. He does a lot of subtle things well. Tapes of his game could be used to illustrate hustling on backchecks to knock the puck away from an attacker, attacking in the neutral zone without committing yourself, playing strong along the wall, and keeping your man out of the play. Dackell is a last-minute man, one of the guys put on the ice in the final minute of a period or game to protect a lead. He kills penalties and protects the puck well.

He has a decent, accurate shot that he could utilize more, but his offense was less of a factor last season than ever before. He seems to score timely goals, and is a shorthanded threat on the penalty kill.

Dackell doesn't have blazing speed but works hard to be where he's supposed to be. He's very smart and hard to knock off the puck.

THE PHYSICAL GAME

Dackell isn't very big and he's not a banger, but he'll make checks and won't be intimidated. He could be the toughest 30-PIM-a-year player in the NHL.

THE INTANGIBLES

Much of what Dackell contributes to a team is subtle, but he is a valuable role player on the Canadiens. He gives his team an honest 14 minutes a night. The Habs seem to have soured on him a bit and he might be expendable. He would make a good role player pickup.

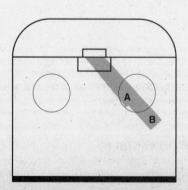

KARL DYKHUIS

Yrs. of NHL service: 10
Born: Sept-Iles, Que.; July 8, 1972
Position: right defense
Height: 6-3
Weight: 214
Uniform no.: 28
Shoots: left

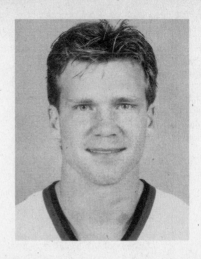

Career statistics:

GP	G	A	TP	PIM
635	42	91	133	493

1999-2000 statistics:

GP	G	A	TP	+/-	PIM	PP	SH	GW	GT	S	PCT
72	7	13	20	-5	46	3	1	0	0	69	10.1

2000-2001 statistics:

GP	G	A	TP	+/-	PIM	PP	SH	GW	GT	S	PCT
67	8	9	17	+9	44	2	0	1	0	66	12.1

2001-2002 statistics:

GP	G	A	TP	+/-	PIM	PP	SH	GW	GT	S	PCT
80	5	7	12	+16	32	0	0	1	0	85	5.9

2002-2003 statistics:

GP	G	A	TP	+/-	PIM	PP	SH	GW	GT	S	PCT
65	1	4	5	-5	34	0	0	0	0	24	4.2

Montreal's kids like Michael Komisarek or Ron Hainsey graduate.

PROJECTION

Dykhuis will not score many points (10 or so), although he will provide sensible defense.

LAST SEASON

Missed 17 games due to coach's decision.

THE FINESSE GAME

Dykhuis has learned the importance of keeping his feet moving, because it helps him stay up with the play. His game edges towards the offensive side, but he also uses his finesse skills well in his own end. He keeps the passes short, accurate, and crisp and banks the puck off the boards or glass if that's the only option available to clear the zone.

He is a natural for penalty killing and four-on-four play because he has fine mobility and quickness, with a quick shift of gears that allows him to get up the ice in a hurry. Smart, with good hands for passing or drilling shots from the point, Dykhuis also leans towards conservatism. He won't venture down low unless the decision to pinch is a sound one.

THE PHYSICAL GAME

Although tall and rangy, Dykhuis isn't a heavyweight. But he goes out of his way to screen off opposing forecheckers and to buy time for his partner. There are times, on a regular basis, when his physical aspect is almost non-existent. He is strong and makes solid contact on those occasions when he does hit, though. He's also such a good skater that he can break up a play, dig out the loose puck and be off in just a stride or two to start an odd-man rush. He also uses his reach to break up plays.

THE INTANGIBLES

Dykhuis saw his role reduced last season and he will either become a part-timer or be moved if some of

RON HAINSEY

Yrs. of NHL service: 0
Born: Bolton, Conn.; Mar. 24, 1981
Position: left defense
Height: 6-3
Weight: 200
Uniform no.: 65
Shoots: left

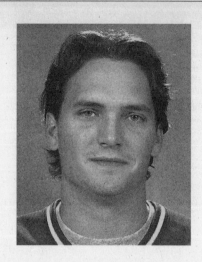

Career statistics:

GP	G	A	TP	PIM
21	0	0	0	2

2002-2003 statistics:

GP	G	A	TP	+/-	PIM	PP	SH	GW	GT	S	PCT
21	0	0	0	-1	2	0	0	0	0	12	0.0

LAST SEASON

Will be entering first full NHL season. Appeared in 33 games with Hamilton (AHL), scoring 2-11 — 13 with 36 PIM.

THE FINESSE GAME

It's been a long time since Montreal has had a top-notch offensive defenseman. Hainsey won't be an elite point-producer, but he's an excellent puck-mover.

Hainsey's skating is exceptional. He's a good-sized guy, but he's a good skater who can start the rush from behind his own net. He's a powerful skater with a good acceleration, a smooth stride, and a good change of direction.

Hainsey sees the ice well. He is pretty poised and will be able to move the puck out of his zone quickly to prevent the opposition from setting up shop.

Hainsey will probably evolve into a solid power-play quarterback. He has a quick and accurate slap-shot and can one-time the puck, which is a big plus for a point man.

THE PHYSICAL GAME

Hainsey will never be a big hitter. He is not at all aggressive, but he has to add enough sand to his game to move people out of his crease with authority. He has added about 30 pounds since his draft year (2000) but what good is it if he doesn't use it?

THE INTANGIBLES

Hainsey had an impressive training camp in 2003 and is expected to challenge for a full-time job this season. If he does, he should see second-unit power-play time.

PROJECTION

Montreal is trying to make its defense younger and more mobile, and Hainsey should be part of that movement. He will probably break in on the third pair and could develop into a No. 4 defenseman in time. Expect around 20 points if he gets a full first season.

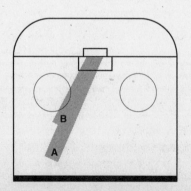

MARCEL HOSSA

Yrs. of NHL service: 1
Born: Ilava, Slovenia; Oct. 12, 1981
Position: left wing
Height: 6-1
Weight: 211
Uniform no.: 81
Shoots: left

Career statistics:

GP	G	A	TP	PIM
44	9	8	17	16

2001-2002 statistics:

GP	G	A	TP	+/-	PIM	PP	SH	GW	GT	S	PCT
10	3	1	4	+2	2	0	0	0	0	20	15.0

2002-2003 statistics:

GP	G	A	TP	+/-	PIM	PP	SH	GW	GT	S	PCT
34	6	7	13	+3	14	2	0	1	0	51	11.8

LAST SEASON

First NHL season. Appeared in 36 games with Hamilton (AHL), scoring 18-12 — 30.

THE FINESSE GAME

Hossa is a good skater who is strong and balanced. He is clever with the puck and has good hockey vision. He is more of a playmaker than a passer at this point, but he has a good array of shots. Hossa needs to shoot more and also be more determined in battling his way into the hard areas of the ice.

Hossa is the younger brother of Ottawa's Marian, and talent runs in the family. Several scouts don't think he will become the same elite player Marian is, but this kid brother is very skilled. Hossa's likely future is as a second-line set-up man. Montreal played him on the left wing mostly in his brief audition but he is a natural center and that is where he will end up, possibly as a No. 2 behind Saku Koivu.

As is the case with a lot of young players, Hossa needs to improve his defensive play and his consistency on a nightly basis.

THE PHYSICAL GAME

Hossa has good size but doesn't use it in an authoritative manner. The Habs would like to see a little more fire in his game.

THE INTANGIBLES

Hossa will always suffer by comparison to his older brother. He's simply not that good. But he is good enough to be a top-six forward in the NHL if he can put the pieces together. He made a pretty good impression in his 34-game stay with Montreal last season but needs to raise his intensity another notch.

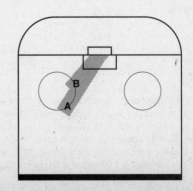

PROJECTION

Hossa could score 30 points if he wins a job.

JOE JUNEAU

Yrs. of NHL service: 11
Born: Pont-Rouge, Que.; Jan. 5, 1968
Position: center
Height: 6-0
Weight: 195
Uniform no.: 90
Shoots: left

Career statistics:

GP	G	A	TP	PIM
758	151	406	557	252

1999-2000 statistics:

GP	G	A	TP	+/-	PIM	PP	SH	GW	GT	S	PCT
65	13	24	37	+3	22	2	0	2	0	126	10.3

2000-2001 statistics:

GP	G	A	TP	+/-	PIM	PP	SH	GW	GT	S	PCT
69	10	23	33	-2	28	5	0	3	1	100	10.0

2001-2002 statistics:

GP	G	A	TP	+/-	PIM	PP	SH	GW	GT	S	PCT
70	8	28	36	-3	10	1	0	1	1	96	8.3

2002-2003 statistics:

GP	G	A	TP	+/-	PIM	PP	SH	GW	GT	S	PCT
72	6	16	22	-10	20	0	0	2	0	88	6.8

LAST SEASON

Missed eight games with shoulder injury. Missed two games with concussion.

THE FINESSE GAME

Juneau's game has become so heavily weighted on the defensive side in recent seasons that it's best to describe him now as a checking center. Juneau has excellent finesse skills, which he uses to prevent scoring chances rather than create them. He has good hockey vision and sense and anticipates plays. He is fine on draws and penalty kills.

When Juneau gets involved in the attack, he is not just a perimeter player. He will go into traffic, and is bigger than he looks on-ice. His quick feet and light hands make him seem smaller because he is so crafty with the puck. Laterally, Juneau is among the best skaters in the NHL. He has an extra gear that allows him to pull away from people. He does not have breakaway speed, but he gets the jump on a defender with his first few steps.

A natural center, Juneau gravitates to the left wing and generates most of his scoring chances from there. He varies his play selection. He will take the puck to the net on one rush, then pull up at the top of the circle and hit the trailer late on the next rush.

Juneau doesn't shoot the puck enough and gets a little intimidated when there is a scramble for a loose puck in front of the net. He is not always willing to sacrifice his body that way. He shoots a tad prematurely. When he could wait and have the goalie down and out, he unloads quickly, because he hears footsteps. His best shot is a one-timer from the left circle.

Juneau is a better playmaker than scorer.

THE PHYSICAL GAME

Juneau has improved his toughness and willingness to take a hit to make a play, but he is still a featherweight. You can almost see him psych himself up to make or take a hit. It doesn't come naturally to him.

THE INTANGIBLES

Juneau had the usual array of nagging injuries. He tends to skate with his head down and that has resulted in several concussions.

PROJECTION

We wouldn't expect much more than 25 points from Juneau, especially since he has missed from 10 to 26 games in each of the last five seasons.

CHAD KILGER

Yrs. of NHL service: 8
Born: Cornwall, Ont.; Nov. 27, 1976
Position: left wing
Height: 6-4
Weight: 224
Uniform no.: 25
Shoots: left

Career statistics:

GP	G	A	TP	PIM
459	63	76	139	208

1999-2000 statistics:

GP	G	A	TP	+/-	PIM	PP	SH	GW	GT	S	PCT
40	3	2	5	-6	18	0	0	0	0	32	9.4

2000-2001 statistics:

GP	G	A	TP	+/-	PIM	PP	SH	GW	GT	S	PCT
77	14	18	32	-8	51	2	1	1	0	103	13.6

2001-2002 statistics:

GP	G	A	TP	+/-	PIM	PP	SH	GW	GT	S	PCT
75	8	15	23	-7	27	0	1	2	0	87	9.2

2002-2003 statistics:

GP	G	A	TP	+/-	PIM	PP	SH	GW	GT	S	PCT
60	9	7	16	-4	21	0	0	1	0	60	15.0

PROJECTION

Kilger needs to have a regular role and not be a part-timer. To become a regular, he has to prove he's worthy of the minutes. Anything less than a 15-goal season is unacceptable.

LAST SEASON

Missed five games with knee injury. Missed two games with finger injury.

THE FINESSE GAME

Kilger plays an intelligent, poised, unexceptional game. He sees the ice well and is a good passer. The release on his shot is too slow for him to be much of an impact scorer in the NHL. He has a long reach, which works to his advantage in dangling the puck away from defenders.

His size and skating ability are NHL caliber. Few big players skate as well as Kilger. He is at his best when he accelerates through the neutral zone. When he gets the puck, if he wants it, he can get a lot of chances by busting through.

Kilger has bounced around a lot. He's 27 and Montreal is his fifth team. The damage done by rushing him into the league at 18 has never been completely undone, but he is an okay depth forward for a team like Montreal.

THE PHYSICAL GAME

Big and physical, Kilger has developed a better knack for getting involved, but it takes a concerted effort on his part and does not come naturally. He needs to consistently exhibit a better work ethic and finish his checks, playing well at both ends of the ice.

THE INTANGIBLES

Montreal likes Kilger enough as a role player (even though they've had problems finding a role for him) that they quickly re-signed him as soon as the free agency period opened in July, albeit at a reduced salary.

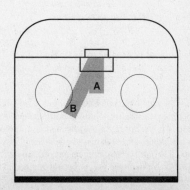

SAKU KOIVU

Yrs. of NHL service: 8
Born: Turku, Finland; Nov. 23, 1974
Position: center
Height: 5-10
Weight: 181
Uniform no.: 11
Shoots: left

Career statistics:

GP	G	A	TP	PIM
429	106	237	343	290

1999-2000 statistics:

GP	G	A	TP	+/-	PIM	PP	SH	GW	GT	S	PCT
24	3	18	21	+7	14	1	0	0	1	53	5.7

2000-2001 statistics:

GP	G	A	TP	+/-	PIM	PP	SH	GW	GT	S	PCT
54	17	30	47	+2	40	7	0	3	2	113	15.0

2001-2002 statistics:

GP	G	A	TP	+/-	PIM	PP	SH	GW	GT	S	PCT
3	0	2	2	0	0	0	0	0	0	2	0.0

2002-2003 statistics:

GP	G	A	TP	+/-	PIM	PP	SH	GW	GT	S	PCT
82	21	50	71	+5	72	5	1	5	0	147	14.3

LAST SEASON

Led team in assists, points, and game-winning goals. Second on team in shooting percentage. Third on team in goals and plus-minus. Tied for third on team in penalty minutes. Career highs in goals and assists. One of three Canadiens to appear in all 82 games.

THE FINESSE GAME

Koivu not only came back from missing nearly an entire season with cancer (non-Hodgkin's lymphoma), he was at the top of his game all season.

A highly skilled, versatile player, Koivu brings brilliance and excitement to every shift. Considered one of the world's best playmakers, he makes things happen with his speed and intimidates by driving the defense back, then uses the room to create scoring chances.

He has great hands and can handle the puck at a fast pace. He stickhandles through traffic and reads plays well. He is intelligent and involved. He is a far superior playmaker than goal-scorer.

Koivu has a variety of shots. He has a slick backhand for shooting or passing. He also has a strong wrist shot and is deadly accurate. He is one of the most dazzling players in the league. And one of the bravest.

THE PHYSICAL GAME

The lone knock on Koivu is his lack of size. He loves to play a physical game, but he just can't. Koivu somehow made it through last season without missing a game. He takes a beating, gets shoved around, and frequently broken. He plays through pain, but the Habs need to keep him from getting damaged. He won't be intimidated, though, and uses his stick as an equalizer, as his high PIM totals will attest.

THE INTANGIBLES

Gritty, gifted, inspirational, and determined, Koivu is revered by his teammates. You can't help but root for this guy. Koivu was an unrestricted free agent after the season.

PROJECTION

Koivu should again be near the 25-goal, 60-assist mark we set for him last season. Too bad he lacks a better supporting cast.

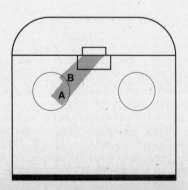

MICHAEL KOMISAREK

Yrs. of NHL service: 0
Born: Islip Terrace, N.Y.; Jan. 19, 1982
Position: right defense
Height: 6-4
Weight: 240
Uniform no.: 8
Shoots: right

Career statistics:

GP	G	A	TP	PIM
21	0	1	1	28

2002-2003 statistics:

GP	G	A	TP	+/-	PIM	PP	SH	GW	GT	S	PCT
21	0	1	1	-6	28	0	0	0	0	26	0.0

LAST SEASON

Will be entering first full NHL season. Appeared in 55 games with Hamilton (AHL), scoring 4-28 — 32 with 75 PIM.

THE FINESSE GAME

Komisarek plays his best when he keeps the game simple. He often tries to start doing his partner's job when he should worry about his own.

Komisarek is definitely in his element in his own zone. He has good puck-moving skills and foot speed which is adequate for the NHL level, but it's not good enough for him to get involved much offensively. When he finds himself on the point, he does have a decent slap shot, but don't expect him to see much power-play time.

He has a history of raising his level of play when the stakes get higher, which is a sign of his intensity.

THE PHYSICAL GAME

Komisarek is big, strong, and likes to hit. Quite a few scouts have even described him as mean. He is learning that it's a lot harder to scare guys in the pros than it was in college. Komisarek is fit and will be able to handle a lot of minutes.

THE INTANGIBLES

Komisarek has been compared to Colin White, a prediction that would probably make Habs fans swoon if it came true. Montreal has been a pretty easy team to push around in the last few years. Komisarek is going to see what he can do to change that. He's a stud.

PROJECTION

There are a lot of job openings on Montreal's blueline, and with Komisarek's size, the Canadiens would love for him to fill one. Don't plan on seeing much offense from him. That's not his gig. He will probably start the season on the third D-pair, but by the All-Star break he will be in the top four.

Komisarek will probably see his fair share of scraps, too, so he could be a sleeper pick in the PIM department if your pool includes that category.

ANDREI MARKOV

Yrs. of NHL service: 3
Born: Vosresensk, Russia; Dec. 20, 1978
Position: left defense
Height: 6-0
Weight: 208
Uniform no.: 79
Shoots: left

Career statistics:

GP	G	A	TP	PIM
198	24	60	84	76

2000-2001 statistics:

GP	G	A	TP	+/-	PIM	PP	SH	GW	GT	S	PCT
63	6	17	23	-6	18	2	0	0	0	82	7.3

2001-2002 statistics:

GP	G	A	TP	+/-	PIM	PP	SH	GW	GT	S	PCT
56	5	19	24	-1	24	2	0	1	0	73	6.8

2002-2003 statistics:

GP	G	A	TP	+/-	PIM	PP	SH	GW	GT	S	PCT
79	13	24	37	+13	34	3	0	2	0	159	8.2

LAST SEASON

Led team defensemen in points and plus-minus. Second on team in average ice time. Third on team in shots. Tied for third on team in assists. Missed two games with knee injury; one game with thigh injury.

THE FINESSE GAME

Markov is mobile and is the kind of power-play quarterback the Canadiens have been waiting for. They can expect him to be their first-unit power-play point man for a long time to come.

Markov has good offensive upside; he is mobile and loves to join the rush. Markov is quick and intelligent and knows what to do with the puck. He doesn't have an Al MacInnis-type slap shot. He is more like Brian Leetch. He has good lateral movement and will release a shot that may not be heavy but has a lot of movement. Markov is also a very accurate shooter.

Markov is able to make a crisp outlet pass out of the zone or he can carry the puck himself.

THE PHYSICAL GAME

Markov is not very big by today's standards, but he is sturdy and he competes. He will draw many more penalties than he commits. Markov spent parts of two seasons in the minors because he had to improve his positional play, especially his coverage of forwards down low. He is not a very emotional player.

THE INTANGIBLES

Markov learned to speak English last season and felt far more comfortable around his teammates. That and better communication contributed to a big step in his development.

PROJECTION

It's been a long time since Montreal has developed a defensive star. Here is one in the making. We would expect Markov to score in the 45-point range.

YANIC PERREAULT

Yrs. of NHL service: 9
Born: Sherbrooke, Que.; Apr. 4, 1971
Position: center
Height: 5-11
Weight: 185
Uniform no.: 94
Shoots: left

Career statistics:

GP	G	A	TP	PIM
602	179	197	376	274

1999-2000 statistics:

GP	G	A	TP	+/-	PIM	PP	SH	GW	GT	S	PCT
58	18	27	45	+3	22	5	0	4	0	114	15.8

2000-2001 statistics:

GP	G	A	TP	+/-	PIM	PP	SH	GW	GT	S	PCT
76	24	28	52	0	52	5	0	2	0	134	17.9

2001-2002 statistics:

GP	G	A	TP	+/-	PIM	PP	SH	GW	GT	S	PCT
82	27	29	56	-3	40	6	0	7	2	156	17.3

2002-2003 statistics:

GP	G	A	TP	+/-	PIM	PP	SH	GW	GT	S	PCT
73	24	22	46	-11	30	7	0	4	0	145	16.5

LAST SEASON

Led team in shots. Second on team in goals and power-play goals. Tied for second on team in game-winning goals. Third on team in points. Missed eight games with groin injury.

THE FINESSE GAME

Perreault is the NHL's face-off king, leading his fellow centermen for the third consecutive season with 62.88 per cent. That's nothing. Some nights he wins 70 or even 80 or 90 per cent of his draws.

Perreault's skating speed is marginal for the NHL level. He tries to compensate with his intelligence, and that alone will keep earning him NHL jobs as a checking center until he decides to pack it in.

Perreault has very good hands and always has his head up, looking for openings. While he doesn't have open-ice speed, he works hard to put on a quick burst in the offensive zone, to gain a half-step on a defender. Once he is open for the shot he waits for the goalie to commit, or he makes a patient pass.

Tricky and solid on his feet, Perreault works the half-boards on the power play. He has an accurate shot with a quick release, and he slithers around to get in the best position for the shot.

THE PHYSICAL GAME

Perreault lacks the size for one-on-one battles in the attacking zone. Defensively, he can't do much except harass a puck carrier with his stick. He is an in-betweener, and if forced to carry the play in any zone his flaws become apparent.

THE INTANGIBLES

Perreault had to carry a lot of the offensive load in 2001-02 during Saku Koivu's cancer battle, and the job he did was nothing short of amazing. Last season, with a healthy Koivu in the lineup, Perreault went back to doing what he does best.

PROJECTION

Perreault was still able to post impressive numbers offensively. Perreault scored only five goals in the second half of the season. He might have been slowed by the groin injury, or he might be slowing, period. It would be wise to scale back expectations to 20 goals and 40 points, which is still good production from a defensive player.

STEPHANE QUINTAL

Yrs. of NHL service: 15
Born: Boucherville, Que.; Oct. 22, 1968
Position: right defense
Height: 6-3
Weight: 231
Uniform no.: 5
Shoots: right

Career statistics:

GP	G	A	TP	PIM
964	60	175	235	1238

1999-2000 statistics:

GP	G	A	TP	+/-	PIM	PP	SH	GW	GT	S	PCT
75	2	14	16	-10	77	0	0	1	0	102	2.0

2000-2001 statistics:

GP	G	A	TP	+/-	PIM	PP	SH	GW	GT	S	PCT
72	1	18	19	-9	60	0	0	0	0	109	0.9

2001-2002 statistics:

GP	G	A	TP	+/-	PIM	PP	SH	GW	GT	S	PCT
75	6	10	16	-7	87	1	0	1	0	85	7.1

2002-2003 statistics:

GP	G	A	TP	+/-	PIM	PP	SH	GW	GT	S	PCT
67	5	5	10	-4	70	0	0	0	0	73	6.8

LAST SEASON

Missed nine games with hamstring injury. Missed four games with finger injury. Missed two games with virus.

THE FINESSE GAME

Quintal's game is limited by his labored skating. He has some nice touches, including a decent point shot, and a good head and hands for passing, but his best moves have to be executed at a virtual standstill. He needs to be paired with a quick skater or his shifts will be spent solely in the defensive zone.

Fortunately, Quintal is aware of his flaws. He plays a smart positional game and doesn't get involved in low-percentage plays in the offensive zone. He won't step up in the neutral zone to risk an interception but will fall back into a defensive mode. He takes up a lot of ice with his body and stick, and when he doesn't overcommit, he reduces the space available to a puck carrier. Quintal should not carry the puck. He tends to get a little panicky under pressure.

Although he can exist as an NHL regular in the five-on-five mode, Quintal is a risky proposition for any specialty-team play.

THE PHYSICAL GAME

Strong on his skates, Quintal thrives on contact and works hard along the boards and in front of the net. He hits hard without taking penalties and is a tough and willing fighter if he has to do it. He has the strength to clear the crease and is a good skater for his size.

THE INTANGIBLES

Quintal is thrilled to be playing in his native Montreal and it shows in his play.

PROJECTION

Quintal can score 20 to 25 points and he is a serviceable, third-pairing defenseman if he is paired with a mobile partner. He has to play in the top four with Montreal, and that's a stretch for him.

CRAIG RIVET

Yrs. of NHL service: 7
Born: North Bay, Ont.; Sept. 13, 1974
Position: right defense
Height: 6-2
Weight: 207
Uniform no.: 52
Shoots: right

Career statistics:

GP	G	A	TP	PIM
437	22	67	89	531

1999-2000 statistics:

GP	G	A	TP	+/-	PIM	PP	SH	GW	GT	S	PCT
61	3	14	17	+11	76	0	0	1	1	71	4.2

2000-2001 statistics:

GP	G	A	TP	+/-	PIM	PP	SH	GW	GT	S	PCT
26	1	2	3	-8	36	0	0	0	0	22	4.6

2001-2002 statistics:

GP	G	A	TP	+/-	PIM	PP	SH	GW	GT	S	PCT
82	8	17	25	+1	76	0	0	0	0	90	8.9

2002-2003 statistics:

GP	G	A	TP	+/-	PIM	PP	SH	GW	GT	S	PCT
82	7	15	22	+1	71	3	0	2	0	118	5.9

LAST SEASON

Third on team in average ice time. One of three Canadiens to appear in all 82 games.

THE FINESSE GAME

There is little that Rivet does not do well. His primary asset is his hockey sense. It has been slow to develop at the NHL level, but gradually Rivet has become an extremely reliable player in his own zone. He is a willing shot-blocker. He is an efficient skater. He passes well and moves the puck quickly out of his zone with low-risk plays.

Rivet's offensive upside is high, although his production slid last season. He has been concentrating on the defensive end of the game more, but he has the skating ability, the hands, and the shot to get more involved in the attack. He is a smart offensive player. He could become a poor-man's Ray Bourque.

Rivet also kills penalties well. He competes hard and is a natural leader.

THE PHYSICAL GAME

The physical part of the game comes naturally to Rivet. He is a willing hitter, not necessarily mean, but he takes his man out with authority. He has good size and knows how to use it. Rivet is strong on his skates and finishes his checks. Not many opposing forwards relish coming into his corner.

THE INTANGIBLES

While he will never be an elite defenseman, he could be a No. 2 on anyone's team except for the league's elite half-dozen teams now, and he might not be far from that rank soon. It's easy to overlook the quiet contributions of a player like this. Rivet shows up in the big spots. He enjoyed a healthy season last year, and that gave a better indication of the kind of player Rivet truly is. He's a great team guy who will help the incoming corps of young Habs defensemen to learn the game.

PROJECTION

Rivet is going to be one of Montreal's top pair. He is capable of scoring in the 25- to 30-point range.

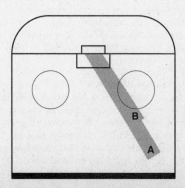

NIKLAS SUNDSTROM

Yrs. of NHL service: 8
Born: Ornskoldsvik, Sweden; June 6, 1975
Position: right wing
Height: 6-0
Weight: 190
Uniform no.: 37
Shoots: left

Career statistics:

GP	G	A	TP	PIM
629	103	211	314	208

1999-2000 statistics:

GP	G	A	TP	+/-	PIM	PP	SH	GW	GT	S	PCT
79	12	25	37	+9	22	2	1	2	3	90	13.3

2000-2001 statistics:

GP	G	A	TP	+/-	PIM	PP	SH	GW	GT	S	PCT
82	10	39	49	+10	28	4	1	0	0	100	10.0

2001-2002 statistics:

GP	G	A	TP	+/-	PIM	PP	SH	GW	GT	S	PCT
73	9	30	39	+7	50	0	1	0	1	74	12.2

2002-2003 statistics:

GP	G	A	TP	+/-	PIM	PP	SH	GW	GT	S	PCT
80	7	19	26	-1	30	0	0	1	0	71	9.9

PROJECTION

Sundstrom will likely play on the third line in Montreal in his first full season. Things went off-kilter early last season in San Jose and Sundstrom adapted well to the change. In 33 games with Montreal, he was 5-9 — 14 and was +3. Expect 10 12 goals.

LAST SEASON

Acquired from San Jose on January 23, 2003, with a third-round draft pick in 2003 for Jeff Hackett.

THE FINESSE GAME

Sundstrom is a defensive forward who possesses some finishing capabilities. As a scorer, he is opportunistic, but he doesn't have the feel for goal scoring or the drive to pay the price around the net.

A deceptively fast skater with good balance and a strong stride, Sundstrom plays a smart game and does a lot of subtle things well.

A puck magnet, he applies his skills to the defensive game. He reads plays very well, is aware defensively and always makes the safe decision. And when he forechecks, especially when killing penalties, he usually comes up with the puck in a one-on-one battle.

THE PHYSICAL GAME

Sundstrom will not get much bigger and has to stay strong. He is persistent and consistently physical. One of the Swede's talents is lifting an opponent's blade to steal the puck. He absorbs far more punishment than he dishes out (since he doesn't punish anybody). He can handle a lot of minutes.

THE INTANGIBLES

Because he doesn't throw big hits or make flashy plays on the ice, and because he is almost constantly smiling off of it, Sundstrom gets taken lightly a lot more than he should. He is committed to playing, and playing well. He is also committed to winning, and is enormously respected in the dressing room.

JOSE THEODORE

Yrs. of NHL service: 5
Born: Laval, Que.; Sept. 13, 1976
Position: goaltender
Height: 5-11
Weight: 182
Uniform no.: 60
Catches: right

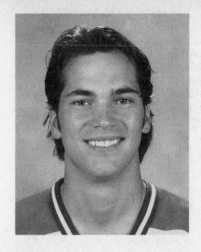

Career statistics:

GP	MIN	GA	SO	GAA	A	PIM
248	13979	604	17	2.59	5	14

1999-2000 statistics:

GP	MIN	GAA	W	L	T	SO	GA	S	SAPCT	PIM
30	1655	2.10	12	13	2	5	58	717	.919	0

2000-2001 statistics:

GP	MIN	GAA	W	L	T	SO	GA	S	SAPCT	PIM
59	3298	2.57	20	29	5	2	141	1546	.909	6

2001-2002 statistics:

GP	MIN	GAA	W	L	T	SO	GA	S	SAPCT	PIM
67	3864	2.11	30	24	10	7	136	1972	.931	6

2002-2003 statistics:

GP	MIN	GAA	W	L	T	SO	GA	S	SAPCT	PIM
57	3419	2.90	20	31	6	2	165	1797	.908	6

LAST SEASON

Missed two games with hip injury.

THE PHYSICAL GAME

Theodore is technically a very sound goalie. One of his best assets is his ability to control rebounds. He doesn't just try to kick the puck away, but he is able to deaden the shot, absorb the shock, and have it land in a spot where he is better able to control it.

It also helps Theodore to be a lefty goalie. There aren't many in the NHL, and for shooters it's like having to face a lefty tennis player. The stick side and glove side of Theodore are opposite to what shooters are accustomed to seeing.

Theodore has excellent reflexes. While he is not quite as extreme as Dominik Hasek, his flexibility and tenacity in not giving up on a shot are very similar.

Theodore's stickhandling is better than average.

What went awry with Theodore last season had more to do with his head than his body.

THE MENTAL GAME

Theodore was a dual trophy winner in 2002 and was exalted to a kind of rock star status in Montreal. He received a hefty pay raise and it was reasonable to think it would all come crashing in on him. It did.

In his great run in 2001-02, he came on very late in the season and played with little pressure behind a Canadiens team that no one gave a chance to make the playoffs. They did, and even won a round, but the expectations for him last season with a team that might have been even worse than the previous season were too much for him to handle.

THE INTANGIBLES

Added to Theodore's what-have-you-done-for-us-lately woes came the investigation of several of his close relatives (including his father and brothers) because of their alleged involvement in loan sharking. While Theodore himself is clear of any charges, this won't make his life any easier.

PROJECTION

Montreal is unlikely to improve much, and Theodore will have to be brilliant to earn more than 22 wins.

JASON WARD

Yrs. of NHL service: 4
Born: Chapleau, Ont.; Jan. 16, 1979
Position: right wing
Height: 6-3
Weight: 200
Uniform no.: 17
Shoots: right

Career statistics:

GP	G	A	TP	PIM
52	5	3	8	22

1999-2000 statistics:

GP	G	A	TP	+/-	PIM	PP	SH	GW	GT	S	PCT
32	2	1	3	-1	10	1	0	0	0	24	8.3

2000-2001 statistics:

GP	G	A	TP	+/-	PIM	PP	SH	GW	GT	S	PCT
12	0	0	0	+3	12	0	0	0	0	4	0.0

2002-2003 statistics:

GP	G	A	TP	+/-	PIM	PP	SH	GW	GT	S	PCT
8	3	2	5	+3	0	0	0	0	0	10	30.0

LAST SEASON

Will be entering first full NHL season. Appeared in 69 games with Hamilton (AHL), scoring 31-41 — 72 with 78 PIM.

THE FINESSE GAME

Montreal drafted Ward in the hopes he would be a power forward. What they have on their hands instead is a powerful third-line winger. Not what they envisioned, but he will turn out to be a very useful sort.

Not many checking-line forwards have hands as soft as Ward's. He has a good, long reach and is strong on his stick. The release time on his shot is what will probably prevent him from being an impact scorer at this level.

Ward is an energy player and tempo changer. He forechecks tenaciously and intelligently. He has a wide skating stance and is tough to knock off-balance. He could stand to improve his foot speed a little. Basically, Ward is a grinder with some offensive upside.

THE PHYSICAL GAME

Ward plays hard and since he's not all that big — he's tall but very weedy — he tends to get dinged up. It wouldn't be a surprise to see him miss 10-15 games per season with injuries. If he could add about 10-15 more pounds of muscle that would help. Ward has tried but he just doesn't have the frame for it. He plays with an edge.

THE INTANGIBLES

Ward is probably not skilled enough to play in the top six, but he should see some power-play time on the second unit.

PROJECTION

Ward ended up as the leading scorer for Hamilton (AHL) despite his mid-March promotion to the parent club. Minor-league scoring doesn't always translate at the NHL level, but Ward has a nose for the net and could score 15-20 goals in a third line role. He could be doing it for many seasons to come in Montreal.

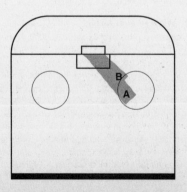

RICHARD ZEDNIK

Yrs. of NHL service: 6
Born: Bystrica, Slovakia; Jan. 6, 1976
Position: left wing
Height: 6-0
Weight: 200
Uniform no.: 20
Shoots: left

Career statistics:

GP	G	A	TP	PIM
431	119	100	219	345

1999-2000 statistics:

GP	G	A	TP	+/-	PIM	PP	SH	GW	GT	S	PCT
69	19	16	35	+6	54	1	0	2	3	179	10.6

2000-2001 statistics:

GP	G	A	TP	+/-	PIM	PP	SH	GW	GT	S	PCT
74	19	25	44	-4	71	5	0	3	1	178	10.7

2001-2002 statistics:

GP	G	A	TP	+/-	PIM	PP	SH	GW	GT	S	PCT
82	22	22	44	-3	59	4	0	3	0	249	8.8

2002-2003 statistics:

GP	G	A	TP	+/-	PIM	PP	SH	GW	GT	S	PCT
80	31	19	50	+4	79	9	0	2	1	250	12.4

PROJECTION

Last season we said, "Zednik should score in the range of 25-30 goals. He will score in the range of 20 to 25 goals." Instead, Zednik found the "on" switch. Having Saku Koivu healthy and eager was a huge boost. Zednik should score 30 goals and may surpass that. There's no reason to stop now.

LAST SEASON

Led team in goals, power-play goals, and shots. Career high in goals. Second on team in points. Third on team in shooting percentage. Missed two games with groin injuries.

THE FINESSE GAME

Zednik has the skating speed and hand skills to mark him as a top-six forward, and he cemented that status last season.

Very good down low, Zednik can control the game and go to the net; he has nice hands and is not shy about shooting. Zednik has a very low crouch and gets a lot on his shot. He is a dynamic player and gained more confidence last season, which is why his production was so much better.

Zednik used to struggle on the power play. Maybe it was pressure, maybe it was not bearing down enough. He improved this year but with the amount of time he sees with the man advantage, he should be scoring even more. When his goal slumps occur, he works hard to snap out of his drought.

THE PHYSICAL GAME

Although he is not big, Zednik is strong. Coming off the wing, he just about carries defenders on his back. Solid and sturdy on his skates, he likes to get involved and isn't rattled by physical play. Zednik gets good leg drive to power his skating and doesn't mind going into the corners for puck battles.

THE INTANGIBLES

Finally, Zednik's potential is starting to shine.

NASHVILLE PREDATORS

Players' Statistics 2001-2002

POS.	NO.	PLAYER	GP	G	A	PTS	+/-	PIM	PP	SH	GW	GT	S	PCT
C	11	DAVID LEGWAND	64	17	31	48	-2	34	3	1	4	1	167	10.2
D	44	KIMMO TIMONEN	72	6	34	40	-3	46	4				144	4.2
L	21	ANDREAS JOHANSSON	56	20	17	37	-4	22	10			1	124	16.1
L	25	DENIS ARKHIPOV	79	11	24	35	-18	32	3		1	1	148	7.4
D	5	ANDY DELMORE	71	18	16	34	-17	28	14		6		149	12.1
R	17	SCOTT HARTNELL	82	12	22	34	-3	101	2		2		221	5.4
R	24	SCOTT WALKER	60	15	18	33	2	58	7		5		124	12.1
L	33	VLADIMIR ORSZAGH	78	16	16	32	-1	38	3		3		152	10.5
L	15	REM MURRAY	85	12	19	31	-2	22	2	1	1		143	8.4
R	18	*ADAM HALL	79	16	12	28	-8	31	8		2		146	10.9
R	14	OLEG PETROV	70	9	18	27	-6	18	2		2		124	7.3
R	43	VITALI YACHMENEV	62	5	15	20	7	12			1		68	7.3
D	27	JASON YORK	74	4	15	19	13	52	2			1	107	3.7
C	22	GREG JOHNSON	38	8	9	17	7	22					55	14.5
L	20	TODD WARRINER	49	6	10	16	1	32			1		72	8.3
C	10	CLARKE WILM	82	5	11	16	-11	36					108	4.6
D	3	KARLIS SKRASTINS	82	3	10	13	-18	44		1			86	3.5
C	16	DENIS PEDERSON	43	4	6	10	2	39				1	64	6.3
D	4	MARK EATON	50	2	7	9	1	22				1	52	3.8
D	32	CALE HULSE	80	2	6	8	-11	121			1		82	2.4
L	19	MARTIN ERAT	27	1	7	8	-9	14	1				39	2.6
C	38	*VERNON FIDDLER	19	4	2	6	2	14			1		20	20.0
D	23	BILL HOULDER	82	2	4	6	-2	46			1		51	3.9
L	41	BRENT GILCHRIST	41	1	2	3	-11	14					41	2.4
C	46	WYATT SMITH	11	1		1	-1						8	12.5
R	7	*SCOTTIE UPSHALL	8	1		1	2					1	6	16.7
L	12	REID SIMPSON	26		1	1	-4	56					11	
R	28	CAMERON MANN	4				-2						5	
D	26	ANDY BERENZWEIG	4				0						5	
C	9	GREG CLASSEN	8				-3	4					2	
C	39	DOMENIC PITTIS	2				0	2					1	
D	27	PASCAL TREPANIER	1				0						1	
D	28	TOMAS KLOUCEK	3				1	2					1	
R	54	*DARREN HAYDAR	2				-1						1	
G	34	WADE FLAHERTY	1				0							
G	29	TOMAS VOKOUN	69				0	28						
R	20	*NATHAN PERROTT	1				0	5						
G	31	CHRIS MASON	1				0							
D	36	*ROBERT SCHNABEL	1				0							
G	31	BRIAN FINLEY	1				0							
G	35	JAN LASAK	3				0							

GP = games played; G = goals; A = assists; PTS = points; +/- = goals-for minus goals-against while player is on ice; PIM = penalties in minutes; PP = power-play goals; SH = shorthanded goals; GW = game-winning goals; GT = game-tying goals; S = no. of shots; PCT = percentage of goals to shots; * = rookie

DENIS ARKHIPOV

Yrs. of NHL service: 3
Born: Kazan, Russia; May 19, 1979
Position: left wing
Height: 6-3
Weight: 214
Uniform no.: 25
Shoots: left

Career statistics:

GP	G	A	TP	PIM
201	37	53	90	52

2000-2001 statistics:

GP	G	A	TP	+/-	PIM	PP	SH	GW	GT	S	PCT
40	6	7	13	0	4	0	0	0	0	42	14.3

2001-2002 statistics:

GP	G	A	TP	+/-	PIM	PP	SH	GW	GT	S	PCT
82	20	22	42	-18	16	7	0	6	1	118	17.0

2002-2003 statistics:

GP	G	A	TP	+/-	PIM	PP	SH	GW	GT	S	PCT
79	11	24	35	-18	32	3	0	1	1	148	7.4

PROJECTION

Arkhipov needs to score 20-25 goals to keep his job on one of the top two lines.

LAST SEASON

Third on team in goals. Worst plus-minus on team. Missed one game with bruised shoulder. Missed two games due to coach's decision.

THE FINESSE GAME

Arkhipov is a power player with a decent scoring touch, although he took a step back from his big 20-goal season. And since Arkhipov wasn't scoring, he let it affect other areas of his game, which was a big mistake. His play away from the puck was indifferent, which led to his terrible plus-minus.

The Predators need Arkhipov to step up his game and take some of the pressure off of David Legwand.

On the nights when he's on, Arkhipov plays so hard and with so much presence that you will come away from the rink thinking Arkhipov is a much bigger player. He isn't short, but he's not very thick. He doesn't look imposing. He simply plays a determined style. Arkhipov is entrusted with playing against some of the league's power centers, like Bobby Holik.

Arkhipov possesses good size, very good hands, good vision, and passing skills. He has good speed and lateral mobility.

THE PHYSICAL GAME

He needs to get a little stronger, but Arkhipov shows the willingness to play an involved game and that bodes well. He is very competitive.

THE INTANGIBLES

Arkhipov is one of the foundation players for Nashville's future. Last year was a contract year (he became a restricted free agent) and there are players who don't handle that well, which may have been a factor in his decline.

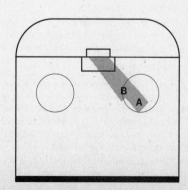

ADAM HALL

Yrs. of NHL service: 1
Born: Kalamazoo, Mich.; Aug. 14, 1980
Position: right wing
Height: 6-3
Weight: 205
Uniform no.: 18
Shoots: right

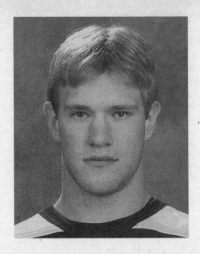

Career statistics:

GP	G	A	TP	PIM
80	16	13	29	31

2001-2002 statistics:

GP	G	A	TP	+/-	PIM	PP	SH	GW	GT	S	PCT
1	0	1	1	0	0	0	0	0	0	2	0.0

2002-2003 statistics:

GP	G	A	TP	+/-	PIM	PP	SH	GW	GT	S	PCT
79	16	12	28	-8	31	8	0	2	0	146	10.9

LAST SEASON

First NHL season. Led NHL rookies in power-play goals. Third among NHL rookies in shots. Tied for fourth among NHL rookies in shooting percentage. Fifth among NHL rookies in goals. Ninth among NHL rookies in points. Appeared in one game with Milwaukee (AHL), scoring 0-0 — 0 with 2 PIM.

THE FINESSE GAME

Hall is a good-sized forward with good hand skills. He will be a better finisher than a playmaker, which has been the case at every level he has risen to. Hall is strong on his stick and on his skates and battles for position in the crease. He has really good hands in tight for picking up loose pucks or tipping in shots.

Hall needs to improve on his play away from the puck and in learning to do other things that can help his team win when he is not scoring goals. The slumps will come, and Hall just has to figure out how to contribute when they do. Playing on the checking line as he did much of last season helped Hall develop a better all-around game. He is smart and coachable.

Hall is at his best on the power play. He seems to intensify his play and half of his 16 goals last season came with the man advantage.

THE PHYSICAL GAME

Hall is naturally aggressive and will assert himself physically around the net. He is a quiet guy, but he plays with passion and he's leadership material.

THE INTANGIBLES

The Predators had planned on giving Hall some seasoning in the minors, which is where he was assigned at the beginning of the season, but injuries forced his recall and Hall never went back. He set a franchise record for goals by a rookie, and while the franchise is young, the record he broke was David Legwand's.

For some reason, Hall didn't get a lot of recognition despite being among the best of the 2003 freshman class. He slumped badly at the end of the season (no goals in the last 19 games), which probably cost him Calder Trophy buzz.

PROJECTION

Hall broke in on the third line but has top-six potential. He could improve to the 20-goal range.

DAN HAMHUIS

Yrs. of NHL service: 0
Born: Smithers, B.C.; Dec. 13, 1982
Position: left defense
Height: 6-0
Weight: 208
Uniform no.: n.a.
Shoots: left

Career (minor league) statistics:

GP	G	A	TP	PIM
68	6	21	27	81

2002-2003 minor league statistics:

GP	G	A	TP	PIM
68	6	21	27	81

LAST SEASON

Will be entering his first NHL season. Appeared in 68 games with Milwaukee (AHL), scoring 6-21 — 27 with 81 PIM.

THE FINESSE GAME

Hamhuis struggled a bit in his first pro year, but it was nothing the Predators didn't expect as part of his learning experience since he was only 19. Hamhuis is developing into a top-four defenseman who can play an all-around game. He is a smaller version of Wade Redden.

Hamhuis is an accomplished passer. He moves the puck well out of his zone. He doesn't have a wicked point shot, but like Redden, uses a sneaky-strong wrist shot that you don't notice until someone has tipped it into the net. Hamhuis doesn't rush the puck sense-lessly on every shift. He is very smart and knows when to pick his spots.

Hamhuis is a mobile defenseman, a very agile skater with a seamless shift of speed. Hamhuis could be one of the best pure skaters among the new crop of defensemen. He understands the game well. He plays his angles and is tough to beat one on one.

THE PHYSICAL GAME

If Hamhuis were a few inches taller and a few pounds heavier, he would be a fearsome checker. He is a will-ing and able open-ice hitter. He gets a lot of drive from his strong legs but he won't be able to jolt big guys because he just won't have the beef. Players bet-ter not have their heads down through the neutral zone against him, though. Hamhuis may have one of the best hip-checks in the NHL. Hamhuis can sometimes get too involved in the thrill of the chase and needs to be reined in when he gets out of position looking to make hits.

THE INTANGIBLES

Nashville culled a lot of their older, pricier defense-men to make room for kids like Hamhuis. If he steps up in training camp, he should win a top-four job and earn some power-play time.

PROJECTION

Hamhuis will most likely concentrate on the defensive aspects of the job, but he has offensive upside. For a rookie D-man, 20 points would be a very good start.

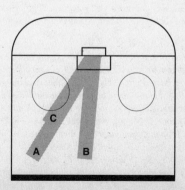

SCOTT HARTNELL

Yrs. of NHL service: 3
Born: Regina, Sask.; Apr. 18, 1982
Position: right wing
Height: 6-2
Weight: 208
Uniform no.: 17
Shoots: left

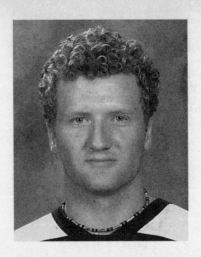

Career statistics:

GP	G	A	TP	PIM
232	28	63	91	260

2000-2001 statistics:

GP	G	A	TP	+/-	PIM	PP	SH	GW	GT	S	PCT
75	2	14	16	-8	48	0	0	0	0	92	2.2

2001-2002 statistics:

GP	G	A	TP	+/-	PIM	PP	SH	GW	GT	S	PCT
75	14	27	41	+5	111	3	0	4	0	162	8.6

2002-2003 statistics:

GP	G	A	TP	+/-	PIM	PP	SH	GW	GT	S	PCT
82	12	22	34	-3	101	2	0	2	0	221	5.4

LAST SEASON

Led team in shots. Second on team in penalty minutes. One of five Predators to appear in all 82 games.

THE FINESSE GAME

Hartnell is a prototypical power forward. He can play with finesse players — his junior linemates were Milan Kraft and Michal Sivek — and he adds character and heart to a squad.

The knock on Hartnell is his skating speed, but he has good power. And here's the main thing about his skating: he wants to get there. He is always digging hard and keeping his feet in motion. He is an up-and-down winger who crashes and gets inside. He is strong on the forecheck and plays with a lot of energy.

Hartnell has very good hockey sense. He has good hands, can make plays with the puck, can drive the net, and have the poise to pull up and find an open man. If Hartnell is guilty of anything in a game, it's of trying to do too much. He has to recognize and play within his limitations.

THE PHYSICAL GAME

Hartnell plays a hard-nosed game. He is gritty around the net. He hits and, when he has to, he will fight.

THE INTANGIBLES

Hartnell is a natural leader who is respected by his peer group as well as veteran players. The Predators believe he will be their future captain. Hartnell's progress hasn't been entirely smooth. There are stretches where his game takes a step backwards. He will become more consistent and is part of the Preds' core group of young players

PROJECTION

The goals won't always be pretty or come easy. Hartnell will earn his way on to one of the top two lines but to stay there he has to produce 20 goals.

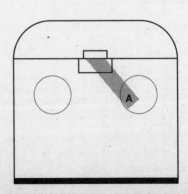

GREG JOHNSON

Yrs. of NHL service: 10
Born: Thunder Bay, Ont.; Mar. 16, 1971
Position: center
Height: 5-11
Weight: 202
Uniform no.: 22
Shoots: left

Career statistics:

GP	G	A	TP	PIM
635	120	198	318	302

1999-2000 statistics:

GP	G	A	TP	+/-	PIM	PP	SH	GW	GT	S	PCT
82	11	33	44	-15	40	2	0	1	0	133	8.3

2000-2001 statistics:

GP	G	A	TP	+/-	PIM	PP	SH	GW	GT	S	PCT
82	15	17	32	-6	46	1	0	4	0	97	15.5

2001-2002 statistics:

GP	G	A	TP	+/-	PIM	PP	SH	GW	GT	S	PCT
82	18	26	44	-14	38	3	0	2	1	145	12.4

2002-2003 statistics:

GP	G	A	TP	+/-	PIM	PP	SH	GW	GT	S	PCT
38	8	9	17	+7	22	0	0	0	0	55	14.5

LAST SEASON

Missed 44 games with a concussion.

THE FINESSE GAME

Johnson can be used in many playing situations thanks to his speed, which is explosive. A small center, he has fine finesse skills. He's also a smart and creative passer, though he doesn't shoot enough, especially given the amount of ice time he receives. When he chooses, he has an accurate wrist shot. He isn't a hard player but he competes well.

On a stronger team Johnson might be pegged as a checking forward, but he has more ice time and more responsibility with Nashville.

Johnson can play four-on-four, kill penalties, and work on the power play. He has been increasing his shot totals but still needs to improve in that area.

THE PHYSICAL GAME

Johnson is small and gets bounced around a lot. Being one of the faster skaters in the league allows him to avoid some situations where he can be outmuscled. He keeps himself in great shape, although last year's head injury obviously made things difficult for him.

THE INTANGIBLES

Johnson had been one of the more durable small players in the NHL. The concussion he suffered in October ended a consecutive games-played streak at 251. Johnson returned to action in late January and didn't miss a game through the end of the season. He is the team's captain, and it's a role he doesn't take lightly.

PROJECTION

With Johnson's speed and decent hands, he should be a 20-goal scorer. History says he isn't likely to score many more than 15. But if you want assists, he's your man in Nashville. We expect the Predators to be getting a little better up front, which may see Johnson's assists rise to around 30.

TOMAS KLOUCEK

Yrs. of NHL service: 3
Born: Prague, Czech.; Mar.7, 1980
Position: left defense
Height: 6-2
Weight: 205
Uniform no.: 28
Shoots: left

Career statistics:

GP	G	A	TP	PIM
98	2	7	9	213

2000-2001 statistics:

GP	G	A	TP	+/-	PIM	PP	SH	GW	GT	S	PCT
43	1	4	5	-3	74	0	0	0	0	22	4.6

2001-2002 statistics:

GP	G	A	TP	+/-	PIM	PP	SH	GW	GT	S	PCT
52	1	3	4	-2	137	0	0	0	0	21	4.8

2002-2003 statistics:

GP	G	A	TP	+/-	PIM	PP	SH	GW	GT	S	PCT
3	0	0	0	+1	2	0	0	0	0	1	0.0

LAST SEASON

Acquired from N.Y. Rangers with Rem Murray and Marek Zidlicky on December 12, 2002, for Mike Dunham. Appeared in 20 games with Hartford (AHL), scoring 3-4 — 7 with 102 PIM. Appeared in 34 games with Milwaukee (AHL), scoring 0-6 — 6 with 80 PIM.

THE FINESSE GAME

Kloucek reads the play well and makes a good enough first pass to show that he can be an everyday top-four defenseman. What sets Kloucek apart is his fearsome and fearless physical play. But simply walloping people isn't enough to keep a player in uniform.

He is still a little young with the puck at times. He will get panicky and throw the puck away under pressure, but that appears to be a factor of inexperience. Kloucek is so eager to strut his stuff when he gets a shift that he has a tendency to try to do too much. Once he relaxes, his game will flow much more effortlessly.

His skating is NHL caliber. Kloucek is the kind of defenseman who can develop into an excellent complement for the most highly skilled defender on the team.

THE PHYSICAL GAME

Kloucek worked hard to come back from reconstructive knee surgery only to suffer a separated shoulder in the minors. He is an amazing physical specimen — massive and rock-hard. Kloucek needs to curb his reckless hitting, because even some of his clean checks are mistaken by referees for penalties.

THE INTANGIBLES

Nashville may become Bashville if Kloucek sticks with the top-four defensemen, as projected. Kloucek is still a project, but the Predators will be happy to swap his learning mistakes for the amazing physical presence he can give a team.

PROJECTION

None of Kloucek's contributions are offensive. He is a tough, physical, momentum-changing defenseman who won't have many quiet nights.

DAVID LEGWAND

Yrs. of NHL service: 4
Born: Detroit, Mich.; Aug. 17, 1980
Position: center
Height: 6-2
Weight: 190
Uniform no.: 11
Shoots: left

Career statistics:

GP	G	A	TP	PIM
280	54	93	147	156

1999-2000 statistics:

GP	G	A	TP	+/-	PIM	PP	SH	GW	GT	S	PCT
71	13	15	28	-6	30	4	0	2	0	111	11.7

2000-2001 statistics:

GP	G	A	TP	+/-	PIM	PP	SH	GW	GT	S	PCT
81	13	28	41	+1	38	3	0	3	0	172	7.6

2001-2002 statistics:

GP	G	A	TP	+/-	PIM	PP	SH	GW	GT	S	PCT
63	11	19	30	+1	54	1	1	1	0	121	9.1

2002-2003 statistics:

GP	G	A	TP	+/-	PIM	PP	SH	GW	GT	S	PCT
64	17	31	48	-2	34	3	1	4	1	167	10.2

LAST SEASON

Led team in points. Second on team in assists and shots. Third on team in goals and game-winning goals. Career highs in goals, assists, and points. Missed 18 games with broken collarbone.

THE FINESSE GAME

Legwand's all-around game continues to improve to the point where he is starting to dominate games on many nights. Think of him as a young Steve Yzerman, without the history of the 100-point seasons. He will become a better player even if he doesn't put up the splashy numbers to draw attention.

Legwand handles the puck well in traffic and shoots well in stride. He wants the puck when the game is on the line, because he has that goal-scorer's mentality that the team is better off when the puck is on his stick rather than anyone else's. He has the ability to carry it up-ice. He isn't totally unselfish and is a good passer, but his first option will always be to take the shot. Legwand is very strong on the puck. He just has to find his shot and utilize his outside speed better. He also needs to be more consistent in following up his shot to the net rather than just breezing on by.

Legwand is an absolutely dynamic skater. He could be one of the best breakaway scorers in the league among his age group. Legwand needs to continue to improve his defensive game. Face-offs remain a weakness.

THE PHYSICAL GAME

He has been compared to Mike Modano in style, but physically and mentally Legwand is years away from being a Modano-type of player. Legwand is still boyish in build and needs to get a lot stronger to be able to compete in the NHL. He has to improve his battle skills. He has a strong lower body and needs to develop the upper body. Remember, it took Modano years to become the all-round player and leader he is now. Legwand was much more aggressive last season. He was injury-free until early March when he suffered a broken collarbone that ended his season.

THE INTANGIBLES

Legwand is still young, still maturing, and still learning what it takes to be an NHL player. He has done nothing wrong yet. Legwand was a restricted free agent after last season.

PROJECTION

Legwand scored the 45 points we projected for him and was actually on pace to score 60, which is what we will expect of him assuming he doesn't miss training camp or lose playing time because of a contract hassle.

VLADIMIR ORSZAGH

Yrs. of NHL service: 4
Born: Banska Bystrica, CZE
Position: right wing
Height: 5-11
Weight: 193
Uniform no.: 33
Shoots: left

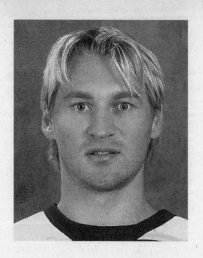

Career statistics:

GP	G	A	TP	PIM
191	34	39	73	106

1999-2000 statistics:

GP	G	A	TP	+/-	PIM	PP	SH	GW	GT	S	PCT
11	2	1	3	+1	4	0	0	0	0	16	12.5

2000-2001 statistics:

Did not play in NHL

2001-2002 statistics:

GP	G	A	TP	+/-	PIM	PP	SH	GW	GT	S	PCT
79	15	21	36	-15	56	5	0	3	0	113	13.3

2002-2003 statistics:

GP	G	A	TP	+/-	PIM	PP	SH	GW	GT	S	PCT
78	16	16	32	-1	38	3	0	3	0	152	10.5

LAST SEASON

Third on team in shots. Missed two games with bruised shoulder.

THE FINESSE GAME

Orszagh is a left-handed shot who plays the right wing. Playing the off-wing opens up one-timers for Orszagh. Once he gets over the blueline he won't be looking to force a pass. He won't back up and make a play. Orszagh will shoot. He has a good selection of shots.

Orszagh is a good skater. He doesn't have blazing speed but he is quick and he's strong on his feet. He can hold off a defender with one arm and keep advancing the puck. He battles for his patch of ice.

He thinks the game well and has good hockey sense.

THE PHYSICAL GAME

Even though he isn't very big, Orszagh is a tough customer. He plays with an edge and he is unfazed by match-ups against bigger, stronger, more famous players. Orszagh could always stand to add some muscle, which can be done, and height, which can't.

THE INTANGIBLES

Orszagh had trouble finding chemistry as linemates were juggled around him. That is probably the biggest reason why his point production didn't jump the way it should have.

PROJECTION

Orszagh figures prominently in Nashville's top-six forward plans again as the No. 2 right wing. A jump to 45 points is logical.

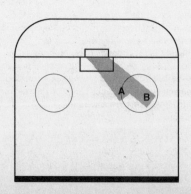

KIMMO TIMONEN

Yrs. of NHL service: 5
Born: Kuopio, Finland; Mar. 18, 1975
Position: left defense
Height: 5-10
Weight: 196
Uniform no.: 44
Shoots: left

Career statistics:

GP	G	A	TP	PIM
337	43	109	152	180

1999-2000 statistics:

GP	G	A	TP	+/-	PIM	PP	SH	GW	GT	S	PCT
51	8	25	33	-5	26	2	1	2	0	97	8.2

2000-2001 statistics:

GP	G	A	TP	+/-	PIM	PP	SH	GW	GT	S	PCT
82	12	13	25	-6	50	6	0	3	0	151	7.9

2001-2002 statistics:

GP	G	A	TP	+/-	PIM	PP	SH	GW	GT	S	PCT
82	13	29	42	+2	28	9	0	1	0	154	8.4

2002-2003 statistics:

GP	G	A	TP	+/-	PIM	PP	SH	GW	GT	S	PCT
72	6	34	40	-3	46	4	0	0	0	144	4.2

LAST SEASON

Led team defensemen in points for fourth consecutive season. Led team in assists with career high. Led team in average ice time (22:24). Second on team in points. Missed four games with bruised ankle. Missed eight games with bruised calf.

THE FINESSE GAME

Timonen has good quickness and adds a lot of skill to the Nashville backline, which doesn't have much in that department. He has been their best defenseman for the past few seasons. He is not a defensive liability, and has worked to improve the defensive aspects of his game.

With Andy Delmore dealt to Buffalo, the scoring pressure will be back on Timonen this season. He has good ability in all offensive areas. He is not elite class, but he moves the puck and sees the ice well. Timonen has excellent hockey sense. He gets first-unit power-play time (28 of his 40 points came on the power play last season). He could also kill penalties, but Nashville does need to give him a breather now and then.

Timonen is one of the smaller defensemen in the league, and in Finland several seasons ago was the partner of New Jersey's Brian Rafalski. Timonen is a lot like Rafalski, although he lacks his ex-teammate's explosive speed and thick build. He does have quickness, however. He reads and jumps into the rush well to create offense.

THE PHYSICAL GAME

Somewhat on the small side, Timonen is not very strong. He isn't going to get bigger, so he has to try to get stronger. He has a powerful lower body.

THE INTANGIBLES

Timonen is one of the first players other teams ask about when seeking a deal with Nashville, but he is quite valuable in this spot. While he would be a complementary player elsewhere, he is as close as the Preds have to a No. 1 defenseman. He was a restricted free agent after last season.

PROJECTION

Timonen scored 40 points last season. That is probably close to his top end. If he can produce 40-45 points a season on a consistent basis, he will have a successful career.

SCOTTIE UPSHALL

Yrs. of NHL service: 0
Born: Fort McMurray, Alta.; Oct. 7, 1983
Position: right wing
Height: 6-0
Weight: 184
Uniform no.: 7
Shoots: left

Career statistics:

GP	G	A	TP	PIM
8	1	0	1	0

2002-2003 statistics:

GP	G	A	TP	+/-	PIM	PP	SH	GW	GT	S	PCT
8	1	0	1	+2	0	0	0	0	1	6	16.7

LAST SEASON

Will be entering first full NHL season. Appeared in 42 games with Kamloops (WHL), scoring 25-31 — 56 with 113 PIM. Appeared in 2 games with Milwaukee (AHL), scoring 1-0 — 1 with 2 PIM.

THE FINESSE GAME

The puck seems to follow Upshall around. It's because he has such a good head for the game, and always skates to the right spot.

Upshall should become a factor on both special teams, although Nashville might limit his penalty killing at first until he gets accustomed to the NHL grind. Upshall will probably start off in a third-line role, since he is such a smart and responsible player, but he has definite offensive upside and he could move up to a second line.

Upshall plays with intensity, sometimes too much. He can get frustrated and goaded into taking bad penalties. Upshall has drawn comparisons to Darcy Tucker for his in-your-face style, but he is more skilled than Tucker. He is not an elite skater or scorer, but he gets by, and everything is enhanced by his desire to win.

THE PHYSICAL GAME

Upshall needs to get stronger to compete at the NHL level. Right now, it seems to be the only thing holding him back. His size is a question mark, but not his heart. It will be a rare night when you don't notice him on the ice. One of the most promising things about Upshall is that the more important the game, the better he plays.

THE INTANGIBLES

Nashville cut loose a number of older players in order to let the next generation step in. Upshall essentially made the team out of training camp last year, but was sent back to junior. He had a solid season and an impressive World Junior Championship for Canada, for which he was team captain. Upshall could be ready to step in. Nashville has a number of skilled forwards but not many with Upshall's sandpaper.

PROJECTION

Upshall is getting less attention than a lot of the other stars set to kick off their careers this season, so he could make a nice sleeper rookie pick for your pool. Expect him to see power-play time and score 30 points (he'll be higher in assists than goals).

TOMAS VOKOUN

Yrs. of NHL service: 5
Born: Karolovy Vary, Czech Republic; July 2, 1976
Position: goaltender
Height: 6-0
Weight: 195
Uniform no.: 29
Catches: right

Career statistics:

GP	MIN	GA	SO	GAA	A	PIM
206	11386	484	9	2.55	2	40

1999-2000 statistics:

GP	MIN	GAA	W	L	T	SO	GA	S	SAPCT	PIM
33	1879	2.78	9	20	1	1	87	908	.904	8

2000-2001 statistics:

GP	MIN	GAA	W	L	T	SO	GA	S	SAPCT	PIM
37	2088	2.44	13	17	5	2	85	940	.910	2

2001-2002 statistics:

GP	MIN	GAA	W	L	T	SO	GA	S	SAPCT	PIM
29	1471	2.69	5	14	4	2	66	678	.903	2

2002-2003 statistics:

GP	MIN	GAA	W	L	T	SO	GA	S	SAPCT	PIM
69	3974	2.20	25	31	11	3	146	1771	.918	28

LAST SEASON

Led NHL goalies in penalty minutes (28). Third among NHL goalies in minutes played.

THE PHYSICAL GAME

Vokoun isn't a spectacular goalie. He plays a very economical style with little flair. He plays his angles well. He deadens the puck when it hits him so he allows few rebounds. Vokoun has wonderful reflexes. He has worked hard to improve his skating and his foot speed.

He is largely a standup goalie although he incorporates some butterfly technique. He has a quick glove. He is not very active with his stick. Vokoun makes good use of his size. He makes the shooter work for his openings.

Vokoun maintains his focus to watch the puck through screens and scrambles. He is pretty good against the breakaway. He faced five penalty shots last season (an NHL record), allowing two. One of the guys that scored on him was Pavel Bure.

Vokoun has matured a lot in his approach to the job in the past few years. Marriage and a family sometimes has that effect on a player. He is a well-conditioned athlete, flexible, strong, and is remarkably durable considering how much work he gets.

THE MENTAL GAME

Very little seems to faze Vokoun. He is pretty low-maintenance for a goalie. Mike Dunham was traded at 5 p.m. on a game day and Vokoun stepped in even though he wasn't expected to start and earned a 2-2 tie against St. Louis. He bounced back from a bad game with a good one. He isn't critical of his teammates, even though they frequently deserve it, so it's no wonder they love playing for him.

THE INTANGIBLES

Would he be a No. 1 goalie on a better (or richer) team than Nashville? Probably not. But Vokoun is good enough to get Nashville to the next level to contend for a playoff spot, at least until goalie prospect Brian Finley is ready. Nobody noticed, but Vokoun posted some pretty stingy numbers last season.

PROJECTION

Vokoun will get close to 70 starts and if Nashville is just a wee bit better to give him improved scoring support, he could get 30 wins. Combined with his low GAA and high save percentage, he's a nice sleeper pick for your pool.

SCOTT WALKER

Yrs. of NHL service: 8
Born: Montreal, Que.; July 19, 1973
Position: right wing
Height: 5-10
Weight: 196
Uniform no.: 24
Shoots: right

Career statistics:

GP	G	A	TP	PIM
499	76	132	208	801

1999-2000 statistics:

GP	G	A	TP	+/-	PIM	PP	SH	GW	GT	S	PCT
69	7	21	28	-16	90	0	1	0	1	98	7.1

2000-2001 statistics:

GP	G	A	TP	+/-	PIM	PP	SH	GW	GT	S	PCT
74	25	29	54	-2	66	9	3	1	1	159	15.7

2001-2002 statistics:

GP	G	A	TP	+/-	PIM	PP	SH	GW	GT	S	PCT
28	4	5	9	-13	18	1	0	0	0	46	8.7

2002-2003 statistics:

GP	G	A	TP	+/-	PIM	PP	SH	GW	GT	S	PCT
60	15	18	33	+2	58	7	0	5	0	124	12.1

LAST SEASON

Second on team game-winning goals. Tied for second on team in shooting percentage. Third on team in penalty minutes. Missed one game with torn rib cartilage. Missed four games with sprained right knee.

THE FINESSE GAME

Few players have reinvented themselves so thoroughly, or successfully, as Walker has done. Walker played defense in junior and seemed to be on the fast track to becoming an enforcer type, but he was switched to right wing in his early days with Vancouver. He continues to develop along power forward lines.

He can still be dropped back on defense in an emergency. Walker is actually versatile enough to play all three forward positions, too. No one's asked him to try goal yet.

Walker has very good speed. He is an excellent penalty killer. He grinds and gets his nose in and doesn't quit on the puck. He doesn't have great hands, but he works hard for his scoring chances and creates off the forecheck. He gets involved in traffic.

THE PHYSICAL GAME

His game is feisty, but instead of just stirring things up, Walker has concentrated on being more of a hockey player, so his penalty minutes have dropped. He wants to stay on the ice. Walker can be a pain to play against. He is courageous and gritty, and he fights. When he does drop the gloves, it's against the big guys, and he holds his own.

THE INTANGIBLES

Walker made a big comeback last season after a concussion the previous year, but was still socked by nagging injuries. He always seems to bounce back. Walker is a role player who can add energy and flexibility to a lineup. Walker would be an excellent third-line player elsewhere. For Nashville, he is a key top-six forward.

PROJECTION

Walker may be back on track, and with the power-play time he gets, we expect 25 goals this season.

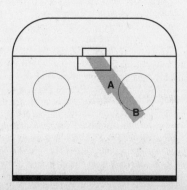

JASON YORK

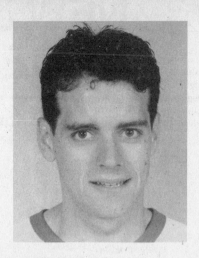

Yrs. of NHL service: 9
Born: Ottawa, Ont.; May 20, 1970
Position: right defense
Height: 6-1
Weight: 208
Uniform no.: 27
Shoots: right

Career statistics:

GP	G	A	TP	PIM
641	39	167	206	525

1999-2000 statistics:

GP	G	A	TP	+/-	PIM	PP	SH	GW	GT	S	PCT
79	8	22	30	-3	60	1	0	1	0	159	5.0

2000-2001 statistics:

GP	G	A	TP	+/-	PIM	PP	SH	GW	GT	S	PCT
74	6	16	22	+7	72	3	0	2	0	133	4.5

2001-2002 statistics:

GP	G	A	TP	+/-	PIM	PP	SH	GW	GT	S	PCT
74	5	20	25	-11	60	3	0	2	0	104	4.8

2002-2003 statistics:

GP	G	A	TP	+/-	PIM	PP	SH	GW	GT	S	PCT
74	4	15	19	+13	52	2	0	0	1	107	3.7

LAST SEASON

Acquired from Anaheim on October 23, 2002, for future considerations. Led team in plus-minus. Third on team in average ice time. Missed eight games due to coach's decision.

THE FINESSE GAME

York's finesse skills are fine. He is a good skater with a hard point shot, and he can handle the point on the second power-play unit — though he isn't quite good enough to step up to the first five. He's a fine penalty killer. He reads plays well (his offensive reads are far superior to his defensive reads) and has the skating ability to spring some shorthanded chances. He can be used in any game situation.

York is a smart, all-round defenseman who concentrated on learning the defensive part of the game first at the NHL level. Once he gained some confidence, his offensive contributions increased. He is never going to be the kind of player who can dominate a game but he is also fairly panic-proof. He's a low risk player, with moderate rewards.

THE PHYSICAL GAME

York made a conscious decision to add a physical element to his game in order to earn more ice time. He plays with some zip now. He is not a big checker but employs positional play to angle attackers to the boards, using his stick to sweep-check or poke pucks. Once he gains control of the puck, he moves it quickly with no panicky mistakes. He doesn't have a polished defensive game but he does work hard. He plays through injuries and is fairly durable.

THE INTANGIBLES

York has shown gradual, steady improvement in his game over the past few seasons. While he will never be an elite NHL defenseman, he is a reliable blueliner who could fit into the second pair on almost anyone's team. He does a lot of little things well and his energy and enthusiasm for the game are apparent. York was a nice pickup by Nashville, and set a franchise record for best plus-minus in a season.

PROJECTION

York is capable of a 30-point season while losing nothing from his defensive game.

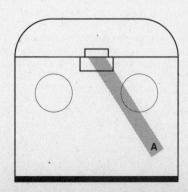

NEW JERSEY DEVILS

Players' Statistics 2001-2002

POS.	NO.	PLAYER	GP	G	A	PTS	+/-	PIM	PP	SH	GW	GT	S	PCT
C	26	PATRIK ELIAS	81	28	29	57	17	22	6		4	1	255	11.0
R	15	JAMIE LANGENBRUNNER	78	22	33	55	17	65	5	1	5		197	11.2
C	23	SCOTT GOMEZ	80	13	42	55	17	48	2		4	1	205	6.3
L	12	JEFF FRIESEN	81	23	28	51	23	26	3		4	1	179	12.8
C	25	JOE NIEUWENDYK	80	17	28	45	10	26	3		4		201	8.4
C	11	JOHN MADDEN	80	19	22	41	13	26	2	2	3		207	9.2
D	28	BRIAN RAFALSKI	79	3	37	40	18	14	2				178	1.7
D	27	SCOTT NIEDERMAYER	81	11	28	39	23	62	3		3		164	6.7
R	29	GRANT MARSHALL	76	9	23	32	-11	78	3		2		113	8.0
R	14	BRIAN GIONTA	58	12	13	25	5	23	2		3		129	9.3
R	24	TURNER STEVENSON	77	7	13	20	7	115					85	8.2
D	4	SCOTT STEVENS	81	4	16	20	18	41			2		113	3.5
C	18	SERGEI BRYLIN	52	11	8	19	-2	16	3	1	1		86	12.8
C	21	PASCAL RHEAUME	77	8	10	18	-5	32		3	2		93	8.6
L	20	JAY PANDOLFO	68	6	11	17	12	23		1	4		92	6.5
D	5	COLIN WHITE	72	5	8	13	19	98			1		81	6.2
D	10	OLEG TVERDOVSKY	50	5	8	13	2	22	2		1		76	6.6
D	2	RICHARD SMEHLIK	55	2	11	13	-5	16					49	4.1
L	19	JIM MCKENZIE	76	4	8	12	3	88			2		42	9.5
R	9	*JIRI BICEK	44	5	6	11	7	25	1		1		63	7.9
L	17	*CHRISTIAN BERGLUND	38	4	5	9	3	20					50	8.0
D	3	KEN DANEYKO	69	2	7	9	6	33					38	5.3
R	16	*MICHAEL RUPP	26	5	3	8	0	21	2		3		34	14.7
D	6	TOMMY ALBELIN	37	1	6	7	10	6		1			30	3.3
C	22	MIKE DANTON	17	2		2	0	35					18	11.1
C	8	STEPHEN GUOLLA	12	2		2	1	2					6	33.3
D	7	RAYMOND GIROUX	11		1	1	-2	6					20	
C	9	CRAIG DARBY	3		1	1	-1						1	
G	30	MARTIN BRODEUR	73				0	10						
G	35	COREY SCHWAB	11				0							
G	1	J-F DAMPHOUSSE					0							
G	40	SCOTT CLEMMENSEN					0							

GP = games played; G = goals; A = assists; PTS = points; +/- = goals-for minus goals-against while player is on ice; PIM = penalties in minutes; PP = power-play goals; SH = shorthanded goals; GW = game-winning goals; GT = game-tying goals; S = no. of shots; PCT = percentage of goals to shots; * = rookie

MARTIN BRODEUR

Yrs. of NHL service: 10
Born: Montreal, Que.; May 6, 1972
Position: goaltender
Height: 6-2
Weight: 210
Uniform no.: 30
Catches: left

Career statistics:

GP	MIN	GA	SO	GAA	A	PIM
665	38957	1419	64	2.19	23	50

1999-2000 statistics:

GP	MIN	GAA	W	L	T	SO	GA	S	SAPCT	PIM
72	4312	2.24	43	20	8	6	161	1797	.910	16

2000-2001 statistics:

GP	MIN	GAA	W	L	T	SO	GA	S	SAPCT	PIM
72	4297	2.32	42	17	11	9	166	1762	.906	14

2001-2002 statistics:

GP	MIN	GAA	W	L	T	SO	GA	S	SAPCT	PIM
73	4347	2.15	38	26	9	4	156	1655	.906	8

2002-2003 statistics:

GP	MIN	GAA	W	L	T	SO	GA	S	SAPCT	PIM
73	4374	2.02	41	23	9	9	147	1706	.914	10

LAST SEASON

Won 2003 Vezina Trophy. Named to NHL First All-Star Team. Tied for 2003 Jennings Trophy. Finalist for 2003 Hart Trophy. Recorded 35 or more wins for seventh consecutive season. Led NHL goalies in wins and shutouts. Fourth among NHL goalies in goals-against average. Second among NHl goalies in minutes played.

THE PHYSICAL GAME

Amid all the talk of goalie guru Francois Allaire's impact on the game (his disciples include Patrick Roy and J-S Giguere) a little-known story was revealed of how Brodeur walked out of an Allaire camp after only a few days, telling himself the butterfly style was not for him. Brodeur may be the lone French-Canadian goalie of his era who is not a strict butterfly practitioner. Brodeur does incorporate elements of that style into his game, but his is a successful hybrid of the butterfly and the stand-up schools.

Brodeur makes the most of his generous size. He stands upright in the net and squares himself so well to the shooter that he looks enormous. He is probably the best in the game at using his stick around the net. He breaks up passes and will make a quick jab to knock the puck off an opponent's stick. He will also whack players in the ankles or jab them behind the knees to protect his turf.

Opponents want to get Brodeur's feet moving — wraparound plays, rebounds, anything involving his skates exposes his weaknesses. Because of his puck control, he prevents a lot of scrambles and minimizes his flaws. When he falls into bad streaks, it is usually because of his footwork.

Brodeur has improved his play out of the net — if the league ever legislates against goalies handling the puck it will have to be known as the Brodeur Rule. He has to guard against cockiness, though. He gets carried away with clearing shots through the middle of the ice. One of the reasons why he was more effective at home during the playoffs (most noticeably in the Stanely Cup Final, when he lost all three games on the road but won all four in New Jersey) is because he relies so heavily on his expert puckhandling off the boards that he can be undone by unfamiliar nooks and crannies of a road rink. Most of the time he handles the puck intelligently and is effective on the penalty kill, sending the puck up-ice, acting as a third defenseman and frustrating the opponents' power play.

THE MENTAL GAME

Despite personal problems that became public in the second round of the playoffs — a nasty divorce and a dose of scandal — Brodeur remained utterly unshaken. Bad games and bad goals don't rattle Brodeur for long. Although he has a tendency to show his frustration on-ice, he also bounces back quickly with strong efforts. He concentrates and doesn't lose his intensity throughout a game. Brodeur exudes confidence and even a bit of defiance through the layers of padding and his mask. When he is on, his glove saves are snappy and he bounces on his feet with flair.

THE INTANGIBLES

Brodeur finally received individual recognition when he was awarded his first Vezina Trophy and was voted to the NHL First All-Star Team for the first time in his career. Yet despite setting a playoff record with seven shutouts, he lost out to losing goalie Giguere for the Conn Smythe as playoff MVP. Getting his name on the Cup for the third time was sufficient consolation.

PROJECTION

Roy's retirement leaves Brodeur as the top goalie in the league. End of discussion. He is likely to top that 35-win mark again.

PATRIK ELIAS

Yrs. of NHL service: 6
Born: Trebic, Czech Republic; Apr. 13, 1976
Position: left wing
Height: 6-1
Weight: 195
Uniform no.: 26
Shoots: left

Career statistics:

GP	G	A	TP	PIM
477	169	209	378	231

1999-2000 statistics:

GP	G	A	TP	+/-	PIM	PP	SH	GW	GT	S	PCT
72	35	37	72	+16	58	9	0	9	1	183	19.1

2000-2001 statistics:

GP	G	A	TP	+/-	PIM	PP	SH	GW	GT	S	PCT
82	40	56	96	+45	51	8	3	6	1	220	18.2

2001-2002 statistics:

GP	G	A	TP	+/-	PIM	PP	SH	GW	GT	S	PCT
75	29	32	61	+4	36	8	1	8	0	199	14.6

2002-2003 statistics:

GP	G	A	TP	+/-	PIM	PP	SH	GW	GT	S	PCT
81	28	29	57	+17	22	6	0	4	1	255	11.0

LAST SEASON

Led team in points for fourth consecutive season. Led team in goals, power-play goals, and shots. Tied for second on team in game-winning goals. Missed one game due to back injury.

THE FINESSE GAME

Elias was among the game's most exciting forwards two years ago. That was before the Devils traded away his two linemates, Jason Arnott and Petr Sykora, and before Elias's confidence eroded.

Elias is one of the best transition forwards in the game. He is quick enough to be in a defensive posture when the opponent has the puck, and savvy enough to read the play, knock down a pass, or sprint when one of his teammates gains control of the puck and looks to send him flying.

Elias has a quick, low release on his shot, especially on his wrister, and can shoot on the fly or fake a shot and stickhandle in close for a backhander. He is not quite a power forward, though he is strong enough to muscle his way into traffic areas for scoring chances. He has superb hockey vision and brings a center's vision and passing skills to the wing. The Devils played him at center on occasion last season, but he is really much better suited as a winger.

Elias works both special teams. He is reliable defensively, enjoys killing penalties, and is a threat to create scoring chances off shorthanded rushes. He takes draws on the PK and holds his own. Elias wants the puck when the game is on the line. Elias seldom makes a poor decision with the puck, even under pressure.

THE PHYSICAL GAME

Elias has good upper-body strength for work along the boards and good lower-body strength for skating speed and balance. He is tough to knock off his skates and plays with controlled aggression. He doesn't take many bad penalties, but will bring his stick up or take a swing if he believes he is being taken advantage of. Elias can't be intimidated. He never backs down and frequently initiates. He plays with attitude and is as quietly tough a forward as you can find in the NHL.

THE INTANGIBLES

Devils' coach Pat Burns was equally hard on Elias as he was on frequent linemate Scott Gomez. Elias did not always handle the hounding well. His demeanor might improve greatly with Grant Marshall (a trade-deadline acquisition) as his right wing on a set line all season, as all of the line juggling played havoc with Elias's mindset.

PROJECTION

Elias is capable of better, but it might be wiser to set more modest goals for him next season — in the 30-goal, 60-point range.

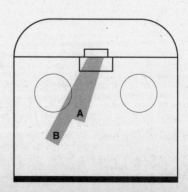

JEFF FRIESEN

Yrs. of NHL service: 9
Born: Meadow Lake, Sask.; Aug. 5, 1976
Position: left wing
Height: 6-0
Weight: 215
Uniform no.: 12
Shoots: left

Career statistics:

GP	G	A	TP	PIM
689	191	265	456	396

1999-2000 statistics:

GP	G	A	TP	+/-	PIM	PP	SH	GW	GT	S	PCT
82	26	35	61	-2	47	11	3	7	0	191	13.6

2000-2001 statistics:

GP	G	A	TP	+/-	PIM	PP	SH	GW	GT	S	PCT
79	14	34	48	+5	66	4	0	1	0	149	9.4

2001-2002 statistics:

GP	G	A	TP	+/-	PIM	PP	SH	GW	GT	S	PCT
81	17	26	43	-1	44	1	1	0	0	161	10.6

2002-2003 statistics:

GP	G	A	TP	+/-	PIM	PP	SH	GW	GT	S	PCT
81	23	28	51	+23	26	3	0	4	1	179	12.8

LAST SEASON

Tied for team lead in plus-minus and shooting percentage. Tied for second on team in game-winning goals. Second on team in goals. Missed one game due to illness.

THE FINESSE GAME

Friesen is a fast, strong skater who handles the puck well and has the size to go with those qualities. He is a better finisher than playmaker. He needs to play with linemates who have a lot of patience and the ability to hold on to the puck for a long time. Friesen can get into holes with his speed for the pass. He has a quick, strong release on his snap or wrist shot, and is shifty with a smooth change of speed. Carrying the puck doesn't slow him down. He is not a natural goal-scorer and probably will never be an elite one, but he works hard and earns his goals.

Friesen never seems to get rattled or forced into making bad plays. In fact, he's the one who forces opponents into panic moves with his pressure. He draws penalties by keeping his feet moving as he drives to the net or digs for the puck along the boards. He is strong on face-offs.

A pure goal-scorer in junior, Friesen developed first as a checking-line winger in his rookie year before becoming a complete player. He deserves a lot of credit for making himself into an all-around player.

THE PHYSICAL GAME

Friesen has dedicated himself to his strength and conditioning. He doesn't have much of a mean streak, but he plays tough and honest with a very long fuse. Don't mistake his patience for a lack of competitiveness.

THE INTANGIBLES

The move to New Jersey couldn't have come at a better time for Friesen, who was lost after his 2001 trade from San Jose (the team that drafted him) to Anaheim. The Devils gave him job security and he proved to be a huge part of their Cup run, scoring four game-winning goals.

PROJECTION

We predicted a 25/50 season for Friesen and he was pretty much on the mark. Friesen is an uncomplaining competitor who will do just about anything the coach asks — in short, the perfect Devil. A 25/50 target is realistic for him again this season. He will never be an elite scorer.

BRIAN GIONTA

Yrs. of NHL service: 2
Born: Rochester, NY; Jan. 18, 1979
Position: right wing
Height: 5-7
Weight: 175
Uniform no.: 14
Shoots: right

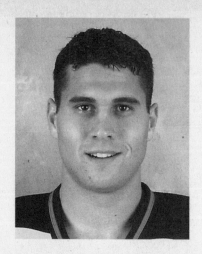

Career statistics:

GP	G	A	TP	PIM
91	16	20	36	31

2001-2002 statistics:

GP	G	A	TP	+/-	PIM	PP	SH	GW	GT	S	PCT
33	4	7	11	+10	8	0	0	0	0	58	6.9

2002-2003 statistics:

GP	G	A	TP	+/-	PIM	PP	SH	GW	GT	S	PCT
58	12	13	25	+5	23	2	0	3	0	129	9.3

LAST SEASON

Second NHL season. Missed 24 games due to leg and ankle injuries.

THE FINESSE GAME

Think Gionta is too small to play in the NHL? Just try saying that to his face, even if you have to bend down a little to look him in the eye. Listed at a generous five-foot-seven, Gionta is a smart, slick forward whose creativity and competitive nature earned him a regular role with the Devils well ahead of schedule. Playing in the NHL is something people have been telling him he couldn't do ever since he was a little(r) guy.

Gionta is a natural goal-scorer. He reads other players very well, especially Sergei Brylin, who became his linemate late in the season and in the playoffs after both players recovered from injuries. He is an instinctive player, and is usually one mental step ahead of most of the other players on the ice. Gionta beats his man off the boards frequently. He wins puck battles against bigger players by getting good body position. Gionta is a nifty skater. He doesn't have great breakaway speed but he is agile and quick. He has excellent hand skills for shooting or passing.

Gionta was a standout player in college (Boston College) and in junior competitions at the international level. One of his frequent linemates in tournament play was Scott Gomez, a Devils' teammate. They were drafted in the same year (1998).

THE PHYSICAL GAME

Gionta competes hard. He throws his body around like a tiny torpedo, and because he is so squarely built, he can surprise people by knocking them off the puck. He won't bowl people over, but he will impede their progress, and because he has a low center of gravity, he is hard to budge. He has a little cockiness to his game, which is a good thing. Size doesn't always matter. Gionta plays with a big heart.

THE INTANGIBLES

Gionta plays like a shark instead of a shrimp. He would have had an even better regular season if it hadn't been for his injuries.

PROJECTION

Gionta will keep a spot on one of the Devils' top two lines. A healthy season could see him move up into the 30-40 point range. He will see second-unit power-play time.

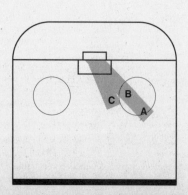

SCOTT GOMEZ

Yrs. of NHL service: 4
Born: Anchorage, AK; Dec. 23, 1979
Position: center
Height: 5-11
Weight: 200
Uniform no.: 23
Shoots: left

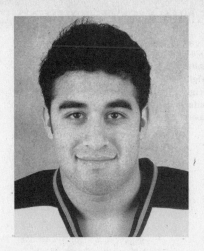

Career statistics:

GP	G	A	TP	PIM
314	56	180	236	208

1999-2000 statistics:

GP	G	A	TP	+/-	PIM	PP	SH	GW	GT	S	PCT
82	19	51	70	+14	78	7	0	1	2	204	9.3

2000-2001 statistics:

GP	G	A	TP	+/-	PIM	PP	SH	GW	GT	S	PCT
76	14	49	63	-1	46	2	0	4	0	155	9.0

2001-2002 statistics:

GP	G	A	TP	+/-	PIM	PP	SH	GW	GT	S	PCT
76	10	38	48	-4	36	1	0	1	0	156	6.4

2002-2003 statistics:

GP	G	A	TP	+/-	PIM	PP	SH	GW	GT	S	PCT
80	13	42	55	+17	48	2	0	4	1	205	6.3

LAST SEASON

Led team in assists. Tied for second on team in points and game-winning goals. Third on team in shots. Missed two games due to coach's decision.

THE FINESSE GAME

Gomez's ability to use the space behind the net to shield himself from defenders and set-up plays is almost Wayne Gretzky-like. He has terrific vision and patience with the puck, and can thread a pass through what seems like the eye of a needle to find a teammate. Anyone playing with Gomez has to be alert, because he is adept at finding seams that others don't even know exist.

He has a very good wrist shot, not a heavy one, but accurate. You might think with his assists-to-goals ratio that Gomez doesn't shoot enough, but his shot totals was up by almost 50 over the previous season, indicating that Gomez has been intensifying that part of his game. He is just not as gifted a goal-scorer as he is a passer. However, he makes excellent use of the extra room on a power play.

The Devils frequently move him to the wing because of his defensive shortcomings. Gomez needs to be in the middle of the ice. He is not as effective along the boards.

Gomez is not a good skater. He needs to be constantly reminded to keep his feet moving and not to glide. He is strong on his skates, though, tough to knock off his feet and willing to work in the dirty areas for pucks. He lacks outside speed but can put on a short burst to get a jump on the defense. Face-offs continue to be a weak area for Gomez.

THE PHYSICAL GAME

As easy-going as Gomez is off-ice, he is just as competitive on it. At his best, Gomez is like a young Claude Lemeiux: chippy, chirpy, tough around the net, and picks up clutch points. When he is in that zone, he is irritating to play against. He won't back down from a scuffle and isn't shy about starting one. He is solid and durable.

THE INTANGIBLES

Gomez still has some rough edges, but his raw talent and desire to succeed are evident, even if he has to be benched now and then to get his attention. Coach Pat Burns was exceptionally hard on him, and there is some friction there that could lead to a personnel decision this season if things come to a head.

PROJECTION

Gomez finally established some chemistry with Patrik Elias and Grant Marshall late in the season, but a setup man like Gomez really needs a sniper on the right wing, something the Devils lack. He should score 60 points, with a heavy emphasis on assists.

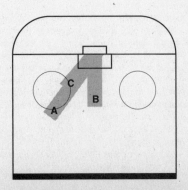

JAMIE LANGENBRUNNER

Yrs. of NHL service: 7
Born: Duluth, Minn.; July 24, 1975
Position: right wing
Height: 6-1
Weight: 200
Uniform no.: 15
Shoots: right

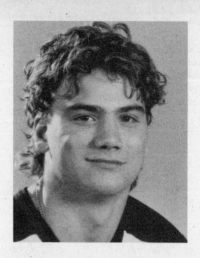

Career statistics:

GP	G	A	TP	PIM
524	115	181	296	449

1999-2000 statistics:

GP	G	A	TP	+/-	PIM	PP	SH	GW	GT	S	PCT
65	18	21	39	+16	68	4	2	6	0	153	11.8

2000-2001 statistics:

GP	G	A	TP	+/-	PIM	PP	SH	GW	GT	S	PCT
53	12	18	30	+4	57	3	2	4	0	104	11.5

2001-2002 statistics:

GP	G	A	TP	+/-	PIM	PP	SH	GW	GT	S	PCT
82	13	19	32	-9	77	0	1	4	0	163	8.0

2002-2003 statistics:

GP	G	A	TP	+/-	PIM	PP	SH	GW	GT	S	PCT
78	22	33	55	+17	65	5	1	5	0	197	11.2

LAST SEASON

Led Devils in game-winning goals. Tied for second on team in points. Third on team in goals, assists, and shooting percentage. Missed four games due to viral infection.

THE FINESSE GAME

Langenbrunner is among the best in the league at getting the puck off the wall or the end boards and creating a scoring chance. He proved to be a crunch-time scorer for the Devils, especially in the playoffs, where he led the Devils with 11 goals (four of those game-winners). He did a lot of the damage playing on a so-called checking line with John Madden and Jay Pandolfo.

An average skater, Langenbrunner won't be coming in with speed and driving a shot off the wing. He is not dynamic at all. But he does have a strong short game; his offense is generated within 15 to 20 feet of the net and he has a quick release on his shot. Any deficiencies he may have are offset by his desire to compete and succeed.

Langenbrunner is a plumber, but one who is talented enough to play with more creative centers when the Devils shuffle lines. He is an aggressive forechecker who creates turnovers for his linemates.

Langenbrunner has very good hand skills. He is intelligent and poised with the puck. He has good hockey vision and can pick his spots for shots. He is also a smart passer on either his forehand or backhand.

THE PHYSICAL GAME

Langenbrunner plays an intense game, bigger than his size allows. He will wear down physically. Last season he managed to stay intact, but that isn't always the case. He competes hard in the dirty areas of the ice, to either get a puck or get himself into a space to get the puck. He lacks the size to be a power forward, but he is one of the gritty types who are annoying to play against. He won't just hang on the perimeter and won't back down — he'll even try to stir things up.

THE INTANGIBLES

Langenbrunner is one of the game's most significant unsung heroes, not just for his talent but for his smarts, his energy, and his attitude. The Devils made a lot of changes going into the 2002-2003 season, but Langenbrunner adjusted easily after the trade (in March 2002) and started last year's training camp as if he had been a Devil forever. Langenbrunner carried the Devils through the early part of the season, when goals were scarce, and stepped up again in the playoffs.

PROJECTION

Langenbrunner's goal-scoring range is 20-25. He will see significant ice time again this season for the Devils.

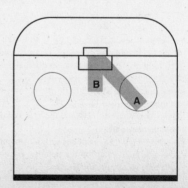

JOHN MADDEN

Yrs. of NHL service: 4
Born: Barrie, Ont.; May 4, 1975
Position: center
Height: 5-11
Weight: 190
Uniform no.: 11
Shoots: left

Career statistics:

GP	G	A	TP	PIM
320	73	55	128	69

1999-2000 statistics:

GP	G	A	TP	+/-	PIM	PP	SH	GW	GT	S	PCT
74	16	9	25	+7	6	0	6	3	0	115	13.9

2000-2001 statistics:

GP	G	A	TP	+/-	PIM	PP	SH	GW	GT	S	PCT
80	23	15	38	+24	12	0	3	4	1	163	14.1

2001-2002 statistics:

GP	G	A	TP	+/-	PIM	PP	SH	GW	GT	S	PCT
82	15	8	23	+6	25	0	0	2	1	170	8.8

2002-2003 statistics:

GP	G	A	TP	+/-	PIM	PP	SH	GW	GT	S	PCT
80	19	22	41	+13	26	2	2	3	0	207	9.2

LAST SEASON

Finalist for 2003 Selke Trophy. Second on team in shorthanded goals and shots. Missed two games due to groin injury.

THE FINESSE GAME

Bobby who? After the Devils lost Bobby Holik to free agency after the 2001-02 season, it appeared there would be too much of a burden placed on Madden to try to handle checking assignments against the league's bigger centers. Madden thrives on a challenge, though, and he did an exceptional job elevating his game, especially in the playoffs, where he was an MVP candidate.

Madden is the perfect example of how offense can be created from defense. Madden lacks creativity and doesn't have a great scoring touch. Madden doesn't have a lot of finesse. His goals come through hard work and his quick burst of speed. Madden's acceleration comes in an eye-blink. He is like a sprinter — he gets an edge out of the blocks in a few powerful strides. Madden can also stop and change direction and put on another skating burst. He is an aggressive forechecker. When he kills penalties, which he does often and well, he puts the heat on the point men and knocks down a lot of point-to-point passes.

Madden needs to improve his work on face-offs. He works hard at it, but his hands just aren't quick enough. He will tie up an opposing center if the draw isn't won from him cleanly.

THE PHYSICAL GAME

Madden is a blocky, stocky guy. On the short side, he can be outmuscled by bigger opposing forwards, but he has the tenacity of a pit bull. If Madden can't stop someone, he will at least slow him down.

Madden plays with an edge. He is always yapping and getting players to retaliate, but he has to guard against taking bad penalties himself. He plays through injury and it takes a lot to knock him out of the lineup.

THE INTANGIBLES

Madden is so critical of his own play that there isn't anything a coach can tell him that Madden doesn't already know. He thinks the game well and studies his opponents' weaknesses to gain any advantage.

PROJECTION

Madden is a checking center who is always good for scoring around 20 goals and preventing about 20 by the opposition.

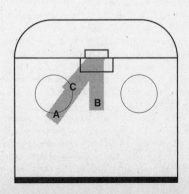

SCOTT NIEDERMAYER

Yrs. of NHL service: 11
Born: Edmonton, Alta.; Aug. 31, 1973
Position: right defense
Height: 6-1
Weight: 200
Uniform no.: 27
Shoots: left

Career statistics:

GP	G	A	TP	PIM
811	98	324	422	434

1999-2000 statistics:

GP	G	A	TP	+/-	PIM	PP	SH	GW	GT	S	PCT
71	7	31	38	+19	48	1	0	0	0	109	6.4

2000-2001 statistics:

GP	G	A	TP	+/-	PIM	PP	SH	GW	GT	S	PCT
57	6	29	35	+14	22	1	0	5	0	87	6.9

2001-2002 statistics:

GP	G	A	TP	+/-	PIM	PP	SH	GW	GT	S	PCT
76	11	22	33	+12	30	2	0	6	0	129	8.5

2002-2003 statistics:

GP	G	A	TP	+/-	PIM	PP	SH	GW	GT	S	PCT
81	11	28	39	+23	62	3	0	3	0	164	6.7

LAST SEASON

Led team in ice time (24:29). Tied for team lead in plus-minus. Second among team defensemen in points. Missed one game due to coach's decision.

THE FINESSE GAME

Niedermayer is an exceptional skater, one of the best-skating defensemen in the NHL. He has it all: speed, balance, agility, mobility, lateral movement, and strength. Plus he has an unbelievable edge for turns and eluding pursuers. Yet Niedermayer doesn't seem to have the vision the great ones have, or the snaky lateral movement that makes a point shot so dangerous. The missing component may be more mental than physical. He has nights when he is "on," and he is spectacular. Those nights tend to come against high-profile teams, or in the playoffs, when he is more interested in his surroundings. But he takes a lot of nights off, when the challenge fails to excite him. Niedermayer's efficient skating style allows him to handle a lot of minutes and not wear down physically.

Those lapses have prevented Niedermayer from joining the ranks of the league's elite "offensemen." While it's true he also has had to heel to the Devils' defensive system, which may have cut into his point production, Niedermayer doesn't have the fire or the flair of a Sandis Ozolinsh or a Brian Leetch. It's time to stop faulting him for that.

Niedermayer is a far better defensive player than many of the other top scorers at his position. Even when he makes a mistake in the offensive zone, he can get back so quickly his partner is seldom outnumbered. He is simply one of the best two-way defensemen in the game...when he chooses to be.

THE PHYSICAL GAME

An underrated body checker because of the focus on the glitzier aspects of his game, Niedermayer has continued to improve his strength and is a willing, if not vicious, hitter. Niedermayer's skating ability helps him tremendously, giving more impetus to his open-ice checks. He makes rub-outs along the wall. He would rather be in open ice, but will pay the price in the trenches. He knows the defensive game well. He has a quiet toughness and won't be intimidated.

THE INTANGIBLES

He is happier without the attention, but he nearly blew it when he was nearly flawless in the playoffs and captured the attention of a lot of hockey experts. No player was more consistent at a high level of competition than Niedermayer was throughout the playoffs.

PROJECTION

Niedermayer may be the league's top all-around defenseman, but he will not be among the league's leading defenseman scorers. Niedermayer's range is around 40 points.

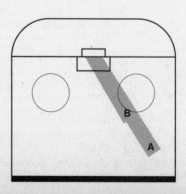

JOE NIEUWENDYK

Yrs. of NHL service: 16
Born: Oshawa, Ont.; Sept. 10, 1966
Position: center
Height: 6-1
Weight: 205
Uniform no.: 25
Shoots: left

Career statistics:

GP	G	A	TP	PIM
1113	511	501	1012	601

1999-2000 statistics:

GP	G	A	TP	+/-	PIM	PP	SH	GW	GT	S	PCT
48	15	19	34	-1	26	7	0	2	0	110	13.6

2000-2001 statistics:

GP	G	A	TP	+/-	PIM	PP	SH	GW	GT	S	PCT
69	29	23	52	+5	30	12	0	4	0	166	17.5

2001-2002 statistics:

GP	G	A	TP	+/-	PIM	PP	SH	GW	GT	S	PCT
81	25	33	58	0	22	6	0	6	1	189	13.2

2002-2003 statistics:

GP	G	A	TP	+/-	PIM	PP	SH	GW	GT	S	PCT
80	17	28	45	+10	56	3	0	4	0	201	8.4

LAST SEASON

Tied for second on Devils in game-winning goals. Missed one game due to illness. Missed one game due to coach's decision.

THE FINESSE GAME

Hands down, Nieuwendyk has the best hands in the NHL for tipping pucks in front of the net. This skill is priceless on power plays. He has fantastic hand-eye coordination. He not only gets his blade on the puck, he acts as if he knows where he's directing it. He also has a long, powerful reach for snaring loose pucks around the crease. Those same hand skills make Nieuwendyk one of the league's best in the face-off department. He was third in the NHL on draws last season (58.49 per cent).

He is aggressive, tough, and aware around the net. He can finish or make a play down low. He has the vision, poise, and hand skills to make neat little passes through traffic. He's a better playmaker than finisher, but he never doubts that he will convert his chances. He has good anticipation and uses his long stick to break up passes.

One of his best moves comes on the rush, when Nieuwendyk cuts wide to the right-wing boards then pulls the puck to his forehand for a dangerous shot.

THE PHYSICAL GAME

Nieuwendyk does not initiate, but he will take punishment around the net and stand his ground. He won't be intimidated — but he won't scare anyone, either. He stayed healthy last season until the playoffs, when a rib injury prevented him from playing in the seven-game Finals.

THE INTANGIBLES

Nieuwendyk needs to play with grinding, energy wingers to do the dirty work he is physically incapable of doing. Teammates need to be alert enough to polish off a pass that can come anytime, from anywhere. Nieuwendyk became an unrestricted free agent after last season. He is no longer a No. 1 center or even a 1A, but he could still do the job on the second line in the right circumstances.

PROJECTION

We expected a decline in numbers for Nieuwendyk last season (he was down 13 points) and would expect that trend to continue.

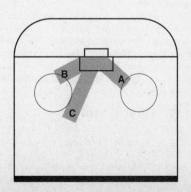

JAY PANDOLFO

Yrs. of NHL service: 7
Born: Winchester, Mass.; Dec. 27, 1974
Position: left wing
Height: 6-1
Weight: 190
Uniform no.: 20
Shoots: left

Career statistics:

GP	G	A	TP	PIM
406	42	65	107	78

1999-2000 statistics:

GP	G	A	TP	+/-	PIM	PP	SH	GW	GT	S	PCT
71	7	8	15	0	4	0	0	0	0	86	8.1

2000-2001 statistics:

GP	G	A	TP	+/-	PIM	PP	SH	GW	GT	S	PCT
63	4	12	16	+3	16	0	0	0	0	57	7.0

2001-2002 statistics:

GP	G	A	TP	+/-	PIM	PP	SH	GW	GT	S	PCT
65	4	10	14	+12	15	0	1	0	0	72	5.6

2002-2003 statistics:

GP	G	A	TP	+/-	PIM	PP	SH	GW	GT	S	PCT
68	6	11	17	+12	23	0	1	4	0	92	6.5

LAST SEASON

Tied for second on team in game-winning goals. Missed 10 games with groin injuries. Missed four games due to slight concussion.

THE FINESSE GAME

If the puck is five feet inside your own blue line, Pandolfo is the man to get it out. Maybe that's a small asset, but on a team like the Devils, a team that is designed to make every little play count, Pandolfo is a prized role player.

Pandolfo is purely a defensive forward. It's hard to believe Pandolfo led the Hockey East League in goals when he played for Boston University back in 1995-96. Pandolfo is like Brian Rolston, but with worse hands. Pandolfo has a knack of making his goals count, though. Four of his six goals in the regular season were game-winners, and he scored six goals in the postseason (seven, if you count the one all the officials missed).

For the time being, though, it looks like Pandolfo is not going to break his defensive mold. He is a terrific penalty killer, usually working in tandem with Selke Trophy finalist John Madden. Pandolfo has good speed — both in short bursts and on the long straightaway — to create shorthanded chances, but he just can't finish.

THE PHYSICAL GAME

Pandolfo always gets involved. He has a little bit of an edge, but mostly it's his willingness to pay the price to help his team win that has Pandolfo bruised and bloodied much of the season. He came back from a concussion without showing any fear of getting in traffic again.

THE INTANGIBLES

Pandolfo does a lot of the little things to help a team win, especially defensively, and he's a quiet, solid team guy.

PROJECTION

He's the glue, not the glitter. Pandolfo has never scored more than 27 points in an NHL season. We doubt he's going to improve on that much.

BRIAN RAFALSKI

Yrs. of NHL service: 4
Born: Dearborn, MI; Sept. 28, 1973
Position: right defense
Height: 5-9
Weight: 190
Uniform no.: 28
Shoots: right

Career statistics:

GP	G	A	TP	PIM
308	24	147	171	86

1999-2000 statistics:

GP	G	A	TP	+/-	PIM	PP	SH	GW	GT	S	PCT
75	5	27	32	+21	28	1	0	1	0	128	3.9

2000-2001 statistics:

GP	G	A	TP	+/-	PIM	PP	SH	GW	GT	S	PCT
78	9	43	52	+36	26	6	0	1	1	142	6.3

2001-2002 statistics:

GP	G	A	TP	+/-	PIM	PP	SH	GW	GT	S	PCT
76	7	40	47	+15	18	2	0	4	1	125	5.6

2002-2003 statistics:

GP	G	A	TP	+/-	PIM	PP	SH	GW	GT	S	PCT
79	3	37	40	+18	14	2	0	0	0	178	1.7

LAST SEASON

Led team defensemen in points. Second on team in assists and ice time (23:08). Career high in games played. Missed three games due to rib injury.

THE FINESSE GAME

Rafalski's greatest asset is his ability to get the puck out of the zone. It sounds so simple, but watch other teams' defense struggle with clearing the puck and you'll appreciate what Rafalski can do by skating the puck out of danger, making a smart pass, or just banging it off the boards. He doesn't look for the highlight play. He makes the smart one, which usually turns into a highlight.

Rafalski is an excellent skater. He's not quite in the class of teammate Scott Niedermayer, but he is similar, and he allows the Devils the luxury of placing one smooth-skating, puckhandling defenseman with a slower, physical partner. In Rafalski's case, that is usually captain Scott Stevens, and Stevens benefits as much from Rafalski's presence as Rafalski does in playing alongside one of the league's premier defensive defensemen.

He has the speed and the hands to get involved in the attack, and does so willingly. Knowing he has Stevens as a backup, Rafalski is confident when he pinches or joins the rush. He has a good shot from the point and sees significant power-play time.

THE PHYSICAL GAME

The downside to being Stevens's partner is that teams want to stay away from the right wing on the attack (Stevens plays left defense) and will overload on the left side, meaning Rafalski has to fight more than his share of physical battles. He is small and makes the best use of his finesse skills in a defensive mode, but he will also get his body in the way. He is durable and strong on his skates. Rafalski is very thick through his upper body and shoulders, so his small appearance can be deceptive.

THE INTANGIBLES

Rafalski is intelligent, poised and utterly unflappable. His panic point is minuscule. Along with Stevens, he routinely handles match-ups against other teams' best forwards and relishes the assignments. He is confident in his ability to tackle a challenge and is usually at his peak at crunch time.

PROJECTION

Rafalski should score in the 40-point range; more if they acquire some offensive juice up front to make better use of Rafalski's point play.

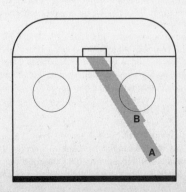

MICHAEL RUPP

Yrs. of NHL service: 1
Born: Cleveland, Ohio; Jan. 13, 1980
Position: center
Height: 6-5
Weight: 235
Uniform no.: 16
Shoots: left

Career statistics:

GP	G	A	TP	PIM
26	5	3	8	21

2002-2003 statistics:

GP	G	A	TP	+/-	PIM	PP	SH	GW	GT	S	PCT
26	5	3	8	0	21	2	0	3	0	34	14.7

LAST SEASON

First NHL season. Missed three games due to illness. Missed three games due to coach's decision. Appeared in 47 games with Albany (AHL), scoring 8-11 — 19 with 21 PIM.

THE FINESSE GAME

Rupp is a power forward with all the strength, but not all of the drive. His size is the first thing you notice. He is tall, rangy, and has a huge wingspan. He looks like he is moving slower than he is because he has such a big stride, but he's not an ungainly skater. He has decent speed and acceleration and not a bad turning radius for such a large dude. It's surprising because Rupp started playing hockey a lot later than many NHL players.

Rupp has very good hands for passing or shooting. He is more of a bang-bang, reactionary kind of player who excels when he is in tight. The closer he gets to the net, the more intense Rupp becomes. Rupp has a heavy shot with a quick release.

Rupp is hard to part from the puck. He protects the puck well with his body and a player has to reach a long way in to knock it off his stick. More likely, the defender will take a penalty and give Rupp a chance to go to work on the power play.

Rupp needs to improve his work on face-offs and his defensive play. The Devils are pretty demanding that way.

THE PHYSICAL GAME

Rupp doesn't back down, but he doesn't initiate enough. He has to show more desire to play through people, which he is strong enough to do. He is a factor on the power play when he puts his big body in front of the goalie.

THE INTANGIBLES

No rookie scored a bigger goal last season than Rupp, who is credited with scoring the Cup-clinching goal for the Devils (the first goal in a 3-0 win in Game 7).

That's a tough act to follow. It will be even tougher for Rupp should the Devils re-sign Joe Nieuwendyk during the off-season, since he was the player Rupp filled in for at center in the playoffs. If they don't, then he could be shifted to either wing.

PROJECTION

Rupp has a shot at earning a top-six role with the Devils. Based on his brief stints, a 20-goal season would be likely.

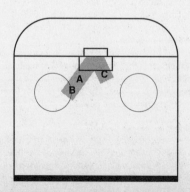

282

SCOTT STEVENS

Yrs. of NHL service: 21
Born: Kitchener, Ont.; Apr. 1, 1964
Position: left defense
Height: 6-2
Weight: 215
Uniform no.: 4
Shoots: left

Career statistics:

GP	G	A	TP	PIM
1597	193	703	896	2763

1999-2000 statistics:

GP	G	A	TP	+/-	PIM	PP	SH	GW	GT	S	PCT
78	8	21	29	+30	103	0	1	1	0	133	6.0

2000-2001 statistics:

GP	G	A	TP	+/-	PIM	PP	SH	GW	GT	S	PCT
81	9	22	31	+40	71	3	0	2	0	171	5.3

2001-2002 statistics:

GP	G	A	TP	+/-	PIM	PP	SH	GW	GT	S	PCT
82	1	16	17	+15	44	0	0	1	0	121	0.8

2002-2003 statistics:

GP	G	A	TP	+/-	PIM	PP	SH	GW	GT	S	PCT
81	4	16	20	+18	41	0	0	2	0	113	3.5

LAST SEASON

Third on team in ice time (23:04). Missed one game due to coach's decision.

THE FINESSE GAME

Every year Stevens gets a little older. Every year, he fails to show many signs of slowing down. Part of that is due to the Devils' superior system, but much is due to Stevens's conditioning and hockey instincts.

Stevens is secure and strong in his skating, capable both forwards and backwards and with good lateral mobility. He is not overly agile, though, and more and more players on the rush are able to beat him one-on-one in open ice. He has a tendency to overhandle the puck in the defensive zone. Instead of quickly banging the puck off the boards to clear the zone, it seems to take him an unusual amount of time to get the puck teed up, and it's often kept in by the attacking team. Stevens then digs in twice as hard to win the puck back, but he often creates more work for himself.

Stevens has a tremendous work ethic that more than makes up for some of his shortcomings (most of those are sins of commission rather than omission). He is a bear on penalty killing because he just won't quit, and a fearless shot-blocker.

Opponents used to delight in goading a young, immature Stevens into taking bad penalties. The tactic can still be effective, but only occasionally. Stevens is a smart player who recognizes the challenges presented to him every night and rarely fails to meet them. He works best paired with a mobile partner. Brian Rafalski is an especially complementary player, although Stevens also meshes well with Scott Niedermayer.

THE PHYSICAL GAME

Stevens is one of the most punishing open-ice hitters. Just ask Paul Kariya, who was rocked by Stevens in the Stanley Cup Final (even though Kariya survived and scored a goal in the game).

Stevens has the skating ability to line up the puck carrier, and the size and strength to explode on impact. Stevens is also effective in small spaces. He shovels most opponents out from in front of the net and crunches them along the boards. He prides himself on his conditioning and can handle a lot of minutes, although the Devils are wise not to overuse him.

THE INTANGIBLES

Stevens plays in as many games as possible, even when the Devils have healthy leads in the standings. Stevens isn't a rah-rah, speechmaking kind of guy, but leads by example. He works harder than almost anyone on the team in practice. Attention to nutrition and fitness has helped Stevens maintain his peak, but the clock eventually winds down for everyone, and Stevens's time is coming. This could be his last peak season.

PROJECTION

Stevens is all defense now. Don't expect his point totals to be much above 20.

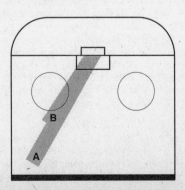

OLEG TVERDOVSKY

Yrs. of NHL service: 9
Born: Donetsk, Ukraine; May 18, 1976
Position: left defense
Height: 6-0
Weight: 205
Uniform no.: 10
Shoots: left

Career statistics:

GP	G	A	TP	PIM
615	74	216	290	244

1999-2000 statistics:

GP	G	A	TP	+/-	PIM	PP	SH	GW	GT	S	PCT
82	15	36	51	+5	30	5	0	5	0	153	9.8

2000-2001 statistics:

GP	G	A	TP	+/-	PIM	PP	SH	GW	GT	S	PCT
82	14	39	53	-11	32	8	0	3	2	188	7.4

2001-2002 statistics:

GP	G	A	TP	+/-	PIM	PP	SH	GW	GT	S	PCT
73	6	26	32	0	31	2	0	1	0	147	4.1

2002-2003 statistics:

GP	G	A	TP	+/-	PIM	PP	SH	GW	GT	S	PCT
50	5	8	13	+2	22	2	0	1	0	76	6.6

LAST SEASON

Missed 28 games due to viral infection/post-concussion syndrome. Missed four games due to coach's decision.

THE FINESSE GAME

Tverdovsky has Brian Leetch potential. Now that he's playing for a solid team for the first time in his nine-year NHL career, we may get to see Tverdovsky reach his peak. He's an explosive skater and he can carry the puck at high tempo. He works the point on the power play, utilizing a nice lateral slide along the blueline, and he kills penalties. He also sees his options and makes his decisions at lightning speed.

Tverdovsky is an impressive talent who passes the puck well and shoots bullets. He is clearly an "offenseman,'" but he has worked at improving his decision-making process. His defensive play is a lot less high-risk than it was his first few years in the league. It's an impressive development, because until last season, Tverdovsky did not have a veteran defenseman to mentor him along.

He can still get lazy defensively, casually moving the puck around the wall or banging it off the glass. He prefers to grab the puck and go, or look for a streaking forward. He's among the best in the league at the headman pass and he works exceptionally well in tandem with a speedy winger.

THE PHYSICAL GAME

Some of Tverdovsky's defensive weaknesses occur because he sometimes plays the puck instead of the man, or tries to poke-check without backing it up with his body. Physically, when he makes the right deci-sion, he can eliminate the man, and he looks to be improving in this area by at least tying up his man.

THE INTANGIBLES

Tverdovsky had a rocky season due to a hit in November that resulted in the viral-like symptoms that came and went. It made it difficult for Tverdovsky to get into a comfortable playing groove.

If Tverdovsky had started his career with a team like the Devils, he might have been All-Star material. He will be part of a strong defense corps that has a good mix of steady, stay-at-home types who can anchor the riskier likes of Tverdovsky, Scott Niedermayer, and Brian Rafalski.

PROJECTION

If he can stay healthy this season, Tverdovsky should be a No. 5 defenseman for the Devils and see more power-play time. A 50-point season could be in the offing.

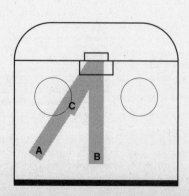

COLIN WHITE

Yrs. of NHL service: 3
Born: New Glasgow, N.S.; Dec. 12, 1977
Position: left defense
Height: 6-4
Weight: 215
Uniform no.: 5
Shoots: left

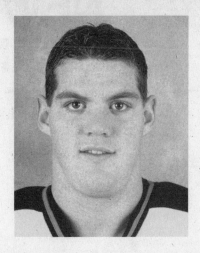

Career statistics:

GP	G	A	TP	PIM
248	10	31	41	426

1999-2000 statistics:

GP	G	A	TP	+/-	PIM	PP	SH	GW	GT	S	PCT
21	2	1	3	+3	40	0	0	1	0	29	6.9

2000-2001 statistics:

GP	G	A	TP	+/-	PIM	PP	SH	GW	GT	S	PCT
82	1	19	20	+32	155	0	0	1	0	114	0.9

2001-2002 statistics:

GP	G	A	TP	+/-	PIM	PP	SH	GW	GT	S	PCT
73	2	3	5	+6	133	0	0	0	0	81	2.5

2002-2003 statistics:

GP	G	A	TP	+/-	PIM	PP	SH	GW	GT	S	PCT
72	5	8	13	+19	98	0	0	1	0	81	6.2

LAST SEASON

Second on team in penalty minutes. Third on team in plus-minus. Missed seven games due to knee injury. Missed two games due to neck injury. Missed one game due to coach's decision.

THE FINESSE GAME

The Devils groomed White to become one of their foundation defensemen for when Scott Stevens would finally retire. There was concern when White took something of a step back in development in his sophomore season, but last year White blossomed.

White isn't a very fast skater, but he has a long stride and is balanced. White has learned to play within his limits, which tends to keep him out of trouble. He can't go chasing better skaters around, nor can he make risky pinches. There are still nights when this occurs, but it happened with far less regularity last season.

White is a fearsome bodychecker. He has excellent size, which he uses to his full advantage. White is not agile enough to throw open-ice body bombs like Stevens, but along the wall and in front of the net he is punishing. He blocks shots and was used on some penalty kills when the regulars needed a break.

White is a good passer who moves the puck quickly. He does not make many low-percentage plays. He has obviously been well-schooled in the Devils' system and uses the boards and his partner (most frequently the nimble Scott Niedermayer) well. White has a decent shot from the point, although he is not very slick with the puck along the blueline. White is unafraid to make a foray into the other team's attacking zone and he usually picks his spots well.

THE PHYSICAL GAME

White has worked on cutting his PIM totals down over the last three seasons and understands that he can be just as intimidating by threatening to snap than actually going berserk and taking a dumb penalty. He will react when the time is right, a great improvement from jumping in at the least provocation.

THE INTANGIBLES

White counts Dave Manson and Wendel Clark as his idols, and he plays with the toughness and the mean streak those two athletes possessed. He is becoming a feared and respected defenseman.

PROJECTION

White will be a top-four defenseman for the Devils again this season. He is progressing in every area of his game. White will never show much on the scoresheet, but should be good for around 20 points and 100 PIM per season.

NEW YORK ISLANDERS

Players' Statistics 2001-2002

POS.	NO.	PLAYER	GP	G	A	PTS	+/-	PIM	PP	SH	GW	GT	S	PCT
C	79	ALEXEI YASHIN	81	26	39	65	-12	32	14		7	1	274	9.5
L	55	JASON BLAKE	81	25	30	55	16	58	3	1	4		253	9.9
R	37	MARK PARRISH	81	23	25	48	-11	28	9		5		147	15.6
C	38	DAVE SCATCHARD	81	27	18	45	9	108	5		2	1	165	16.4
C	17	SHAWN BATES	74	13	29	42	-9	52		6	1	1	126	10.3
C	27	MICHAEL PECA	66	13	29	42	-4	43	4	2	2		117	11.1
D	4	ROMAN HAMRLIK	73	9	32	41	21	87	3		2		151	6.0
D	3	ADRIAN AUCOIN	73	8	27	35	-5	70	5		1		175	4.6
R	45	ARRON ASHAM	78	15	19	34	1	57	4		1		114	13.1
D	44	JANNE NIINIMAA	76	5	29	34	-9	80	3				101	5.0
C	28	JASON WIEMER	81	9	19	28	5	116		1	2		139	6.5
C	12	OLEG KVASHA	69	12	14	26	4	44		1	2		121	9.9
D	29	KENNY JONSSON	71	8	18	26	-8	24	3	1		1	108	7.4
R	11	*MATTIAS WEINHANDL	47	6	17	23	-2	10	1				66	9.1
C	25	RANDY ROBITAILLE	51	6	14	20	5	10	2		2		69	8.7
D	2	MATTIAS TIMANDER	80	3	13	16	-2	24			1		83	3.6
D	24	RADEK MARTINEK	66	2	11	13	15	26			1		67	3.0
C	16	*JUSTIN PAPINEAU	16	3	3	6	0	4			2		23	13.0
D	33	ERIC CAIRNS	60	1	4	5	-7	124					31	3.2
L	16	*RAFFI TORRES	17		5	5	0	10					12	
C	26	*JUSTIN MAPLETOFT	11	2	2	4	-1	2	1				12	16.7
D	44	SVEN BUTENSCHON	37		4	4	-6	26					19	
R	21	*TRENT HUNTER	8		4	4	5	4					19	
C	10	ERIC MANLOW	8	2	1	3	2	4	1				7	28.6
R	20	STEVE WEBB	49	1		1	-5	75					27	3.7
R	49	*ERIC GODARD	19				-3	48					6	
D	32	ALAN LETANG	4				-1						2	
D	6	BRANDON SMITH	3				-2						1	
D	36	RAY SCHULTZ	4				-1	28					1	
G	30	GARTH SNOW	43				0	24						
D	59	ALAIN NASREDDINE	3				0	2						
G	34	STEPHEN VALIQUETTE					0							
G	39	RICK DIPIETRO	10				0	2						
D	8	*TOMI PETTINEN	2				1							

GP = games played; G = goals; A = assists; PTS = points; +/- = goals-for minus goals-against while player is on ice; PIM = penalties in minutes; PP = power-play goals; SH = shorthanded goals; GW = game-winning goals; GT = game-tying goals; S = no. of shots; PCT = percentage of goals to shots; * = rookie

ARRON ASHAM

Yrs. of NHL service: 4
Born: Portage La Prairie, Man.; Apr. 13, 1978
Position: right wing
Height: 5-11
Weight: 209
Uniform no.: 45
Shoots: right

Career statistics:

GP	G	A	TP	PIM
199	26	28	54	195

1999-2000 statistics:

GP	G	A	TP	+/-	PIM	PP	SH	GW	GT	S	PCT
33	4	2	6	-7	24	0	1	1	0	29	13.8

2000-2001 statistics:

GP	G	A	TP	+/-	PIM	PP	SH	GW	GT	S	PCT
46	2	3	5	-9	59	0	0	0	0	32	6.3

2001-2002 statistics:

GP	G	A	TP	+/-	PIM	PP	SH	GW	GT	S	PCT
35	5	4	9	+7	55	0	0	0	0	30	16.7

2002-2003 statistics:

GP	G	A	TP	+/-	PIM	PP	SH	GW	GT	S	PCT
78	15	19	34	+1	57	4	0	1	0	114	13.1

LAST SEASON

Third on team in shooting percentage. Career high in goals. Missed five games due to coach's decision.

THE FINESSE GAME

Asham is a gritty forward who makes space for himself by his willingness to play a fierce game. He isn't big, but he is always willing to fight and lets his opponents know it. He has good hands for either scrapping or scoring.

Although his natural position is center, Asham is a better right wing. He doesn't see the ice well and isn't a good passer. His job is to disturb the defensemen into making mistakes and then make a beeline for the net for rebounds and screens. Asham is strong along the boards.

Asham has terrific hockey sense, desire, and the skating speed to compete at the NHL level. He is usually in the right place at the right time. The Isles even played him at times alongside Alexei Yashin.

THE PHYSICAL GAME

He doesn't just throw himself about wildly. Asham knows when to hit and when to take the edge off. He plays a smart forechecking game and doesn't go head-hunting. Experience is only going to make him a more dangerous and more valuable role player.

THE INTANGIBLES

Asham reminds some onlookers of a young Mike Keane. He was inspired by playing with a former Hab, Shayne Corson, whose combination of toughness and scoring touch was the perfect role model for Asham. Asham lacks Corson's size, but is undeterred by the disadvantage. Asham has given the Islanders some much-needed honest toughness.

PROJECTION

We pegged Asham for 15 goals last season and he hit that mark. There is no reason why he can't do so again.

ADRIAN AUCOIN

Yrs. of NHL service: 8
Born: Ottawa, Ont.; July 3, 1973
Position: right defense
Height: 6-2
Weight: 214
Uniform no.: 3
Shoots: right

Career statistics:

GP	G	A	TP	PIM
521	70	131	201	402

1999-2000 statistics:

GP	G	A	TP	+/-	PIM	PP	SH	GW	GT	S	PCT
57	10	14	24	+7	30	4	0	1	0	126	7.9

2000-2001 statistics:

GP	G	A	TP	+/-	PIM	PP	SH	GW	GT	S	PCT
73	4	24	28	+5	45	2	0	0	0	159	2.5

2001-2002 statistics:

GP	G	A	TP	+/-	PIM	PP	SH	GW	GT	S	PCT
81	12	22	34	+23	62	7	0	1	0	232	5.2

2002-2003 statistics:

GP	G	A	TP	+/-	PIM	PP	SH	GW	GT	S	PCT
73	8	27	35	-5	70	5	0	1	0	175	4.6

LAST SEASON

Second among NHL players in average ice time (29:00). Tied for third on team in power-play goals. Missed eight games due to groin injury. Missed one game due to coach's decision.

THE FINESSE GAME

Aucoin is a mobile, agile skater who moves well with the puck. He doesn't have breakaway speed, which is what prevents him from being an elite offensive defenseman, but he jumps alertly into the play. On the power play, he smartly switches off with a forward to cut in deep, and he has good hands for shots in-tight. He also has a good point shot and is very intelligent with his shot selection.

Once considered strictly an offensive defensemen, Aucoin has worked hard to improve the defensive side of his game. He puts his finesse skills to great use as a defender. He's among the league's best one-on-one in open ice. Even a shifty puck carrier like Pavel Bure has trouble getting past Aucoin on a mano-a-mano rush. Aucoin doesn't fall for the deke, he keeps his feet moving and his body aligned, and simply pokes the puck away. He makes it look so easy against the game's most elusive forwards.

Aucoin developed into the Islanders' most valuable weapon on the power play. He is a very good point man, with lateral movement along the blueline and a quick, accurate one-timer. He also kills penalties.

THE PHYSICAL GAME

Aucoin is a strong, good-sized defenseman who often plays smaller. Aucoin isn't a big hitter, and along the boards may fail to stick and pin his man. He has no mean streak to speak of. Opponents know he can be pushed around and they take advantage of that. What Aucoin does do well is position his body effectively to cut down on passing lanes in the defensive zone. Aucoin is in top physical condition and can handle a lot of minutes (he was second in the league to Nicklas Lidstrom). Paired most often with Kenny Jonsson, Aucoin often handles duties against the other team's top line.

THE INTANGIBLES

Just because Aucoin can handle those excessive minutes doesn't mean he should. The Isles give him an absurd workload, especially in the playoffs. Cutting him back to 25 or 26 minutes a game would be beneficial to all parties.

PROJECTION

We called for 30 points for Aucoin last season, and he should be in the 30-40 range again.

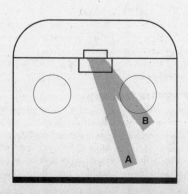

ERIC CAIRNS

Yrs. of NHL service: 7
Born: Oakville, Ont.; June 27, 1974
Position: left defense
Height: 6-6
Weight: 230
Uniform no.: 33
Shoots: left

Career statistics:

GP	G	A	TP	PIM
334	7	25	32	864

1999-2000 statistics:

GP	G	A	TP	+/-	PIM	PP	SH	GW	GT	S	PCT
67	2	7	9	-5	196	0	0	0	0	55	3.6

2000-2001 statistics:

GP	G	A	TP	+/-	PIM	PP	SH	GW	GT	S	PCT
45	2	2	4	-18	106	0	0	0	0	21	9.5

2001-2002 statistics:

GP	G	A	TP	+/-	PIM	PP	SH	GW	GT	S	PCT
74	2	5	7	-2	176	0	0	1	0	34	5.9

2002-2003 statistics:

GP	G	A	TP	+/-	PIM	PP	SH	GW	GT	S	PCT
60	1	4	5	-7	124	0	0	0	0	31	3.2

LAST SEASON

Led team in penalty minutes. Missed 20 games with dislocated shoulder. Missed two games due to coach's decision.

THE FINESSE GAME

It is natural to think a player as big as Cairns would be clumsy, and he does have some footwork issues. He also possesses some smarts with the puck and enough skill to skate the puck out of the defensive zone. Occasionally he can beat a forechecker, but Cairns knows better than to make a habit of that. He doesn't have great foot speed and can get caught flat-footed.

With the puck, Cairns favors backhand moves that allow him to use his body to shield the puck from defenders. He is content to get the puck deep in the zone and let the forwards do the offensive work, but his point shot is accurate when he elects to use it. Out of his own zone, he makes an accurate outlet pass.

Although not a great skater, Cairns turns pretty smoothly and makes up for any shortcomings in speed by using his size and reach. He may look like someone who can be beaten easily to the outside, but he generally does a nice job of angling a puck carrier to less dangerous ice. Cairns works every off-season to improve his footwork.

THE PHYSICAL GAME

Cairns is a willing fighter and plays policeman if any opponent starts taking liberties with his teammates. He likes the big hits and mean rubouts, but does a pretty good job of avoiding the cheap hooking and holding penalties big defensemen always seem to get against smaller, quicker forwards. He has become a legitimate NHL fighter and one who doesn't need to prove himself anymore at every challenge, which means he can concentrate more on actually playing.

THE INTANGIBLES

Cairns has become a solid No. 5 or 6 defenseman, which appears to be his niche, and the Isles have developed the right depth at that position to let him settle into his role.

PROJECTION

Cairns will never be a star and he isn't going to score much, but he has made himself into a decent NHL defenseman. He's still a project, and he will forever be a player who has to work at his game on a daily basis. His size, strength, and reach, sensibly packaged and deployed, are a commodity in the NHL. If he plays his cards right he can have a good career as a dependable stay-at-home, and as a partner for the offensive guy who's going to be up-ice all night.

RICK DIPIETRO

Yrs. of NHL service: 1
Born: Lewiston, ME; Sept. 19, 1981
Position: goaltender
Height: 5-11
Weight: 185
Uniform no.: 39
Catches: right

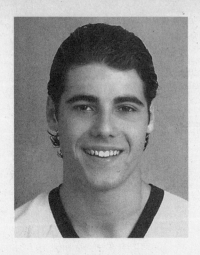

Career statistics:

GP	MIN	GA	SO	GAA	A	PIM
30	1668	92	0	3.31	0	2

2000-2001 statistics:

GP	MIN	GAA	W	L	T	SO	GA	S	SAPCT	PIM
20	1083	3.49	3	15	1	0	63	515	.878	6

2002-2003 statistics:

GP	MIN	GAA	W	L	T	SO	GA	S	SAPCT	PIM
10	585	2.97	2	5	2	0	29	273	.894	2

LAST SEASON

Appeared in 34 games with Bridgeport (AHL), with a 16-10-8 record and 2.14 GAA.

THE PHYSICAL GAME

DiPietro is absolutely phenomenal handling the puck. There is a chance he may become every bit as good as Martin Brodeur. However, DiPietro first has to learn how to stop it.

DiPietro certainly has the build. He is very quick, and has good mechanics. He was rushed to the NHL in 2000-2001, and both his confidence and his technique suffered as he was bounced around to the minors. DiPietro has to recover his focus and his angles.

The Isles' defense will be thrilled when he does win a No. 1 job because of his ability to wing the puck off the glass for a breakout, or just settle it and move it along gently behind the goal line to help the defense on the breakout. Teams will think more about keeping the puck away from him and alter their game, which is what Brodeur does to his opponents, especially on the power play.

DiPietro was usually thinking too far ahead last season instead of playing the game logically. Stop puck, control rebound, then think about playing it. In that order.

THE MENTAL GAME

DiPietro has a refreshing brashness that is just shy of being too cocky. Arrogance is not a bad thing to have in an elite-level player, which DiPietro may well be, as long as he doesn't think he's smarter than his coaches. The rough start to his pro career may have humbled him just enough.

THE INTANGIBLES

The Islanders traded Chris Osgood at the trade deadline, which will leave Garth Snow as his goaltending partner. Since Snow still wants to be the No. 1 goalie, we think a more non-threatening veteran would be a better fit to help bring DiPietro along.

PROJECTION

The Islanders have been through too many "goalies of the future" already. This looms as the make-or-break season for DiPietro. If he doesn't earn the No. 1 job here, it will be with some other organization — although Jean-Sebastien Giguere remains a cautionary tale for giving up on a goalie too soon.

ROMAN HAMRLIK

Yrs. of NHL service: 11
Born: Gottwaldov, Czech Republic; Apr. 12, 1974
Position: left defense
Height: 6-2
Weight: 200
Uniform no.: 4
Shoots: left

Career statistics:

GP	G	A	TP	PIM
792	110	302	412	917

1999-2000 statistics:

GP	G	A	TP	+/-	PIM	PP	SH	GW	GT	S	PCT
80	8	37	45	+1	68	5	0	0	1	180	4.4

2000-2001 statistics:

GP	G	A	TP	+/-	PIM	PP	SH	GW	GT	S	PCT
76	16	30	46	-20	92	5	1	4	0	232	6.9

2001-2002 statistics:

GP	G	A	TP	+/-	PIM	PP	SH	GW	GT	S	PCT
70	11	26	37	+7	78	4	1	1	0	169	6.5

2002-2003 statistics:

GP	G	A	TP	+/-	PIM	PP	SH	GW	GT	S	PCT
73	9	32	41	+21	87	3	0	2	0	151	6.0

LAST SEASON

Led team defensemen in points for third consecutive season. Led team in plus-minus. Second on team in average ice time (26:34) and assists. Missed six games due to shoulder injury. Missed three games due to coach's decision.

THE FINESSE GAME

Hamrlik is better defensively than some people think, and not as good offensively as some other people think. He has turned into a solid two-way defenseman whose game doesn't have many valleys or peaks. He has established a solid, consistent game when he stays healthy.

He can handle marathon ice time and has the desire to dominate a game. He has all the tools. He is a fast, strong skater — forwards and backwards.

A mobile defenseman with a solid shot and good passing skills, Hamrlik is not creative. But he knows how to outsmart and not just overpower attackers. He loves to get involved offensively, despite not having elite skills. He has an excellent shot with a quick release. He could be smarter about taking some velocity off his shot in order to get a less blockable shot through.

Hamrlik has learned to make less risky plays in his own zone. He makes a great first pass out of the zone. Defensively, he runs into problems when he is trying to move the puck out of his zone and when he is forced to handle the puck on his backhand, but that is about the only way the opposition can cope with him.

THE PHYSICAL GAME

Hamrlik is aggressive and likes physical play, though he is not a huge, splashy hitter. He usually keeps himself in good condition and can handle a lot of minutes.

THE INTANGIBLES

Hamrlik returned to the Islanders' good graces with a big rebound season and is part of a solid top-four defense corps. Over the course of the full season, Hamrlik was probably the Isles' best two-way defenseman.

PROJECTION

Hamrlik should be a 10-goal, 40-point scorer.

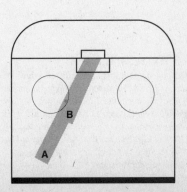

KENNY JONSSON

Yrs. of NHL service: 9
Born: Angelholm, Sweden; Oct. 6, 1974
Position: left defense
Height: 6-3
Weight: 217
Uniform no.: 29
Shoots: left

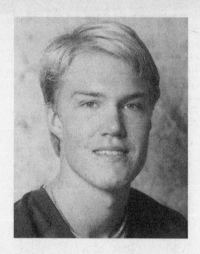

Career statistics:

GP	G	A	TP	PIM
607	58	180	238	276

1999-2000 statistics:

GP	G	A	TP	+/-	PIM	PP	SH	GW	GT	S	PCT
65	1	24	25	-15	32	1	0	0	0	84	1.2

2000-2001 statistics:

GP	G	A	TP	+/-	PIM	PP	SH	GW	GT	S	PCT
65	8	21	29	-22	30	5	0	0	0	91	8.8

2001-2002 statistics:

GP	G	A	TP	+/-	PIM	PP	SH	GW	GT	S	PCT
76	10	22	32	+15	26	2	1	0	0	107	9.4

2002-2003 statistics:

GP	G	A	TP	+/-	PIM	PP	SH	GW	GT	S	PCT
71	8	18	26	-8	24	3	1	0	1	108	7.4

LAST SEASON

Missed three games due to virus. Missed one game with strained knee. Missed five games with sprained knee. Missed three games due to illness.

THE FINESSE GAME

Jonsson is not overly creative, nor is he a risk taker. He reads the ice and passes the puck very well. He makes a good first pass out of the zone, but he will also bank it off the boards if that's the safer play. He doesn't shoot for the home-run pass on every shift, but will recognize the headman play when it's there.

Jonsson moves the puck up and plays his position. He always makes sure he has somebody beaten before he makes a pass. He can be used in almost every game situation. He kills penalties, works the point on the power play, plays four-on-four, and is used in the late stages of a period or a game to protect a lead. Jonsson is not elite in any one role, but he is very good in many of them. He's reliable and coachable.

Jonsson is a talented skater, big and mobile, yet tends to leave himself open after passes and gets nailed.

THE PHYSICAL GAME

Jonsson is smart and plays with an edge. He and Adrian Aucoin were almost exclusively matched up night after night against the opposition's top line and were seldom outplayed. The knock on him earlier in his career was that he was a bit soft and didn't like to play through traffic, but that has changed. He competes hard every night and in the hard areas of the ice. He can handle all the minutes he gets.

THE INTANGIBLES

Jonsson dislikes the spotlight, but he accepts the responsibility of being a team leader on and off the ice. Injuries major and minor continue to nag him. While he isn't a true No. 1 defenseman, he is a solid No. 2 on his best nights and even a No. 3 when he's just a little off.

PROJECTION

Jonsson still has several prime years left. He should score in the 25-point range and be a conservative defenseman as part of the Isles' top four unit.

OLEG KVASHA

Yrs. of NHL service: 5
Born: Moscow, Russia; July 26, 1978
Position: left wing
Height: 6-5
Weight: 230
Uniform no.: 12
Shoots: right

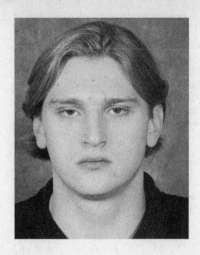

Career statistics:

GP	G	A	TP	PIM
348	53	81	134	249

1999-2000 statistics:

GP	G	A	TP	+/-	PIM	PP	SH	GW	GT	S	PCT
78	5	20	25	+3	34	2	0	0	0	110	4.5

2000-2001 statistics:

GP	G	A	TP	+/-	PIM	PP	SH	GW	GT	S	PCT
62	11	9	20	-15	46	0	0	0	0	118	9.3

2001-2002 statistics:

GP	G	A	TP	+/-	PIM	PP	SH	GW	GT	S	PCT
71	13	25	38	-4	80	2	0	3	0	119	10.9

2002-2003 statistics:

GP	G	A	TP	+/-	PIM	PP	SH	GW	GT	S	PCT
69	12	14	26	+4	44	0	1	2	0	121	9.9

LAST SEASON

Missed 10 games due to foot injuries. Missed three games due to coach's decision.

THE FINESSE GAME

The word "enigmatic" has been used to describe Kvasha more times than the Islanders care to remember. He's a big guy, with a world of skill, who only puts the whole package together once every eight to 10 games.

Kvasha has good speed and great hands. He can make a lot of things happen with the puck in full stride. He can also play center, and he brings a center's vision to the left wing. He has terrific hockey sense and vision. He anticipates well and sees holes a split second before they open.

With big-time skills, Kvasha has to improve his play away from the puck. He never seems to put himself in the right position at the right time, and his defensive lapses usually mean he ends up riding the bench in a tight game.

Kvasha could use his shot more. He has an excellent wrist shot that is his best weapon.

THE PHYSICAL GAME

With his strength and good size, Kvasha will drive to the net. He is not above crashing the goalie. But he can be intimidated, and on those nights he is way too big and talented to be as invisible as he tries to be.

THE INTANGIBLES

Who is the real Oleg Kvasha? The slacker forward who gets booed every time he touched the puck? Or the guy who showed up with a four-point game in Detroit when the Isles were still in danger of missing the playoffs?

PROJECTION

We know what Kvasha is capable of. He has the skill level to be a 20-goal, 50-point player. Like everyone else, we're waiting for that "click" where his game falls neatly into place. If it happens, it is likely to occur in another rink, since the Islanders have pretty much run out of patience.

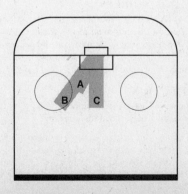

RADEK MARTINEK

Yrs. of NHL service: 2
Born: Havilickuv Brod, Czech Reublic; Aug. 31, 1976
Position: right defense
Height: 6-1
Weight: 200
Uniform no.: 24
Shoots: right

Career statistics:

GP	G	A	TP	PIM
89	3	15	18	42

2001-2002 statistics:

GP	G	A	TP	+/-	PIM	PP	SH	GW	GT	S	PCT
23	1	4	5	+5	16	0	0	1	0	25	4.0

2002-2003 statistics:

GP	G	A	TP	+/-	PIM	PP	SH	GW	GT	S	PCT
66	2	11	13	+15	26	0	0	1	0	67	3.0

LAST SEASON

Third on team in plus-minus. Missed four games with rib injury. Missed eight games due to coach's decision. Appeared in three games with Bridgeport (AHL), scoring 0-3 — 3 with 2 PIM.

THE FINESSE GAME

Martinek continues to develop as a blue-chip prospect despite injuries that have slowed his progress in the last two seasons. He is rock-solid defensively, and is confident in his finesse skills. Martinek was not afraid to jump up into the play from his first shift in his first NHL game.

Martinek is smart. He is a good passer, making the first smooth move out of the zone, or he can carry it himself. He's not a great skater, but he's NHL-caliber.

Martinek is only average-sized, but he holds up physically against the game's best power forwards.

THE PHYSICAL GAME

Martinek can play against other teams' top lines on a nightly basis. He is strong on his skates and he patrols his own end of the ice with authority. Martinek clears out space in front of his net. He competes hard, every night, every shift.

THE INTANGIBLES

Although he lost only four games to injury, Martinek soldiered on through most of the season on a sore knee. We're eager to see Martinek at 100 per cent. He figures into the Isles' top-four defensemen and could eventually move into the top pair.

PROJECTION

Martinek can score 20-25 points and be a big-play defenseman if he gets and stays healthy.

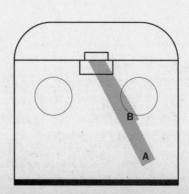

JANNE NIINIMAA

Yrs. of NHL service: 7
Born: Raahe, Finland; May 22, 1975
Position: right defense
Height: 6-1
Weight: 220
Uniform no.: 44
Shoots: left

Career statistics:

GP	G	A	TP	PIM
555	42	230	272	547

1999-2000 statistics:

GP	G	A	TP	+/-	PIM	PP	SH	GW	GT	S	PCT
81	8	25	33	+14	89	2	2	0	0	133	6.0

2000-2001 statistics:

GP	G	A	TP	+/-	PIM	PP	SH	GW	GT	S	PCT
82	12	34	46	+6	90	8	0	1	0	122	9.8

2001-2002 statistics:

GP	G	A	TP	+/-	PIM	PP	SH	GW	GT	S	PCT
81	5	39	44	+13	80	1	0	2	0	119	4.2

2002-2003 statistics:

GP	G	A	TP	+/-	PIM	PP	SH	GW	GT	S	PCT
76	5	29	34	-9	80	3	0	0	0	101	5.0

LAST SEASON

Acquired from Edmonton on March 11, 2003, with a second-round draft pick in 2003 for Brad Isbister and Raffi Torres. Third on Isles in average ice time (26:09).

THE FINESSE GAME

The best news about Niinimaa's play in the last few seasons is his consistency. He makes fewer of the boneheaded decisions that marred his early career. He remains a gambler at heart, though, which often pays off with his creative offensive moves.

In the past, Niinimaa would get too active in a confined area. In his own end, he would sometimes get a guy pinned and there would be too much movement. He had to learn to be patient and just pin the guy. Once he works the puck free, Niinimaa is good at jumping into the play and getting up-ice. He sometimes gets impatient. Niinimaa wants to create things offensively and when there isn't anything there, he gets into trouble.

A nimble, agile player, Niinimaa sets his feet wide apart for outstanding drive, power and balance, and uses a long stride and long reach to win races to the puck. He can turn the corners at near top speed and doesn't have to slow down when carrying the puck. When the opportunity to jump into the play presents itself, he is gone in a vapor trail.

Niinimaa is a dynamic player with elite skills. A left-handed shot who plays the right side, he has excellent skating and puckhandling skills, which allow him to handle the amount of body shifting necessary to open his body to the rink and keep the forehand available as often as possible. He is a first-rate power-play quarterback and puck carrier.

Niinimaa does a great job of "framing" his stick and giving his teammates a passing target. He keeps the blade on the ice and available, his body position saying, "Put it here, so I can do something with it." He knows he can create just as much offensive danger by merely flipping a puck towards the net instead of taking the full-windup slap shot every time. Although his one-timers can be blistering, he doesn't always shoot to score. Sometimes he shoots to create a rebound or deflection. He does a good job of looking for lanes to get the puck through to the net instead of just blasting away with shots that can be blocked.

THE PHYSICAL GAME

Niinimaa plays a fairly physical game, though he is not aggressive. He bumps and jolts, and makes opponents pay a price for every inch of important ice gained. He seems to relish one-on-one battles. He wants the puck and does whatever is necessary to win control of it. He is in very good physical shape and can handle a lot of minutes.

THE INTANGIBLES

Niinimaa is just a cut below the game's elite defensemen, but his addition has given the Isles a very solid top four.

PROJECTION

Niinimaa will score in the 40-point range.

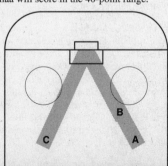

MARK PARRISH

Yrs. of NHL service: 5
Born: Edina, Minn. Feb. 2, 1977
Position: right wing
Height: 5-11
Weight: 200
Uniform no.: 37
Shoots: right

Career statistics:

GP	G	A	TP	PIM
383	120	99	219	152

1999-2000 statistics:

GP	G	A	TP	+/-	PIM	PP	SH	GW	GT	S	PCT
81	26	18	44	+1	39	6	0	3	0	152	17.1

2000-2001 statistics:

GP	G	A	TP	+/-	PIM	PP	SH	GW	GT	S	PCT
70	17	13	30	-27	28	6	0	3	0	123	13.8

2001-2002 statistics:

GP	G	A	TP	+/-	PIM	PP	SH	GW	GT	S	PCT
78	30	30	60	+10	32	9	1	6	0	162	18.5

2002-2003 statistics:

GP	G	A	TP	+/-	PIM	PP	SH	GW	GT	S	PCT
81	23	25	48	-11	28	9	0	5	0	147	15.6

LAST SEASON

Second on team in power play goals, game-winning goals, and shooting percentage. Third on team in points. Worst plus-minus on team. Missed one game due to flu.

THE FINESSE GAME

With his good outside speed and reads, Parrish is able to wiggle past such top one-on-one defenders as Brian Leetch for scoring chances. He is a goal-scorer by skill and by nature. He goes to the net hard because he knows he has to score to stay in the lineup.

Parrish has terrific hands and a great shot, and he has started thinking like a finisher. He will get a lot of first-unit power-play time. He does some of his best work around the front of the net. He loves to score.

Parrish is a player who goes in streaks and slumps. That is pretty much Parrish's pattern, and he needs to snap out of it to take his place among the league's top goal-scorers. He's 26 now, just coming into his prime, but consistency continues to elude him.

THE PHYSICAL GAME

Parrish doesn't have great size but he doesn't avoid the high-traffic areas. He is not afraid of anything or anybody. Parrish works in all of the dirty areas in the attacking zone, and not just around the net. He will absorb a blow just to chip the puck in safely rather than make a high-risk play. His defensive awareness has improved. The Isles even used him on the occasional penalty-killing shift, and he scored his first career shorthanded goal.

THE INTANGIBLES

Parrish missed Michael Peca, who contributed mightily to Parrish's 30-goal season in 2001-02. He is developing into a quiet leader and character player, so with the right attitude he can be a huge asset for the Isles. Parrish is still developing a goal-scorer's confidence, and remains a streaky, slumping player. His playoffs weren't impressive for the second straight year.

PROJECTION

Unless Parrish develops more consistency, he should score goals in the mid-20s range again.

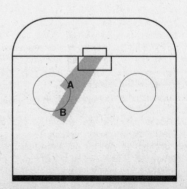

MICHAEL PECA

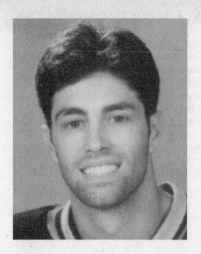

Yrs. of NHL service: 9
Born: Toronto, Ont.; March 26, 1974
Position: center
Height: 5-11
Weight: 190
Uniform no.: 27
Shoots: right

Career statistics:

GP	G	A	TP	PIM
546	140	191	331	489

1999-2000 statistics:

GP	G	A	TP	+/-	PIM	PP	SH	GW	GT	S	PCT
73	20	21	41	+6	67	2	0	3	0	144	13.9

2000-2001 statistics:

Did not play in NHL

2001-2002 statistics:

GP	G	A	TP	+/-	PIM	PP	SH	GW	GT	S	PCT
80	25	35	60	+19	62	3	6	5	1	168	14.9

2002-2003 statistics:

GP	G	A	TP	+/-	PIM	PP	SH	GW	GT	S	PCT
66	13	29	42	-4	43	4	2	2	0	117	11.1

LAST SEASON

Second on team in shorthanded goals. Missed 25 games due to knee surgery. Missed one game due to coach's decision.

THE FINESSE GAME

Everything Peca does, he does with intensity, which only enhances his talent. Peca is a strong, sure skater who plays every shift as if a pink slip will be waiting on the bench if he slacks off. He's good with the puck in traffic and has the timing and the nice hands to create time and space for his linemates. He does a lot of the little things — especially when forechecking — that create turnovers and scoring chances. His goals come from his quickness and his effort. He challenges anyone for the puck.

While he will never be a 100-point guy, Peca seldom looks out of place playing with or against the elite-level players in the league. His hustle and attitude have earned him his NHL job and league-wide respect. Peca thinks the game well and can be used in all situations. Peca is still ideally suited as a two-way defensive center, but the Isles need him to be much more than that and he tries to oblige.

Peca creates breakaway chances with his reads and anticipation. He is smart at disrupting plays and knows what to do once he has control of the puck.

THE PHYSICAL GAME

The biggest obstacle for Peca to overcome last season was a return from knee surgery (the result of Darcy Tucker's cheap shot in the 2002 playoffs). Typically, Peca made it back to the lineup well ahead of schedule, although the knee continued to be a concern most of the season.

Peca plays much bigger than his size. He's gritty and honest, and is always trying to add more weight. He has a tough time even keeping an extra five pounds on, and with all of the ice time he gets, he can wear down. Although he lacks the size to match up with some of the league's bigger forwards, he is tireless in his pursuit and effort.

He's among the best open-ice hitters in the league. Peca launches successful strikes against bigger players because of his timing, balance, and leg strength. He will also drop the gloves and go after even the biggest foe. He is prickly and in-your-face, although opponents are less impressed with his diving skills.

THE INTANGIBLES

Peca's presence on and off the ice was sorely missed last season, and he needs to be 100 per cent from the get-go this year if the team is to improve its status.

PROJECTION

Expect a 50-60 point season from Peca if he can stay healthy.

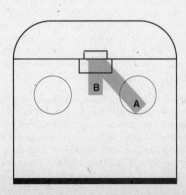

MATTIAS WEINHANDL

Yrs. of NHL service: 1
Born: Ljungby, Sweden; June 1, 1980
Position: right wing
Height: 6-0
Weight: 183
Uniform no.: 11
Shoots: right

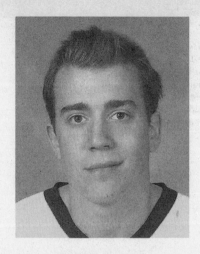

Career statistics:

GP	G	A	TP	PIM
47	6	17	23	10

2002-2003 statistics:

GP	G	A	TP	+/-	PIM	PP	SH	GW	GT	S	PCT
47	6	17	23	-2	10	1	0	0	0	66	9.1

LAST SEASON

Missed eight games with shoulder injury. Missed eight games due to coach's decision. Appeared in 23 games with Bridgeport (AHL) scoring 9-12 — 21 with 14 PIM.

THE FINESSE GAME

Weinhandl's NHL career nearly ended before it ever had a chance to begin, due to a serious eye injury he suffered while playing in Sweden. Weinhandl has made it back in very good form.

Weinhandl has some excellent offensive skills. He has terrific hands and will take the puck into high traffic areas. He goes into the hard areas of the ice for his scoring chances or will work along the boards. Weinhandl doesn't just sit back and wait for someone to do the dirty work for him.

He has good speed and balance. Weinhandl has all the looks of a big-time, big-game goal scorer. He is a pure sniper who was a linemate of Henrik and Daniel Sedin in Sweden several years ago. He is creative and has good hockey vision. He will work best on a second line and teamed with a playmaker. His defensive game needs some work but it's far from tragic.

THE PHYSICAL GAME

Weinhandl is physically mature, has a quiet toughness, and won't be intimidated. He plays hard. He needs to improve his physical conditioning because he wore down whenever he saw a streak of games where he played a lot of minutes. Weinhandl has shown us flashes. Now he needs to show more consistency.

THE INTANGIBLES

The Islanders have auditioned just about everyone on the team to play alongside Alexei Yashin, and Weinhandl was the only player who even remotely looked like a comfortable fit. New Isles coach Steve Sterling is familiar with Weinhandl from coaching him in the minors, and that may help his chances in training camp. Weinhandl was selected to play in the 2003 Young Stars game, which was a confidence booster. He would have earned some playing time in the postseason but suffered a broken toe.

PROJECTION

If Weinhandl can win that coveted spot in Yashin's line, he could score in the 20-25 goal range. He would make a nice sleeper pick in the pool.

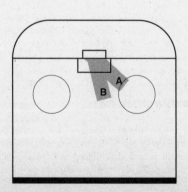

JASON WIEMER

Yrs. of NHL service: 9
Born: Kimberley, B.C.; Apr. 14, 1976
Position: left wing/center
Height: 6-1
Weight: 225
Uniform no.: 28
Shoots: left

Career statistics:

GP	G	A	TP	PIM
602	80	96	176	1187

1999-2000 statistics:

GP	G	A	TP	+/-	PIM	PP	SH	GW	GT	S	PCT
64	11	11	22	-10	120	2	0	3	0	104	10.6

2000-2001 statistics:

GP	G	A	TP	+/-	PIM	PP	SH	GW	GT	S	PCT
65	10	5	15	-15	177	3	0	1	1	76	13.2

2001-2002 statistics:

GP	G	A	TP	+/-	PIM	PP	SH	GW	GT	S	PCT
70	11	20	31	-4	178	5	1	1	0	115	9.6

2002-2003 statistics:

GP	G	A	TP	+/-	PIM	PP	SH	GW	GT	S	PCT
81	9	19	28	+5	116	0	1	2	0	139	6.5

LAST SEASON

Second on team in penalty minutes. Missed one game due to coach's decision.

THE FINESSE GAME

Wiemer has the build and the touch for standing in the traffic areas and picking pucks out of scrambles. He also has a touch of meanness that merits him some room and time to execute. His release has improved, but he does not have an NHL-calibre shot that will make him a power forward who can post big numbers. Wiemer has to grind out his goals, and is willing to.

He does the dirty work in the corners, but Wiemer needs to play with some skilled linemates because he doesn't have the finesse or creativity to make any pretty plays. He can finish off what someone with more vision opens up for him, however.

Wiemer's major shortcoming is his skating, but it is not enough of a problem to prevent him from becoming an impact player. He is very strong and well balanced for work around the net. He relies on his strength and his reach. Wiemer is quite adept at using his feet to kick a puck free or pin it along the wall for a draw. He is a good enough two-way player who can be given a checking assignment to shadow a star center. He can be a physical force and go toe-to-toe with guys like Ed Jovanovski. Wiemer is used on the power play and to kill penalties.

THE PHYSICAL GAME

Wiemer relishes body contact and initiates checks to intimidate. He is very strong and can hit to hurt. He drives to the net and pushes defenders back. He isn't shy about dropping his gloves or raising his elbows.

He functions as the grinder. He will scrap along the boards and in the corners for the puck. He can complement almost any linemate. Wiemer is passionate, plays with an edge, and makes his teammates braver.

THE INTANGIBLES

Despite his modest skills, Wiemer is a two-way forward. Wiemer is dependable and rarely takes a shift off. He can be put on the ice to protect a lead or help his team tie a game up late.

PROJECTION

Wiemer should score in the 15-goal range as he continues in his third-line role and picks up some second-unit power-play time.

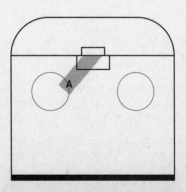

ALEXEI YASHIN

Yrs. of NHL service: 9
Born: Sverdlovsk, Russia; Nov. 5, 1973
Position: center
Height: 6-3
Weight: 225
Uniform no.: 79
Shoots: right

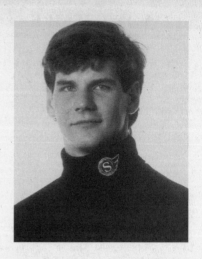

Career statistics:

GP	G	A	TP	PIM
663	276	355	631	279

1999-2000 statistics:

Missed NHL season.

2000-2001 statistics:

GP	G	A	TP	+/-	PIM	PP	SH	GW	GT	S	PCT
82	40	48	88	+10	30	13	2	10	1	263	15.2

2001-2002 statistics:

GP	G	A	TP	+/-	PIM	PP	SH	GW	GT	S	PCT
78	32	43	75	-3	25	15	0	5	0	239	13.4

2002-2003 statistics:

GP	G	A	TP	+/-	PIM	PP	SH	GW	GT	S	PCT
81	26	39	65	-12	32	14	0	7	1	274	9.5

LAST SEASON

Led team in assists, points, power-play goals, game-winning goals, and shots. Second on team in goals. Missed one game due to coach's decision.

THE FINESSE GAME

Yashin's skills are world class — on par with those of any other player of his generation. He has great hands and size. As he stickhandles in on the rush, he can put the puck through the legs of two or three defenders en route to the net.

Yashin doesn't have pure breakaway speed, but he is shifty, powerful, and balanced. He doesn't utilize his teammates well. He wants the puck a lot and has to play with unselfish linemates. He is at his best with the open ice that the power play provides, and more than half of his goals came on the man advantage.

Yashin isn't a flashy skater, but he has drawn comparisons to Ron Francis with his quiet effectiveness, and he is spectacular at times. He doesn't go all-out every shift, though, and on those occasions it looks like he's either pacing himself or he's fatigued. Because it looks as if he isn't trying, when things go poorly for him people assume he's loafing. Because he has such a chilly demeanor, people think he doesn't care. It's a tough image to counteract.

THE PHYSICAL GAME

Yashin is big and rangy and he protects the puck well. He has stepped up his desire to play through checks and pays the price in traffic. He is also smart and skilled enough to avoid unnecessary wallops. Because he has a long fuse, Yashin was once thought of as a timid player.

THE INTANGIBLES

The Isles have spent two years auditioning compatible wingers for Yashin and have yet to find the right fit. Yashin struggled so badly at times last season that he was put on a fourth line. Is that Yashin's fault, or the Islanders'?

It doesn't help Yashin's cause that the Islanders, in their eagerness to re-establish themselves as legitimate contenders, gave him a 10-year deal in 2001 that averages $8.7 million. When your $8 million guy is outhustled by players like Jason Blake making $600,000, there is considerable fodder for criticism. Maybe it's time to stop thinking of him as a great player. He's just a good one who makes a great amount of money.

PROJECTION

Yashin's early-season struggles last year could be chalked up to the absence of Michael Peca and increased checking pressure on Yashin. He should be a point-a-game player.

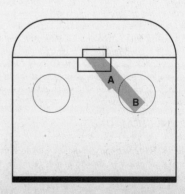

NEW YORK RANGERS

Players' Statistics 2001-2002

POS.	NO.	PLAYER	GP	G	A	PTS	+/-	PIM	PP	SH	GW	GT	S	PCT
R	27	ALEX KOVALEV	78	37	40	77	-9	70	11		3	1	271	13.7
R	22	ANSON CARTER	79	26	34	60	-11	26	10		1	1	193	13.5
C	93	PETR NEDVED	78	27	31	58	-4	64	8	3	4	1	205	13.2
C	88	ERIC LINDROS	81	19	34	53	5	141	9		3		235	8.1
D	3	TOM POTI	80	11	37	48	-6	58	3		2		148	7.4
C	11	MARK MESSIER	78	18	22	40	-2	30	8	1	5	1	117	15.4
R	36	MATTHEW BARNABY	79	14	22	36	9	142	1		1	1	104	13.5
C	16	BOBBY HOLIK	64	16	19	35	-1	52	3		2		213	7.5
R	9	PAVEL BURE	39	19	11	30	4	16	5	1	3	1	136	14.0
D	2	BRIAN LEETCH	51	12	18	30	-3	20	5		2	1	150	8.0
C	26	*JAMIE LUNDMARK	55	8	11	19	-3	16					78	10.3
D	23	VLADIMIR MALAKHOV	71	3	14	17	-7	52	1				131	2.3
D	29	BORIS MIRONOV	56	6	10	16	2	56	2			1	70	8.6
R	10	SANDY MCCARTHY	82	6	9	15	-4	81			1		81	7.4
R	38	RONALD PETROVICKY	66	5	9	14	-12	77	2	1	1		65	7.7
D	6	DARIUS KASPARAITIS	80	3	11	14	5	85			1		84	3.6
D	5	DALE PURINTON	58	3	9	12	-2	161					50	6.0
L	39	DAN LACOUTURE	68	3	6	9	-4	72					47	6.4
D	18	*ALES PISA	51	1	3	4	12	24	1				37	2.7
L	8	TED DONATO	49	2	1	3	-1	6					30	6.7
R	42	*JOHN TRIPP	9	1	2	3	1	2					16	6.3
D	24	SYLVAIN LEFEBVRE	35		2	2	-7	10					14	
D	33	DAVE KARPA	19		2	2	-1	14					13	
L	12	DIXON WARD	8				-2	2					7	
R	44	BILLY TIBBETTS	11				-2	12					6	
C	28	ROMAN LYASHENKO	2				-2						4	
G	35	MIKE RICHTER	13				0							
G	30	MIKE DUNHAM	58				0							
D	22	MIKE WILSON	1				1							
G	40	JOHAN HOLMQVIST	1				0							
G	34	JASON LABARBERA					0							
L	47	BARRETT HEISTEN					0							
G	31	DAN BLACKBURN	32				0	2						

GP = games played; G = goals; A = assists; PTS = points; +/- = goals-for minus goals-against while player is on ice; PIM = penalties in minutes; PP = power-play goals; SH = shorthanded goals; GW = game-winning goals; GT = game-tying goals; S = no. of shots; PCT = percentage of goals to shots; * = rookie

MATTHEW BARNABY

Yrs. of NHL service: 10
Born: Ottawa, Ont.; May 4, 1973
Position: right wing
Height: 6-0
Weight: 189
Uniform no.: 36
Shoots: left

Career statistics:

GP	G	A	TP	PIM
631	88	136	224	2100

1999-2000 statistics:

GP	G	A	TP	+/-	PIM	PP	SH	GW	GT	S	PCT
64	12	12	24	+3	197	0	0	3	0	80	15.0

2000-2001 statistics:

GP	G	A	TP	+/-	PIM	PP	SH	GW	GT	S	PCT
76	5	8	13	-10	265	1	0	0	0	67	7.5

2001-2002 statistics:

GP	G	A	TP	+/-	PIM	PP	SH	GW	GT	S	PCT
77	8	13	21	-10	214	0	0	1	0	69	11.6

2002-2003 statistics:

GP	G	A	TP	+/-	PIM	PP	SH	GW	GT	S	PCT
79	14	22	36	+9	142	1	0	1	1	104	13.5

LAST SEASON

Second on team in plus-minus and penalty minutes. Missed three games with sprained right knee.

THE FINESSE GAME

Barnaby's offensive skills are minimal. He gets some room because of his reputation, and that buys him a little time around the net to get a shot away. He is utterly fearless and dives right into the thick of the action, going for loose pucks. But he has no hands — for scoring goals, that is.

No one hires Barnaby for his scoring touch. His game is marked by his fierce intensity. He hits anyone, but especially loves going after the other teams' big names. He is infuriating to play against.

He skates well enough not to look out of place and is strong and balanced on his feet. He will do anything to win. If he could develop a better scoring touch he would start reminding people of Dale Hunter.

THE PHYSICAL GAME

Barnaby is a human bobblehead doll. A little breeze from an opponent's stick and Barnaby's head snaps back to try to draw a penalty.

Barnaby brings a lot of energy to the game. Considering his size, it's a wonder he survives the season. He has to do some cheap stuff to survive, which makes him an even more irritating opponent. Big guys especially hate him because it's a no-win when a big bruiser takes on the poor underdog Barnaby. But he's so obnoxious they just can't help it.

THE INTANGIBLES

The Rangers were in such a state of disarray last season that Barnaby was actually their top right winger. He shouldn't even be playing on a second line, hard though he may try. He simply lacks the offensive instincts. But he has a knack for stirring up loose pucks as well as trouble, and loves the game so much that you can seldom fault his effort.

PROJECTION

Barnaby far exceeded our expectations for productivity and also cut down on unnecessary penalties. Another 35-point, 150 PIM season would be a plus.

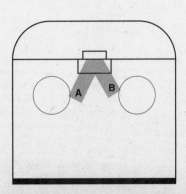

PAVEL BURE

Yrs. of NHL service: 12
Born: Moscow, Russia; Mar. 31, 1971
Position: right wing
Height: 5-10
Weight: 189
Uniform no.: 9
Shoots: left

Career statistics:

GP	G	A	TP	PIM
702	437	342	779	484

1999-2000 statistics:

GP	G	A	TP	+/-	PIM	PP	SH	GW	GT	S	PCT
74	58	36	94	+25	16	11	2	14	0	360	16.1

2000-2001 statistics:

GP	G	A	TP	+/-	PIM	PP	SH	GW	GT	S	PCT
82	59	33	92	-2	58	19	5	8	3	384	15.4

2001-2002 statistics:

GP	G	A	TP	+/-	PIM	PP	SH	GW	GT	S	PCT
68	34	35	69	-5	62	12	1	2	1	287	11.8

2002-2003 statistics:

GP	G	A	TP	+/-	PIM	PP	SH	GW	GT	S	PCT
39	19	11	30	+4	16	5	1	3	1	136	14.0

LAST SEASON

Second on team in shooting percentage. Tied for third on team in game-winning goals. Missed 31 games due to knee surgery on both knees. Missed nine games due to right knee injury.

THE FINESSE GAME

Bure needs to play with linemates who move the puck to him quickly and let him do the work. Bure is a selfish player, in the positive sense of the word. He is a gifted scorer, so he should shoot and not look for a pass. Let his assists come from rebounds off the goalies' pads or teammates recovering one of his bullet shots off the glass. Bure averages four shots on goal per game and six to eight that whistle wide.

Goalies never know when Bure's shot is going to come. He keeps his legs churning and the shot is on net before the keeper knows it. He does not telegraph his shot by breaking stride, and it's an awesome sight. He has great balance and agility; he moves equally well both with the puck and without it. Bure is always lurking and looking for the headman pass.

The Russian Rocket's quickness — and his control of the puck at supersonic speed — means anything is possible. He intimidates with his skating, driving back defenders who must play off him or risk being deked out of their skates at the blueline. He opens up tremendous ice for his teammates and will leave a drop pass or, more often, try to do it himself. However, multiple knee surgeries now on both of his legs over the past few years raise a huge red flag about Bure's ability to return at full speed.

Bure doesn't do much defensively. All he cares about is the scoring half of the ice. When he is going through a slump he doesn't do the other little things that can make a player useful until the scoring starts to kick in again. He is a shorthanded threat because of his speed and anticipation. He is one of the best breakaway scorers in the league. His explosive skating comes from his thick, powerful thighs, which look like a speed skater's.

THE PHYSICAL GAME

Bure has a little nasty edge to him, and will make solid hits for the puck, though he doesn't apply himself as enthusiastically in a defensive role. He has to play a reckless game to drive to the net and score goals. He takes a lot of punishment getting there and that's what makes him vulnerable to injuries.

THE INTANGIBLES

When Bure is healthy and motivated, he is one of the most dynamic players in the game. We're just not sure Bure will be either of those this season.

PROJECTION

Can Bure return to 50-goal, 100-point status at age 32? Can he even play 50 games? Too many questions, and not enough answers. Caution is advised.

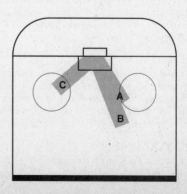

ANSON CARTER

Yrs. of NHL service: 7
Born: Toronto, Ont.; June 6, 1974
Position: right wing
Height: 6-1
Weight: 200
Uniform no.: 22
Shoots: right

Career statistics:

GP	G	A	TP	PIM
452	143	167	310	150

1999-2000 statistics:

GP	G	A	TP	+/-	PIM	PP	SH	GW	GT	S	PCT
59	22	25	47	+8	14	4	0	1	1	144	15.3

2000-2001 statistics:

GP	G	A	TP	+/-	PIM	PP	SH	GW	GT	S	PCT
61	16	26	42	+1	23	7	1	4	0	102	15.7

2001-2002 statistics:

GP	G	A	TP	+/-	PIM	PP	SH	GW	GT	S	PCT
82	28	32	60	+3	25	12	0	6	0	181	15.5

2002-2003 statistics:

GP	G	A	TP	+/-	PIM	PP	SH	GW	GT	S	PCT
79	26	34	60	-11	26	10	0	1	1	193	13.5

with the Rangers.

PROJECTION

Carter should score 25 goals, but with the Rangers in such disarray, it's hard to guess exactly what his role will be this season.

LAST SEASON

Acquired from Edmonton with Ales Pisa on March 11, 2003, for Cory Cross and Radek Dvorak. Second on Rangers in points and power-play goals. Third on team in goals. Tied for third on team in assists.

THE FINESSE GAME

Carter is a deceptive skater with a long, rangy, loping stride, but he isn't a bit awkward in turns. What really sets him apart, though, is his hockey intelligence. He thinks the game well in all zones. He is capable of playing center but is better utilized as a winger.

Carter has pushed himself hard to improve his skating and shooting, and both skills are now polished. He is worthy of handling key ice time on the top two forward lines and now he has the production to match his effort.

Carter drives to the net well. He has good balance and is hard to knock off his skates. He isn't a power forward per se, but he goes into the high-traffic areas and has soft hands for receiving passes and releasing a quick shot. As well as working the power play, Carter is a smart penalty killer.

THE PHYSICAL GAME

A late bloomer physically, Carter still needs to add some muscle but he is not afraid to hit, not afraid to take a hit and, like Peter Forsberg, will make a preemptive hit while carrying the puck. He's not dirty or mean, just honestly tough.

THE INTANGIBLES

Carter came to the Rangers and immediately his play fell off a cliff. Carter had only one goal in 11 games

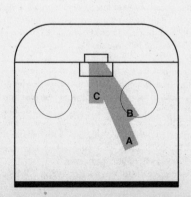

GREG DE VRIES

Yrs. of NHL service: 7
Born: Sundridge, Ont.; Jan. 4, 1973
Position: left defense
Height: 6-3
Weight: 215
Uniform no.: 7
Shoots: left

Career statistics:

GP	G	A	TP	PIM
500	30	69	99	459

1999-2000 statistics:

GP	G	A	TP	+/-	PIM	PP	SH	GW	GT	S	PCT
69	2	7	9	-7	73	0	0	0	0	40	5.0

2000-2001 statistics:

GP	G	A	TP	+/-	PIM	PP	SH	GW	GT	S	PCT
79	5	12	17	+23	51	0	0	0	0	76	6.6

2001-2002 statistics:

GP	G	A	TP	+/-	PIM	PP	SH	GW	GT	S	PCT
82	8	12	20	+18	57	1	1	3	0	148	5.4

2002-2003 statistics:

GP	G	A	TP	+/-	PIM	PP	SH	GW	GT	S	PCT
82	6	26	32	+15	70	0	0	2	0	112	5.3

LAST SEASON

One of four Avalanche players to appear in all 82 games.

THE FINESSE GAME

De Vries has spent a lot of years playing in the shadow of name defensemen like Ray Bourque and Rob Blake in Colorado, but now that he has become a free agent, that is about to change.

Don't expect a splash, because de Vries isn't a flashy kind of player. What he is, is smart and safe. De Vries is much better than Blake, for example, at knowing when to pinch and get involved offensively and when to back off. His shot isn't scary, but de Vries has an accurate slap from the point and also uses a long wrister effectively. He is a heads-up passer.

De Vries is a fine skater in all directions, agile, mobile, and with decent foot speed. He won't intimidate defenders to back off him on the rush. He is tough to beat one-on-one. He is a sound penalty killer. De Vries seldom gets panicky with the puck. He is poised and his defensive reads are fine. He can be used in all game situations. De Vries can handle second-unit power-play time and play four-on-four.

THE PHYSICAL GAME

De Vries is a solid player who will take the body. He doesn't make spectacular open-ice hits, but he takes care of the hard areas around his crease and in the corners. He is durable and in good condition and can handle a lot of minutes.

THE INTANGIBLES

De Vries will prove to be the best value among the available free-agent defensemen on the market last summer. He is a solid top-four defenseman. He will give as many quality minutes as Derian Hatcher and almost as many points, but for about half the paycheck.

PROJECTION

In the right spot, de Vries will earn 20-plus minutes of ice time per night and score 30 points.

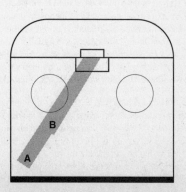

MIKE DUNHAM

Yrs. of NHL service: 7
Born: Johnson City, N.Y.; June 1, 1972
Position: goaltender
Height: 6-3
Weight: 200
Uniform no.: 30
Catches: left

Career statistics:

GP	MIN	GA	SO	GAA	A	PIM
301	16747	733	16	2.63	4	16

1999-2000 statistics:

GP	MIN	GAA	W	L	T	SO	GA	S	SAPCT	PIM
52	3077	2.85	19	27	6	0	146	1584	.908	6

2000-2001 statistics:

GP	MIN	GAA	W	L	T	SO	GA	S	SAPCT	PIM
48	2810	2.28	21	21	4	4	107	1381	.923	2

2001-2002 statistics:

GP	MIN	GAA	W	L	T	SO	GA	S	SAPCT	PIM
58	3316	2.61	23	24	9	3	144	1525	.906	2

2002-2003 statistics:

GP	MIN	GAA	W	L	T	SO	GA	S	SAPCT	PIM
58	3286	2.50	21	26	7	5	137	1626	.916	0

LAST SEASON

Acquired from Nashville on December 12, 2002, for Rem Murray, Tomas Kloucek, and Marek Zidlicky. Missed two games with groin injury. Missed one game with hamstring injury.

THE PHYSICAL GAME

Dunham is built well for the stand-up style he favors. He injects some butterfly elements, but for the most part he makes the best use of his size by staying upright and letting the puck hit him. He has to stay on his feet or his knees since he does not have great reflexes for close-in scrambles.

Dunham handles the puck fairly well. He is no Martin Brodeur, but he has obviously learned a great deal from being Brodeur's teammate for two years in New Jersey, and he helps out his defense by moving the puck. Dunham is easily the best puckhandling goalie the Rangers have ever had. He also uses his stick well to break up passes around the crease.

Dunham has some streaks of inconsistency, which may be more due to his frequent injuries than inexperience, since he is a rather seasoned goalie. He gives his team a chance to win every night by not allowing very many soft goals. There were a number of games last season that Dunham won all by his lonesome.

THE MENTAL GAME

Dunham is a poised performer, and has matured a lot over the years. He is very competitive and his years as Nashville's No. 1 goalie have given him the confidence that he can handle the job.

Injuries have been a factor over the past few years. The Rangers gave him very few nights off, and it had been awhile since he handled that kind of workload, a reason why he wore down later in the season.

This season will bring a new quandary for Dunham. If Mike Richter returns, and if the Rangers want to get young Dan Blackburn into more games, what becomes of Dunham? He finished last season as the No. 1 goalie, and deserves to be considered the same as training camp starts, but he could be put into an uncomfortable situation.

PROJECTION

Assuming a similar workload and a slightly improved Rangers team, Dunham could reach 30 wins.

BOBBY HOLIK

Yrs. of NHL service: 13
Born: Jihlava, Czech Republic; Jan. 1, 1971
Position: center
Height: 6-4
Weight: 230
Uniform no.: 16
Shoots: right

Career statistics:

GP	G	A	TP	PIM
942	256	330	586	1006

1999-2000 statistics:

GP	G	A	TP	+/-	PIM	PP	SH	GW	GT	S	PCT
79	23	23	46	+7	106	7	0	4	1	257	8.9

2000-2001 statistics:

GP	G	A	TP	+/-	PIM	PP	SH	GW	GT	S	PCT
80	15	35	50	+19	97	3	0	3	0	206	7.3

2001-2002 statistics:

GP	G	A	TP	+/-	PIM	PP	SH	GW	GT	S	PCT
81	25	29	54	+7	97	6	0	3	2	270	9.3

2002-2003 statistics:

GP	G	A	TP	+/-	PIM	PP	SH	GW	GT	S	PCT
64	16	19	35	-1	52	3	0	2	0	213	7.5

LAST SEASON

Third on team in shots. Missed 18 games due to hip injury.

THE FINESSE GAME

Few players combine brute strength and skill as well as Holik does. Holik is limited as a creative playmaker because he lacks vision. He plays a fairly straightforward power game and needs to play with wingers who do the same. He does not play well when forced to carry the puck. His best formula is to dump-and-chase, cycle, and create off the forecheck.

Holik has a terrific shot, a bullet drive he gets away quickly from a rush down the left side. He has great hands for working in-tight, in traffic, and off the backhand. On the backhand, Holik uses his bulk to obscure the vision of his defenders, protecting the puck and masking his intentions. He has a fair wrist shot.

He's a powerful skater with good balance, but lacks jump and agility. Once he starts churning, though, Holik can get up a good head of steam. He is more responsible defensively, and the Rangers used him to kill penalties, which he seldom did in his nine-year Devils career.

Holik is a face-off ace. When he doesn't win a draw cleanly, he almost always ties up his opposing number and prevents him from getting involved in the play. He ranked fifth in the NHL (58.2 per cent) among players who took more than 1,000 draws last season.

THE PHYSICAL GAME

Holik is just plain big. And mean. He's a serious hitter who can hurt and who applies his bone-jarring body checks at the appropriate times. And at inappropriate times. Holik takes a lot of bad penalties, a flaw that was masked on the Devils, who always had strong penalty killing. It is a far more disastrous weakness on the Rangers, whose PK was 29th among the 30 NHL teams last season.

Holik can be easily frustrated when he feels he is being hooked and held and the opposition isn't penalized. Holik plays with a smirk that is absolutely infuriating. He plays at his best when he is given a checking assignment to focus on, especially if he is matched against another physical center.

THE INTANGIBLES

Holik signed a lucrative five-year, $45 million free-agent deal with the Rangers in 2002. Holik is blunt and plain-spoken, and cares more about winning than making friends. This came as a great shock to the rest of the Rangers.

PROJECTION

Expect a better season — 20-25 goals and 50 points from Holik.

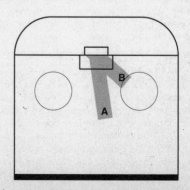

DARIUS KASPARAITIS

Yrs. of NHL service: 11
Born: Elektrenai, Lithuania; Oct. 16, 1972
Position: right defense
Height: 5-11
Weight: 212
Uniform no.: 6
Shoots: left

Career statistics:

GP	G	A	TP	PIM
728	24	119	143	1204

1999-2000 statistics:

GP	G	A	TP	+/-	PIM	PP	SH	GW	GT	S	PCT
73	3	12	15	-12	146	1	0	1	0	76	3.9

2000-2001 statistics:

GP	G	A	TP	+/-	PIM	PP	SH	GW	GT	S	PCT
77	3	16	19	+11	111	1	0	0	0	81	3.7

2001-2002 statistics:

GP	G	A	TP	+/-	PIM	PP	SH	GW	GT	S	PCT
80	2	12	14	0	142	0	0	0	0	81	2.5

2002-2003 statistics:

GP	G	A	TP	+/-	PIM	PP	SH	GW	GT	S	PCT
80	3	11	14	+5	85	0	0	1	0	84	3.6

LAST SEASON

Tied for second on team in plus-minus. Missed one game with rib injury. Missed one game with flu.

THE FINESSE GAME

Kasparaitis is a strong, powerful skater and he can accelerate in all directions. You can run but you can't hide from this defenseman, who accepts all challenges. He is aggressive in the neutral zone, often overly so, stepping up to break up a team's attack when he would be wiser to back off.

He has the skills to occasionally get involved in the offense, although it's not Kasparaitis's concern or his strength. He will make a sharp outlet pass and then follow up into the play. He also has good offensive instincts, moves the puck well and, if he plays on his off-side, will open up his forehand for the one-timer. He concentrates heavily on the physical part of his game, and would be happy going through the season without a point if he could wreak havoc elsewhere.

Kasparaitis has infectious enthusiasm, which is an inspiration to the rest of his team. He's highly competitive.

THE PHYSICAL GAME

It's always borderline interference with Kasparaitis, who uses his stick liberally, waiting three or four seconds after a victim has gotten rid of the puck to apply the lumber. Cross-check, butt-end, high stick — through the course of a single game Kasparaitis will usually illustrate all of the stick infractions.

His timing isn't always the best, and he has to think about the good of the team rather than indulging in his own vendettas. Kasparaitis is legitimately tough. It doesn't matter whose name is on back of the jersey — Tkachuk, Modano, Yashin — he will goad the stars and the heavyweights equally. He yaps, too, and is as irritating as a car alarm at 3 a.m.

THE INTANGIBLES

Kasparaitis played a very high-risk game with the Rangers and isn't the smartest of defensemen. He is best suited on a third defensive pairing but the Rangers often needed him in a more prominent role.

PROJECTION

Chalk up 80 PIM and maybe 20 points.

ALEXEI KOVALEV

Yrs. of NHL service: 11
Born: Togliatti, Russia; Feb. 24, 1973
Position: right wing
Height: 6-1
Weight: 220
Uniform no.: 27
Shoots: left

Career statistics:

GP	G	A	TP	PIM
771	278	357	635	836

1999-2000 statistics:

GP	G	A	TP	+/-	PIM	PP	SH	GW	GT	S	PCT
82	26	40	66	-3	94	9	2	4	1	254	10.2

2000-2001 statistics:

GP	G	A	TP	+/-	PIM	PP	SH	GW	GT	S	PCT
79	44	51	95	+12	96	12	2	9	1	307	14.3

2001-2002 statistics:

GP	G	A	TP	+/-	PIM	PP	SH	GW	GT	S	PCT
67	32	44	76	+2	80	8	1	3	2	266	12.0

2002-2003 statistics:

GP	G	A	TP	+/-	PIM	PP	SH	GW	GT	S	PCT
78	37	40	77	-9	70	11	0	3	1	271	13.7

LAST SEASON

Aqcuired from Pittsburgh with Janne Laukkanen, Dan LaCouture, and Mike Wilson on February 10, 2003, for Joel Bouchard, Rico Fata, Mikael Samuelsson, and Richard Lintner. Led Rangers in goals, assists, points, power-play goals, and shots. Third on team in ice time (22:51) and shooting percentage. Tied for third on team in game-winning goals.

THE FINESSE GAME

Kovalev managed to turn back into the same frustrating player he had been when he started his career with the Rangers from the minute he pulled the sweater back on after the trade. Kovalev did produce 10 goals (and three assists) in 24 games with the Rangers to finish the season, but never appeared to be the same wondrous player he had been in Pittsburgh.

You don't often see hands or feet as quick as Kovalev's on a player of his size. He has the dexterity, puck control, strength, balance, and speed to beat the first forechecker coming out of the zone or the first line of defense once he crosses the attacking blueline. Former linemate (and boss) Mario Lemieux called Kovalev the best stickhandler he has ever seen. He is one of the few players in the NHL agile and balanced enough to duck under a check at the sideboards and maintain possession of the puck. Exceptional hands allow him to make remarkable moves, but his hockey thought process doesn't always allow him to finish them off well. Kovalev has a deceptive wrist shot with a lightning release.

On many occasions, Kovalev's slithery moves don't do enough offensive damage. Many times he overhandles, then turns the puck over. Too many times, he fails to get the puck deep. He hates to surrender the puck even when dump-and-chase is the smartest option, and as a result he causes turnovers at the blueline and has to chase any number of opposition breakaways to his team's net. Every time Kovalev seems rid of these bad habits, they come sneaking back into his game.

Kovalev is often used on the point on the power play because of his excellent shot, but he is too much of a risk there and creates a lot of shorthanded chances for the other team.

THE PHYSICAL GAME

The chippier the game, the happier Kovalev is. He'll bring his stick up and wade into the fray. He can be sneaky dirty. He'll run goalies over and try to make it look as if he was pushed into them by a defender. He's so strong and balanced on his skates that when he goes down, odds are it's a dive. At the same time, he absorbs all kinds of physical punishment, legal and illegal, and rarely receives the benefit of the doubt from the referees.

Kovalev has very good size and is a willing hitter. He likes to make highlight-reel hits that splatter people. Because he is such a strong skater, he is very hard to knock down unless he's leaning. He makes extensive use of his edges because he combines balance and a long reach to keep the puck well away from his body, and from a defender's. But there are moments when he seems at a 45-degree angle and then he can be nudged over.

THE INTANGIBLES

The Rangers need to find complementary forwards for Kovalev and a better defensive system to make him less of a risk factor.

PROJECTION

Kovalev should be a point-a-game player.

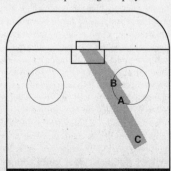

BRIAN LEETCH

Yrs. of NHL service: 15
Born: Corpus Christi, Tex.; Mar. 3, 1968
Position: left defense
Height: 6-1
Weight: 190
Uniform no.: 2
Shoots: left

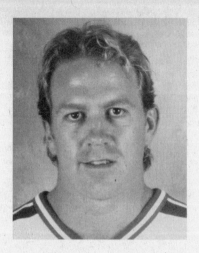

Career statistics:

GP	G	A	TP	PIM
1072	227	718	945	501

1999-2000 statistics:

GP	G	A	TP	+/-	PIM	PP	SH	GW	GT	S	PCT
50	7	19	26	-16	20	3	0	2	1	124	5.6

2000-2001 statistics:

GP	G	A	TP	+/-	PIM	PP	SH	GW	GT	S	PCT
82	21	58	79	-18	34	10	1	3	1	241	8.7

2001-2002 statistics:

GP	G	A	TP	+/-	PIM	PP	SH	GW	GT	S	PCT
82	10	45	55	+14	28	1	0	3	0	202	4.9

2002-2003 statistics:

GP	G	A	TP	+/-	PIM	PP	SH	GW	GT	S	PCT
51	12	18	30	-3	20	5	0	2	1	150	8.0

LAST SEASON

Led team in average ice time (26:05). Missed 31 games due to ankle injury.

THE FINESSE GAME

Leetch is a premier passer who sees the ice clearly, identifies the passing option on the move and hits his target with a forehand or backhand pass. He is terrific at picking passes out of the air and keeping clearing passes from getting by him at the point.

He has a fine first step that sends him close to top speed almost instantly. He can be posted at the point, then see an opportunity to jump into the play down low and bolt into action. His anticipation is superb. He seems to be thinking about five seconds ahead of everyone else. He instantly makes a transition from defense to offense, and always seems to make the right decision to pass or skate with the puck.

Leetch has a remarkable knack for getting his point shot through traffic and to the net. He even uses his eyes to fake. He is adept at looking and/or moving in one direction, then passing the opposite way.

He smartly jumps into holes to make the most of an odd-man rush, and he's quick enough to hop back on defense if the puck goes the other way. Leetch has astounding lateral movement, leaving forwards completely out of room when it looked like there was open ice to get past him. He uses this as a weapon on offense to open up space for his teammates.

Leetch has a range of shots. He'll use a slapper from the point, usually through a screen because it won't overpower any NHL goalie, but he'll also use a wrist shot from the circle. He is gifted with the one-on-one moves that help him wriggle in front for 10-footers on the forehand or backhand.

THE PHYSICAL GAME

Not a thumping hitter, Leetch is still capable of taking the body. He competes for the puck and is a first-rate penalty killer. He blocks shots. Leetch's major problem is overwork. The best thing to happen to him was the ankle injury, which resulted in a fresh Leetch for the late part of the season.

THE INTANGIBLES

Leetch played out his contract last season and Rangers GM Glen Sather played a little game of chicken with him. It was hardly a smart move by Sather.

PROJECTION

On a better team, Leetch would be a 70-point player. On the Rangers, he should score 50.

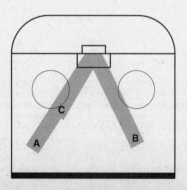

ERIC LINDROS

Yrs. of NHL service: 11
Born: London, Ont.; Feb. 28, 1973
Position: center
Height: 6-4
Weight: 240
Uniform no.: 88
Shoots: right

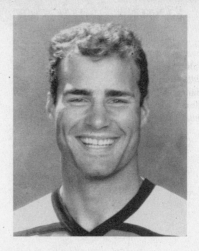

Career statistics:

GP	G	A	TP	PIM
639	346	439	785	1225

1999-2000 statistics:

GP	G	A	TP	+/-	PIM	PP	SH	GW	GT	S	PCT
55	27	32	59	+11	83	10	1	2	1	187	14.4

2000-2001 statistics:

Did not play in NHL

2001-2002 statistics:

GP	G	A	TP	+/-	PIM	PP	SH	GW	GT	S	PCT
72	37	36	73	+19	138	12	1	4	0	196	18.9

2002-2003 statistics:

GP	G	A	TP	+/-	PIM	PP	SH	GW	GT	S	PCT
81	19	34	53	+5	141	9	0	3	0	235	8.1

LAST SEASON

Second on team in shots. Tied for second on team in plus-minus. Third on team in penalty minutes and power-play goals. Tied for third on team in assists and game-winning goals. Missed one game due to NHL suspension.

THE FINESSE GAME

Lindros is not the physical presence he once was. After all of the concussions he has suffered through the years, he can't afford to be. Lindros has tried to survive by playing a perimeter game, and some nights, that's enough. Barely.

He is still big enough and skilled enough to demand a lot of room on the ice. He has a very good passing touch, which is underrated, and a shot that weighs a ton. Lindros has the balance and soft hands to control the puck in extremely tight quarters and make those nimble moves at the high speed he reaches quickly. That said, it remains more his nature to muscle the puck to a teammate or to the front of the net, and to let his strength do most of the work.

To offset the torque his arms can generate, the stick Lindros uses has an extremely firm shaft with only a slight curve to the blade. That helps on face-offs, adds velocity to his wrist and snap shots, and makes his backhand shot a significant weapon, both for its speed and its accuracy to the upper corners from close range.

THE PHYSICAL GAME

The notion that a player this big and as inherently mean as Lindros needs a bodyguard is absurd. Lindros can best help himself by keeping his head up. You would have thought he would have learned by now, but Lindros still looks down at his feet when he is steaming across the blueline, a perfect vulnerable position for another crushing blow.

Lindros takes some of the dumbest penalties at the worst times.

THE INTANGIBLES

Lindros can't afford to play scared, but he often does. The Rangers were looking to move him after last season, but he's a tough sell now.

PROJECTION

Lindros will get about 60 quiet points.

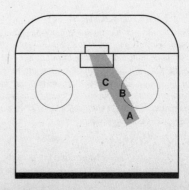

JAMIE LUNDMARK

Yrs. of NHL service: 1
Born: Edmonton, Alta.; Jan. 16, 1981
Position: center
Height: 6-0
Weight: 174
Uniform no.: 26
Shoots: right

Career statistics:

GP	G	A	TP	PIM
55	8	11	19	16

2002-2003 statistics:

GP	G	A	TP	+/-	PIM	PP	SH	GW	GT	S	PCT
55	8	11	19	-3	16	0	0	0	0	78	10.3

LAST SEASON

First NHL season. Missed one game with flu. Missed two games due to coach's decision. Appeared in 22 games with Hartford (AHL), scoring 9-9 — 18 with 18 PIM.

THE FINESSE GAME

Every quality Lundmark has is enhanced by his character and work ethic. He is an all-around player who could be a poor man's Steve Yzerman.

Lundmark does just about everything well, even though he is exceptional in no particular area. He is a strong skater, very well-balanced on his skates, with good speed. Lundmark has good lateral movement and agility and will be able to beat a defender one-on-one. He has very nice hands for passing. His shot is accurate with a decent release. He has to shoot more. Lundmark has a pretty hard slap shot.

He is a center by trade but played wing most of last season with Bobby Holik. His game is pretty advanced defensively for a young player. Lundmark uses his linemates well but Holik doesn't, which didn't make this duo very compatible. Lundmark would be a better player at center. Lundmark will develop into a player who can be used in all game situations. He can enhance a power play, kill penalties, and do the job at even strength or even four-on-four.

THE PHYSICAL GAME

Lundmark has been adding some much-needed muscle since his draft year (1999) and will need to continue to work on his strength and conditioning. He is tough in his own way, but not very aggressive, although he has a feisty streak that crops up every now and again. Lundmark won't be intimidated. He is getting harder to take off the puck and he is starting to initiate some hits now as well.

THE INTANGIBLES

Lundmark is a quiet kid who seems a bid awed by the presence of the Rangers veterans. This is not an easy team for a kid to break in with. Lundmark was yo-yoed to the minors through the first 50 games or so and was always one of the first players benched when things got tough. The Rangers will soon learn that Lundmark is a gamer.

PROJECTION

Lundmark can be expected to continue in a third-line role, which is likely his NHL future anyway. Should the Rangers give him more responsibility and minutes, he could step up his production to 30 points or so. He is likely to develop into a checking line player who can score 15 goals a season, which is not a bad asset. There is potential for him to develop into a second-line center but he will never be a big scorer.

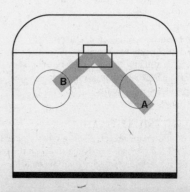

VLADIMIR MALAKHOV

Yrs. of NHL service: 11
Born: Ekaterinburg, Russia; Aug. 30, 1968
Position: left defense
Height: 6-4
Weight: 230
Uniform no.: 23
Shoots: left

Career statistics:

GP	G	A	TP	PIM
621	79	239	318	616

1999-2000 statistics:

GP	G	A	TP	+/-	PIM	PP	SH	GW	GT	S	PCT
24	1	4	5	+1	23	1	0	1	0	18	5.6

2000-2001 statistics:

GP	G	A	TP	+/-	PIM	PP	SH	GW	GT	S	PCT
3	0	2	2	0	4	0	0	0	0	6	0.0

2001-2002 statistics:

GP	G	A	TP	+/-	PIM	PP	SH	GW	GT	S	PCT
81	6	22	28	+10	83	1	0	0	0	145	4.1

2002-2003 statistics:

GP	G	A	TP	+/-	PIM	PP	SH	GW	GT	S	PCT
71	3	14	17	-7	52	1	0	0	0	131	2.3

LAST SEASON

Missed seven games due to shoulder injury. Missed four games due to back spasms.

THE FINESSE GAME

Malakhov has an absolute bullet of a shot; one of the hardest shots in the league. He rifles off a one-timer or shoots on the fly, and has outstanding offensive instincts for both shooting and playmaking. He moves the puck and jumps into the play alertly.

Malakhov is so talented he never looks like he's trying hard. Some nights he's not. He seems discouraged at times when things aren't going smoothly. If he tries a few plays early in a game that don't work, you might as well put him on the bench for the rest of the night. If he has a few good shifts early, especially offensively, odds are he'll be one of the three stars.

Defensively, Malakhov is in love with the poke check, and uses his long reach to cut down passing lanes. Malakhov can be used on both special teams. He is a mobile skater, with good agility and balance. He has a huge stride, and is fast but not necessarily agile. He can be easily turned the wrong way by a shifty attacker.

THE PHYSICAL GAME

Malakhov is a big guy and when he is inspired, he sticks and pins his man. He has a little bit of a mean streak. He doesn't fight often, but he is capable of winning a bout when he does get fired up. Malakhov blocks shots willingly.

THE INTANGIBLES

Malakhov always seems to be on the verge of becoming one of the game's top defensemen. He will just as quickly take a step back and play games where he is just about invisible. It's inexcusable for a player of his size and talent.

PROJECTION

Malakhov should be in the 40-point range but injuries have been a big factor the past few years. At 35, he may be just too brittle to be counted on for a full, healthy season any more.

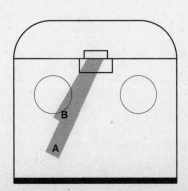

MARK MESSIER

Yrs. of NHL service: 24
Born: Edmonton, Alta.; Jan. 18, 1961
Position: center
Height: 6-1
Weight: 210
Uniform no.: 11
Shoots: left

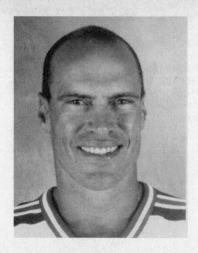

Career statistics:

GP	G	A	TP	PIM
1680	676	1168	1844	1868

1999-2000 statistics:

GP	G	A	TP	+/-	PIM	PP	SH	GW	GT	S	PCT
66	17	37	54	-15	30	6	0	4	0	131	13.0

2000-2001 statistics:

GP	G	A	TP	+/-	PIM	PP	SH	GW	GT	S	PCT
82	24	43	67	-25	89	12	3	2	0	131	18.3

2001-2002 statistics:

GP	G	A	TP	+/-	PIM	PP	SH	GW	GT	S	PCT
41	7	16	23	-1	32	2	0	2	0	69	10.1

2002-2003 statistics:

GP	G	A	TP	+/-	PIM	PP	SH	GW	GT	S	PCT
78	18	22	40	-2	30	8	1	5	1	117	15.4

LAST SEASON

Led Rangers in game-winning goals and shooting percentage. Missed one game with neck spasms. Missed one game with foot injury. Missed one game with left arm contusion. Missed one game with sprained ribs.

THE FINESSE GAME

Messier is strong on his skates. He changes directions, pivots, bursts into open ice, and, when his game is at its peak, does it all with or without the puck. He still has tremendous acceleration and a powerful burst of straightaway speed, which is tailor-made for killing penalties and scoring shorthanded goals — even if he cheats into the neutral zone, looking for a breakaway pass, too often.

Messier's shot of choice is a wrister off the back (his "wrong") foot from the right-wing circle, which is where he always seems to gravitate. It's a trademark, and it still fools many a goalie. He also makes good use of the backhand, for passing and shooting. Messier will weave to the right-wing circle, fake a pass to the center of the ice, get the goalie to cheat away from the post, then flip a backhand under the crossbar. He shoots from almost anywhere and is unpredictable in his shot selection when the back-foot wrister is not available.

Messier has always been better at making the utmost use of his teammates, rather than trying one-on-one moves. His hallmark is his bottomless determination to win, which prevents his more skilled — but less brave — cohorts from faltering. He just drags them right to the front lines with him. Defensively, Messier has become a liability.

THE PHYSICAL GAME

The Messier mean streak is legendary, but less frequently evident. He is a master of the pre-emptive strike, the elbows, or stick held teeth-high when a checker is coming towards him. The more ice time Messier saw in a game last season, the worse the result, but it's hard to tell this proverbial 800-pound gorilla to take a seat.

THE INTANGIBLES

There are few better big-game players in NHL history than Messier, but the past is the past. Messier was an unrestricted free agent after last season.

PROJECTION

Messier is at best a third-line forward. It's just a question of whether this great player can mentally accept a part-time role.

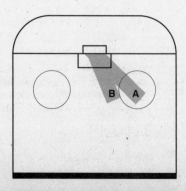

PETR NEDVED

Yrs. of NHL service: 12
Born: Liberec, Czech Republic; Dec. 9, 1971
Position: center
Height: 6-3
Weight: 195
Uniform no.: 93
Shoots: left

Career statistics:

GP	G	A	TP	PIM
808	282	352	634	564

1999-2000 statistics:

GP	G	A	TP	+/-	PIM	PP	SH	GW	GT	S	PCT
76	24	44	68	+2	40	6	2	4	0	201	11.9

2000-2001 statistics:

GP	G	A	TP	+/-	PIM	PP	SH	GW	GT	S	PCT
79	32	46	78	+10	54	9	1	5	0	230	13.9

2001-2002 statistics:

GP	G	A	TP	+/-	PIM	PP	SH	GW	GT	S	PCT
78	21	25	46	-8	36	6	1	3	1	175	12.0

2002-2003 statistics:

GP	G	A	TP	+/-	PIM	PP	SH	GW	GT	S	PCT
78	27	31	58	-4	64	8	3	4	1	205	13.2

LAST SEASON

Led team in shorthanded goals. Second on team in goals and game-winning goals. Third on team in points. Missed four games due to hip injury.

THE FINESSE GAME

When he gets in a slump, Nedved quickly reverts to his old bad habit of overpassing. Too often he gets in the best position to shoot and instead forces a pass that is knocked down or picked off. Nedved makes use of time and space. He has an excellent wrist shot with a hair-trigger release and radar-like accuracy. He likes to go high on the glove side, picking the corner.

He plays best with linemates who are well-schooled in European-style hockey. The Rangers occasionally use him as a power-play quarterback, which is all wrong. He lacks a heavy shot from the point and a shooter's confidence, and is better up front on the half-boards.

Tall but slightly built, he is good at handling the puck in traffic or in open ice at tempo. He sees the ice well and has a creative mind. Good on attacking-zone draws, Nedved knows his way around a face-off. He has good hand quickness and cheats well. On offensive-zone draws, he turns his body so that he's almost facing the boards. That's about it for his defensive contribution, though he can kill penalties because of his quickness and anticipation. Nedved frequently gets confused in his defensive assignments.

THE PHYSICAL GAME

Nedved was motivated to atone for his previous poor season and stepped up his game a notch last year. He is built along fairly willowy lines, which prevents him from playing any sort of domination game. He isn't exactly soft, nor is he as averse to contact as his reputation indicates. Nedved is simply not very aggressive.

THE INTANGIBLES

After being booed every time he touched the puck in the Garden in 2001-02, Nedved responded by becoming the Rangers' most consistent forward (and we mean consistently good — there were a number of consistently bad ones last year).

PROJECTION

Nedved is a 60-point scorer and his trade value is about the best on the Rangers — which could see him on the move this season.

TOM POTI

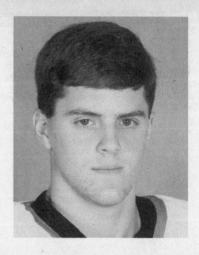

Yrs. of NHL service: 5
Born: Worcester, Mass.; Mar. 22, 1977
Position: left defense
Height: 6-3
Weight: 215
Uniform no.: 3
Shoots: left

Career statistics:

GP	G	A	TP	PIM
376	39	122	161	269

1999-2000 statistics:

GP	G	A	TP	+/-	PIM	PP	SH	GW	GT	S	PCT
76	9	26	35	+8	65	2	1	1	0	125	7.2

2000-2001 statistics:

GP	G	A	TP	+/-	PIM	PP	SH	GW	GT	S	PCT
81	12	20	32	-4	60	6	0	3	0	161	7.4

2001-2002 statistics:

GP	G	A	TP	+/-	PIM	PP	SH	GW	GT	S	PCT
66	2	23	25	-10	44	2	0	1	0	109	1.8

2002-2003 statistics:

GP	G	A	TP	+/-	PIM	PP	SH	GW	GT	S	PCT
80	11	37	48	-6	58	3	0	2	0	148	7.4

LAST SEASON

Tied for eighth among NHL defensemen in points. Led team defensemen in points. Second on team in ice time and assists. Missed one game with flu. Missed one game with neck injury.

THE FINESSE GAME

Poti is a good — but not great — "offenseman." He doesn't score enough points to compensate for his defensive lapses, which are major and plentiful. If he fails to either up his production or cut down on his defensive miscues, he is trouble to have in a lineup.

Early in his Edmonton career, Poti was likened to a young Paul Coffey. That comparison was never fair, and it looks like Poti will not become an elite offensive defenseman, but at least he has a good role model in New York in Brian Leetch, his frequent defense partner.

Poti is a fine puckhandler and passer. He has good vision and can spring to teammates with headman passes. He carries the puck with speed and disguises his intentions. He is an excellent skater. Poti uses a low shot from the point that isn't a rocket, so teammates can take advantage of it for tip-ins. He needs to work on his defense to become a better all-round player. He is intelligent and should keep developing.

THE PHYSICAL GAME

What don't we like? Well, Poti is soft. He has decent size but doesn't use it well. He is still adding some muscle and needs to throw his weight around a bit more and add some grit to his game. He prefers to use his stick instead of his body to do the defensive work. He has to deal with a medical condition, a severe food allergy, which forces him to pay strict attention to his nutrition and condition. His effortless skating style helps him handle a lot of minutes.

Leetch, until he gets worn down late in a season, can play with an edge, block shots, and at least play the body. Poti needs to watch and learn.

THE INTANGIBLES

Poti carried a lot of the minutes while Leetch was out last season. Poti is a smart, likable guy, and a good team man, but his defensive deficiencies are maddening.

PROJECTION

He'll score 50 points but he'll still manage to be a minus player.

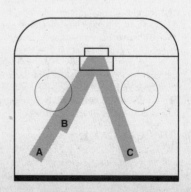

OTTAWA SENATORS

Players' Statistics 2001-2002

POS.	NO.	PLAYER	GP	G	A	PTS	+/-	PIM	PP	SH	GW	GT	S	PCT
R	18	MARIAN HOSSA	80	45	35	80	8	34	14		10	1	229	19.6
R	11	DANIEL ALFREDSSON	78	27	51	78	15	42	9		6		240	11.3
C	28	TODD WHITE	80	25	35	60	19	28	8	1	5		144	17.4
L	9	MARTIN HAVLAT	67	24	35	59	20	30	9		4		179	13.4
C	14	RADEK BONK	70	22	32	54	6	36	11		4	2	146	15.1
C	21	BRYAN SMOLINSKI	68	21	25	46	0	20	6	1	8		176	11.9
D	6	WADE REDDEN	76	10	35	45	23	70	4		3		154	6.5
D	3	ZDENO CHARA	74	9	30	39	29	116	3		2		168	5.3
C	12	MIKE FISHER	74	18	20	38	13	54	5	1	3		142	12.7
L	20	MAGNUS ARVEDSON	80	16	21	37	13	48	2		4		138	11.6
C	22	SHAUN VAN ALLEN	78	12	20	32	17	66	2	2	3		53	22.6
D	23	KAREL RACHUNEK	58	4	25	29	23	30	3		1		110	3.6
L	15	PETER SCHAEFER	75	6	17	23	11	32			1		93	6.4
C	39	*JASON SPEZZA	33	7	14	21	-3	8	3				65	10.8
R	26	VACLAV VARADA	55	9	10	19	1	31	2				81	11.1
L	19	PETR SCHASTLIVY	33	9	10	19	3	4	5		2		68	13.2
D	4	CHRIS PHILLIPS	78	3	16	19	7	71	2		1		97	3.1
D	24	*ANTON VOLCHENKOV	57	3	13	16	-4	40					75	4.0
R	16	JODY HULL	70	3	8	11	-3	14			1		42	7.1
R	25	CHRIS NEIL	68	6	4	10	8	147					62	9.7
D	34	SHANE HNIDY	67		8	8	-1	130					58	
D	7	CURTIS LESCHYSHYN	54	1	6	7	11	18					30	3.3
D	2	BRIAN POTHIER	14	2	4	6	11	6			1		23	8.7
R	38	BRAD SMYTH	12	3	1	4	-2	15	2				16	18.8
R	10	*TONI DAHLMAN	12	1		1	-1				1		5	20.0
R	33	*JOSH LANGFELD	12		1	1	2	4					16	
R	32	ROB RAY	46				-5	96					14	
R	27	DENNIS BONVIE	12				-1	29					3	
R	36	JOEY TETARENKO	4				-1	9					3	
G	40	PATRICK LALIME	67				0	6						
G	35	SIMON LAJEUNESSE					0							
G	31	MARTIN PRUSEK	18				0							
G	1	RAY EMERY	3				0							

GP = games played; G = goals; A = assists; PTS = points; +/- = goals-for minus goals-against while player is on ice; PIM = penalties in minutes; PP = power-play goals; SH = shorthanded goals; GW = game-winning goals; GT = game-tying goals; S = no. of shots; PCT = percentage of goals to shots; * = rookie

DANIEL ALFREDSSON

Yrs. of NHL service: 8
Born: Grums, Sweden; Dec. 11, 1972
Position: right wing
Height: 5-11
Weight: 195
Uniform no.: 11
Shoots: right

Career statistics:

GP	G	A	TP	PIM
552	187	301	488	235

1999-2000 statistics:

GP	G	A	TP	+/-	PIM	PP	SH	GW	GT	S	PCT
57	21	38	59	+11	28	4	2	0	0	164	12.8

2000-2001 statistics:

GP	G	A	TP	+/-	PIM	PP	SH	GW	GT	S	PCT
68	24	46	70	+11	30	10	0	3	1	206	11.7

2001-2002 statistics:

GP	G	A	TP	+/-	PIM	PP	SH	GW	GT	S	PCT
78	37	34	71	+3	45	9	1	4	2	243	15.2

2002-2003 statistics:

GP	G	A	TP	+/-	PIM	PP	SH	GW	GT	S	PCT
78	27	51	78	+15	42	9	0	6	0	240	11.3

LAST SEASON

Tied for 10th in NHL in assists. Led team in assists and shots. Second on team in goals and points. Third on team in game-winning goals. Tied for third on team in power-play goals. Missed three games with back injury. Missed one game with hip injury.

THE FINESSE GAME

Considering that Alfredsson hasn't played with a No. 1 center most of his career in Ottawa, he has compiled some pretty remarkable numbers.

Alfredsson's release is hair-trigger, and he has one of the best shots in the league. He also has a solid work ethic. He didn't make it to the NHL by being on cruise control. Alfredsson has to work for his space. One of the reasons why he is so good on the power play is because of his work in open ice. Alfredsson can work the power play off the half-boards but the Senators frequently use him at the point. He has excellent vision and hands. He can be quiet an entire game and then kill a team with two shots. Think of Alfredsson as a stealth bomber.

Alfredsson likes to play a puck-control game and needs to work with other forwards who will distribute the puck. Alfredsson is well schooled in the defensive aspects of the game, and he works diligently along the wall. He is a constant shorthanded threat when killing penalties because of his speed and anticipation. There are few better players in the league one-on-one or on the breakaway. He has reduced the curve of his blade a bit for improved puck control.

THE PHYSICAL GAME

Alfredsson has a very thick and powerful lower body to fuel his skating. He is fearless and takes a lot of abuse to get into the high-scoring areas. He will skate up the wall and cut to the middle of the ice. He might get nailed by the off-side defenseman, but on the next rush he will try it again. He won't be scared off, and on the next chance he may get the shot away and in.

THE INTANGIBLES

The talent around Alfredsson keeps getting deeper and their presence is elevating his game.

PROJECTION

Alfredsson is a point-a-game player, respected by teammates and opponents alike.

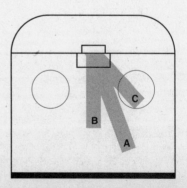

MAGNUS ARVEDSON

Yrs. of NHL service: 6
Born: Karlstad, Sweden; Nov. 25, 1971
Position: left wing
Height: 6-2
Weight: 198
Uniform no.: 20
Shoots: left

Career statistics:

GP	G	A	TP	PIM
393	92	118	210	229

1999-2000 statistics:

GP	G	A	TP	+/-	PIM	PP	SH	GW	GT	S	PCT
47	15	13	28	+4	36	1	1	4	1	91	16.5

2000-2001 statistics:

GP	G	A	TP	+/-	PIM	PP	SH	GW	GT	S	PCT
51	17	16	33	+23	24	1	2	4	0	79	21.5

2001-2002 statistics:

GP	G	A	TP	+/-	PIM	PP	SH	GW	GT	S	PCT
74	12	27	39	+27	35	0	0	1	0	121	9.9

2002-2003 statistics:

GP	G	A	TP	+/-	PIM	PP	SH	GW	GT	S	PCT
80	16	21	37	+13	48	2	0	4	0	138	11.6

PROJECTION

Arvedson is a checking forward who can produce 15-20 goals. A valuable combination.

LAST SEASON

Missed one game due to knee injury. Missed one game due to personal reasons.

THE FINESSE GAME

Arvedson has great speed and is strong on the puck. He wasn't much of a scorer coming up to the NHL and that isn't about to change now. Arvedson has a good shot but he doesn't use it enough. He is unselfish and will usually look to set up a teammate. He is an accurate shooter when he does fire.

Arvedson has some offensive upside, but he just doesn't seem interested in pushing the envelope. He is good and smart enough to play on one of the top two lines, maybe in a defensive-minded, Jere Lehtinen type of role, although he is probably best suited to play on a third line.

He is good enough defensively that he was a Selke Trophy candidate in only his second NHL season. He kills penalties and can be used as a checking center.

THE PHYSICAL GAME

Arvedson is big and strong and able to handle the rigours of an NHL schedule. He can handle a checking assignment to cover the top players, kill penalties, and contribute offensively.

THE INTANGIBLES

Arvedson became an unrestricted free agent after last season. If the Senators lose him, that will leave a conspicuous hole on their left side. Arvedson isn't a gaudy player, but he does a lot of little things well and doesn't look out of place, even on a skilled team like the Sens.

RADEK BONK

Yrs. of NHL service: 9
Born: Krnov, Czech Republic; Jan. 9, 1976
Position: center
Height: 6-3
Weight: 210
Uniform no.: 14
Shoots: left

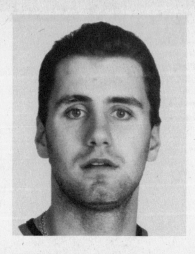

Career statistics:

GP	G	A	TP	PIM
623	140	215	355	335

1999-2000 statistics:

GP	G	A	TP	+/-	PIM	PP	SH	GW	GT	S	PCT
80	23	37	60	-2	53	10	0	5	1	167	13.8

2000-2001 statistics:

GP	G	A	TP	+/-	PIM	PP	SH	GW	GT	S	PCT
74	23	36	59	+27	52	5	2	3	0	139	16.5

2001-2002 statistics:

GP	G	A	TP	+/-	PIM	PP	SH	GW	GT	S	PCT
82	25	45	70	+3	52	6	2	5	0	170	14.7

2002-2003 statistics:

GP	G	A	TP	+/-	PIM	PP	SH	GW	GT	S	PCT
70	22	32	54	+6	36	11	0	4	2	146	15.1

LAST SEASON

Second on team in power-play goals and shooting percentage. Missed eight games due to chest injuries. Missed two games with lower back injury. Missed two games with thigh injury.

THE FINESSE GAME

Considering the flaws in his game — his lack of foot speed being the biggest thing holding him back — Bonk is a competent No. 2 center. The problem is the Senators employ him as a No. 1. You have to give Bonk high marks for trying, and you can't blame him when he is bested because of the talent gap.

Bonk's skating is fine when he gets a good head of steam up, but he doesn't explode in his first two strides (the way Joe Sakic does, for example). Bonk can't utilize his skills when he can't accelerate away from stick-checks. His skating is the primary reason why he has not been able to be an impact scorer in the NHL as he was in the minors.

Bonk makes the best of the situation, especially when he is situated between Marian Hossa, one of the most gifted young forwards in the game, and Magnus Arvedson. The trio does a good job of cycling the puck low. Bonk protects the puck well and is responsible defensively.

Bonk is a puck magnet; the puck always seems to end up on his stick in the slot. He scores the majority of his goals from work in-tight, getting his stick free. He has a heavy shot but doesn't have a quick release. He is a smart and creative passer and plays well in advance of his years, with a great deal of poise.

Defensively, Bonk keeps improving. He is decent on face-offs, and can be used to kill penalties because of his anticipation. He is a poor-man's Bobby Holik when he plays with a little edge.

THE PHYSICAL GAME

Although Bonk has good size, he does not show signs of becoming a power forward. He is aggressive only in pursuit of the puck. He goes into the corners and wins many one-on-one battles because of his strength and hand skills. He can lose his cool and will take the occasional bad penalty.

THE INTANGIBLES

Bonk has overachieved for so long now that he's taken for granted, but given how hard Bonk had to work to get this good, he deserves a lot of credit.

PROJECTION

Bonk can be expected to score an assist-heavy 60 points.

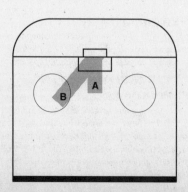

ZDENO CHARA

Yrs. of NHL service: 6
Born: Trencin, Slovakia; Mar. 18, 1977
Position: right defense
Height: 6-9
Weight: 255
Uniform no.: 3
Shoots: left

Career statistics:

GP	G	A	TP	PIM
380	25	66	91	619

1999-2000 statistics:

GP	G	A	TP	+/-	PIM	PP	SH	GW	GT	S	PCT
65	2	9	11	-27	57	0	0	1	1	47	4.3

2000-2001 statistics:

GP	G	A	TP	+/-	PIM	PP	SH	GW	GT	S	PCT
82	2	7	9	-27	157	0	1	0	0	83	2.4

2001-2002 statistics:

GP	G	A	TP	+/-	PIM	PP	SH	GW	GT	S	PCT
75	10	13	23	+30	156	4	1	2	0	105	9.5

2002-2003 statistics:

GP	G	A	TP	+/-	PIM	PP	SH	GW	GT	S	PCT
74	9	30	39	+29	116	3	0	2	0	168	5.3

LAST SEASON

Led team in plus-minus. Second on team in average ice time (24:57). Third on team in penalty minutes. Missed eight games with chest injury.

THE FINESSE GAME

For a player of his height, Chara is very well-coordinated. He has worked on his foot speed which enables him to get in a better position for his checks. Chara's number of hits has risen because he is able to line up players and stay in motion. If he is out of position at all, his hits are sure to be called high sticks and elbows, for the simple reason that he is so much taller than everyone else — their faces just happen to be in the wrong place. By keeping his hands down and his feet moving, Chara can avoid taking needless penalties. He can also register a more jarring legal check.

Chara has to keep the game simple, and he has to stay alert. If Chara does start losing body position, opposing teams can start a scramble in his zone and Chara has to work hard just to recover.

Chara moves the puck well but he has a tendency to admire his passes, like a baseball player waiting to break into a slow home-run jog around the bases. This leaves him open to hits when he is off-balance.

With his long arms, long stick, and long body, Chara makes a daunting screen up front on the power play, where the Senators often used him.

THE PHYSICAL GAME

Chara is solid, with a good center of gravity that is rare to find in a player of his altitude. Players simply bounce off him. He goes through phases when he loses his edge, though. When he starts getting those high-sticking calls he has a tendency to back down for a while. He doesn't mind a good scrap, and he has awfully long arms to tag a combatant. He routinely handles assignments against other teams' top lines. He loves to hit.

THE INTANGIBLES

Chara is often his own worst enemy because he demands so much of himself. He has a great reputation as a gamer, and as a kid who is coachable and willing to work to improve his game. At six-foot-nine, he is the tallest defenseman in NHL history. He and Chris Phillips worked well together last season as Ottawa's top defensive pair.

PROJECTION

Chara far surpassed the 25 points we projected for him last season. Considering his role on the offensively skilled Senators, we're going to upgrade the prediction to 40 points.

MIKE FISHER

Yrs. of NHL service: 4
Born: Peterborough, Ont.; June 5, 1980
Position: center
Height: 6-1
Weight: 193
Uniform no.: 12
Shoots: right

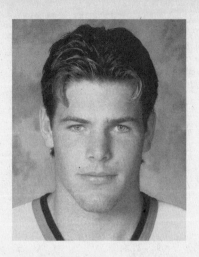

Career statistics:

GP	G	A	TP	PIM
224	44	46	90	170

1999-2000 statistics:

GP	G	A	TP	+/-	PIM	PP	SH	GW	GT	S	PCT
32	4	5	9	-6	15	0	0	1	0	49	8.2

2000-2001 statistics:

GP	G	A	TP	+/-	PIM	PP	SH	GW	GT	S	PCT
60	7	12	19	-1	46	0	0	3	0	83	8.4

2001-2002 statistics:

GP	G	A	TP	+/-	PIM	PP	SH	GW	GT	S	PCT
58	15	9	24	+8	55	0	3	4	0	123	12.2

2002-2003 statistics:

GP	G	A	TP	+/-	PIM	PP	SH	GW	GT	S	PCT
74	18	20	38	+13	54	5	1	3	0	142	12.7

LAST SEASON

Career highs in goals, assists, and points. Missed five games with shoulder injury. Missed two games with knee injury. Missed one game with flu.

THE FINESSE GAME

Power forwards take a long time to develop, so Senators fans should be patient. Fisher is right on target. Ottawa has a lot of highly skilled, creative forwards, but the Sens also need a guy who'll crash the net to score, and Fisher is that player.

None of Fisher's skills are elite, but he has a very good all-round game and is rapidly developing into a very reliable forward who can play center or wing. Fisher is a good skater. He puts his speed and agility to work on a smart forechecking game. He is well-balanced and shifty on his feet. He possesses good instincts and intelligence; he reads plays well in all zones.

Fisher is developing into a keen penalty killer because of his speed and anticipation. He plays a good puck-control game and creates time and space for his linemates with his patience with the puck. He has a deft passing touch. Fisher doesn't have a great shot. His scoring chances come from his desire and his willingness to drive to the front of the net. Fisher's work pays off with some close-range goals. Fisher can't quite dominate against NHL defensemen the way he did when he was a high-scoring junior player, but he is showing a taste for the battle now.

THE PHYSICAL GAME

Amid a finesse-laden lineup in Ottawa, Fisher stands out because of his willingness to play a physical game.

He plays an in-your-face style and uses speed as an aggressive weapon. He wins most of his battles for loose pucks. He has decent size but is still growing. Fisher is very competitive and will sacrifice his body to make a play. Fisher finishes his checks and plays with high energy on a consistent basis. As he gains confidence, he will become more of a force. He has a pretty long fuse, and won't be goaded into taking too many meaningless penalties.

THE INTANGIBLES

Fisher had a disappointing playoffs, but it was revealed afterward that he had played with an injured right wrist that required surgery. In another season or two, Fisher may take his place among the league's top power forwards.

PROJECTION

It seems whenever Fisher gets on a roll, he gets put back on the shelf again with another injury. We wouldn't bank on Fisher for much more than 60 games, and 30 points, until he gets past the injury bug.

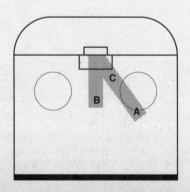

MARTIN HAVLAT

Yrs. of NHL service: 3
Born: Mlada Boleslav, Czech Republic; Apr. 19, 1981
Position: right wing
Height: 6-1
Weight: 190
Uniform no.: 9
Shoots: left

Career statistics:

GP	G	A	TP	PIM
212	65	86	151	116

2000-2001 statistics:

GP	G	A	TP	+/-	PIM	PP	SH	GW	GT	S	PCT
73	19	23	42	+8	20	7	0	5	0	133	14.3

2001-2002 statistics:

GP	G	A	TP	+/-	PIM	PP	SH	GW	GT	S	PCT
72	22	28	50	-7	66	9	0	6	1	145	15.2

2002-2003 statistics:

GP	G	A	TP	+/-	PIM	PP	SH	GW	GT	S	PCT
67	24	35	59	+20	30	9	0	4	0	179	13.4

LAST SEASON

Tied for second on team in assists. Third on team in shots. Tied for third on team in power-play goals. Missed 12 games with groin injuries. Missed two games with elbow injury.

THE FINESSE GAME

Havlat is an excellent, speedy skater with a huge reserve of confidence. He has superb one-on-one moves, and can leave far more experienced players in a tangle as he dipsy-doodles past them. By the way, he loves to do that. He'd rather make pretzels out of defenders than take a more direct route to the net.

Havlat could develop along Claude Lemieux lines, thanks to the way he plays with an edge. He is a catalyst, and plays the game hard both ways. He has the hand skills to back up his brash style. He tends to score big, clutch goals. Havlat is grating enough to goad even smart players into taking a retaliatory penalty. To rub it in, Havlat will go out and score on the power play.

A creative player, Havlat also combines well with his teammates rather than trying to make everything a solo effort. They have to read off him, though, because Havlat has a lot of tricks up his sleeve and is happy to make use of all of them in a single attack. He loves to shoot, but he is also a totally unselfish player who uses his teammates well.

THE PHYSICAL GAME

Havlat is average-sized but plays much bigger. He is game-tough. Havlat has a powerful lower body that allows him a burst of acceleration in his skating. Teammate Marian Hossa would probably win a rink-long dash, but for sprints, Havlat's the man.

THE INTANGIBLES

Havlat has been bugged by groin injuries for two seasons, or else his numbers could put him among the league leaders.

PROJECTION

Havlat will surpass the 30-goal, 70-point mark if he stays healthy.

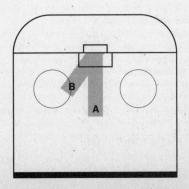

MARIAN HOSSA

Yrs. of NHL service: 5
Born: Stara Lubovna, Slovakia; Jan. 12, 1979
Position: right wing
Height: 6-1
Weight: 199
Uniform no.: 18
Shoots: left

Career statistics:

GP	G	A	TP	PIM
386	152	156	308	197

1999-2000 statistics:

GP	G	A	TP	+/-	PIM	PP	SH	GW	GT	S	PCT
78	29	27	56	+5	32	5	0	4	0	240	12.1

2000-2001 statistics:

GP	G	A	TP	+/-	PIM	PP	SH	GW	GT	S	PCT
81	32	43	75	+19	44	11	2	7	0	249	12.9

2001-2002 statistics:

GP	G	A	TP	+/-	PIM	PP	SH	GW	GT	S	PCT
80	31	35	66	+11	50	9	1	4	1	278	11.1

2002-2003 statistics:

GP	G	A	TP	+/-	PIM	PP	SH	GW	GT	S	PCT
80	45	35	80	+8	34	14	0	10	1	229	19.6

LAST SEASON

Fourth in NHL in goals. Third in NHL in game-winning goals. Fourth in NHL in shooting percentage. Led team in goals, points, power-play goals, game-winning goals, and shooting percentage. Second on team in shots. Tied for second on team in assists. Missed two games due to flu.

THE FINESSE GAME

Hossa has the kind of rink-long speed that can throw an opposing team's defense into utter chaos. Defensemen see Hossa flying and know they have to get their feet moving or they'll be turned into human pylons. If a defenseman cheats to the outside, Hossa will deftly cut inside. He would prefer to take the shortest route to the net anyway.

Hossa is a pure goal-scorer, with excellent hands that keep pace with his flashing blades. He owns the kind of instincts that cannot be taught or drilled into a player. He is nothing short of brilliant on the attack, and destined to be a great, great scorer. His ability to finish is without equal in his age group.

Hossa is a swift and mobile skater, always dangerous one-on-one. Hossa works hard in the offensive zone, but needs to work on his defensive game and his play without the puck. He also needs to be more consistent in his effort. He is used to kill penalties and is a shorthanded threat.

Hossa works down low, has keen hockey sense, excellent vision, size, and skating ability. This guy is the complete offensive package.

THE PHYSICAL GAME

Hossa uses his size well — better in the offensive zone than the rest of the ice. He isn't shy about physical play at all. But Ottawa is still a pretty soft team and he gets bounced around a lot more than he should.

THE INTANGIBLES

Hossa is only going to get better. He is one of the most exciting young players in the NHL.

PROJECTION

This is the year Hossa gets the Rocket Richard Trophy. We expect 50 to 55 goals from Hossa, which should be enough to do it.

PATRICK LALIME

Yrs. of NHL service: 7
Born: St. Bonaventure, Que.; July 7, 1974
Position: goaltender
Height: 6-3
Weight: 185
Uniform no.: 40
Catches: left

Career statistics:

GP	MIN	GA	SO	GAA	A	PIM
265	15229	611	28	2.41	3	31

1999-2000 statistics:

GP	MIN	GAA	W	L	T	SO	GA	S	SAPCT	PIM
38	2038	2.33	19	14	3	3	79	834	.905	4

2000-2001 statistics:

GP	MIN	GAA	W	L	T	SO	GA	S	SAPCT	PIM
60	3607	2.35	36	19	5	7	141	1640	.914	2

2001-2002 statistics:

GP	MIN	GAA	W	L	T	SO	GA	S	SAPCT	PIM
61	3583	2.48	27	24	8	7	148	1521	.903	19

2002-2003 statistics:

GP	MIN	GAA	W	L	T	SO	GA	S	SAPCT	PIM
67	3943	2.16	39	20	7	8	142	1591	.911	6

LAST SEASON

Second in NHL in wins with career high. Tied for second in NHL in shutouts with career high. Fifth in NHL in goals-against average. Fourth in NHL in minutes played. Missed one game with flu.

THE PHYSICAL GAME

Lalime plays an almost classic stand-up style and has very good technique. His reflexes aren't great, so he is careful to make the best use of his height and take away the angle.

Even when he faces a barrage of shots, Lalime never looks like he is getting panicky. Like Martin Brodeur, Lalime plays behind a solid defense, and he probably doesn't get the credit he deserves. He isn't the best puckhandler, but he is adequate.

Lalime bears up well under the crease-crashing that has become epidemic, and he doesn't get off his game. He has a temper, though, and he will come out swinging when he's had enough.

THE MENTAL GAME

Lalime established his role as Ottawa's No. 1 goalie last season, and seemed to grow larger in goal just with the confidence he developed. The team has more faith in him as well, and that affects the way everyone plays.

THE INTANGIBLES

Lalime is good enough for now, but he is not among the game's elite goalies and there is serious doubt that he will be. For the Senators to become a serious Cup contender, Lalime will either have to be replaced or will have to take his game to a level we haven't seen yet. Lalime erased a lot of doubts by getting the Senators to the Eastern Conference Finals last season, but a lot of people expected even more of the Senators. Right or wrong, a goalie isn't considered great until he wins the Cup. Just ask Curtis Joseph.

PROJECTION

Lalime showed more resiliency than we gave him credit for. He goes into the season secure as Ottawa's No. 1 goalie but still has something to prove. His 39 wins last season will be hard to top but he should be in the 35-win range with a GAA under 2.00.

CHRIS PHILLIPS

Yrs. of NHL service: 6
Born: Fort McMurray, Alta.; Mar. 9, 1978
Position: left defense
Height: 6-3
Weight: 215
Uniform no.: 4
Shoots: left

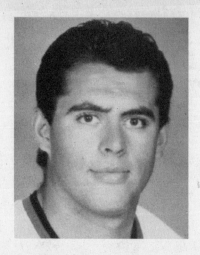

Career statistics:

GP	G	A	TP	PIM
385	24	72	96	240

1999-2000 statistics:

GP	G	A	TP	+/-	PIM	PP	SH	GW	GT	S	PCT
65	5	14	19	+12	39	0	0	1	0	96	5.2

2000-2001 statistics:

GP	G	A	TP	+/-	PIM	PP	SH	GW	GT	S	PCT
73	2	12	14	+8	31	2	0	0	0	77	2.6

2001-2002 statistics:

GP	G	A	TP	+/-	PIM	PP	SH	GW	GT	S	PCT
63	6	16	22	+5	29	1	0	1	0	103	5.8

2002-2003 statistics:

GP	G	A	TP	+/-	PIM	PP	SH	GW	GT	S	PCT
78	3	16	19	+7	71	2	0	1	0	97	3.1

LAST SEASON

Missed three games with knee injury. Missed one game due to personal reasons.

THE FINESSE GAME

Phillips is a very good skater for his size. He has all of the attributes (decent speed, lateral mobility, balance, and agility), and he skates well backwards and has a small turning radius. Carrying the puck doesn't slow him down much. He is skilled enough to be used up front in a pinch, although it confused his development as a younger player.

Phillips still has trouble making defensive reads, but he has improved in that area as well and has taken his place among Ottawa's top-four defensemen.

He will never post Ray Bourque numbers, but Phillips can handle Bourque-like ice time. He has a feel for the offensive part of the game. He joins the attack intelligently and has a hard shot from the point, as well as a good wrist shot when he goes in deep. He is not a great skater: he has a short stride and is not fluid. He doesn't move the puck well and lacks vision.

THE PHYSICAL GAME

There are very few question marks about Phillips's honest brand of toughness. He is solidly built and likes to hit, and just has to learn to do so more consistently. He is mobile enough to catch a defender and drive with his legs to pack a wallop in his checks.

THE INTANGIBLES

Phillips was partnered with Zdeno Chara. The duo saw most of the action against other teams' top lines. Phillips will be remembered most fondly by Sens fans for his OT goal in Game 6 of the Eastern Conference Finals last season that sent the Senators to a Game 7 against the Devils.

PROJECTION

Phillips has become a consistent, reliable defenseman whose fame is most heavily weighted to the defensive aspect of the game. Phillips isn't as interested in scoring points, which means you can expect about 20-25 points from him.

WADE REDDEN

Yrs. of NHL service: 7
Born: Lloydminster, Sask.; June 12, 1977
Position: left defense
Height: 6-2
Weight: 205
Uniform no.: 6
Shoots: left

Career statistics:

GP	G	A	TP	PIM
548	61	182	243	338

1999-2000 statistics:

GP	G	A	TP	+/-	PIM	PP	SH	GW	GT	S	PCT
81	10	26	36	-1	49	3	0	2	1	163	6.1

2000-2001 statistics:

GP	G	A	TP	+/-	PIM	PP	SH	GW	GT	S	PCT
78	10	37	47	+22	49	4	0	0	0	159	6.3

2001-2002 statistics:

GP	G	A	TP	+/-	PIM	PP	SH	GW	GT	S	PCT
79	9	25	34	+22	48	4	1	1	0	156	5.8

2002-2003 statistics:

GP	G	A	TP	+/-	PIM	PP	SH	GW	GT	S	PCT
76	10	35	45	+23	70	4	0	3	0	154	6.5

LAST SEASON

Led team defensemen in points for fourth consecutive season. Led team in average ice time (25:24). Tied for second on team in assists and plus-minus. Missed three games with hip injury. Missed two games with viral infection. Missed one game with bruised foot.

THE FINESSE GAME

Redden is a good skater who can change gears swiftly and smoothly, and his superb rink vision enables him to get involved in his team's attack. He has a high skill level. His shot is hard and accurate and he is a patient and precise passer. Redden's ability to move the puck without panic is one of his best assets.

Redden was mature when he broke into the game. He is smart and his level rises with the level of competition. His poise is exceptional.

Redden's work habits and attitude are thoroughly professional. He is a player who is willing to learn in order to improve his game.

THE PHYSICAL GAME

Redden is not a big hitter, and the coaching staff has to continually ride him to finish his checks. What he lacks in aggressiveness he makes up for with his quietly competitive nature. He can handle a lot of ice time. He plays an economical game without a lot of wasted effort; he is durable and can skate all night long. He would move up a step if he dished it out instead of just taking it. Redden has a very long fuse, but his coaches wouldn't mind seeing a little more fire.

THE INTANGIBLES

Redden has a laid-back nature, but he raises his game when something is on the line. Redden became a restricted free agent at the end of the season and did nothing to hurt his contract position.

PROJECTION

Redden is finding the right balance between contributing to the team's offense and playing it safe on defense. His scoring range should be 35-40 points, and he should remain among the team's plus-minus leaders.

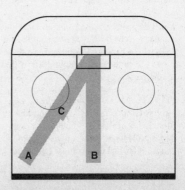

BRYAN SMOLINSKI

Yrs. of NHL service: 10
Born: Toledo, Ohio; Dec. 27, 1971
Position: center / right wing
Height: 6-1
Weight: 208
Uniform no.: 21
Shoots: right

Career statistics:

GP	G	A	TP	PIM
749	212	276	488	454

1999-2000 statistics:

GP	G	A	TP	+/-	PIM	PP	SH	GW	GT	S	PCT
79	20	36	56	+2	48	2	0	0	2	160	12.5

2000-2001 statistics:

GP	G	A	TP	+/-	PIM	PP	SH	GW	GT	S	PCT
78	27	32	59	+10	40	5	3	5	0	183	14.8

2001-2002 statistics:

GP	G	A	TP	+/-	PIM	PP	SH	GW	GT	S	PCT
80	13	25	38	+7	56	4	1	0	2	187	6.9

2002-2003 statistics:

GP	G	A	TP	+/-	PIM	PP	SH	GW	GT	S	PCT
68	21	25	46	0	20	6	1	8	0	176	11.9

LAST SEASON

Acquired from Los Angeles on March 11, 2003, for Tim Gleason and future considerations. Second on team in game-winning goals. Missed 11 games with eye injury. Missed two games due to personal reasons.

THE FINESSE GAME

Smolinski has been shuffled from center to wing during his career, but works much better in the middle, where he makes good use of the open ice. That is where the Senators have slotted him. Smolinski has a quick release and an accurate shot, and, on nights when he brings his "A" game, he works to get himself into quality shooting areas. Confidence is a big factor. He has a history of being a streaky, slumpy player.

Smolinski's skating is adequate, but it could improve with some lower-body work. He has good balance and lateral movement but he is not quick. He has a railroad-track skating base and is tough to knock over.

Smolinski has the smarts to be an asset on both specialty teams, and he has really stepped up as a penalty killer. He has good defensive awareness — his play away from the puck is sound. He is good in-tight with the puck.

THE PHYSICAL GAME

Smolinski has a thick, blocky build, and he can be a solid hitter. He doesn't have much of an aggressive nature on a nightly basis, but it shows up sporadically, and on those nights he is at his most effective.

THE INTANGIBLES

Smolinski has a lot going for him physically, but he's rather easy-going and needs a fire lit under him from time to time. Teams get frustrated with him because of his lack of drive and intensity. He was a solid veteran pickup for the Senators and had a good playoffs.

The first evidence of an infusion of cash from new owner Eugene Melnyk was displayed when Smolinski was re-signed to a four-year deal worth $10 million. Instead of becoming a walk-away rental player, Smolinski will be around to enhance Ottawa's depth at center.

PROJECTION

Smolinski bounced back with a 20-goal season. He should be able to improve those numbers playing on such an offensively gifted team. He scored eight points in 10 games after the trade to the Senators.

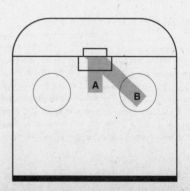

JASON SPEZZA

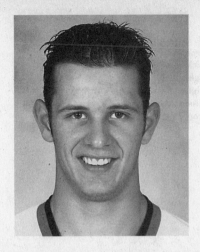

Yrs. of NHL service: 1
Born: Mississauga, Ont.; June 13, 1983
Position: center
Height: 6-2
Weight: 214
Uniform no.: 39
Shoots: right

Career statistics:

GP	G	A	TP	PIM
33	7	14	21	8

2001-2002 junior statistics:

GP	G	A	TP	PIM
53	42	63	105	42

2002-2003 statistics:

GP	G	A	TP	+/-	PIM	PP	SH	GW	GT	S	PCT
33	7	14	21	-3	8	3	0	0	0	65	10.8

LAST SEASON

First NHL season. Appeared in 43 games with Binghamton (AHL), scoring 22-32 — 54 with 71 PIM. Missed three games due to coach's decision.

THE FINESSE GAME

Spezza has been compared to Pierre Turgeon for his playmaking ability and, like Turgeon in his early days, Spezza has a tendency to melt a little under pressure. He spent about half of the season in the minors playing under a good teaching coach (John Paddock), and the education served him well. Spezza was called up during the playoffs and showed enough flashes to make the Senators believe he will be graduating this season.

Spezza has slick moves and a big shot, but he would rather make the pass. He will have to learn to mix up his play selection. He can toast a defender one-on-one. Spezza will make his presence known on the power play. He had 12 power-play points in only 33 games, which is only four fewer than rookie leader Rick Nash had in 74 games. He has good hockey sense and vision. Spezza seems to see the play two moves ahead of everybody else.

While Spezza has drawn raves for his passing, he also has a first-rate snap shot and a big slap shot, both of which he needs to employ more often.

Spezza needs to improve his defensive play and his skating. Those were the two areas targeted when he was sent down to the farm.

THE PHYSICAL GAME

Spezza has good size, but don't look for him to get involved. Spezza doesn't consistently compete hard, especially in big spots, which is why his stock dipped slightly in his draft year. He could be a future Lady Byng winner.

THE INTANGIBLES

Spezza has been under intense scrutiny since he was 16, and he hasn't always handled it well. It is difficult for a young player (especially one in Canada) to be a high first-round pick (second overall in 2001) and not be a star from the get-go. The Senators are a patient franchise, and Spezza will benefit from the cautious handling. Spezza showed more maturity last season. He didn't sulk when he was dispatched to the minors after training camp, but instead worked hard to earn a chance at a promotion.

PROJECTION

Spezza will be technically a rookie this season, and we would expect rookie-type numbers until he gets incorporated fully into the lineup. A 15-goal, 30-assist year would not surprise.

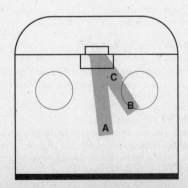

SHAUN VAN ALLEN

Yrs. of NHL service: 10
Born: Calgary, Alta.; Aug. 29, 1967
Position: center
Height: 6-1
Weight: 205
Uniform no.: 22
Shoots: left

Career statistics:

GP	G	A	TP	PIM
721	82	175	257	401

1999-2000 statistics:

GP	G	A	TP	+/-	PIM	PP	SH	GW	GT	S	PCT
75	9	19	28	+20	37	0	2	4	0	75	12.0

2000-2001 statistics:

GP	G	A	TP	+/-	PIM	PP	SH	GW	GT	S	PCT
59	7	16	23	+5	16	0	2	3	0	51	13.7

2001-2002 statistics:

GP	G	A	TP	+/-	PIM	PP	SH	GW	GT	S	PCT
73	8	13	21	0	26	0	1	1	0	48	16.7

2002-2003 statistics:

GP	G	A	TP	+/-	PIM	PP	SH	GW	GT	S	PCT
78	12	20	32	+17	66	2	2	3	0	53	22.6

PROJECTION

Van Allen is a valuable role player who can be useful in the right spot. His optimum production is 30 points.

LAST SEASON

Led team in shorthanded goals. Career highs in goals, assists, and points. Missed four games with surgery to remove kidney stones.

THE FINESSE GAME

Van Allen always posted huge numbers in the minors, but like so many minor-league scoring stars he couldn't transfer his touch to the big leagues. The flaw in Van Allen's case is his skating. It is marginally NHL caliber, and it forced him to change his profile from that of an offensive player to a defensive one.

When Van Allen does accomplish something offensively, it's because of his intelligence and hard work. He is a very good face-off man. If he controls the draw in the offensive zone, he knows how to set up an attack.

Although he has become more of a defensive specialist, Van Allen can lend a hand on the power play. Ottawa has so many high-octane players that he seldom gets the chance. Van Allen rarely plays a poor game because his intensity level is usually high.

THE PHYSICAL GAME

Van Allen's solid defensive play is enhanced by his work ethic. He's not a banger but he will get in the way. He seldom forgets what it takes for him to keep a job in the NHL.

THE INTANGIBLES

Van Allen happily re-upped with the Senators and is a perfect fit for their system. He may not score a lot of goals, but they tend to be clutch ones when he does.

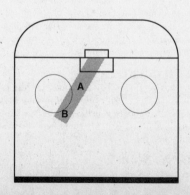

VACLAV VARADA

Yrs. of NHL service: 6
Born: Vsetin, Czech Republic; Apr. 26, 1976
Position: right wing
Height: 6-0
Weight: 208
Uniform no.: 26
Shoots: left

Career statistics:

GP	G	A	TP	PIM
387	48	104	152	334

1999-2000 statistics:

GP	G	A	TP	+/-	PIM	PP	SH	GW	GT	S	PCT
76	10	27	37	+12	62	0	0	0	0	140	7.1

2000-2001 statistics:

GP	G	A	TP	+/-	PIM	PP	SH	GW	GT	S	PCT
75	10	21	31	-2	81	2	0	2	0	112	8.9

2001-2002 statistics:

GP	G	A	TP	+/-	PIM	PP	SH	GW	GT	S	PCT
76	7	16	23	-7	82	1	0	1	0	138	5.1

2002-2003 statistics:

GP	G	A	TP	+/-	PIM	PP	SH	GW	GT	S	PCT
55	9	10	19	+1	31	2	0	0	0	81	11.1

LAST SEASON

Acquired from Buffalo on February 25, 2003, with a fifth-round draft pick in 2003 for Jakub Klepis. Missed 24 games due to knee injuries.

THE FINESSE GAME

Varada has developed into a two-way forward with heavy emphasis on the defensive side of the puck.

Varada is the mold of a power forward, but he lacks the kind of scoring touch and desire to score that the role demands. When he is on, he plays with such intensity and reckless abandon that by the end of the game his face is cut and scraped, as if he had been attacked by crazed weasels.

With excellent size and great hands, Varada is wonderful with the puck — a superb stickhandler. He can also make plays, though his strength lies in crashing the net and getting someone else to get the puck through to him. He has a good wrist and slap shot. He needs to be an involved player and not stay on the perimeter. He has a passion for scoring and drives to the net for his best chances. He handles himself well in traffic. He is a solidly balanced skater and an effective forechecker.

THE PHYSICAL GAME

Varada is thick: thick arms, thick legs, thick thighs. He is much more powerful than he looks. He gives the Senators some desperately needed size on the right side. He can be gritty and hard to play against. Varada needs to do that every night.

The biggest knock on Varada is his intensity level. If he brings his game up every night, he will be a star, even on this team of stars. Even a checking guy has to score now and again. Varada looked like an astute pickup by Ottawa GM John Muckler but injuries prevented Varada from being the kind of impact player the Senators needed him to be in the playoffs.

PROJECTION

Varada once looked like a 30-goal scorer but it looks as if even he has stopped believing that will happen. Ten to 15 goals would be an improvement.

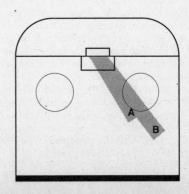

ANTON VOLCHENKOV

Yrs. of NHL service: 1
Born: Moscow, Russia; Feb. 25, 1982
Position: left defense
Height: 6-0
Weight: 209
Uniform no.: 24
Shoots: left

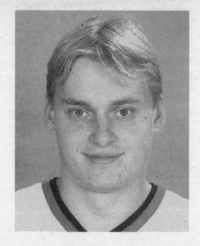

Career statistics:

GP	G	A	TP	PIM
57	3	13	16	40

2002-2003 statistics:

GP	G	A	TP	+/-	PIM	PP	SH	GW	GT	S	PCT
57	3	13	16	-4	40	0	0	0	0	75	4.0

LAST SEASON

First NHL season. Missed seven games with shoulder injury. Missed five games with groin injury. Missed one game with dental surgery. Missed 12 games due to coach's decision.

THE FINESSE GAME

Volchenkov still has some rough edges, but the Senators guessed right when they thought the young defenseman would benefit more from playing in the NHL than the minors. Except for a slump in the first half of the season, Volchenkov did not look out of place on Ottawa's third defense pair. He will be a top four in another few seasons.

Volchenkov has a lot of skill. He is an agile and balanced skater, and he has more offensive upside than he has shown so far. For now, he is concentrating on the defensive aspect of the game, which is the right way to develop. He is sound positionally and he is tough to beat one-on-one.

Volchenkov is conservative by nature. He will make the short outlet pass or the chip off the wall to get out of trouble instead of a more flashy play.

THE PHYSICAL GAME

Volchenkov is an absolutely terrifying hitter. If he isn't there yet, he will soon be named in the class of Scott Stevens and Rob Blake among players who can deliver devastating, clean open-ice checks. He dished out memorable pops on Jonas Hoglund, Jiri Bicek, and Christian Berglund last season. Volchenkov is naturally aggressive and he looks like he loves to play the game.

Anyone can hit along the boards, in a contained area, but it takes skill to do so in open ice. No wonder he has already earned the nickname "The A Train."

He needs to take a more professional approach to the game by working on his strength and conditioning. Yes, he can become even more powerful.

THE INTANGIBLES

Ottawa has had a reputation the past few years of being a soft team. Volchenkov is doing a lot to change that image. He is the kind of hitter than can set the tone for an entire game, and that is a rare commodity. The fact that Volchenkov adapted to North America as quickly as he did despite knowing little English was also impressive.

PROJECTION

We wouldn't worry too much about Volchenkov's point totals yet. If he can score 20 points and dominate physically the way he started to do last season, that would be huge.

PHILADELPHIA FLYERS

Players' Statistics 2001-2002

POS.	NO.	PLAYER	GP	G	A	PTS	+/-	PIM	PP	SH	GW	GT	S	PCT
C	97	JEREMY ROENICK	79	27	32	59	20	75	8	1	6	2	197	13.7
R	8	MARK RECCHI	79	20	32	52	0	35	8	1	3	1	171	11.7
R	11	TONY AMONTE	72	20	31	51	0	28	7	1	5	1	207	9.7
C	25	KEITH PRIMEAU	80	19	27	46	4	93	6		4	1	171	11.1
C	26	MICHAL HANDZUS	82	23	21	44	13	46	1	1	9		133	17.3
D	5	KIM JOHNSSON	82	10	29	39	11	38	5		2		159	6.3
D	37	ERIC DESJARDINS	79	8	24	32	30	35	1		2		197	4.1
R	24	SAMI KAPANEN	71	10	21	31	-18	18	5		2	1	189	5.3
L	10	JOHN LECLAIR	35	18	10	28	10	16	8		4	1	99	18.2
L	12	SIMON GAGNE	46	9	18	27	20	16	1	1	3	1	115	7.8
C	39	MARTY MURRAY	76	11	15	26	-1	13	1	1			105	10.5
L	87	DONALD BRASHEAR	80	8	17	25	5	161			1		99	8.1
R	14	JUSTIN WILLIAMS	41	8	16	24	15	22			2		105	7.6
D	2	ERIC WEINRICH	81	2	18	20	16	40	1	1			103	1.9
R	20	*RADOVAN SOMIK	60	8	10	18	9	10		1	2		95	8.4
C	13	CLAUDE LAPOINTE	80	8	8	16	2	36			1		87	9.2
D	28	MARCUS RAGNARSSON	68	3	13	16	7	62	1				79	3.8
D	22	DMITRY YUSHKEVICH	83	3	11	14	-9	46					75	4.0
D	36	*DENNIS SEIDENBERG	58	4	9	13	8	20	1				123	3.3
C	19	*ERIC CHOUINARD	28	4	4	8	2	8	1				45	8.9
D	6	CHRIS THERIEN	67	1	6	7	10	36					93	1.1
R	18	TOMI KALLIO	24	2	4	6	-10	14					28	7.1
L	15	JOE SACCO	34	1	5	6	0	20			1		48	2.1
L	29	TODD FEDORUK	63	1	5	6	1	105					33	3.0
L	18	JAMIE WRIGHT	23	2	2	4	0	16					18	11.1
D	23	*JIM VANDERMEER	24	2	1	3	9	27					22	9.1
C	27	ANDRE SAVAGE	16	2	1	3	2	4			1		13	15.4
R	9	MARK GREIG	5	1	1	1	1	2					2	
C	18	*PATRICK SHARP	3				0	2					3	
C	34	*IAN MACNEIL	2			1							2	
R	21	*MIKE SIKLENKA	1				0						1	
G	35	NEIL LITTLE					0							
G	33	MAXIME OUELLET					0							
D	0	JOHN SLANEY					0							
G	42	ROBERT ESCHE	30				0	6						
R	47	*KIRBY LAW	2				0	2						
G	32	ROMAN CECHMANEK	58				0	8						

GP = games played; G = goals; A = assists; PTS = points; +/- = goals-for minus goals-against while player is on ice; PIM = penalties in minutes; PP = power-play goals; SH = shorthanded goals; GW = game-winning goals; GT = game-tying goals; S = no. of shots; PCT = percentage of goals to shots; * = rookie

TONY AMONTE

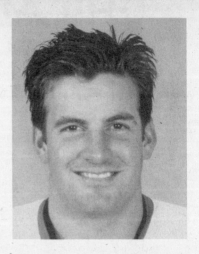

Yrs. of NHL service: 12
Born: Hingham, Mass.; Aug. 2, 1970
Position: right wing
Height: 6-0
Weight: 200
Uniform no.: 11
Shoots: left

Career statistics:

GP	G	A	TP	PIM
933	372	403	775	631

1999-2000 statistics:

GP	G	A	TP	+/-	PIM	PP	SH	GW	GT	S	PCT
82	43	41	84	+10	48	11	5	2	1	260	16.5

2000-2001 statistics:

GP	G	A	TP	+/-	PIM	PP	SH	GW	GT	S	PCT
82	35	29	64	-22	54	9	1	3	1	256	13.7

2001-2002 statistics:

GP	G	A	TP	+/-	PIM	PP	SH	GW	GT	S	PCT
82	27	39	66	+11	67	6	1	4	0	232	11.6

2002-2003 statistics:

GP	G	A	TP	+/-	PIM	PP	SH	GW	GT	S	PCT
72	20	31	51	0	28	7	1	5	1	207	9.7

LAST SEASON

Acquired from Phoenix on March 10, 2003, for Guilliaume Lefebvre, a third-round draft pick in 2003, and a second-round draft pick in 2004. Led Flyers in shots. Third on team in assists, points, and game-winning goals. Tied for third on team in goals. Missed eight games due to rib injury, ending NHL's longest consecutive games-played ironman streak at 453. Missed one game due to coach's decision.

THE FINESSE GAME

Amonte is blessed with exceptional speed and acceleration. His timing is accurate and his anticipation keen. He has good balance and he can carry the puck at a pretty good clip, though he is more effective when streaking down the wing and getting the puck late. Playing on the left side leaves his forehand open for one-timers, but Amonte is equally secure on the right wing. He uses his speed to drive wide around the defense to the net. His speed intimidates.

Amonte has a quick release on his wrist shot. He likes to go top shelf, just under the crossbar, and he can also go to the backhand shot or a wrist shot off his back foot, like a fadeaway jumper in basketball. He is a top power-play man, since he is always working himself into open ice. He is better utilized down low on a power play than on the point. An accurate shooter, and one who takes a lot of shots, Amonte is also creative in his playmaking. He passes very well and is conscious of where his teammates are; he usually makes the best percentage play. He has confidence in his shot and wants the puck when the game is on the line.

Amonte is a smart player away from the puck, which makes him a favorite with the demanding coach, Ken Hitchcock. He sets picks and creates openings for his teammates. He is an aggressive penalty killer and a shorthanded threat.

THE PHYSICAL GAME

Amonte's speed and movement keep him out of a lot of trouble zones, but he will also drive to the front of the net and take punishment there if that's the correct play. He loves to score, he loves to help his linemates score, and although he is outweighed by a lot of NHL defensemen, he is seldom outworked. He's intense and is not above getting chippy and rubbing his glove in someone's face. Amonte plays through pain, as evidenced by his ironman streak.

Amonte takes a lot of abuse and plays through the checks. He seldom takes bad retaliatory penalties. He just keeps his legs driving and draws calls with his nonstop skating.

THE INTANGIBLES

Amonte struggled in Phoenix, which signed him as a free agent in 2002, but he was a point-a-game player (7-8 — 15 in 13 games) after the trade to the Flyers. Amonte had a woeful playoffs, though, with only one goal in 13 games, so he has a lot to atone for this season.

PROJECTION

Amonte is a good fit on a veteran Flyers squad and should be the team's leading scorer, possibly in the 80-point range.

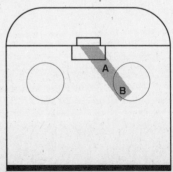

ERIC DESJARDINS

Yrs. of NHL service: 15
Born: Rouyn, Que.; June 14, 1969
Position: right defense
Height: 6-1
Weight: 205
Uniform no.: 37
Shoots: right

Career statistics:

GP	G	A	TP	PIM
1050	131	408	539	673

1999-2000 statistics:

GP	G	A	TP	+/-	PIM	PP	SH	GW	GT	S	PCT
81	14	41	55	+20	32	8	0	4	1	207	6.8

2000-2001 statistics:

GP	G	A	TP	+/-	PIM	PP	SH	GW	GT	S	PCT
79	15	33	48	-3	50	6	1	4	1	187	8.0

2001-2002 statistics:

GP	G	A	TP	+/-	PIM	PP	SH	GW	GT	S	PCT
65	6	19	25	-1	24	2	1	0	0	117	5.1

2002-2003 statistics:

GP	G	A	TP	+/-	PIM	PP	SH	GW	GT	S	PCT
79	8	24	32	+30	35	1	0	2	0	197	4.1

LAST SEASON

Led team in plus-minus. Second on team in average ice time (22:54). Tied for second on team in shots. Missed two games with back injury. Missed one game with bruised knee.

THE FINESSE GAME

Desjardins is a competent two-way defenseman. He has the puckhandling skills and poise to beat the first forechecker and carry the puck out of the defensive zone. He makes accurate breakout passes and has enough savvy to keep the play simple, gain the redline and dump the puck deep in attacking ice if no other option is available. He makes the smart, safe play all the time.

Stable and capable enough to handle power-play duty, Desjardins is wise enough to realize only the ultra-elite overpower NHL goalies with point shots. Although he has a strong one-timer, his slap shot is not always accurate. He is much more dangerous offensively when he uses his wrist shot, or simply flips deflectable pucks toward the net.

A fine skater with light, agile feet, and a small turning radius, Desjardins goes up-ice well with the play, keeping the gap to the forwards small and remaining in good position to revert to defense if there is a turnover. A long reach helps him challenge puck carriers to make plays more quickly, change their minds or shoot from a lower-percentage angle. He keeps his stick active while killing penalties, sweeping it on the ice to contest passing lanes and intercept pucks.

THE PHYSICAL GAME

Desjardins is particularly effective when penalty killing in front of the net. He immobilizes the opponent's stick first, then ties up the body — which separates him from the huge percentage of defensemen who are satisfied to do one or the other, but not both. He plays a hard game more than a punishing one, but uses his strength in more subtle ways to gain position in front of both goals. On offense, he will venture to the corners from time to time and will beat his check to the front of the net after winning a battle for the puck. Desjardins is quietly tough. He will wear down if his minutes are not watched. He rebounded well from off-season shoulder surgery in 2002.

THE INTANGIBLES

The Flyers nearly tempted fate by letting Desjardins become an unrestricted free agent, but re-signed him the day before he hit the market. The Flyers have employed him for years as a top-two defenseman, which is beyond his scope, but he gives it his best. With a couple of young defensive prospects on the way, Desjardins will be valuable to have as a mentor.

A quiet leader on-ice and in the dressing room, Desjardins plays a clean, controlled game and rarely takes stupid penalties. He always seems to be where he is most needed, does not panic, and does not fight. He is steady and professional and easy to underappreciate.

PROJECTION

Desjardins gives a lot of steady minutes, and can score in the 30-point range.

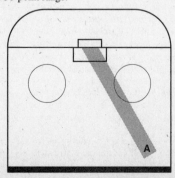

SIMON GAGNE

Yrs. of NHL service: 4
Born: Ste. Foy, Que.; Feb. 29, 1980
Position: left wing
Height: 6-0
Weight: 190
Uniform no.: 12
Shoots: left

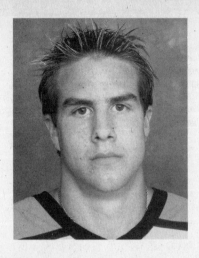

Career statistics:

GP	G	A	TP	PIM
274	89	111	200	88

1999-2000 statistics:

GP	G	A	TP	+/-	PIM	PP	SH	GW	GT	S	PCT
80	20	28	48	+11	22	8	1	4	0	159	12.6

2000-2001 statistics:

GP	G	A	TP	+/-	PIM	PP	SH	GW	GT	S	PCT
69	27	32	59	+24	18	6	0	7	1	191	14.1

2001-2002 statistics:

GP	G	A	TP	+/-	PIM	PP	SH	GW	GT	S	PCT
79	33	33	66	+31	32	4	1	7	0	199	16.6

2002-2003 statistics:

GP	G	A	TP	+/-	PIM	PP	SH	GW	GT	S	PCT
46	9	18	27	+20	16	1	1	3	1	115	7.8

LAST SEASON

Tied for second on team in plus-minus. Missed 29 games with groin injuries. Missed five games due to concussion. Missed two games with abdominal strain.

THE FINESSE GAME

Gagne, for the first time in his four-year NHL career, hit his first roadblock last season. Much of the backslide stemmed from the injuries he had to deal with, which combined to make him a little less confident, a little less aggressive, and a little less fit.

If he can return to his previous form, Gagne is an effortless skater. He can be as effective in the closing shifts of the game, when his team is desperate for a goal, as he is in the opening minutes. He doesn't seem to tire. Sleek and fluid, with seamless changes of direction and pace, he can carry the puck without slowing one whit. He plays a strong puck-control game and is one of those puck magnets — he always seems to be involved in the play with the puck.

Gagne is an unselfish player, and works best when teamed with pure finishers. He can score on his own, too, and is a natural goal scorer with an excellent wrist shot. He is outstanding on the power play. He always has his head up and senses his best options. Gagne has improved his defensive game immensely.

THE PHYSICAL GAME

Gagne will get his body in the way but he is not a physical player. He has some problems when the Flyers are facing a team that is big and strong. Gagne isn't a big player and injuries take a toll on him. Gagne will always need to devote himself to fitness and conditioning year-round.

THE INTANGIBLES

Scouts who told us that Gagne would prove to be the best player of the strong rookie crop of 2000 obviously knew what they were talking about.

PROJECTION

Gagne should score 30 goals over the course of a healthy season. He had a better playoffs than most of his teammates — which isn't saying a whole lot, but it might be a sign that Gagne can bounce back this season.

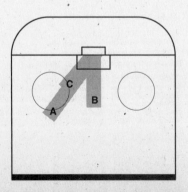

JEFF HACKETT

Yrs. of NHL service: 13
Born: London, Ont.; June 1, 1968
Position: goaltender
Height: 6-1
Weight: 198
Uniform no.: 30
Catches: left

Career statistics:

GP	MIN	GA	SO	GAA	A	PIM
473	26495	1296	23	2.93	5	60

1999-2000 statistics:

GP	MIN	GAA	W	L	T	SO	GA	S	SAPCT	PIM
56	3301	2.40	23	25	7	3	132	1543	.914	4

2000-2001 statistics:

GP	MIN	GAA	W	L	T	SO	GA	S	SAPCT	PIM
19	998	3.25	4	10	2	0	54	477	.887	0

2001-2002 statistics:

GP	MIN	GAA	W	L	T	SO	GA	S	SAPCT	PIM
15	717	3.18	5	5	2	0	38	395	.904	2

2002-2003 statistics:

GP	MIN	GAA	W	L	T	SO	GA	S	SAPCT	PIM
36	2054	2.86	15	17	2	1	98	1106	.911	2

LAST SEASON

Signed as free agent by Philadelphia on July 1, 2003. Previously acquired by Boston with Jeff Jillson on January 23, 2003, from San Jose for Kyle McLaren and a fourth-round pick in the 2004. Previously acquired by San Jose from Montreal on January 23, 2003, for Niklas Sundstrom and a third-round pick in 2004. Missed 10 games with broken finger.

THE PHYSICAL GAME

Hackett is a student of goaltending. His technique could provide a textbook for any young goalie. His positional play is strong. He knows when to challenge a shooter at the top of the crease and he plays his angles well.

One of the hardest-working players on any team he has ever been on, Hackett probably overdoes it and has to be urged to conserve his energy. He is an active goalie and he's not the most robust guy in the world. Fortunately he makes the game easier for himself by simply stopping the puck and controlling his rebounds.

Hackett has decent reflexes for bang-bang plays around the net. His glove is a great asset. He can play conservatively, holding the puck for a draw to cool off the action until the refs warn him about moving it.

His stickhandling has improved slightly but it's a major flaw.

THE MENTAL GAME

Hackett is very competitive but he hasn't been a No. 1 goalie since 1999-2000. Boston acquired him for a run into the playoffs but he was injured after the deal and he came into the postseason off a layoff, so it's hard to judge his effectiveness at an elite level. Hackett hasn't played for a serious contender in a long time. This will be a different kind of pressure for him to handle. It's one thing to go out and play gallantly for a team that has no hope of winning, and quite another to actually win the games.

THE INTANGIBLES

After the theatrics of Roman Cechmanek, the Flyers players will probably be relieved to play in front of a guy who just does his job and doesn't make a habit of stopping pucks with his head. But as competitive as Hackett is, we wonder about Philadelphia GM Bobby Clarke's habit of placing the least importance on the game's most critical position.

PROJECTION

Hackett will probably think he's in heaven playing behind such a solid defensive team. He's 35 and the Flyers will have to limit him to around 60 starts, of which at least 30 should be wins.

KIM JOHNSSON

Yrs. of NHL service: 4
Born: Malmo, Sweden; Mar. 16, 1976
Position: left defense
Height: 6-1
Weight: 205
Uniform no.: 5
Shoots: left

Career statistics:

GP	G	A	TP	PIM
315	32	95	127	166

1999-2000 statistics:

GP	G	A	TP	+/-	PIM	PP	SH	GW	GT	S	PCT
76	6	15	21	-13	46	1	0	1	0	101	5.9

2000-2001 statistics:

GP	G	A	TP	+/-	PIM	PP	SH	GW	GT	S	PCT
75	5	21	26	-3	40	4	0	0	0	104	4.8

2001-2002 statistics:

GP	G	A	TP	+/-	PIM	PP	SH	GW	GT	S	PCT
82	11	30	41	+12	42	5	0	1	0	150	7.3

2002-2003 statistics:

GP	G	A	TP	+/-	PIM	PP	SH	GW	GT	S	PCT
82	10	29	39	+11	38	5	0	2	0	159	6.3

LAST SEASON

Led team defensemen in points for second consecutive season. Led team in average ice time (24:05). One of three Flyers to appear in all 82 games.

THE FINESSE GAME

Johnsson isn't a very dynamic player, but he's a mobile skater and puck mover. Never underestimate the value of a defender who does the job of getting the puck out of his zone so efficiently. It keeps the opposition from setting up and reduces the strain on his goaltender.

When Johnsson is playing with confidence, he eagerly joins the rush. Johnsson works the point on the first power-play unit. He has a good shot from the point. It is not overpowering, but he releases it quickly and he keeps it low and on net. He is not afraid to venture into the circles because he knows his skating can help him recover and prevent odd-man rushes against. He brings a little cockiness to his game that makes him try some creative plays. Where Johnson must improve most is in his play without the puck.

Quite reliable defensively, Johnsson plays his position well and makes smart defensive reads. He has a long reach for making sweep and poke checks and tying up an opponent's stick. If he continues to work on the defensive part of his game, he could become a poor man's Nick Lidstrom.

THE PHYSICAL GAME

Just average size, Johnsson is not very physical or aggressive, and he needs to get stronger to win more one-on-one battles. His lack of strength around his net is a drawback, and he must work on playing firmer in his own end.

THE INTANGIBLES

Johnsson was "The Kid," the only regular under age 30 among the Flyers' regular defensemen last season. The Philadelphia defense is in desperate need of an overhaul, and Johnsson can be expected to be the cornerstone of that group. There isn't much special about him, but he's a steady player with an offensive touch.

PROJECTION

Johnsson made major progress to become a 40-point scorer, but we don't see him moving into much better company than that.

SAMI KAPANEN

Yrs. of NHL service: 8
Born: Vantaa, Finland; June 14, 1973
Position: left wing
Height: 5-10
Weight: 195
Uniform no.: 24
Shoots: left

Career statistics:

GP	G	A	TP	PIM
548	149	212	361	111

1999-2000 statistics:

GP	G	A	TP	+/-	PIM	PP	SH	GW	GT	S	PCT
76	24	24	48	+10	12	7	0	5	2	229	10.5

2000-2001 statistics:

GP	G	A	TP	+/-	PIM	PP	SH	GW	GT	S	PCT
82	20	37	57	-12	24	7	0	4	0	223	9.0

2001-2002 statistics:

GP	G	A	TP	+/-	PIM	PP	SH	GW	GT	S	PCT
77	27	42	69	+9	23	11	0	4	1	248	10.9

2002-2003 statistics:

GP	G	A	TP	+/-	PIM	PP	SH	GW	GT	S	PCT
71	10	21	31	-18	18	5	0	2	1	189	5.3

LAST SEASON

Acquired from Carolina with Ryan Bast on February 7, 2003, for Pavel Brendl and Bruno St. Jacques. Worst plus-minus on Flyers. Missed 11 games with groin injuries. Missed one game due to coach's decision.

THE FINESSE GAME

Kapanen is one of the swiftest skaters in the league. He plays a smart small-man's game. Kapanen is a skilled forward who is always moving. He handles the puck well while in motion, though like a lot of European forwards he tends to hold the puck a tad too long. He will shoot on the fly, however, and has an NHL shot when he does release it. He has a fine wrist shot and he can score off the rush.

Kapanen has quickness, good balance, and good strength. He makes few mistakes. He knows where to be on the ice and how to use big players as picks and screens. He sticks to the perimeter until he darts into holes. He takes care of his defensive assignments, and even though he's too small to body check, he is able to harass opponents by lifting up a stick and swiping the puck. Kapanen is strong on the puck.

Kapanen uses a short stick to keep the puck in-close to his body. He loses a bit off his shot because of it, but he can create some great scoring chances with his passing because of his control. It also means defenders are forced to reach in for the puck, and that's when he's clever at drawing penalties.

THE PHYSICAL GAME

Kapanen plays without fear and draws a lot of penalties with his speed. He is lean without much muscle mass. He plays a spunky game and picks up the team on its quieter nights because he sprints to the pucks and tries on every shift.

THE INTANGIBLES

Kapanen took a huge step back after his five 20-plus goal seasons with Carolina. Maybe it was due to injuries (a groin injury is especially detrimental to a fleet skater like Kapanen) or to the 'Canes' hangover that seems to hit teams that get to the Finals, unexpectedly, and then lose. He is a clone of Montreal's Saku Koivu. Kapanen is an exciting player and had decent production in the postseason.

PROJECTION

Kapanen scored 13 points in 28 games after his trade to the Flyers, which indicates he should return to 60-point form. The Flyers wasted little time in signing him to a new contract after the season was over.

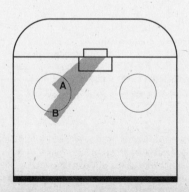

CLAUDE LAPOINTE

Yrs. of NHL service: 12
Born: Lachine, Que.; Oct. 11, 1968
Position: center
Height: 5-9
Weight: 188
Uniform no.: 13
Shoots: left

Career statistics:

GP	G	A	TP	PIM
837	122	175	297	689

1999-2000 statistics:

GP	G	A	TP	+/-	PIM	PP	SH	GW	GT	S	PCT
76	15	16	31	-22	60	2	1	3	0	129	11.6

2000-2001 statistics:

GP	G	A	TP	+/-	PIM	PP	SH	GW	GT	S	PCT
80	9	23	32	-2	56	1	1	1	1	94	9.6

2001-2002 statistics:

GP	G	A	TP	+/-	PIM	PP	SH	GW	GT	S	PCT
80	9	12	21	-9	60	0	3	0	0	74	12.2

2002-2003 statistics:

GP	G	A	TP	+/-	PIM	PP	SH	GW	GT	S	PCT
80	8	8	16	+2	36	0	0	1	0	87	9.2

LAST SEASON

Acquired from N.Y. Islanders on March 9, 2003, for a fifth-round draft pick in 2003. Missed two games with sprained ankle.

THE FINESSE GAME

Lapointe is one of those useful veteran forwards who will always find a spot in a lineup because of his intelligence, yet he'll always be worried about his job because he doesn't do anything special.

He drives to the front of the net, knowing that that's where good things happen. He has good acceleration and quickness with the puck, but he has no hands whatsoever. All of his goals have to be willed in by him. He isn't blessed with great vision, but he doesn't take unnecessary chances, either, and can be used in clutch situations.

Quick and smart, Lapointe gets a breakaway every other game, but he doesn't have the scoring touch to finish off his chances. He is heady and aggressive. As a low draft pick (234th overall in 1988), he has always had to fight for respect. His effort is what has kept him around this long.

Lapointe was used as a checking-line winger, where he can use his speed. He is an effective penalty killer and is strong on defensive-zone draws.

THE PHYSICAL GAME

Small but solidly built, Lapointe uses his low center of gravity and good balance to bump people much bigger than he is; he surprises some by knocking them off the puck. He doesn't quit and is dogged in the corners and in front of the net. He is gritty and hard-working.

THE INTANGIBLES

Lapointe is used as a checker, an energy guy, a penalty killer, and on face-offs. He doesn't score many goals but the ones he does score tend to be big. He is an excellent team man. Lapointe became a free agent after the season but re-signed with the Flyers, whose system suits him well.

PROJECTION

Lapointe is a role-playing forward who can get 10 goals and play 13-15 hard minutes every night.

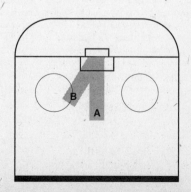

JOHN LECLAIR

Yrs. of NHL service: 12
Born: St. Albans, VT; July 5, 1969
Position: left wing
Height: 6-3
Weight: 226
Uniform no.: 10
Shoots: left

Career statistics:

GP	G	A	TP	PIM
798	359	347	706	377

1999-2000 statistics:

GP	G	A	TP	+/-	PIM	PP	SH	GW	GT	S	PCT
82	40	37	77	+8	36	13	0	7	2	249	16.1

2000-2001 statistics:

GP	G	A	TP	+/-	PIM	PP	SH	GW	GT	S	PCT
16	7	5	12	+2	0	3	0	2	0	48	14.6

2001-2002 statistics:

GP	G	A	TP	+/-	PIM	PP	SH	GW	GT	S	PCT
82	25	26	51	+5	30	4	0	6	1	220	11.4

2002-2003 statistics:

GP	G	A	TP	+/-	PIM	PP	SH	GW	GT	S	PCT
35	18	10	28	+10	16	8	0	4	1	99	18.2

LAST SEASON

Led team in shooting percentage. Tied for team lead in power-play goals. Missed 47 games due to shoulder surgery.

THE FINESSE GAME

You rarely find a player who shoots as often as LeClair does and who has such a good shooting percentage. Most snipers waste a lot of shots, and high-percentage shooters are more selective. LeClair combines the two by working to get into the highest-quality scoring areas and using a terrific shot with a quick release.

A team can defend against LeClair all night long, then lose position on him once and the puck is in the net. He knows his job is to score goals and he doesn't let up — from the opening whistle to the final second of the game.

He is big enough to post up in front and drive through the melees for all the rebounds, deflections, and garbage goals his teammates can create. He also has enough power in his skating and confidence in his strength to cut in from the wing and drive to the net. But the left wing's attributes as a scorer far outweigh his abilities as a puckhandler. If the puck were a football, you could imagine him putting it under his arm, lowering his head, and ramming it across the goal line.

THE PHYSICAL GAME

LeClair is one of the strongest men in the NHL and is nearly impossible to push off the puck legally. He wants to win the puck, wants the puck in the net, and will use every ounce of his strength to try to put it there. He always draws the attention of at least one defender, but accepts his role willingly. Because of a long reach and a big body, LeClair is able to place himself between the puck and the defender. When he has a defender under each arm behind the net, he will kick the puck to the front.

The frequent disappointment is that LeClair, who puts so much into winning the puck behind the goal line, doesn't really have the deft touch to make a smooth relay to someone who might be driving to the net. His passing skills are dubious, his puckhandling skills erratic. Teams try to neutralize him by forcing him to carry the puck and make plays.

For all his size and positioning, LeClair isn't a true power forward. He lacks the mean streak around the net that the elite power forwards possess. LeClair is more like Dave Andreychuk. You can hack and whack him, but as his low PIM totals suggest, he rarely fights back.

THE INTANGIBLES

LeClair was finally rid of his back injuries, only to suffer a shoulder injury that required surgery. He may also be rid of Philadelphia, as he okayed a trade to one of four approved teams after the season.

PROJECTION

Lower your expectations and pencil LeClair in for 30 goals instead of 40 to 50.

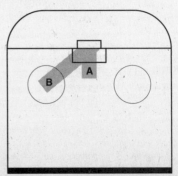

JONI PITKANEN

Yrs. of NHL service: 0
Born: Oulu, Finland; Sept. 19, 1983
Position: defense
Height: 6-3
Weight: 200
Uniform no.: n.a.
Shoots: left

Career (European) statistics:

GP	G	A	TP	PIM
105	9	30	39	57

2002-2003 European statistics:

GP	G	A	TP	PIM
35	5	15	20	38

LAST SEASON

Will be entering first NHL season.

THE FINESSE GAME

Pitkanen is one of the most highly regarded defensive prospects in a long time, and certainly one of the best blueline hopefuls the Flyers have unearthed in ages.

Pitkanen has a lot going for him, starting with size. When you're as big as Pitkanen is — and you can skate and handle the puck and pass — opponents are going to back off and give you a lot of room. Pitkanen is an intelligent player and should have no problem adjusting to the pace of the North American game. Certainly the physical play won't bother him.

One thing Pitkanen lacks is an effective point shot. He has a bullet slap shot, but he has absolutely no idea where it's going. The NHL will be happy it legislated end-zone netting once Pitkanen makes the league. He would be more useful on the point if he sacrificed some m.p.h. for accuracy.

THE PHYSICAL GAME

He's big. He's mean. He was born to be a Flyer. Pitkanen won't make the splashy open-ice hits, but he will be at his best in the trenches. Toe-to-toe, Pitkanen will be a fearsome opponent along the boards and in front of the crease.

THE INTANGIBLES

The reason the Flyers didn't throw money around courting high-priced defensemen in the free agent market is because of players in the pipeline like Pitkanen and Jeff Woywitka. One red flag is that Pitkanen has been injury-prone in his developmental years and has already had a serious shoulder injury and (minor) knee surgery.

PROJECTION

Pitkanen will get every chance to win a spot in training camp. It will be a few seasons before he's an impact player in the NHL, but he is expected to develop into a top-pair defenseman.

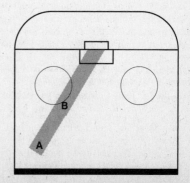

KEITH PRIMEAU

Yrs. of NHL service: 13
Born: Toronto, Ont.; Nov. 24, 1971
Position: center
Height: 6-5
Weight: 220
Uniform no.: 25
Shoots: left

Career statistics:

GP	G	A	TP	PIM
846	258	332	590	1455

1999-2000 statistics:

GP	G	A	TP	+/-	PIM	PP	SH	GW	GT	S	PCT
23	7	10	17	+10	31	1	0	1	0	51	13.7

2000-2001 statistics:

GP	G	A	TP	+/-	PIM	PP	SH	GW	GT	S	PCT
71	34	39	73	+17	76	11	0	4	1	165	20.6

2001-2002 statistics:

GP	G	A	TP	+/-	PIM	PP	SH	GW	GT	S	PCT
75	19	29	48	-3	128	5	0	3	0	151	12.6

2002-2003 statistics:

GP	G	A	TP	+/-	PIM	PP	SH	GW	GT	S	PCT
80	19	27	46	+4	93	6	0	4	1	171	11.1

LAST SEASON

Third on team in penalty minutes. Missed two games with ankle injury.

THE FINESSE GAME

Primeau has to be judged harshly at center although, in fairness to him, he should really be playing wing but teams insist on putting him in the middle. He is modestly effective there because of his size and skating, but he doesn't have the good playmaking skills, vision, or sense to make the most of the center-ice position. He doesn't have the puck on his stick much, nor does he use his wingers well or establish much chemistry.

Primeau's assets — his strength, his speed, his work along the boards — would serve him much better as a winger. There is less contact in the middle, and he limits himself by thinking more like a scorer than a power forward.

Primeau has a huge stride with a long reach. A left-handed shot, he will steam down the right side, slide the puck to his backhand, get his feet wide apart for balance, then shield the puck with his body and use his left arm to fend off the defenseman before shoveling the puck to the front of the net. He's clever enough to accept the puck at top speed and, instead of wondering what to do with it, he makes a move.

Primeau has worked hard on all aspects of his game and can be used in almost any role, including penalty killing and four-on-four play.

THE PHYSICAL GAME

It's not that Primeau doesn't like to hit, because he does. When he plays with a little bit of an edge he can dominate for a period or an entire game. He has a fiery temper and can lose control. Emotion is a desirable quality, but he has become too valuable a player to spend too much time in the penalty box. He can't be overly tame, either. He needs to wig out once in a while to scare people. Primeau has acquired considerable presence.

THE INTANGIBLES

The Flyers are becoming disenchanted with Primeau and it's likely he will be dealt before the end of the season — but only if the Flyers can find or develop another center to play behind Jeremy Roenick.

PROJECTION

We downgraded Primeau to 50 points last season and he fell shy of that. Expect his numbers to continue a gradual decline.

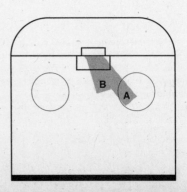

MARCUS RAGNARSSON

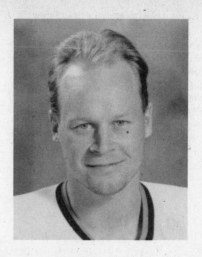

Yrs. of NHL service: 8
Born: Ostervala, Sweden; Aug. 13, 1971
Position: left defense
Height: 6-1
Weight: 215
Uniform no.: 28
Shoots: left

Career statistics:

GP	G	A	TP	PIM
562	30	131	161	424

1999-2000 statistics:

GP	G	A	TP	+/-	PIM	PP	SH	GW	GT	S	PCT
63	3	13	16	+13	38	0	0	0	0	60	5.0

2000-2001 statistics:

GP	G	A	TP	+/-	PIM	PP	SH	GW	GT	S	PCT
68	3	12	15	+2	44	1	0	0	0	74	4.1

2001-2002 statistics:

GP	G	A	TP	+/-	PIM	PP	SH	GW	GT	S	PCT
70	5	15	20	+4	44	2	0	3	0	68	7.3

2002-2003 statistics:

GP	G	A	TP	+/-	PIM	PP	SH	GW	GT	S	PCT
68	3	13	16	+7	62	1	0	0	0	79	3.8

LAST SEASON

Acquired from San Jose for Dan McGillis on December 6, 2002. Third on Flyers in average ice time (22:33). Missed 13 games with pinched nerve in back.

THE FINESSE GAME

Ragnarsson has a lot of poise, plus hand skills, and skating ability. He has quick feet and he moves the puck well. He makes a good first pass and some good decisions at the blueline to get the puck through. He is so calm he seems just about bomb-proof. Other players get rattled under pressure but Ragnarsson can very quietly get the puck out of danger.

Ragnarsson controls a lot of the breakouts and he makes smart choices in the neutral zone. He is given a lot of responsibility on the power play, and while he is not in the elite class of quarterbacks, he has a decent, if not outstanding, point shot. He needs to shoot more, but he seems content to focus on the defensive aspect of his game.

Defensively, Ragnarsson uses his body positionally to take up space, but isn't much of a hitter. He is more effective when paired with a more physical type of defenseman, even though that means the opposing team will prefer to flood Ragnarsson's side of the ice.

THE PHYSICAL GAME

Built solidly, Ragnarsson will play a physical game, though finesse is his forte. He can handle a lot of ice time. He conserves his energy by being in the right place and not being forced to scramble. He is not soft, just not very aggressive.

THE INTANGIBLES

Ragnarsson is a little less intense than the type of player GM Bobby Clarke usually shops for. He didn't seem to find anyone in Philadelphia with whom he had the same chemistry he did with Mike Rathje in San Jose.

PROJECTION

Ragnarsson's offensive game has more upside, but he has found a comfort zone and won't score much more than 25 points.

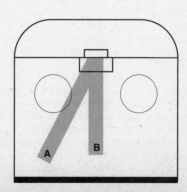

MARK RECCHI

Yrs. of NHL service: 14
Born: Kamloops, B.C.; Feb. 1, 1968
Position: right wing
Height: 5-10
Weight: 185
Uniform no.: 8
Shoots: left

Career statistics:

GP	G	A	TP	PIM
1091	430	696	1126	733

1999-2000 statistics:

GP	G	A	TP	+/-	PIM	PP	SH	GW	GT	S	PCT
82	28	63	91	+20	50	7	1	5	1	223	12.6

2000-2001 statistics:

GP	G	A	TP	+/-	PIM	PP	SH	GW	GT	S	PCT
69	27	50	77	+15	33	7	1	8	0	191	14.1

2001-2002 statistics:

GP	G	A	TP	+/-	PIM	PP	SH	GW	GT	S	PCT
80	22	42	64	+5	46	7	2	4	0	205	10.7

2002-2003 statistics:

GP	G	A	TP	+/-	PIM	PP	SH	GW	GT	S	PCT
79	20	32	52	0	35	8	1	3	1	171	11.7

LAST SEASON

Tied for team lead in assists and power-play goals. Second on team in points. Tied for third on team in goals. Missed two games with flu. Missed one game due to coach's decision.

THE FINESSE GAME

Recchi is one of the top small players in the game. He's a feisty and relentless worker in the offensive zone. Recchi busts into open ice, finding the holes almost before they open, and excels at the give-and-go. His vision and patience with the puck make him the ideal man to find in open ice on the power play. Recchi can play the point and is dangerous off the right wing half-boards with his unerring ability to find Jeremy Roenick or Simon Gagne parked at the left side of the crease.

Recchi can score goals, too. He has a dangerous shot from the off-wing. Although he is not as dynamic as Maurice Richard, he likes to use the Richard cut-back while rifling a wrist shot back across. It's heavy, it's on net, and it requires no backswing. He follows his shot to the net for a rebound. He has excellent hands, vision, and anticipation for any scoring opportunity.

Recchi has worked hard to improve his defensive play, although he will still make mental errors. He kills penalties well because he hounds the point men aggressively and knocks the puck out of the zone. Then he heads off on a breakaway or forces the defender to pull him down.

He isn't a pretty skater but he always keeps his feet moving. While other players are coasting, Recchi's blades are in motion, and he draws penalties. He is ready to spring into any play. He is a puck magnet. He protects the puck well, keeping it close to his feet.

THE PHYSICAL GAME

Recchi gets chopped at because he doesn't hang around the perimeter. He accepts the punishment to get the job done. He is a solid player with a low center of gravity, and he is tough to knock off the puck.

THE INTANGIBLES

Recchi is an unselfish player and team leader. If his points continue to fall off, he will have to continue to do the little things that can help his team win hockey games. His strong work ethic just continues to intensify. With seven goals, Recchi was one of the few Flyers who had a playoffs worth writing home about.

PROJECTION

Injuries to John LeClair are no excuse, but Recchi simply hasn't found a winger with whom he has the same dynamic chemistry. Recchi is no longer a point-a-game player. His top is now in the 55-point range.

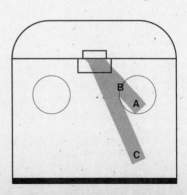

JEREMY ROENICK

Yrs. of NHL service: 14
Born: Boston, Mass.; Jan. 17, 1970
Position: center
Height: 6-1
Weight: 207
Uniform no.: 97
Shoots: right

Career statistics:

GP	G	A	TP	PIM
1062	456	617	1073	1283

1999-2000 statistics:

GP	G	A	TP	+/-	PIM	PP	SH	GW	GT	S	PCT
75	34	44	78	+11	102	6	3	12	1	192	17.7

2000-2001 statistics:

GP	G	A	TP	+/-	PIM	PP	SH	GW	GT	S	PCT
80	30	46	76	-1	114	13	0	7	1	192	15.6

2001-2002 statistics:

GP	G	A	TP	+/-	PIM	PP	SH	GW	GT	S	PCT
75	21	46	67	+32	74	5	0	3	0	167	12.6

2002-2003 statistics:

GP	G	A	TP	+/-	PIM	PP	SH	GW	GT	S	PCT
79	27	32	59	+20	75	8	1	6	2	197	13.7

LAST SEASON

Led team in goals and points. Tied for team lead in assists and power-play goals. Second on team in game-winning goals. Tied for second on team in plus-minus and shots. Third on team in shooting percentage. Missed two games due to NHL suspension. Missed one game due to coach's decision.

THE FINESSE GAME

Roenick commands a lot of attention on the ice because of his effort. He draws away defenders to open up ice for his teammates. He has good acceleration and can turn quickly, change directions or burn a defender with a surprising outside burst of speed. A defenseman who plays aggressively against him will be left staring at the back of Roenick's jersey as he skips by en route to the net. He has to be forced into the high-traffic areas, where his lack of size and strength are the only things that derail him.

Roenick is tough to handle one-on-one. He won't make the same move or take the same shot twice in a row. He has a variety of shots and can score from almost anywhere on the ice. He can rifle a wrist shot from 30 feet away, or else wait until the goalie is down and lift in a backhand from in-tight. He has a drag-and-pull move to his backhand that is highly deceptive, and it also keeps the goalie guessing because he is able to show a backhand but pull it quickly to his forehand once he has frozen the goalie.

Roenick is reliable defensively.

THE PHYSICAL GAME

Roenick remains one of the peskier centers to play against. He can take some stupid penalties. They are nearly all of the aggressive ilk — smashing people into the boards, getting his elbows up — and he never backs down. He plays through pain and is highly competitive. Roenick plays with passion and with such a headlong style that injuries are routine.

The Flyers have been careful to monitor Roenick's ice time as he does tend to wear down. Roenick doesn't know how to play this game easy.

THE INTANGIBLES

Roenick is a lightning rod. He will take heat for his teammates, or direct it towards a target, even if it's himself. Roenick is the Flyers' go-to guy on the ice and in the room.

PROJECTION

Expect Roenick to score around 70 points and again be one of the Flyers' core players.

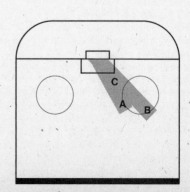

DENNIS SEIDENBERG

Yrs. of NHL service: 1
Born: Schwenningen, Germany; July 18, 1981
Position: left defense
Height: 6-0
Weight: 180
Uniform no.: 36
Shoots: left

Career statistics:

GP	G	A	TP	PIM
58	4	9	13	20

2002-2003 statistics:

GP	G	A	TP	+/-	PIM	PP	SH	GW	GT	S	PCT
58	4	9	13	+8	20	1	0	0	0	123	3.3

LAST SEASON

First NHL season. Missed six games due to coach's decision. Appeared in 19 games with Philadelphia (AHL), scoring 5-6 — 11.

THE FINESSE GAME

Seidenberg impressed many of the veteran Flyers with his poise. He played three seasons in Germany before making the jump to the NHL, and handled the transition to both the NHL game and North American lifestyle well.

Seidenberg has good offensive upside. He is accurate with his point shot, and has a lot of velocity on it to create rebounds. He isn't shy about shooting, nor does he just fire blindly. Seidenberg looks up and times his shots to get through open lanes rather than getting them blocked. That gives his teammates the confidence to be more aggressive driving to the net for loose pucks.

Seidenberg is an excellent skater and moves the puck up-ice well. He will dump the puck in if that's the right decision, or will make a play in the neutral zone and follow the rush. Like a lot of European players who have soccer training, Seidenberg is very quick with his feet and can kick the puck up to his stick, barely breaking stride to do so.

THE PHYSICAL GAME

Seidenberg is not a very big or physical player, and he has to improve his conditioning to handle the rigors of the NHL schedule.

Seidenberg started his sophomore slump a little early, slowing down in the second half. That's not unusual for first-year players from European leagues, because the season there is under 60 games. The Flyers sent Seidenberg down to the minors at the end of the season, so he did not see any playing time during the Stanley Cup playoffs.

PROJECTION

Seidenberg will get a chance to become part of the top-four defense corps, although he is likely to start off the season as a No. 5 defenseman. He could score 30 points over the course of a full season.

CHRIS THERIEN

Yrs. of NHL service: 9
Born: Ottawa, Ont.; Dec. 14, 1971
Position: left defense
Height: 6-5
Weight: 235
Uniform no.: 6
Shoots: left

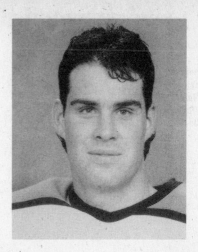

Career statistics:

GP	G	A	TP	PIM
650	28	117	145	499

1999-2000 statistics:

GP	G	A	TP	+/-	PIM	PP	SH	GW	GT	S	PCT
80	4	9	13	+11	66	1	0	1	0	126	3.2

2000-2001 statistics:

GP	G	A	TP	+/-	PIM	PP	SH	GW	GT	S	PCT
73	2	12	14	+22	48	1	0	0	0	103	1.9

2001-2002 statistics:

GP	G	A	TP	+/-	PIM	PP	SH	GW	GT	S	PCT
77	4	10	14	+16	30	0	2	3	0	105	3.8

2002-2003 statistics:

GP	G	A	TP	+/-	PIM	PP	SH	GW	GT	S	PCT
67	1	6	7	+10	36	0	0	0	0	93	1.1

LAST SEASON

Missed four games due to concussion. Missed five games with back injury. Missed four games with upper body injury. Missed one game due to coach's decision.

THE FINESSE GAME

Although not particularly quick, Therien is a fluid skater for his size and has average offensive instincts. He handles the puck well and looks to move it as his first option, but he can skate it out of the defensive zone and make a crisp pass while in motion. If that option is not available, he keeps it simple and bangs the puck off the boards.

Good balance allows Therien to maximize his size when, rather than use the typical big-man play and slide on the ice, he takes a stride, drops to one knee and keeps his stick flat on the ice — making himself a larger and wider obstacle.

Therien doesn't have much lateral speed, but he is a strong, straight-ahead skater who can get up-ice in a hurry. He also has enough offensive sense that he can play the point on the power play on the second unit.

THE PHYSICAL GAME

Therien uses his reach to good advantage. He can dominate, and physically punishes opposing forwards in front of the net in penalty-killing situations. Extremely alert away from the puck, he dedicates himself to gaining body position and making sure his man doesn't get it.

Therien knows big defensemen can be penalty magnets, but he keeps much of his game within the rules. He keeps the elbows down, and plays an effec-tive, clean physical game. Therien has low PIM totals for a player as involved in hitting as he is. When he hits along the boards or battles in the corners, he tends to lower his body position and use his weight to smear an opponent along the boards. Other big defensemen are too upright in those situations or try to use their arms to pin opponents, which isn't as effective. Therien makes his heft and bulk work for him.

THE INTANGIBLES

Therien is a top-four defenseman in Philadelphia and handles a lot of ice time, but he is not a dominating rearguard. Therien needs to play with a mobile defenseman. He is a bit exposed when he doesn't get to play with a fluid partner. Therien needs to be motivated at times.

PROJECTION

Therien's offensive instincts do not translate into points because he usually takes only one or two shots per game. He tends to score big goals when he does score, though. He plays fairly mistake-free hockey and has channelled his enthusiasm into dogged, effective play, making him a key contributor. He is a fairly typical journeyman who would be better off as a No. 5 defenseman than a top four.

ERIC WEINRICH

Yrs. of NHL service: 13
Born: Roanoke, Va.; Dec. 19, 1966
Position: right defense
Height: 6-1
Weight: 213
Uniform no.: 2
Shoots: left

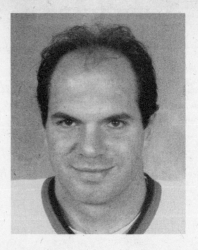

Career statistics:

GP	G	A	TP	PIM
1002	65	287	352	727

1999-2000 statistics:

GP	G	A	TP	+/-	PIM	PP	SH	GW	GT	S	PCT
77	4	25	29	+4	39	2	0	0	0	120	3.3

2000-2001 statistics:

GP	G	A	TP	+/-	PIM	PP	SH	GW	GT	S	PCT
82	7	24	31	-9	44	3	0	2	1	109	6.4

2001-2002 statistics:

GP	G	A	TP	+/-	PIM	PP	SH	GW	GT	S	PCT
80	4	20	24	+27	26	0	0	2	0	102	3.9

2002-2003 statistics:

GP	G	A	TP	+/-	PIM	PP	SH	GW	GT	S	PCT
81	2	18	20	+16	40	1	1	0	0	103	1.9

LAST SEASON

Missed one game due to coach's decision.

THE FINESSE GAME

Weinrich's skating is above average. He accelerates quickly and has good straightaway speed, though he doesn't have great balance for pivots or superior leg drive for power. He jumps into the rush and has an efficient style that allows him to play a lot of minutes.

Shooting and passing hard, he is strong on the puck. Weinrich can still handle second-unit power-play time. He has a low, accurate shot that he gets away quickly. He will not gamble down low, but will sometimes sneak into the top of the circle for a one-timer. Weinrich has composure with the puck in all zones. He is an outstanding penalty killer and shot-blocker.

Weinrich plays better with an offensive-minded partner. He used to be a more offensive defenseman, but as he has matured; his finesse skills have become more valuable on the defensive side of the puck. He is more useful when he is the support player who can move the puck up and shift into the play. Weinrich is a steady influence for a younger defenseman.

THE PHYSICAL GAME

A good one-on-one defender, Weinrich has reached an age (37 this season) where he needs to watch his minutes. Although not a soft player (a criticism that dogged him early in his career), Weinrich is not mean by any stretch of the imagination. He will stand up for himself or a teammate, and won't get pushed around. His experience playing with Chris Chelios in Chicago taught him to battle hard and he has incorporated that into his game.

THE INTANGIBLES

Weinrich became a free agent at the end of the season and is likely to look for one more year before the labor war of 2004. He would make a valuable contributor to a team that is deep on defense and could use him on the third defense pair. He is such a good team guy that younger defensemen will find him to be a virtual playing assistant coach.

PROJECTION

Weinrich should score in the 20-point range.

PHOENIX COYOTES

Players' Statistics 2001-2002

POS.	NO.	PLAYER	GP	G	A	PTS	+/-	PIM	PP	SH	GW	GT	S	PCT
R	12	MIKE JOHNSON	82	23	40	63	9	47	8		3	1	178	12.9
R	19	SHANE DOAN	82	21	37	58	3	86	7		2		225	9.3
L	17	LADISLAV NAGY	80	22	35	57	17	92	8		6		209	10.5
C	11	DAYMOND LANGKOW	82	20	32	52	20	56	4	2	2		196	10.2
C	77	CHRIS GRATTON	80	15	30	45	-16	107	4		2	1	215	7.0
C	24	JAN HRDINA	61	14	29	43	4	42	11		4		86	16.3
D	27	TEPPO NUMMINEN	78	6	24	30	0	30	2		1	1	108	5.6
R	29	*BRANKO RADIVOJEVIC	79	12	15	27	-2	63	1		3	1	109	11.0
D	23	PAUL MARA	73	10	15	25	-7	78	1				95	10.5
D	55	DANNY MARKOV	64	4	16	20	2	36	2			1	105	3.8
D	7	DERON QUINT	51	7	10	17	-5	20	2				85	8.2
L	49	BRIAN SAVAGE	43	6	10	16	-4	22	1		1	1	68	8.8
R	28	LANDON WILSON	31	6	8	14	1	26			3		92	6.5
R	16	KELLY BUCHBERGER	79	3	9	12	0	109		1			32	9.4
L	18	PAUL RANHEIM	68	3	8	11	-8	16					71	4.2
D	2	TODD SIMPSON	66	2	7	9	7	135					67	3.0
D	45	BRAD FERENCE	75	2	7	9	-3	146					49	4.1
D	4	OSSI VAANANEN	67	2	7	9	1	82					49	4.1
D	15	RADOSLAV SUCHY	77	1	8	9	2	18	1				48	2.1
L	38	SCOTT PELLERIN	43	1	4	5	-8	16	1				37	2.7
C	14	*JEFF TAFFE	20	3	1	4	-4	4	1		1		18	16.7
L	44	ANDREI NAZAROV	59	3		3	-9	135	2				35	8.6
D	5	DRAKE BEREHOWSKY	7	1	2	3	0	27					8	12.5
C	36	KRYSTOFER KOLANOS	2				0						8	
R	34	FRANK BANHAM	5				-1	2					5	
G	1	SEAN BURKE	22				0	4						
G	35	ZAC BIERK	16				0	2						
G	33	BRIAN BOUCHER	45				0							
G	40	JEAN-MARC PELLETIER	2				0							
D	52	*MARTIN GRENIER	3				-1							
C	21	*JASON JASPERS	2				-1							

GP = games played; G = goals; A = assists; PTS = points; +/- = goals-for minus goals-against while player is on ice; PIM = penalties in minutes; PP = power-play goals; SH = shorthanded goals; GW = game-winning goals; GT = game-tying goals; S = no. of shots; PCT = percentage of goals to shots; * = rookie

SEAN BURKE

Yrs. of NHL service: 15
Born: Windsor, Ont.; Jan. 29, 1967
Position: goaltender
Height: 6-4
Weight: 210
Uniform no.: 1
Catches: left

Career statistics:

GP	MIN	GA	SO	GAA	A	PIM
715	40799	2023	33	2.98	21	278

1999-2000 statistics:

GP	MIN	GAA	W	L	T	SO	GA	S	SAPCT	PIM
7	418	2.58	2	5	0	0	18	208	.913	2

2000-2001 statistics:

GP	MIN	GAA	W	L	T	SO	GA	S	SAPCT	PIM
62	3644	2.27	25	22	13	4	138	1766	.922	16

2001-2002 statistics:

GP	MIN	GAA	W	L	T	SO	GA	S	SAPCT	PIM
60	3587	2.29	33	21	6	5	137	1711	.920	14

2002-2003 statistics:

GP	MIN	GAA	W	L	T	SO	GA	S	SAPCT	PIM
22	1248	2.12	12	6	2	2	44	632	.930	4

LAST SEASON

Missed 29 games with sprained ankle. Missed 19 games with knee injury. Missed seven games with groin injury. Missed one game with flu.

THE PHYSICAL GAME

Burke is a big goalie and when he is on his game, he challenges the shooter well and comes out to the top of his crease. He worked extensively with a goalie coach and has learned to make the game easier on himself. Burke is much better technically than he was at the start of his career, and it's why he has played at such a high level at an older age.

Burke handles the puck well. He is confident and active on the dump-ins. He gives his defensemen a chance to handle the puck more easily and break out of the zone with less effort.

Burke fills up the net and is very quick for a net-minder of his size. He has a quick glove hand, but when he gets into slumps he will drop it and give the shooter the top corner over his left shoulder.

THE MENTAL GAME

Burke had to work very hard to win a full-time role again in the NHL and he takes nothing for granted. At 36, though, his body has started to turn on him. He missed a total of 56 games last year, almost all due to lower body injuries. Burke is smarter and mellower but still highly competitive.

THE INTANGIBLES

Several teams were inquiring about Burke, who will make $4.5 million on the last year of his contract. That is No. 1 goalie money, but given Burke's streak of serious injuries last year, he would be a high-risk acquisition for a team hoping to make a serious Cup run.

PROJECTION

Phoenix always plays better when Burke is between the pipes (14-6-2 with him in the lineup vs. 17-29-9-5 with another goalie) but his recent injury history makes him a gamble for much more than 20 wins.

SHANE DOAN

Yrs. of NHL service: 8
Born: Halkirk, Alta.; Oct. 10, 1976
Position: right wing
Height: 6-2
Weight: 223
Uniform no.: 19
Shoots: right

Career statistics:

GP	G	A	TP	PIM
569	115	168	283	541

1999-2000 statistics:

GP	G	A	TP	+/-	PIM	PP	SH	GW	GT	S	PCT
81	26	25	51	+6	66	1	1	4	0	221	11.8

2000-2001 statistics:

GP	G	A	TP	+/-	PIM	PP	SH	GW	GT	S	PCT
76	26	37	63	0	89	6	1	6	1	220	11.8

2001-2002 statistics:

GP	G	A	TP	+/-	PIM	PP	SH	GW	GT	S	PCT
81	20	29	49	+11	61	6	0	2	0	205	9.8

2002-2003 statistics:

GP	G	A	TP	+/-	PIM	PP	SH	GW	GT	S	PCT
82	21	37	58	+3	86	7	0	2	0	225	9.3

LAST SEASON

Led team in shots. Second on team in assists and points. Third on team in goals. One of three Coyotes to appear in all 82 games.

THE FINESSE GAME

Doan's game is speed. He is fast and strong, and forechecks aggressively and intelligently along the wall and in the corners. He intimidates with his skating because he gets in on a defenseman fast. Once he gains control of the puck he finds the open man in front of the net. He isn't overly creative, nor does he have great hands, but will thrive on the dump-and-chase play, where he can just skate on his wing and race for the puck.

Doan has acceptable wrist and slap shots and has gained a great deal of confidence in using them. That has elevated his game. He has stopped thinking purely like a checker and drives to the net instead of turning away from the play.

Mike Johnson's rapid development took some of the pressure off of Doan, who is best suited as a No. 2 winger. He is an excellent penalty killer and adds a huge dimension to his game when he gets in a scoring groove.

THE PHYSICAL GAME

Doan is strong and a very good body checker. He seems to have a mean streak lurking under his exterior. He will lay some hard hits on people. He plays with a little edge but doesn't take many bad penalties.

THE INTANGIBLES

Doan needs to play with grinding-type linemates and Chris Gratton may be a good fit with him, especially since Doan can compensate for Gratton's lack of foot speed. People look at Doan's size and speed and want 40 goals from him, but it's not going to happen.

Not many forwards score 25 goals and play as well defensively and physically as Doan. He is well-respected by teammates and coaches and could be a future captain of the Coyotes.

PROJECTION

Doan can develop into a Jere Lehtinen type of forward who can consistently score 20-25 goals a season.

BRAD FERENCE

Yrs. of NHL service: 3
Born: Calgary, Alta.; Apr. 2, 1979
Position: right defense
Height: 6-3
Weight: 210
Uniform no.: 45
Shoots: right

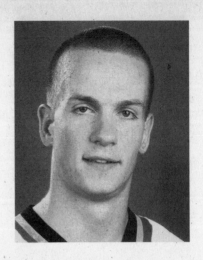

Career statistics:

GP	G	A	TP	PIM
182	4	25	29	460

1999-2000 statistics:

GP	G	A	TP	+/-	PIM	PP	SH	GW	GT	S	PCT
13	0	2	2	+2	46	0	0	0	0	10	-

2000-2001 statistics:

GP	G	A	TP	+/-	PIM	PP	SH	GW	GT	S	PCT
14	0	1	1	-10	14	0	0	0	0	5	0.0

2001-2002 statistics:

GP	G	A	TP	+/-	PIM	PP	SH	GW	GT	S	PCT
80	2	15	17	-13	254	0	0	0	0	65	3.1

2002-2003 statistics:

GP	G	A	TP	+/-	PIM	PP	SH	GW	GT	S	PCT
75	2	7	9	-3	146	0	0	0	0	49	4.1

LAST SEASON

Acquired from Florida on March 8, 2003, for Darcy Hordichuk and a second-round draft pick in 2003. Led team in penalty minutes.

THE FINESSE GAME

Ference is one tough customer, but when he's not in the penalty box, he can be a different kind of force. One of the best skills Ference possesses is his shot from the point. He's not Al MacInnis, but he's pretty smart with the puck on the point. He hardly ever has his shot blocked. He makes sure that if he doesn't get the puck on net, at least he gets it deep.

Ference was a little on the lean side when he broke into the pros, but he has added a lot of useful muscle.

Ference is a good skater. He shows an ability to get involved in the offensive side of the game. He handles the puck and passes fairly well. Ference has an upbeat attitude and wants to learn and improve.

THE PHYSICAL GAME

Ference is mean and his short fuse can get him into trouble — with the refs, with the league, and with his own coach. Ference's minor penalties aren't for holding or tripping. They're for cross-checking and roughing. He is not intimidated by other team's top lines. Ference needs to learn to keep his composure. He already has a pretty fierce reputation around the NHL. Ference doesn't have to uphold it every night.

THE INTANGIBLES

Ference has a long way to go, but he's been compared to Chris Pronger. He made a good impression with Phoenix after the trade. He will make them a little tougher to get two points off of this season.

PROJECTION

Ference has an upside and should get enough ice time to make the most of it. He could score 20 points, and accumulate more than 200 PIM.

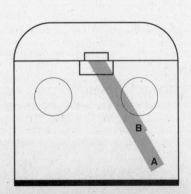

CHRIS GRATTON

Yrs. of NHL service: 10
Born: Brantford, Ont.; July 5, 1975
Position: center
Height: 6-4
Weight: 225
Uniform no.: 77
Shoots: left

Career statistics:

GP	G	A	TP	PIM
770	161	277	438	1240

1999-2000 statistics:

GP	G	A	TP	+/-	PIM	PP	SH	GW	GT	S	PCT
72	15	34	49	-23	136	4	0	1	1	202	7.4

2000-2001 statistics:

GP	G	A	TP	+/-	PIM	PP	SH	GW	GT	S	PCT
82	19	21	40	0	102	5	0	5	1	156	12.2

2001-2002 statistics:

GP	G	A	TP	+/-	PIM	PP	SH	GW	GT	S	PCT
82	15	24	39	0	75	1	0	5	0	139	10.8

2002-2003 statistics:

GP	G	A	TP	+/-	PIM	PP	SH	GW	GT	S	PCT
80	15	30	45	-16	107	4	0	2	1	215	7.0

LAST SEASON

Acquired from Buffalo on March 10, 2003, with a fourth-round draft pick in 2004 for Daniel Briere and a third-round draft pick in 2004. Third on Coyotes in shots. Missed two games with concussion.

THE FINESSE GAME

Gratton was among the face-off kings last season, finishing second only to Montreal's Yanic Perreault with a 58.57 winning percentage.

Gratton does a lot of things well, but not well enough or consistently enough to keep coaches and GMs from going grey. There are times when he can dominate a game, or step in to help an embattled teammate. And there are times when he takes shifts, nights, and weeks off. For a player of his skill level and experience, those lapses are unforgivable. It's what keeps Gratton on the move from the fourth line to the first.

Of course, for a player of his size, much more is expected. He was supposed to be a power center, and he is happier playing in the middle than the wing, but Gratton is clearly overmatched in the middle against other team's top units. One of the major reasons is his lack of foot speed, which hurts him despite a lot of work in this area.

Gratton's game is meat and potatoes. He's a grinder and needs to work hard every shift, every night, to make an impact. He has a hard shot, which he needs to use more. He gets his goals from digging around the net and there's some Cam Neely in him, but he lacks the long, strong stride Neely used in traffic. He has good hand-eye coordination and can pick passes out of midair for a shot. He has a big, noisy, but not always effective, slap shot.

An unselfish playmaker, Gratton is not the prettiest of passers, but he has some poise with the puck and he knows when to pass and when to shoot.

THE PHYSICAL GAME

On his good nights, Gratton is hard-working and doesn't shy from contact, but he has to initiate more. If his skating improves, he will be able to establish a more physical presence. He doesn't generate enough speed from leg drive to be much of a checker. He won't be an impact player in the NHL unless he does.

THE INTANGIBLES

Gratton was traded, to no one's surprise. He has landed in a good spot in Phoenix, and his style meshes well with the speedy Shane Doan. He scored only one point — an assist — in 14 games with the Coyotes though. Gratton was a restricted free agent after the season.

PROJECTION

Gratton is likely to score in the 15-goal range, and that appears to be his top end. Enough of the promise. That's the reality.

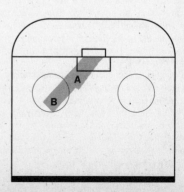

JAN HRDINA

Yrs. of NHL service: 5
Born: Hradec Kralove, Czech Republic; Feb. 5, 1976
Position: center
Height: 6-0
Weight: 206
Uniform no.: 24
Shoots: right

Career statistics:

GP	G	A	TP	PIM
370	79	152	231	223

1999-2000 statistics:

GP	G	A	TP	+/-	PIM	PP	SH	GW	GT	S	PCT
70	13	33	46	+13	43	3	0	1	0	84	15.5

2000-2001 statistics:

GP	G	A	TP	+/-	PIM	PP	SH	GW	GT	S	PCT
78	15	28	43	+19	48	3	0	1	1	89	16.9

2001-2002 statistics:

GP	G	A	TP	+/-	PIM	PP	SH	GW	GT	S	PCT
79	24	33	57	-7	50	6	0	6	0	115	20.9

2002-2003 statistics:

GP	G	A	TP	+/-	PIM	PP	SH	GW	GT	S	PCT
61	14	29	43	+4	42	11	0	4	0	86	16.3

LAST SEASON

Acquired from Pittsburgh with Francois Leroux on March 11, 2003, for Ramzi Abid, Dan Focht, and Guillaume Lefebvre. Led Coyotes in power-play goals and shooting percentage. Second on team in game-winning goals. Missed 11 games with hip injuries. Missed two games with back spasms.

THE FINESSE GAME

Hrdina is a highly skilled center who does everything well. He is a very good skater with the ability to shift gears and directions effortlessly. He doesn't shoot enough, but when he does he has a quick and accurate wrist shot. It would be a terrific weapon if he used it more often, but Hrdina is more likely to be guilty of overpassing the puck.

Hrdina is a highly intelligent player in all areas, and it looked like he was going to settle into a comfort zone where he would be a strictly defensive forward. He needs to be nudged to keep his offensive aspirations higher. Hrdina has fine offensive sense and touch, although he doesn't shoot enough. He is also versatile enough to play center or left wing.

THE PHYSICAL GAME

Hrdina is slightly less than average height but he has a wide body. He fights for the puck and is tough to knock off his feet. He is excellent on draws. Not only does he have quick hands, he is able to tie up the opposing center's stick, and he uses his feet. He cheats a bit on draws, but usually gets away with it. Between him and Chris Gratton, the Coyotes could absolutely dominate a game on draws.

THE INTANGIBLES

Phoenix played Hrdina as a No. 2 left wing behind Ladislav Nagy.

PROJECTION

Hrdina would have scored in the 55-point range if it hadn't been for injuries. That could be his ceiling, although he won't see the power-play time in Phoenix that he did in Pittsburgh.

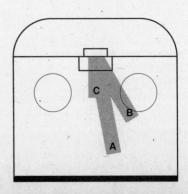

MIKE JOHNSON

Yrs. of NHL service: 6
Born: Scarborough, Ont.; Oct. 3, 1974
Position: right wing
Height: 6-2
Weight: 200
Uniform no.: 12
Shoots: right

Career statistics:

GP	G	A	TP	PIM
469	99	176	275	207

1999-2000 statistics:

GP	G	A	TP	+/-	PIM	PP	SH	GW	GT	S	PCT
80	21	26	47	+6	27	6	1	3	0	132	15.9

2000-2001 statistics:

GP	G	A	TP	+/-	PIM	PP	SH	GW	GT	S	PCT
76	13	30	43	-10	42	4	1	0	1	124	10.5

2001-2002 statistics:

GP	G	A	TP	+/-	PIM	PP	SH	GW	GT	S	PCT
57	5	22	27	+14	28	1	2	0	0	73	6.8

2002-2003 statistics:

GP	G	A	TP	+/-	PIM	PP	SH	GW	GT	S	PCT
82	23	40	63	+9	47	8	0	3	1	178	12.9

LAST SEASON

Led team in goals, assists, and points with career highs. Second on team in shooting percentage. Tied for second on team in power-play goals. Third on team in plus-minus and game-winning goals. One of three Coyotes to appear in all 82 games.

THE FINESSE GAME

Johnson has an advanced knowledge of how to use the ice offensively and defensively. Why it took until he was 28 for him to put all the pieces together will remain a mystery, but he has arrived. Finally.

Johnson protects the puck on the boards. When he's down low in his own end on defensive-zone coverage, he's strong and supports the puck well. In the attacking zone, Johnson will take the puck to the net. He knows when to dart and doesn't just stand around waiting for defenders to tie him up. He moves into scoring positions. His puck movement on the power play is exceptional. He doesn't have a strong shot, but he has a quick release.

Johnson is a terrific skater with the kind of speed that will always earn him an NHL job. He will be a 10-year pro. He can tarry puck carriers when killing penalties and has the one-step quickness to be a short-handed threat.

THE PHYSICAL GAME

Johnson added about 20 pounds of much-needed muscle over the past few seasons, and was able to do so without it affecting his speed.

THE INTANGIBLES

Talk about your overnight successes. Toronto gave up waiting to see this kind of performance again from Johnson, whose last notable season came in 1998-99. Then Tampa Bay tried him out. He came to Phoenix in the Nikolai Khabibulin trade in a salary dump that has worked out pretty well for the Coyotes. Johnson was a restricted free agent after the season.

PROJECTION

It's one thing to catch everyone by surprise. It's quite another to perform well after you've raised the bar. Anything less than a 25-goal, 65-point season would be a letdown.

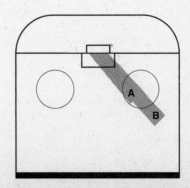

KRYSTOFER KOLANOS

Yrs. of NHL service: 2
Born: Calgary, Alta.; July 27, 1981
Position: center
Height: 6-3
Weight: 205
Uniform no.: 36
Shoots: right

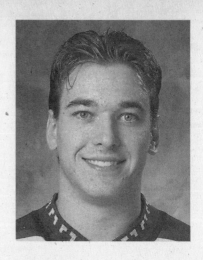

Career statistics:

GP	G	A	TP	PIM
59	11	11	22	48

2001-2002 statistics:

GP	G	A	TP	+/-	PIM	PP	SH	GW	GT	S	PCT
57	11	11	22	+6	48	0	0	5	0	81	13.6

2002-2003 statistics:

GP	G	A	TP	+/-	PIM	PP	SH	GW	GT	S	PCT
2	0	0	0	0	0	0	0	0	0	8	0.0

LAST SEASON
Missed 80 games due to concussion.

THE FINESSE GAME
Kolanos may turn into a special kind of goal-scorer. He is one of those players that always seems to attract the puck. He knows where the play is going to go and anticipates. Most importantly, Kolanos wants the puck when the game is on the line.

Kolanos made the jump right out of college with an impressive training camp in 2001. He scored the overtime goal that won the NCAA title for Boston College. His confidence had to carry him through his first test — getting a contract with the Coyotes.

Kolanos was on target to develop into a very good second-line center before he suffered the first of two concussions at the end of his rookie season (the second occurred in training camp last September). He is smart and has very good hand skills. His skating is NHL caliber. Kolanos was fifth among the league's rookie scorers at the time of his injury in 2001-02.

THE PHYSICAL GAME
Kolanos wasn't a very aggressive player even before suffering the first head injury. He shows a lot of guts, though, in returning for the final two games of last season.

THE INTANGIBLES
Kolanos impressed the Coyotes enough in his freshman year so that the team traded away the talented Michal Handzus.

PROJECTION
Kolanos remains a very high-risk player because of the severity and the timing of his two head injuries. If Kolanos is able to return symptom-free, he is capable of 15-20 goals and 15-20 assists.

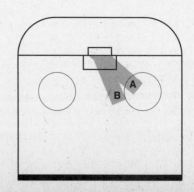

DAYMOND LANGKOW

Yrs. of NHL service: 7
Born: Edmonton, Alberta; Sept. 27, 1976
Position: center
Height: 5-11
Weight: 180
Uniform no.: 11
Shoots: left

Career statistics:

GP	G	A	TP	PIM
544	115	187	302	334

1999-2000 statistics:

GP	G	A	TP	+/-	PIM	PP	SH	GW	GT	S	PCT
82	18	32	50	+1	56	5	0	7	0	222	8.1

2000-2001 statistics:

GP	G	A	TP	+/-	PIM	PP	SH	GW	GT	S	PCT
71	13	41	54	+12	50	3	0	2	0	190	6.8

2001-2002 statistics:

GP	G	A	TP	+/-	PIM	PP	SH	GW	GT	S	PCT
80	27	35	62	+18	36	6	3	2	1	171	15.8

2002-2003 statistics:

GP	G	A	TP	+/-	PIM	PP	SH	GW	GT	S	PCT
82	20	32	52	+20	56	4	2	2	0	196	10.2

LAST SEASON

Led team in plus-minus and shorthanded goals. One of three Coyotes to appear in all 82 games.

THE FINESSE GAME

Langkow's primary drawback is his size. We're seeing more and more small men succeed in the NHL, and it appears Langkow could be one of them, especially if the Coyotes get just a little bigger to support him. He has terrific hockey sense, which is probably his chief asset, to go along with his stickhandling ability and shot. He is a fine passer with good vision, and he is patient with the puck. He is not shy about shooting and possesses an effective wrist shot and slap shot.

Langkow has good speed, spies his options quickly, and works hard. He knows what's going to happen before it does, which is the mark of an elite playmaker. He will harass opponents on the forecheck and create turnovers. Langkow is a solid two-way forward and likes to play in a system with aggressive forechecking. His defensive awareness is above average, but his face-off ability is less than average.

THE PHYSICAL GAME

Langkow is a spunky, fast, in-your-face kind of player. He has some sandpaper in his game, which gives him an edge over other small forwards who only rely on their finesse skills. He doesn't mind aggravating people, and he'll throw punches at far bigger men. He won't be intimidated and does his scoring in the trenches despite getting hit. He has a high pain threshold. For a guy who plays as hard as he does every night, Langkow can handle a surprisingly heavy workload as far as ice time goes.

THE INTANGIBLES

Langkow shows all the signs of being one of those indispensable forwards that other teams dislike playing against. He was a restricted free agent after the season.

PROJECTION

While Langkow is best suited as a third-line forward, he's destined to be a top six in Phoenix for the foreseeable future. He is a solid 20-goal, 50-point player.

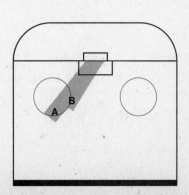

PAUL MARA

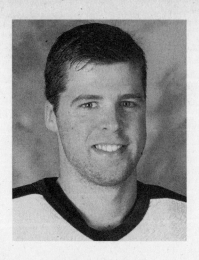

Yrs. of NHL service: 4
Born: Ridgewood, NJ; Sept. 7, 1979
Position: left defense
Height: 6-4
Weight: 210
Uniform no.: 23
Shoots: left

Career statistics:

GP	G	A	TP	PIM
265	31	58	89	263

1999-2000 statistics:

GP	G	A	TP	+/-	PIM	PP	SH	GW	GT	S	PCT
54	7	11	18	-27	73	4	0	1	0	78	9.0

2000-2001 statistics:

GP	G	A	TP	+/-	PIM	PP	SH	GW	GT	S	PCT
62	6	14	20	-16	54	2	0	1	0	78	7.7

2001-2002 statistics:

GP	G	A	TP	+/-	PIM	PP	SH	GW	GT	S	PCT
75	7	17	24	-6	58	2	0	0	1	112	6.3

2002-2003 statistics:

GP	G	A	TP	+/-	PIM	PP	SH	GW	GT	S	PCT
73	10	15	25	-7	78	1	0	0	0	95	10.5

LAST SEASON

Third on team in average ice time (21:06). Career highs in goals and points. Missed nine games with sprained shoulder.

THE FINESSE GAME

Mara is primarily an offensive defenseman. His point shot is a weapon not because of its velocity — he is no Al MacInnis — but because he gets it away quickly and keeps it low and on net. He creates chances for tip-ins and scrambles off his rebounds. He can run a power play.

Mobile for his size, Mara's skating is quite smooth and powerful. He is also one of those efficient skaters who can stay as strong late in the game as he was on his first few shifts.

He has good vision and is an excellent passer. He is also quick to move the puck out of his zone and will jump up and join the rush. Mara is used in more crunch-time situations. Mara's progress has been steady. He has good hockey intelligence.

THE PHYSICAL GAME

Mara makes take-outs, but he is not a punishing hitter. He is tall but lean, and needs to fill out more because he will need more strength to compete in the trenches. Mara was not in the best of shape when he arrived from Tampa Bay in a trade (in 2001 in the Nikolai Khabibulin deal), but he has improved.

THE INTANGIBLES

Mara is a top-four defenseman with Phoenix but how will the loss of partner Danny Markov (in an off-season trade to Carolina) affect him?

PROJECTION

Mara should be a consistent scorer in the 30- to 35-point range.

LADISLAV NAGY

Yrs. of NHL service: 3
Born: Preslov, Slovakia; June 1, 1979
Position: center
Height: 5-11
Weight: 194
Uniform no.: 17
Shoots: left

Career statistics:

GP	G	A	TP	PIM
211	55	67	122	166

1999-2000 statistics:

GP	G	A	TP	+/-	PIM	PP	SH	GW	GT	S	PCT
11	2	4	6	+2	2	1	0	0	0	15	13.3

2000-2001 statistics:

GP	G	A	TP	+/-	PIM	PP	SH	GW	GT	S	PCT
46	8	9	17	-2	22	2	0	2	0	64	12.5

2001-2002 statistics:

GP	G	A	TP	+/-	PIM	PP	SH	GW	GT	S	PCT
74	23	19	42	+6	50	5	0	5	0	187	12.3

2002-2003 statistics:

GP	G	A	TP	+/-	PIM	PP	SH	GW	GT	S	PCT
80	22	35	57	+17	92	8	0	6	0	209	10.5

PROJECTION

We thought last year might be the breakout season for Nagy. Maybe now that the Tony Amonte experiment has failed, Nagy will get more ice time and will become the 30-goal sniper we think he is destined to be.

LAST SEASON

Led team in power-play goals. Second on team in goals and plus-minus. Tied for second on team in power-play goals. Third on team in assists, points, and shots. Career highs in assists and points. Missed two games with an infection.

THE FINESSE GAME

Nagy is a very skilled player. He has great hands and a good sense for the game.

His overall speed is just about average but what sets him apart is his initial burst of quickness, cheetah-like, for the first 10 feet. He jumps into holes and reads the openings very well. He is good at taking the puck to the net with his quickness and his deft touch.

Nagy has a confidence to him, almost a cockiness, which good scorers have to have. He is creative and willing to try moves that other players either can't do or would hesitate to even attempt. Nagy is not afraid to shoot the puck or walk off the half-boards on a power play.

THE PHYSICAL GAME

Nagy is on the small side and does not play a physical game, although he is by no means a perimeter player. You will find Nagy playing in traffic.

THE INTANGIBLES

Nagy has a tremendous offensive upside. Nagy is one of the players Phoenix received in exchange for Keith Tkachuk in 2001.

TYSON NASH

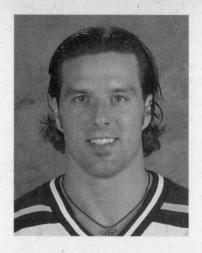

Yrs. of NHL service: 4
Born: Edmonton, Alta.; Mar. 11, 1975
Position: left wing
Height: 6-0
Weight: 185
Uniform no.: 9
Shoots: left

Career statistics:

GP	G	A	TP	PIM
255	24	26	50	479

1999-2000 statistics:

GP	G	A	TP	+/-	PIM	PP	SH	GW	GT	S	PCT
66	4	9	13	+6	150	0	1	1	0	68	5.9

2000-2001 statistics:

GP	G	A	TP	+/-	PIM	PP	SH	GW	GT	S	PCT
57	8	7	15	+8	110	0	1	0	0	113	7.1

2001-2002 statistics:

GP	G	A	TP	+/-	PIM	PP	SH	GW	GT	S	PCT
64	6	7	13	+2	100	0	0	1	0	66	9.1

2002-2003 statistics:

GP	G	A	TP	+/-	PIM	PP	SH	GW	GT	S	PCT
66	6	3	9	0	114	1	0	2	0	77	7.8

LAST SEASON

Missed 12 games with ankle injury. Missed four games due to coach's decision.

THE FINESSE GAME

Nash likes to make things happen, but injuries over the past three seasons have robbed him of some of his jump. The operations included a reconstructive knee surgery as well as two sports hernias. Just when Nash seemed to be getting past those, he missed the first dozen games of this season with an ankle injury.

This was highly frustrating for a player like Nash, because he couldn't make things happen the way he likes to, or anticipate. Nash is a forechecking force, and agitator. But by losing a step, Nash can't get in on his man, or do anything if he did get there.

Nash is a high-energy player who can lift the bench and the building with his effort. He lacks the skill level to rise above much more than a fourth-line role, but boy, does he try. St. Louis gave him the occasional fling on the power play, and he scored his first career power-play goal.

THE PHYSICAL GAME

Nash still looks like a frustrated player, and the emotion sometimes boils over into bad penalties. He's much less of an impact player than he wants to be.

THE INTANGIBLES

Nash is anxious to prove himself. This could be a critical season for him, especially since he finished last season as a restricted free agent, if he can ever return to his rookie season (1999-2000) form. He's a good energy guy to have in the lineup, which is why the Blues will give him a chance again.

PROJECTION

Nash's point totals will never be very high. He might break 20 over a full season. He is pretty much a safe bet for triple digit PIM totals.

ANDREI NAZAROV

Yrs. of NHL service: 9
Born: Chelyabinsk, Russia; May 22, 1974
Position: left wing
Height: 6-5
Weight: 241
Uniform no.: 44
Shoots: right

Career statistics:

GP	G	A	TP	PIM
536	52	69	121	1278

1999-2000 statistics:

GP	G	A	TP	+/-	PIM	PP	SH	GW	GT	S	PCT
76	10	22	32	+3	78	1	0	1	0	110	9.1

2000-2001 statistics:

GP	G	A	TP	+/-	PIM	PP	SH	GW	GT	S	PCT
79	2	4	6	-23	229	0	0	0	0	63	3.2

2001-2002 statistics:

GP	G	A	TP	+/-	PIM	PP	SH	GW	GT	S	PCT
77	6	5	11	+5	215	0	0	0	0	56	10.7

2002-2003 statistics:

GP	G	A	TP	+/-	PIM	PP	SH	GW	GT	S	PCT
59	3	0	3	-9	135	2	0	0	0	35	8.6

LAST SEASON

Missed two games due to NHL suspension. Missed 21 games due to coach's decision.

THE FINESSE GAME

Nazarov isn't overly creative with the puck, but with his size, does he have to be? This giant has decent hand skills around the net, though he does have some trouble fishing out loose pucks from his feet in goal-mouth scrambles, presumably because his head is so far from the ice it's tough to see.

The biggest improvement in Nazarov's game is in his skating. He is not at his best handling the puck for long and is insecure if forced to rush with it. Defenders brave enough to venture close have a relatively easy time stripping it from him because the puck is so far from his feet. He plops himself in front of the net on power plays and creates a wall that is nearly impossible for the goalie to see around. Nazarov needs to play with linemates who will get him the puck. He has decent hands and can shoot.

Nazarov is smart and understands the game well. He is aware of his limitations and won't try to do too much. He has an obvious love for the game.

THE PHYSICAL GAME

When he first broke into the league with San Jose, he quickly developed a reputation as a scary-mean player. He is a good, hard, physical player, but he isn't the sort who goes looking to hurt people. Nazarov is just so big and strong that the injuries kind of happen. He'll fight when he has to, and his long reach makes him tough for even some of the league's best brawlers to cope with. He will protect his teammates and provide an emotional spark.

THE INTANGIBLES

Nazarov is with his sixth NHL team in a very short span. It seems that no one can quite contain this bull in the china shop style. Nazarov is raw and rough. He certainly gets a lot of room to work on his puck-handling skills.

PROJECTION

Forget points. Although Nazarov will continue to work on being more than a fourth-line player, his value lies in your fantasy league with a category for PIM. A sensational year for him would be 10 goals.

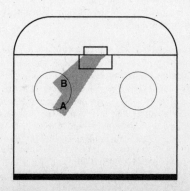

TEPPO NUMMINEN

Yrs. of NHL service: 15
Born: Tampere, Finland; July 3, 1968
Position: left defense
Height: 6-2
Weight: 199
Uniform no.: 27
Shoots: right

Career statistics:

GP	G	A	TP	PIM
1098	108	426	534	405

1999-2000 statistics:

GP	G	A	TP	+/-	PIM	PP	SH	GW	GT	S	PCT
79	8	34	42	+21	16	2	0	2	0	126	6.3

2000-2001 statistics:

GP	G	A	TP	+/-	PIM	PP	SH	GW	GT	S	PCT
72	5	26	31	+9	36	1	0	2	0	109	4.6

2001-2002 statistics:

GP	G	A	TP	+/-	PIM	PP	SH	GW	GT	S	PCT
76	13	35	48	+13	20	4	0	6	0	117	11.1

2002-2003 statistics:

GP	G	A	TP	+/-	PIM	PP	SH	GW	GT	S	PCT
78	6	24	30	0	30	2	0	1	1	108	5.6

LAST SEASON

Led team defensemen in points for sixth consecutive season. Led team in average ice time (23:51). Missed four games with bruised ankle.

THE FINESSE GAME

Smart and reserved, Numminen's agility and anticipation make him look much faster than he is. A graceful skater with a smooth change of direction, he never telegraphs what he is about to do. His skating makes him valuable on the first penalty-killing unit. He will not get caught out of position and is seldom bested one-on-one.

If he is under pressure, Numminen is not afraid to give up the puck on a dump-and-chase, rather than force a neutral-zone play. He works best with a partner with some offensive savvy. Otherwise, he takes too much of the offensive game on himself, and his plays look forced. He would rather dish off than rush with the puck. Numminen is a crisp passer, he moves the puck briskly and seldom overhandles it. He is terrific at making the first pass to move the puck out of the zone.

Numminen is not a finisher. He joins the play but doesn't lead it. Most of his offense is generated from point shots or passes in-deep. He works the right point on the power play. He is uncannily adept at keeping the puck in at the point, frustrating opponents who try to clear it out around the boards. He intentionally shoots the puck wide for tip-ins by his sure-handed forwards. He is not afraid to pinch, either.

THE PHYSICAL GAME

For a scrawny guy, Numminen plays an acceptable physical game, and he plays hurt. He can be intimidated and doesn't scare attackers who will attempt to drive through him to the net. Opponents get a strong forecheck on him to neutralize his smart passing game. He'll employ his body as a last resort, but would rather use his stick and gain the puck. He is even-tempered and not at all nasty. He averaged close to 24 minutes per game again last season and faced other teams' top lines night after night. At 35, that's a bit taxing, and the Coyotes need to trim his minutes.

THE INTANGIBLES

Numminen is slowing down and might be seeing his final season as a top-pair defenseman. It's the last year of his contract and it could be his final season, period. He was still the team's most reliable defenseman.

PROJECTION

Numminen is a complete, if not elite, defenseman and capable of again scoring 30 points.

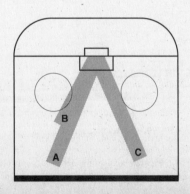

BRANKO RADIVOJEVIC

Yrs. of NHL service: 1
Born: Piestany, Slovakia; Nov. 24, 1980
Position: right wing
Height: 6-1
Weight: 209
Uniform no.: 29
Shoots: right

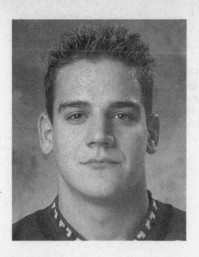

Career statistics:

GP	G	A	TP	PIM
97	16	17	33	67

2001-2002 statistics:

GP	G	A	TP	+/-	PIM	PP	SH	GW	GT	S	PCT
18	4	2	6	+1	4	0	0	1	0	19	21.0

2002-2003 statistics:

GP	G	A	TP	+/-	PIM	PP	SH	GW	GT	S	PCT
79	12	15	27	-2	63	1	0	3	1	109	11.0

LAST SEASON

First NHL season. Tied for fourth among NHL rookies in shooting percentage. Tied for seventh among NHL rookies in goals. Tied for 10th among NHL rookies in points. Third on team in shooting percentage. Missed three games due to coach's decision.

THE FINESSE GAME

Radivojevic's primary asset is his foot speed. He has really quick feet and is an agile skater for a good-sized guy.

Radivojevic is aggressive on the forecheck and forces turnovers. He protects the puck well when he in controlling it. Radivojevic doesn't waste his speed on useless forays all over the ice. He is intelligent and seems to have a game plan on every shift.

Radivojevic will probably see a lot of second-unit power-play ice time. He works to jump in and out of holes and drives to the net well. He has good hand skills, especially in tight. He is a creative playmaker.

Radivojevic has performed well in pressure spots earlier in his career and could develop into a solid power forward and go-to guy. Radivojevic was originally drafted by Colorado in 1999 but went unsigned. Phoenix picked him up as a free agent and he's proving to be a diamond in the rough.

THE PHYSICAL GAME

Radivojevic is a high energy player. He needs to get a little stronger to play a better power game, which is the style he thrives on. He is not naturally aggressive. Radivojevic has probably added 20 pounds since his draft year and now needs to put it to good use on a consistent basis.

THE INTANGIBLES

If you ask us, hockey needs more guys with names like Branko.

PROJECTION

Radivojevic may move up to the second line this season. Expect to see him hit the 20-goal mark.

365

JEFF TAFFE

Yrs. of NHL service: 0
Born: Hastings, Minn.; Feb. 19, 1981
Position: center
Height: 6-3
Weight: 195
Uniform no.: 14
Shoots: left

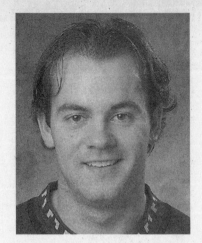

Career statistics:

GP	G	A	TP	PIM
20	3	1	4	4

2002-2003 statistics:

GP	G	A	TP	+/-	PIM	PP	SH	GW	GT	S	PCT
20	3	1	4	-4	4	1	0	1	0	18	16.7

LAST SEASON

Will be entering first full NHL season. Appeared in 57 games with Springfield (AHL), scoring 23-26 — 49 with 44 PIM.

THE FINESSE GAME

Taffe led the farm team in scoring even though he spent 20 games with the parent club in three different stints. He obviously has an offensive flair which looks like it will be able to translate to the NHL level.

Taffe is a skater with a fluid, graceful stride. He is agile and has the confidence to try to beat a defender with one-on-one moves. He has good hockey vision and intelligence.

He is equally good at scoring and playmaking. Taffe has developed a lot of faith in his ability to score goals. He is especially dangerous on the power play. Taffe needs a lot of work on his defensive play.

THE PHYSICAL GAME

What sets Taffe apart is his heart and effort, which was questioned early in his career. He has been gradually adding about 15 pounds of muscle over the years since he was drafted (in the first round in 2000 by St. Louis), which will make him stronger. He doesn't initiate much, although he plays with a little edge and won't get pushed around.

THE INTANGIBLES

Taffe may get caught up in a numbers game at center. If he has a good enough camp, the always cost-conscious Coyotes will make room for him.

PROJECTION

Taffe is likely to become a second-line center in the NHL, but it might not happen this season. If it does, he is capable of a 40-point season and possible Calder Trophy consideration.

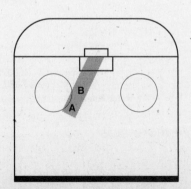

DAVID TANABE

Yrs. of NHL service: 4
Born: Minneapolis, Minn.; July 19, 1980
Position: right defense
Height: 6-1
Weight: 190
Uniform no.: 21
Shoots: right

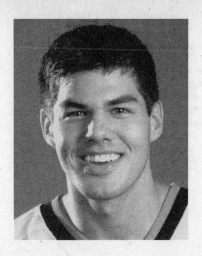

Career statistics:

GP	G	A	TP	PIM
251	15	47	62	115

1999-2000 statistics:

GP	G	A	TP	+/-	PIM	PP	SH	GW	GT	S	PCT
31	4	0	4	-4	14	3	0	0	0	28	14.3

2000-2001 statistics:

GP	G	A	TP	+/-	PIM	PP	SH	GW	GT	S	PCT
74	7	22	29	-9	42	5	0	1	0	130	5.4

2001-2002 statistics:

GP	G	A	TP	+/-	PIM	PP	SH	GW	GT	S	PCT
78	1	15	16	-13	35	0	0	0	0	113	0.9

2002-2003 statistics:

GP	G	A	TP	+/-	PIM	PP	SH	GW	GT	S	PCT
68	3	10	13	-27	24	2	0	0	0	104	2.9

LAST SEASON

Acquired from Carolina with Igor Knyazev on June 21, 2003, for Danny Markov and and fourth-round draft pick in 2003. Worst plus-minus on team. Missed 14 games with shoulder injuries.

THE FINESSE GAME

Tanabe is a terrific skater who may turn into one of the best-skating defensemen of his generation. The only question mark is his hockey sense, because he doesn't seem to be able to make as many good things happen as he should. Tanabe is still a very high-risk player.

He can make a good first pass out of his zone or rush the puck end-to-end. He has a hard shot from the point. His defensive reads need a lot of work. Tanabe looks good on the power play, but he has to make a living at working five-on-five.

Tanabe has taken a page out of Scott Niedermayer's book. Like the highly skilled Devils' defenseman, Tanabe hustles back on defense after he has made an offensive-zone play. One thing Tanabe has to remember is never to lose momentum. When he keeps his feet moving, he can cover the entire ice surface effortlessly.

THE PHYSICAL GAME

Tanabe needs to improve his conditioning and his strength. He is built on the lean side, and is easily muscled off the puck. Tanabe has to be tougher to play through. He battles asthma and has to use an inhaler during games.

THE INTANGIBLES

Paul Coffey, who played with Tanabe in Carolina, is now with the Coyotes and was one of the reasons why Tanabe was traded to Phoenix. Coffey is a big booster of this offensive defenseman, and it won't hurt for Tanabe to be schooled by Coffey.

PROJECTION

We expected more out of Tanabe last season. He battled with nagging upper-body injuries, and the whole team slumped after Rod Brind'Amour was lost to injury. But Tanabe needs to score 35-40 points to make it worth a team's while to put him in the lineup. Expect him to be a top-four defenseman in Phoenix.

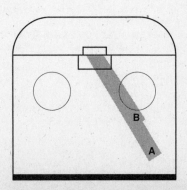

OSSI VAANANEN

Yrs. of NHL service: 3
Born: Vantaa, Finland; Aug. 18, 1980
Position: left defense
Height: 6-4
Weight: 215
Uniform no.: 4
Shoots: left

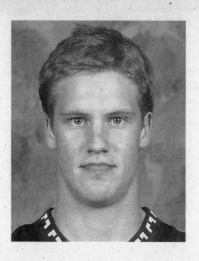

Career statistics:

GP	G	A	TP	PIM
224	8	31	39	246

2000-2001 statistics:

GP	G	A	TP	+/-	PIM	PP	SH	GW	GT	S	PCT
81	4	12	16	+9	90	0	0	2	0	69	5.8

2001-2002 statistics:

GP	G	A	TP	+/-	PIM	PP	SH	GW	GT	S	PCT
76	2	12	14	+6	74	0	1	0	0	41	4.9

2002-2003 statistics:

GP	G	A	TP	+/-	PIM	PP	SH	GW	GT	S	PCT
67	2	7	9	+1	82	0	0	0	0	49	4.1

LAST SEASON

Missed 14 games with sprained knee. Missed one game with bruised foot.

THE FINESSE GAME

Vaananen handles a lot of the grunt work, like making hits and blocking shots.

Most of what Vaananen does well occurs in his own end of the ice. He takes away passing lanes and clears out the front of his net. He is big and strong and sturdy on his skates. If he is guilty of anything, it is on nights when he tries to do too much.

Vaananen is a smart player and a quick study. He has never been a scorer at any level of his development, and it isn't going to happen in the NHL. He digs in around his own net, though, and is gritty in all the right areas. He moves the puck very well.

THE PHYSICAL GAME

Vaananen has good size and strength and plays a zesty game. He is tall and has a very long reach for tying up attackers. He handles a lot of ice time. Once he got into the lineup after opening night he was impossible to pry off the ice. He doesn't take many bad penalties. He plays hard and clean.

Vaananen has added a few pounds (about 10-12) since his rookie year but it's not likely he'll get overly bulky.

THE INTANGIBLES

Vaananen didn't play with the same zest that characterized his first two seasons, and was less effective on a nightly basis as a result.

PROJECTION

Vaananen is colorful and just plain fun to watch. He will never score many points. He needs to put some life back in his game.

PITTSBURGH PENGUINS

Players' Statistics 2001-2002

POS.	NO.	PLAYER	GP	G	A	PTS	+/-	PIM	PP	SH	GW	GT	S	PCT
C	66	MARIO LEMIEUX	67	28	63	91	-25	43	14		4		235	11.9
C	82	MARTIN STRAKA	60	18	28	46	-18	12	7		4		136	13.2
D	32	DICK TARNSTROM	61	7	34	41	-11	50	3				115	6.1
R	95	ALEKSEY MOROZOV	27	9	16	25	-3	16	6		2	1	46	19.6
R	37	MIKAEL SAMUELSSON	80	10	14	24	-21	40	2	1	2	1	154	6.5
L	10	VILLE NIEMINEN	75	9	12	21	-25	93		2	1		86	10.5
L	19	RICO FATA	63	7	12	19	-7	16					79	8.9
L	34	*RAMZI ABID	33	10	8	18	-4	32	4		3		59	16.9
C	20	MATHIAS JOHANSSON	58	5	10	15	-14	16	2				70	7.1
D	39	JOEL BOUCHARD	34	5	8	13	0	14	1		2		47	10.6
C	14	MILAN KRAFT	31	7	5	12	-8	10			1		50	14.0
L	43	*TOMAS SUROVY	26	4	7	11	0	10	1		2		47	8.5
L	23	STEVE MCKENNA	79	9	1	10	-18	128	5		3		59	15.3
D	28	MICHAL ROZSIVAL	53	4	6	10	-5	40	1				61	6.6
R	11	ALEXANDRE DAIGLE	33	4	3	7	-10	8	1				48	8.3
C	26	KENT MANDERVILLE	82	2	5	7	-22	46			1		72	2.8
R	72	ERIC MELOCHE	13	5	1	6	-2	4	2		1	1	34	14.7
D	6	RICHARD LINTNER	29	4	2	6	-14	10	2			1	45	8.9
C	12	*MICHAL SIVEK	38	3	3	6	-5	14	1				45	6.7
L	33	*GUILLAUME LEFEBVRE	26	2	4	6	2	4					19	10.5
D	8	HANS JONSSON	63	1	4	5	-23	36					40	2.5
D	3	JAMIE PUSHOR	76	3	1	4	-28	76					54	5.6
C	15	BRIAN HOLZINGER	14	1	3	4	-5	8			1		23	4.3
D	57	SHAWN HEINS	47	1	2	3	-4	42			1		38	2.6
D	4	*DAN FOCHT	22		3	3	-9	29					12	
R	36	*TOM KOSTOPOULOS	8		1	1	-4						6	
C	16	KRIS BEECH	12		1	1	-3	6					6	
L	19	VLADIMIR VUJTEK	5		1	1	-4						3	
D	2	JOSEF MELICHAR	8				-2	2					6	
L	48	*KONSTANTIN KOLTSOV	2				-2						4	
D	34	*ROSS LUPASCHUK	3				-3	4					3	
D	29	*BROOKS ORPIK	6				-5	2					2	
G	31	SEBASTIEN CARON	24				0	6						
G	1	JOHAN HEDBERG	41				0	18						
G	30	J-SEBASTIEN AUBIN	21				0	2						

GP = games played; G = goals; A = assists; PTS = points; +/- = goals-for minus goals-against while player is on ice; PIM = penalties in minutes; PP = power-play goals; SH = shorthanded goals; GW = game-winning goals; GT = game-tying goals; S = no. of shots; PCT = percentage of goals to shots; * = rookie

JOHAN HEDBERG

Yrs. of NHL service: 2
Born: Leksand, Sweden; May 5, 1973
Position: goaltender
Height: 6-0
Weight: 184
Uniform no.: 1
Catches: left

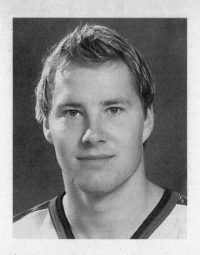

Career statistics:

GP	MIN	GA	SO	GAA	A	PIM
116	6832	328	7	2.88	3	40

2000-2001 statistics:

GP	MIN	GAA	W	L	T	SO	GA	S	SAPCT	PIM
9	545	2.64	7	1	1	0	24	253	.905	0

2001-2002 statistics:

GP	MIN	GAA	W	L	T	SO	GA	S	SAPCT	PIM
66	3877	2.75	25	34	7	6	178	1851	.904	22

2002-2003 statistics:

GP	MIN	GAA	W	L	T	SO	GA	S	SAPCT	PIM
41	2410	3.14	14	22	4	1	126	1197	.895	18

LAST SEASON

Missed 14 games with fractured clavicle.

THE PHYSICAL GAME

Hedberg is a classic butterfly goalie. He has very good reflexes, moves well laterally across the crease and has a quick glove hand. He stays square to the shooter and, while he will occasionally allow a bad-angle goal, he doesn't beat himself often.

A little too aggressive at the start of his NHL career, Hedberg would charge out of his net thinking he could play pucks in the slot. He has learned to be more conservative. It doesn't help him that the Penguins are not very solid defensively. Often, Hedberg will have to do too much to help his defense out.

Hedberg is pretty good with his stick, moving the puck and using his stick to break up passes around the crease. He is very level-headed and doesn't get flustered under pressure. Hedberg freezes the puck a lot for draws. His centers are good on face-offs, and his defensemen have trouble moving the puck, so Hedberg likes to settle things down. The NHL has been talking about a crackdown on this, and if delay of game penalties start being called more tightly on goalies, Hedberg could run into some problems.

THE MENTAL GAME

Hedberg wants to play with the game and the season on the line. While he is not an elite-level goalie, he is just a notch below the NHL netminding stars. This will be an interesting season for him since he is likely to be challenged for the No. 1 role by Sebastien Caron, who stepped up his game while Hedberg was sidelined.

Hedberg's injury was also a factor in the second half, as he went 2-12-1 after returning from the broken collarbone.

THE INTANGIBLES

Hedberg had to wait a long time to get his NHL break (at age 28) and he does not take winning the job lightly. He plays with an upbeat attitude. His teammates want to play hard in front of him, and he gives them a chance to win every night.

PROJECTION

There is a good chance the Penguins will have an even worse season than they did last year, and there is no guarantee Hedberg will win the No. 1 job. Twenty wins would be an optimistic prediction.

MILAN KRAFT

Yrs. of NHL service: 3
Born: Plzen, Czech.; Jan. 17, 1980
Position: center
Height: 6-3
Weight: 211
Uniform no.: 14
Shoots: right

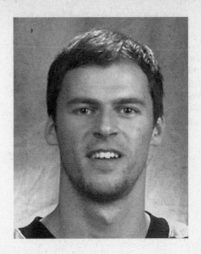

Career statistics:

GP	G	A	TP	PIM
141	22	20	42	34

2000-2001 statistics:

GP	G	A	TP	+/-	PIM	PP	SH	GW	GT	S	PCT
42	7	7	14	-6	8	1	1	1	1	63	11.1

2001-2002 statistics:

GP	G	A	TP	+/-	PIM	PP	SH	GW	GT	S	PCT
68	8	8	16	-9	16	1	0	2	1	103	7.8

2002-2003 statistics:

GP	G	A	TP	+/-	PIM	PP	SH	GW	GT	S	PCT
31	7	5	12	-8	10	0	0	1	0	50	14.0

LAST SEASON

Missed five games with groin injury. Appeared in 40 games with Wilkes-Barre (AHL), scoring 13-24 — 37 with 28 PIM.

THE FINESSE GAME

Kraft has a high skill level. He is a good skater, not an outstanding one, but there is no doubt he can compete at the NHL level. Kraft's primary asset is his stick-handling. He is a good playmaker, but needs to take more shots to make his game less predictable. He will work best with a finishing winger who likes to get the puck late. In his stints with the Pens, Kraft often played on the third or fourth lines. He needs to be a top-six forward to maximize his potential. Kraft has yet to show the kind of desire to earn even a top-nine role.

His biggest weakness is draws. He has learned to keep his hands lower on his stick and get into a better crouch, and he has improved somewhat. He still needs a lot of work in that department, however. He needs to improve his overall defense as well.

THE PHYSICAL GAME

Kraft needs to get stronger, especially if he is going to be handling the anticipated amount of ice time this season. He is rangy and needs to develop a more muscular frame.

THE INTANGIBLES

There are going to be a lot of job openings in training camp this year, and Kraft has to win one. As a first-round pick (in 1998), he is getting a lot of second chances, but those may run out this season.

PROJECTION

It's a Catch-22 (or Catch-14) for Kraft. He needs to score to play on one of the top two lines, but in order to play on one of the top two lines, he had better score at least 20 goals this season.

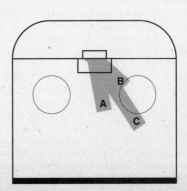

MARIO LEMIEUX

Yrs. of NHL service: 16
Born: Montreal, Que.; Oct. 5, 1965
Position: center
Height: 6-4
Weight: 230
Uniform no.: 66
Shoots: right

Career statistics:

GP	G	A	TP	PIM
879	682	1010	1692	812

2000-2001 statistics:

GP	G	A	TP	+/-	PIM	PP	SH	GW	GT	S	PCT
43	35	41	76	+15	18	16	1	5	0	171	20.5

2001-2002 statistics:

GP	G	A	TP	+/-	PIM	PP	SH	GW	GT	S	PCT
24	6	25	31	0	14	2	0	0	0	75	8.0

2002-2003 statistics:

GP	G	A	TP	+/-	PIM	PP	SH	GW	GT	S	PCT
67	28	63	91	-25	43	14	0	4	0	235	11.9

LAST SEASON

Third in NHL in assists. Eighth in NHL in points. Led team in goals, assists, points, power-play goals, game-winning goals, and shots. Second on team in average ice time (23:04) and shooting percentage. Missed 10 games with groin injury. Missed two games with back injury. Missed three games due to coach's decision.

THE FINESSE GAME

Injuries and age have robbed him of some of the magic, and the fact that he had to strip his team for financial reasons forces him to play with Martin Straka and 16 Wilkes-Barre Penguins. It is amazing that Lemieux stayed in the scoring race for as long as he did last season, at a 1.35 points per game pace.

Lemieux is still sneaky-good in his best moments. He can seem to be no factor in a game for 58 minutes and then beat a team with two plays, whether it is with a creative assist or one of his heavy and deceptive shots. Lemieux looks like he is cruising, but his first step to the puck is so huge and effortless that he can still make defensemen look silly by controlling the puck and then swooping around them. Step up to challenge Lemieux when he is carrying the puck, and he will use his long reach to pull the puck through a defender's legs. Back off him, and he will use the open ice to wheel tightly and put the puck on the tape of the breaking teammate.

Even though it appears he is slowing the game down to a molasses pace, Lemieux can do everything at a high tempo. He has spectacular vision, hands, and grace, and is one of the rare athletes still capable of dominating a game completely.

Discipline-minded Philadelphia coach Ken Hitchcock said he would have no trouble having Lemieux on his team, "He's the best defensive player in the league. He always has the puck."

THE PHYSICAL GAME

Lemieux needs to come back at full strength but play fewer minutes. It can't be an easy decision for the coaching staff to keep Lemieux on the bench, though, not when he's the owner and the rest of the Penguins' lineup has been exhausted of talent.

THE INTANGIBLES

Lemieux isn't likely to make a big fuss over it, but this is likely to be his Farewell Tour. Catch it if you can.

PROJECTION

Figure Lemieux to play in about 60 games and score about 80 points.

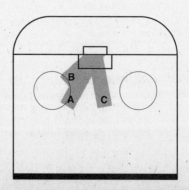

STEVE MCKENNA

Yrs. of NHL service: 6
Born: Toronto, Ont.; Aug. 21, 1973
Position: left wing
Height: 6-8
Weight: 255
Uniform no.: 23
Shoots: left

Career statistics:

GP	G	A	TP	PIM
324	17	12	29	739

1999-2000 statistics:

GP	G	A	TP	+/-	PIM	PP	SH	GW	GT	S	PCT
46	0	5	5	+3	125	0	0	0	0	14	0.0

2000-2001 statistics:

GP	G	A	TP	+/-	PIM	PP	SH	GW	GT	S	PCT
54	1	1	2	-4	119	0	0	0	0	19	5.3

2001-2002 statistics:

GP	G	A	TP	+/-	PIM	PP	SH	GW	GT	S	PCT
54	2	1	3	0	144	1	0	1	0	17	11.8

2002-2003 statistics:

GP	G	A	TP	+/-	PIM	PP	SH	GW	GT	S	PCT
79	9	1	10	-18	128	5	0	3	0	59	15.3

LAST SEASON

Led team in penalty minutes. Career highs in goals and points. Missed one game with elbow injury. Missed one game with flu. Missed one game due to coach's decision.

THE FINESSE GAME

McKenna is all rough edges, and it has been a long-term project for this lifetime defenseman to be converted into a very physical left wing. He sticks his nose in and plays hard.

He plays mainly on the fourth line at even strength, but the Penguins also made good use of his huge frame up front on the power play. He is just about impossible to budge, and with the man advantage, he does a good job of letting people hack at him without taking a retaliatory penalty to blow the power play. McKenna sees the occasional shift with better players, who play a little bolder with him around.

McKenna's skating is a drawback, but he has good lower-body strength and works hard. He's been progressing steadily and has a solid work ethic. His game isn't pretty but he thinks the game pretty well. He just needs his feet and hands to react quickly enough for the NHL level. When he has the time, he knows what to do with the puck and can make a play.

McKenna has good leadership qualities. He is a heart-and-soul player, even if he only gets seven or eight minutes a game.

THE PHYSICAL GAME

McKenna is as tough as he is tall. He has a long reach. He will take on anybody, and, most often, he'll win. He's a serious pugilist who always sticks up for his teammates. He's a hard 255 pounds, has a mean streak and can deliver punishing hits. Be afraid. Be very afraid.

THE INTANGIBLES

McKenna was the perfect guy to have around on a team that played an entire season without much hope. He has an upbeat attitude and can help keep a room loose. He is a team player. He is tough and not intimidated by anyone. McKenna approaches every game as if his team has a chance to win, even if in his heart he knows they are hopelessly overmatched.

PROJECTION

Nine goals and only one assist? How crazy a stat is that? Count on triple-digit PIM and maybe 15 points.

ALEXEI MOROZOV

Yrs. of NHL service: 6
Born: Moscow, Russia; Feb. 16, 1977
Position: right wing
Height: 6-1
Weight: 202
Uniform no.: 95
Shoots: left

Career statistics:

GP	G	A	TP	PIM
376	68	101	169	74

1999-2000 statistics:

GP	G	A	TP	+/-	PIM	PP	SH	GW	GT	S	PCT
68	12	19	31	+12	14	0	1	0	0	101	11.9

2000-2001 statistics:

GP	G	A	TP	+/-	PIM	PP	SH	GW	GT	S	PCT
66	5	14	19	-8	6	0	0	1	0	72	6.9

2001-2002 statistics:

GP	G	A	TP	+/-	PIM	PP	SH	GW	GT	S	PCT
72	20	29	49	-7	16	7	0	3	0	162	12.4

2002-2003 statistics:

GP	G	A	TP	+/-	PIM	PP	SH	GW	GT	S	PCT
27	9	16	25	-3	16	6	0	2	1	46	19.6

LAST SEASON

Third on team in power-play goals. Missed 55 games with fractured wrist.

THE FINESSE GAME

With a very sneaky, deceptive selection of shots, Morozov looks like he will be a big-goal scorer — in terms of importance, if not numbers. He tries to be too cute and make the extra play instead of shooting, but when he uses his hard and accurate shot to his advantage, he is extremely effective. He is a good stickhandler and has a good sense of timing with his passes.

Morozov was a gangly, awkward player who took some time to develop. Now the Penguins are reaping the rewards. Morozov is never better than when he gets to play on a line with Mario Lemieux. That could apply to just about anyone, but Morozov has the skill level that best complements Lemieux.

Morozov became a little more selfish last season, taking more shots, and that paid off with power-play ice time. Morozov has a very quick release on his shot and a high degree of accuracy.

THE PHYSICAL GAME

Morozov is a little on the stringy side. He'll never be confused with a power forward, though the Penguins are a little shy on size up front and need him to be more of a presence.

THE INTANGIBLES

With the departure of Alexei Kovalev, Morozov is set to inherit the No. 1 right wing job.

PROJECTION

We were hoping for another big step forward by Morozov last season, but a broken wrist suffered in November knocked him out for the rest of the season. He should be a 20-goal scorer.

Morozov is definitely a guy to have on your roster if you're playing the New Jersey Devils. He has 12 career goals against N.J. in 25 regular-season games.

BROOKS ORPIK

Yrs. of NHL service: 0
Born: Amherst, N.Y.; Sept. 26, 1980
Position: left defense
Height: 6-2
Weight: 222
Uniform no.: 29
Shoots: left

Career statistics:

GP	G	A	TP	PIM
6	0	0	0	2

2002-2003 statistics:

GP	G	A	TP	+/-	PIM	PP	SH	GW	GT	S	PCT
6	0	0	0	-5	2	0	0	0	0	2	0.0

LAST SEASON

Appeared in 71 games with Wilkes-Barre (AHL), scoring 4-14 — 18 with 105 PIM.

THE FINESSE GAME

Orpik is a steady, stay-at-home defenseman who can provide a calming influence on the ice. He had a six-game stint with the Penguins in December and did not look out of place.

Orpik is very steady and strong on his skates. He has never produced much offensively at any level of his development, so don't expect him to be running Pittsburgh's power plays.

Orpik has improved most in defensive reads and decision-making. Orpik shows signs of becoming a sound positional player who will not try to attempt too much. He plays within his limits, and he should develop into a safe defenseman with a long career.

THE PHYSICAL GAME

A lot of scouts pegged Orpik as a devastating, open-ice hitter when he was drafted (18th overall in 2000). One Penguins scout compared him to Darius Kasparaitis, but it was pretty evident from his brief NHL exposure that he will not become that type of player. That's not a knock. Orpik is still a solid checker, but he will do most of his work clearing out the front of his crease and along the boards. He could stand to add just a bit more upper-body strength for his one-on-one battles in tight.

THE INTANGIBLES

It must have just about killed the Penguins to keep Orpik in the minors while everything was going haywire with the big club, but they'll be happy they were patient. Orpik has now had two solid seasons in the minors (after three years of college). He was very consistent in the minors and the Pens will be looking for the same from him in the NHL.

One drawback is that Orpik (and the other budding Penguins defensemen) could use a solid veteran blue-liner to learn from, but the Pens don't have one.

PROJECTION

Orpik is likely to win a top-six role with the Pens and it's just a matter of time before he becomes a top four.

MICHAL ROZSIVAL

Yrs. of NHL service: 4
Born: Vlasim, Czech.; Sept. 3, 1978
Position: right defense
Height: 6-1
Weight: 208
Uniform no.: 28
Shoots: right

Career statistics:

GP	G	A	TP	PIM
237	18	47	65	161

1999-2000 statistics:

GP	G	A	TP	+/-	PIM	PP	SH	GW	GT	S	PCT
75	4	17	21	+11	48	1	0	1	0	73	5.5

2000-2001 statistics:

GP	G	A	TP	+/-	PIM	PP	SH	GW	GT	S	PCT
30	1	4	5	+3	26	0	0	0	0	17	5.9

2001-2002 statistics:

GP	G	A	TP	+/-	PIM	PP	SH	GW	GT	S	PCT
79	9	20	29	-6	47	4	0	4	0	89	10.1

2002-2003 statistics:

GP	G	A	TP	+/-	PIM	PP	SH	GW	GT	S	PCT
53	4	6	10	-5	40	1	0	0	0	61	6.6

LAST SEASON

Missed 15 games with separated shoulder. Missed 10 games due to thumb injuries. Missed three games due to "precautionary" reason. Missed one game with groin injury.

THE FINESSE GAME

While Rozsival isn't a No. 1 defenseman; he is a poised, low-risk blueliner who affords the Penguins a sense of stability in their top four. He has developed into Pittsburgh's steadiest defenseman.

Rozsival is hardly elite in any aspect of his game. He ranks "good" in a number of skill areas: skating, passing, playmaking, and hockey sense, and doesn't have any crucial flaws. He is a strong skater and is tough to beat one-on-one.

It seemed that every time Rozsival got going last season, he was dinged up again. The longest consecutive stretch he was able to play was from mid-December to mid-February.

THE PHYSICAL GAME

Rozsival doesn't play with much of an edge. He plays a containment game, and is not much of a hitter. Rozsival is good-sized and pretty strong and needs to assert himself more. He would be best playing with a physical, aggressive defensemen, if the Penguins can find one. Rozsival keeps himself well-conditioned (at least aerobically) and can handle a lot of minutes. He was second among Pittsburgh defensemen in average ice time last season (20:25).

THE INTANGIBLES

Rozsival would make a nice second- or third-pair defenseman on a number of teams. Pittsburgh is stretched so thin at the position that he will probably be asked again to overachieve in the top-pair role.

PROJECTION

Rozsival should produce around 20 points if he can stay healthy over the course of a full season.

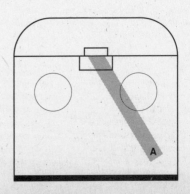

MARTIN STRAKA

Yrs. of NHL service: 11
Born: Plzen, Czech Republic; Sept. 3, 1972
Position: center
Height: 5-9
Weight: 178
Uniform no.: 82
Shoots: left

Career statistics:

GP	G	A	TP	PIM
676	182	322	504	252

1999-2000 statistics:

GP	G	A	TP	+/-	PIM	PP	SH	GW	GT	S	PCT
71	20	39	59	+24	26	3	1	2	0	146	13.7

2000-2001 statistics:

GP	G	A	TP	+/-	PIM	PP	SH	GW	GT	S	PCT
82	27	68	95	+19	38	7	1	4	1	185	14.6

2001-2002 statistics:

GP	G	A	TP	+/-	PIM	PP	SH	GW	GT	S	PCT
13	5	4	9	+3	0	1	0	1	0	33	15.1

2002-2003 statistics:

GP	G	A	TP	+/-	PIM	PP	SH	GW	GT	S	PCT
60	18	28	46	-18	12	7	0	4	0	136	13.2

LAST SEASON

Led team in shooting percentage. Second on team in goals, points, and power-play goals. Third on team in assists and shots. Missed 11 games with back injury. Missed 11 games with recurring hamstring injury.

THE FINESSE GAME

Straka has elite skills that he applies with the work ethic of a third-line grinder. The only thing that keeps him from being in the same class as a Jaromir Jagr or Pavel Bure is his shot, which isn't in the same class as his skating or hockey sense. Most of his goals come from breakaways, where Straka uses his speed, or by pouncing on loose pucks and rebounds.

He plays the left point on the power play (the Pens often use a five-man forward unit) not because of his shot, but because of his heady puck movement.

Straka can do a lot of things. He is a water bug with imagination. He makes clever passes that always land on the tape and give the recipient time to do something with the puck. He draws people to him and creates open ice for his linemates, or he intimidates with his speed to hurry the defender into a giveaway.

Straka doesn't have the outside speed to burn defenders, but creates space for himself with his wheeling in tight spaces. He has good balance and is tough to knock off his feet, even though he's not big. Not a great defensive player, Straka is effective in five-on-five situations. He is a perpetual threat.

THE PHYSICAL GAME

Straka is small and avoids corners and walls, and has to be teamed with more physical linemates to give him some room. He needs to learn to protect the puck better with his body and buy some time. The beating he took physically over the past two seasons may cost him speed and agility and could affect him mentally as well.

THE INTANGIBLES

Straka is one of the last valuable commodities left on the Penguins, which makes him almost a sure bet to be traded.

PROJECTION

Straka was well off the point-a-game pace we anticipated, but injuries were a major factor. If he can somehow manage to stay healthy, he could raise his production to around 70 points.

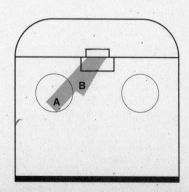

TOMAS SUROVY

Yrs. of NHL service: 1
Born: Banska Bystrica, Slovakia; Sept. 24, 1981
Position: left wing
Height: 6-0
Weight: 187
Uniform no.: 43
Shoots: left

Career statistics:

GP	G	A	TP	PIM
26	4	7	11	10

2002-2003 statistics:

GP	G	A	TP	+/-	PIM	PP	SH	GW	GT	S	PCT
26	4	7	11	0	10	1	0	2	0	47	8.5

LAST SEASON
Appeared in 39 games with Wilkes-Barre (AHL), scoring 19-20 — 39 with 18 PIM.

THE FINESSE GAME
Surovy has a great shot, and has drawn some (admittedly premature) parallels to Peter Bondra. Surovy lacks Bondra's explosive speed, and hasn't yet shown the Uzi-like ability to fire pucks on net.

Surovy played on a line with Mario Lemieux, although former coach Rick Kehoe was reluctant to do so, because he wanted Surovy to shoot rather than be intimidated into passing to big No.66, who also happens to own the team. It is Surovy's natural tendency to try to make a play rather than shoot it himself, and it's a habit if he will have to shake.

Surovy is very patient with the puck and has good poise, keeping his head up to look for passing options. It appears he will have little trouble adjusting to the pace of the NHL game. Skating may be what holds him back from becoming more of an impact player. He does have great hands, but they're much faster than his feet.

THE PHYSICAL GAME
Surovy has good size and strength, but he is not very aggressive and is not yet willing or able to overpower his opponents.

THE INTANGIBLES
No less an authority than Lemieux is solidly in this young Czech star's corner, which means he'll get every chance to win a top-six role in training camp and will probably see a considerable amount of ice time on the power play.

PROJECTION
Based on what we saw of Surovy after his February call-up, we would expect 15-20 goals as he breaks in for his first full NHL season.

378

SAN JOSE SHARKS

Players' Statistics 2001-2002

POS.	NO.	PLAYER	GP	G	A	PTS	+/-	PIM	PP	SH	GW	GT	S	PCT
R	8	TEEMU SELANNE	82	28	36	64	-6	30	7		5	1	253	11.1
C	25	VINCENT DAMPHOUSSE	82	23	38	61	-13	66	15		6		176	13.1
C	12	PATRICK MARLEAU	82	28	29	57	-10	33	8	1	3	1	172	16.3
L	19	MARCO STURM	82	28	20	48	9	16	6		2		208	13.5
C	18	MIKE RICCI	75	11	23	34	-12	53	5	1	2		101	10.9
D	2	MIKE RATHJE	82	7	22	29	-19	48	3		1		147	4.8
C	10	ALYN MCCAULEY	80	9	16	25	1	20	3				108	8.3
D	22	SCOTT HANNAN	81	3	19	22	0	61	1				103	2.9
L	17	SCOTT THORNTON	41	9	12	21	-7	41	4		1		64	14.1
D	21	*JIM FAHEY	43	1	19	20	-3	33					66	1.5
R	13	TODD HARVEY	76	3	16	19	5	74					64	4.7
L	9	ADAM GRAVES	82	9	9	18	-14	32	1				118	7.6
C	15	WAYNE PRIMEAU	77	6	12	18	-28	55	1				114	5.3
R	14	*JONATHAN CHEECHOO	66	9	7	16	-5	39			3	1	94	9.6
C	16	MARK SMITH	75	4	11	15	1	64					68	5.9
D	7	BRAD STUART	36	4	10	14	-6	46	2		1		63	6.3
R	23	*NICHOLAS DIMITRAKOS	21	6	7	13	-7	8	3			1	34	17.6
D	4	KYLE MCLAREN	33		8	8	-10	30					43	
D	5	JEFF JILLSON	26		6	6	-7	9					22	
R	28	MATT BRADLEY	46	2	3	5	-1	37					21	9.5
C	26	*LYNN LOYNS	19	3		3	-4	19					12	25.0
D	38	*ROB DAVISON	15	1	2	3	4	22					15	6.7
R	46	*MIROSLAV ZALESAK	10	1	2	3	-2						8	12.5
C	41	RYAN KRAFT	7		1	1	2						1	
D	4	JOHN JAKOPIN	12				0	11					3	
D	53	*JESSE FIBIGER	16				-5	2					2	
L	49	*CHAD WISEMAN	4				-2	4					1	
G	20	EVGENI NABOKOV	55				0	10						
G	29	VESA TOSKALA	11				0							
G	37	MIIKKA KIPRUSOFF	22				0							

GP = games played; G = goals; A = assists; PTS = points; +/- = goals-for minus goals-against while player is on ice; PIM = penalties in minutes; PP = power-play goals; SH = shorthanded goals; GW = game-winning goals; GT = game-tying goals; S = no. of shots; PCT = percentage of goals to shots; * = rookie

BRAD BOYES

Yrs. of NHL service: 0
Born: Mississauga, Ont.; Apr. 17, 1982
Position: center
Height: 6-0
Weight: 181
Uniform no.: n.a.
Shoots: right

Career (minor league) statistics:

GP	G	A	TP	PIM
80	30	34	64	66

2002-2003 minor league statistics:

GP	G	A	TP	PIM
80	30	34	64	66

LAST SEASON

Acquired from Toronto on March 5, 2003, with Alyn McCauley and a first-round draft pick in 2003, for Owen Nolan. Appeared in 65 games with St. John's (AHL), scoring 23-28 — 51 with 45 PIM. Appeared in 15 games with Cleveland (AHL), scoring 7-6 — 13 with 21 PIM.

THE FINESSE GAME

Boyes will need to improve on his skating if he is going to make an impact in the NHL. Boyes was expected to work with a skating coach during the off-season. It will be absolutely essential for him to get better.

Boyes is a clever playmaker. He senses where his linemates are and makes a lot of no-look passes in deep. He has highly tuned offensive instincts and fabulous hands.

Boyes has succeeded at the junior and minor league levels because his creativity sets him apart from anyone else on the ice. He may be one of the smartest players in this year's rookie crop. He will be dynamite on the power play, where the open ice will allow him that extra fraction of a second to find the teammate with the best scoring option. If it's him, Boyes will take the shot, but he is a better playmaker than finisher.

Boyes has great hands for draws, too.

THE PHYSICAL GAME

Boyes has character and heart and talent, but what's lacking is size. He will willingly go into traffic and will even initiate fights for the puck. Although he is not aggressive, neither is he timid.

THE INTANGIBLES

Anyone who thinks Toronto got the better of the Nolan deal may want to reassess that opinion in a season or two. Boyes may have been the key to the deal, if he can make the skating grade.

PROJECTION

San Jose may have some job openings at center. Expect Boyes to challenge and start out the season in a part-time role, with an eye on one of the top two slots. If he starts the season in the minors, he might be back by midseason. He could start off with a 30-point season, about equally distributed between goals and assists, if he sticks.

JONATHAN CHEECHOO

Yrs. of NHL service: 1
Born: Moose Factory, Ont.; July 15, 1980
Position: right wing
Height: 6-0
Weight: 205
Uniform no.: 14
Shoots: right

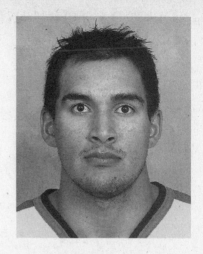

Career statistics:

GP	G	A	TP	PIM
66	9	7	16	39

2002-2003 statistics:

GP	G	A	TP	+/-	PIM	PP	SH	GW	GT	S	PCT
66	9	7	16	-5	39	0	0	3	1	94	9.6

LAST SEASON

First NHL season. Missed nine games due to coach's decision. Appeared in 9 games with Cleveland (AHL), scoring 3-4 — 7 with 16 PIM.

THE FINESSE GAME

On a team that was loaded with European-style forwards, Cheechoo stood out for his determination to go into the corners, work along the boards, and drive to the front of the net. His point totals will be more heavily weighted towards goals. He has a quick release on his shot and will score most of his goals from in tight. He likes to shoot and will take a chance from almost any area of the ice to force the goalie to handle it. Cheechoo has a dangerous backhand, which is just about a dying art. His hand-eye coordination is perfect for tipping point shots. Cheechoo's own slap shot is good enough that he can see some point duty on the power play. He has a flair for the dramatic and will probably score some key goals for the Sharks in seasons to come.

Cheechoo isn't much of a playmaker although he is a decent puckhandler. His assists will come from rebounds off of his shots.

Cheechoo is a strong, balanced skater. He's had to work on getting faster and developing some one-step quickness to get an edge on a defender. He has improved a great deal. While Cheechoo will never leave any vapor trials, he now has NHL caliber speed.

Cheechoo has had to become more consistent in his play. That was the message that went with his first-half demotion to the minors and he used that as motivation, rather than a reason to sulk. Cheechoo has to remember that on nights when he isn't scoring, there will be other things he can do to help his team win.

THE PHYSICAL GAME

Cheechoo is solidly built and is a fearsome forechecker. He is not fighter, but he is a strong hitter and can develop into an intimidating threat when he hones in on a puck-carrier. He is an enthusiastic player who avoids taking dumb penalties.

THE INTANGIBLES

Cheechoo has had the odds stacked against him as a native player who grew up on a reservation in Canada. He takes nothing for granted and will work hard to earn and keep an NHL job. How can you not root for a player from Moose Factory?

PROJECTION

After a first half that was a learning experience for Cheechoo, he was demoted and then promoted again from the minors and played steadily from mid-December on. He may start out on a third line as a tempo-changing forward but he will also see some power-play time and we wouldn't be shocked to see him chip in 10-15 goals.

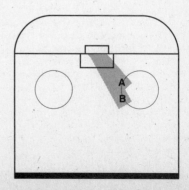

VINCENT DAMPHOUSSE

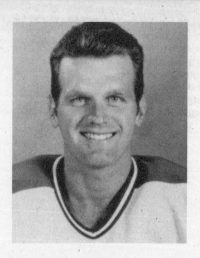

Yrs. of NHL service: 17
Born: Montreal, Que.; Dec. 17, 1967
Position: center
Height: 6-1
Weight: 200
Uniform no.: 25
Shoots: left

Career statistics:

GP	G	A	TP	PIM
1296	420	744	1164	1124

1999-2000 statistics:

GP	G	A	TP	+/-	PIM	PP	SH	GW	GT	S	PCT
82	21	49	70	+4	58	3	1	1	1	204	10.3

2000-2001 statistics:

GP	G	A	TP	+/-	PIM	PP	SH	GW	GT	S	PCT
45	9	37	46	+17	62	4	0	3	0	101	8.9

2001-2002 statistics:

GP	G	A	TP	+/-	PIM	PP	SH	GW	GT	S	PCT
82	20	38	58	+8	60	7	2	4	1	172	11.6

2002-2003 statistics:

GP	G	A	TP	+/-	PIM	PP	SH	GW	GT	S	PCT
82	23	38	61	-13	66	15	0	6	0	176	13.1

LAST SEASON

Led Sharks in assists, power-play goals, and game-winning goals. Second on Sharks in points and penalty minutes. Third on Sharks in shots and shooting percentage. One of five Sharks to appear in all 82 games.

THE FINESSE GAME

Cool in-tight, Damphousse has a marvellous back-hand shot he can roof. He creates opportunities down low by shaking and faking checkers with his skating. He likes to set up behind the net to make plays. Goalies need to be on the alert when he is on the attack because he is unafraid to take shots from absurd angles. He just likes to get a shot on net and get the goalie and defense scrambling. It's an effective tactic.

Damphousse shows poise with the puck. He has become more of a playmaker than a finisher. His puck control and passing touch are superb. He's a superb player in four-on-four situations. He has sharp offensive instincts and is good in traffic.

He won't leave any vapor trails with his skating in open ice, but Damphousse is quick around the net, especially with the puck. His lack of foot speed isn't as much of a detriment on a team that has skaters who can drive the defense back and give Damphousse more time and space for his shot. He has exceptional balance to hop through sticks and checks. In open ice he uses his weight to shift and change direction, making it appear as if he's going faster than he is — and he can juke without losing the puck while looking for his passing and shooting options.

THE PHYSICAL GAME

Damphousse uses his body to protect the puck, but he is not much of a grinder and loses most of his one-on-one battles. He has to be supported by physical linemates who will get him the puck. He'll expend a great deal of energy in the attacking zone, but little in his own end of the ice, though he is more diligent about this in crunch times.

A well-conditioned athlete who can handle long shifts and lots of ice time, Damphousse has a pretty high pain threshold. He is not shy about using his stick.

THE INTANGIBLES

Damphousse became an unrestricted free agent after last season.

PROJECTION

We'll stick with the same projection as last year (which Damphousse met) of 60 points.

JIM FAHEY

Yrs. of NHL service: 1
Born: Boston, Mass.; May 11, 1979
Position: right defense
Height: 6-0
Weight: 215
Uniform no.: 21
Shoots: right

Career statistics:

GP	G	A	TP	PIM
43	1	19	20	33

2002-2003 statistics:

GP	G	A	TP	+/-	PIM	PP	SH	GW	GT	S	PCT
43	1	19	20	-3	33	0	0	0	0	66	1.5

LAST SEASON

First NHL season. Seventh among NHL rookies in assists. Missed two games with head injury. Missed 10 games due to coach's decision. Appeared in 25 games with Cleveland (AHL), scoring 3-14 — 17 with 42 PIM.

THE FINESSE GAME

A valuable right-handed shooting point man, Fahey's rapid development allowed the Sharks to trade another highly regarded prospect in Jeff Jillson. Fahey may be set to become San Jose's best offensive defenseman.

Fahey was drafted in the ninth round in 1998, but improved by leaps and bounds through his college career at Northeastern. At first he seemed destined to be a one-way offenseman like Sandis Ozolinsh, but Fahey concentrated on learning the defensive part of the game and he will be a better player for it. It may mean the difference between an NHL career and a life in the minors.

Fahey's skating speed is adequate for the NHL. He is very strong on his skates, and very strong on the puck. He protects the puck well with his body. He has a good passing touch, good hockey sense, and decent vision. Fahey is learning when to gamble deep, and when to stay back on defense. In his own end, he makes a good first pass. He will use the boards to chip the puck out or even to pass the puck to a teammate. The latter is a unique tactic that Fahey excels at.

Fahey can still be a little high-risk at the point, but he should settle down with more experience and confidence. Fahey led all NHL rookies in power-play assists with 13, and had three fewer power-play points than rookie leader Rick Nash, and Fahey appeared in 29 fewer games.

THE PHYSICAL GAME

Scouts have raved about Fahey's character. He pays close attention to his conditioning. He is quick to get involved to aid a teammate. He is not a fighter by nature, but is an honest, tough player.

THE INTANGIBLES

Last season was Fahey's first as a pro (he played college hockey for Northeastern) and he sure grew up fast. Fahey is the kind of kid who may turn out to be an NHL captain. He is a leader by example and a good team guy. Fahey was about the only good thing to happen to the Sharks last season. He still needs a lot of coaching but he is open to it because he wants to improve.

PROJECTION

Fahey led all NHL rookie defensemen in points, playing only half a season in the bigs. He could well be San Jose's leading scorer on defense next season with around 35 points.

ADAM GRAVES

Yrs. of NHL service: 15
Born: Toronto, Ont.; Apr. 12, 1968
Position: left wing
Height: 6-0
Weight: 205
Uniform no.: 9
Shoots: left

Career statistics:

GP	G	A	TP	PIM
1152	329	287	616	1224

1999-2000 statistics:

GP	G	A	TP	+/-	PIM	PP	SH	GW	GT	S	PCT
77	23	17	40	-15	14	11	0	4	0	194	11.9

2000-2001 statistics:

GP	G	A	TP	+/-	PIM	PP	SH	GW	GT	S	PCT
82	10	16	26	-16	77	1	0	1	0	136	7.3

2001-2002 statistics:

GP	G	A	TP	+/-	PIM	PP	SH	GW	GT	S	PCT
81	17	14	31	+11	51	1	3	1	0	139	12.2

2002-2003 statistics:

GP	G	A	TP	+/-	PIM	PP	SH	GW	GT	S	PCT
82	9	9	18	-14	32	1	0	0	0	118	7.6

LAST SEASON

One of five Sharks to appear in all 82 games.

THE FINESSE GAME

While his timing has eroded, Graves remains a short-game player who scores a high percentage of his goals off deflections, rebounds, and slam dunks. A shot from the top of the circle is a long-distance effort for him. He favors the wrist shot. His rarely used slap shot barely exists. He is much better when working on instinct because, when he has time to make plays, he will outthink himself.

Although not very fast in open ice and something of an awkward skater, Graves's balance and strength are good and he can get a few quick steps on a rival. He is smart with the puck. He protects it with his body and is strong enough to fend off a checker with one arm and shovel the puck to a linemate with the other. He needs to play on a line with scorers, because he is a grinder first, a scorer second. He will drive to the net to screen the goalie and dig for rebounds, so he needs to play with someone who shoots to make the most of his efforts.

Graves is a former center who can step in on draws. He is an intelligent penalty killer.

THE PHYSICAL GAME

Graves is a role player. It is a job he accepts willingly. He is great with young players and veterans alike. He is never critical of a teammate. He is as loyal as a St. Bernard, but he can play like a junkyard dog.

THE INTANGIBLES

On those nights when the points aren't coming, Graves never hurts his club and finds other ways to contribute. He's a frequent winner of "Players' Player" awards, such is the respect he has earned. Off the ice, the absurdly modest Graves is one of the genuine good guys. Graves was an unrestricted free agent after last season.

PROJECTION

Graves should score in the 20-point range on a third line.

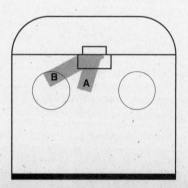

TODD HARVEY

Yrs. of NHL service: 9
Born: Hamilton, Ont.; Feb. 17, 1975
Position: right wing
Height: 6-0
Weight: 200
Uniform no.: 13
Shoots: right

Career statistics:

GP	G	A	TP	PIM
561	82	125	207	880

1999-2000 statistics:

GP	G	A	TP	+/-	PIM	PP	SH	GW	GT	S	PCT
71	11	7	18	-11	140	2	0	0	0	90	12.2

2000-2001 statistics:

GP	G	A	TP	+/-	PIM	PP	SH	GW	GT	S	PCT
69	10	11	21	+6	72	1	0	2	0	66	15.1

2001-2002 statistics:

GP	G	A	TP	+/-	PIM	PP	SH	GW	GT	S	PCT
69	9	13	22	+16	73	0	0	1	0	66	13.6

2002-2003 statistics:

GP	G	A	TP	+/-	PIM	PP	SH	GW	GT	S	PCT
76	3	16	19	+5	74	0	0	0	0	64	4.7

LAST SEASON

Led Sharks in penalty minutes. Second on Sharks in plus-minus. Missed four games with neck injury. Missed two games due to personal reasons.

THE FINESSE GAME

Harvey's skating is rough. In fact, it's pretty choppy, and as a result he lacks speed. To make up for that, he has good anticipation and awareness. He's clever and his hands are very good. When Harvey gets the puck, he plays it with patience and strength. He is not a legitimate first-line player, but he can fit in with skilled players if asked because of his effort, but only on a short-term basis.

The goals Harvey gets are ugly ones. He works the front of the net with grit. He goes to the net and follows up shots with second and third efforts. He always has his feet moving and has good hand-eye coordination. He doesn't have the greatest shot, but he battles to get into the prime scoring areas.

Harvey needs to play big every night to maximize his abilities, but he also has to become smarter in picking his spots. It's not going to do his career any good to spend half the season in the trainer's room.

THE PHYSICAL GAME

Harvey's talent level rises when he gets more involved. He's not big enough to be a legitimate NHL heavyweight, but he doesn't back down from challenges. When he's at his best, he gets inside other people's jerseys and heads.

THE INTANGIBLES

Harvey can be an effective, chippy fourth-liner and get spot power-play duty. He tends to get dinged up and miss 10-15 games a season although he was fairly healthy last year. Harvey became an unrestricted free agent after last season.

PROJECTION

Harvey will give you a hard 10 minutes a night but his offensive production has dwindled to just about zero.

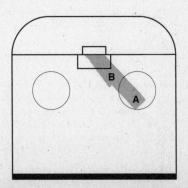

PATRICK MARLEAU

Yrs. of NHL service: 6
Born: Swift Current, Sask.; Sept. 15, 1979
Position: center
Height: 6-2
Weight: 210
Uniform no.: 12
Shoots: left

Career statistics:

GP	G	A	TP	PIM
478	125	145	270	169

1999-2000 statistics:

GP	G	A	TP	+/-	PIM	PP	SH	GW	GT	S	PCT
81	17	23	40	-9	36	3	0	3	0	161	10.6

2000-2001 statistics:

GP	G	A	TP	+/-	PIM	PP	SH	GW	GT	S	PCT
81	25	27	52	+7	22	5	0	6	0	146	17.1

2001-2002 statistics:

GP	G	A	TP	+/-	PIM	PP	SH	GW	GT	S	PCT
79	21	23	44	+9	40	3	0	5	0	121	17.4

2002-2003 statistics:

GP	G	A	TP	+/-	PIM	PP	SH	GW	GT	S	PCT
82	28	29	57	-10	33	8	1	3	1	172	16.3

LAST SEASON

Led team in shooting percentage. Tied for team lead in goals. Second on team in power-play goals. Third on team in assists and points. One of six Sharks to appear in all 82 games.

THE FINESSE GAME

Because of Marleau's quickness and intelligence, some scouts have described him as a bigger version of Paul Kariya. Marleau has great first- and second-step acceleration, with an extra gear.

Marleau plays an advanced offensive game. His defensive game still lags. He should become a high-level, two-way center, but his game is still tilted on the offensive side. He pounces on a loose puck and is a scoring threat every time he has it. His offensive reads are outstanding. He anticipates plays and has excellent hands. He is a terrific finisher and a fine playmaker. He has a quick release with an accurate touch, he's a valuable power-play weapon.

Marleau was more consistent last season and took over as the No. 1 center for the Sharks.

THE PHYSICAL GAME

Marleau is an imposing athlete. He skates through his checks and when he hits you, you know it. He has a thick build. He does not go looking to run people, but he will battle to get into traffic for the puck. He will take a check to make a play.

THE INTANGIBLES

Marleau is so polished it's easy to forget he's just 24 years old. He had to endure a tough season in San Jose. He may face some more changes depending on the free agents the Sharks keep or cut loose.

PROJECTION

Marleau should hit the 30-goal mark this season.

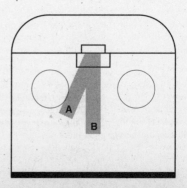

ALYN MCCAULEY

Yrs. of NHL service: 6
Born: Brockville, Ont.; May 29, 1977
Position: center
Height: 5-11
Weight: 190
Uniform no.: 10
Shoots: left

Career statistics:

GP	G	A	TP	PIM
320	36	56	92	56

1999-2000 statistics:

GP	G	A	TP	+/-	PIM	PP	SH	GW	GT	S	PCT
45	5	5	10	-6	10	1	0	0	0	41	12.2

2000-2001 statistics:

GP	G	A	TP	+/-	PIM	PP	SH	GW	GT	S	PCT
14	1	0	1	0	0	0	0	0	0	13	7.7

2001-2002 statistics:

GP	G	A	TP	+/-	PIM	PP	SH	GW	GT	S	PCT
82	6	10	16	+10	18	0	1	1	0	95	6.3

2002-2003 statistics:

GP	G	A	TP	+/-	PIM	PP	SH	GW	GT	S	PCT
80	9	16	25	+1	20	3	0	0	0	108	8.3

PROJECTION

McCauley will be a top-six forward with the Sharks. He scored 3-7 — 10 in 16 games after the trade. A 20-goal season may be in the offing.

LAST SEASON

Acquired from Toronto with Brad Boyes on March 5, 2003, for Owen Nolan.

THE FINESSE GAME

McCauley's skating, scoring touch, and vision make him an exciting player to watch. Injuries, serious ones like a concussion, and a knee injury in his second NHL season cost him considerable development time.

McCauley is a fine transition player. He has a good shot and is a terrific playmaker. He has nice hands, sharp instincts, and he sees his options and finds people around the net. McCauley peaks in an up-tempo game because he handles the puck well while skating at a brisk pace.

McCauley's hand-eye coordination is unreal. He is adept at picking pucks out of the air for scoring chances. McCauley concentrated hard on defense early in his career and is now a fine two-way forward.

THE PHYSICAL GAME

McCauley is a small, stocky player without much ferocity. McCauley has learned to play a small man's game and deserves high marks for battling back after his injuries.

THE INTANGIBLES

McCauley is very hard on himself. He wants to be a top player and a leader. He has very good work habits but he can get moody when things aren't going well, mostly because he wants so much to help his team win. He was a restricted free agent after the season.

KYLE MCLAREN

Yrs. of NHL service: 8
Born: Humbolt, Sask.; June 18, 1977
Position: left defense
Height: 6-4
Weight: 230
Uniform no.: 4
Shoots: left

Career statistics:

GP	G	A	TP	PIM
450	34	98	132	400

1999-2000 statistics:

GP	G	A	TP	+/-	PIM	PP	SH	GW	GT	S	PCT
71	8	11	19	-4	67	2	0	3	0	142	5.6

2000-2001 statistics:

GP	G	A	TP	+/-	PIM	PP	SH	GW	GT	S	PCT
58	5	12	17	-5	53	2	0	0	1	91	5.5

2001-2002 statistics:

GP	G	A	TP	+/-	PIM	PP	SH	GW	GT	S	PCT
38	0	8	8	-4	19	0	0	0	0	57	0.0

2002-2003 statistics:

GP	G	A	TP	+/-	PIM	PP	SH	GW	GT	S	PCT
33	0	8	8	-10	30	0	0	0	0	43	0.0

LAST SEASON

Acquired from Boston on January 23, 2003, with a fourth-round draft pick in 2004 for Jeff Hackett and Jeff Jillson. Missed 49 games due to contract dispute. Third on team in average ice time.

THE FINESSE GAME

McLaren is big and mobile. His puckhandling is well above average, and he moves the puck out of the zone quickly and without panicking. He can rush with the puck or make the cautious bank off the boards to clear the zone. McLaren jumps eagerly into the play.

He can play either right or left defense, and his advanced defensive reads allow him to adapt, which is very hard to do for a young player.

McLaren is an effective penalty killer because he is fearless. He blocks shots and takes away passing lanes. He can also play on the power play, and probably will improve in this area because he plays heads-up and has a hard and accurate slap shot with a quick release. As he gains more confidence he will become more of an offensive factor, but frequently he puts the cart before the horse and goes on the attack — before he has taken care of his own end of the ice.

THE PHYSICAL GAME

McLaren is a mean, punishing hitter. He is almost scary in his fierce checking ability. He is tough and aggressive, but he doesn't go looking for fights and doesn't take foolish penalties. When he does scrap, he can go toe-to-toe and has already earned some respect around the league as a player you don't want to tick off. He is strong on the puck, strong on the wall, and doesn't allow loitering in front of his crease.

McLaren has a tendency to lose his edge and get too freewheeling and offensive. Every time he lapses into this bad habit, the coaching staff have to rein him in and bring him back to a simple game.

THE INTANGIBLES

Last season was a virtual washout due to the long holdout. McLaren will become part of a solid top four in San Jose with Mike Rathje, Brad Stuart, and last season's rookie surprise Jim Fahey.

PROJECTION

The less McLaren thinks about getting points, the more easily he will score. Keep expectations low until you get a look at how McLaren starts off the season. Even in a good year, 25 points may be his max.

EVGENI NABOKOV

Yrs. of NHL service: 3
Born: Ust-Kamenogorsk, Kazakhstan; July 25, 1975
Position: goaltender
Height: 6-0
Weight: 200
Uniform no.: 20
Catches: left

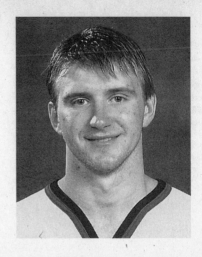

Career statistics:

GP	MIN	GA	SO	GAA	A	PIM
199	11242	445	17	2.38	5	32

1999-2000 statistics:

GP	MIN	GAA	W	L	T	SO	GA	S	SAPCT	PIM
11	414	2.17	2	2	1	1	15	166	.910	0

2000-2001 statistics:

GP	MIN	GAA	W	L	T	SO	GA	S	SAPCT	PIM
66	3700	2.19	32	21	7	6	135	1582	.915	8

2001-2002 statistics:

GP	MIN	GAA	W	L	T	SO	GA	S	SAPCT	PIM
67	3901	2.29	37	24	5	7	149	1818	.918	14

2002-2003 statistics:

GP	MIN	GAA	W	L	T	SO	GA	S	SAPCT	PIM
55	3227	2.71	19	28	8	3	146	1561	.906	10

LAST SEASON

Missed seven games in contract dispute. Missed four games with back injury.

THE PHYSICAL GAME

The most impressive skill Nabokov has is his recovery. When he does drop down into a butterfly, it seems like his pads never stay on the ice long, if at all. He goes into a textbook butterfly, but is back on his feet and in his stance immediately. It's one of the quickest moves in the game.

His glove is always perfectly positioned, like one of those goalies in a tabletop hockey game. Nabokov's glove isn't noisy. He's not flapping it all over the place. He makes the tough gloves saves look easy, unlike some goalies who give even a routine save a flourish. What might be a Statue of Liberty save for Patrick Roy is a simple snap of the glove and hold for a face-off for Nabokov. Nabokov's glove is always cocked and ready. He is very consistent.

Nabokov's play with the puck has improved, but it still remains one of the weaker parts of his game.

THE MENTAL GAME

Nabokov is very coachable and, despite still practicing his English, he integrated himself well with his teammates. They seem to like playing for him and want to play hard in front of him. Nabokov doesn't need to showboat. He is that good, and that's good enough for the Sharks.

THE INTANGIBLES

It's tough for any player who misses training camp to get his groove back, and it's especially difficult for a goaltender. Nabokov was never in sync at any point in the season.

PROJECTION

Nabokov is signed so he won't be missing camp again. He needs to get his game in gear. Nabokov is a 30-win goalie.

MIKE RATHJE

Yrs. of NHL service: 10
Born: Mannville, Alta.; May 11, 1974
Position: left defense
Height: 6-5
Weight: 245
Uniform no.: 2
Shoots: left

Career statistics:

GP	G	A	TP	PIM
591	25	111	136	393

1999-2000 statistics:

GP	G	A	TP	+/-	PIM	PP	SH	GW	GT	S	PCT
66	2	14	16	-2	31	0	0	0	0	46	4.3

2000-2001 statistics:

GP	G	A	TP	+/-	PIM	PP	SH	GW	GT	S	PCT
81	0	11	11	+7	48	0	0	0	0	89	0.0

2001-2002 statistics:

GP	G	A	TP	+/-	PIM	PP	SH	GW	GT	S	PCT
52	5	12	17	+23	48	4	0	0	0	56	8.9

2002-2003 statistics:

GP	G	A	TP	+/-	PIM	PP	SH	GW	GT	S	PCT
82	7	22	29	-19	48	3	0	1	0	147	4.8

LAST SEASON

Second on team in average ice time (24:06). One of six Sharks to appear in all 82 games.

THE FINESSE GAME

A stay-at-home type of defenseman, Rathje has great quickness for a player his size. He is a lot like Ken Morrow, the kind of player who is so quiet that you have to watch him every game to appreciate how good he is. He is strong enough to play against the league's power forwards and quick enough to deal with skilled, faster players. Rathje is routinely matched up against other teams' top lines and just as routinely smothers them. Rathje didn't find a comfortable defense partner after Marcus Ragnarsson was traded to Philadelphia in early December. Rathje was -3 before the trade and -16 after it.

Rathje has the ability to get involved in the attack, but is prized primarily for his defense. He combines his lateral mobility with a good low shot to get the puck on the net without being blocked.

With great poise, Rathje helps to get the puck out of the zone quickly. He can either carry the puck out and make a smart headman pass and then follow the play, or he can make a safe move and chip the puck out along the wall.

THE PHYSICAL GAME

Rathje has good size and strength. He plays with controlled aggression. He has a little bit of mean in him, and he likes to hit. He has unbelievable strength and good mobility for his size. His penalty minutes look low because he plays hard without taking bad penalties. Rathje doesn't hit with Scott Stevens-like force, but he is well-respected by opponents.

THE INTANGIBLES

The cornerstone of the Sharks' blueline, Rathje has become a franchise defenseman.

PROJECTION

Rathje can get 25-30 points and keep other teams' forward lines off the board.

MIKE RICCI

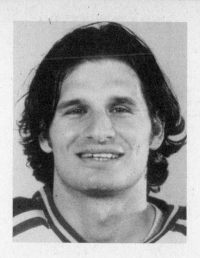

Yrs. of NHL service: 13
Born: Scarborough, Ont.; Oct. 27, 1971
Position: center
Height: 6-0
Weight: 190
Uniform no.: 18
Shoots: left

Career statistics:

GP	G	A	TP	PIM
943	226	336	562	861

1999-2000 statistics:

GP	G	A	TP	+/-	PIM	PP	SH	GW	GT	S	PCT
82	20	24	44	+14	60	10	0	5	0	134	14.9

2000-2001 statistics:

GP	G	A	TP	+/-	PIM	PP	SH	GW	GT	S	PCT
81	22	22	44	+3	60	9	2	4	0	141	15.6

2001-2002 statistics:

GP	G	A	TP	+/-	PIM	PP	SH	GW	GT	S	PCT
79	19	34	53	+9	44	5	2	0	0	115	16.5

2002-2003 statistics:

GP	G	A	TP	+/-	PIM	PP	SH	GW	GT	S	PCT
75	11	23	34	-12	53	5	1	2	0	101	10.9

LAST SEASON

Missed seven games with back injuries.

THE FINESSE GAME

Ricci looks like he shaves with a cheese grater. He usually has a black eye or stitches. Some of his teeth have been missing since the Reagan administration. His is the face of old-school hockey.

Ricci is a two-way forward whose game is tilting more heavily towards defense now. He has good hand skills, combined with his hockey sense and a tireless work ethic. He always seems to be in the right place, poised to make the right play. He sees his passing options well and is patient with the puck. He can rifle it as well. Ricci has a good backhand shot that is a useful weapon in tight.

Ricci's major flaw is his lack of foot speed. It prevented him from being more of an offensive force, but Ricci has long been an efficient forechecker and he never seems that out of place among his NHL brethren because he wants to get from Point A to Point B more than a lot of other guys do.

Very slick at face-offs, Ricci has good hand speed and hand-eye coordination for winning draws outright. He will battle to tie up the opposing center and use his feet to kick the puck to a teammate. He's a determined penalty killer. He pressures the points and blocks shots, and he has excellent anticipation. He's a checking forward with some offensive capabilities.

THE PHYSICAL GAME

Ricci is annoying to play against. He will antagonize and draw penalties. Ricci will fearlessly accept checking assignments against other team's top lines and star players. He isn't huge but he is big and sturdy. It's not unusual to see him cutting to the front of the net and dragging a defender like a big floppy anchor. He will play hurt, as he did last season through back problems. Ricci keeps himself in good condition and can handle a lot of ice time.

THE INTANGIBLES

Ricci is a character guy and a team leader. He considers it his job to make sure the kids are comfortable and is well-respected by the veterans. He is upbeat off the ice and his versatility is a plus. Ricci has long been a favorite of this publication and he is one of our foxhole guys, but his back ailment has to be a concern now that he is 32. Ricci was an unrestricted free agent after last season and could help a playoff-ready team.

PROJECTION

Ricci may drop to 30 points but he will contribute in ways that don't show up on the scoresheet.

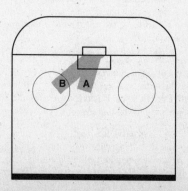

BRAD STUART

Yrs. of NHL service: 4
Born: Rocky Mountain House, Alta.; Nov. 6, 1979
Position: left defense
Height: 6-2
Weight: 215
Uniform no.: 7
Shoots: left

Career statistics:

GP	G	A	TP	PIM
277	25	77	102	173

1999-2000 statistics:

GP	G	A	TP	+/-	PIM	PP	SH	GW	GT	S	PCT
82	10	26	36	+3	32	5	1	3	0	133	7.5

2000-2001 statistics:

GP	G	A	TP	+/-	PIM	PP	SH	GW	GT	S	PCT
77	5	18	23	+10	56	1	0	2	1	119	4.2

2001-2002 statistics:

GP	G	A	TP	+/-	PIM	PP	SH	GW	GT	S	PCT
82	6	23	29	+13	39	2	0	2	0	96	6.3

2002-2003 statistics:

GP	G	A	TP	+/-	PIM	PP	SH	GW	GT	S	PCT
36	4	10	14	-6	46	2	0	1	0	63	6.3

LAST SEASON

Missed 16 games in contract dispute. Missed 21 games with concussion. Missed eight games with ankle injury. Missed one game with flu.

THE FINESSE GAME

Stuart is an offensive-minded defenseman. His primary asset is his ability to make a smart first pass. He gets the puck out of the zone intelligently and quickly and opens up the rink for the Sharks. He finds the open man. He plays the point on the first power-play unit.

Stuart is a powerful skater. He is speedy and mobile and can lead a rush or join the attack as the trailer. He is a good one-on-one defender. Poised and smart, he will soon have the ability to dominate games with his skating and puck possession.

His defensive reads overall are good, although he is still learning. He is intelligent and will work to better his game. Stuart has started applying his skills more to the defensive part of the game, which will be the next step towards making him an all-around defenseman.

THE PHYSICAL GAME

Well-conditioned, Stuart is a natural at playing physically. He is strong along the wall and in front of the net and doesn't take bad penalties. He can (and does) handle a lot of ice time.

THE INTANGIBLES

Stuart missed training camp over a contract hassle and very little went right after he finally agreed to terms in mid-November. He suffered a season-ending concussion in a game on February 21 when he was jumped by Columbus goon Jody Shelley, who received a whopping two-game suspension for the attack.

PROJECTION

Stuart was on the fast track to becoming one of the best-scoring defensemen in the NHL, but he's a question mark due to the head injury.

MARCO STURM

Yrs. of NHL service: 6
Born: Dingolfing, Germany; Sept. 8, 1978
Position: left wing
Height: 6-0
Weight: 195
Uniform no.: 19
Shoots: left

Career statistics:

GP	G	A	TP	PIM
466	101	115	216	190

1999-2000 statistics:

GP	G	A	TP	+/-	PIM	PP	SH	GW	GT	S	PCT
74	12	15	27	+4	22	2	4	3	0	120	10.0

2000-2001 statistics:

GP	G	A	TP	+/-	PIM	PP	SH	GW	GT	S	PCT
81	14	18	32	+9	28	2	3	5	0	153	9.1

2001-2002 statistics:

GP	G	A	TP	+/-	PIM	PP	SH	GW	GT	S	PCT
77	21	20	41	+23	32	4	3	5	0	174	12.1

2002-2003 statistics:

GP	G	A	TP	+/-	PIM	PP	SH	GW	GT	S	PCT
82	28	20	48	+9	16	6	0	2	0	208	13.5

PROJECTION

Wow, we were hoping for this kind of breakthrough season from Sturm, but we were beginning to wonder if it was ever going to happen. There is little doubt he can be a consistent 30-goal scorer. Sturm is the complete package.

LAST SEASON

Led team in game-winning goals. Tied for team lead in goals. Second on team in shots and shooting percentage. Career highs in goals and points. One of six Sharks to appear in all 82 games.

THE FINESSE GAME

Sturm may be the best all-round player on the Sharks, and last season his offense finally started closing the gap on the defensive aspect of his game. A versatile skater who can play all three forward positions, Sturm doesn't require a lot of maintenance. He knows where to be without the puck.

He is also a fine skater with smooth acceleration. Sturm has good hands for stickhandling and shooting. Sturm really stepped it up in taking shots last season and could improve even more.

Sturm is extremely intelligent and hardworking. He is not afraid to block shots. He is going to be the kind of player who scores important goals and makes key plays that determine the outcome of games. He is the third-liner playing on a first or second line, and he could give the Sharks what Jere Lehtinen gives the Dallas Stars.

THE PHYSICAL GAME

Sturm is not big but he competes every night. He is chippy and feisty, and plays bigger than he is.

THE INTANGIBLES

The most complete, reliable forward on the team, Sturm finally started producing. He did it under difficult circumstances, too.

ST. LOUIS BLUES

Players' Statistics 2001-2002

POS.	NO.	PLAYER	GP	G	A	PTS	+/-	PIM	PP	SH	GW	GT	S	PCT
R	38	PAVOL DEMITRA	78	36	57	93	0	32	11		4	1	205	17.6
D	2	AL MACINNIS	80	16	52	68	22	61	9	1	2		299	5.3
L	61	CORY STILLMAN	79	24	43	67	12	56	6		4		157	15.3
C	39	DOUG WEIGHT	70	15	52	67	-6	52	7		3		182	8.2
R	19	SCOTT MELLANBY	80	26	31	57	1	176	13		4	1	132	19.7
L	7	KEITH TKACHUK	56	31	24	55	1	139	14		5		185	16.8
C	33	ERIC BOGUNIECKI	80	22	27	49	22	38	3	1	5		117	18.8
L	26	PETR CAJANEK	51	9	29	38	16	20	2	2	1		90	10.0
D	29	ALEXANDER KHAVANOV	81	8	25	33	-1	48	2	1	2		90	8.9
R	10	DALLAS DRAKE	80	20	10	30	-7	66	4	1	2	1	113	17.7
L	22	MARTIN RUCINSKY	61	16	14	30	-1	38	4	4	3	1	135	11.9
R	13	VALERI BURE	51	5	23	28	-13	10	3		2		161	3.1
D	5	*BARRET JACKMAN	82	3	16	19	23	190					66	4.5
C	12	STEVE MARTINS	42	5	6	11	-5	28		1			38	13.2
L	25	SHJON PODEIN	68	4	6	10	7	28	1				52	7.7
D	27	BRYCE SALVADOR	71	2	8	10	7	95	1				73	2.7
L	9	TYSON NASH	66	6	3	9	0	114	1		2		77	7.8
D	46	CHRISTIAN LAFLAMME	47		9	9	1	45					44	
C	17	RYAN JOHNSON	75	2	5	7	-13	38					67	3.0
R	21	JAMAL MAYERS	15	2	5	7	1	8					26	7.7
R	34	REED LOW	79	2	4	6	3	234			1		48	4.2
D	6	TOM KOIVISTO	22	2	4	6	1	10			1		26	7.7
R	18	STEVE DUBINSKY	28		6	6	3	4					23	
D	37	JEFF FINLEY	64	1	3	4	-2	46			1		30	3.3
D	44	CHRIS PRONGER	5	1	3	4	-2	10					11	9.1
D	43	MIKE VAN RYN	20		3	3	3	8					21	
L	15	*PETER SEJNA	1	1		1	0		1				3	33.3
D	28	*MATT WALKER	16		1	1	0	38					13	
R	20	ERIC NICKULAS	8		1	1	-2	6					3	
L	23	SERGEI VARLAMOV	3				1						5	
D	55	*CHRISTIAN BACKMAN	4				-3						4	
G	30	TOM BARRASSO	6				0							
D	47	RICHARD PILON					0							
G	30	CHRIS OSGOOD	46				0	12						
G	40	FRED BRATHWAITE	30				0							
G	35	BRENT JOHNSON	38				0	2						
C	15	DANIEL CORSO	1				-1							
G	45	CODY RUDKOWSKY	1				0							
G	1	CURTIS SANFORD	8				0							
G	50	REINHARD DIVIS	2				0							

GP = games played; G = goals; A = assists; PTS = points; +/- = goals-for minus goals-against while player is on ice; PIM = penalties in minutes; PP = power-play goals; SH = shorthanded goals; GW = game-winning goals; GT = game-tying goals; S = no. of shots; PCT = percentage of goals to shots; * = rookie

PETR CAJANEK

Yrs. of NHL service: 1
Born: Zlinia, Czech Republic; Aug. 18, 1975
Position: center
Height: 5-11
Weight: 176
Uniform no.: 26
Shoots: left

Career statistics:

GP	G	A	TP	PIM
51	9	29	38	20

2002-2003 statistics:

GP	G	A	TP	+/-	PIM	PP	SH	GW	GT	S	PCT
51	9	29	38	+16	20	2	2	1	0	90	10.0

LAST SEASON

First NHL season. Missed 24 games with fractured leg. Missed seven games with facial laceration.

THE FINESSE GAME

Cajanek had a terrific first half (7-23 — 30 in 41 games) before his second half was obliterated by injuries. Cajanek is a strong player in all zones. His complete game allowed him to step right in with the Blues when injuries hit at the start of the season.

Cajanek is primarily a playmaker. He has excellent hands for passing. He is very patient with the puck. Like a lot of players making the transition to North American hockey, he is reluctant to play a dump-and-chase game. He is also very shy about shooting.

He protects the puck well and recognizes his passing options quickly. He is not just a perimeter player. Cajanek is willing to take the puck into traffic or go into the corners.

Cajanek is a very good skater. He doesn't always play with intensity and needs to keep his consistency level up.

THE PHYSICAL GAME

Cajanek isn't very big, but he is solidly built and will take a hit to make a play.

THE INTANGIBLES

Cajanek was an overage draft pick by St. Louis in 2001 after being named MVP of the Czech Elite League. He doesn't have much upside since he is probably already as good as it gets, but his best is decent enough to be a solid two-way center who has top-six skills. His facial injury forced him to miss all but two games of the playoffs, so it was impossible to get a read on what kind of postseason player he will turn out to be.

PROJECTION

Playing time at center is a little tough to come by after Pavol Demitra and Doug Weight, but Cajanek should continue to see second-unit power-play time and should score 45 assist-heavy points.

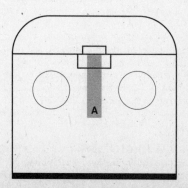

PAVOL DEMITRA

Yrs. of NHL service: 9
Born: Dubnica, Slovakia; Nov. 29, 1974
Position: center
Height: 5-11
Weight: 203
Uniform no.: 38
Shoots: left

Career statistics:

GP	G	A	TP	PIM
485	193	268	461	152

1999-2000 statistics:

GP	G	A	TP	+/-	PIM	PP	SH	GW	GT	S	PCT
71	28	47	75	+34	8	8	0	4	0	241	11.6

2000-2001 statistics:

GP	G	A	TP	+/-	PIM	PP	SH	GW	GT	S	PCT
44	20	25	45	+27	16	5	0	5	0	124	16.1

2001-2002 statistics:

GP	G	A	TP	+/-	PIM	PP	SH	GW	GT	S	PCT
82	35	43	78	+13	46	11	0	10	0	212	16.5

2002-2003 statistics:

GP	G	A	TP	+/-	PIM	PP	SH	GW	GT	S	PCT
78	36	57	93	0	32	11	0	4	1	205	17.6

LAST SEASON

Tied for fourth in NHL in assists. Sixth in NHL in points. Led team in goals, assists, and points. Second on team in shots. Third on team in power-play goals. Career highs in assists and points. Tied for third on team in game-winning goals. Missed four games with chicken pox.

THE FINESSE GAME

Demitra has made a complete adjustment to being a No. 1 center. Demitra's speed makes things happen. He has great moves one-on-one, and he finds a way to get in the holes. He has good stick skills and loves to shoot. He can really find the top of the net, especially with his one-timer. He is well-versed at picking the top corners, and he can do it at speed.

Demitra is a creative and exceptional puckhandler, with a quick, deceptive shot. He's not shy about letting the puck go. He likes to drag the puck into his skates and then shoot it through a defenseman's legs. The move gets the rearguard to move up a little bit, and Demitra gets it by him on net.

Coming in off his right (off) side, Demitra will move to the middle on his forehand and throw the puck back against the grain. He needs to work on his puck-protection skills. Sometimes he exposes the puck too much and what should be a scoring chance for him gets knocked away. Defensively, he's reliable.

Face-offs are still not his strong suit, but he works hard at it.

THE PHYSICAL GAME

Demitra is not very big but he has built up his body over the past several years. He is very competitive and durable. He can take the heat and the ice time. Having Doug Weight around for a full season eased some of the checking pressure for him.

THE INTANGIBLES

Credit linemate Keith Tkachuk with some of Demitra's success. Demitra is by nature a modest and reserved player, but Tkachuk urged Demitra to step up and be a leader. Tkachuk demands the puck, and they feed off of one another. Demitra has arrived as an NHL star. He wants to succeed and appears to be willing to pay the price to succeed in the NHL. He is a pretty low-maintenance star, too. Demitra was a restricted free agent after last season.

PROJECTION

We thought Pronger's absence would cost Demitra some points. Instead, he blew right past our expectations and had an exceptional season. He could be a 100-point scorer.

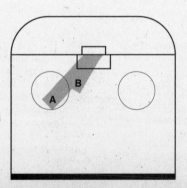

DALLAS DRAKE

Yrs. of NHL service: 11
Born: Trail, B.C.; Feb. 4, 1969
Position: right wing
Height: 6-1
Weight: 187
Uniform no.: 10
Shoots: left

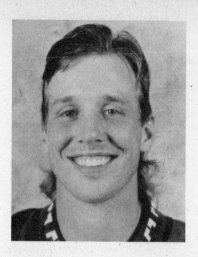

Career statistics:

GP	G	A	TP	PIM
743	153	245	398	682

1999-2000 statistics:

GP	G	A	TP	+/-	PIM	PP	SH	GW	GT	S	PCT
79	15	30	45	+11	62	0	2	5	0	127	11.8

2000-2001 statistics:

GP	G	A	TP	+/-	PIM	PP	SH	GW	GT	S	PCT
82	12	29	41	+18	71	2	0	3	0	142	8.4

2001-2002 statistics:

GP	G	A	TP	+/-	PIM	PP	SH	GW	GT	S	PCT
80	11	15	26	+8	87	1	3	2	0	116	9.5

2002-2003 statistics:

GP	G	A	TP	+/-	PIM	PP	SH	GW	GT	S	PCT
80	20	10	30	-7	66	4	1	2	1	113	17.7

LAST SEASON

Third on team in shooting percentage. Career high in goals. Missed one game with ankle injury. Missed one game with flu.

THE FINESSE GAME

Drake is best suited to a third-line role, and he knows it even though in the past he has played with some top-line guys. In a pinch, Drake can be used to play with more highly skilled players and he can handle power-play assignments. Because he is so involved and so intelligent, he is better than the average grinder. He is an aggressive forechecker, strong along the boards and in front of the net. He's not huge, but he sure plays big. He doesn't stand in and take a bashing, but he'll jump in and out of traffic to fight for the puck or bounce in on rebounds.

Quick and powerful in his skating, Drake will get outmuscled but not outhustled. His scoring chances come in-deep. Drake doesn't have great hands. He needs to bang around for his pucks.

He shouldn't start thinking like a scorer, though — he has to keep doing the same dirty things that got him this far. He is the kind of player needed in a championship mix. Drake is an excellent penalty killer and is always a threat to create something shorthanded.

THE PHYSICAL GAME

Drake gets noticed because he runs right over people. He is limited by his size, but he will give a team whatever he's got. He's feisty enough to get the other team's attention, and he works to keep himself in scoring position. He has a mean streak.

THE INTANGIBLES

Drake is at his best at crunch time — in the closing minutes of a game, in a playoff stretch drive, in the postseason. If he isn't putting points on the board, he is disrupting the other team's attack. Drake is all heart.

PROJECTION

Drake's 20 goals were a pleasant surprise last season but we don't expect a repeat. Fifteen goals would do nicely. He'd better not start thinking like a goal-scorer, either.

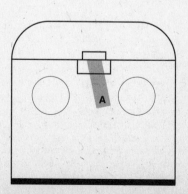

BARRET JACKMAN

Yrs. of NHL service: 1
Born: Trail, B.C.; Mar. 5, 1981
Position: left defense
Height: 6-1
Weight: 200
Uniform no.: 5
Shoots: left

Career statistics:

GP	G	A	TP	PIM
83	3	16	19	190

2001-2002 statistics:

GP	G	A	TP	+/-	PIM	PP	SH	GW	GT	S	PCT
1	0	0	0	0	0	0	0	0	0	1	0.0

2002-2003 statistics:

GP	G	A	TP	+/-	PIM	PP	SH	GW	GT	S	PCT
82	3	16	19	+23	190	0	0	0	0	66	4.5

LAST SEASON

Won 2003 Calder Trophy. Named to NHL All-Rookie Team. Led team in plus-minus. Second on team in penalty minutes. One Blues player to appear in all 82 games.

THE FINESSE GAME

Jackman has the brain of a 35-year-old defenseman in a 22-year-old's body. The St. Louis defense looked on the brink of collapse in training camp with the prospect of having to play without Norris Trophy winner Chris Pronger, but up stepped Jackman to partner Al MacInnis and look like an All-Star himself while doing it.

Jackman's game is so complete, so rock-solid, that it was incredible to think he was a first-year player (and only a second-year pro). Strength on the puck? Check. Positioning? Check. Intelligence? Check. Checking? Check.

Jackman is a smooth skater with above-average NHL speed. He has a great passing touch, either in an offensive mode or to make the first pass out of the zone. He will never be much of a factor on the power play, though, and his offensive contributions will be modest.

Jackman doesn't panic under pressure and plays odd-man rushes wisely, seldom getting suckered out of position. Jackman didn't just play last season. He faced opposing teams' top lines night after night. He was sent out in crucial game situations. He had to grow up in a hurry.

THE PHYSICAL GAME

MacInnis saw the promise in Jackman, and in the 2001 off-season urged him to work out with some of the other Blues with a fitness and nutrition consultant. MacInnis has made this gesture only once previously — to a very young Pronger. Jackman wisely heeded the advice. Reportedly, Jackman's body fat dropped from 18 to 8.5 per cent on the program.

Jackman isn't huge, but he is strong, tough, and aggressive. He will fight if he has to, and he's not scared of league heavyweights, although he isn't one himself. If he were about three inches taller we could be looking at a dominating defenseman.

THE INTANGIBLES

Jackman is a franchise defenseman and a future Norris Trophy candidate.

PROJECTION

Jackman will be a top-four defenseman but he will be limited offensively. Sacrifice the points (he'll probably score in the 25-point range, tops) and keep the physical play, leadership, and character.

398

ALEXANDER KHAVANOV

Yrs. of NHL service: 3
Born: Moscow, Russia; Jan 30, 1972
Position: defense
Height: 6-0
Weight: 187
Uniform no.: 29
Shoots: left

Career statistics:

GP	G	A	TP	PIM
236	18	62	80	155

2000-2001 statistics:

GP	G	A	TP	+/-	PIM	PP	SH	GW	GT	S	PCT
74	7	16	23	+16	52	2	0	0	0	92	7.6

2001-2002 statistics:

GP	G	A	TP	+/-	PIM	PP	SH	GW	GT	S	PCT
81	3	21	24	+9	55	0	0	0	0	87	3.5

2002-2003 statistics:

GP	G	A	TP	+/-	PIM	PP	SH	GW	GT	S	PCT
81	8	25	33	-1	48	2	1	2	0	90	8.9

LAST SEASON

Second on team in average ice time (21:56). Career highs in goals, assists, and points. Missed one game due to coach's decision.

THE FINESSE GAME

Khavanov is a very skilled player who doesn't get rattled with the puck. He came to North America as an older player (this will be his fourth season and he is 31 years old), so he was pretty poised when he stepped in.

Khavanov shows his biggest improvement in his sense of urgency. He rushed the puck more, dictated the play, and got more involved. Khavanov earned his increased ice time, and his presence was needed when Chris Pronger lost so much of the season due to injury.

Khavanov is valuable because he can be used on the right or left side, although he is better on the left, which is where he was stationed when Pronger returned.

He is pretty poised with the puck and doesn't get rattled easily.

THE PHYSICAL GAME

Khavanov is tall but a little on the light side. He can handle 22 minutes a game because he has a quietly efficient skating style. He is not very physical.

THE INTANGIBLES

Khavanov was a pleasant surprise for the Blues last season, but with a couple of young defensemen getting ready to make an impact, he could battle for a role in the top four.

PROJECTION

If Khavanov sees the amount of ice time he did last season, he will score around 30 assist-heavy points.

AL MACINNIS

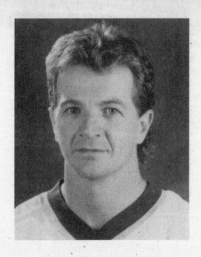

Yrs. of NHL service: 21
Born: Inverness, N.S.; July 11, 1963
Position: right defense
Height: 6-2
Weight: 209
Uniform no.: 2
Shoots: right

Career statistics:

GP	G	A	TP	PIM
1413	340	932	1272	1505

1999-2000 statistics:

GP	G	A	TP	+/-	PIM	PP	SH	GW	GT	S	PCT
61	11	28	39	+20	34	6	0	7	0	245	4.5

2000-2001 statistics:

GP	G	A	TP	+/-	PIM	PP	SH	GW	GT	S	PCT
59	12	42	54	+23	52	6	1	3	0	218	5.5

2001-2002 statistics:

GP	G	A	TP	+/-	PIM	PP	SH	GW	GT	S	PCT
71	11	35	46	+3	52	6	0	4	1	231	4.8

2002-2003 statistics:

GP	G	A	TP	+/-	PIM	PP	SH	GW	GT	S	PCT
80	16	52	68	+22	61	9	1	2	0	299	5.3

LAST SEASON

Finalist for 2003 Norris Trophy. Named to NHL First All-Star Team. Led NHL defensemen in points and assists. Tied for 10th in NHL in assists. Tied for fourth in NHL in shots. Led team in average ice time (26:54). Led team in shots. Second on team in points. Tied for second on team in assists and plus-minus. Missed one game with back spasms. Missed one game due to coach's decision.

THE FINESSE GAME

What makes MacInnis's shot so good is that he knows the value of a change-up, and he changes his shot according to the situation. From the point, he will try to keep his shot low. It will be a screaming shot if he thinks he can beat the goalie cleanly, but he will take a few m.p.h. off it if there are teammates there to tip the shot. If he dances to the top of the circles or closer, MacInnis will go top-shelf. And as much as he likes to shoot, he will also fake a big wind-up, which freezes the defenders, then make a quick slap-pass to an open teammate. There aren't too many better defensemen than MacInnis on the power play.

MacInnis knows when to jump into the play and when to back off. He can start a rush with a rink-wide pass, then be quick enough to burst up-ice and be in position for a return pass. Even when he merely rings the puck off the boards he's a threat, since there is so much on the shot the goaltender has to be careful to stop it. MacInnis has a hard shot even when he's moving backwards.

He skates well with the puck. MacInnis is not very agile, but he gets up to speed in a few strides and can hit his outside speed to beat a defender one-on-one. He will gamble and is best paired with a defensively alert partner, though he has improved his defensive play and is very smart against a two-on-one.

THE PHYSICAL GAME

MacInnis uses his finesse skills in a defensive posture, always looking for the counterattack. He reads defenses alertly, and positions himself to tie up attackers rather than try to knock them down. In his own way, he is a tough competitor who will pay the price to win. MacInnis managed to avoid wearing down last season despite a staggering amount of ice time. Chris Pronger's return should ease his workload.

THE INTANGIBLES

The impact MacInnis had on his partner Barret Jackman winning the Calder Trophy can't be exaggerated, and it sure didn't hurt the ice-gobbling, 40-year-old veteran to have a young pup by his side.

PROJECTION

The apparently ageless MacInnis led all defensemen in points despite Pronger's prolonged absence. It's hard not to pick him for another 60 points at least.

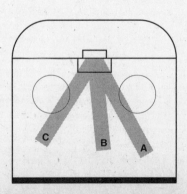

JAMAL MAYERS

Yrs. of NHL service: 5
Born: Toronto, Ont.; Oct. 24, 1974
Position: center / right wing
Height: 6-1
Weight: 212
Uniform no.: 21
Shoots: right

Career statistics:

GP	G	A	TP	PIM
288	30	42	72	356

1999-2000 statistics:

GP	G	A	TP	+/-	PIM	PP	SH	GW	GT	S	PCT
79	7	10	17	0	90	0	0	0	0	99	7.1

2000-2001 statistics:

GP	G	A	TP	+/-	PIM	PP	SH	GW	GT	S	PCT
77	8	13	21	-3	117	0	0	0	0	132	6.1

2001-2002 statistics:

GP	G	A	TP	+/-	PIM	PP	SH	GW	GT	S	PCT
77	9	8	17	+9	99	0	1	0	0	105	8.6

2002-2003 statistics:

GP	G	A	TP	+/-	PIM	PP	SH	GW	GT	S	PCT
15	2	5	7	+1	8	0	0	0	0	26	7.7

LAST SEASON

Missed 61 games with knee surgery.

THE FINESSE GAME

Mayers has played center but is better suited as a winger. He gets too busy on the ice as a center. When he comes in off the wing and forechecks, the defenseman doesn't have time to move the puck. Whether he hits or not, he is on the puck so quickly that the defender is hurried into throwing the puck around the boards or making another mistake. Mayers has to keep reminding himself that he can really rush a play on the forecheck. He is sharp on face-offs and will often take draws even though he is not playing center.

Speed is his biggest asset, or it was until he suffered a torn ACL that required surgery. Mayers is starting to learn how to position himself. Sometimes it is tough for a player with his energy and his speed to do anything but charge around full-tilt. Sometimes he has to slow down and get the other player into an angle or into a pocket to close him out instead of going right at him, and Mayers has begun to recognize that.

Mayers doesn't have a great scoring touch. He has to work hard by driving to the net. Sometimes he thinks he can play a finesse game. He can't.

THE PHYSICAL GAME

Mayers is a solidly built player and dedicates himself to conditioning year-round. He is really fit, and if his game develops to where he gets more ice time (he averaged just over 14 minutes last season before the injury) he can take it. Mayers loves the physical part of the game. He is a willing and powerful hitter.

THE INTANGIBLES

Mayers will need to come back from his knee surgery at 100 per cent because his powerful, swift skating was at the heart of his NHL career.

PROJECTION

Mayers was on such a positive career track before the injury, but he has to be a question mark this season, both for the Blues and for pool players.

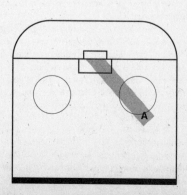

SCOTT MELLANBY

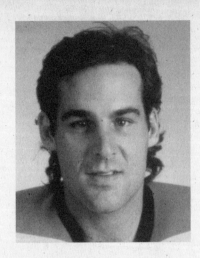

Yrs. of NHL service: 17
Born: Montreal, Que,; June 11, 1966
Position: right wing
Height: 6-1
Weight: 205
Uniform no.: 19
Shoots: right

Career statistics:

GP	G	A	TP	PIM
1223	326	413	739	2285

1999-2000 statistics:

GP	G	A	TP	+/-	PIM	PP	SH	GW	GT	S	PCT
77	18	28	46	+14	126	6	0	2	1	134	13.4

2000-2001 statistics:

GP	G	A	TP	+/-	PIM	PP	SH	GW	GT	S	PCT
63	11	10	21	-13	71	3	0	0	0	95	11.6

2001-2002 statistics:

GP	G	A	TP	+/-	PIM	PP	SH	GW	GT	S	PCT
64	15	26	41	-5	93	8	0	2	0	137	10.9

2002-2003 statistics:

GP	G	A	TP	+/-	PIM	PP	SH	GW	GT	S	PCT
80	26	31	57	+1	176	13	0	4	1	132	19.7

LAST SEASON

Tied for Fourth in NHL in shooting percentage. Led team in shooting percentage. Second on team in power-play goals. Third on team in goals and penalty minutes. Tied for third on team in game-winning goals. Missed one game with flu. Missed one game due to coach's decision.

THE FINESSE GAME

Not having a great deal of speed or agility, Mellanby generates most of his effectiveness in tight spaces where he can use his size. On the power play, he sets up below the hash marks for a one-timer. He works for screens and tips. He doesn't have many moves, but he can capitalize on a loose puck with some good hands in-tight. Goals don't come naturally to him; however, he's determined and pays the price in front of the net.

Mellanby has developed a quicker release and more confidence in his shot. Coaches through the years have wanted Mellanby to shoot more because he is so accurate with it.

He has become more of a two-way player in his golden years, though he no longer sees many penalty-killing shifts. He is not much of a shorthanded threat. He lacks the speed and scoring instincts to convert turnovers into dangerous chances. His skating was never his strong suit and he has become slower, but he will still give his best effort on a nightly basis.

THE PHYSICAL GAME

Mellanby forechecks aggressively, using his body well to hit and force mistakes in the attacking zone. He engages in one-on-one battles in tight areas and tries to win his share. He is also willing to mix it up and take penalties of aggression. He seldom misses an opportunity to rub his glove in an opponent's face.

He's very strong along the boards and uses his feet when battling for the puck.

THE INTANGIBLES

Mellanby adds leadership to the Blues. He has played through pain, both physical and personal. Mellanby is a gamer, and every successful team needs a heart and soul guy just like him. We thought he might be playing his final NHL season, but he scored his first career hat trick — he's got to come back for an encore.

PROJECTION

Last year Mellanby scored the most goals in a season since the 1996-97 season. More importantly, he kept the Blues from feeling sorry for themselves for being without Chris Pronger most of the season. Does he have one more 20-goal season in him? We're going to think positively.

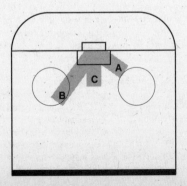

CHRIS OSGOOD

Yrs. of NHL service: 10
Born: Peace River, Alta.; Nov. 26, 1972
Position: goaltender
Height: 5-10
Weight: 175
Uniform no.: 30
Catches: left

Career statistics:

GP	MIN	GA	SO	GAA	A	PIM
501	28742	1180	38	2.46	12	101

1999-2000 statistics:

GP	MIN	GAA	W	L	T	SO	GA	S	SAPCT	PIM
53	3148	2.40	30	14	8	6	126	1349	.907	18

2000-2001 statistics:

GP	MIN	GAA	W	L	T	SO	GA	S	SAPCT	PIM
52	2834	2.69	25	19	4	1	127	1310	.903	8

2001-2002 statistics:

GP	MIN	GAA	W	L	T	SO	GA	S	SAPCT	PIM
66	3743	2.50	32	25	6	4	156	1727	.910	10

2002-2003 statistics:

GP	MIN	GAA	W	L	T	SO	GA	S	SAPCT	PIM
46	2525	2.95	21	17	6	4	124	1153	.892	12

LAST SEASON

Acquired from N.Y. Islanders on March 11, 2003, with a third-round draft pick in 2003 for Justin Papineau and a second-round draft pick in 2003. Missed 19 games with sprained ankle.

THE PHYSICAL GAME

Osgood is a small goalie, and he gets into trouble when he stops challenging shooters and stays too deep in his net. When Osgood is playing well, he plays his angles textbook-style. But Osgood has a streak in him where he relies on his reflexes too much. While his reaction time is excellent, he tends to lose the puck in scrambles around (especially behind) his net and ends up looking foolish on wraparounds.

Osgood has a superb glove and he's tough to beat high. His problems arise when he loses his concentration and his angles, and fails to square himself to the shooter. He will sometimes allow a ludicrous goal from 90 feet. On nights when he's on, he controls his rebounds well and doesn't have to scramble for too many second or third shots. His lateral movement is very good.

Osgood can handle the puck. He also uses his stick effectively to poke pucks off attackers' sticks around the net. He's no Martin Brodeur, however, and he tends to get overambitious. Sometimes less is more.

THE MENTAL GAME

Osgood has always had a bit of an attitude which never endears him to his teammates but sustains him through rough patches. He has won a Cup (with Detroit) but doesn't get the respect most Cup-winning goalies receive. He will be the No. 1 goalie in St. Louis this season.

THE INTANGIBLES

The Blues went through eight (EIGHT!) goalies last season. Osgood was a trade deadline pickup as a rental for the playoffs and despite a first-round playoff exit (in seven games), St. Louis wasted little time in re-signing him.

PROJECTION

The Blues are a solid team and Osgood should return to the 30-win ranks.

SHJON PODEIN

Yrs. of NHL service: 11
Born: Rochester, Minn.; Mar. 5, 1968
Position: left wing
Height: 6-2
Weight: 200
Uniform no.: 25
Shoots: left

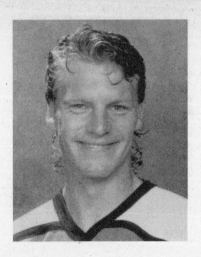

Career statistics:

GP	G	A	TP	PIM
699	100	106	206	439

1999-2000 statistics:

GP	G	A	TP	+/-	PIM	PP	SH	GW	GT	S	PCT
75	11	8	19	+12	29	0	1	3	0	104	10.6

2000-2001 statistics:

GP	G	A	TP	+/-	PIM	PP	SH	GW	GT	S	PCT
82	15	17	32	+7	68	0	0	3	0	137	10.9

2001-2002 statistics:

GP	G	A	TP	+/-	PIM	PP	SH	GW	GT	S	PCT
64	8	10	18	+2	41	0	1	2	0	67	11.9

2002-2003 statistics:

GP	G	A	TP	+/-	PIM	PP	SH	GW	GT	S	PCT
68	4	6	10	+7	28	1	0	0	0	52	7.7

PROJECTION
Podein is a strictly defensive player now. His passion outpaces his production.

LAST SEASON
Missed 17 games due to coach's decision.

THE FINESSE GAME
Podein is a laborer. He works hard, loves his job, and uses his size well. He started out as a center, but he is better suited as a winger because his hands aren't great and his passing skills are average at best. He is happiest in a dump-and-chase game, where he can use his straightaway speed to bore in on the puck carrier. Podein's work ethic makes him a mainstay on the penalty kill.

A mucker, Podein is not a fancy scorer. He gets most of his goals, and there aren't a lot of them, from digging around the net for rebounds and loose pucks. He doesn't have particularly good hockey sense, but he is determined.

Podein is not an agile skater but he is sturdy for work along the boards, and he can work up a pretty good head of steam. Just don't ask him to turn.

THE PHYSICAL GAME
Podein is antagonistic, with a bit of a mean streak, and he tends to be a bit careless with his stick. He can take bad penalties because of that tendency.

THE INTANGIBLES
Podein plays well on a checking line. He is a high-energy player and a penalty killer who can lift the bench with a strong shift. He has taken a long route to the NHL and works to stay here. Podein became an unrestricted free agent after last season. He won't have trouble finding work anywhere as a role player.

CHRIS PRONGER

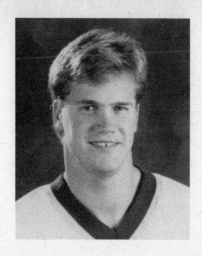

Yrs. of NHL service: 10
Born: Dryden, Ont.; Oct. 10, 1974
Position: left defense
Height: 6-6
Weight: 220
Uniform no.: 44
Shoots: left

Career statistics:

GP	G	A	TP	PIM
642	80	266	346	1010

1999-2000 statistics:

GP	G	A	TP	+/-	PIM	PP	SH	GW	GT	S	PCT
79	14	48	62	+52	92	8	0	3	2	192	7.3

2000-2001 statistics:

GP	G	A	TP	+/-	PIM	PP	SH	GW	GT	S	PCT
51	8	39	47	+21	75	4	0	0	1	121	6.6

2001-2002 statistics:

GP	G	A	TP	+/-	PIM	PP	SH	GW	GT	S	PCT
78	7	40	47	+23	120	4	1	3	0	204	3.4

2002-2003 statistics:

GP	G	A	TP	+/-	PIM	PP	SH	GW	GT	S	PCT
5	1	3	4	-2	10	0	0	0	0	11	9.1

LAST SEASON

Missed 77 games with wrist and knee surgery.

THE FINESSE GAME

Pronger is lanky with a powerful skating stride for angling his man to the boards for a take-out. He blends his physical play with good offensive instincts and skills. His skating is so fluid and his strides so long and efficient that he looks almost lazy, but he is faster than he looks and covers a lot of ground.

He also handles the puck well when skating and is always alert for passing opportunities. Pronger's vision shows in his work on the power play. He patrols the point smartly, using a low, tippable shot. Like many tall defensemen, he doesn't get his slap shot away quickly, but he compensates with a snap shot that he uses liberally. He has good enough hands for a big guy and the Blues occasionally use him up front on the power play.

Pronger not only jumps into the rush, he knows when to, which is an art. He'll back off if the opportunity is not there. Playing with Al MacInnis, one of the game's great offensive defensemen, has helped Pronger in this area. Pronger makes unique plays that make him stand out, great breakout passes, and clever feeds through the neutral zone. He is also wise enough to dump-and-chase rather than hold on to the puck and force a low-percentage pass. Pronger focuses more on his defensive role, but there is considerable upside to his offense.

Disciplined away from the puck and alert defensively, Pronger shows good anticipation, going where the puck is headed before it's shot there. He is very confident with the puck in his own end. His defensive reads are excellent.

THE PHYSICAL GAME

Pronger finishes every check with enthusiasm and shows something of a nasty streak with his stick. He makes his stand between the blueline and the top of the circle, forcing the forward to react. His long reach helps to make that style effective. He also uses his stick and reach when killing penalties.

THE INTANGIBLES

Pronger worked hard to get back in time for the playoffs but was clearly not the same player after missing nearly the entire season with injuries that prevented him from keeping in good aerobic condition. He will be one of the dominating defensemen in the league if he can return to form.

PROJECTION

Pronger's health bears watching in training camp. If he looks like he's ready to go, pencil him in for 45-50 points.

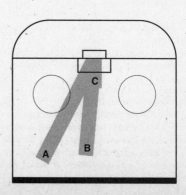

BRYCE SALVADOR

Yrs. of NHL service: 3
Born: Brandon, Man.; Feb. 11, 1976
Position: defense
Height: 6-2
Weight: 215
Uniform no.: 27
Shoots: left

Career statistics:

GP	G	A	TP	PIM
212	9	23	32	242

2000-2001 statistics:

GP	G	A	TP	+/-	PIM	PP	SH	GW	GT	S	PCT
75	2	8	10	-4	69	0	0	1	0	60	3.3

2001-2002 statistics:

GP	G	A	TP	+/-	PIM	PP	SH	GW	GT	S	PCT
66	5	7	12	+3	78	1	0	2	0	37	13.5

2002-2003 statistics:

GP	G	A	TP	+/-	PIM	PP	SH	GW	GT	S	PCT
71	2	8	10	+7	95	1	0	0	0	73	2.7

LAST SEASON

Missed four games with hamstring injuries. Missed two games with shoulder injury. Missed three games due to coach's decision.

THE FINESSE GAME

Salvador could become a poor man's Kevin Lowe. At his best, he is a steady, stay-at-home type of defender and he likes the physical part of the game. He will never be the kind of big open-ice hitter like Scott Stevens, another player he has been compared to, but it would be fine with the Blues if he learns to block shots, kill penalties, and bulldoze the front of the cage the way Stevens does. After all, Stevens was a member of the Blues — for one season.

Salvador has enough dedicated players around him on defense, particularly Chris Pronger, that he doesn't have to look far to find a solid example to follow. Salvador won't be a Pronger-type of player, since he lacks the finesse skills to get as involved offensively. He has an okay shot from the point and makes some pretty smart reads, so he's not a total waste on the power play, when he merits second-unit assignments. Salvador's feet are pretty good. He is a decent skater with good balance and isn't easy to beat one-on-one.

Salvador is getting closer to being a reliable and consistent defender. His lapses and lulls are fewer and don't occur as often.

THE PHYSICAL GAME

Salvador is not overly aggressive but he can play a very in-your-face style of game. He needs to do that more often, but it doesn't seem to come naturally. He needs to make it tougher for teams to wrest two points from the Blues. Salvador is fairly tall and solidly built.

THE INTANGIBLES

It's not likely that Salvador will develop into a top-two defenseman the Blues had hoped — rookie Barret Jackman shot right past him last season — but he has a likely future as a solid second-pair defenseman. Salvador was a restricted free agent after last season.

PROJECTION

Salvador won't get a lot of points, but if he starts earning upwards of 20 minutes a game, he could surprise with 20 points.

KEITH TKACHUK

Yrs. of NHL service: 11
Born: Melrose, Mass.; Mar. 28, 1972
Position: left wing
Height: 6-2
Weight: 225
Uniform no.: 7
Shoots: left

Career statistics:

GP	G	A	TP	PIM
781	398	363	761	1778

1999-2000 statistics:

GP	G	A	TP	+/-	PIM	PP	SH	GW	GT	S	PCT
50	22	21	43	+7	82	5	1	1	0	183	12.0

2000-2001 statistics:

GP	G	A	TP	+/-	PIM	PP	SH	GW	GT	S	PCT
76	35	44	79	+3	122	17	0	5	2	271	12.9

2001-2002 statistics:

GP	G	A	TP	+/-	PIM	PP	SH	GW	GT	S	PCT
73	38	37	75	+21	117	13	0	7	1	244	15.6

2002-2003 statistics:

GP	G	A	TP	+/-	PIM	PP	SH	GW	GT	S	PCT
56	31	24	55	+1	139	14	0	5	0	185	16.8

LAST SEASON

Led team in power-play goals. Tied for team lead in game-winning goals. Second on team in goals. Third on team in shots. Missed nine games with wrist injury. Missed 11 games with fractured foot. Missed two games due to personal reasons. Missed four games due to NHL suspension.

THE FINESSE GAME

In front of the net Tkachuk will bang and crash, but he also has soft hands for picking pucks out of skates and flicking strong wrist shots. He can also kick at the puck with his skates without going down. He has a quick release. He looks at the net, not down at the puck on his stick, and finds the openings. He has a great feel for the puck. From the hash marks in, he is one of the most dangerous forwards in the NHL. Eliminating the man-in-the-crease rule has increased his effectiveness and his production because the trenches are where he does his best work. He doesn't just stand in the slot, either, but moves in and out.

Tkachuk has improved his one-step quickness and agility. He is powerful and balanced, and often drives through bigger defensemen. Because of his size and strength, he is frequently used to take draws, and it's a rare face-off where the opposing center doesn't end up getting smacked by him.

THE PHYSICAL GAME

Volatile and mean as a scorpion, Tkachuk takes bad penalties. And since he has a reputation around the league for getting his stick up and retaliating for hits with a quick rabbit-punch to the head, referees keep a close eye on him. Tkachuk needs to stay on the ice. He can be tough without buying a time-share in the penalty box or serving a suspension, as he did last season for a cross-check on Wes Walz.

Tkachuk can dictate the physical tempo of a game with his work in the corners and along the boards. He comes in hard with big-time hits on the forecheck.

THE INTANGIBLES

Tkachuk has good chemistry with Pavol Demitra. His personal life was in turmoil last season because of a daughter born in fragile health.

PROJECTION

Injuries took a toll and prevented Tkachuk from being a 75-point player.

MATT WALKER

Yrs. of NHL service: 0
Born: Beaverlodge, Alta.; Apr. 7, 1980
Position: right defense
Height: 6-2
Weight: 222
Uniform no.: 28
Shoots: right

Career statistics:

GP	G	A	TP	PIM
16	0	1	1	38

2002-2003 statistics:

GP	G	A	TP	+/-	PIM	PP	SH	GW	GT	S	PCT
16	0	1	1	0	38	0	0	0	0	13	0.0

LAST SEASON

Will be entering first full NHL season. Missed three games with eye injury. Missed 11 games due to coach's decision. Appeared in 40 games with Worcester (AHL), scoring 1-8 — 9 with 58 PIM.

THE FINESSE GAME

Mention Matt Walker's name to anyone with the St. Louis Blues, and you'll see a glint in their eye.

Walker is a classic throwback. He's a rough, tough, stay-at-home kid who wouldn't look out of place playing back in the old six-team league.

Walker is powerful. He patrols the front of his net with a true presence. He rocks people along the wall and in the corners.

His offensive contributions will be minimal to nonexistent. This doesn't mean he is unskilled. Walker is a good skater and he makes a good first pass out of the zone. He needs to improve on his defensive reads and his reaction time, or else the pace of the NHL game will be beyond him.

THE PHYSICAL GAME

Curb your enthusiasm. Walker loves to hit so much that he will get overanxious and start running around, leaving his position and leaving his partner out-manned. Discipline will be his mantra. If anyone wants to throw 'em down, he will find a willing dance partner in Walker. His teammates feel a little bigger and braver with Walker around.

THE INTANGIBLES

Walker has made an impression (actually, he's probably made dents) in training camp and in his brief stints with the Blues last season. He has some elite defensemen to mentor him in St. Louis. He will probably play on the third defense pair with his future as a No. 4 defenseman.

PROJECTION

Walker is raw, but probably ready to start being worked into the St. Louis lineup. He will never score a lot of points, but will pile up some PIMs.

DOUG WEIGHT

Yrs. of NHL service: 12
Born: Warren, Mich.; Jan. 21, 1971
Position: center
Height: 5-11
Weight: 200
Uniform no.: 39
Shoots: left

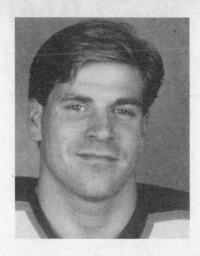

Career statistics:

GP	G	A	TP	PIM
837	210	553	763	697

1999-2000 statistics:

GP	G	A	TP	+/-	PIM	PP	SH	GW	GT	S	PCT
77	21	51	72	+6	54	3	1	4	0	167	12.6

2000-2001 statistics:

GP	G	A	TP	+/-	PIM	PP	SH	GW	GT	S	PCT
82	25	65	90	+12	91	8	0	3	2	188	13.3

2001-2002 statistics:

GP	G	A	TP	+/-	PIM	PP	SH	GW	GT	S	PCT
61	15	34	49	+20	40	3	0	1	0	131	11.4

2002-2003 statistics:

GP	G	A	TP	+/-	PIM	PP	SH	GW	GT	S	PCT
70	15	52	67	-6	52	7	0	3	0	182	8.2

LAST SEASON

Tied for second on team in assists. Third on team in average ice time. Tied for third on team in points. Missed 10 games with fractured bone in face. Missed two games with bruised ankle.

THE FINESSE GAME

Playmaking is Weight's strong suit. He has good vision and passes well to either side. His hands are soft and sure. He has quick and accurate wrist and snap shots. He handles the puck well in traffic, is strong on the puck, and creates a lot of scoring chances. Weight is an outstanding one-on-one player, but doesn't have to challenge all the time. He will trail the play down the right wing (his preferred side) and jump into the attack late. On the power play, Weight does his best work off the right-wing half-boards. He always seems to find a passing seam.

Weight won't win many footraces. Everybody thinks he's faster than he is because he keeps his legs pumping and he often surprises people on the rush who think they have him contained, only to see him push his way past. He frequently draws penalties. He has decent quickness, good balance, and a fair change of direction. Every asset Weight owns is enhanced by his competitive nature. Even when he isn't scoring, he is making other players around him better.

Weight has improved his defensive play slightly; he is like an offensive Doug Risebrough. His point production is amazingly consistent. He seldom slumps unless he is playing hurt, which he frequently does.

THE PHYSICAL GAME

Weight shows flashes of grit but doesn't bring it to the ice every night, maybe because he gets banged up so easily. Still, he is built like a fire hydrant, and on the nights he's on he hits with enthusiasm, finishing every check. He initiates and annoys. Weight has a mean streak when riled. He's also a bit of a trash talker, yapping and playing with a great deal of spirit. He has worked on his strength and conditioning and can handle a lot of ice time. He is strong on his skates and hard to knock off the puck.

THE INTANGIBLES

Weight has relaxed slightly in St. Louis after the initial pressure of his salary dump trade from Edmonton and big new contract (which has three years, $23 million remaining). Pavol Demitra's ability to handle the transition to center also made things easier on Weight, who can now just concern himself with doing his job instead of everyone else's.

PROJECTION

Weight had a decent bounce-back season and would have flirted with 80 points if he hadn't been injured. Since we anticipate him missing at least a dozen games with injuries, we'd expect around 15 goals, 45 assists.

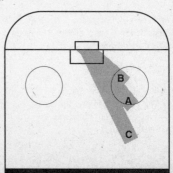

TAMPA BAY LIGHTNING

Players' Statistics 2001-2002

POS.	NO.	PLAYER	GP	G	A	PTS	+/-	PIM	PP	SH	GW	GT	S	PCT
C	20	VACLAV PROSPAL	80	22	57	79	9	53	9		4		134	16.4
C	4	VINCENT LECAVALIER	80	33	45	78	0	39	11	2	3	1	274	12.0
C	19	BRAD RICHARDS	80	17	57	74	3	24	4		2		277	6.1
R	26	MARTIN ST. LOUIS	82	33	37	70	10	32	12	3	5	3	201	16.4
D	22	DAN BOYLE	77	13	40	53	9	44	8		1	1	136	9.6
L	33	FREDRIK MODIN	76	17	23	40	7	43	2	1	4	1	179	9.5
L	25	DAVE ANDREYCHUK	72	20	14	34	-12	34	15		3	2	170	11.8
L	17	RUSLAN FEDOTENKO	76	19	13	32	-7	44	6		6		114	16.7
D	13	PAVEL KUBINA	75	3	19	22	-7	78					139	2.2
L	7	BEN CLYMER	65	6	12	18	-2	57	1		1		103	5.8
R	36	ANDRE ROY	62	10	7	17	0	119			2		85	11.8
D	37	BRAD LUKOWICH	70	1	14	15	4	46					52	1.9
D	21	CORY SARICH	82	5	9	14	-3	63			2		79	6.3
C	27	TIM TAYLOR	82	4	8	12	-13	38			1		95	4.2
C	16	*ALEXANDER SVITOV	63	4	4	8	-4	58	1				69	5.8
D	23	JANNE LAUKKANEN	19	2	6	8	-2	8					12	16.7
D	44	NOLAN PRATT	67	1	7	8	-6	35					38	2.6
R	28	SHELDON KEEFE	37	2	5	7	-1	24					51	3.9
D	25	MARC BERGEVIN	70	2	5	7	-11	36					27	7.4
R	15	NIKITA ALEXEEV	37	4	2	6	-6	8	1		1	1	52	7.7
D	2	STAN NECKAR	70	1	4	5	-6	43			1		38	2.6
D	5	JASSEN CULLIMORE	28	1	3	4	3	31					23	4.3
L	11	CHRIS DINGMAN	51	2	1	3	-11	91					41	4.9
L	18	JIMMIE OLVESTAD	37		3	3	-2	16					30	
D	38	DARREN RUMBLE	19				-2	6					10	
G	35	NIKOLAI KHABIBULIN	65				0	8						
G	30	KEVIN HODSON	7				0	2						
G	47	JOHN GRAHAME	40				0	11						
R	25	SHANE WILLIS					0							
C	0	MARTIN CIBAK					0							
G	1	EVGENY KONSTANTINOV	1				0	2						

GP = games played; G = goals; A = assists; PTS = points; +/- = goals-for minus goals-against while player is on ice; PIM = penalties in minutes; PP = power-play goals; SH = shorthanded goals; GW = game-winning goals; GT = game-tying goals; S = no. of shots; PCT = percentage of goals to shots; * = rookie

NIKITA ALEXEEV

Yrs. of NHL service: 2
Born: Murmansk, Russia; Dec. 27, 1981
Position: right wing
Height: 6-5
Weight: 210
Uniform no.: 15
Shoots: left

Career statistics:

GP	G	A	TP	PIM
81	8	6	14	16

2001-2002 statistics:

GP	G	A	TP	+/-	PIM	PP	SH	GW	GT	S	PCT
44	4	4	8	-9	8	1	0	1	0	47	8.5

2002-2003 statistics:

GP	G	A	TP	+/-	PIM	PP	SH	GW	GT	S	PCT
37	4	2	6	-6	8	1	0	1	1	52	7.7

LAST SEASON

Missed one game due to coach's decision. Appeared in 36 games with Springfield (AHL), scoring 7-5 — 12.

THE FINESSE GAME

Alexeev is big, strong, and skilled. His skating is average, but he will probably be able to get by with it in the NHL. He has good size and great, soft hands and should be able to find a home on one of Tampa Bay's top-two lines this season or next.

Alexeev was rushed to the pros before he was really ready, but sometimes bad teams don't believe they have any other option. At least it looked like Alexeev will survive. His confidence doesn't appear irreparably harmed.

Alexeev has a lot of offensive upside. Like many young players, he needs to bring a more consistent effort to the rink every night. He has the tools to become a dominant player.

THE PHYSICAL GAME

Alexeev is six-foot-five but he has none of the clumsiness or lack of coordination that sometimes afflicts big kids. He needs to get stronger. Alexeev isn't very physical. People see this hulking player and assume he will be tossing guys aside with one arm, but it's not in his nature. Alexeev will have to pick his physical game up a notch. He can't be effective playing a perimeter game. He has to put in the effort on a nightly basis, and not just when the mood strikes him.

THE INTANGIBLES

The Lightning envision Alexeev as a linemate for Vincent Lecavalier. Alexeev needs to adopt a more serious approach to his job. He has yet to approach this opportunity like a job, and that may be a serious character flaw that costs him an NHL career unless he matures.

PROJECTION

Consistency eludes him, but Tampa Bay still believes Alexeev will be a 25-goal scorer soon.

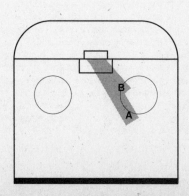

DAN BOYLE

Yrs. of NHL service: 3
Born: Ottawa, Ont.; July 12, 1976
Position: right defense
Height: 5-11
Weight: 190
Uniform no.: 22
Shoots: right

Career statistics:

GP	G	A	TP	PIM
247	28	84	112	121

1999-2000 statistics:

GP	G	A	TP	+/-	PIM	PP	SH	GW	GT	S	PCT
13	0	3	3	-2	4	0	0	0	0	9	-

2000-2001 statistics:

GP	G	A	TP	+/-	PIM	PP	SH	GW	GT	S	PCT
69	4	18	22	-14	28	1	0	0	0	83	4.8

2001-2002 statistics:

GP	G	A	TP	+/-	PIM	PP	SH	GW	GT	S	PCT
66	8	18	26	-16	39	3	0	1	1	99	8.1

2002-2003 statistics:

GP	G	A	TP	+/-	PIM	PP	SH	GW	GT	S	PCT
77	13	40	53	+9	44	8	0	1	1	136	9.6

LAST SEASON

Fifth among NHL defensemen in points. Led team in average ice time (24:30). Led team defensemen in points. Career highs in goals, assists, and points. Missed four games with fractured finger. Missed one game due to coach's decision.

THE FINESSE GAME

It's rare to see an NHL defenseman improve his offensive production as radically as Boyle did last season without damaging the defensive part of his game. What is most amazing about him is that he became a better defensive player while piling up the points.

Boyle was a high-scoring defenseman in college but his limited defensive ability made him a bubble boy in the NHL. Boyle completely dedicated himself to learning the defensive game, to the point of severely limiting his involvement in the attack, but now he is competent and confident in all zones.

Boyle lacks the size to be a dominating defenseman, and doesn't have the brilliant speed to be an offensive defenseman. He has, however, become a player who positions himself well and can use his finesse skills in a defensive role. He is also a pretty good power-play quarterback. He keeps his point shot low and its velocity makes it perfect for tip-ins and re-directs. He will mix up the attack with a rush here, a wheel, and a pass there. Boyle is occasionally guilty of getting too mesmerized and leaving his point open when he cheats down low.

THE PHYSICAL GAME

Boyle is a pipsqueak alongside some of the NHL's bigger defensemen. He competes hard, and he will put his body in the way. His best defense is getting to the puck first and getting it out of the zone. Boyle pays a lot of attention to his conditioning and handles a lot of minutes without wearing down.

THE INTANGIBLES

Boyle repeatedly handled tough checking assignments against other teams' top lines. Boyle couldn't have picked a better time to have a big year. He became a restricted free agent at the end of the season.

PROJECTION

Tampa Bay is woefully understocked on defense, meaning Boyle will draw major power play and ice time again. He should score an assist-heavy 50 points.

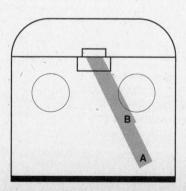

BEN CLYMER

Yrs. of NHL service: 4
Born: Edina, Minn.; Apr. 11, 1978
Position: left wing
Height: 6-1
Weight: 199
Uniform no.: 7
Shoots: right

Career statistics:

GP	G	A	TP	PIM
229	27	39	66	201

1999-2000 statistics:

GP	G	A	TP	+/-	PIM	PP	SH	GW	GT	S	PCT
60	2	6	8	-26	87	2	0	0	0	98	2.0

2000-2001 statistics:

GP	G	A	TP	+/-	PIM	PP	SH	GW	GT	S	PCT
23	5	1	6	-7	21	3	0	0	0	25	20.0

2001-2002 statistics:

GP	G	A	TP	+/-	PIM	PP	SH	GW	GT	S	PCT
81	14	20	34	-10	36	4	0	2	0	151	9.3

2002-2003 statistics:

GP	G	A	TP	+/-	PIM	PP	SH	GW	GT	S	PCT
65	6	12	18	-2	57	1	0	1	0	103	5.8

LAST SEASON

Missed 16 games with groin injuries. Missed one game due to coach's decision.

THE FINESSE GAME

Clymer is a former defenseman who has been converted to a checking-line winger by the Lightning, with surprisingly good results.

Good size and decent skating ability made him a high second-round draft pick by the Boston Bruins in 1997. When the Bruins failed to sign him, Tampa Bay nabbed him as a free agent in 1999. He struggled on defense at the NHL level, so the Lightning tried their experiment. He played almost exclusively up front last season, although he's a handy guy to have in the lineup because he can slide back on defense in case of injuries or penalties.

Clymer has a strong stride and good speed. His offensive skills are good enough that he can create something offensively when he forces a turnover. Clymer has little trouble with defensive-zone coverage.

THE PHYSICAL GAME

Clymer plays with an edge. One of his idols is Chris Chelios, and Clymer can play with a similar mean streak. He is a willing hitter and his skating gives him the ability to crunch. Clymer does a lot of the dirty work and is fearless.

THE INTANGIBLES

Clymer is one of those good-soldier types that is integral to a team's success. That fact that he is so versatile is another plus. He may need to produce more than six goals to avoid being a bubble boy, but nagging groin injuries last season probably slowed him down. Clymer does a lot of little things to help his team win, and those don't show up on the scoresheet.

PROJECTION

Assuming injuries were what held Clymer back offensively last season, we would expect 10-15 goals in a third-line role.

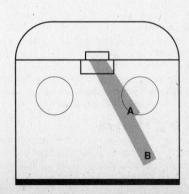

JASSEN CULLIMORE

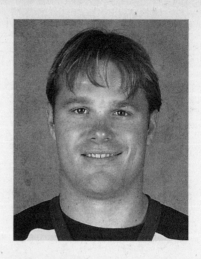

Yrs. of NHL service: 9
Born: Simcoe, Ont.; Dec. 4, 1972
Position: left defense
Height: 6-5
Weight: 244
Uniform no.: 5
Shoots: left

Career statistics:

GP	G	A	TP	PIM
445	17	42	59	446

1999-2000 statistics:

GP	G	A	TP	+/-	PIM	PP	SH	GW	GT	S	PCT
46	1	1	2	-12	66	0	0	0	0	23	4.3

2000-2001 statistics:

GP	G	A	TP	+/-	PIM	PP	SH	GW	GT	S	PCT
74	1	6	7	-6	80	0	0	0	0	56	1.8

2001-2002 statistics:

GP	G	A	TP	+/-	PIM	PP	SH	GW	GT	S	PCT
78	4	9	13	-1	58	0	0	1	0	84	4.8

2002-2003 statistics:

GP	G	A	TP	+/-	PIM	PP	SH	GW	GT	S	PCT
28	1	3	4	+3	31	0	0	0	0	23	4.3

PROJECTION

Cullimore is completely keyed on using his finesse skills on defense, so 12-15 points would be a safe and conservative bet.

LAST SEASON

Missed 54 games with shoulder surgery.

THE FINESSE GAME

Cullimore is big and rangy, and a good skater for his size. He jumps smartly into the play, using a big stride and a big reach. He makes smart pinches and doesn't gamble too often.

He is a good enough skater to hustle back if he does make a mistake in judgement. Cullimore is a good passer but not creative. He will chip the puck off the boards if that's the right play, but he is also ready to break a forward with a smooth outlet pass. He is a low-risk, stabilizing defenseman.

Cullimore is intelligent and diligent in his approach to the game. He will always be after the coaches to analyze plays. He routinely draws the checking assignments against other team's top forward line, and he always does his homework.

THE PHYSICAL GAME

Not big or mean, but determined, Cullimore takes his man out effectively in front of the net. He gets good leg drive to power his checks. He blocks a lot of shots. He was able to return from shoulder surgery in February and was not reluctant to use the healed shoulder for body work. Cullimore has a pretty long fuse and won't take dumb penalties.

THE INTANGIBLES

Cullimore is a quiet, blue-collar defenseman who accepts every responsibility against other team's top lines as part of Tampa Bay's top defense pair.

NIKOLAI KHABIBULIN

Yrs. of NHL service: 9
Born: Sverdlovsk, Russia; Jan. 13, 1973
Position: goaltender
Height: 6-1
Weight: 203
Uniform no.: 35
Catches: left

Career statistics:

GP	MIN	GA	SO	GAA	A	PIM
421	23833	1050	32	2.64	11	82

1999-2000 statistics:

Missed NHL season.

2000-2001 statistics:

GP	MIN	GAA	W	L	T	SO	GA	S	SAPCT	PIM
2	123	2.93	1	1	0	0	6	69	.913	0

2001-2002 statistics:

GP	MIN	GAA	W	L	T	SO	GA	S	SAPCT	PIM
70	3896	2.36	24	32	10	7	153	1914	.920	6

2002-2003 statistics:

GP	MIN	GAA	W	L	T	SO	GA	S	SAPCT	PIM
65	3787	2.47	30	22	11	4	156	1760	.911	8

LAST SEASON

Tied for third among NHL goalies in assists. Reached 30 wins for first time since 1998-99.

THE PHYSICAL GAME

Khabibulin is a butterfly-style goalie who positions himself like a shortstop. He gets down low and always gets his body behind the shot, and he stays on his feet and moves with the shooter. He may perform the best split-save in the league; it's stunningly graceful and athletic, and his legs look about five feet long. He leaves only the tiniest five-hole because he also gets the paddle of his stick down low across the front of the crease. Shooters have to go upstairs on him, but he doesn't give away a lot of net.

Solid in his fundamentals, Khabibulin plays well out on the top of his crease, which is unusual for Russian goalies, who tend to stay deep in their net. He is aggressive but patient at the same time, and waits for the shooter to commit first. He has an excellent glove hand.

Khabibulin's biggest flaw remains his stickhandling, although with hard work by the coaching staff, this has improved to where it no longer hurts his team.

THE MENTAL GAME

Khabibulin has trouble maintaining his focus and concentration. Maybe it's because he played so many seasons for bad teams that he just wore down having to be the savior night after night just to keep his team from getting embarrassed. Or maybe it's because he just couldn't handle the pressure once Tampa Bay actually became a contending team.

THE INTANGIBLES

Although he was largely responsible for the Lightning getting into the playoffs, Khabibulin wasn't the same dazzling, dominating goaltender in the postseason. As hard as it might be to believe, there was talk during the off-season that the Lightning would entertain trade rumors for him, since a lot of teammates were unhappy with his attitude and his performance in the playoffs.

PROJECTION

Khabibulin is an enigma. Can he earn 30 wins again? Will it happen with the Lightning?

PAVEL KUBINA

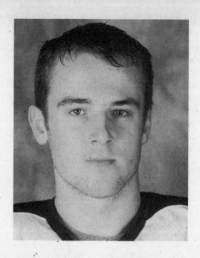

Yrs. of NHL service: 5
Born: Vsetin, Czech Republic; Sept. 10, 1979
Position: right defense
Height: 6-4
Weight: 230
Uniform no.: 13
Shoots: right

Career statistics:

GP	G	A	TP	PIM
374	43	93	136	482

1999-2000 statistics:

GP	G	A	TP	+/-	PIM	PP	SH	GW	GT	S	PCT
69	8	18	26	-19	93	6	0	3	0	128	6.3

2000-2001 statistics:

GP	G	A	TP	+/-	PIM	PP	SH	GW	GT	S	PCT
70	11	19	30	-14	103	6	1	1	0	128	8.6

2001-2002 statistics:

GP	G	A	TP	+/-	PIM	PP	SH	GW	GT	S	PCT
82	11	23	34	-22	106	5	2	3	0	189	5.8

2002-2003 statistics:

GP	G	A	TP	+/-	PIM	PP	SH	GW	GT	S	PCT
75	3	19	22	-7	78	0	0	0	0	139	2.2

LAST SEASON

Second on team in average ice time (21:24). Third on team in penalty minutes. Missed three games with neck injury and headaches. Missed one game with bruised foot. Missed three games due to coach's decision.

THE FINESSE GAME

Kubina isn't a great skater. He is big and somewhat upright in his stance, and he takes short strides. He lacks lateral quickness, though he has shown improvement. He is very strong on his skates.

The key to his game is his passing. He has fair offensive instincts. Kubina has a big shot, but not a great one. Because his shot is so heavy, he has been given some power-play chances in the past, but he lacks the lateral movement for the slide along the blueline that makes those kind of shots harder to block or save.

Kubina struggled defensively last season. He receives a lot of ice time and a lot of responsibility, but the coaching staff seemed to lose faith in him and often gave the tougher assignments to other defensive pairings. Kubina is a good shot-blocker.

THE PHYSICAL GAME

Kubina has good size and he uses it well. He has a bit of an edge to him. All in all, a solid package.

THE INTANGIBLES

Kubina did not continue the progress he had shown through his first few sink-or-swim seasons with the Lightning. Kubina was a healthy scratch on several occasions, and went from being a crowd darling to being booed, which had to dent his confidence. He has to be nagged to keep at his conditioning and to work on his off-ice habits. He is likely to carry another heavy workload.

PROJECTION

Kubina's offensive output simply plunged. There is no reason why he shouldn't be producing in the 30-point range. It's too early to give up on him, but this could be the season that determines just how much Kubina wants a job as a top-four defenseman in the NHL.

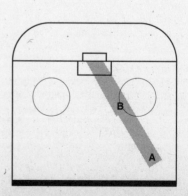

VINCENT LECAVALIER

Yrs. of NHL service: 5
Born: Ile Bizard, Que.; Apr. 21, 1980
Position: center
Height: 6-4
Weight: 205
Uniform no.: 4
Shoots: left

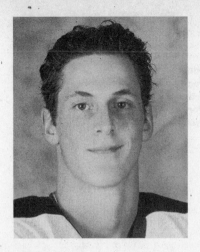

Career statistics:

GP	G	A	TP	PIM
386	114	147	261	232

1999-2000 statistics:

GP	G	A	TP	+/-	PIM	PP	SH	GW	GT	S	PCT
80	25	42	67	-25	43	6	0	3	1	166	15.1

2000-2001 statistics:

GP	G	A	TP	+/-	PIM	PP	SH	GW	GT	S	PCT
68	23	28	51	-26	66	7	0	3	0	165	13.9

2001-2002 statistics:

GP	G	A	TP.	+/-	PIM	PP	SH	GW	GT	S	PCT
76	20	17	37	-18	61	5	0	3	1	164	12.2

2002-2003 statistics:

GP	G	A	TP	+/-	PIM	PP	SH	GW	GT	S	PCT
80	33	45	78	0	39	11	2	3	1	274	12.0

LAST SEASON

Tied for team lead in goals. Second on team in points, shorthanded goals, and shots. Third on team in assists and power-play goals. Career highs in goals, assists, and points. Missed two games with sprained knee.

THE FINESSE GAME

Last season was Lecavalier's coming-out. He played in the NHL All-Star Game and led his team into the playoffs for the first time since 1996.

Lecavalier's puck skills proved everything they were advertised to be when the Lightning drafted him first overall in 1998. He is an elite playmaker. His passing skills are world class, and he has gained more confidence in his moves, even making daring spin-o-ramas. Like Wayne Gretzky and Mario Lemieux, the two great centers with whom he has been compared, Lecavalier will invent moves lesser players don't even dream of. His linemates have to be constantly aware that he can get the puck to them at any time.

Like many young players, Lecavalier will need to focus on his defensive play, but he has a good foundation for that already and should be an apt pupil. He is a shifty skater who can catch a defenseman flat-footed. His speed is major league. He can burst to the outside with the puck and beat a defenseman one-on-one.

THE PHYSICAL GAME

A tall, skinny kid who has to keep working in the weight room in order to do battle against the league's heavyweights, Lecavalier has worked with a personal trainer. He is still a bit coltish. He has a nasty streak in him, and is just as quick to answer a hit with a whack of the stick.

THE INTANGIBLES

Lecavalier had some heated duels with coach John Tortorella, and emerged a better, more mature player for it. After being rushed into the NHL and expected to become the next Lemieux, Lecavalier realized it was important to first become Vincent Lecavalier. Tortorella took the captain's "C" away from Lecavalier, which might have looked like an insult but ended up taking pressure off. Adding veterans like Dave Andreychuk and Tim Taylor to the roster also played a key role in helping Lecavalier settle down.

PROJECTION

This is what we said about Lecavalier last year: "If he doesn't score 70 points this season, it might be time to reconsider his future." The future is now.

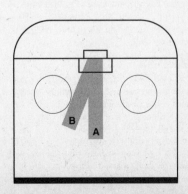

FREDRIK MODIN

Yrs. of NHL service: 7
Born: Sundsvall, Sweden; Oct. 8, 1974
Position: left wing
Height: 6-4
Weight: 225
Uniform no.: 33
Shoots: left

Career statistics:

GP	G	A	TP	PIM
503	123	128	251	227

1999-2000 statistics:

GP	G	A	TP	+/-	PIM	PP	SH	GW	GT	S	PCT
80	22	26	48	-26	18	3	0	5	0	167	13.2

2000-2001 statistics:

GP	G	A	TP	+/-	PIM	PP	SH	GW	GT	S	PCT
76	32	24	56	-1	48	8	0	4	0	217	14.8

2001-2002 statistics:

GP	G	A	TP	+/-	PIM	PP	SH	GW	GT	S	PCT
54	14	17	31	0	27	2	0	4	1	141	9.9

2002-2003 statistics:

GP	G	A	TP	+/-	PIM	PP	SH	GW	GT	S	PCT
76	17	23	40	+7	43	2	1	4	1	179	9.5

LAST SEASON

Third on team in plus-minus. Tied for third on team in game-winning goals. Missed four games with back spasms/rib contusion. Missed two games with groin injury.

THE FINESSE GAME

Modin's shot is so heavy that it can physically knock the breath out of even the most well-padded goalie. He is dangerous as soon as he crosses the blueline.

He would be even more of a constant threat if he took more shots. With his speed and release, Modin should be close to 300 shots over a full season, but he still looks to pass too much.

He clicks beautifully with Brad Richards. In the past, Modin was always looking to set up a shooter, but now Richards looks to set Modin up. If Modin plays with Richards again this season, that positive trend should continue.

Modin has a bit of a knock-kneed skating style and isn't pretty to watch, but he does have NHL-calibre speed and is strong on his skates. Modin is fairly aware defensively.

THE PHYSICAL GAME

Modin has a powerful upper body for muscling through plays when he has a notion to, though he will still drift once in awhile. On nights when he gets it into his head to play a physical game, Modin drives to the net with better intent and is far more effective.

Modin has very good size and could have developed into a power forward. That is not likely to happen this late in his career.

THE INTANGIBLES

Modin carried his disappointing regular-season performance into the playoffs. If he doesn't snap out of it, he will lose a job on the top two lines. There wasn't really a threat of that happening before, but Tampa Bay will get a little deeper. Modin needs to answer a lot of questions this season.

PROJECTION

Modin has all the makings of a consistent 30-goal scorer, which made last season's 17 so baffling. It might have been the stress of impending (restricted) free agency. Some players simply don't handle the heat well when they're playing for a new contract.

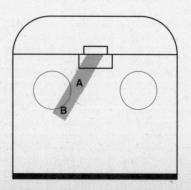

BRAD RICHARDS

Yrs. of NHL service: 3
Born: Montague, P.E.I.; May 2, 1980
Position: center/left wing
Height: 6-1
Weight: 198
Uniform no.: 19
Shoots: left

Career statistics:

GP	G	A	TP	PIM
244	58	140	198	51

2000-2001 statistics:

GP	G	A	TP	+/-	PIM	PP	SH	GW	GT	S	PCT
82	21	41	62	-10	14	7	0	3	0	179	11.7

2001-2002 statistics:

GP	G	A	TP	+/-	PIM	PP	SH	GW	GT	S	PCT
82	20	42	62	-18	13	5	0	0	1	251	8.0

2002-2003 statistics:

GP	G	A	TP	+/-	PIM	PP	SH	GW	GT	S	PCT
80	17	57	74	+3	24	4	0	2	0	277	6.1

LAST SEASON

Tied for fourth in NHL in assists. Led team in shots. Tied for team lead in assists. Third on team in points and average ice time (19:56). Missed two games due to personal reasons.

THE FINESSE GAME

Nothing about Richards's game is outstanding. He is only average size, isn't a dazzling skater, and doesn't have great hands. But what Richards possesses is a Mario Lemieux-like ability to slow the game down to his own pace. He certainly isn't the next Lemieux, but he is deceptive and calm with his playmaking, and that fools a lot of people.

Richards is a very smart player. To compare him to another great player, Wayne Gretzky, Richards seems to think the game on a completely different level. He is calm and poised. Richards needs to shoot more because now teams realize he is pressing to set up plays and they can sag off him. Even with that, he tied for the league lead in power-play assists (34).

Richards improved in the two areas in which he had been weakest: the defensive game and face-offs.

THE PHYSICAL GAME

He needs to get stronger. Richards continues to work in the off-season to better his upper-body strength. He is willing to scrap along the boards for the puck. Richards also needs to continue to improve his skating. He is a fit player and can handle a lot of minutes (he led Tampa Bay forwards in ice time for the second consecutive season).

THE INTANGIBLES

The only problem with Richards is that there is only one of him. Richards upgrades the level of any winger who gets to play alongside him. A lot of people thought it was Lecavalier who made Richards look so good in junior. It might have been just the opposite. Richards was a restricted free agent after the season.

PROJECTION

Richards scored 12 points more than he did during his breakout season in 2001-02. This is about his ceiling.

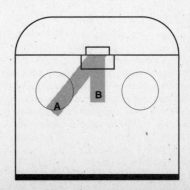

CORY SARICH

Yrs. of NHL service: 4
Born: Saskatoon, Sask.; Aug. 16, 1978
Position: right defense
Height: 6-3
Weight: 204
Uniform no.: 21
Shoots: right

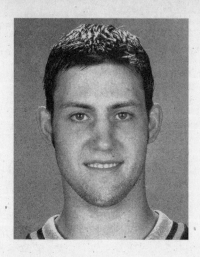

Career statistics:

GP	G	A	TP	PIM
290	6	34	40	351

1999-2000 statistics:

GP	G	A	TP	+/-	PIM	PP	SH	GW	GT	S	PCT
59	0	6	6	-6	77	0	0	0	0	69	0.0

2000-2001 statistics:

GP	G	A	TP	+/-	PIM	PP	SH	GW	GT	S	PCT
73	1	8	9	-25	106	0	0	1	0	66	1.5

2001-2002 statistics:

GP	G	A	TP	+/-	PIM	PP	SH	GW	GT	S	PCT
72	0	11	11	-4	105	0	0	0	0	55	0.0

2002-2003 statistics:

GP	G	A	TP	+/-	PIM	PP	SH	GW	GT	S	PCT
82	5	9	14	-3	63	0	0	2	0	79	6.3

LAST SEASON

One of three Lightning players to appear in all 82 games. Career highs in goals and points.

THE FINESSE GAME

Sarich is a stay-at-home defenseman who has developed into an extremely steady and reliable bedrock for the Tampa Bay defense. He has NHL skating ability, with decent lateral movement, pivots, and balance. He moves the puck very well. Being big and strong and being able to get the puck out of the zone quickly and safely already has Sarich ahead of some NHL players with much more experience than he has.

Sarich does not get involved in the attack. He knows his game is defense. There isn't much fanciness to him.

Sarich has improved his positional play and that has resulted in less scrambling in the defensive zone. He is playing a much more efficient and poised game.

THE PHYSICAL GAME

Sarich has pro size and a mean streak, but he held it in check while concentrating on learning the game. Now that he has gained some confidence (and gotten over his concussion from October 2001), he has become more aggressive. That's a good thing. His skating is powerful enough to help him line up opponents for some pretty big hits. Sarich has to be careful not to get carried away with the joy of splattering people.

THE INTANGIBLES

Sarich faced a critical year last season and handled it beautifully. He was one of the steadier Tampa Bay players and took the kind of strides you like to see in a young defenseman who may be about to hit his peak.

PROJECTION

Sarich will probably not put many more than 15 points on the board.

MARTIN ST. LOUIS

Yrs. of NHL service: 4
Born: Laval, Que., Canada June 18, 1975
Position: center/right wing
Height: 5-9
Weight: 185
Uniform no.: 15
Shoots: left

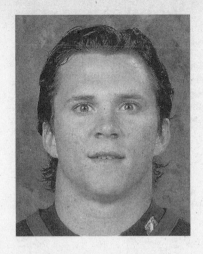

Career statistics:

GP	G	A	TP	PIM
282	71	94	165	96

1998-1999 statistics:

GP	G	A	TP	+/-	PIM	PP	SH	GW	GT	S	PCT
13	1	1	2	-2	10	0	0	0	0	14	7.1

1999-2000 statistics:

GP	G	A	TP	+/-	PIM	PP	SH	GW	GT	S	PCT
56	3	15	18	-5	22	0	0	1	0	73	4.1

2000-2001 statistics:

GP	G	A	TP	+/-	PIM	PP	SH	GW	GT	S	PCT
78	18	22	40	-4	12	3	3	4	0	141	12.8

2002-2003 statistics:

GP	G	A	TP	+/-	PIM	PP	SH	GW	GT	S	PCT
82	33	37	70	+10	32	12	3	5	3	201	16.4

LAST SEASON

Led team in plus-minus and shorthanded goals. Tied for team lead in goals. Career highs in goals, assists, and points. Second on team in power-play goals and game-winning goals. Tied for second on team in shooting percentage. Third on team in shots. One of three Lightning players to appear in all 82 games.

THE FINESSE GAME

Of course he's small. But how many times have you watched a bigger guy go through the motions on the ice and wish he played the game as hard as St. Louis does?

St. Louis gives that effort because he has to, every shift. It's not the work ethic that is so startling about St. Louis, though, it's the way he convinced the Tampa Bay coaches (and himself) that he shouldn't be pigeon-holed as a high-octane checking forward.

He was a scorer at the college level (Vermont, where he was a three-time Hobey Baker finalist), but started his career with Calgary as a checker and penalty killer. Once he signed on with the Lightning as a free agent in 2000, St. Louis started showing that his hands could be just as quick as his nimble feet. St. Louis has a hair-trigger release on his shot.

He excels on the power play, where he has that extra bit of open ice to work with. St. Louis is equally likely to shoot as pass, which makes him difficult to defend against.

THE PHYSICAL GAME

St. Louis is not going to win any weightlifting contests, but he has a solid build and a low center of gravity that not only gives him great balance but puts him a lot closer to the puck than a defender.

THE INTANGIBLES

St. Louis has given hope to every player who was ever told he was too small to compete. If there were an award for The Biggest Surprise in the NHL, or maybe The Biggest Little Surprise, the trophy would go to St. Louis. And it would probably be bigger than he is.

PROJECTION

St. Louis brought his game up another notch in the playoffs, which is the mark of a good NHL player. He won't be catching anyone off-guard this season, though, and we expect his point production to slack off a bit from 70.

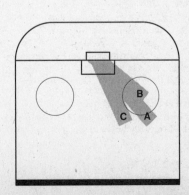

CORY STILLMAN

Yrs. of NHL service: 8
Born: Peterborough, Ont.; Dec. 20, 1970
Position: left wing
Height: 6-0
Weight: 194
Uniform no.: 61
Shoots: left

Career statistics:

GP	G	A	TP	PIM
564	159	195	354	290

1999-2000 statistics:

GP	G	A	TP	+/-	PIM	PP	SH	GW	GT	S	PCT
37	12	9	21	-9	12	6	0	3	1	59	20.3

2000-2001 statistics:

GP	G	A	TP	+/-	PIM	PP	SH	GW	GT	S	PCT
78	24	28	52	-8	51	10	0	4	0	174	13.8

2001-2002 statistics:

GP	G	A	TP	+/-	PIM	PP	SH	GW	GT	S	PCT
80	23	22	45	+8	36	6	0	4	0	140	16.4

2002-2003 statistics:

GP	G	A	TP	+/-	PIM	PP	SH	GW	GT	S	PCT
79	24	43	67	+12	56	6	0	4	0	157	15.3

LAST SEASON

Acquired from St. Louis on June 21, 2003, for a second-round draft pick in 2003. Tied for third on Blues in points. Career highs in assists and points. Missed three games with knee injury.

THE FINESSE GAME

A natural center, Stillman brings a pivot's playmaking ability to the wing. He's intelligent and has sound hockey instincts, but doesn't have that extra notch of speed an elite player at the NHL level needs. Since he's not very big (which hampers his odds of playing center), he needs every advantage he can get. St. Louis used him at left wing last season.

Stillman has a good enough point shot to be used on the power play. He can beat a goalie with his shot from just inside the blueline. He has good hands and a keen understanding of the game. He possesses great patience and puckhandling skills, and is efficient in small areas. He has the potential to become an effective player if he is supported by gifted forwards.

A goal scorer, Stillman possesses a kind of selfishness that is intrinsic to good scorers. He wants the puck, and he wants to shoot it. He creates off the forecheck, not with his size but with his anticipation. Stillman's major flaw is his lack of consistency.

THE PHYSICAL GAME

Stillman is thick and sturdy enough to absorb some hard hits. He is not overly aggressive but will protect the puck.

THE INTANGIBLES

Stillman has worked hard to be an NHL player. He is not an overwhelming player, just a useful sort. St. Louis may miss him more than they realize. Stillman was a restricted free agent after last season.

PROJECTION

Stillman can score in the 20-goal range and he should see significant power-play time with Tampa Bay.

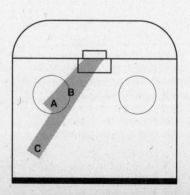

ALEXANDER SVITOV

Yrs. of NHL service: 1
Born: Omsk, Russia; Nov. 3, 1982
Position: center
Height: 6-3
Weight: 198
Uniform no.: 16
Shoots: left

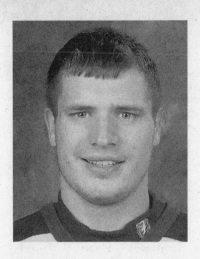

Career statistics:

GP	G	A	TP	PIM
63	4	4	8	58

2002-2003 statistics:

GP	G	A	TP	+/-	PIM	PP	SH	GW	GT	S	PCT
63	4	4	8	-4	58	1	0	0	0	69	5.8

LAST SEASON

Missed five games due to coach's decision. Appeared in 11 games with Springfield (AHL), scoring 4-5 — 9.

THE FINESSE GAME

Svitov is a physically imposing specimen with a nasty streak that gets him into hot water. It also gets him a lot of open ice.

Svitov is snarly enough to scare some players away from him, and when that happens, he can make the most of his decent hands and puck skills. He is a very good skater with a fluid stride, and he has good hockey sense.

Svitov is projected as a top-two center. Svitov's game is well-rounded. There isn't much missing from his game. He can skate, shoot, pass, backcheck, forecheck, and win draws. He will be able to kill penalties, block shots, and jam up front on the power play. He is a smart, smart player.

THE PHYSICAL GAME

Svitov took a number of bad penalties last season and needs to curb his natural aggression (dare we call it viciousness?) in order to get ice time. He can't keep hurting his team by sitting in the penalty box, but it's tough to ask a scorpion to play nice. He has been compared to Bobby Holik, although he probably has more offensive upside.

THE INTANGIBLES

Svitov is still rough around the edges, and we do mean rough, but with some polish and maturity he will be a gale force in the NHL in just a few seasons. He has the capability to become a dominating player. Svitov is still getting a handle on the English language, and that may help him feel more comfortable once he does.

PROJECTION

Svitov still has some growing up to do, at least mentally. Physically, he is ready to rock and roll. This might not be his breakout season, but we should see signs of improvement and maybe 15 goals.

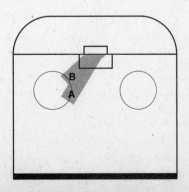

TORONTO MAPLE LEAFS

Players' Statistics 2001-2002

POS.	NO.	PLAYER	GP	G	A	PTS	+/-	PIM	PP	SH	GW	GT	S	PCT
R	89	ALEXANDER MOGILNY	73	33	46	79	4	12	5	3	9		165	20.0
C	13	MATS SUNDIN	75	37	35	72	1	58	16	3	8	1	223	16.6
R	11	OWEN NOLAN	75	29	25	54	-3	107	13	3	5		221	13.1
D	15	TOMAS KABERLE	82	11	36	47	20	30	4	1	2	1	119	9.2
C	80	NIK ANTROPOV	72	16	29	45	11	124	2	1	6		102	15.7
D	67	ROBERT SVEHLA	82	7	38	45	13	46	2		1		110	6.4
C	21	ROBERT REICHEL	81	12	30	42	7	26	1	1	1		111	10.8
C	16	DARCY TUCKER	77	10	26	36	-7	119	4	1	2		108	9.3
R	19	MIKAEL RENBERG	67	14	21	35	5	36	7		1		137	10.2
R	14	JONAS HOGLUND	79	13	19	32	2	12	2		3		157	8.3
C	93	DOUG GILMOUR	62	11	19	30	-6	36	3				85	12.9
R	28	TIE DOMI	79	15	14	29	-1	171	4				91	16.5
D	96	PHIL HOUSLEY	58	6	23	29	6	26	2		2		137	4.4
C	39	TRAVIS GREEN	75	12	12	24	2	67	2	1	3		86	13.9
D	24	BRYAN MCCABE	75	6	18	24	9	135	3		1		149	4.0
D	25	JYRKI LUMME	73	6	11	17	10	46	1		3		72	8.3
R	12	TOM FITZGERALD	66	4	13	17	10	57					89	4.5
L	27	SHAYNE CORSON	46	7	8	15	-5	49					69	10.1
D	8	AKI BERG	78	4	7	11	3	28			2		49	8.2
D	22	GLEN WESLEY	70	1	10	11	-2	44	1				77	1.3
R	26	PAUL HEALEY	44	3	7	10	8	16	1				43	7.0
R	2	WADE BELAK	55	3	6	9	-2	196					33	9.1
L	7	GARY ROBERTS	14	5	3	8	-2	10	3				22	22.7
D	29	*KAREL PILAR	17	3	4	7	-7	12	1		1		22	13.6
L	23	ALEXEI PONIKAROVSKY	13		3	3	4	11					13	
D	55	RICHARD JACKMAN	42		2	2	-10	41					35	
C	9	JOSH HOLDEN	5	1		1	-2	2					6	16.7
C	41	*MATTHEW STAJAN	1	1		1	1						1	100.0
C	10	AARON GAVEY	5		1	1	1						8	
D	45	*CARLO COLAIACOVO	2		1	1	0						1	
D	44	ANDERS ERIKSSON	4				1						7	
G	37	TREVOR KIDD	19				0							
G	20	ED BELFOUR	62				0	24						
G	99	MIKAEL TELLQVIST	3				0							

GP = games played; G = goals; A = assists; PTS = points; +/- = goals-for minus goals-against while player is on ice; PIM = penalties in minutes; PP = power-play goals; SH = shorthanded goals; GW = game-winning goals; GT = game-tying goals; S = no. of shots; PCT = percentage of goals to shots; * = rookie

NIK ANTROPOV

Yrs. of NHL service: 4
Born: Vost, Kazakhstan; Feb. 18, 1980
Position: center
Height: 6-5
Weight: 203
Uniform no.: 80
Shoots: left

Career statistics:

GP	G	A	TP	PIM
201	35	59	94	199

1999-2000 statistics:

GP	G	A	TP	+/-	PIM	PP	SH	GW	GT	S	PCT
66	12	18	30	+14	41	0	0	2	0	89	13.5

2000-2001 statistics:

GP	G	A	TP	+/-	PIM	PP	SH	GW	GT	S	PCT
52	6	11	17	+5	30	0	0	1	0	71	8.5

2001-2002 statistics:

GP	G	A	TP	+/-	PIM	PP	SH	GW	GT	S	PCT
11	1	1	2	-1	4	0	0	0	0	12	8.3

2002-2003 statistics:

GP	G	A	TP	+/-	PIM	PP	SH	GW	GT	S	PCT
72	16	29	45	+11	124	2	1	6	0	102	15.7

Antropov was a restricted free agent after the season.

PROJECTION

Maybe he's back, but he still makes a risky pool pick. If you believe in Antropov's upside, he might progress to 20 goals.

LAST SEASON

Third on team in plus-minus, penalty minutes, and game-winning goals. Missed 10 games due to knee injuries.

THE FINESSE GAME

Antropov has a long reach and is a smart player positionally. Foot speed is a serious flaw. He has a long stride but it takes him a few beats to get moving.

Antropov is prone to tunnel vision. He handles the puck well and has a nice passing touch, but he doesn't always recognize his best options. He is also too reluctant to shoot.

Antropov started his career as a center, but the Leafs used him primarily as a left wing last season and it was a better fit for him because of his defensive deficiencies.

THE PHYSICAL GAME

Antropov is very tall and rangy. He has good strength for puck battles around the net and has started to show some flashes of assertiveness. Antropov has spent several seasons battling serious knee injuries and it's understandable that it will take even more time to stop being afraid of re-injury. Antropov did have some recurring knee problems last season, but they were not as serious.

THE INTANGIBLES

We wrote Antropov off last season because it looked like injuries took their toll on both his confidence and his development. While last season's production wasn't exactly stunning, it was big step forward. Maybe a new contract served as a motivator, since

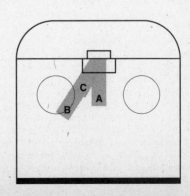

ED BELFOUR

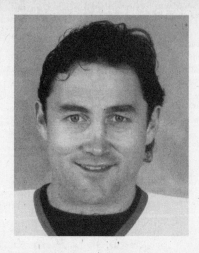

Yrs. of NHL service: 14
Born: Carman, Man.; Apr. 21, 1965
Position: goaltender
Height: 5-11
Weight: 192
Uniform no.: 20
Catches: left

Career statistics:

GP	MIN	GA	SO	GAA	A	PIM
797	46066	1884	65	2.45	26	344

1999-2000 statistics:

GP	MIN	GAA	W	L	T	SO	GA	S	SAPCT	PIM
62	3620	2.10	32	21	7	4	127	1571	.919	10

2000-2001 statistics:

GP	MIN	GAA	W	L	T	SO	GA	S	SAPCT	PIM
63	3687	2.34	35	20	7	8	144	1508	.905	4

2001-2002 statistics:

GP	MIN	GAA	W	L	T	SO	GA	S	SAPCT	PIM
60	3467	2.65	21	27	11	1	153	1458	.895	12

2002-2003 statistics:

GP	MIN	GAA	W	L	T	SO	GA	S	SAPCT	PIM
62	3738	2.26	37	20	5	7	141	1816	.922	24

LAST SEASON

Third among NHL goalies in wins. Tied for fifth among NHL goalies in shutouts. Tied for third among NHL goalies in penalty minutes. Missed four games with an infected finger.

THE PHYSICAL GAME

Belfour's style relies more on athleticism than technique. He is always on his belly, his side, his back. Last season he took over from the then retired Dominik Hasek as the best goalie with the worst style in the NHL.

He has great instincts and reads the play well. Belfour plays in butterfly stance, giving the five-hole but usually taking it away from the shooter with his quick reflexes. He is very aggressive and often comes so far out of his crease that he gets tangled with his own defenders and runs interference on opponents. He knows he is well-padded and is not afraid to use his body, though injuries have made him less aggressive than in the past. In fact, Belfour uses his body more than his stick or glove, and that is part of his problem. He tries to make the majority of saves with his torso, making the routine saves more difficult.

Belfour tends to keep his glove low. The book on him is to shoot high, but that's the case with most NHL goalies — and a lot of NHL shooters have trouble picking that spot. He sometimes gives up bad rebounds, but the Toronto defense is so good and so quick they will swoop in on the puck before the opposition gets a second or third whack.

He has a lot of confidence and an impressive ability to handle the puck, though he sometimes overdoes it. He uses his body to screen when handling the puck for a 15-foot pass, and often sets picks for his forwards.

THE MENTAL GAME

Belfour is such a battler, such a competitor. Sometimes he goes overboard, but it's easier to cool an athlete off than fire him up. His teammates believe in him fully, and he has supreme confidence, even arrogance, in his abilities. Off the ice is another issue.

THE INTANGIBLES

Belfour was greeted rudely in Toronto. He is not the most charismatic fellow, and he was blamed for not being Curtis Joseph, as if that were Belfour's fault. If he didn't replace Joseph's in the fans' hearts, he sure did in the nets.

PROJECTION

We didn't give Belfour the credit he deserved last season. He should reach the 30-win mark. We're keeping the estimate low because it looks like the Leafs are a team in decline.

AKI-PETTERI BERG

Yrs. of NHL service: 7
Born: Turku, Finland; July 28, 1977
Position: left defense
Height: 6-3
Weight: 220
Uniform no.: 8
Shoots: left

Career statistics:

GP	G	A	TP	PIM
452	13	55	68	278

1999-2000 statistics:

GP	G	A	TP	+/-	PIM	PP	SH	GW	GT	S	PCT
70	3	13	16	-1	45	0	0	0	0	70	4.3

2000-2001 statistics:

GP	G	A	TP	+/-	PIM	PP	SH	GW	GT	S	PCT
59	3	4	7	-3	45	3	0	1	0	43	7.0

2001-2002 statistics:

GP	G	A	TP	+/-	PIM	PP	SH	GW	GT	S	PCT
81	1	10	11	+14	46	0	0	0	0	66	1.5

2002-2003 statistics:

GP	G	A	TP	+/-	PIM	PP	SH	GW	GT	S	PCT
78	4	7	11	+3	28	0	0	2	0	49	8.2

THE INTANGIBLES

Unless Berg improves his conditioning to the point where he can handle more ice time, he is going to slip out of the top six and become a spare defenseman.

PROJECTION

We're not sure what Berg's role will be with the Leafs this season. Best to keep offensive expectations low.

LAST SEASON

Missed three games due to injury. Missed one game due to coach's decision.

THE FINESSE GAME

Berg has a pleasing combination of offensive and defensive skills. His skating is topnotch. He has a powerful stride with great mobility and balance. And he gets terrific drive from perfect leg extension and deep knee bends.

He sees the ice well and has excellent passing skills. His skating ability and his ability to make the first pass out of the zone are solid. Berg jumps into the play and moves to open ice. He handles the puck well, but lacks the vision and creativity to be a first-unit power-play quarterback. He does have some offensive upside and has developed into a solid two-way defenseman.

Berg has improved defensive-zone reads, but he still needs the coaching staff to stay on his case.

THE PHYSICAL GAME

Berg is big and strong, and has the mobility to lay down some serious open-ice checks. He is almost the same size as Rob Blake, and Berg is capable of the same style of punishing checks that Blake and Scott Stevens have doled out. Berg, though, hasn't shown the same taste for hitting that Blake and Stevens do, and he has to be constantly ridden to use his size and strength. Berg is not tough.

Berg tends to wear down when he gets too much ice time, and coaches have to watch his minutes.

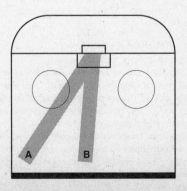

TOM FITZGERALD

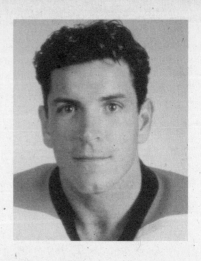

Yrs. of NHL service: 15
Born: Melrose, Mass.; Aug. 28, 1968
Position: right wing / center
Height: 6-0
Weight: 195
Uniform no.: 12
Shoots: right

Career statistics:

GP	G	A	TP	PIM
957	128	174	302	684

1999-2000 statistics:

GP	G	A	TP	+/-	PIM	PP	SH	GW	GT	S	PCT
82	13	9	22	-18	66	0	3	1	0	119	10.9

2000-2001 statistics:

GP	G	A	TP	+/-	PIM	PP	SH	GW	GT	S	PCT
82	9	9	18	-5	71	0	2	2	0	135	6.7

2001-2002 statistics:

GP	G	A	TP	+/-	PIM	PP	SH	GW	GT	S	PCT
78	8	12	20	-7	39	0	2	0	0	125	6.4

2002-2003 statistics:

GP	G	A	TP	+/-	PIM	PP	SH	GW	GT	S	PCT
66	4	13	17	+10	57	0	0	0	0	89	4.5

LAST SEASON

Missed eight games with upper body injury. Missed six games with leg injury. Missed two games due to coach's decision.

THE FINESSE GAME

Fitzgerald is a defensive specialist, a checker, and penalty killer who elevates his game with clutch performances.

He is quick and uses his outside speed to take the puck to the net. He doesn't shoot often. He doesn't have the fastest release and a goalie can usually adjust himself in time despite Fitzgerald's foot speed. He isn't very creative. Fitzgerald's chances emerge from his hard work digging around the net. He is defensively aware and can play as a safety-valve winger when he gets a chance on one of the top two lines.

Fitzgerald is versatile and can be played at any of the three forward positions. He is more effective on the wing. He is only average on draws. His hands aren't very quick and he tends to be overwhelmed by bigger centers.

THE PHYSICAL GAME

Fitzgerald is gritty and wiry-strong. He has fairly good size and he uses it along the boards and in front of the net. Although he's a pesky checker who gets people teed off, his own discipline keeps him from taking many cheap penalties. He gives his team some bang and pop and energy, and he finishes his checks. He is durable, handles a lot of minutes, and is a tough guy to keep out of the lineup. Fitzgerald is getting a little older, and the nagging injuries are starting to mount up.

THE INTANGIBLES

Fitzgerald is a quiet leader on a team where a lot of the other guys get a lot more attention. That doesn't faze Fitzgerald. He is strictly a blue-collar guy and an important role player who usually gives a team everything he's got.

PROJECTION

Fitzgerald brings effort, not points. In continued third-line duty with Toronto, he can score around 25 points if he stays healthy.

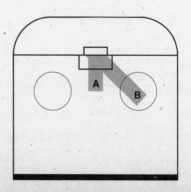

TRAVIS GREEN

Yrs. of NHL service: 11
Born: Castlegar, B.C.; Dec. 20, 1970
Position: center
Height: 6-2
Weight: 200
Uniform no.: 39
Shoots: right

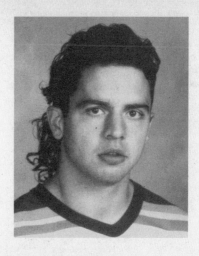

Career statistics:

GP	G	A	TP	PIM
793	171	244	415	591

1999-2000 statistics:

GP	G	A	TP	+/-	PIM	PP	SH	GW	GT	S	PCT
78	25	21	46	-4	45	6	0	2	1	157	15.9

2000-2001 statistics:

GP	G	A	TP	+/-	PIM	PP	SH	GW	GT	S	PCT
69	13	15	28	-11	63	3	0	0	0	113	11.5

2001-2002 statistics:

GP	G	A	TP	+/-	PIM	PP	SH	GW	GT	S	PCT
82	11	23	34	+13	61	3	0	2	0	119	9.2

2002-2003 statistics:

GP	G	A	TP	+/-	PIM	PP	SH	GW	GT	S	PCT
75	12	12	24	+2	67	2	1	3	0	86	13.9

LAST SEASON

Missed six games with rib injury. Missed one game due to coach's decision.

THE FINESSE GAME

Green deserves a lot of credit for reinventing himself as a hockey player. Considered a pure scorer in minor and junior league, Green was taken in hand several years ago by Islanders minor-league coach Butch Goring — whose defensive play was a key factor in all four of the team's Stanley Cups — and he added a completely new dimension to Green's game. Green's keen defensive awareness and ability to win draws (he won at a 53 per cent clip last season) make him a valuable third-line center. Green's game has made almost a complete 180, though, since his offensive contributions continue to dwindle.

Green is on the ice in the waning seconds of the period or the game to protect a lead. His skating is flawed. He can stop pushing and stop moving so there's no glide to him, and his skating really falls off. He has decent balance and agility with some quickness, though he lacks straight-ahead speed.

He controls the puck well. He plays more of a finesse game than a power game. An unselfish player, Green passes equally well to either side. He sees the ice well, but he has a very heavy shot. His release is sluggish, which he why he was never the scorer at the NHL level that he was in the minors. His goals are usually the result of sheer effort, not natural ability.

Green is good on face-offs. He has quick hands and he uses his body to tie up an opponent, enabling his linemates to skate in for the puck.

THE PHYSICAL GAME

Green has good size and is competitive, but hockey courage doesn't come naturally to him. He talks himself into going into the corners and around the net, knowing he has to get to dirty areas to produce. He uses his body to get in the way. He wants to be on the ice and has learned to pay the price to be there.

THE INTANGIBLES

Green's skating is what keeps him from ascending to a higher level; keeping him from playing alongside top-notch players. His perceived lack of fire is another reason why he is frequently changing addresses.

PROJECTION

Green is a third-line player who can give around 10-15 goals and 30 points.

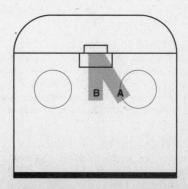

JONAS HOGLUND

Yrs. of NHL service: 7
Born: Hammaro, Sweden; Aug. 29, 1972
Position: right wing
Height: 6-3
Weight: 215
Uniform no.: 14
Shoots: right

Career statistics:

GP	G	A	TP	PIM
545	117	145	262	112

1999-2000 statistics:

GP	G	A	TP	+/-	PIM	PP	SH	GW	GT	S	PCT
82	29	27	56	-2	10	9	1	3	0	215	13.5

2000-2001 statistics:

GP	G	A	TP	+/-	PIM	PP	SH	GW	GT	S	PCT
82	23	26	49	+1	14	5	0	5	2	196	11.7

2001-2002 statistics:

GP	G	A	TP	+/-	PIM	PP	SH	GW	GT	S	PCT
82	13	34	47	+11	26	1	1	4	0	199	6.5

2002-2003 statistics:

GP	G	A	TP	+/-	PIM	PP	SH	GW	GT	S	PCT
79	13	19	32	+2	12	2	0	3	0	157	8.3

PROJECTION

Hoglund has 30-goal ability, 15-goal results. No wonder teams get fed up with him.

LAST SEASON

Missed two games due to injury, ending consecutive games-played streak at 272. Missed one game due to coach's decision.

THE FINESSE GAME

Hoglund has natural goal-scoring instincts but has never made his mark at the NHL level. He has a good, hard slap shot and half-wrister. Every time he gets the puck he has a chance to score. So why doesn't he score more? A major part of this is that he doesn't shoot enough. Someone with his skill level should be putting 250 shots on goal a season.

He lacks a goal-scorer's mentality but he has a goal-scorer's tools. Goal-scorers have a confidence, almost an arrogance, about them, and Hoglund lacks that. Instead, Hoglund looks for the pass almost every time.

Hoglund has adapted well to North American hockey in his defensive and positional play.

Hoglund skates well for a big man. He's no speed skater, but his skating is NHL caliber.

THE PHYSICAL GAME

Hoglund is a big guy but doesn't play a physical game. He has a long reach, which he uses instead of his body to try to win control of the puck or slow down an opponent. He's never been very fond of hitting or getting hit. Intensity also seems to be a foreign concept.

THE INTANGIBLES

Hoglund became an unrestricted free agent after last season.

TOMAS KABERLE

Yrs. of NHL service: 5
Born: Rakovnik, Czech Republic; Mar. 2, 1978
Position: left defense
Height: 6-2
Weight: 200
Uniform no.: 15
Shoots: left

Career statistics:

GP	G	A	TP	PIM
372	38	155	193	92

1999-2000 statistics:

GP	G	A	TP	+/-	PIM	PP	SH	GW	GT	S	PCT
82	7	33	40	+3	24	2	0	0	0	82	8.5

2000-2001 statistics:

GP	G	A	TP	+/-	PIM	PP	SH	GW	GT	S	PCT
82	6	39	45	+10	24	0	0	1	0	96	6.3

2001-2002 statistics:

GP	G	A	TP	+/-	PIM	PP	SH	GW	GT	S	PCT
69	10	29	39	+5	2	5	0	3	1	85	11.8

2002-2003 statistics:

GP	G	A	TP	+/-	PIM	PP	SH	GW	GT	S	PCT
82	11	36	47	+20	30	4	1	2	1	119	9.2

LAST SEASON

Led team in average ice time (24:50) and plus-minus. Led team defensemen in points. Career highs in goals and points. Third on team in assists. One of two Leafs to appear in all 82 games.

THE FINESSE GAME

Kaberle brings all the skills expected of a good European defenseman and combines them with a taste for the North American style of play. It's an impressive package. Kaberle has not joined the NHL's elite corps of defensemen, and he might never, but he is a solid No. 3.

One of the things that keeps Kaberle from being even more productive is his hesitation with the puck on the point. He will often hold up and look for a play instead of taking the shot. Penalty killers know they can press him aggressively.

Kaberle is a mobile skater who makes a smart first pass; he's an excellent puck-moving defenseman. He is always looking to join the rush, and he likes to create offense. He can get too fancy at times when he should be making the simple play instead, and will occasionally get into trouble in his own zone because of that tendency. That is where plus-minus stats can be misleading. Even though he led the Leafs in plus-minus, he is pretty adventurous in his own end.

Kaberle is still learning and has already made great strides. His panic point is a lot higher than it was. He is poised and seldom gives up the puck under pressure.

THE PHYSICAL GAME

Kaberle comes to compete hard every night, but he's just not strong enough to handle some one-on-one battles. He is well-conditioned and handles a lot of ice time. Kaberle faces a lot of the opposing team's top lines every night.

THE INTANGIBLES

Kaberle is a solid top four on anyone's team and he is in the upper tier of the second pairings in the league, with the potential to improve that status. He could develop along Scott Niedermayer-like lines — which is to say he will never be a star, and should remain just a notch below the league's elite offensive defensemen.

PROJECTION

We asked for 50 points from Kaberle last season and he just missed. Given the amount of quality ice time he receives, 50 points should be his standard.

BRYAN MARCHMENT

Yrs. of NHL service: 13
Born: Toronto, Ont.; May 1, 1969
Position: left defense
Height: 6-1
Weight: 200
Uniform no.: 20
Shoots: left

Career statistics:

GP	G	A	TP	PIM
814	38	137	175	2126

1999-2000 statistics:

GP	G	A	TP	+/-	PIM	PP	SH	GW	GT	S	PCT
49	0	4	4	+3	72	0	0	0	0	51	-

2000-2001 statistics:

GP	G	A	TP	+/-	PIM	PP	SH	GW	GT	S	PCT
75	7	11	18	+15	204	0	1	3	1	73	9.6

2001-2002 statistics:

GP	G	A	TP	+/-	PIM	PP	SH	GW	GT	S	PCT
72	2	20	22	+22	178	0	0	0	0	68	2.9

2002-2003 statistics:

GP	G	A	TP	+/-	PIM	PP	SH	GW	GT	S	PCT
81	2	12	14	+2	141	0	0	0	0	84	2.4

LAST SEASON

Signed as free agent by Toronto on July 11, 2003. Previously acquired by Colorado from San Jose on March 8, 2003, for third- and fifth-round draft picks in 2003. Led Avs in penalty minutes.

THE FINESSE GAME

Because of Marchment's (deserved) reputation as a crippling hitter, his skills are often overshadowed. They are fairly sound for a big man. He loves to play and he loves to get involved from the first shift. He's never happier than when there's some blood on his jersey, even if it's his own.

Marchment makes good decisions, with or without the puck. He knows when it is appropriate to step up in the neutral zone, when to pinch in the offensive zone, or when to backpedal. Marchment lacks the skating ability to compensate when he does make a bad choice, however.

He has a decent point shot and can drill a one-timer or snap a long quick shot on net, although offense has never been his forte and is even less of a factor now late in his career. He is not much of a passer, since he doesn't sense when he should feather a pass to a teammate or rifle a puck to a receiver.

Marchment's sins are usually of aggression. Where he doesn't make many mistakes is in his down-low coverage. He is a solid penalty-killer.

THE PHYSICAL GAME

This is what Marchment has built a career on. He is a dangerous, low hitter with a history of controversial checks that damage knees and end careers. One scout describes Marchment as "the ultimate leg breaker."

He also hits high, so instead of forcing early retirement with a knee injury, he can do so by causing a concussion.

Marchment can hit tough and clean when he wants to, by keeping his shoulder down and his feet on the ice. But even those checks, when legal, create a buzz because Marchment doesn't care who he hits. If it's a marquee name, a young star, a shrimp, or a stud, all are fair game.

Marchment is also a good fighter, although few people care to test him anymore unless they are retaliating for a hit on a teammate. He finishes every check, blocks shots, and uses his upper body well. He would be a more effective hitter but he lacks drive from his legs and is not a well-balanced skater.

THE INTANGIBLES

Teammates have called Marchment an odd guy. They tend to like him, just not understand him, and he can be a tough fit in the dressing room. This might not make him an ideal Leaf.

PROJECTION

Marchment will get your pool team a healthy dose of PIM when he is not sitting out with a suspension (although he managed to escape Colin Campbell's wrath last season).

BRYAN MCCABE

Yrs. of NHL service: 8
Born: St. Catharines, Ont.; June 8, 1975
Position: left defense
Height: 6-2
Weight: 213
Uniform no.: 24
Shoots: left

Career statistics:

GP	G	A	TP	PIM
633	60	157	217	1176

1999-2000 statistics:

GP	G	A	TP	+/-	PIM	PP	SH	GW	GT	S	PCT
79	6	19	25	-8	139	2	0	2	0	119	5.0

2000-2001 statistics:

GP	G	A	TP	+/-	PIM	PP	SH	GW	GT	S	PCT
82	5	24	29	+16	123	3	0	2	0	159	3.1

2001-2002 statistics:

GP	G	A	TP	+/-	PIM	PP	SH	GW	GT	S	PCT
82	17	26	43	+16	129	8	0	1	0	157	10.8

2002-2003 statistics:

GP	G	A	TP	+/-	PIM	PP	SH	GW	GT	S	PCT
75	6	18	24	+9	135	3	0	1	0	149	4.0

LAST SEASON

Third on team in average ice time (23:38). Missed seven games with fractured foot.

THE FINESSE GAME

McCabe is an unorthodox skater. He doesn't have a fluid, classic stride. He is okay going from his right to his left, but suspect going from his left to his right. When he has the puck or is jumping into the play he has decent speed, but his lack of mobility defensively is one of his flaws. He is hesitant in his own zone when reading the rush and will get caught.

He also doesn't have great puck-moving skills, which is a tremendous defect for a defenseman. His passes don't go tape-to-tape. They go off the glass, or down the rink for an icing, or worse, are picked off by a defender. He kills penalties well and blocks shots.

Toronto thought enough of McCabe's offensive skills to trade away Danny Markov in 2001, and McCabe fulfilled the roll in 2001-02 with 43 points, but his offensive game took a major step backwards last season. Maybe it was a confidence issue. McCabe has a heavy, major-league slap shot.

THE PHYSICAL GAME

McCabe is willing to drop his gloves and can handle himself in a bout, though it's not a strong part of his game. He is strong but not mean. McCabe understands that the physical part of the game is a major element of his success. McCabe is in good physical condition and can handle a lot of ice time.

THE INTANGIBLES

He is not an elite defenseman but he is not far below that. He routinely handles checking assignments against other team's top lines. Like the rest of his teammates, McCabe had an abysmal playoffs.

PROJECTION

Is McCabe a consistent 25-point scorer? Or is 40 points his norm? We're leading towards the former.

ALEXANDER MOGILNY

Yrs. of NHL service: 14
Born: Khabarovsk, Russia; Feb. 18, 1969
Position: right wing
Height: 6-0
Weight: 200
Uniform no.: 89
Shoots: left

Career statistics:

GP	G	A	TP	PIM
919	453	524	977	414

1999-2000 statistics:

GP	G	A	TP	+/-	PIM	PP	SH	GW	GT	S	PCT
59	24	20	44	+3	20	5	1	1	2	161	14.9

2000-2001 statistics:

GP	G	A	TP	+/-	PIM	PP	SH	GW	GT	S	PCT
75	43	40	83	+10	43	12	0	7	0	240	17.9

2001-2002 statistics:

GP	G	A	TP	+/-	PIM	PP	SH	GW	GT	S	PCT
66	24	33	57	+1	8	5	0	4	0	188	12.8

2002-2003 statistics:

GP	G	A	TP	+/-	PIM	PP	SH	GW	GT	S	PCT
73	33	46	79	+4	12	5	3	9	0	165	20.0

LAST SEASON

Won 2003 Lady Byng Trophy. Tied for second in NHL in shooting percentage. Tied for fourth in NHL in game-winning goals. Led team in assists, points, and shooting percentage. Tied for team lead in short-handed goals. Second on team in goals. Third on team in shots. Missed five games due to injury. Missed three games due to coach's decision.

THE FINESSE GAME

When he is healthy and in a groove, skating is the basis of Mogilny's game. He has a burst of speed from a standstill and hits his top speed in just a few strides. When he streaks down the ice, there is a good chance you'll see something new that you didn't expect. He is creative, unpredictable, and unbelievably quick.

Mogilny's anticipation sets him apart from players who are merely fast. He is about as good a player as there is in the league at the transition game. He waits for a turnover and a chance to get a jump on the defenseman, with a preferred move to the outside. He's not afraid to go inside either, so a defenseman intent on angling him to the boards could just as easily get burned inside.

Mogilny can beat you in so many ways. He has a powerful and accurate wrist shot from the tops of the circles in. He shoots without breaking stride. He can work a give-and-go that is a thing of beauty. He one-times with the best of them. And everything is done at racehorse speed. The game comes easy to Mogilny, and he plays it with insolence.

THE PHYSICAL GAME

Mogilny intimidates with his speed but will also add a physical element. He has great upper-body strength and will drive through a defender to the net.

THE INTANGIBLES

Mogilny had a second straight solid postseason performance. Mogilny did not show up to collect his Lady Byng Trophy, since he doesn't believe in personal achievements.

PROJECTION

Mogilny fell a bit off the 40-goal pace we predicted for him last season. Accordingly, we'll drop our expectations to 30 goals.

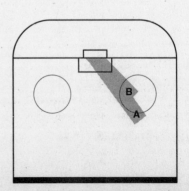

OWEN NOLAN

Yrs. of NHL service: 13
Born: Belfast, N. Ireland; Sept. 22, 1971
Position: right wing
Height: 6-1
Weight: 210
Uniform no.: 11
Shoots: right

Career statistics:

GP	G	A	TP	PIM
850	330	357	687	1490

1999-2000 statistics:

GP	G	A	TP	+/-	PIM	PP	SH	GW	GT	S	PCT
78	44	40	84	-1	110	18	4	6	2	261	16.9

2000-2001 statistics:

GP	G	A	TP	+/-	PIM	PP	SH	GW	GT	S	PCT
57	24	25	49	0	75	10	1	4	1	191	12.6

2001-2002 statistics:

GP	G	A	TP	+/-	PIM	PP	SH	GW	GT	S	PCT
75	23	43	66	+7	93	8	2	2	1	217	10.6

2002-2003 statistics:

GP	G	A	TP	+/-	PIM	PP	SH	GW	GT	S	PCT
75	29	25	54	-3	107	13	3	5	0	221	13.1

LAST SEASON

Acquired from San Jose on March 5, 2003, for Alyn McCauley, Brad Boyes, and a first-round draft pick in 2003. Tied for team lead in shorthanded goals. Second on team in power-play goals and shots. Third on team in goals and points. Missed five games due to injury. Missed one game due to coach's decision.

THE FINESSE GAME

Nobody knows where Nolan's shot is headed, except Nolan. A pure shooter with good hands, he rips one-timers from the circle with deadly speed and accuracy. Nolan needs to be selfish because he is a pure goal-scorer.

He has an amazing knack for letting the puck go at just the right moment. Nolan has a little move in-tight to the goal with a forehand-to-backhand, and around the net he is about as good as anyone in the game. On the power play, he is just about unstoppable.

Nolan is a strong skater with good balance and fair agility. He is quick straight-ahead but won't split the defense when carrying the puck. He's better without the puck, driving into open ice for the pass and quick shot. Defensively, he has improved tremendously, though it is still not his strong suit.

THE PHYSICAL GAME

Nolan is as strong as a bull and since he's capable of snapping at any time, opponents are wary of him.

THE INTANGIBLES

Nolan needed a change of scene and Toronto looked like the perfect fit. Nolan sure did tear things up after the trade, with seven goals and five assists in 14 regular-season games, but he was brutal in the play-offs, with just two assists in seven games. Since the Leafs obtained him for the postseason, the early report on the trade reads "Bust."

PROJECTION

Nolan's numbers are declining slightly, and we would be reluctant to recommend expecting more than 30 goals. Although he will sure have something to prove for that playoff letdown.

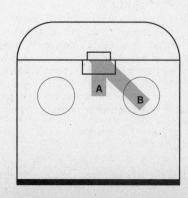

KAREL PILAR

Yrs. of NHL service: 1
Born: Prague, Czech Republic; Dec. 23, 1977
Position: right defense
Height: 6-3
Weight: 210
Uniform no.: 29
Shoots: right

Career statistics:

GP	G	A	TP	PIM
40	4	7	11	20

2001-2002 statistics:

GP	G	A	TP	+/-	PIM	PP	SH	GW	GT	S	PCT
23	1	3	4	+3	8	0	0	0	0	32	3.1

2002-2003 statistics:

GP	G	A	TP	+/-	PIM	PP	SH	GW	GT	S	PCT
17	3	4	7	-7	12	1	0	1	0	22	13.6

LAST SEASON

Will be entering first full NHL season. Appeared in seven games with St. John's (AHL), scoring 2-5 — 7.

THE FINESSE GAME

Pilar is a big defenseman whose chief asset is his puck-moving ability. But even at that, he's not elite. He takes a little too much time making the outlet pass. Pilar is still adjusting to the faster NHL pace.

His skating is bit awkward for this level, making it tough for him to jump into the play, which is something he really likes to do. He was a purely offensive defenseman (and one of the best) in the Czech League but it's unlikely he will succeed in the NHL as that kind of player. He needs to learn to use his finesse skills in a defensive role and improve his play away from the puck.

THE PHYSICAL GAME

Pilar had good leg drive and lower body strength to generate power into his checks. He won't be a big open-ice hitter, and he's not very assertive. He has a lot less physical presence than a player of his size should exhibit.

THE INTANGIBLES

Toronto fully expected Pilar to come into training camp last fall and earn a starting job. He had a terrible camp, and the acquisition of Robert Svehla bumped him down the depth chart a bit. After he was sent to the minors, Pilar developed a virus that knocked him out for 45 games and pretty much made his whole season a washout. It was a setback in his development and he will have a lot to prove in order to earn a top-four role this season.

PROJECTION

Pilar should see second-unit power-play time and get his share of points (20 to 25) if he can make the team. Nothing he does excites us much, but Toronto still thinks he has some potential.

ROBERT REICHEL

Yrs. of NHL service: 13
Born: Litvinov, Czech Republic; June 25, 1971
Position: center
Height: 5-10
Weight: 185
Uniform no.: 21
Shoots: left

Career statistics:

GP	G	A	TP	PIM
159	32	61	93	52

1999-2000 statistics:

Did not play in NHL.

2000-2001 statistics:

Did not play in NHL

2001-2002 statistics:

GP	G	A	TP	+/-	PIM	PP	SH	GW	GT	S	PCT
78	20	31	51	+7	26	1	0	3	0	152	13.2

2002-2003 statistics:

GP	G	A	TP	+/-	PIM	PP	SH	GW	GT	S	PCT
81	12	30	42	+7	26	1	1	1	0	111	10.8

LAST SEASON

Missed one game due to coach's decision.

THE FINESSE GAME

Reichel's strength is as a playmaker. He thinks "pass" first and needs to play on a line with a pure finisher. He is one of those gifted passers who can make a scoring opportunity materialize when there appears to be no hole. His wingers have to be alert because the puck will find its way to their tape. He has great control of the puck in open ice or in scrums.

Reichel will certainly take the shot when he's got it, but he won't force a pass to someone who is in a worse scoring position than he is. Nor will he pay a price to worm his way into a high-percentage scoring area. He has an explosive shot with a lot of velocity on it. He pursues loose pucks in front and wheels around to the back of the net to look for an open teammate.

At least that's how Reichel plays when things are going well. He's just as likely to go into a slump or a pout, and he doesn't add much to a team when he isn't piling up points. He's moody and is just as inclined to sulk as he is to go on a scoring streak.

THE PHYSICAL GAME

Reichel is small but sturdy. He is not a big fan of contact and there are some who question his hockey courage. He's not a player other teams are afraid to play against. He is well-conditioned and can handle a lot of ice time.

THE INTANGIBLES

Reichel is a costly bomb. We've long questioned his desire and motivation and don't think he can be part of the core of any team wanting to be a champion. He is the opposite of clutch. We are mystified by Toronto's relentless pursuit of players who have quit on their teams or the NHL. Reichel is one of those, as is Robert Svehla and Mikael Renberg. Maybe that's why there haven't been many Cup parades in Toronto lately.

PROJECTION

Reichel is skilled and can get 45 points but who really cares? He is an impactless player.

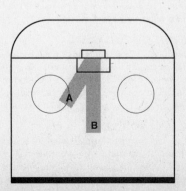

MIKAEL RENBERG

Yrs. of NHL service: 8
Born: Pitea, Sweden; May 5, 1972
Position: right wing
Height: 6-2
Weight: 218
Uniform no.: 19
Shoots: left

Career statistics:

GP	G	A	TP	PIM
602	178	261	439	322

1999-2000 statistics:

GP	G	A	TP	+/-	PIM	PP	SH	GW	GT	S	PCT
72	10	25	35	-1	32	3	0	1	0	122	8.2

2000-2001 statistics:

Did not play in NHL

2001-2002 statistics:

GP	G	A	TP	+/-	PIM	PP	SH	GW	GT	S	PCT
71	14	38	52	+11	36	4	0	3	0	130	10.8

2002-2003 statistics:

GP	G	A	TP	+/-	PIM	PP	SH	GW	GT	S	PCT
67	14	21	35	+5	36	7	0	1	0	137	10.2

PROJECTION

Renberg's output continues to decline. We think 15 goals, 30 points is about his speed now.

LAST SEASON

Third on team in power-play goals. Missed 11 games with hand infection. Missed four games with rib injury.

THE FINESSE GAME

Renberg has a long, strong stride and excellent balance, but only average speed. Anticipation is the key that gives him a head start on the defense.

He drives to the net, and is strong enough to shrug off a lot of checks, or even shovel a one-handed shot or pass if one arm is tied up. He likes to come in on the off-wing, especially on the power play, and snap a strong shot off his back foot. He sees the ice well and is always looking for a teammate he can hit with a pass. He is more of a set-up guy than a finisher, always looking for his partner instead of taking the shot himself.

Renberg's best shots are his quick-release wristers or snaps with little backswing. He is defensively aware and is a solid two-way forward who can be on the ice in almost any situation.

THE PHYSICAL GAME

Renberg doesn't fight, but he is extremely strong, has a nasty streak, and likes to hit hard. He won't be intimidated. Since he isn't a great skater, his adjustment to the smaller ice surfaces actually helped his game.

THE INTANGIBLES

Renberg has become too fragile and his production too erratic to maintain a top-six role in Toronto, especially after the arrival of Owen Nolan which bumped him down on the depth chart.

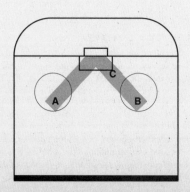

MATS SUNDIN

Yrs. of NHL service: 13
Born: Bromma, Sweden; Feb. 13, 1971
Position: center
Height: 6-4
Weight: 220
Uniform no.: 13
Shoots: right

Career statistics:

GP	G	A	TP	PIM
1005	434	580	1014	817

1999-2000 statistics:

GP	G	A	TP	+/-	PIM	PP	SH	GW	GT	S	PCT
73	32	41	73	+16	46	10	2	7	0	184	17.4

2000-2001 statistics:

GP	G	A	TP	+/-	PIM	PP	SH	GW	GT	S	PCT
82	28	46	74	+15	76	9	0	6	1	226	12.4

2001-2002 statistics:

GP	G	A	TP	+/-	PIM	PP	SH	GW	GT	S	PCT
82	41	39	80	+6	94	10	2	9	2	262	15.6

2002-2003 statistics:

GP	G	A	TP	+/-	PIM	PP	SH	GW	GT	S	PCT
75	37	35	72	+1	58	16	3	8	1	223	16.6

LAST SEASON

Fifth in NHL in power-play goals. Led team in goals, power-play goals, and shots. Tied for team lead in shorthanded goals. Second on team in points, game-winning goals, and shooting percentage. Missed six games with upper-body injury. Missed one game with facial injury.

THE FINESSE GAME

Sundin is a big skater who looks huge, as he uses an ultralong stick that gives him a broad wingspan. For a big man he is an agile and well-balanced skater. He has good lower-body strength, supplying drive for battles along the boards. He's evasive, and once he is on the fly he is hard to stop. He is less effective when carrying the puck. His best play is to get up a head of steam, jump into the holes, and take a quick shot.

Sundin plays center but attacks from the off (left) wing, where he can come off the boards with speed. He protects the puck along the wall and makes it hard for people to reach in without taking him down for a penalty. He gets the puck low in his own end. People can move to him right away, and he has to move the puck. If a checker stays with him, Sundin can't get the puck back.

Sundin can take bad passes in stride, either kicking an errant puck up onto his stick or reaching behind to corral it. He isn't a clever stickhandler. His game is power and speed. He doesn't look fast, but he has ground-eating strides that allow him to cover in two strides what other skaters do in three or four. He is quick, too, and can get untracked in a heartbeat.

Sundin's shot is excellent. He can use a slap shot,

one-timer, wrister, or backhand. The only liability to his reach is that he will dangle the puck well away from his body and he doesn't always control it, which makes him vulnerable to a poke-check when he is in open ice. He has developed into one of the league's better face-off men.

THE PHYSICAL GAME

Sundin is big and strong. His conditioning is excellent; he can skate all night. He has even shown a touch of meanness, but mostly with his stick. Sundin is consistent and durable.

THE INTANGIBLES

Sundin always looks like he's ready to bust out, but always comes up a little short when it counts, like in the playoffs.

PROJECTION

Sundin can be expected to have his usual 75-point season again.

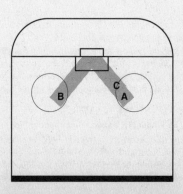

ROBERT SVEHLA

Yrs. of NHL service: 8
Born: Martin, Slovakia; Jan. 2, 1969
Position: right defense
Height: 6-1
Weight: 210
Uniform no.: 67
Shoots: right

Career statistics:

GP	G	A	TP	PIM
655	68	267	335	649

1999-2000 statistics:

GP	G	A	TP	+/-	PIM	PP	SH	GW	GT	S	PCT
82	9	40	49	+23	64	3	0	1	0	143	6.3

2000-2001 statistics:

GP	G	A	TP	+/-	PIM	PP	SH	GW	GT	S	PCT
82	6	22	28	-8	76	0	0	0	0	121	5.0

2001-2002 statistics:

GP	G	A	TP	+/-	PIM	PP	SH	GW	GT	S	PCT
82	7	22	29	-19	87	3	0	0	0	119	5.9

2002-2003 statistics:

GP	G	A	TP	+/-	PIM	PP	SH	GW	GT	S	PCT
82	7	38	45	+13	46	2	0	1	0	110	6.4

LAST SEASON

Second on team in average ice time (23:44), assists, and points. One of two Leafs to appear in all 82 games. Has appeared in 382 consecutive games.

THE FINESSE GAME

Svehla is among the best in the NHL at the lost art of the sweep-check. If he does lose control of the puck, and an attacker has a step or two on him on a breakaway, Svehla has the poise to dive and use his stick to knock the puck away without touching the man's skates.

He is a terrific skater. No one, not even Jaromir Jagr, can beat Svehla wide, because he skates well backwards and laterally. He plays a quick transition. He is among the best NHL defensemen one-on-one in open ice. He pinches aggressively and intelligently and makes high-risk plays. Unfortunately for the Panthers, he gambles too often in his own zone. Svehla also has the uncanny knack of making a change at the worst time. But then he is off the ice, so his plus-minus doesn't suffer. Because of his skating, Svehla is an effective open-ice hitter.

Svehla works on the first power play, moving to the left point. He uses a long wrist shot from the point to make sure the puck will get through on net. When he kills penalties, he makes safe plays off the boards.

THE PHYSICAL GAME

With an admirable ironman streak going, you might think Svehla avoids contact, but that isn't the case. Svehla is not that strong or naturally aggressive, but he competes. He gets into the thick of things by battling along the wall and in the corners for the puck. He is not a huge checker, but he pins his man and doesn't allow him back into the play. He is in peak condition and needs little recovery time between shifts, so he can handle a lot of ice time. Svehla sacrifices his body but somehow manages to avoid serious injury.

THE INTANGIBLES

Svehla "retired" from Florida in 2002, only to unretire after being traded to Toronto. He threatened to retire again after last season, mostly because he wants a bump in salary raise to $5 million. Toronto might just be desperate enough to give it to him.

PROJECTION

Svehla's top end is probably 45 points. That's a little over $500,000 per point.

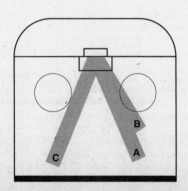

DARCY TUCKER

Yrs. of NHL service: 7
Born: Castor, Alberta; Mar. 15, 1975
Position: center
Height: 5-11
Weight: 185
Uniform no.: 16
Shoots: left

Career statistics:

GP	G	A	TP	PIM
545	106	160	266	947

1999-2000 statistics:

GP	G	A	TP	+/-	PIM	PP	SH	GW	GT	S	PCT
77	21	30	51	-12	163	1	2	5	0	138	15.2

2000-2001 statistics:

GP	G	A	TP	+/-	PIM	PP	SH	GW	GT	S	PCT
82	16	21	37	+6	141	2	0	4	0	122	13.1

2001-2002 statistics:

GP	G	A	TP	+/-	PIM	PP	SH	GW	GT	S	PCT
77	24	35	59	+24	92	7	0	5	0	124	19.4

2002-2003 statistics:

GP	G	A	TP	+/-	PIM	PP	SH	GW	GT	S	PCT
77	10	26	36	-7	119	4	1	2	0	108	9.3

LAST SEASON

Missed five games due to NHL suspension.

THE FINESSE GAME

Tucker is a pesky forward with a scoring touch. He brings an offensive awareness that enhances his role as a third-line checking center. He has decent hands, and a knack for scoring big goals.

Like Tomas Holmstrom, Tucker is a player who is wasted on a non-playoff team. Tucker is the kind of player to keep no matter what his points are, just to have him on hand for a pressure game. He is the kind of role player who needs a specific assignment. Every night he brings a level of intensity to his game that supplements — and some might suggest, surpasses — his talent.

Tucker was a scorer in junior (137 points in his last year at Kamloops of the WHL) and the minors (93 points with Fredericton of the AHL in 1995-96). His major drawback is that he lacks big-league speed. He is a good forechecker who will hound the puck carrier, and he can do something with the puck once it's on his stick. He is good on draws and will tie up his opposing center. He will block shots. He will fill the water bottles. Whatever it takes to win, Tucker is there.

THE PHYSICAL GAME

Tucker crossed the line when he went from being an annoying, pesky guy to a cheap-shot artist. He was handed a five-game suspension for punching Ottawa's Chris Neil (who was on the bench while Tucker was on the ice).

THE INTANGIBLES

Tucker's got spunk. He cares. He wants to make his team better. Like Claude Lemieux, Tucker is able to take some of the heat off the other players in the room by handling media attention. It's almost impossible to watch a Leafs game and not notice Tucker.

PROJECTION

Tucker's production tailed off even more drastically than we expected after his career year in 2001-02. Points aren't why teams keep a player like Tucker around for, but he should still be in the 40-point range.

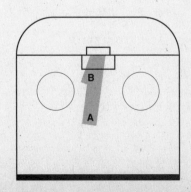

VANCOUVER CANUCKS

Players' Statistics 2001-2002

POS.	NO.	PLAYER	GP	G	A	PTS	+/-	PIM	PP	SH	GW	GT	S	PCT
L	19	MARKUS NASLUND	82	48	56	104	6	52	24		12	1	294	16.3
R	44	TODD BERTUZZI	82	46	51	97	2	144	25		7	1	243	18.9
C	7	BRENDAN MORRISON	82	25	46	71	18	36	6	2	8		167	15.0
D	55	ED JOVANOVSKI	67	6	40	46	19	113	2		1	1	145	4.1
C	24	MATT COOKE	82	15	27	42	21	82	1	4			118	12.7
C	16	TREVOR LINDEN	71	19	22	41	-1	30	4	1	1		116	16.4
C	33	HENRIK SEDIN	78	8	31	39	9	38	4	1	1	1	81	9.9
D	3	BRENT SOPEL	81	7	30	37	-15	23	6		1		167	4.2
L	22	DANIEL SEDIN	79	14	17	31	8	34	4		2		134	10.4
D	6	SAMI SALO	79	9	21	30	9	10	4		1	1	126	7.1
R	26	TRENT KLATT	82	16	13	29	10	8	3		2		127	12.6
D	2	MATTIAS OHLUND	59	2	27	29	1	42					100	2.0
R	10	TREVOR LETOWSKI	78	11	14	25	8	36	1	1	2		136	8.1
C	13	ARTEM CHUBAROV	62	7	13	20	4	6	1		1		78	9.0
D	8	MAREK MALIK	79	7	13	20	20	68	1	1	2	1	77	9.1
L	25	MATS LINDGREN	54	5	9	14	-2	18		2	1		51	9.8
D	5	BRYAN ALLEN	48	5	3	8	8	73			1		43	11.6
L	32	BRAD MAY	23	3	4	7	4	42					25	12.0
D	23	MURRAY BARON	78	2	4	6	13	62					34	5.9
C	14	*BRANDON REID	7	2	3	5	4						15	13.3
L	37	JARKKO RUUTU	36	2	2	4	-7	66			1		36	5.6
D	4	NOLAN BAUMGARTNER	8	1	2	3	4	4	1				7	14.3
R	18	*JASON KING	8		2	2	0						12	
R	15	*PAT KAVANAGH	3	1		1	2	2			1		4	25.0
L	20	DARREN LANGDON	54		1	1	-2	159					19	
L	81	*FEDOR FEDOROV	7		1	1	0	4					2	
D	27	*MIKKO JOKELA	1				0						3	
D	28	BRYAN HELMER	2				1						2	
G	30	TYLER MOSS	1				0							
G	39	DAN CLOUTIER	57				0	24						
G	1	PETER SKUDRA	23				0							
L	21	*ZENITH KOMARNISKI	1				0	2						
R	38	BRAD LEEB					0							
G	35	ALEXANDER AULD	7				0							

GP = games played; G = goals; A = assists; PTS = points; +/- = goals-for minus goals-against while player is on ice; PIM = penalties in minutes; PP = power-play goals; SH = shorthanded goals; GW = game-winning goals; GT = game-tying goals; S = no. of shots; PCT = percentage of goals to shots; * = rookie

BRYAN ALLEN

Yrs. of NHL service: 2
Born: Kingston, Ont.; Aug. 21, 1980
Position: left defense
Height: 6-4
Weight: 215
Uniform no.: 5
Shoots: left

Career statistics:

GP	G	A	TP	PIM
65	5	3	8	79

2000-2001 statistics:

GP	G	A	TP	+/-	PIM	PP	SH	GW	GT	S	PCT
6	0	0	0	0	0	0	0	0	0	2	0.0

2001-2002 statistics:

GP	G	A	TP	+/-	PIM	PP	SH	GW	GT	S	PCT
11	0	0	0	+1	6	0	0	0	0	4	0.0

2002-2003 statistics:

GP	G	A	TP	+/-	PIM	PP	SH	GW	GT	S	PCT
48	5	3	8	+8	73	0	0	1	0	43	11.6

PROJECTION

If Allen wins a job, he won't score much, but this could be the defining year for him as an NHL defenseman.

LAST SEASON

Missed 28 games due to coach's decision. Missed one game with flu. Appeared in seven games with Manitoba (AHL), scoring 0-1 — 1 with 4 PIM.

THE FINESSE GAME

Vancouver wanted Allen to claim a full-time job last season, but despite an open door because of injuries to Ed Jovanovski and Mattias Ohlund, Allen just wasn't up to the task.

Allen is mostly a stay-at-home defenseman. He is a very good skater, which is his primary asset. Although he lacks lateral mobility, his leg drive allows him to unleash some solid checks. He doesn't have a great shot and lacks the vision that would help him more offensively, but he is a decent passer. Allen is poised and patient with the puck.

Allen needs to improve his defensive reads and has to make quicker decisions with the puck. He has shown steady progress and is showing signs of developing into a reliable second-pair defenseman.

THE PHYSICAL GAME

Sturdy and strong, Allen lacks the mean streak that comes naturally to the game's punishing hitters. He will work hard along the boards and around the net with take-out hits. He's Derian Hatcher minus the snarl. He has the size and strength to go to war with just about any of the game's biggest forwards.

THE INTANGIBLES

Allen seems finally ready to challenge for a top-four role. The Canucks don't want to keep him here as a third-pair defensemen, which means he had better show up in training camp hungry for a top spot. Allen was a restricted free agent after last season.

TODD BERTUZZI

Yrs. of NHL service: 8
Born: Sudbury, Ont.; Feb. 2, 1975
Position: right wing
Height: 6-3
Weight: 235
Uniform no.: 44
Shoots: left

Career statistics:

GP	G	A	TP	PIM
559	181	217	398	789

1999-2000 statistics:

GP	G	A	TP	+/-	PIM	PP	SH	GW	GT	S	PCT
80	25	25	50	-2	126	4	0	2	0	173	14.5

2000-2001 statistics:

GP	G	A	TP	+/-	PIM	PP	SH	GW	GT	S	PCT
79	25	30	55	-18	93	14	0	3	0	203	12.3

2001-2002 statistics:

GP	G	A	TP	+/-	PIM	PP	SH	GW	GT	S	PCT
72	36	49	85	+21	110	14	0	3	0	203	17.7

2002-2003 statistics:

GP	G	A	TP	+/-	PIM	PP	SH	GW	GT	S	PCT
82	46	51	97	+2	144	25	0	7	1	243	18.9

LAST SEASON

Named to NHL First All-Star Team. Led NHL in power-play goals. Third in NHL in goals. Fifth in NHL in points. Led team in shooting percentage. Second on team in goals, assists, points, penalty minutes, and shots. Third on team in game-winning goals. Career highs in points and goals. One of five Canucks to appear in all 82 games.

THE FINESSE GAME

Bertuzzi has developed into a premier power forward. For a big man, he's quick and mobile, and he's got a soft pair of hands to complement his skating. With the puck, Bertuzzi can walk over people. He is effective in the slot area, yet he's also creative with the puck and can make some plays. He can find people down low and make things happen on the power play. Bertuzzi has keen offensive instincts.

Bertuzzi has physically dominating skills, but he doesn't have great vision. He has a tendency to roam all over the ice and doesn't think the game well. What he won't become is a physical, tough, aggressive fighter. It's not in his makeup, but he can be an energetic player. He has worked on his defensive game.

Bertuzzi is without a doubt the best dumb player in the NHL. He failed to stay disciplined at the most important times in the playoffs. He managed to lead all players in penalty minutes (60) in the playoffs even though the Canucks were ousted in the second round, largely as a result of Bertuzzi's brainless and/or selfish play.

THE PHYSICAL GAME

Bertuzzi often wanders around and doesn't finish his checks with authority. He's a solid physical specimen who shows flashes of aggression and an occasional mean streak, but he really has to be pushed and aggravated to reach a boiling point. Then again, there will be games where he snaps completely and takes either bad aggressive penalties or peculiarly lazy ones, or even a suspension.

THE INTANGIBLES

Bertuzzi needs to be handled gently by the coaching staff, with an arm around his shoulder and a kick to the butt administered at the right times. He is now a top-line player with the Canucks, and should gain confidence from that. He's also a fan favorite.

PROJECTION

Bertuzzi should again score in the range of 40-50 goals. He owes his teammates after those playoffs.

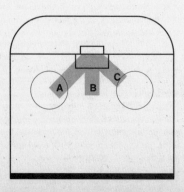

DAN CLOUTIER

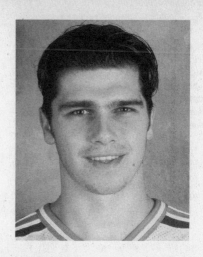

Yrs. of NHL service: 5
Born: Mont-Laurier, Que.; Apr. 22, 1976
Position: goaltender
Height: 6-1
Weight: 182
Uniform no.: 39
Catches: left

Career statistics:

GP	MIN	GA	SO	GAA	A	PIM
245	12937	591	10	2.74	3	88

1999-2000 statistics:

GP	MIN	GAA	W	L	T	SO	GA	S	SAPCT	PIM
52	2492	3.49	9	30	3	0	145	1258	.885	29

2000-2001 statistics:

GP	MIN	GAA	W	L	T	SO	GA	S	SAPCT	PIM
0	0	0.00	0	0	0	0	0	0	-	-

2001-2002 statistics:

GP	MIN	GAA	W	L	T	SO	GA	S	SAPCT	PIM
62	3502	2.43	31	22	5	7	142	1440	.901	20

2002-2003 statistics:

GP	MIN	GAA	W	L	T	SO	GA	S	SAPCT	PIM
57	3376	2.42	33	16	7	2	136	1477	.908	24

PROJECTION

Cloutier is not an elite No. 1 goalie, but Vancouver is so good he will probably pass 30 wins again.

LAST SEASON

Career high in wins. Missed 13 games with knee injuries.

THE PHYSICAL GAME

Cloutier is an athletic, stand-up goalie — surprising in an era of so many Patrick Roy butterfly clones. He doesn't have the reflexes to excel with a less technical style.

He follows the play well and squares his body to the shooter. He will learn to play his angles better with more NHL experience, but he has good size to take away a lot of the net from the shooter.

Cloutier's skills are still a little raw. He doesn't control his rebounds well off his pads, and his stick-handling could use work. But he is an eager student who would benefit from a veteran backup goalie (which the Canucks didn't have last season) and a full-time, quality goalie coach.

THE MENTAL GAME

Cloutier is combative and emotional. He has to learn to channel his aggression better, because it often gets the best of him. The fight in him extends to his desire to succeed at the NHL level. He is as competitive on the ice as he is easygoing off it. Once again he had a disappointing playoffs (3.24 GAA).

THE INTANGIBLES

Cloutier is good enough for the regular season, but we doubt he will get the Canucks to the promised land in the postseason. Cloutier was a restricted free agent after the season.

MATT COOKE

Yrs. of NHL service: 5
Born: Belleville, Ont.; Sept. 7, 1978
Position: center
Height: 5-11
Weight: 205
Uniform no.: 24
Shoots: left

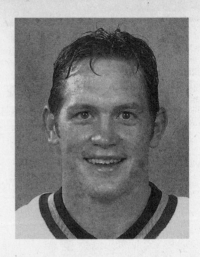

Career statistics:

GP	G	A	TP	PIM
326	47	69	116	353

1999-2000 statistics:

GP	G	A	TP	+/-	PIM	PP	SH	GW	GT	S	PCT
51	5	7	12	+3	39	0	1	1	0	58	8.6

2000-2001 statistics:

GP	G	A	TP	+/-	PIM	PP	SH	GW	GT	S	PCT
81	14	13	27	+5	94	0	2	0	0	121	11.6

2001-2002 statistics:

GP	G	A	TP	+/-	PIM	PP	SH	GW	GT	S	PCT
82	13	20	33	+4	111	1	0	2	0	103	12.6

2002-2003 statistics:

GP	G	A	TP	+/-	PIM	PP	SH	GW	GT	S	PCT
82	15	27	42	+21	82	1	4	0	0	118	12.7

LAST SEASON

Tied for third in NHL in shorthanded goals. Led team in plus-minus and shorthanded goals. Career highs in goals, assists, and points. One of five Canucks to appear in all 82 games.

THE FINESSE GAME

Just think of Cooke as the Pacific Time Zone version of Darcy Tucker. Cooke plays with attitude (although he has yet to make a name for himself as a cheap-shot artist). He will do whatever it takes to help his team win. He'll yap; he'll dive, he'll kill penalties, he'll score a shorthanded goal, he'll shadow an opposing forward. Just give him an assignment and he's happy.

Cooke has been a competent scorer at the minor league level. He's not going to bring much to the table offensively. He has average hands and an average shot, but he makes the most of what he's got with a relentless work ethic.

Cooke is very aware defensively. He developed as a center, and can move to that position if needed, although Vancouver used him mostly on the left side last season. Most of all, he's got spunk.

THE PHYSICAL GAME

Cooke is a small guy with an irritating, abrasive style. Being a pest comes naturally to him, and he'll do what he can to aggravate opposing players into taking a whack at him. Given Vancouver's proficiency on the power play, being able to draw penalties is a pretty powerful weapon.

THE INTANGIBLES

Cooke has found his role as an energetic checking forward.

PROJECTION

Cooke looks like he has cemented the third-line left-wing slot, which is perfect for a player of his energy and limitations. He can score 15 goals a year in that role.

ED JOVANOVSKI

Yrs. of NHL service: 8
Born: Windsor, Ont.; June 26, 1976
Position: left defense
Height: 6-2
Weight: 210
Uniform no.: 55
Shoots: left

Career statistics:

GP	G	A	TP	PIM
587	71	190	261	963

1999-2000 statistics:

GP	G	A	TP	+/-	PIM	PP	SH	GW	GT	S	PCT
75	5	21	26	-3	54	1	0	1	0	109	4.6

2000-2001 statistics:

GP	G	A	TP	+/-	PIM	PP	SH	GW	GT	S	PCT
79	12	35	47	-1	102	4	0	2	2	193	6.2

2001-2002 statistics:

GP	G	A	TP	+/-	PIM	PP	SH	GW	GT	S	PCT
82	17	31	48	-7	101	7	1	3	1	202	8.4

2002-2003 statistics:

GP	G	A	TP	+/-	PIM	PP	SH	GW	GT	S	PCT
67	6	40	46	+19	113	2	0	1	1	145	4.1

LAST SEASON

Led team defensemen in points for fourth consecutive season. Second on team in average ice time (24:14). Third on team in plus-minus and penalty minutes. Missed 14 games with heel injury. Missed one game with flu.

THE FINESSE GAME

Jovanovski's skating is the one aspect that prevents him from being an elite NHL defenseman. He has worked hard to improve and it has become above-average. He can get up to full steam and streak through the neutral zone like a freight train. He sure isn't pretty, but he's powerful.

Strong on his feet with a dynamic stride, Jovanovski is quicker than most big men, perhaps because of early soccer training, and he can use his feet to move the puck if his stick is tied up. His powerful hitting is made more wicked because he gets so much speed and leg drive. He can make plays, too. He gets a little time because his speed forces the opposition to back off, and he has a nice passing touch. Jovanovski plays in all game situations, and plays the point on the first power-play unit. He is very patient with the puck and has become more confident in his ability to make plays.

Jovanovski is developing along the lines of a Scott Stevens, a defenseman who can dominate in all zones. He still gives the impression of being more raw than polished; he could get even better.

THE PHYSICAL GAME

Jovanovski is among the best open-ice hitters in the NHL. He hits to hurt. Because of his size and agility, Jovanovski able to catch people right where he wants them. They aren't dirty hits, but they're old-time hockey throwbacks, administered by a modern-sized defenseman.

Jovanovski has to continue to play smarter. Jovanovski can still be diverted from his game by smaller, peskier players. He is so easy to distract that this must be at the top of every team's game plan against the Canucks.

THE INTANGIBLES

Jovanovski has become a big-time, crunch-time player.

PROJECTION

We projected Jovanovski as a potential 50-point scorer last season and he would have hit it if he hadn't been injured. He could do it this time.

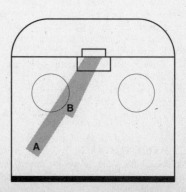

TREVOR LINDEN

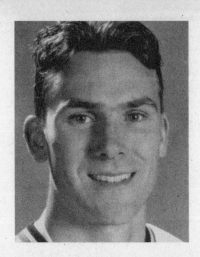

Yrs. of NHL service: 15
Born: Medicine Hat, Alta.; Apr. 11, 1970
Position: center / right wing
Height: 6-4
Weight: 215
Uniform no.: 16
Shoots: right

Career statistics:

GP	G	A	TP	PIM
1079	335	443	778	805

1999-2000 statistics:

GP	G	A	TP	+/-	PIM	PP	SH	GW	GT	S	PCT
50	13	17	30	-3	34	4	0	3	0	87	14.9

2000-2001 statistics:

GP	G	A	TP	+/-	PIM	PP	SH	GW	GT	S	PCT
69	15	22	37	0	60	6	0	3	0	126	11.9

2001-2002 statistics:

GP	G	A	TP	+/-	PIM	PP	SH	GW	GT	S	PCT
80	13	24	37	-5	71	3	0	2	0	141	9.2

2002-2003 statistics:

GP	G	A	TP	+/-	PIM	PP	SH	GW	GT	S	PCT
71	19	22	41	-1	30	4	1	1	0	116	16.4

LAST SEASON

Second on team in shooting percentage. Missed six games with sprained knee. Missed five games with eye injury.

THE FINESSE GAME

Not a graceful skater, Linden at times looks awkward, and he's not as strong on his skates as a player of his size should be. Despite his heavy feet, his agility is satisfactory, but he lacks first-step quickness and doesn't have the all-out speed to pull away from a checker. He has a big turning radius. If only he would keep his feet moving, Linden would be so much more commanding. Instead, he can be angled off the play fairly easily because he will not battle for better ice.

Linden has improved his release, but it is not quick. He has a long reach, although unlike, say, Dave Andreychuk's, (who is built along similar lines) his short game is not as effective as it should be.

Linden is a well-rounded player who can kill penalties, work on the power play, and is very sound at even strength. He sees a lot less power-play time now because the Canucks have superior offensive players. Linden is unselfish and makes quick, safe passing decisions that help his team break smartly up the ice, often creating odd-man rushes. He has improved in his defensive coverage. He is very good on face-offs.

Linden can play center or right wing; he's better on the wing.

THE PHYSICAL GAME

Linden is big but doesn't always play tough, and so doesn't make good use of his size. He will attack the blueline and draw the attention of both defensemen, but will pull up rather than try to muscle through and earn a holding penalty. There are people he should nullify who still seem able to get away from him. He does not skate through the physical challenges along the boards. When he plays big, he is a big, big player.

When Linden is throwing his weight around, he drives to the net and drags a defender or two with him, opening up a lot of ice for his teammates. He creates havoc in front of the net on the power play, planting himself for screens and deflections. When the puck is at the side boards, he's smart enough to move up higher, between the circles, forcing the penalty killers to make a decision. If the defenseman on that side steps up to cover him, space will open behind the defenseman; if a forward collapses to cover him, a point shot will open up.

THE INTANGIBLES

Linden is a character guy and a reliable performer. Vancouver liked him enough to sign him to a three-year contract extension in January.

PROJECTION

Linden is a support player now. He will get 15 goals and 35 to 40 points.

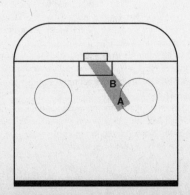

MAREK MALIK

Yrs. of NHL service: 7
Born: Ostrava, Czech.; June 24, 1975
Position: left defense
Height: 6-5
Weight: 215
Uniform no.: 8
Shoots: left

Career statistics:

GP	G	A	TP	PIM
386	24	71	95	343

1999-2000 statistics:

GP	G	A	TP	+/-	PIM	PP	SH	GW	GT	S	PCT
57	4	10	14	+13	63	0	0	1	0	57	7.0

2000-2001 statistics:

GP	G	A	TP	+/-	PIM	PP	SH	GW	GT	S	PCT
61	6	14	20	-4	34	1	0	1	0	72	8.3

2001-2002 statistics:

GP	G	A	TP	+/-	PIM	PP	SH	GW	GT	S	PCT
82	4	19	23	+8	88	0	0	0	0	91	4.4

2002-2003 statistics:

GP	G	A	TP	+/-	PIM	PP	SH	GW	GT	S	PCT
79	7	13	20	+20	68	1	1	2	1	77	9.1

LAST SEASON

Acquired from Carolina on November 1, 2002, for Harold Druken and Jan Hlavac. Second on team in plus-minus. Career high in goals and points. Missed two games due to coach's decision.

THE FINESSE GAME

Malik will never develop into the star he was once projected to be, but at least he has progressed to becoming a top-four defenseman, and for a time that was in doubt.

Malik is a good skater for his towering size, though he is a straight-legged skater and not quick. He uses his range mostly as a defensive tool and is not much involved in the attack. He has a fairly high skill level in all areas.

Malik is poised with the puck. He is a good passer and playmaker, and moves the puck out of his own end quickly. He won't try to do too much himself but will utilize his teammates well. He's big, but does a lot of little things well, which makes him a solid defensive player. He limits his offensive contributions to a shot from the point. However, he may yet develop better skills as a playmaker.

THE PHYSICAL GAME

Malik has begun to fill out his once-weedy frame to be able to handle some of the NHL's big boys one-on-one. Like Kjell Samuelsson, he takes up a lot of space with his arms and stick, and is more of an octopus-type defenseman than a solid hitter. He is strong in front of his net. He has some aggressiveness in him, but he is not a fighter.

THE INTANGIBLES

The biggest step Malik has taken over the past few seasons is in his consistency. He takes fewer nights off. Malik is starting to grasp the concept of the NHL game.

PROJECTION

Malik will fight for a job with Vancouver's top four. It looks like 25 points is his top end as far as offensive contributions are concerned. His defense comes first.

BRENDAN MORRISON

Yrs. of NHL service: 5
Born: North Vancouver, B.C.; Aug. 12, 1975
Position: center
Height: 5-11
Weight: 190
Uniform no.: 7
Shoots: left

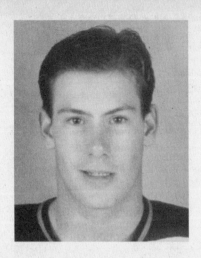

Career statistics:

GP	G	A	TP	PIM
389	89	193	282	140

1999-2000 statistics:

GP	G	A	TP	+/-	PIM	PP	SH	GW	GT	S	PCT
56	7	28	35	+12	18	2	0	1	0	96	7.3

2000-2001 statistics:

GP	G	A	TP	+/-	PIM	PP	SH	GW	GT	S	PCT
82	16	38	54	+2	42	3	2	3	3	179	8.9

2001-2002 statistics:

GP	G	A	TP	+/-	PIM	PP	SH	GW	GT	S	PCT
82	23	44	67	+18	26	6	0	4	0	183	12.6

2002-2003 statistics:

GP	G	A	TP	+/-	PIM	PP	SH	GW	GT	S	PCT
82	25	46	71	+18	36	6	2	8	0	167	15.0

LAST SEASON

Second on team in game-winning goals. Tied for second on team in shorthanded goals. Third on team in goals, assists, points, and shots. Tied for third on team in power-play goals. Career highs in goals, assists, and points. One of five Canucks to appear in all 82 games.

THE FINESSE GAME

Morrison's hockey sense and vision are outstanding. Morrison may not be a classic No. 1 NHL center, but he doesn't look out of place between Markus Naslund and Todd Bertuzzi. Morrison plays a key role in the line's dominance.

Morrison has a world of confidence in his abilities, almost to the point of cockiness, and he will try some daring and creative moves. He has soft hands for passing and he uses a selection of deceptively heavy and accurate shots. He can work low on the power play or at the point, and he sees all of his options quickly. He doesn't panic and is poised with the puck.

He is a strong skater, with balance, quickness, agility, and breakaway speed. Morrison has no trouble with NHL speed, except when it comes to defensive decisions, although he is adjusting. Morrison is a quick and savvy penalty killer.

THE PHYSICAL GAME

Small but wise enough to stay out of trouble, Morrison has wiry strength for playing in the high-traffic areas. He loves to create plays from behind the net. He plays with a little edge to him that shows he will not be intimidated. He is strong on his skates and tough to knock off balance.

THE INTANGIBLES

We're not sold on Morrison as a first-line center. The important thing is that he is. We think he'd be a better No. 2 but he's the best Vancouver has.

PROJECTION

Morrison hit the target we expected for him last season, and 70-75 points is probably his ceiling.

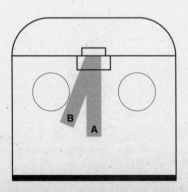

MARKUS NASLUND

Yrs. of NHL service: 10
Born: Ornskoldsvik, Sweden; July 30, 1973
Position: left wing
Height: 5-11
Weight: 195
Uniform no.: 19
Shoots: left

Career statistics:

GP	G	A	TP	PIM
712	255	290	545	455

1999-2000 statistics:

GP	G	A	TP	+/-	PIM	PP	SH	GW	GT	S	PCT
82	27	38	65	-5	64	6	2	3	1	271	10.0

2000-2001 statistics:

GP	G	A	TP	+/-	PIM	PP	SH	GW	GT	S	PCT
72	41	34	75	-2	58	18	1	5	0	277	14.8

2001-2002 statistics:

GP	G	A	TP	+/-	PIM	PP	SH	GW	GT	S	PCT
81	40	50	90	+22	50	8	0	6	1	302	13.3

2002-2003 statistics:

GP	G	A	TP	+/-	PIM	PP	SH	GW	GT	S	PCT
82	48	56	104	+6	52	24	0	12	1	294	16.3

LAST SEASON

Finalist for 2003 Hart Trophy. Named to NHL First All-Star Team. Led NHL in power-play points (54) and game-winning goals. Second in NHL in points, goals, and power-play goals. Tied for eighth in NHL in assists. Led team in goals, assists, points, and shots. Second on team in power-play goals. Career highs in goals, assists, and points. One of five Canucks to appear in all 82 games.

THE FINESSE GAME

Naslund has joined the NHL's elite. As good as his numbers are, he is a better two-way player than he is given credit for. He's a player who can be relied upon in the closing minutes of the game, either to make a big play that results in a goal, or to protect a lead.

Naslund is a pure sniper. He has excellent snap and wrist shots and can score in just about every way imaginable, including the backhand in-tight. He has quick hands and an accurate touch. He needs to play with people who will get him the puck, although he has become far more aggressive and consistent in his puck pursuit. He is a jitterbug on the ice and can keep up with the fastest linemates. He is also confident with the puck, and loves to toast defensemen with an inside-outside move. Naslund's wrister is one of the finest in the league.

Naslund quarterbacks the Vancouver power play, which was third-best in the NHL last season. He has flawless offensive instincts and hockey vision. Above all Naslund is remarkably consistent in his effort. There are a lot of peaks but few valleys. Naslund knows what it takes to succeed and is willing to pay the price.

A lot was expected of Naslund early in his career. He started out in the Pittsburgh system and bounced around in the minors before finding his niche with the Canucks and especially with Todd Bertuzzi on Vancouver's top line.

THE PHYSICAL GAME

There is a lot of heart in this Hart finalist. Naslund has good conditioning habits and is a tireless worker. He is not a major physical presence, but he makes something of a pest out of himself. Naslund recovered well from a badly broken leg that required surgery and ended his 2000-01 season prematurely. He plays through injuries.

THE INTANGIBLES

Being named captain meant a great deal to Naslund, and he wears the "C" well. He takes it seriously, and has developed into the kind of captain who will not only lead by his sterling example, but will challenge his team, publicly if necessary, to step up to his level. He is a consummate team player and a lightning rod. He will accept blame and deflect credit. He is consistent and confident.

PROJECTION

Naslund should be a 100-point scorer again.

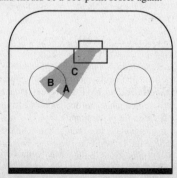

MATTIAS OHLUND

Yrs. of NHL service: 6
Born: Pitea, Sweden; Sept. 9, 1976
Position: left defense
Height: 6-2
Weight: 220
Uniform no.: 2
Shoots: left

Career statistics:

GP	G	A	TP	PIM
398	40	138	178	327

1999-2000 statistics:

GP	G	A	TP	+/-	PIM	PP	SH	GW	GT	S	PCT
42	4	16	20	+6	24	2	1	1	0	63	6.3

2000-2001 statistics:

GP	G	A	TP	+/-	PIM	PP	SH	GW	GT	S	PCT
65	8	20	28	-16	46	1	1	4	0	136	5.9

2001-2002 statistics:

GP	G	A	TP	+/-	PIM	PP	SH	GW	GT	S	PCT
81	10	26	36	+16	56	4	1	3	0	193	5.2

2002-2003 statistics:

GP	G	A	TP	+/-	PIM	PP	SH	GW	GT	S	PCT
59	2	27	29	+1	42	0	0	0	0	100	2.0

LAST SEASON

Led team in average ice time (25:23). Career high in assists. Missed five games with sprained knee/flu. Missed 18 games with knee injury.

THE FINESSE GAME

Ohlund has a high skill level and a big body to go with it. He is a lovely, fluid skater with splendid agility for his size. He's very confident with the puck. Because of his skating and his reach, he is difficult to beat one-on-one. He isn't fooled by dekes, either. He plays the crest and maintains his position.

A good power-play player from the right point, Ohlund gets significant power-play time. He uses an effective, short backswing on his one-timer. He makes a sharp first pass out of the defensive zone, and gets involved in the attack by moving up into the rush (but he won't get caught deep very often).

Injuries over the years, especially a serious eye injury, has hurt Ohlund's development and may have prevented him from being an "A" defenseman, but he's a very good "B."

THE PHYSICAL GAME

Ohlund is big and powerful. He is assertive, won't be intimidated, and finishes his checks. He clears out the front of the net and works the boards and corners. For a player considered to be a finesse defenseman, he plays an involved game. He has an iron constitution and can handle a lot of ice time.

THE INTANGIBLES

Ohlund has fought to come back from a career-threatening eye injury and surgery, so his development has been delayed. He was healthy last season and at 27 is just coming into his prime.

PROJECTION

Ohlund can score 40 points if he can avoid injury.

BRANDON REID

Yrs. of NHL service: 0
Born: Kirkland, Que.; Mar. 9, 1981
Position: center
Height: 5-8
Weight: 165
Uniform no.: 14
Shoots: right

Career statistics:

GP	G	A	TP	PIM
7	2	3	5	0

2002-2003 statistics:

GP	G	A	TP	+/-	PIM	PP	SH	GW	GT	S	PCT
7	2	3	5	+4	0	0	0	0	0	15	13.3

LAST SEASON

Will be entering first full NHL season. Appeared in 73 games with Manitoba (AHL), scoring 18-36 — 54 with 18 PIM.

THE FINESSE GAME

Maybe that crackdown on obstruction-type penalties is working after all. How else to explain the NHL careers of little big men like Tampa Bay's Martin St. Louis and New Jersey's Brian Gionta?

Next to join the fraternity may be this dynamite. Reid made enough of an impression in his limited stint in the regular season and playoffs to indicate the Canucks may make room for him on their roster. And he takes up so little space!

The key to Reid's game is his playmaking. He's a real skeeter, darting every which way with amazing one-step quickness. That sprint helps him avoid lumbering checkers (Reid makes all but the most agile defensemen look a little clumsy).

Reid has good hockey sense, vision, and terrific hands. He is a pure setup man. His passes are on the money, even through traffic. His shot, when he uses it, is accurate and he has a good release, but he is not a goal-scorer by nature. His defensive awareness is sound.

THE PHYSICAL GAME

Reid's lack of size is obviously a drawback, but someone at every stage of his career has told him he can't take the next step and Reid plays as if he is determined to prove them all wrong. He will get in the way. He will throw what few pounds he has at the opponent. He probably can't handle a lot of minutes because he plays so hard, but he is likely destined for a part-time role this season anyway. There will be very few nights when anyone outworks him.

THE INTANGIBLES

Reid won't be a top-nine forward this season, but the recent trend in the league is to have more skill players and fewer goons on the fourth line, so he could be quite useful. He could see some second-unit power-play time.

PROJECTION

Reid has a great attitude and will do what he can to get into the Vancouver lineup. Based on what we saw in his brief NHL experience, 25 points wouldn't be a surprise.

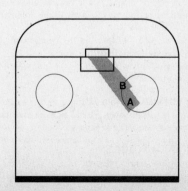

SAMI SALO

Yrs. of NHL service: 5
Born: Turku, Finland; Sept. 2, 1974
Position: right defense
Height: 6-3
Weight: 215
Uniform no.: 6
Shoots: right

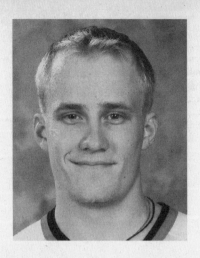

Career statistics:

GP	G	A	TP	PIM
274	28	71	99	60

1999-2000 statistics:

GP	G	A	TP	+/-	PIM	PP	SH	GW	GT	S	PCT
37	6	8	14	+6	2	3	0	1	0	85	7.1

2000-2001 statistics:

GP	G	A	TP	+/-	PIM	PP	SH	GW	GT	S	PCT
31	2	16	18	+9	10	1	0	0	0	61	3.3

2001-2002 statistics:

GP	G	A	TP	+/-	PIM	PP	SH	GW	GT	S	PCT
66	4	14	18	+1	14	1	1	2	0	122	3.3

2002-2003 statistics:

GP	G	A	TP	+/-	PIM	PP	SH	GW	GT	S	PCT
79	9	21	30	+9	10	4	0	1	1	126	7.1

THE INTANGIBLES

Salo enjoyed his first relatively injury-free season in four years and it made a huge difference.

PROJECTION

A healthy Salo should score in the 35-point range.

LAST SEASON

Acquired from Ottawa for Peter Schaefer on September 21, 2002. Career highs in goals and points. Missed two games with shoulder injury. Missed one game with groin injury.

THE FINESSE GAME

Salo is highly skilled. He has very quick feet and good mobility which, combined with his long reach, make him hard to beat one-on-one. He also possesses an extremely hard shot. He likes to get involved offensively, and steps up into the play alertly. He is still growing into his NHL job and as he gains confidence, his offensive contributions will increase. He can handle second-unit power-play time.

Salo has good hands for passing or receiving the puck, and he makes a crisp first pass out of the zone. He has a good head for the game, and is calm with the puck under pressure. He reads plays well and moves the puck without mistakes. The epitome of a low-risk defenseman, he is a classic crunch-time defenseman for protecting a lead.

Salo was well-schooled in the Ottawa defensive system before being traded to Vancouver. He fit in well as a top-four defenseman, stepping up when there were injuries.

THE PHYSICAL GAME

Salo won't punish anyone. He is more of a positional defenseman who will ride guys out. Salo has good size and is strong on his skates but he doesn't play with an edge.

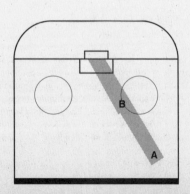

DANIEL SEDIN

Yrs. of NHL service: 3
Born: Ornskoldsvik, Sweden; Sept. 26, 1980
Position: left wing
Height: 6-1
Weight: 200
Uniform no.: 22
Shoots: left

Career statistics:

GP	G	A	TP	PIM
233	43	54	97	90

2000-2001 statistics:

GP	G	A	TP	+/-	PIM	PP	SH	GW	GT	S	PCT
75	20	14	34	-3	24	10	0	3	0	127	15.8

2001-2002 statistics:

GP	G	A	TP	+/-	PIM	PP	SH	GW	GT	S	PCT
79	9	23	32	+1	32	4	0	2	0	117	7.7

2002-2003 statistics:

GP	G	A	TP	+/-	PIM	PP	SH	GW	GT	S	PCT
79	14	17	31	+8	34	4	0	2	0	134	10.4

LAST SEASON

Missed three games due to coach's decision.

THE FINESSE GAME

This is supposed to be the finisher of the pair of Sedin twins, but Daniel has yet to prove he can be an impact scorer at the NHL level. We know this much: He won't be a power forward. Sedin plays too much of a perimeter game. Even goal-scorers who rely on their speed and skills are willing to go into traffic. Sedin doesn't.

Sedin has outstanding hockey sense. He is one of those natural goal-scorers to whom shooting and shot selection is a reflex. He doesn't have to think about where the puck is going. He knows what he is going to do with it before it's on his stick. He moves the puck quickly. He has very good hockey vision and intelligence. Primarily an offensive player, he needs to improve on his defensive duties.

Daniel is fast and strong on his skates. Although he is a shooter first, he also has good playmaking skills. He has adequate defensive awareness.

THE PHYSICAL GAME

Daniel's immediate need will be to beef up, not only in size but in intensity. Considering the size of the typical NHL defenseman these days, Sedin needs to do some upper-body work for the battles in the trenches. And just how badly does he want a job in the NHL? Sedin will need to show a lot more than he has in his first three seasons.

THE INTANGIBLES

Third-liners are routinely scoring 15 goals a season now. Sedin was a second-line left winger last season and if Markus Naslund hadn't had such an outstanding year offensively, there would have been a lot more pressure on Sedin to score. Sedin was a restricted free agent after the season, as was his twin.

PROJECTION

Unless Sedin shows some spark in training camp, pool players would be wise to steer clear.

HENRIK SEDIN

Yrs. of NHL service: 3
Born: Ornskoldsvik, Sweden; Sept. 26, 1980
Position: center
Height: 6-2
Weight: 200
Uniform no.: 33
Shoots: left

Career statistics:

GP	G	A	TP	PIM
242	33	71	104	112

2000-2001 statistics:

GP	G	A	TP	+/-	PIM	PP	SH	GW	GT	S	PCT
82	9	20	29	-2	38	2	0	1	0	98	9.2

2001-2002 statistics:

GP	G	A	TP	+/-	PIM	PP	SH	GW	GT	S	PCT
82	16	20	36	+9	36	3	0	1	1	78	20.5

2002-2003 statistics:

GP	G	A	TP	+/-	PIM	PP	SH	GW	GT	S	PCT
78	8	31	39	+9	38	4	1	1	1	81	9.9

LAST SEASON

Career highs in assists and points. Missed three games with shoulder injury. Missed one game with hand injury.

THE FINESSE GAME

Henrik, the playmaker, is better suited to the NHL style of play than his twin, Daniel, the scorer. Henrik is a little bigger than his brother, and a little grittier. He doesn't have a great, soft touch with the puck, but he works hard to complete his plays.

Sedin needs to develop more confidence in his own ability to shoot and score. If he remains too shot-shy, then opposing defenders can always sag off him and wait for him to try to force a pass to one of his wingers.

Sedin is a very good, powerful skater, though he doesn't have great acceleration, and he will need to work on his footwork. His defensive game is advanced, but he will need to continue to improve his work on draws. He has very good hockey sense. Sedin sees significant penalty-killing shifts and is a willing shot-blocker.

Sedin is strong on the puck and protects it well with his body. He may develop into a poor man's Peter Forsberg.

THE PHYSICAL GAME

Henrik has NHL size and NHL temperament. Feisty by nature, the physical side of the game comes naturally to him. He is solid on his skates and well-balanced.

THE INTANGIBLES

Sedin has yet to attain the kind of consistency to earn a spot on Vancouver's top line, which is where the Canucks desperately want him to play. Coach Marc Crawford won't give it to him, though, until Sedin earns it. He was a restricted free agent after last season.

PROJECTION

Sedin's progress continues to be painfully slow. Will this be the breakout year? If it is, expect an assist-heavy 65 points.

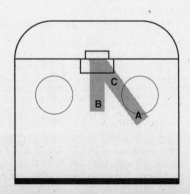

BRENT SOPEL

Yrs. of NHL service: 3
Born: Calgary, Alta.; Jan. 7, 1977
Position: defense
Height: 6-1
Weight: 205
Uniform no.: 3
Shoots: right

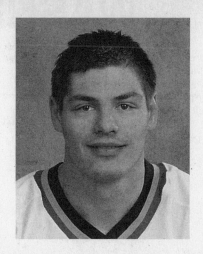

Career statistics:

GP	G	A	TP	PIM
222	22	61	83	93

1999-2000 statistics:

GP	G	A	TP	+/-	PIM	PP	SH	GW	GT	S	PCT
18	2	4	6	+9	12	0	0	1	0	11	18.2

2000-2001 statistics:

GP	G	A	TP	+/-	PIM	PP	SH	GW	GT	S	PCT
52	4	10	14	+4	10	0	0	1	0	57	7.0

2001-2002 statistics:

GP	G	A	TP	+/-	PIM	PP	SH	GW	GT	S	PCT
66	8	17	25	+21	44	1	0	3	0	116	6.9

2002-2003 statistics:

GP	G	A	TP	+/-	PIM	PP	SH	GW	GT	S	PCT
81	7	30	37	-15	23	6	0	1	0	167	4.2

LAST SEASON

Third on team in average ice time (21:41). Worst plus-minus on team. Missed one game with ankle injury.

THE FINESSE GAME

Sopel went from being a +21 player a season ago to -15 last season. That is just about a mathematical impossibility unless a player is traded to a team like Atlanta, but Sopel stayed on the same strong Canucks team. The decline was especially baffling since Sopel was developing a reputation as being a pretty savvy guy in his own end.

Most likely the problems started at the other team's blueline, with Sopel getting too carried away at the offensive point and making ill-timed pinches and turnovers.

Sopel is a good skater. He skates well backwards and has good lateral movement. He makes a firm outlet pass, or if he has to, he can skate the puck out of his own zone.

THE PHYSICAL GAME

Sopel has good size but certainly isn't too big by today's standards. He is stronger than he looks. Sopel has added about 15 pounds since his draft year (1995). Sopel is a containment hitter. He doesn't make big open-ice checks, but he will keep his man tied up in the corners, along the wall or in front of the net.

THE INTANGIBLES

Sopel's favorite player growing up was Mathieu Schneider, and Sopel resembles Schneider in more than a few ways. He is developing into a defenseman who won't be flashy, but at the end of the night you'll realize he did a lot more things to help his team win than some of the stars. At least that's what we thought after the 2001-02 season. Now he is going to have a tough fight for a top-four role on Vancouver's defense.

PROJECTION

Sopel needs to forget about scoring points and get back to playing basic defensive hockey. Keep it simple, Sopel.

WASHINGTON CAPITALS

Players' Statistics 2001-2002

POS.	NO.	PLAYER	GP	G	A	PTS	+/-	PIM	PP	SH	GW	GT	S	PCT
R	68	JAROMIR JAGR	75	36	41	77	5	38	13	2	9		290	12.4
C	20	ROBERT LANG	82	22	47	69	12	22	10		2	1	146	15.1
D	55	SERGEI GONCHAR	82	18	49	67	13	52	7		2	1	224	8.0
C	92	MICHAEL NYLANDER	80	17	43	60	3	40	7		2		161	10.6
R	12	PETER BONDRA	76	30	26	56	-3	52	9	2	4		256	11.7
C	14	KIP MILLER	72	12	38	50	-1	18	3		4		89	13.5
L	94	SERGEI BEREZIN	75	23	17	40	7	12	5		2		199	11.6
R	9	DAINIUS ZUBRUS	63	13	22	35	15	43	2				104	12.5
C	11	JEFF HALPERN	82	13	21	34	6	88	1	2	2		126	10.3
R	25	MIKE GRIER	82	15	17	32	-14	36	2	2	2		133	11.3
L	22	STEVE KONOWALCHUK	77	15	15	30	3	71	2		3		119	12.6
L	27	IVAN CIERNIK	47	8	10	18	6	24			2	1	61	13.1
D	2	KEN KLEE	70	1	16	17	22	89					67	1.5
D	6	CALLE JOHANSSON	82	3	12	15	9	22	1				77	3.9
D	19	BRENDAN WITT	69	2	9	11	12	106					80	2.5
C	46	*BRIAN SUTHERBY	72	2	9	11	7	93					38	5.3
D	54	JASON DOIG	55	3	5	8	-3	108			1		41	7.3
C	21	GLEN METROPOLIT	23	2	3	5	4	6			1		22	9.1
L	8	JOSH GREEN	45	1	4	5	-3	21					43	2.3
C	16	ANDREAS SALOMONSSON	32	1	4	5	-1	14				1	20	5.0
D	29	*JOEL KWIATKOWSKI	54		5	5	3	18					56	
D	4	RICK BERRY	43	2	1	3	-3	87			1		40	5.0
C	23	TRENT WHITFIELD	14	1	1	2	1	6			1		4	25.0
D	44	*STEVE EMINGER	17		2	2	-3	24					6	
D	39	*JOSEF BOUMEDIENNE	6	1		1	-1				1		7	14.3
R	51	STEPHEN PEAT	27	1		1	-3	57					7	14.3
D	58	JEAN-FRANCOIS FORTIN	33		1	1	-3	22					20	
L	45	*ALEX HENRY	41				-5	80					8	
L	36	COLIN FORBES	5				-2						3	
R	41	*MICHAEL FARRELL	4				1	2					2	
G	1	CRAIG BILLINGTON	5			0								
D	3	SYLVAIN COTE	1			0		4						
G	37	OLAF KOLZIG	66			0								
G	35	S. CHARPENTIER	17			0								
D	0	NOLAN YONKMAN				0								
L	18	MATT PETTINGER	1			0								
D	34	JAKUB CUTTA				0								

GP = games played; G = goals; A = assists; PTS = points; +/- = goals-for minus goals-against while player is on ice; PIM = penalties in minutes; PP = power-play goals; SH = shorthanded goals; GW = game-winning goals; GT = game-tying goals; S = no. of shots; PCT = percentage of goals to shots; * = rookie

RICK BERRY

Yrs. of NHL service: 2
Born: Brandon, On.; Nov. 4, 1978
Position: defense
Height: 6-2
Weight: 210
Uniform no.: 4
Shoots: left

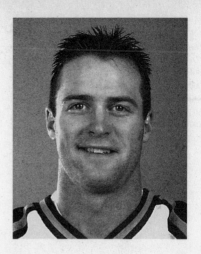

Career statistics:

GP	G	A	TP	PIM
132	2	7	9	206

2000-2001 statistics:

GP	G	A	TP	+/-	PIM	PP	SH	GW	GT	S	PCT
19	0	4	4	+5	38	0	0	0	0	10	0.0

2001-2002 statistics:

GP	G	A	TP	+/-	PIM	PP	SH	GW	GT	S	PCT
70	0	2	2	-3	81	0	0	0	0	49	0.0

2002-2003 statistics:

GP	G	A	TP	+/-	PIM	PP	SH	GW	GT	S	PCT
43	2	1	3	-3	87	0	0	1	0	40	5.0

PROJECTION

Berry hasn't been much of a scorer at any level. More than 20 points would be a pleasant surprise.

LAST SEASON

Acquired from Pittsburgh on waivers on October 4, 2002. Missed 39 games due to coach's decision.

THE FINESSE GAME

Berry has some really top-notch finesse skills, and he applies them almost exclusively to the defensive part of the game.

Berry is a very good skater, forward and back. He has good lateral mobility and is quite agile. He makes a good first pass out of the defensive zone, or he can skate the puck out himself and get a rush started. Berry won't pinch or gamble too deep into the offensive zone, even though he is such a good skater he could scramble back and recover defensively.

Berry has good hockey sense and a pretty good point shot. He could be involved more in the attack as he becomes more comfortable. Right now he seems more intent on learning his defensive positioning, and that's not a bad thing. It will give him a better foundation for what looks like a promising future.

THE PHYSICAL GAME

Berry is a good-sized defenseman who relishes the physical part of the game. Because he is such a good skater, he can generate some good leg drive for his hits. Berry has a naturally aggressive streak.

THE INTANGIBLES

Berry spent most of the season as a spare defenseman with the Caps, which made it a tough learning season for him. Washington is expected to move out some of its older, pricier defensemen, which may open up a job for Berry. Berry was a restricted free agent after last season.

PETER BONDRA

Yrs. of NHL service: 13
Born: Luck, Ukraine; Feb. 7, 1968
Position: right wing
Height: 6-0
Weight: 200
Uniform no.: 12
Shoots: left

Career statistics:

GP	G	A	TP	PIM
907	451	339	790	657

1999-2000 statistics:

GP	G	A	TP	+/-	PIM	PP	SH	GW	GT	S	PCT
62	21	17	38	+5	30	5	3	5	0	187	11.2

2000-2001 statistics:

GP	G	A	TP	+/-	PIM	PP	SH	GW	GT	S	PCT
82	45	36	81	+8	60	22	4	8	0	305	14.7

2001-2002 statistics:

GP	G	A	TP	+/-	PIM	PP	SH	GW	GT	S	PCT
77	39	31	70	-2	80	17	1	8	1	333	11.7

2002-2003 statistics:

GP	G	A	TP	+/-	PIM	PP	SH	GW	GT	S	PCT
76	30	26	56	-3	52	9	2	4	0	256	11.7

LAST SEASON

Tied for team lead in shorthanded goals. Second on team in goals and shots. Third on team in power-play goals. Tied for third on team in game-winning goals. Missed three games with back spasms.

THE FINESSE GAME

Bondra is an explosive skater. He has a wide skating stance for balance, a deep knee bend, and a powerful kick, like a sprinter out of the starting blocks. Bondra skates as fast with the puck as without it, and he wants the puck early. He cuts in on the off-wing and shoots in stride. He has a very good backhand shot and likes to cut out from behind the net and make things happen in-tight. He mixes up his shots. He will fire quickly — not many veteran European players have this good a slap shot — or drive in close, deke and wrist a shot.

At his best, Bondra is in the category of players you would pay to watch play. His speed is exceptional, and he makes intelligent offensive plays. He accelerates quickly and smoothly and drives defenders back because they have to play off his speed. If he gets hooked to the ice he doesn't stay down, but jumps back to his skates and gets involved in the play again, often after the defender has forgotten about him.

Bondra lives to score goals. He has a real scorer's mentality. But don't underestimate his defensive awareness. He quickly grasped the concept that better defensive positioning helps his offense. That's not so odd when you think of the game in terms of gap control.

Bondra, with 35 shorthanded goals in the past nine seasons, is a dangerous shorthanded threat. He makes opposing teams' power plays jittery because of his anticipation and breakaway speed, and he follows up his shots to the net and is quick to pounce on rebounds.

THE PHYSICAL GAME

Bondra isn't strong, but he will lean on people. He can't be intimidated.

THE INTANGIBLES

Bondra suffered from the loss of Adam Oates (to free agency in 2002) and never clicked with either Robert Lang or Michael Nylander.

PROJECTION

Bondra is 35 and maybe his days as a 40-goal scorer are over. They sure are unless the Caps find him a linemate who understands Bondra's sense of timing.

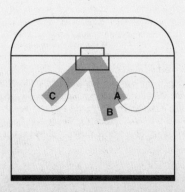

STEVE EMINGER

Yrs. of NHL service: 0
Born: Woodbridge, Ont.; Oct. 31, 1983
Position: right defense
Height: 6-1
Weight: 196
Uniform no.: 44
Shoots: right

Career statistics:

GP	G	A	TP	PIM
17	0	2	2	24

2002-2003 statistics:

GP	G	A	TP	+/-	PIM	PP	SH	GW	GT	S	PCT
17	0	2	2	-3	24	0	0	0	0	6	0.0

LAST SEASON

Will be entering first full NHL season. Appeared in 23 games with Kitchener (OHL), scoring 2-27 — 29 with 40 PIM.

THE FINESSE GAME

The Caps' breakout should improve dramatically once Eminger becomes an NHL regular. He is a handsome package. Eminger makes a sharp first pass, he is a very good skater, he handles the puck well, he has good hockey vision, and he competes.

Eminger will be a major factor on the power play. He will graduate to be a quality point man. He probably won't be in the exceptional Brian Leetch class, but he is like Leetch in that he likes to start the power play by carrying the puck out of his own end.

Eminger has to learn to use his teammates better. He is so used to doing so many things by himself in junior. At the NHL level, the level of the quality of talent around him is higher and he will learn to trust their abilities as well as his own.

Eminger is still pretty young but shows signs of becoming a solid two-way defenseman.

THE PHYSICAL GAME

Eminger isn't considered a physical defenseman, but he plays with an edge and there are games where he even exhibits a bit of a mean streak. He has good size, and will make effective takeouts. Eminger won't make highlight-reel hits, but he will finish his checks and won't play a shy game.

THE INTANGIBLES

Rather than have Eminger spend time in junior, the Caps kept him up for three months basically just working out with their coaches and players. Washington has invested the time in him and it should pay off with a top-four job this season, especially with the Caps shedding a couple of veteran defensemen to clear room.

PROJECTION

Eminger is likely to concentrate on nailing down the defensive game first, but he has some offensive upside.

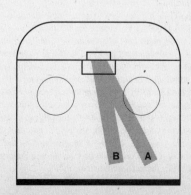

SERGEI GONCHAR

Yrs. of NHL service: 9
Born: Chelyabinsk, Russia; Apr. 13, 1974
Position: left defense
Height: 6-2
Weight: 208
Uniform no.: 55
Shoots: left

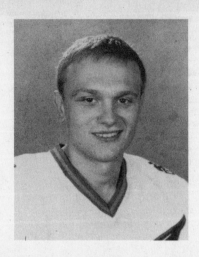

Career statistics:

GP	G	A	TP	PIM
598	137	230	367	473

1999-2000 statistics:

GP	G	A	TP	+/-	PIM	PP	SH	GW	GT	S	PCT
73	18	36	54	+26	52	5	0	3	0	181	9.9

2000-2001 statistics:

GP	G	A	TP	+/-	PIM	PP	SH	GW	GT	S	PCT
76	19	38	57	+12	70	8	0	2	0	241	7.9

2001-2002 statistics:

GP	G	A	TP	+/-	PIM	PP	SH	GW	GT	S	PCT
76	26	33	59	-1	58	7	0	2	0	216	12.0

2002-2003 statistics:

GP	G	A	TP	+/-	PIM	PP	SH	GW	GT	S	PCT
82	18	49	67	+13	52	7	0	2	1	224	8.0

LAST SEASON

Tied for first among NHL defensemen in goals. Second among NHL defensemen in points. Led team in average ice time (26:34) and assists. Third on team in points, plus-minus, and shots. One of five Caps to appear in all 82 games.

THE FINESSE GAME

Even though the Caps asked Gonchar to take his offensive game down a notch and concentrate more on his own end, Gonchar was still among the scoring leaders among NHL defensemen. It's difficult to believe that Gonchar developed as a defensive defenseman in Russia. He sees the ice well and passes well, but he never put up any big offensive numbers before coming into the NHL. Now he ranks among the game's elite offensive defensemen, but he is not high-risk. He has also become among the best two-way defensemen in the game.

He jumps up into the play willingly and intelligently. Gonchar has a natural feel for the flow of a game and makes tape-to-tape feeds through people — even under pressure. He sees first-unit power-play time on the point and makes a first-rate quarterback. He plays heads-up. He doesn't have the blazing speed that some elite defensemen have when carrying the puck, but he will gain the zone with some speed. He is an excellent passer.

Gonchar's shot is accurate enough, but it won't terrorize any goalies. He doesn't push the puck forward and step into it like Al MacInnis. Most of the time he is content with getting it on the net, though he is not reluctant to shoot.

THE PHYSICAL GAME

Strong on his skates, Gonchar has worked hard on his off-ice conditioning and he can handle a lot of quality minutes. His defense is based more on reads and positional play than on a physical element. He is not an overly aggressive player. Teams like to target him early to scare him off his best effort.

THE INTANGIBLES

Gonchar's 103 goals are the most scored by any NHL defenseman during the past four seasons. He is a coach's delight because he is completely no-fuss and low-maintenance.

PROJECTION

Gonchar is a consistent scorer in the 60-point range and is underrated defensively.

MIKE GRIER

Yrs. of NHL service: 7
Born: Detroit, Mich.; Jan. 5, 1975
Position: right wing
Height: 6-1
Weight: 227
Uniform no.: 25
Shoots: right

Career statistics:

GP	G	A	TP	PIM
530	96	119	215	328

1999-2000 statistics:

GP	G	A	TP	+/-	PIM	PP	SH	GW	GT	S	PCT
65	9	22	31	+9	68	0	3	2	0	115	7.8

2000-2001 statistics:

GP	G	A	TP	+/-	PIM	PP	SH	GW	GT	S	PCT
74	20	16	36	+11	20	2	3	2	1	124	16.1

2001-2002 statistics:

GP	G	A	TP	+/-	PIM	PP	SH	GW	GT	S	PCT
82	8	17	25	+1	32	0	2	3	0	112	7.1

2002-2003 statistics:

GP	G	A	TP	+/-	PIM	PP	SH	GW	GT	S	PCT
82	15	17	32	-14	36	2	2	2	0	133	11.3

LAST SEASON

Acquired from Edmonton on October 7, 2002, for a second-round and third-round draft pick in 2003. Tied for team lead in shorthanded goals. Worst plus-minus on team. One of five Caps to appear in all 82 games.

THE FINESSE GAME

Grier is a hockey player in a football player's body — an aggressive forechecker who bores in on the unfortunate puck carrier with all the intensity of a lineman blitzing a quarterback. But Grier doesn't waste energy. He is intelligent about when to come in full-tilt or when to back off a bit and pick off a hasty pass. He frightens a lot of people into mistakes, and the savvier he gets at reading their reactions, the better he'll be.

Grier definitely believes that the most direct route to the net is the best path to choose. He won't hesitate to bull his way through two defensemen to get there.

The knock on Grier has always been his skating. He has a slow first couple of strides, but he then gets into gear and is strong and balanced with fair agility. He scores his goals like Adam Deadmarsh does, by driving to the net after loose pucks. Grier was a scorer at the collegiate level and has decent hands. Since he always keeps his legs pumping, he draws a good share of penalties. He is also a sound penalty killer and a shorthanded scoring threat.

THE PHYSICAL GAME

Grier can't be too bulky or he won't be agile enough for his pursuit. Grier is tough but he isn't a fighter. It takes a lot to provoke him. He's just an honest, rugged, physical winger.

THE INTANGIBLES

Grier is an unsung hero who will do just about anything the coaches ask. He played on the third line with Jeff Halpern and Steve Konowalchuk last season. Grier was a restricted free agent after last season.

PROJECTION

Grier is a defensive forward who can handle some second-unit power-play time. He can chip in 15-18 goals.

JEFF HALPERN

Yrs. of NHL service: 4
Born: Potomac, Maryland; May 3, 1976
Position: center
Height: 6-0
Weight: 201
Uniform no.: 11
Shoots: right

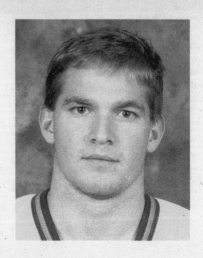

Career statistics:

GP	G	A	TP	PIM
289	57	67	124	216

1999-2000 statistics:

GP	G	A	TP	+/-	PIM	PP	SH	GW	GT	S	PCT
79	18	11	29	+21	39	4	0	2	1	118	10.2

2000-2001 statistics:

GP	G	A	TP	+/-	PIM	PP	SH	GW	GT	S	PCT
80	21	21	42	+13	60	2	1	5	2	110	19.1

2001-2002 statistics:

GP	G	A	TP	+/-	PIM	PP	SH	GW	GT	S	PCT
48	5	14	19	-9	29	0	0	4	0	74	6.8

2002-2003 statistics:

GP	G	A	TP	+/-	PIM	PP	SH	GW	GT	S	PCT
82	13	21	34	+6	88	1	2	2	0	126	10.3

PROJECTION

Halpern should continue to develop into a solid two-way center, with emphasis on the checking side. He scored 21 goals in his rookie season, and if he can do that again, the Caps would be thrilled.

LAST SEASON

Tied for team lead in shorthanded goals. Third on team in penalty minutes. One of five Caps to appear in all 82 games.

THE FINESSE GAME

Halpern is a very smart player without the puck. He doesn't have great speed, but he is very aware positionally. Halpern is the kind of guy you would like to have on the ice all night long. You never have to worry about him. He makes big plays. And he makes little plays.

Halpern is a reliable, low-risk forward at even strength. His job as a "goal preventer" is advanced and he is learning to take pride in this checking role. Halpern can play center or wing, though he's more effective in the middle, which is where he played most of last season between Steve Konowalchuk and Mike Grier.

Halpern used to be something of a liability on draws, but he studied Adam Oates when that face-off specialist was with the Caps and he has improved. He is used to kill penalties.

THE PHYSICAL GAME

Halpern isn't big, but he plays with a quiet kind of toughness.

THE INTANGIBLES

Last year was an important comeback season for Halpern after battling back from injuries, including major knee surgery in January, 2002. He is expected to be the Caps' third-line center again and should be more effective this season.

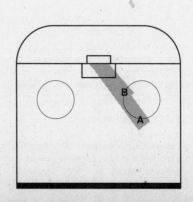

JAROMIR JAGR

Yrs. of NHL service: 13
Born: Kladno, Czech Republic; Feb. 15, 1972
Position: right wing
Height: 6-2
Weight: 234
Uniform no.: 68
Shoots: left

Career statistics:

GP	G	A	TP	PIM
950	506	729	1235	661

1999-2000 statistics:

GP	G	A	TP	+/-	PIM	PP	SH	GW	GT	S	PCT
63	42	54	96	+25	50	10	0	5	1	290	14.5

2000-2001 statistics:

GP	G	A	TP	+/-	PIM	PP	SH	GW	GT	S	PCT
81	52	69	121	+19	42	14	1	10	1	317	16.4

2001-2002 statistics:

GP	G	A	TP	+/-	PIM	PP	SH	GW	GT	S	PCT
69	31	48	79	0	30	10	0	3	0	197	15.7

2002-2003 statistics:

GP	G	A	TP	+/-	PIM	PP	SH	GW	GT	S	PCT
75	36	41	77	+5	38	13	2	9	0	290	12.4

LAST SEASON

Led team in goals, points, power-play goals, game-winning goals, and shots. Missed six games with wrist injury. Missed one game with groin injury.

THE FINESSE GAME

Jagr's exceptional skating and extraordinary ice time make him tough to shadow. Jagr is as close to a perfect skater as there is in the NHL. He keeps his body centered over his skates, giving him a low center of gravity and making it tough for anyone to knock him off the puck. He has a deep knee bend, for quickness and power. His strokes are long and sure, and he has control over his body and exceptional lateral mobility. He dazzles with his footwork and handles the puck at high tempo. If he's affected by lower body injuries, Jagr's game is severely compromised. He can score, but he can't dominate the way he does when he's 100 per cent.

Jagr loves — and lives — to score. He's poetry in motion with his beautifully effortless skating style. And, with his Mario Lemieux-like reach, Jagr can dangle the puck while he's gliding and swooping. He fakes the backhand and goes to his forehand in a flash. He is also powerful enough to drag a defender with him to the net and push off a strong one-handed shot. He has a big slap shot and can drive it on the fly or fire it with a one-timer off a pass.

Jagr plays on the penalty kill not because of his defensive play, which can be indifferent, but because he is a shorthanded threat with his breakaway speed.

Jagr has lost his status as one of the game's most dangerous offensive weapons. Whether it's the lack of a supporting cast in Washington, declining skills, or complete disinterest is impossible to say.

THE PHYSICAL GAME

Earlier in his career he could be intimidated physically; he still doesn't like to get hit, but he's not as wimpy as he used to be. Jagr is confident, almost cocky, and tough to catch. When he feels like it, anyway.

THE INTANGIBLES

The Caps signed free agent Robert Lang in 2002 and auditioned him as a center for Jagr but it didn't really take. Then they acquired Michael Nylander, but that chemistry wore off shortly after Nylander's arrival. Jagr was held to two goals in six playoff games against Tampa Bay. All right, so he was coming off a wrist injury...but, Tampa Bay?

PROJECTION

Jagr helped get the Caps into the playoffs but Washington isn't too pleased with its investment ($66 million over the next six years, and owner Ted Leonsis has only himself to blame). Jagr's contract prevents Washington from doing much to help the rest of its team, so how does Jagr make more of an impact? We're downgrading Jagr to 80 points.

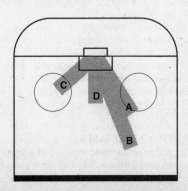

CALLE JOHANSSON

Yrs. of NHL service: 16
Born: Goteborg, Sweden; Feb. 14, 1967
Position: left defense
Height: 5-11
Weight: 203
Uniform no.: 6
Shoots: left

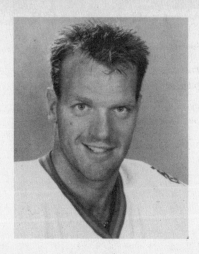

Career statistics:

GP	G	A	TP	PIM
1101	119	410	529	519

1999-2000 statistics:

GP	G	A	TP	+/-	PIM	PP	SH	GW	GT	S	PCT
82	7	25	32	+13	24	1	0	3	0	138	5.1

2000-2001 statistics:

GP	G	A	TP	+/-	PIM	PP	SH	GW	GT	S	PCT
76	7	29	36	+11	26	5	0	0	0	154	4.6

2001-2002 statistics:

GP	G	A	TP	+/-	PIM	PP	SH	GW	GT	S	PCT
11	2	0	2	-4	8	0	0	1	0	18	11.1

2002-2003 statistics:

GP	G	A	TP	+/-	PIM	PP	SH	GW	GT	S	PCT
82	3	12	15	+9	22	1	0	0	0	77	3.9

LAST SEASON

Third on Capitals in average ice time (21:45). One of five Capitals to appear in all 82 games.

THE FINESSE GAME

Johansson has tremendous legs, notably big, strong thighs that generate the power for his shot and his explosive skating. He makes every move look easy. He is agile, mobile, and great at moving up-ice with the play. Speed, balance, and strength allow him to chase a puck behind the net, pick it up without stopping, and make an accurate pass. He is confident, even on the backhand, and likes to have the puck in key spots.

Johansson is not an elite scorer, but he is smart offensively. He moves the puck with a good first pass, then has enough speed and instinct to jump up and be ready for a return pass. He keeps the gap tight as the play enters the attacking zone, which opens up more options. He is available to the forwards if they need him for offense, and closer to the puck if it is turned over to the opposition.

Johansson has a low, accurate shot that can be tipped. He is unselfish to a fault, often looking to pass when he should use his shot.

He has good defensive instincts and reads plays well. His skating gives him the confidence (maybe overconfidence) to gamble and challenge the puck carrier. He has a quick stick for poke- and sweep-checks.

THE PHYSICAL GAME

Although not an aggressive player, Johansson is strong and knows what he has to do with his body in the defensive zone. This part of the game has not come naturally, but he has worked at it. He is not an impact player physically, although he wins his share of the one-on-one battles because he gets so much power from his legs. He stays in good condition and can (and does) give a team a lot of minutes.

THE INTANGIBLES

Johansson is one of the most underrated defensemen in the league, but in a youth and budget movement, the Caps opted not to resign him and he became an unrestricted free agent after last season. He would be very helpful to a team looking to break in some young defensemen, since Johansson was instrumental in Brendan Witt's development in Washington. He's a true glue guy.

PROJECTION

Johansson can still be a serviceable No. 4 defenseman and score 20 points.

OLAF KOLZIG

Yrs. of NHL service: 9
Born: Johannesburg, South Africa; Apr. 9, 1970
Position: goaltender
Height: 6-3
Weight: 225
Uniform no.: 37
Catches: left

Career statistics:

GP	MIN	GA	SO	GAA	A	PIM
481	27678	1162	31	2.52	8	69

1999-2000 statistics:

GP	MIN	GAA	W	L	T	SO	GA	S	SAPCT	PIM
73	4371	2.24	41	20	11	5	163	1957	.917	6

2000-2001 statistics:

GP	MIN	GAA	W	L	T	SO	GA	S	SAPCT	PIM
72	4279	2.48	37	26	8	5	177	1941	.909	14

2001-2002 statistics:

GP	MIN	GAA	W	L	T	SO	GA	S	SAPCT	PIM
71	4131	2.79	31	29	8	6	192	1977	.903	8

2002-2003 statistics:

GP	MIN	GAA	W	L	T	SO	GA	S	SAPCT	PIM
66	3894	2.40	33	25	6	4	156	1925	.919	0

LAST SEASON

Fifth season with 30 or more wins. Missed eight games with hand injuries.

THE PHYSICAL GAME

Kolzig is a big butterfly goalie with sharp reflexes and good skating ability for a player of his size. Rather than just lumber around and let the puck hit him, however, he is active and positions himself well to block as much of the net as possible from the shooter. Kolzig is very good at controlling his rebounds. He still works at this skill almost daily during the season.

Kolzig is aggressive and consistent in his technical play. Although still not regarded as an elite NHL goalie, Kolzig is solidly among the second echelon.

He needs to improve his stickhandling. He could use his stick better to break up plays around the net.

The book on Kolzig is to go high, since he takes away the bottom of the net so well.

THE MENTAL GAME

Kolzig has matured so much. He can still be a bit of a hothead in the course of a game, but for the most part he stays relaxed and focused. He is a good influence in the dressing room and his teammates want to play hard in front of him. Bad goals or bad games don't haunt him. He always gives his team a chance to win, and he steals some games.

THE INTANGIBLES

Kolzig returned to solid form last season. Washington had trouble scoring goals and there were a lot of nights where Kolzig had to be just about perfect for his team to get a point. He was the Caps' MVP and the major reason why they returned to the playoffs.

PROJECTION

Kolzig was able to manage 30 wins despite some nagging injuries and we would expect another 30-win season from him.

STEVE KONOWALCHUK

Yrs. of NHL service: 11
Born: Salt Lake City, Utah; Nov. 11, 1972
Position: left wing
Height: 6-1
Weight: 207
Uniform no.: 22
Shoots: left

Career statistics:

GP	G	A	TP	PIM
687	146	195	341	619

1999-2000 statistics:

GP	G	A	TP	+/-	PIM	PP	SH	GW	GT	S	PCT
82	16	27	43	+19	80	3	0	1	0	146	11.0

2000-2001 statistics:

GP	G	A	TP	+/-	PIM	PP	SH	GW	GT	S	PCT
82	24	23	47	+8	87	6	0	5	0	163	14.7

2001-2002 statistics:

GP	G	A	TP	+/-	PIM	PP	SH	GW	GT	S	PCT
28	2	12	14	-2	23	0	0	0	0	36	5.6

2002-2003 statistics:

GP	G	A	TP	+/-	PIM	PP	SH	GW	GT	S	PCT
77	15	15	30	+3	71	2	0	3	0	119	12.6

LAST SEASON

Third on team in shooting percentage. Missed three games with groin injury. Missed two games with foot injuries.

THE FINESSE GAME

Konowalchuk is a willing guy who plays any role asked of him. He's a digger who has to work hard for his goals, and an intelligent and earnest player who uses every ounce of energy on every shift. He is one of the Caps' most eager forecheckers.

There is nothing fancy about his offense. He just lets his shot rip and drives to the net. He doesn't have the moves and hand skills to beat a defender one-on-one, but he doesn't care; he'll go right through him. His release on his shot is improving.

Konowalchuk is reliable and intelligent defensively. On the draw, he ties up the opposing center if he doesn't win the puck drop outright. He uses his feet along the boards as well as his stick. He's the kind of guy who does all the dirty work that makes the finesse players on his team look even prettier.

THE PHYSICAL GAME

Konowalchuk is very strong. He has some grit in him, too, and will aggravate opponents with his constant effort. He doesn't take bad penalties, but often goads rivals into retaliating. He is very fit and can handle a lot of ice time.

THE INTANGIBLES

Konowalchuk is a heart-and-soul guy. His non-stop intensity makes him one of the Caps' most gutsy and valuable leaders. They are a different team when he is not in the lineup.

PROJECTION

Konowalchuk is a quality guy on the ice or in the dressing room, and he can score 15 to 20 goals.

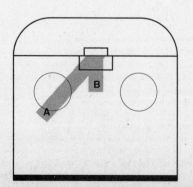

ROBERT LANG

Yrs. of NHL service: 10
Born: Teplice, Czech Republic; Dec. 19, 1970
Position: center
Height: 6-2
Weight: 216
Uniform no.: 20
Shoots: right

Career statistics:

GP	G	A	TP	PIM
577	144	244	388	146

1999-2000 statistics:

GP	G	A	TP	+/-	PIM	PP	SH	GW	GT	S	PCT
78	23	42	65	-9	14	13	0	5	1	142	16.2

2000-2001 statistics:

GP	G	A	TP	+/-	PIM	PP	SH	GW	GT	S	PCT
82	32	48	80	+20	28	10	0	2	0	177	18.1

2001-2002 statistics:

GP	G	A	TP	+/-	PIM	PP	SH	GW	GT	S	PCT
62	18	32	50	+9	16	5	1	3	0	175	10.3

2002-2003 statistics:

GP	G	A	TP	+/-	PIM	PP	SH	GW	GT	S	PCT
82	22	47	69	+12	22	10	0	2	1	146	15.1

LAST SEASON

Led team in shooting percentage. Second on team in assists, points, and power-play goals. One of five Caps to appear in all 82 games.

THE FINESSE GAME

Lang always gives the impression that there's something left in his tank, not exactly the right quality for a first-line player. And with the kind of money the Caps just invested in him, they expect him to be a top-six guy. Lang came up tiny again the playoffs.

Lang is certainly not without skill. He has deceptive quickness and is very solid on his skates, along with great hands, great hockey sense, and the ability to make plays on his forehand or backhand. Players on both wings have to be prepared for a pass that could materialize out of thin air or through a thicket of sticks and skates. Lang has the presence to draw defenders to him to open up ice for his linemates, and he makes good use of them.

Patient with the puck, Lang often holds on too long. He will always pass up a shot if he can make a play instead. Lang is a smart penalty killer because of his anticipation. He lapses defensively at even strength, however.

THE PHYSICAL GAME

Lang will not take a hit to make a play, a glaring flaw for a front-line player. He has to show more willingness to initiate. He'll never trounce anyone, but he has to fight for the puck and fight through checks.

THE INTANGIBLES

Lang's numbers weren't awful and it might have helped him if he didn't play with revolving doors on either wing.

PROJECTION

Lang's top end is probably an assist-heavy 70 points.

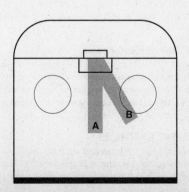

MICHAEL NYLANDER

Yrs. of NHL service: 10
Born: Stockholm, Sweden; Oct. 3, 1972
Position: center
Height: 6-1
Weight: 195
Uniform no.: 92
Shoots: left

Career statistics:

GP	G	A	TP	PIM
630	139	294	433	272

1999-2000 statistics:

GP	G	A	TP	+/-	PIM	PP	SH	GW	GT	S	PCT
77	24	30	54	+6	30	5	0	2	0	122	19.7

2000-2001 statistics:

GP	G	A	TP	+/-	PIM	PP	SH	GW	GT	S	PCT
82	25	39	64	+7	32	4	0	5	0	176	14.2

2001-2002 statistics:

GP	G	A	TP	+/-	PIM	PP	SH	GW	GT	S	PCT
82	15	46	61	+28	50	6	0	2	0	158	9.5

2002-2003 statistics:

GP	G	A	TP	+/-	PIM	PP	SH	GW	GT	S	PCT
80	17	43	60	+3	40	7	0	2	0	161	10.6

LAST SEASON

Acquired from Chicago on November 1, 2002, with a third-round draft pick in 2003 for Andrei Nikolishin and Chris Simon. Third on team in assists. Has appeared in 310 consecutive regular-season games.

THE FINESSE GAME

Nylander's point production has never reflected his high skill level. He can do things with the puck that are magical. He knows all about time and space. If anything, he is guilty of hanging on to the puck too long and passing up quality shots, as he tries to force a pass to a teammate who is in a worse scoring position than he is. In Jaromir Jagr, Nylander was teamed with a finisher. They started out well after Nylander's arrival but the combination was less than magical down the stretch.

An open-ice player, Nylander is an excellent skater and composed with the puck. He's strictly a one-way forward. He needs to play with a go-to guy, but also needs a safety-valve winger who is defensively alert.

THE PHYSICAL GAME

Nylander is on the small side and plays even smaller. He uses his body to protect the puck but he won't fight hard for possession. No wonder he's able to keep his games-played streak intact. He is rarely in danger of being in a position where he can get hurt.

THE INTANGIBLES

Nylander is not a No. 1 center although the Caps tried to shoehorn him into that role (perhaps figuring that Jagr can make any player into a top-line pivot). He is streaky and moody. Nylander won't dominate games.

PROJECTION

Nylander continues to be an erratic player who can look like a star during his hot streaks but who will just as easily be invisible. He will probably produce around 15 goals and 45 assists.

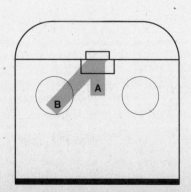

BRIAN SUTHERBY

Yrs. of NHL service: 1
Born: Edmonton, Alta.; Mar. 1, 1982
Position: center
Height: 6-2
Weight: 180
Uniform no.: 46
Shoots: left

Career statistics:

GP	G	A	TP	PIM
79	2	9	11	95

2001-2002 statistics:

GP	G	A	TP	+/-	PIM	PP	SH	GW	GT	S	PCT
7	0	0	0	-3	2	0	0	0	0	3	0.0

2002-2003 statistics:

GP	G	A	TP	+/-	PIM	PP	SH	GW	GT	S	PCT
72	2	9	11	+7	93	0	0	0	0	38	5.3

LAST SEASON

First NHL season. Appeared in five games with
Portland (AHL), scoring 0-5 — 5 with 11 PIM.

THE FINESSE GAME

Sutherby was coached in juniors by Lee Fogilin and
his role model is Mark Messier. Both of those
influences will give you a pretty clear image of the
kind of player Sutherby is and will become.

The Caps were careful not to rush Sutherby and
here is the payoff. He has improved every season, and
raises his game at important moments, like in the
World Junior Championships.

Sutherby is tall and has a long reach. He applies
this well to his intelligent and dogged forechecking.
He is able to reach in and steal a puck from an opponent without taking a penalty. Sutherby also isn't shy
about powering his way in the zone on a forecheck to
stir things up.

He does not have great offensive instincts, but his
skills are above-average. Sutherby passes well and is
likely to be a better playmaker than scorer. He has an
adequate shot but he is reluctant to use it.

THE PHYSICAL GAME

Sutherby has added about 20 pounds since his draft
year (he was a first-rounder in 2000) and he loves to
use it. He is naturally aggressive. Sutherby is a banger
and crasher.

THE INTANGIBLES

Sutherby started off the season with a conditioning
stint in the minors but was a regular fourth-line player
since his November recall. Sutherby is going to be a
top defensive forward, and he may challenge incumbent Jeff Halpern for the checking-line center's job.
He is not offensively skilled enough to take on a top-
two job, although the Caps may give him a tryout
there since they aren't impressive up the middle
(Robert Lang and Michael Nylander). Scouts are very
high on Sutherby's leadership qualities, which are in
short supply in Washington.

PROJECTION

Sutherby's future is as a two-way center who can
score 10-15 goals this season.

BRENDAN WITT

Yrs. of NHL service: 8
Born: Humboldt, Sask.; Feb. 20, 1975
Position: left defense
Height: 6-2
Weight: 229
Uniform no.: 19
Shoots: left

Career statistics:

GP	G	A	TP	PIM
496	17	43	60	771

1999-2000 statistics:

GP	G	A	TP	+/-	PIM	PP	SH	GW	GT	S	PCT
77	1	7	8	+5	114	0	0	0	0	64	1.6

2000-2001 statistics:

GP	G	A	TP	+/-	PIM	PP	SH	GW	GT	S	PCT
72	3	3	6	+2	101	0	0	0	0	87	3.5

2001-2002 statistics:

GP	G	A	TP	+/-	PIM	PP	SH	GW	GT	S	PCT
68	3	7	10	-1	78	0	0	0	0	81	3.7

2002-2003 statistics:

GP	G	A	TP	+/-	PIM	PP	SH	GW	GT	S	PCT
69	2	9	11	+12	106	0	0	0	0	80	2.5

LAST SEASON

Second on team in penalty minutes. Missed three games with groin injury. Missed four games with shoulder injury. Missed six games with upper body injury.

THE FINESSE GAME

Witt's skill level is high, if not elite, and he applies his abilities in his own zone. His skating is capable. He has worked to improve his agility, though his pivots and passing skills remain a bit rough. Still, he does not overhandle the puck, and by making simple plays he keeps himself out of serious trouble. He skates well backwards and has decent lateral mobility.

Witt gets involved somewhat in the attack, but the extent of his contribution is a hard point shot. He won't gamble low and can't run a power play. He won't ever be an offensive force.

One of the steadier, and sometimes scarier, players on the Caps' blueline, Witt is effective without being flashy. His game is maturing.

THE PHYSICAL GAME

A strong physical presence on the ice, Witt can get even stronger. He loses few one-on-one battles. He blocks shots fearlessly, and is naturally aggressive and intimidating. He is a little too eager to fight and can be goaded into the box. Witt is a powerful hitter.

THE INTANGIBLES

Witt has continued to mature slowly and steadily, and is one of the Caps' top-two defensemen. He handles the checking assignments against other team's top lines. He will miss Calle Johansson if the Caps decide not to re-sign that underrated veteran defenseman.

PROJECTION

Witt hasn't reached his best level yet, but he's getting closer. One very positive sign is how much he continues to improve each year. Although he won't score a lot of points, he will get a lot of ice time.

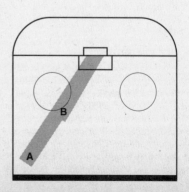

DAINIUS ZUBRUS

Yrs. of NHL service: 7
Born: Elektrenai, Lithuania; June 16, 1978
Position: right wing
Height: 6-4
Weight: 231
Uniform no.: 9
Shoots: left

Career statistics:

GP	G	A	TP	PIM
485	79	137	216	265

1999-2000 statistics:

GP	G	A	TP	+/-	PIM	PP	SH	GW	GT	S	PCT
73	14	28	42	-1	54	3	0	1	0	139	10.1

2000-2001 statistics:

GP	G	A	TP	+/-	PIM	PP	SH	GW	GT	S	PCT
61	13	13	26	-11	37	4	0	0	0	83	15.7

2001-2002 statistics:

GP	G	A	TP	+/-	PIM	PP	SH	GW	GT	S	PCT
71	17	26	43	+5	38	4	0	3	0	138	12.3

2002-2003 statistics:

GP	G	A	TP	+/-	PIM	PP	SH	GW	GT	S	PCT
63	13	22	35	+15	43	2	0	0	0	104	12.5

LAST SEASON

Second on team in plus-minus. Missed 14 games with hand injury and surgery. Missed three games with concussion. Missed two games due to coach's decision.

THE FINESSE GAME

Zubrus has the ability to be a big-time offensive threat. Zubrus plays the game in a north-south direction, goal line to goal line, rather than in the east-west fashion favored by most imports. He is helped in this regard by a long stride that covers lots of ground. His puck control is impressive, as though the puck is on a very short rope that is nailed to his stick. His great ability is to control the puck down low and create scoring chances for himself and his teammates. He is not a natural goal-scorer.

Splendid acceleration is a key component of Zubrus's game. He is both confident in his skating and competent enough to burst between defensemen to take the most direct path to the net. He also features enough power and balance to control a sweep behind the net, pull in front and roof a backhand shot under the crossbar from close range.

Zubrus uses his edges well and is tough to knock off the puck. He is quite willing to zoom in off the wing, use his body to shield the puck from a defender and make something happen. The soft touch in his hands and the quick release of the puck shot complement the power in his legs.

Zubrus still has a way to go to become a complete player. He is a better player in his own zone than he used to be.

THE PHYSICAL GAME

Zubrus will fight his own battles. He uses his size to his advantage, finishes checks with authority and out-muscles as many people as he can. He's gritty in the corners and along the boards, and is adept at using his feet to control the puck if his upper body is tied up. He is a very strong one-on-one player.

THE INTANGIBLES

Zubrus was moved back to right wing and didn't fare as well there as he did when he had the chance to play as Jaromir Jagr's center. His hand surgery (which occurred in midseason) came after a very erratic start.

PROJECTION

We keep waiting for that bust-out, 60-point season from Zubrus. So have a lot of GMs. Maybe 40 points is more his speed.

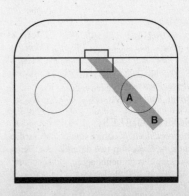

PLAYER INDEX